ACTIVITIES 1929–1931

The Collected Writings of John Maynard Keynes

Keynes in 1929

THE COLLECTED WRITINGS OF
JOHN MAYNARD KEYNES

VOLUME XX

ACTIVITIES 1929–1931
RETHINKING EMPLOYMENT
AND UNEMPLOYMENT POLICIES

EDITED BY

DONALD MOGGRIDGE

MACMILLAN

CAMBRIDGE UNIVERSITY PRESS

FOR THE

ROYAL ECONOMIC SOCIETY

© The Royal Economic Society 1981

Published for the Royal Economic Society

throughout the world, excluding the U.S.A. and Canada, by

THE MACMILLAN PRESS LTD

London and Basingstoke
Associated companies in Delhi Dublin Hong Kong Johannesburg Lagos
Melbourne New York Singapore Tokyo

and throughout the U.S.A. and Canada by

THE PRESS SYNDICATE OF THE UNIVERSITY OF CAMBRIDGE
32 East 57th Street, New York, NY 10022, U.S.A.

Printed in Great Britain at the
University Press, Cambridge

British Library Cataloguing in Publication Data

Keynes, John Maynard, *Baron Keynes*
The collected writings of John Maynard Keynes
Vol. 20: Activities 1929–1931, rethinking employment and unemployment policies

1. Economics
I. Moggridge, Donald Edward
II. Royal Economic Society
330.15'6   HB171

ISBN 0–333–10735–7

CUP ISBN 0–521–23072–1 (the U.S.A. and Canada only)

3-4-82

CONTENTS

GENERAL INTRODUCTION

This new standard edition of *The Collected Writings of John Maynard Keynes* forms the memorial to him of the Royal Economic Society. He devoted a very large share of his busy life to the Society. In 1911, at the age of twenty-eight, he became editor of the *Economic Journal* in succession to Edgeworth: two years later he was made secretary as well. He held these offices without intermittence until almost the end of his life. Edgeworth, it is true, returned to help him with the editorship from 1919 to 1925; Macgregor took Edgeworth's place until 1934, when Austin Robinson succeeded him and continued to assist Keynes down to 1945. But through all these years Keynes himself carried the major responsibility and made the principal decisions about the articles that were to appear in the *Economic Journal*, without any break save for one or two issues when he was seriously ill in 1937. It was only a few months before his death at Easter 1946 that he was elected president and handed over his editorship to Roy Harrod and the secretaryship to Austin Robinson.

In his dual capacity of editor and secretary Keynes played a major part in framing the policies of the Royal Economic Society. It was very largely due to him that some of the major publishing activities of the Society—Sraffa's edition of Ricardo, Stark's edition of the economic writings of Bentham, and Guillebaud's edition of Marshall, as well as a number of earlier publications in the 1930s—were initiated.

When Keynes died in 1946 it was natural that the Royal Economic Society should wish to commemorate him. It was perhaps equally natural that the Society chose to commemorate him by producing an edition of his collected works. Keynes himself had always taken a joy in fine printing, and the Society, with the help of Messrs Macmillan as publishers and the Cambridge University Press as printers, has been anxious to give Keynes's writings a permanent form that is wholly worthy of him.

The present edition will publish as much as is possible of his work in the field of economics. It will not include any private and personal correspondence or publish many letters in the possession of his family. The edition is concerned, that is to say, with Keynes as an economist.

Keynes's writings fall into five broad categories. First there are the books which he wrote and published as books. Second there are collections of articles and pamphlets which he himself made during his lifetime (*Essays in Persuasion* and *Essays in Biography*). Third, there is a very considerable volume of published but uncollected writings—articles written for newspapers, letters to newspapers, articles in journals that have not been included in his two volumes of collections, and various pamphlets. Fourth, there are a few hitherto unpublished writings. Fifth, there is correspondence with economists and concerned with economics or public affairs. It is the intention of this series to publish almost completely the whole of the first four categories listed above. The only exceptions are a few syndicated articles where Keynes wrote almost the same material for publication in different newspapers or in different countries, with minor and unimportant variations. In these cases, this series will publish one only of the variations, choosing the most interesting.

The publication of Keynes's economic correspondence must inevitably be selective. In the day of the typewriter and the filing cabinet and particularly in the case of so active and busy a man, to publish every scrap of paper that he may have dictated about some unimportant or ephemeral matter is impossible. We are aiming to collect and publish as much as possible, however, of the correspondence in which Keynes developed his own ideas in argument with his fellow economists, as well as the more significant correspondence at times when Keynes was in the middle of public affairs.

Apart from his published books, the main sources available to those preparing this series have been two. First, Keynes in his will made Richard Kahn his executor and responsible for his economic papers. They have been placed in the Marshall Library of the University of Cambridge and have been available for this edition. Until 1914 Keynes did not have a secretary and his earliest papers are in the main limited to drafts of important letters that he made in his own handwriting and retained. At that stage most of the correspondence that we possess is represented by what he received rather than by what he wrote. During the war years of 1914–18 and 1940–6 Keynes was serving in the Treasury. With the opening in 1968 of the records under the thirty-year rule, the papers that he wrote then and between the wars have become available. From 1919 onwards, throughout the rest of his life, Keynes had the help of a secretary—for many years Mrs Stephens. Thus for the last twenty-five years of his working life we have in most cases the carbon copies of his own letters as well as the originals of the letters that he received.

There were, of course, occasions during this period on which Keynes wrote himself in his own handwriting. In some of these cases, with the help of his correspondents, we have been able to collect the whole of both sides of some important interchanges and we have been anxious, in justice to both correspondents, to see that both sides of the correspondence are published in full.

The second main source of information has been a group of scrapbooks kept over a very long period of years by Keynes's mother, Florence Keynes, wife of Neville Keynes. From 1919 onwards these scrapbooks contain almost the whole of Maynard Keynes's more ephemeral writing, his letters to newspapers and a great deal of material which enables one to see not only what he wrote but the reaction of others to his writing. Without these very carefully kept scrapbooks the task of any editor or biographer of Keynes would have been immensely more difficult.

The plan of the edition, as at present intended, is this. It will total thirty volumes. Of these the first eight are Keynes's published books from *Indian Currency and Finance*, in 1913, to the *General Theory* in 1936, with the addition of his *Treatise on Probability*. There next follow, as vols. IX and X, *Essays in Persuasion* and *Essays in Biography*, representing Keynes's own collections of articles. *Essays in Persuasion* differs from the original printing in two respects: it contains the full texts of the articles or pamphlets included in it and not (as in the original printing) abbreviated versions of these articles, and it also contains two later pamphlets which are of exactly the same character as those included by Keynes in his original collection. In *Essays in Biography* there have been added a number of biographical studies that Keynes wrote both before and after 1933.

There will follow two volumes, XI–XII, of economic articles and correspondence and a further two volumes, already published, XIII–XIV, covering the development of his thinking as he moved towards the *General Theory*. There are included in these volumes such part of Keynes's economic correspondence as is closely associated with the articles that are printed in them. A supplement to these volumes, XXIX, prints some further material relating to the same issues, which has since been discovered.

The remaining fourteen volumes deal with Keynes's *Activities* during the years from the beginning of his public life in 1905 until his death. In each of the periods into which we divide this material, the volume concerned publishes his more ephemeral writings, all of it hitherto uncollected, his correspondence relating to these activities, and such other material and correspondence as is necessary to the understanding of Keynes's activities. These volumes are edited by Elizabeth Johnson and Donald Moggridge, and it has been their task to trace and interpret Keynes's activities sufficiently to make the material fully intelligible to a later generation. Elizabeth Johnson has been responsible for vols. XV–XVIII, covering Keynes's earlier years and his activities down to the end of World War I reparations and reconstruction. Donald Moggridge is responsible for all the remaining volumes recording Keynes's other activities from 1922 until his death in 1946.

The record of Keynes's activities during World War II is now complete with the publication of volumes XXV–XXVII. It remains to fill the gap between 1922 and 1939 with three volumes of which this is the second; to print certain of Keynes's published articles and the correspondence relating to them which have not appeared elsewhere in this edition, and to publish a volume of his social, political and literary writings.

Those responsible for this edition have been: Lord Kahn, both as Lord Keynes's executor and as a long and intimate friend of Lord Keynes, able to help in the interpreting of much that would be otherwise misunderstood; the late Sir Roy Harrod as the author of his biography; Austin Robinson as Keynes's co-editor on the *Economic Journal* and successor as Secretary of the Royal Economic Society. Austin Robinson has acted throughout as Managing Editor; Donald Moggridge is now associated with him as Joint Managing Editor.

In the early stages of the work Elizabeth Johnson was assisted by Jane Thistlethwaite, and by Mrs McDonald, who was originally responsible for the systematic ordering of the files of the Keynes papers. Judith Masterman for many years worked with Mrs Johnson on the papers. More recently Susan Wilsher, Margaret Butler and Leonora Woollam have continued the secretarial work. Barbara Lowe has been responsible for the indexing. Since 1977 Judith Allen has been responsible for much of the day-to-day management of the edition, as well as seeing the volumes through the press.

EDITORIAL NOTE

This volume is the second of three concerned with Keynes's activities between 1922 and 1939. It concerns itself with Keynes's writings and policy advice between the autumn of 1929 and Britain's departure from the gold standard on 21 September 1931.

The sources for this volume are Keynes's own surviving papers, material available in the Public Record Office and the papers of colleagues and friends. Where the material comes from the Public Record Office, the call numbers for the relevant files appear in the List of Documents Reproduced following page 623.

In this, as in all the similar volumes, in general all of Keynes's own writings are printed in larger type. Keynes's own footnotes are indicated by asterisks or other symbols to distinguish them from the editorial footnotes. All introductory matter and all writings by others than Keynes are printed in smaller type. The only exception to this general rule is that occasional short quotations from a letter from Keynes to his parents or to a friend, used in introductory passages to clarify a situation, are treated as introductory matter and are printed in the smaller type.

Most of Keynes's letters included in this and other volumes are reprinted from the carbon copies that remain among his papers. In most cases he has added his initials to the carbon in the familiar fashion in which he signed to all his friends. We have no certain means of knowing whether the top copy, sent to the recipient of the letter, carried a more formal signature.

Chapter 1

'I AM BECOMING MORE FASHIONABLE AGAIN'[1]

During the autumn of 1929, between the rise in Bank rate in London on 26 September and late October, stock exchange prices in New York remained at high levels even though the trend was slightly downwards. However, in the third week in October the market had a series of bad days culminating in a sharp break on 24 October. Keynes commented to Lydia the next day:

Wall Street *did* have a go yesterday. Did you read about it? The biggest crash ever recorded . . . I have been in a thoroughly financial and disgusting state of mind all day.

It was in this state of mind that he cabled a comment on events for the next day's *New York Evening Post*.

From The New York Evening Post, *25 October 1929*

A BRITISH VIEW OF THE WALL STREET SLUMP

No-one can welcome a Wall Street crash who thinks of it in terms of the individuals involved. But it is easier for an Englishman than it would be for an American to take an objective view of what is happening from the standpoint of world business. Looking at it this way we in Great Britain can't help heaving a big sigh of relief at what seems like the removal of an incubus which has been lying heavily on the business life of the whole world outside America. This is actually reflected already in certain markets on this side. We have had our own troubles affecting certain groups of speculative stocks, but first-class British securities are stronger in the market now than they have

[1] Letter to Lydia, 25 October 1929.

I

been for some time and there is in authoritative circles a new spirit of hopefulness about the future.

Is this a paradox? I do not think so. The extraordinary speculation on Wall Street in past months had driven up the rate of interest to an unprecedented level. Since the gold standard ensures a high degree of mobility of international lending, this meant dear money everywhere. But nothing has happened to enable industry and enterprise outside America to support a higher rate than before. The result is that new enterprise has been damped down in countries thousands of miles from Wall Street and commodity prices have been falling. And this was due to a wholly artificial cause. If the recent high rate of interest had lasted another six months, it would have been a real disaster.

But now, after the drastic and even terrible events of the last few weeks, we see daylight again. There seems a chance of an epoch of cheap money ahead. This will be in the real interests of business all over the world. Money in America has already become very cheap indeed. The Federal Reserve Bank of New York will probably take the first opportunity of putting its rate even lower. If so, I am sure that the Bank of England and the other European central banks will not be slow to follow suit. And then perhaps enterprise throughout the world can get going again. Incidentally commodity prices will recover and farmers will find themselves in better shape.

I may be a bad prophet in speaking this way. But I am sure that I am reflecting the instinctive reaction of English financial opinion to the immediate situation. There will be no serious direct consequences in London resulting from the Wall Street slump except to the limited number of Anglo-American securities which are actively dealt in both here and in New York. On the other hand we find the longer look ahead decidedly encouraging.

I must, however, add the warning that the improvement in world trade must not be expected to follow instantaneously. We shall probably have a bad winter of unemployment in Great

Britain; and the same will very likely be the case in Germany. But this will be the result of the dear money which prevailed during the summer and early autumn. Moreover in Europe we have not yet got the cheap money for which we are hoping. After cheap money has arrived, a few months have to elapse before the business decisions to which it gives rise can materialise in new trade and industrial activity. But if cheap money does come, I do not doubt its remedial efficacy. The world always underestimates the influence of dear money as a depressing influence and of cheap money is a reviving one, precisely because there is a time lag between cause and effect which leads to the real connection being overlooked.

The day before the crash Keynes had spoken to the National Liberal Club on 'The Public Concern as an Alternative to Socialism'. No substantial record of his remarks survives.

On the day of the crash, at Bedford College, London, and on 7 November at the University of Manchester, he lectured on 'The Advisability of Methods other than High Wages as a Means of Improving the Conditions of the Working Class'. The substance of the lectures appeared as 'The Question of High Wages' in the first issue of a new periodical for which Keynes served on the editorial board.

From The Political Quarterly, *January–March 1930*

THE QUESTION OF HIGH WAGES

The earlier generation of economists was extremely suspicious of attempts to raise wages; so much so that they became suspect themselves among certain sections of social idealists. Their general case was that there existed a certain level of wages fixed by external circumstances—by economic law, as they would have expressed it—and that any attempt to lift wages above this level was doomed to failure and would do harm. In particular, they were extremely suspicious of trade unions, and they were inclined to sympathise with the then state of the law, which was designed to hamper their activities in every way.

Some of their arguments are now universally admitted to have been bad arguments—for example, their theory of the wages fund. But quite apart from whether their arguments were good or bad, the tide of events was against them; and their arguments and point of view became discredited irrespective of their merits, and, I think it may be said, out of proportion to their demerits. For one thing the rapid strides of economic progress caused wages to rise substantially. This seemed to contradict their theories, though, of course, in the new circumstances, there was nothing necessarily inconsistent between the theory of a natural wage level and the fact of a rising level of real wages. Apart from the tide of events the growth of democracy and the social conscience made the attitude of the economists seem both impolitic and hard-hearted.

Accordingly, when—fifty years later—we reach the age of Marshall we find a change of heart out of proportion, perhaps, to the amount of change of theory. One of Marshall's earliest publications was a gentle defence and justification of trade unionism as a means of ameliorating the conditions of the working class; and all living economists were brought up to respect and plead for the activities of trade unions as they existed in the latter half of the nineteenth century and before the War.

But to-day, with the present generation of post-war economists, we find an increasingly sharp cleavage of opinion. The more old-fashioned people are disturbed as to whether the long continuance of unemployment may not suggest that there is some disequilibrium between the level of wages and the facts of the external world. For they have not abandoned the belief that there is in some sense what one might call a natural level of wages with which it is unsafe to tamper. Public opinion in modern conditions is so decidedly opposed to a retrograde movement in wages that scarcely anyone, whatever he might think, dares to breathe in public the view that wages may be too high. People grumble under their breath; they maintain that all other solutions of present difficulties are futile; but they are reluctant to put forward their own.

While this is the attitude of some of the more old-fashioned people, there is a growing scepticism abroad as to the psychological and theoretical validity of the orthodox theory of value which leads others to dispute that there is any natural level of wages at all, or, at any rate, one that is rigidly fixed; and this attitude of mind accords much better with popular aspirations. Limits there are, no doubt, this school of thought would admit; but there is a fairly wide margin, they would maintain, within which the determining factor is, not so much what used to be called economic law, as social and political habits and practices, and the trend of public opinion.

Advocates of such views are employing two distinct types of argument. The first of them involves no radical departure from orthodox analysis. It follows from the assumption that the existing efficiency of industry and the existing efficiency of production are decidedly below what is humanly possible with our existing possessions of knowledge and technique; and the only respect in which it departs from the orthodox hypothesis is to be found in the denial that the entrepreneur—the business man—is always making as much profit as he can. For this view goes a long way beyond the old notion that if you pay a man better you will make *him* more efficient. This view expresses the more up-to-date maxim that if you pay a man better you make *his employer* more efficient, by forcing the employer to discard obsolete methods and plant, and by hastening the exit from industry of less efficient employers, and so raising the standard all round. By hustling the employer, and making him pay wages which he cannot afford to pay at the moment if he is to make a normal profit, you will have the effect of increasing the efficiency of what is called, in the language of Marshall's analysis, 'the representative firm'. In short, the average business man is no longer envisaged as the feverishly active and alert figure of the classical economists, who never missed a chance of making a penny if it was humanly possible, and was always in a state of stimulus up to the limit of his capacity. The new view of him seems to be that he is a fellow who is easy-going and content with a given income and does not bestir himself unduly to increase it to what would be for him the maximum attainable. Therefore, in raising wages you bring into activity latent energies in the entrepreneur out of which the additional wages can be paid. Mr J. W. F. Rowe, in his *Wages in Practice and Theory*, has produced some interesting facts and statistics intended to support this point of view.

The second type of critic makes a much more fundamental attack on the old theory. He questions altogether the rigidity of what economists call the theory of distribution. This theory flows from two sets of assumptions: The first is that the supply of a given factor of production responds in a very sensitive way to the absolute reward offered to it; and the other is that there is a possibility of substitution between the factors of production depending upon the relative rewards offered to them. In popular language, you cannot get the services of a factor in sufficient quantity if you offer it less; on the other hand, if you offer it more relatively to the others, then the other factors will tend to be substituted for it as being more economical. The new theory attacks the rigidity of the solution offered on the basis of these assumptions. It would not dispute that such considerations fix limits within which the actual situation must lie; but it contends that these limits are somewhat wide, and that within them the situation is determined first and foremost by historical influences as gradually modified by contemporary social and political forces.

For example, if the nature of man and the technical means at his disposal were to remain quite unchanged, but everyone was suddenly to forget what has been hitherto the usual range of salaries and remuneration for business men, workers, clerks, and so forth, so that it all had to be worked out again *de novo*, these critics contend that there is no reason to expect that the answer would come out the same as it is now. We should not find that the dividends of the shareholders, the salaries of the managerial staff, and the wages of the office boy would work out just in the existing proportions. These relative rates of remuneration are, they contend, the product of historical and social forces. There are no actual physical or psychological laws which compel them to be what they are now; and if they were to be worked out again in a new situation, we should reach a different answer. Accordingly there is a large arbitrary element in the relative rates of remuneration, and the factors of production get what they do, not because in any strict economic sense they precisely earn it, but because past events have led to these rates being customary and usual. So there is nothing sacrosanct about them. If the working class have the political and bargaining power to get a larger share of the product of industry than formerly, well, that is a new historical fact; historical evolution is this time on their side. The business men will have to get less, and that is all there is to it.*

But it is not only in academic circles that the old orthodoxies about the dangers of high wages are being forgotten. How far the old notions are being overlooked even by the orthodox themselves, and in the homes of the orthodox, is shown, I think, by what happened on the occasion of the return to the gold standard in 1925, when it was believed—I think I have proof positive of this—by the Governor of the Bank of England, the Secretary to the Treasury, and the editor of *The Economist*, that it was possible to increase real wages some 10 per cent by an arbitrary act without producing any untoward consequences—a conclusion which would have shocked, more than one can say, their predecessors in these offices of fifty years ago.

Now I am not here concerned to defend the orthodox analysis and the orthodox hypotheses against these attacks. To a large extent I sympathise with the attacks. I think there is a great deal in what the critics say. I believe that the best working theories of the future will own these assailants as their parents. All those,

* For an able advocacy of the theoretical basis of this point of view, see Mr Maurice Dobb's article 'The Sceptical View of Wages' in *The Economic Journal*, December 1929.

who want to improve economic theory and to make a contribution to it, ought to pay a great deal of attention to what Mr
Dobb and Mr Rowe and others are saying.

My present purpose is, rather, to propose certain qualifications which are in my judgement of great practical importance
when it is a question of applying these ideas in the actual world of
today, and to express grave doubts whether an indiscriminate
public opinion, reinforced by the votes of wage earners, in favour
of raising wages, whenever possible, is really the best means
open to us, within the existing framework of society, for attaining
what is presumably the object, namely, the betterment of the
material conditions of the working class.

For the high-wage party forget that we belong not to a closed
system, but to an international system; and to an international
system, moreover, for which we have deliberately contrived a
very high degree of mobility of international lending. What are
the consequences of this? Let me illustrate by an artificial
example.

Let us suppose two countries where the factors of production
are of exactly equal efficiency, with relations between them in
respect of trading goods and lending money much the same as
exist today between, let us say, Germany and England. Let us
suppose that the high-wage party have their way in one
country—England—but not in the other—Germany. It follows
that the capitalist will receive a smaller proportion of the product
here than abroad. His reward for a given amount of energy and
risk will be less. Consequently he will prefer to invest his money
abroad. It may be that the proportion that he gets in both
countries is, in a sense, arbitrary, and the result of historical and
social influences. But if you have extreme mobility of international lending capital resources will tend to flow towards those
countries where the relative remuneration is greatest. If our
currency standard is not an international one the effort to lend
more money abroad would put the exchanges against us, and by
raising English prices, would bring back real wages in England

to the lower level which previously existed. But under the gold standard the consequences are much more complicated. If English business men are finding the employment of their funds in English businesses relatively unprofitable, and endeavour, therefore, to increase the proportion which they employ abroad, the first effect will be a tendency for gold to flow abroad, for the Bank rate to rise, and for enterprise in England to be yet further embarrassed. From this increased unemployment would ensue, and perhaps, if the unemployment goes on long enough and rises to a sufficiently high level, the final result would be that real wages in England would be driven down again to the old parity. The Bank rate, in its internal aspect, is essentially a means of ensuring that there shall be enough unemployment to put effective pressure on wages so as to cause them to fall to a level which is in equilibrium with external conditions; though this may be attended by friction and opposition, and there may be a great waste of the forces of industry before the new equilibrium is finally brought about.

In short, the extent to which one country can move in these matters, independently of other countries, is greatly affected by the mobility of lending which exists between countries having the same monetary standard.

The consequences of the extreme freedom for foreign lending which we actually enjoy has troubled me ever since I first studied economics. In recent times only have I reached a clear-cut opinion on this subject. That opinion I must not stop to elaborate in this place; for it is relevant to wider subjects than that which I am now discussing. But one thing is clear, namely, that the free field for foreign lending means that the capitalist is free to direct his resources to those parts of the world where the proportion of the product he receives is greatest. How much he gets in any particular place may be due more to social than to economic causes; but that is no obstacle to his preferring to invest where his share is the greatest.

This argument also helps us to answer the old question how

far sweated labour abroad may be injurious to labour at home. The old answer which economists used to give maintained that we do not suffer by sweated labour abroad because we gain as consumers. But whether that be true or not, I think it is true to say that if labour gets a less proportion of the product abroad—if its efficiency wages are less—then capital will get more; consequently capital will tend to drift abroad, putting the exchanges against us, and so, through the concatenation of circumstances I have outlined, producing unemployment, the express purpose of which is to bring wages down to a parity with what they are in the outside world.

So I conclude that even if Mr Rowe and Mr Dobb and others are right—one of them as to the possibility of getting more exertion out of the capitalist, and the other as to the possibility of giving him a smaller conventional share of the total product—there are nevertheless very narrow limits to the practical application of these notions unless they are applied internationally, or unless we place obstacles in the way of the mobility of foreign lending.

It is obvious that this analysis, if it is correct, has some application to the existing position in Great Britain. The period of restoring sterling to gold parity, which culminated in the return to the gold standard in 1925, meant a fairly substantial increase in real wages relatively to what was going on elsewhere. The first effect was to make it difficult for us to export at a profit. People have become fairly familiar with that. But there was a second, more delayed consequence which must not be overlooked. The result of this increase in real wages—the result of leaving money wages unchanged—was a fall of profits; a fall so severe as to make many branches of English business definitely unprofitable.

Now the man who has embarked his capital in a business is generally unable to get it out quickly. But that does not apply to the investment of new resources. When, therefore, English business in many of its branches has been for several years unprofitable, and the outlook is discouraging, it inevitably happens that the active investor, striving to get the maximum return, tends to lend his money to enterprises operating abroad. And in our case, this comes on the top of the natural tendency of new countries to be able to offer higher returns to capital than we can. We already had a situation where the tendency of capital to flow abroad was perhaps in excess of our favourable balance of trade. The additional factor—the high wage movement—has consequently provoked an almost chronic tendency in the direction of dear money, the technical object of which has been partly to prevent excessive lending abroad but also, by damping down home enterprise itself, to put pressure on the whole business world against the high wage movement.

Of course, that is not the only reason for the existing situation, which is extremely complex. But perhaps it is the most permanent, the most obstinate influence. Today, this influence is aggravated by other troubles. At other times, perhaps, we can overlook it for a year or two because other factors are helping us. But all the time there is the underlying tendency for a large part of British business to be relatively unprofitable owing to the existing level of wages, compared with the level of wages abroad; hence capital avoids more and more such outlets as there may be at home and seeks outlets elsewhere.

All this relates to the past. So far as the existing disequilibrium is concerned, I believe that it is impracticable and undesirable to seek the remedy of reducing wages. We must contrive somehow or other, first to mitigate the tendency to excessive foreign lending by finding new openings at home at attractive rates; and for the rest we must, as opportunity offers, try to solve what is still left of our problem by squeezing the higher wages out of increased efficiency. It may not be easy. But I believe it to be easier than the alternative.

But what has happened, should, I suggest, be a warning to us for the future. If we want to better the condition of the working class, it is inexpedient to attempt to do it by the method which reduces the rewards of capital below what is obtainable in other countries. Or, at any rate, if we do adopt this method, we must supplement it by abandoning or diminishing the existing freedom of foreign investment. For it never pays to render the entrepreneur poor and seedy. It is impossible in the present order of society to secure the optimum level of output and employment by any other way than by paying the capitalist his full rate, and, if anything, a little over. As a producer be sure that he makes a good income. That will not prevent the application of a sound system of taxation to the recipient of this income as a citizen, *after* the income has been earned. Once a capitalist has embarked on a given business in a given country he is undoubtedly highly squeezable. But this will not encourage the others. To squeeze him in the act of earning his profits is, I suggest, to squeeze him in the wrong place. Unless, therefore, we make radical changes in the internal structure and external relations of our economic system we shall do well to turn to what I should call the liberal solution, or what I have heard Mr Ramsay MacDonald call the socialist solution, of the problem of bettering the working class, as against the trade union solution.

Compare high taxation with high wages in its effect on the incentive to the business man to increase his output. The taxes only fall on profits after he has earned them, and take only a proportion. Thus, broadly speaking, his inducement to earn profits and to raise his output to the socially optimum level is just as great as if the taxes did not exist. But if you force him to pay higher wages then his less profitable business becomes definitely unprofitable, and you necessarily cause him to abandon it—or part of it—and to reduce his output.

In short, we must not starve the goose that lays the golden eggs before we have discovered how to replace her. We must tax her eggs instead.

But there is another and an even more important point. Artificially high wages burden an industry in direct proportion to the amount of labour employed. Businesses which may be earning high profits and employing relatively little labour get off very lightly. In particular, finance and the like escape almost scot-free. Taxes, therefore, spread the cost of bettering the material condition of the working class over a much wider area.

Finally, the taxation of profit does not discriminate against the use of a particular factor of production, as artificially high wages do. They have no tendency to make employers economise in the use of labour and so throw men out of work.

It is therefore, to my way of thinking, a great misfortune that the concerted self-conscious efforts of the working class to better themselves should be so much concentrated on the effort to raise wages, even to the point of being suspicious, as I fancy the trade unions are, of alternative methods of bettering conditions. For the main *raison d'être* of a trade union as a corporate body is gone if the perpetual struggle for higher wages is to be abandoned.

For, once we face the fact that the level of wages which is socially desirable, having regard to justice and charity in the distribution of wealth, may represent a larger share of the total product than is awarded to labour in some other countries—it becomes very clear that to throw the burden of the betterment onto a particular section of employers is to put them at a hopeless disadvantage with their competitors, and calculated to reduce their output and the volume of employment which they can offer. If we decide that the interests of justice and charity require that the income of the working class should be higher than that which they receive from the economic machine, then we must, so to speak, subscribe to that end. Taxation is a method of compulsory subscription, and the subscription must be spread over the whole community. But if that subscription is made to fall solely on a particular body of employers then we must not be surprised if the level of employment and output is below what it should be.

In the decade immediately before the War there was a strong movement in this direction in the shape of social insurance and free education. Since the War we have gone a great deal further,

particularly in increased insurance and pensions, and in subsidies to working class houses, paying for these things by taxes of
a kind which are not specially deterrent to business enterprise.

If we want to better the condition of the working class there
are plenty of alternative ways of doing it, and plenty of ways of
assigning to them a larger proportion of the total national income
than they have enjoyed in the past otherwise than by increasing
their wages.

First, there is social insurance. It is open to the state to make a
much larger contribution than hitherto, even to the point of
bearing the whole cost of insurance for sickness, old age, and
unemployment. The trade unions would do much better to press
for their insurance to be paid out of taxation than for wages
which are higher than their employers can truly afford.

Second, pensions. It would be possible to increase pensions
substantially without raising them to a level disproportionate
with incomes generally.

Third, there is room for a great increase of useful expenditure
by the state on health, and recreation, and education, and the
facilities for travel.

Fourth, we have by no means reached the limit of what it
would be in the social interest to expend on improving the
housing of the working class, by making it possible to provide
houses for the workers at below the economic rent. It is better to
provide houses below the economic rent out of taxation than to
ask employers to pay more than economic wages.

And finally, there is the possibility of children's and family
allowances. In this case I believe that the trade union movement
is actively hostile on the express ground that it fears such
allowances would be what I wish them to be, namely, an
alternative to higher wages. It would be much better that a man
with heavy family burdens to support should receive assistance
out of taxation, which is thrown on profits generally, than that an
attempt should be made to raise wages paid by his employer to a
disproportionate level.

It is commonly held, I know, that higher taxes would be just

as bad for business enterprise as higher wages, if not more so.
Personally I believe that view to be false. Of course, it would be
better for the capitalist to pay both lower wages and lower taxes;
but if it is a question of choosing between the two then I believe
that higher taxes are a better expedient than higher wages.

The real objection to a policy of higher taxes is, of course, the
difficulty of making sure that they would be an alternative and
not an addition to higher wages. If the business man has already
been weakened by higher wages, we should think twice before
adding the burden of higher taxes. What we really need in the
interest of the well-being of the country as a whole is a new
bargain—though I know it is not humanly possible—by which
wages are reduced or stabilised in return for other advantages
procured by means of higher taxation.

I express no opinion as to whether we can, at the present
juncture, afford any further material betterment of the condition
of the working class. It may be that we should postpone the next
important movement forward until after the return of normal
prosperity. Moreover, it is necessary and important to admit that
there is a limit to the level to which taxes can be raised without
reacting injuriously on industry. My present purpose is limited
to expressing a preference for taxation as a method, rather than
to raise wages to what is, internationally, an uneconomic level.

When we have raised wages as high as possible without
driving the investor to invest abroad, and raised taxes as high as
possible without producing other injurious consequences, we
shall have done all that we can—otherwise than by an increase of
efficiency—to better the conditions of the working class within
the existing framework of society. We can do no more without
abolishing the entrepreneur system; and whether *that* is worth
doing must depend on our judgement as to the technical efficiency
and the moral attractiveness of the alternative.

Well, as in the case of some past economic judgements, those
for example of Ricardo, these frank conclusions of an economist
are capable either of a conservative or of a revolutionary
interpretation. The conservative will conclude that his instinct-

ive feeling, that it is exceedingly dangerous and difficult to stir from the ancient paths and that the old dispensation of serious inequalities in the distribution of wealth is rooted in the nature of things, has received in what I have said an ample justification. On the other hand the liberal and the moderate socialist will be pleased to find that they have been right in their suspiciousness towards extreme trade unionism, that the best way is to continue and to amplify the programme of social services initiated in 1906, and that there is still room for substantial progress along these lines. Finally, the revolutionary will learn from this paper that the position is just what he supposed it to be, namely, that there is practically nothing to be done within the existing framework of society, that it is sheer waste of time tinkering with it, and the only thing worth doing is to organise and prepare for re-volutionary changes. So I am hopeful that for once I may have been able to please everybody.

After Keynes gave his lecture in Manchester, a Mr W. S. Jones wrote to *The Manchester Guardian* asking two questions: was the rate of interest in his discussion of foreign lending net of differential degrees of risk, and what would greater nonwage benefits do to working-class character (foresight, thrift and independence)? Keynes replied on 16 November.

To the Editor of The Manchester Guardian, *16 November 1929*

Sir,

By an accident Mr W. S. Jones's questions addressed to me in your issue of November 9 have only now come to my notice.

To his question whether the nominal rate of interest on foreign investment or a net rate [dis]counted for additional risk is the one relevant to my argument I answer that it was the latter I had in mind.

His suggestion, however, that benefits to the working class, other than high wages, would have a harmful effect 'on the character of the individual' reminds me of an answer which I once received from a little girl, when examining in the local examinations, to the question, 'What is it that the Socialists want to do?' Innocence answered: 'The Socialists think it would do the poor good to make them just like the rich. It would not. It would spoil their characters.'

Yours, &c.,

J. M. KEYNES

On 5 November the Chancellor of the Exchequer formally appointed a Committee on Finance and Industry under the chairmanship of H. P. Macmillan, a Scottish judge. Keynes was among the members, who also included Sir Thomas Allen of the Co-operative Wholesale Society; Ernest Bevin, of the Transport and General Workers Union; Lord Bradbury formerly of the Treasury; R. H. Brand of Lazards, the merchant bankers; Professor T. E. Gregory of the London School of Economics; Lennox Lee of the Federation of British Industries; Cecil Lubbock of Whitbreads the brewers, and a former Deputy Governor of the Bank of England; Reginald McKenna of the Midland Bank and a former Chancellor of the Exchequer; J. T. Walton Newbold, editor of *The Social Democrat*; Sir Walter Raine, a coal exporter; J. Frater Taylor of Armstrong Whitworth; and A. R. G. Tulloch of the District Bank. The terms of reference of the Committee were:

To inquire into banking, finance and credit, paying regard to the factors both internal and international which govern their operation, and to make recommendations calculated to enable these agencies to promote the development of trade and commerce and the employment of labour.

The Committee held its first preliminary meeting on 21 November. Keynes's role in its deliberations is the subject of Chapter 2.

Four days later Keynes was invited to a luncheon with the Prime Minister on 2 December. The invitation was the basis of his remark that he was 'becoming fashionable again'. The meeting was to discuss the current industrial situation and ways of improving the information and advice available to the government. The meeting was announced in the press, leading Keynes to expect little from it. As he told Lydia the day before,

I don't know what sort of a party Ramsay's is to be tomorrow. But they are announcing it in the press, and today Garvin's leader in *The Observer* is about nothing else. It probably means that there will be too many people there for anything useful to be said.

At the luncheon, in addition to Keynes, were Lord Weir, Sir Andrew Duncan, Sir Warren Fisher, Walter Layton, G. D. H. Cole, Professor Henry Clay and Thomas Jones. After the discussion, those present were asked to send in memoranda on the topics discussed and to meet again a week later. Keynes obliged with a memorandum.

THE INDUSTRIAL SITUATION

The Prime Minister to announce that he has been considering with the leaders of the financial and business world, with the trade unions and with certain economists whether there is a real justification for a certain atmosphere of business pessimism and lethargy which he seems to detect; or whether, on the contrary, the present may not be a favourable time for a drastic reorganisation and re-equipment of the industry of the country on a considered plan, having regard to what, with reasonable optimism, we can expect to be the economic prospects of the country five or ten years hence; and for a determined and united onslaught by all sections of the community on the problem of unemployment.

The result of these enquiries, backed up by the various statements to be appended, is to persuade him that it is now practicable to attack the problems of the future in a new spirit of optimism and energy.

The Government, wishing for their part to provide the best possible atmosphere for confidence and new developments, think it appropriate at this moment to give certain undertakings to the business world in order to enable industrial leaders to lay their plans in conditions of as much security and freedom from sudden surprises as is in any way possible.

The Government announce, therefore, that without in any way abating their objection in principle or their freedom to introduce modifications at some later date, no change will be made in the McKenna or Safeguarding Duties during the year 1930; that no changes in the coal industry will be introduced during this period which are calculated on balance to worsen the financial situation of the coal mines as compared with the present position;* and that no important new commitments involving taxation, beyond those of which the public already knows, will be entered into between now and the forthcoming Budget.

But if the Government on their side are prepared to do what lies in their power to ease the immediate situation, it is necessary that the business world for their part should tackle the problems which lie to their hand with more energy and enterprise than has been apparent in some quarters in recent months.

In particular, it is important that sound schemes for the rationalisation of industry—especially in the heavy industries and in textiles—should not be obstructed by vested interests or by individuals whose own personal position may possibly be changed for the worse by new schemes. Those in the positions of higher command in business who are no longer in the prime of life should consider whether they should not give place to their successors, and directors who are no longer able to give the same mental energy to their duties as at one time should facilitate in every way the passing of control into other hands.

There should then be subjoined a number of statements as follows from various authorities:

II

First and foremost there should be a declaration [by] the Governor of the Bank of England that in his view the apparent termination of the epoch of dear money in the United States has entirely altered the situation so far as concerns the risks of allowing a general easing of credit conditions in this country. He is therefore ready, without of course committing himself as to the precise level of Bank rate at any given time, and in the absence of any disturbing circumstances of a kind which cannot

---

* Personally I am in favour of a subsidy to miners' wages, equivalent to half the proposed reduction in hours, for a period of two years. This would not cost much (say £2,500,000 a year) but I know that most people think it too shocking to mention.

be foreseen at the moment, to give an assurance to the business world that they can lay their plans with every expectation that during the coming year the available credit will be ample for all requirements. He declares, further, that the Bank of England will be prepared to make itself responsible, failing assistance from other quarters, for supplying any capital which may be required for schemes for the rationalisation of industry which are shown to the satisfaction of the Bank to be well conceived and calculated to attain their object.

III

There would next follow a declaration signed by the chairmen of the Big Five banks to the effect that they concur in the opinion expressed by the Governor of the Bank of England as to the general prospects and giving to the business world assurances that they will do everything in their power to satisfy demands for credit, which are presented to them and are in their opinion satisfactory; particularly those concerned with the rationalisation of existing concerns, with the initiation of new enterprises, and with the development of export markets.

IV

A statement by the leading trade unions, the Federation of British Industries, and the leading employers' associations that they will be content during 1930 with the *status quo* in wages and will observe a truce in regard to labour disputes.

V

A statement on behalf of the leading issue houses that for the present they will give priority to loans for home purposes and to such foreign loans as are directly calculated to lead to important new orders to home industry, and will be mainly governed in making new issues by a consideration of the direct and indirect advantages which they can secure for British business.

VI

A statement on behalf of the leading building societies that the lower rates for money now available should act as an encouragement to new housebuilding and that they have ample funds to assist all new applicants on reasonable terms.

VII

A statement by the chairmen of the four railway companies that the results for the year 1929, having regard to the great economies which have been made, are financially far more satisfactory than those of 1928; that economies in management and personnel have by no means reached their limit; and that the recent negotiations with bus companies have now reached a point which may be considered to have solved the pre-existing conflict of interest between road and rail transport for passengers. Accordingly, they feel that the basis exists for a confident programme, both as regards the development of railway equipment and for co-operation between road and rail facilities.

VIII

The lords mayor of the principal cities and the Chairman of the London County Council should declare that the bodies over which they preside have decided to accelerate all work in prospect which is capable of acceleration without waste; and the Minister of Health, or other appropriate authority, should add a declaration that he will facilitate to the utmost of his power the activities of these and other local authorities in properly completing the equipment of the country so far as it lies within the scope of the local authorities. The Treasury should at the same time announce a reduction in the rates of interest charged on new local loans.

IX

Finally, full statements should be made on behalf of the Central Electricity Board, the Road Board, the proposed London Traffic Board and any other public or semi-public bodies which have development programmes in view, that they are accelerating these programmes to the full extent of their power. Figures should be given wherever possible.

At the next meeting, on 9 December, those attending differed slightly from the previous occasion[2] and the discussion centred much more on the type of body and the kinds of economic advice the Government needed. Again there was a request for memoranda and again a further meeting was planned for the next Monday. Keynes responded the next day.

ECONOMIC GENERAL STAFF

I. *The duties of an Economic General Staff*

(i) To engage in continuous study of current problems affecting national economic policy in regard to the development and organisation of industry and commerce, national finance and the distribution of wealth.

The following are a few examples of the sort of questions which should have been the subject of such study in the last few years.

1. The reactions of currency disturbances abroad on British industry.

2. The effect of tariffs and policies of national self-sufficiency abroad on British trade.

3. The return to the gold standard.

4. The effects of unrestricted foreign investment and the

---

[2] Lord Wier was not present, while additions to the group were Mr J. H. Thomas, Sir Josiah Stamp, Sir Kenneth Stewart, J. A. Hobson, Walter Citrine and Colonel David Carnegie.

possibility of controlling the rate and kind of foreign lending.

5. Credit and industry (including all the questions now to be examined by the Committee on Finance and Industry).

6. The housing problem.

7. The effect of the rating system on industry and on housing.

8. The unemployment problem.

9. The state of agriculture.

10. The staple export trades.

11. The obstacles to the rationalisation of industry and the means of overcoming them—taken industry by industry.

12. The special problems of the coal industry.

13. The bearing of the prospective rate of population growth on education programmes, housing, pensions, etc.

14. The social and business consequences of a high level of direct taxation.

15. The reactions of hours, wages and conditions of labour abroad on similar conditions at home.

16. Trade union restrictions.

17. The public concern.

18. The direction of investment.

Very few of the above are strictly matters of departmental interest until they are actually ripe to be the subject of legislation or administration. But when competent commissions are appointed to study them, their reports generally come too late or represent a compromise between different interests and opinions, rather than a strictly expert analysis based solely on scientific and technical grounds.

The pressing problems of the future may, and of course in many cases will, be on quite different points from the above.

(ii) To co-ordinate and advise as to the collection of statistical and other information required by the Government, by Parliament and by scientific economists.

It should be the duty of the Staff to keep an eye on the completeness and co-ordination of the statistical information collected by Government Departments; but it is not desirable that they should attempt to create a separate statistical department. It should rather be their duty to suggest to the appropriate Government Department (including the Government Actuary) ways of improving and extending their existing statistical work.

(iii) To act on its own initiative in calling the attention of the Prime Minister or of the Cabinet to important tendencies and changes at home or abroad.

(iv) To suggest to the Government plans for solving fundamental economic difficulties, such for instance as the avoidance of chronic unemployment, the development of national resources, the difficulties of the export trades, or the obstacles in the way of rationalising industries.

(v) To supply secretarial and expert assistance to such commissions or committees as may be appointed from time to time, on the lines of the committees now appointed by the Committee of Civil Research, whenever the subject matter is economic in character.

It should be the duty of the Staff to keep in close touch with outside experts of all kinds, and it should have the power, with the assent of the Prime Minister, to set up mixed committees on which outside experts and representatives would sit— sometimes together with Ministers, members of the Staff itself, or other civil servants—to report, sometimes for publication and sometimes for the private information of the Government, on particular problems and projects.

(vi) In addition to temporary *ad hoc* committees, there should be a permanent panel or scientific committee of economists and others, for which the Staff would act as secretariat, which would be expected to give, confidentially, impartial outside advice and assistance on any questions which the Government of the day may wish to submit to it.

(vii) In all its activities it would be a primary duty of the Staff to keep in the closest possible touch with the main Government Departments dealing with economic matters, and to avoid overlapping in any way with the proper functions of the latter. Wherever any sort of administrative or executive action is in question, the Staff should never act except through the appropriate Administrative Department. It should be a purely advisory body with no other responsibilities or powers.

(viii) It is worth considering whether there should not be a permanent Committee of Economic Policy, consisting either of the Cabinet Ministers primarily responsible for economic departments* under the chairmanship of the Prime Minister, or the principal permanent officials of such departments, to which the Chief of the Economic General Staff would act as secretary, and to which all questions of primary importance relating to economic and financial policy would be referred in the first instance.

II. *The status and organisation of the Staff*

The Staff would form a very small separate organ, somewhat like the Cabinet Secretariat—of which indeed it might, in point of form, be considered a branch—closely attached to the Prime Minister and to the Cabinet. Since officials who are not concerned with executive and administrative responsibilities always run the risk of being left out of [in?] the cold, it would be vital to give the Chief of the Staff a position of sufficient prestige and importance to ensure that he could obtain the attention of the Prime Minister and the Cabinet to matters to which he attached importance. That is to say, he should be regarded as a considerable officer of the state.

The higher personnel of the secretariat of the Staff should be very few in number, certainly less than a dozen in the first instance, but should be the best experts available and should be sufficiently well remunerated to ensure that the most suitable persons possible could always be obtained. It might, perhaps, be

---

* E.g. The Prime Minister, the Chancellor of the Exchequer, the President of the Board of Trade, and the Ministers of Labour, Health and Agriculture.

desirable to give a modest annual retaining fee to the members of the proposed permanent Scientific Committee.

Appointments to the Staff should not necessarily be of the same permanent character as in the regular Civil Service, but might sometimes be (e.g.) for periods of five years, or—where special problems had to be examined—purely temporary. This would not prevent permanent civil servants being seconded to the Staff from time to time. For it would be desirable that there should be a considerable amount of interchange between the Staff, economic appointments in the outside academic world, and the chief technical economic posts in regular Government Departments. Members of the Staff might, perhaps, be allowed occasionally not to break entirely their relations with universities or similar bodies, provided these were fully compatible with their carrying out their duties and with their making their Staff work their chief call and main preoccupation; for this would have the positive advantage of keeping touch with the latest academic work and the younger men. But it should, of course, be absolutely forbidden to members of the Staff to maintain relations of any kind with the business and financial world, in respect of which they would be under the strictest Civil Service conditions;—which would also apply to their writing for publication over their own names or appearing in any public capacity.

The object of the above would be to obtain the services— generally for a limited period whilst they are in the prime of their powers—of individuals whose bent and desire is to devote their lives to scientific research, and to guiding from the centre the evolution of the economic structure, rather than to administration or to politics.

III. *The need for such a body*

The advantage to the Prime Minister, in view of the rapidly changing and intensely difficult problems of the modern age, of having at his elbow such a body as is here proposed hardly needs elaborating. Mr Ramsay MacDonald felt it in 1924 and everything which has happened since has emphasised the desirability of creating such an organ as he then contemplated. Indeed the necessities of the situation have already called into existence by devious and anonymous paths the nucleus, and in many ways the model, of the proposed Staff in the shape of the Committee of Civil Research.

The foregoing may be open to the charge of magnifying unduly the functions and importance of what is proposed. But a move along these lines would indeed be an act of statemanship, the importance of which cannot easily be exaggerated. For it would mark a transition in our conceptions of the functions and purposes of the state, and a first measure towards the deliberate and purposive guidance of the evolution of our economic life. It would be a recognition of the enormous part to be played in this by the scientific spirit as distinct from the sterility of the purely party attitude, which is never more out of place than in relation to complex matters of fact and interpretation involving technical difficulty. It would mean the beginning of ways of doing and thinking about political problems which are probably necessary for the efficient working of modern democracy. For it would be an essay in the art of combining representative institutions and the voice of public opinion with the utilisation by Governments of the best technical advice in spheres, where such advice can never, and should not, have the last word or the power, but must be a necessary ingredient in the decisions of those who have been entrusted by the country with the last word and with the power.

J. M. K.

10 December 1929

The final meeting on 16 December had the participants from the previous two meetings plus the Chancellor of the Exchequer, Philip Snowden. It discussed the memoranda from Keynes and others on the functions and status of an advisory committee.

Two days later the Government began formal preparations for an Economic Advisory Council. The Prime Minister announced its formation on 22 January 1930. A Treasury Minute of 27 January set out its terms of reference and its organisation. The Council's purpose was:

> To advise His Majesty's Government in economic matters, to make continuous study of developments in trade and industry and in the use of national and imperial resources, of the effect of legislation and fiscal policy at home and abroad and of all aspects of national, imperial and international economy with a bearing on the prosperity of the country.

The Prime Minister was to chair the Council, and the Chancellor, the President of the Board of Trade, the Lord Privy Seal and the Minister of Agriculture were designated members. Other Ministers might be summoned from time to time. Other members might be chosen 'in virtue of their special knowledge and experience of industry and economics'. On 15 February the Prime Minister announced the Council's non-ministerial members. Besides Keynes, the fifteen names included Sir Arthur Balfour, Managing Director of Arthur Balfour and Co.; Ernest Bevin, General Secretary of the Transport and General Workers' Union; Sir John Cadman, Chairman of Anglo-Persian Oil and Iraq Petroleum; Walter Citrine, General Secretary of the Trades Union Congress; G. D. H. Cole, the Oxford economist; Ernest Debenham, a Director of Lloyds Bank; Sir Andrew Duncan, Chairman of the Central Electricity Generating Board; Sir Alfred Lewis, Chief General-Manager of the National Provincial Bank; Sir William McLintock, the accountant; Sir Josiah Stamp, Chairman of the London, Midland and Scottish Railway; and R. H. Tawney, the economic historian. Hubert Henderson, partly at Keynes's urging, became the senior economist on the permanent staff of the Council, leaving his job with *The Nation* and refusing the offer of a chair at the London School of Economics in consequence. The other permanent staff were Thomas Jones and A. F. Hemming of the Council's predecessor organisation, the Committee of Civil Research, and three economists, H. V. Hodson, Colin Clark and Piers Debenham (the son of Sir Ernest), the last unpaid.

On 4 January 1930, in his second last appearance as editor of *The Nation*, Hubert Henderson wrote an article favouring retention of the McKenna Duties imposed during the war on certain classes of manufactures. The result was a minor political uproar in Liberal circles. Two weeks later, in an unsigned article, Henderson reaffirmed his stand.

The same day *The Evening Standard* in a leading article attributed both of Henderson's articles to Keynes. Keynes, although deeply affected by the illness and death of Frank Ramsay on 18 January, replied in a letter to the editor published on 20 January.

To the Editor of The Evening Standard, *20 January 1930*

Sir

You do me too much honour in ascribing to my pen the recent articles in *The Nation* on the McKenna Duties. I did not write these articles. But I agree with them—together, I believe with the great majority of reasonable free traders. For it is no part of orthodox free trade theory that duties are injurious to the protected industry, or that established tariffs can be suddenly removed without doing any harm.

If Mr Snowden were to take off the existing protectionist duties, I assume that his object in doing this would be to increase the amount of unemployment for the time being, in order to bring further pressure to bear for the reduction of wages, and so enable our other industries to compete more successfully in world markets.

But, personally, I feel that this medicine is too severe for our present circumstances.

J. M. KEYNES

Three weeks later a *Nation* leader attacked Lord Beaverbrook's proposals for Empire Free Trade. The next day, *The Sunday Express*, a Beaverbrook newspaper, vented its fury on 'Professor Keynes, whose knowledge of commerce has been gained from University text-books rather than from practical experience' and accused him of 'even greater myopia' than Lloyd George whom he advised. Keynes replied in a letter published on 16 February.

To the Editor of The Sunday Express, *16 February 1930*

Sir

Your leading article of last Sunday has been brought to my notice. I shall be glad if you will give publicity to the following denials:

(1) I am not and never have been the editor of *The Nation*, and did not write the article you attribute to me;

(2) I am not and never have been a professor;

(3) I do not suffer from myopia.

It does not follow from the above denials that I am an Empire Crusader. On the other hand, I do not think so badly of Professor Beaverbrook as to attribute to him the authorship of your leader.

J. M. KEYNES

On 28 January, Keynes spoke to an informal meeting of the Council for the Preservation of Rural England. The day before he had set his proposals down on paper.

OUTLINE OF FINANCIAL PROPOSALS FOR RURAL PRESERVATION

This plan proceeds from the following assumptions.—

1. It is a matter of *great* urgency to have some scheme put into operation by Central Authority which shall prevent sporadic exploitation of what should be preserved as wild or open country.

2. The areas which it is necessary to protect cover a much wider space than can be looked after by private bodies, or even by local authorities unaided by the central Government.

3. The areas where some precautions are necessary represent a much larger amount of land than it would be advisable for Public Authorities to take into their own possession, at any rate at the present time.

4. Nor is there any need to interfere with the present management and ownership of much of the land, so long as matters proceed much as at present with the lands used in the main for agricultural and sporting purposes, etc.

The financial cost of the following proposal is far less formidable and can be spread over a much longer period than would be the case with a scheme of outright purchase. The scheme is primarily designed for lands which are comparatively barren from the economic point of view such as the South Downs, Dartmoor and Exmoor, the Lakes, etc. But it can also be made applicable to rural preservation in the neighbourhood of towns, where the land is likely to be of greater economic value.

The proposal is as follows:

1. A Committee to be set up to specify all areas which in their opinion ought to be protected from future development, or developed, if at all, under supervision. These areas might be classified in three classes—(*a*) suitable for National Parks (*b*) open agricultural or sporting country (*c*) protected belts in the neighbourhood of towns.

2. This Committee to be followed by a continuing Commission with statutory powers to schedule areas (after an opportunity has been given for objections to be raised). In the case of lands so scheduled no development or other activity to be permitted, which would have the effect of changing materially the outward appearance of such lands, except under licence from the Commission, which shall not be unreasonably withheld.

2. The lands so scheduled to be valued on two bases, namely:

(*a*) Twenty years' purchase of their present Schedule A valuation for income tax exclusive of assessments in respect of buildings (called hereafter their *income value*), and

(*b*) Their value (exclusive of buildings) in the open market at the date of the Act of Parliament which sets this machinery in motion coming into force (called hereafter their *capital value*).

3. Scheduled lands to have the following advantages:

(*a*) The Commission to pay to their owners every year an amount equal to the Schedule A income tax payable in respect of them (exclusive of assessments in respect of buildings), so that they are in effect freed from income tax.

(*b*) Their capital value as assessed above to be exempted from death duties.

4. The Commission to have the right at any time hereafter to purchase scheduled areas or any part of them at their capital value as fixed, once and for all, under 2 (*b*) above, together with the value of the buildings as at the date of the exercise of this right.

5. Where the capital value is more than double the income value on the average of the whole of an area in a single ownership at the date of the Act, the Commission shall have an option:

(a) To exclude any part of the estate from their schedule and recalculate capital and income values on the reduced area.

(b) To purchase outright any part of the estate by paying its capital value and recalculate capital and income values for the balance on the basis of the reduced area; or

(c) In the event of their proceeding to schedule an area having a capital value more than double its income value, they must make an annual payment to the owner of $2\frac{1}{2}$ per cent on the excess of the capital value over twice the income value.

6. The Commission to have powers to release land from schedule at any subsequent time, when the above privileges will also cease; or, either on their own initiative or on the application of any Local Government body or town planning authority, to schedule further areas on the same general terms, subject to modification as to the date at which the valuations are made.

7. The Commission to have placed at its disposal by the Treasury £1,000,000 a year plus the revenues from any land which it may have purchased as below, out of which to meet its expenses, to make payments to owners of land under 3(a) and 5(c) above, and to employ the balance at its discretion to purchase land outright under 4 above or by negotiation. Thus the total cost to the Treasury would be £1,000,000 a year *plus* the cost of the exemption from death duties.

Since a large part of the lands in question would have a very low annual value for Schedule A income tax, the above fund should be sufficient to allow the scheduling of a very large area of wild country and to provide a margin year by year to finance outright purchase for the purpose of gradually forming National Parks and to deal with the most expensive problem of forming protected belts in the neighbourhood of towns.

J. M. KEYNES

27 January 1930

These proposals led to further correspondence with Raymond Unwin, the technical adviser to the Greater London Regional Planning Committee.

From RAYMOND UNWIN, *7 February 1930*

Dear Mr Maynard Keynes,

Since we met at the C.P.R.E. dinner recently, I have been considering your interesting proposal as a means for securing what we all wish in regard to rural preservation and regional planning.

With reference to your proposals, there are one or two points about which I should like further information, as I may easily have misunderstood your intention.

First of all as regards compensation for the excess of the market value of the estate over its value for revenue as indicated by the Schedule A valuation: seeing that the reservation of land from use for building development does not affect the Schedule A value, but does cancel, so long as it remains in force, the difference between that value and the market value, I do not see how the payment of the Schedule A charges can be regarded as even a distant approximation to fair dealing. Assuming that we have three owners A, B and C, that each owns one acre of land which is to be reserved from building use in different situations and that the Schedule A valuations for the three acres are respectively 10/–, 30/– and 60/– per acre and the capital values are £10, £30 and £60; assuming also that there is no excess building value on these plots: there are three other owners A1, B1 and C1 owning similar acres, assessed at the same Schedule A but having values just within your limit, which for the sake of round figures we can take at £20, £60 and £120. To compensate for a loss which in the case of A, B, and C, is purely sentimental, but which in the case of A1, B1 and C1 varies from £10 to £60 capital value, it is proposed, as I understand it, to pay to A and to A1 2/– per annum, to B and to B1 6/– per annum, and to C and to C1 12/– per annum. This seems so detached from the merits of each case, that I do not quite see what is gained by dealing with the matter through Schedule A assessment.

Passing then to the death duties, the case becomes more difficult because death duties are assessed on a varying percentage, which depends not on the value of the single acre of land with which we are concerned, but on the total value of the estate which is left. Taking one case only, that of C1 above; assuming that he leaves an estate of only £500, he will be remitted in effect, by way of compensation for the reservation of his acre of land 2 per cent of £60 or £1.4s. There might, however, be another man D whose conditions agree in every respect with those of C1, but who leaves an estate valued at £2,000,000. In his case the remission for a similar restriction on a similar acre would be 40 per cent on £60, that is £24. If I have rightly understood the working of this arrangement, I do not see that there is any approach to fair dealing sufficiently near to justify the bringing into any proposal all the difficulties which must be involved when the revenue of the Treasury is in any way to be affected.

As regards the alternative proposal which is being seriously considered by the Town Planning Department of the Government, by the Central Landowners Association, the Surveyors' Institution and other similar bodies, I did not of course attempt to make anything like a complete statement of this, and I think from some of your criticisms of it, my statement was not too clear. I should, however, be very glad indeed if you would look over the proposals, because they do not involve any attempt to secure the ordinary increment on land values, and we are rather anxious that the proposals should not be confused with that question.

I am sending you a preliminary printed memorandum, which states the problem generally, and a supplementary typed memorandum, which goes into the question of the means proposed for dealing with the matter. I think there is at present considerable political possibility of getting something along these lines passed. I doubt very much whether there is a good prospect of securing an annual grant from Parliament for the purpose of paying to owners compensation for something which the owners themselves fully admit is not lost to them as a body, which no single owner of all the land affected would need to ask for, and which merely involves some method of adjustment between them. The chief danger politically that I fear is that something in the way of an indiscriminate tax on increment values might be attempted which would not distinguish between the different causes of increment value and might render our problem more difficult, at any rate for a longish period.

Forgive this long letter.

> Believe me,
> Yours sincerely,
> RAYMOND UNWIN

To RAYMOND UNWIN, *12 February 1930*

Dear Mr Unwin,

Many thanks for your letter. I admit great force in your arguments, and have no completely satisfactory logical reply to make to them.

My reason for making a payment based on Schedule A value, even when there was no difference between that value and market value, was intended partly to oil the wheels, partly because the restrictions proposed would certainly do some injury to landowners in restricting their freedom hereafter and their remoter possibilities of profit even though the expectation of this was not very tangibly represented in market value. My reason for making extra payment when the market value was double the Schedule A value was simply a rough and ready one. It seemed to me that up to that point the compensation already being given was adequate, and that supplementary payment only became necessary at about that point. But very probably some more meticulous scale would be preferable.

Nor have I any logical answer to your death duty point. It is quite true that the concessions would be worth much more to the large landowner than to the small. But I think that the large landowner who goes on holding big tracts of country and is prepared to have them sterilised has much to complain about in respect of the present death duties, and that it would be well worth while to get his goodwill for the scheme by doing a little to remedy what he at least feels as an injustice. But on the basis of purely arithmetical calculation I have, as I say, no answer to your point.

The essence of my suggestion lies, of course, not in the particular scale of compensation suggested, but in the idea of making an annual payment to landowners in return for sterilisation (or reservation if that phrase is preferred), whilst leaving the land undisturbed in its present ownership. That is the essential point, to my mind. The precise scale of compensation and the manner of calculating it are further matters, on which my opinion is not worth much. Probably my details are bad. I chose them because they seemed to me to be a rough and ready way of approaching the matter, which would obviously cost comparatively little, and yet would oil the wheels amazingly.

There is another point on which I should be ready to make a concession in my original statement. I think that my scheme is primarily applicable to the wilder open spaces of the country, and not so applicable to belts in the neighbourhood of towns. I

35

should be inclined, therefore, to restrict it to that and to leave the latter to plans such as your own, with the possibility of pooling where this is feasible. But in practice, any kind of pooling will raise endless difficulties, and I confess I am afraid that the whole thing may be held back by the practical opposition which will arise to pooling schemes. It is extremely difficult to prove that a given landlord has benefited by any specific amount through the reservation of areas in his neighbourhood. Nor is it quite correct that the total value of land in the neighbourhood of towns is left unaltered by reservation. If you take away the possibility of developing land which has special amenity value owing to its surroundings, etc., it by no means follows that you add precisely that amount to the amenity value of less attractive sites without similar surroundings.

You will see that I am more anxious to get things done than to bother about what seem to me comparatively minor questions of equity (though *sometimes* I agree pooling is essential if one is to avoid merely giving a present to a neighbouring landlord).

If I publish my scheme, as I shall not do at once, but may do later on, I shall take advantage of the criticisms of yourself and others to modify its details very materially.

Yours sincerely,
[Copy initialled] J. M. K.

From RAYMOND UNWIN, *13 February 1930*

Dear Mr Keynes,

Very many thanks for writing so fully about your scheme. I am inclined to agree with you that the alternative scheme, which we may roughly call 'pooling of interests', is more applicable for land in the neighbourhood of urban development, than for the wide rural areas. It is for that reason that I am particularly interested in your proposals, and very glad to find that you are likely to work them out further.

In giving evidence before the National Parks Committee, I suggested that apart from the reservation of a few outstanding areas, the most promising line for the Committee to take would be to recommend that the National Exchequer should make some contribution to the reservation of large open spaces in regional planning schemes—very much on the lines that the Middlesex County Council do in relation to minor Town Planning Authorities within the County. The Middlesex C.C. have undertaken to contribute 75 per cent of the cost of all open spaces which they consider to have not merely local but regional importance within the County of Middlesex. We anticipate that under new powers, some of which come into force within a month or two, and some we hope to secure in amendments to the Town Planning Act, it would be possible for County Councils to carry out singly or jointly very large regional planning schemes covering protection of amenity and reservation of regional open spaces, leaving the detail schemes still to be dealt with by the Local Authorities. If there were some fund such as you suggest, out of which contributions could be made by some central department, to assist these Regional Planning Authorities in carrying out the large scale reservations, wherever they can be regarded as having some wide national importance, or even as a general means of apportioning some of the cost as national instead of local, I think this would greatly stimulate the kind of work that we want.

I very much hope that you will continue to work at the problem, and I am entirely with you as to the urgency and as to the importance of getting some scheme which can readily be put into operation.

Again thanking you,

> I am,
> Yours sincerely,
> RAYMOND UNWIN

By this stage, however, Keynes was heavily involved in the work of the Macmillan Committee.

Chapter 2

THE MACMILLAN COMMITTEE

After its appointment on 5 November 1929 the Macmillan Committee met for the first time on 21 November. A week later it examined its first witness, Sir Ernest Harvey, the Deputy Governor of the Bank of England. In all, the Committee was to spend 49 days taking oral evidence and, if we are to go by the references in Keynes's appointments book, it met 100 times before Keynes left for America at the end of May 1931. Keynes dominated the proceedings of the Committee, both in examining witnesses and shaping the report. The other active members were Reginald McKenna, T. E. Gregory, R. H. Brand and Ernest Bevin.

Keynes's efforts to shape the work of the Committee led him in February and March 1930 to spend five sessions elaborating his approach to monetary theory and policy, which reflected his work on the final stages of his *Treatise on Money* (*JMK*, vols. V and VI) which was to appear in October 1930. The transcript of this 'private evidence' was discussed in the Treasury, and was also passed to R. G. Hawtrey before he gave evidence to the Committee in April 1930.

Keynes began his presentation at the meeting on 20 February after the Committee had heard nine witnesses.

COMMITTEE ON FINANCE AND INDUSTRY

Note of discussion on
Thursday, 20 February 1930
Present:
The Rt Hon. Lord Macmillan (*Chairman*)

Sir Thomas Allen	Mr Cecil Lubbock
Mr Ernest Bevin	The Rt Hon. Reginald McKenna
The Rt Hon. Lord Bradbury, G.C.B.	Mr J. T. Walton Newbold
The Hon. R. H. Brand, C.M.G.	Sir Walter Raine
Professor T. E. Gregory, D.SC.	Mr J. Frater Taylor
Mr J. M. Keynes, C.B.	Mr A. A. G. Tulloch
Mr Lennox B. Lee	Mr G. Ismay (*Secretary*)

(CHAIRMAN) *I think our arrangement today was that Mr Keynes should discuss the general outlook of our inquiry with us. I imagine that Mr Keynes would welcome interpolations at the various stages?* Yes, Mr Chairman, it would help me very much if members would interrupt me. If their questions belong to some later part of the argument they will excuse me if I postpone them, but apart from that it would help me very much.

You would not wish that it should be a mere monologue, but a discussion in which you should take a leading part. Would you tell us the topics which you think we could usefully discuss? It is an extraordinarily difficult task. What I really want to do is to give some account of the general character of the theory which mainly influences my mind in considering the practical issues which are before us. It is very difficult to give you a part of this theory without mentioning the whole of it; yet, if I were to try to do that I should be excessively prolix.

I have decided that probably the best way will be to begin rather in the middle and then work forwards and backwards, starting from the things that are probably relatively familiar and keeping till the last some of the things which I hold of great importance but which are likely to be less familiar.

I think it will be useful if, first of all we go through the more or less orthodox theory of how Bank rate works, the classical theory of Bank rate as it has existed in this country for the last 50 years.

So long as we are on a gold standard the fundamental principle of our currency management has to be that the difference between our international receipts and payments which we have to meet or receive in gold shall never be very large. We cannot afford to lose large quantities of gold or, at any rate not to lose them continuously. So that the primary task of currency management is to keep an approximate equality between our international receipts and payments. This balance is made up of two parts. There is first of all the balance on income account, the excess of our receipts in respect of interest, exports, freights, and so forth over our outgoings in respect of what we have to pay for imports, etc. On income account that balance is normally in our favour; I do not suppose there has ever been a year when it has not been in our favour. Normally there is a large balance. Secondly, there is the balance on capital account, which is the excess of what we lend foreigners over what we borrow from them, and that normally is adverse to us; that is to say, we are lending on balance in most years. So that the task of the Bank of England is to equate within reasonable limits our favourable balance on income account with our adverse balance on capital account.

(MR BRAND) *By 'lending to foreigners' do you include purchase of securities?* Yes, all transactions of a capital character, all purchases of securities, all purchases of assets situated abroad.

(MR MCKENNA) *Short term as well as long?* Short term as well as long. The useful distinction is between those transactions which you think of as current income transactions and those you think of as capital transactions. Now the balance in our favour on income account depends, broadly speaking, on relative prices at home and abroad. If our prices are higher than other people's we tend to sell less to them and buy more from them. So that it is the comparative price level here and elsewhere which determines the fluctuations in our favourable balance on income account. It is also governed not only by relative prices, but by the absolute prices of those exports of which we make rather a speciality—in particular, freights. For example, at this moment the average of freights is 30 per cent lower than it was a year ago. Our gross receipts from freights are a very big figure—I do not know if anybody knows it—something of the order of £150,000,000 a year; so that quite irrespective of whether our freight is lower than other people's or not, a fall of that degree in the price of one of our specialities is a very serious thing for us. What happened on the other hand during the boom of 1919–20 certainly very much increased our favourable balance on income account.

It is a question of price, partly whether our prices as compared with other people's are competitive prices and partly a question of absolute prices. On the other hand, our dealings in respect of capital transactions depend very little on price; they depend on rates of interest, rates of profit. The movement of short money is not governed by whether prices are higher here or elsewhere, it is governed by whether rates of interest are higher here than elsewhere; and the inclination of the investor to buy American common stocks or British ordinary shares is governed by his estimate of the rate of profit in relation to the price in the two countries. So that those two elements, which have to be kept in approximate equality, fluctuate under quite different sets of influences, one of them under what we can broadly call price influence, the other under what we can broadly call interest influence.

May I suggest 'price level' instead of 'price'? Price level, certainly. And, of course, by interest rates in this connection one has to mean not the actual interest rate, but the net interest rate after allowing for risk, for investment fashions, for whatever attracts or deters people. It is sometimes convenient to say that interest rates have gone higher abroad, when you merely mean that a given rate of interest is more attractive to the investor. For example, when the English investor is afraid of the bonds of South American countries so that he needs a much higher rate of interest to attract him, that operates very much as a low rate of interest would if you were to leave out these other elements of attraction. At the moment, when people are attracted by American securities as against English it may not be the rate of interest—the rate of interest may be higher here than in America—it may be the rate of interest plus all these other elements that attract or repel them in making their investment.

Consequently, the equality between those two elements in our international accounts—the income balance and the capital balance—has to be preserved partly by influencing prices and partly by influencing interest rates. You could not over long periods keep the two approximately equal if you only had the power to influence one of them because the thing would be cumulative. In order to preserve the equality you would have to do absurd things with price levels or with interest rates if you were limited to influencing only one of those two factors.

Now the only normal method which is open to the Bank of England for its currency management is by altering the terms of bank lending. I include in the terms of bank lending both the quantity of credit and the rate of interest charged for it. There has been too much inclination, I think Mr McKenna would agree, in the past to mean by the terms of bank lending nothing more than Bank rate in the narrow sense. I shall often use Bank rate as a convenient shorthand for the terms of lending as a whole including alterations in the quantity of credit as well as in the price for it. So that the only method the Bank of England has of affecting either of these two factors, either the price factor or the interest factor, is by means of the Bank rate. The only thing that they can do is to alter the terms of lending.

The great historic virtue of Bank rate policy is, as we shall see, that it works on both factors in the situation and on both in the right direction. The full reasons for that I shall reach later. If Bank rate is raised it tends to restore equilibrium, partly by diminishing the adverse balance on lending account and partly by increasing the favourable balance on income account; and the beauty of Bank rate is that double effect. If it only affected the capital account it would not be an adequate instrument for preserving long-period equilibrium. But the way it works on the two factors is very materially different. Its influence on lending is rapid, but not permanent. By raising Bank rate we can rapidly diminish the amount of our lending for the time being, but in the long run—this again is something that I shall not deal with fully at the moment—the amount of money which we can invest abroad on balance has to be governed by deeper considerations than the Bank rate. The Bank rate could not restore permanent equilibrium, if it merely affected the short-loan situation. On the other hand, its immediate efficacy on the short position is very great. Its influence on the price factor is much slower, in fact it may be intolerably slow, but when it has produced its final effect on price levels this effect is much more lasting. It is the real change which, in some circumstances, is necessary for the restoration of real equilibrium. So the Bank rate sets in motion rapid forces to diminish the calls on us to lend abroad, and slow forces which will have the effect of increasing our ability to lend abroad by reducing our price level to a more competitive level with the outside world. But the way in which Bank rate does that is very intricate. What I have said about its general effect is a matter of universal agreement. It is the traditional doctrine, I think, that Bank rate not only diminishes lending, but also affects price level in a downward direction, but what the reason is, what the conditions are for doing it rapidly is another matter. I do not want to go further at the moment than to remind you of this generally accepted truth about its principles of operation. Let me turn back for a moment to the question of the price level.

Are you leaving this part of the subject? Not for good.

Do you say it influences the cost of living as well as the wholesale price level? Well, I should like you to postpone that; I am coming back to that.

(CHAIRMAN) *On this general question, what exactly is the meaning of this economic equilibrium? That is the ideal you are striving at?* It is an equilibrium between our favourable balance on income account and our adverse balance on lending account which is necessary in order that we should not perpetually either lose gold or gain gold.

Is it to preserve the gold situation? It is an economic equilibrium in the ordinary sense.

It does not affect the social life of the community? If you are on the gold standard what you commit yourself to is to keep movements of gold within limits. That is what Sir Robert Kindersley the other day called 'the rules of the game'.[1] You so conduct your affairs that you tend neither to gain nor to lose large quantities of gold.

And the gold standard must be worked on such a principle if it is to do its job; that is what we are on now—not the economic outlook.

(MR MCKENNA) *The gold standard, if it implies the maintenance of the stock of gold by a central bank can only be worked—*

(CHAIRMAN) *The present theory of the gold standard.*

(MR MCKENNA) *The gold standard does not necessarily imply the maintenance of a stock of gold of any particular size by a central bank.*

(MR BRAND) *Do you mean the gold exchange standard?*

(MR MCKENNA) *Well, there are so many forms of gold standard besides the gold exchange standard.* The gold exchange standard would give you some latitude. But you could not pile up your foreign balances indefinitely, any more than your stock of gold.

(LORD BRADBURY) *What you set out to do is to secure that given you have a favourable balance on income account you lend that favourable balance to foreign countries and no more?* That is right.

(MR LUBBOCK) *You want to equalise your receipts and payments whether on income or capital account. You would like to keep them together without moving gold at all.*

---

[1] Kindersley had been a witness on 23 and 24 January and 6 February. He introduced the phrase in his answer to Question 1595 on 6 February.

(MR BRAND) *You do actually advance them every day?*

(MR LUBBOCK) *Whenever you are not losing gold, you do.*

(CHAIRMAN) *I understand what you are discussing, it is accepting a certain position, that you have the gold standard.* Which is the actual position. Therefore, it is very important.

(CHAIRMAN) *That involves the actual retention of gold of a certain quantity. Then you say that must be maintained within a certain range or else you dislocate the position. How is it to be maintained?* Our only method is Bank rate policy, and the beauty of Bank rate policy is that it operates on both factors.

(MR BRAND) *Is it not also true that even if you had no gold standard no country can permanently go on lending considerably larger sums to other countries?* That would be true, but if your exchange rate fluctuated you would have another instrument besides Bank rate policy, and the essence of our actual situation is that we have no corrective other than Bank rate.

(PROFESSOR GREGORY) *If I may go to points 3 and 4 of your argument, when you draw a distinction between the income accruing as determined by relative price levels and the balances on capital account which are dependent on rates of interest, you would agree in the long run there is a tendency for those two things to move together?* Only if they are forced. I should say they are remote from one another unless and until they are forcibly brought together.

You would not accept Wicksell's assertion that lending at other than an equilibrium rate of interest expressed in [a] money rate of interest influences the price level? That is largely the way in which Bank rate operates. Leaving Bank rate for the moment I go back to the question of prices. For simplicity of exposition let us concentrate on the effect of lower prices in increasing exports. The argument would apply equally to its effect in decreasing imports. Let us concentrate on its effect on exports. In a given state of economic development of the world the volume of our exports mainly depends on the prices we are asking relatively to the prices which our competitors are asking, so that we cannot increase our exports unless either the activity of world trade as a whole increases, which is something which we can effect very slowly ourselves, and also the steps which we may have to take to increase our share of it, insofar as they mean dearer money will probably operate in the wrong direction. We can only increase our exports if world trade is going up or if there is an extra demand for our specialities—which is something we cannot control or rely on—or if we lower our prices.

This is very important. There are two ways in which we can reduce our prices which it is vital to distinguish. We can reduce our prices either by reducing our cost of production—we may sell cheaper because we are producing cheaper—or we may reduce our prices by selling at a loss or at less than normal profit. Those are very different things. In a good many expositions of this subject people have stopped at the fall of prices and have not inquired whether the fall of prices is due to a fall in the cost of production or merely through business men being caught in a position where they are unable to obtain their usual rate of profit.

(CHAIRMAN) *Or have to meet their revenue charges out of capital?* Yes, that is a right way of putting it.

(MR FRATER TAYLOR) *They are willing to sell at a loss having in view the benefit as a whole?* Yes, it may be once their fixed plant is set up it pays them better to sell at less than the usual price rather than to close down. But whatever the reason is, selling at less than normal business profit is quite a different sort of price fall from one which is based on a real reduction in cost.

(MR BRAND) *And is temporary over a period of years.* We used to think it was.

(MR MCKENNA) *It cannot go on indefinitely.*

(CHAIRMAN) *It may even be worth while to sell some of your commodities at less than economic prices in order to maintain the establishment, on the analogy of the railways it is often better to take one extra passenger on a train at less than an economic fare.* Yes. There are, of course, all sorts of reasons why it pays manufacturers to accept business at less than an economic price rather than close down, but when the fall of price means that they are getting less than the profit expected it is a very different fall of price from what it is when they are genuinely producing at lower costs. It is very important for the development of my argument that those two different factors should be properly appreciated.

(SIR W. RAINE) *May it not be because of the fall in the cost of raw material— for instance, wool—at present time?* Yes; that may be very important.

(SIR T. ALLEN) *There is another matter which you will have to consider, whether it is economically profitable to sell in a sheltered market at a profit at home and simultaneously at a loss abroad.* Yes. If that were part of the normal course of trade and of business—as in rather rare cases it may be, I should not include that as selling below cost of production, if manufacturers did it with their eyes open and went on doing it indefinitely believing it paid them. I only mean this by selling below cost, something which he would not do if he had correctly foreseen the situation.

It is done definitely as a matter of policy by the United States at the present moment. I would not call that selling below the cost of production.

My point is that it has an effect upon our ability and capacity at home to recuperate. Oh! yes, it is one of the forms which foreign competition can take.

(LORD BRADBURY) *Is there not a further price fall—at any rate theoretically—that arises simply by an increase in the value of money?* I am including that in lower costs of production. I am talking of money costs of production.

Quite apart from the commodity cost of production you can have a money cost of production. I know all the difficulty about wages being very difficult to reduce, but supposing the purchasing power of money generally over the whole area can be increased then you can get a fall in prices without any diminution in profits. Yes, but I should say that was due to a fall in money costs of production. Money costs of production may fall because there is a change in the value of money, expressed in a fall of incomes, or may fall because of increased efficiency.

You are including both of them? Yes. You are trying to distinguish two different reasons why money costs of production might fall.

The only point that matters is that a possible fall in the costs of production might be due to a monetary cause, not to an efficiency cause. Certainly. That is the point I am coming to. If you reduce the costs of production that either means that you have got increased efficiency or that you are paying lower money efficiency wages. By efficiency wages I mean wages per unit of output. I should explain that I use 'wages' in a very wide sense, to cover what economists call 'remuneration of the factors of production'. Whether it is business men's efforts, or capital, or whatever it is, the 'remuneration of the factors of production' is very often convenient, though not quite accurate, to cover by the term 'wages'.

(MR BRAND) *Including profits.* Including profits, yes; in the sense of the normal reward that a business man receives—not including windfalls. You may reduce costs of production, either because physical efficiency is increased, or because you are paying the factors of production less money for their efforts. In order to be any good from the competitive point of view any increase of efficiency must take place faster than our competitors'. Presumably we are in the ordinary way doing what we can in that direction, anyhow, and quite apart from monetary management. It is not usually considered part of monetary management to look after the individual efficiency of business men. That certainly has been the traditional view, and it has been expressed to us a good many times in the course of our evidence. I think it is the right view. You do not become efficient in order to preserve international monetary equilibrium. You are efficient irrespective of whether it suits the Bank of England that you should be. And moreover, generally speaking, over the whole average of industry, extra economies which are obtainable by special effort in this direction are probably small and limited in amount. On the other hand, in general theory, it is one of our assumptions that efficiency is as high as we are able to make it in the given conditions. Therefore when the Bank of England is using Bank rate to bring about a better equilibrium, its effect on efficiency will not be of a high order; it will not be efficiency it is aiming at, because it cannot. Therefore when we use Bank rate we have to depend in practice either on reducing money wages or on reducing profits.

The Bank of England has not any direct power to reduce wages. In a Socialist or a Fascist community the governing authority may have such direct power; in Russia or in Italy the Government can decree that wages next morning shall be different from what they were last night; they may use that at times as an instrument for bringing about international equilibrium. But in this country we have no such power. The Bank of England has no direct power to reduce wages, but it has—as we shall see—the power to reduce profits. This is a matter to which I shall return in great detail later, that an increase of Bank rate tends to reduce business profits. That is something I shall hope to prove later on. It is not a paradox, it is something that is readily accepted.

(MR MCKENNA) *I think we shall all be with you before you begin.*

(MR BRAND) *Including bank profits?* The aggregate profits. The Bank rate would fail in its double effect if it did not reduce profits. Granted that an increase of Bank rate tends to reduce profits, the way Bank rate is supposed to work is as follows: First of all, it gives us a breathing space, because by raising the rate of interest it causes us to lend less on balance abroad, and therefore it diminishes our adverse international balance on capital account. That is a temporary relief.

(CHAIRMAN) *Acceleration.* That is the external effect of Bank rate, but the more fundamental result (and the necessary result if it is to do all that we hope) is its internal effect. The internal effect of a higher Bank rate is to render it less attractive to embark on new enterprises and new developments, and to encourage business men to realise stocks which they have produced in the hope of normal profits. The effect of that is to give us another temporary relief, for *entrepreneurs* and business men generally find themselves under pressure to realise stocks which they have bought in the expectation of getting a good price for them, and to sell them at a price less than they expected to get. There is pressure on the business world to sell off stocks, even though it be at a loss.

(MR LUBBOCK) *Will you explain how the pressure impinges on them?* The pressure impinges on them, many people say primarily, I should say secondarily, by the fact that these stocks are very often carried by means of bank money, and there is less willingness to do that. I should say the most important way it impinges on them is that the people whom they were expecting to buy from them do not buy from them because of the curtailment of enterprise, therefore they are either stuck with the stocks or they have to accept lower prices.

46

(CHAIRMAN) *A restriction of markets.* A restriction of their market. There is a great deal of force in what the banks have told us, that they do not put on pressure to call in advances. The man who is prepared to be stuck with his own stock will not find his banker making too much trouble about it, but he is not prepared as a rule to be stuck with his own stock. If the purchaser does not come forward, it is good business practice, as a rule, to sell even though it may be at a less price than was expected.

(MR BRAND) *It works really by limiting capital enterprise?* Yes. And the limitation of capital enterprise means that all kinds of people who would have come forward for goods do not come forward. It is not so much that the bankers are refusing willing borrowers, as that borrowers do not come forward, and that has repercussions throughout the whole economic system, particularly on those people who have been making goods in anticipation of a demand which does not materialise.

(SIR T. ALLEN) *You mean frequently a man wants to borrow and because of the bank's rate of interest he is restrained?* Yes. He need not enter into the new enterprise, and because of the rate of interest he does not.

(MR TULLOCH) *Do you not think the result will be very gradual in that case because of the rise of Bank rate?* I should say not very gradual. There are very few commodities of which people are prepared to hold stocks for three months. If you have a cessation of capital enterprise you rapidly find many types of manufacturers getting less demand for their goods. In the case of other type goods it is slower, because in cases where they are making foods for working class consumption they will not suffer until unemployment sets in.

(SIR T. ALLEN) *In my own experience it is immediate.*

(SIR W. RAINE) *Do you not get the same results sometimes without any regard to the Bank rate? Take the coal trade. The Bank rate has been falling—* In particular industries. There are always some trades going up and some going down, but I should say you only get this on the average of the whole as a result of Bank rate restricting enterprise.

The Bank rate has been falling for the last two or three months, and yet there has been increased pressure on the coal trade, so much so that you have had a reduction of three or four shillings in the price of export coal. I mean a Bank rate which is felt as higher in the circumstances, e.g. owing to the falling tendency of prices. I am not sure whether the Bank rate is not in effect higher today than it was a year ago. However, I will come to that later. What I mean by a high Bank rate—

(MR BEVIN) *How long do you estimate it will be before the working class feel this?* It is difficult to say, because that depends upon how long business men are prepared to go on at a loss before they sack their men. Orthodox theory would have told you some years ago that it was very quick. Recent experience is that it may be a very long time before you will get the full results of

47

unemployment. You get slight results quickly but the business world is so inclined to go on and swallow its losses that I do not think we have yet got the whole of the unemployment due to what happened in 1925.

(MR FRATER TAYLOR) *As a matter of fact in the steel business a manufacturer dare not blow out a blast without very good cause. He sets his teeth and carries on.* Yes. Recent experience shows that the effect is much slower than it was.

Now, this tendency of prices to fall owing to the fact that home buyers do not come forward gives us another secondary relief. The slackening off of enterprise means that we tend to import less rather than more raw material. The willingness of manufacturers to sell at cut prices means a stimulus to export, so we get another temporary relief owing to the depression of enterprise. Thus the Bank rate helps us both on capital account and on income account. There are one or two very good examples of that in the recent history of Germany.

(SIR T. ALLEN) *That temporary relief is a charge upon industry.* Very much so.

Which has to be met by some of us. I did not mean relief to industry; I meant relief to the Bank of England—to the gold position. I agree it is not a relief to industry; it is very much the opposite. This is not a relief which can go on permanently. If you were to close down Lancashire tomorrow we should stop importing raw cotton [but] before long we should stop exporting our cotton goods.

If conditions were so bad that every mill was closed down we should for six months go on exporting goods at cut prices that did not pay us. On the other hand we should stop buying raw cotton. So it would have an excellent effect on the exchanges and would be heartily welcomed by the Bank of England as a relief to the situation. That is one of the ways in which Bank rate is so wonderfully skilful, bringing in this way a rapid relief, but clearly we cannot look at the fall in prices due to such causes as permanent. There would not be the historical approval of Bank rate policy if Bank rate stopped at that.

What is the next stage? *Entrepreneurs* will endeavour to reduce wages, or if, as is the case, wages are governed by long-period agreements, so that they cannot do anything in that direction, they will gradually withdraw from the business, except in so far as they can make further balancing economies of efficiencies in other directions. If they are prevented from reducing wages they will probably withdraw from the business, in some cases immediately, in other cases, if the same state of affairs continues, only over a long period.

(CHAIRMAN) *Is that because wages is the only factor in the cost of production that is not under their control?* Insofar as they have to meet debenture interest and bank interest, that is still less under their control than wages.

The cost of the raw material of the industry is probably controlled by a world price which the individual manufacturer has to submit to. It is a world price; it is not a matter he can regulate. No.

Then there are a certain number of charges which are imposed upon him by Act of Parliament; things that he cannot escape. Yes.

The only matter in which there is any give is wages—using wages in your large term. Or swallowing losses. He can continue to operate without putting aside for depreciation of his plant and so forth, but I call that cutting a loss; I do not call that reducing costs of production.

(MR BRAND) *And if you take debenture interest you lose that in the end, because he has to turn his debentures into shares.* In some types of business he would withdraw very quickly; in other types of business the process would be much delayed. There are some businesses you can close down quickly; in other cases it does not pay to close down unless the closing down is going to last for some time. For instance, the laying up of a ship; you would lay up a ship fairly readily; probably more readily than you would blow out a furnace. You have various time lags running through, but the general effect is that he will withdraw from business particularly where new enterprise is concerned. He may not be able to give up some things he has embarked on already, but he will not go in for anything new. Each year the exhaustion of plant is proceeding; every year a larger and larger percentage of our plant needs replacement; and therefore the mere failure to make good what is wearing out will mean a pretty considerable reduction of activity. So that all this shows itself in increased unemployment. By the time the higher Bank rate has produced unemployment it is bound to be some use, it has achieved part of what it set out to achieve; and if it brings enough unemployment, it makes some progress towards bringing down wages. For the only way we can bring down wages, which is by hypothesis required for the restoration of international equilibrium, is by the pressure of unemployment. It used to be assumed that this happened pretty early, but we were not then thinking of any very large reduction of wages; very often in the nineteenth century all that was needful was the avoidance of an increase. The pressure of the Bank rate, by discouraging new enterprise, would bring about a diminished demand for labour, and that diminished demand for labour would bring about fairly rapidly the small adjustment of one or two per cent which is all that would be required in normal circumstances; and if we are living in an age of progress, as I suppose we are, where efficiency is increasing one or two per cent per annum it may not mean any reduction of wages, but merely that we should pause in the upward movement, and that pause would be brought about by the demand for labour being less than in normal times. That is the natural progress of causation. There is no way by which Bank rate brings down prices except through the increase of unemployment. It brings down prices by causing enterprisers to sell at a loss, but it does not bring them down to the equilibrium price level except by operating through unemployment. Assuming fluidity, this unemployment if it rises high enough and lasts long enough, will cause wages to fall. It used to be the theory that one would not have to wait long, if not for a fall, at least for the cessation of a rise.

(CHAIRMAN) *You interpret unemployment as excess of labour over demand?* At the price; and therefore a means of putting on pressure for the price of labour to fall.

In order to increase the demand again? In order to increase the demand again and enable us to expect a larger surplus on income account.

(SIR T. ALLEN) *Have we not a position where we have acute unemployment rather than a reduction in wages now?* That is what I am coming to. The classical theory of Bank rate assumes that the operation of the Bank rate does not stop at the point of chronic unemployment, and that unemployment does have a sufficient effect on production to bring down the wage level.

(CHAIRMAN) *This rise in Bank rate may be arrested. Take the supply and demand for labour; the wage rates do not respond at once economically to the law of supply and demand because of the legal position with regard to wages and wages agreements extending over a period. The thing does not act entirely in conformity with economic law because of the interferences with economic law which we have produced.*

(SIR T. ALLEN) *It may not respond at all. Take Australia. Today they are having acute unemployment, still the rate of wages is maintained, though by the maintenance of that rate they may get a further increase of unemployment.*

(CHAIRMAN) *We may have from Mr Keynes an elucidation of what is the ideal economic position, but then we have to take along with that a large number of artificial interferences with economic law.* I am not saying this does happen; I am saying this is the assumption of the principle on which we manage our economic affairs.

Economic theory. No, it is assumption. The actual system we use is one which depends for its efficacy on this assumption which I think in pre-War days no one would have contradicted. I remember Mr Brand being very reluctant to depart from that theory. But he was always well aware that it was the fundamental assumption.

(MR BRAND) *If it did not happen.* But you always believed it would happen. That is what everybody believed. It might not happen in six months, but it would happen fairly quickly.

But it did not.

(PROFESSOR GREGORY) *When you say 'did not'—they did come down before the War; they are not coming down now.*

(MR MCKENNA) *The assumption is not true today.* What I am trying to explain is how the assumptions which are required by the actual system under which we are operating are effected.

I agree with all my interruptors completely as to what the actual situation is, but it is of the essence of the classical theory which, as I say, no one would deny before the War, that the way in which our price level was kept in equilibrium with the price level of the outside world was by influencing our costs of production which either kept prices down or checked a rise. The Bank rate operates by putting pressure through unemployment to bring this about. This is the method on which we depended in the past. Let us assume for the moment that it works as for many years it did work. When wages have fallen, and it may be only a very small average fall over the country that is required or merely the absence of an increase, we should then be in a better competitive position. Our exports would increase, we should have a larger balance on income account. We should, therefore, by this time be in a position to lend more on capital account. Therefore the tendency to lend abroad which the Bank rate had temporarily to counteract need no longer be counteracted; the Bank rate can fall back to its previous figure having done its work, and then we are in a new position with our costs of production in complete equilibrium with the rest of the world, so as to enable us to invest abroad that portion of our savings which is attracted by the rate of interest abroad.

(MR BRAND) *Would real wages be the same?* I am coming to that.

(SIR T. ALLEN) *You are claiming now the extension of our capacity to lend abroad as being of significance and importance for us. Are you going to develop further the idea of using more capital at home rather than abroad?* If we have a system of *laissez-faire* the amount we want to lend abroad is governed by the relative attractions of investment abroad and at home which is not a thing which depends very much on prices. The amount we want to invest having been settled by relative interest rates we have to get our costs down to a level which will allow us to export an amount corresponding to that.

I have in my mind the idea of attracting money for industry at home. Yes; I shall be coming to that later on. When we are in this new position of equilibrium money wages will have fallen, but, as Mr Brand has just pointed out, it does not by any means follow that real wages, the buying power of wages, will have fallen to the same extent, even if it falls at all, because as soon as costs of production fall all round the prices of goods will fall and the money wages will buy more than they bought previously, and the fall in real wages will be far less than the fall in money wages, and insofar as there is a fall in real wages it will not really be a result of this Bank rate method. It will simply be a necessary concomitant of the increase of foreign investment while such increase is going on. During the period when we are investing abroad we must have a rather lower cost of production than if we were not. We have to be pressing our goods on the foreigner and that will turn the terms of trade against us, so we shall get a little less for our labour while foreign investment is going on; but that will be compensated later on because when the foreigner has to pay us interest on the loan, and possibly repay us finally, that has an opposite effect. It turns the terms of trade in our favour and causes our real wages to be higher. So the effect of foreign investment is to bring real wages lower than they would be while it is going on and higher after it has occurred. Any fall in real wages that occurs in this position as compared with the old is simply the necessary concomitant of foreign investment, and only a temporary loss, which we shall get back at a subsequent period. I believe in nineteenth century conditions that fall, if any, was very small. I think that in the nineteenth century foreign investment even while it was going on had a very slight adverse effect on wages. I am inclined to think it is now bigger because it is very difficult now to force abroad a greater volume of exports.

I would like to ask the process by which the benefit of investment abroad would ultimately reach the wage earner? In subsequent years when the interest has to be paid and instalments of capital have to be repaid to us, foreigners are more eager sellers to us in order to acquire our currency, just as we are more eager sellers to them while we are investing, and that greater eagerness on their part enables us to make a better bargain. They are in the position of having to reduce their prices to a point that tempts us just as when we are investing abroad we have to reduce our prices to a point which tempts them, so that during that period our exports would bring more back in exchange than they would if we had not a balance of trade in our favour.

(MR BEVIN) *That would depend on a fairly free distribution at home which would enable prices to fall?* It might. This is a thing that takes place over a very long period of years. We are now benefiting from foreign investment which went on over the previous 70 years. It is a very slow thing.

(MR BRAND) *Would you agree with what I have always thought, that the fact that we can maintain apparently a much higher standard of life, for instance, than Belgium and Germany, is largely due to the fact that we have invested £4,000,000,000 abroad?* I do not know that I would say largely, but partly. It only helps the working man insofar as it turns the terms of trade in our favour. I do not think that is a big factor. But it is a very real factor. When our new equilibrium has been produced and we have a lower money wage and lower money costs of production and greater ability to export, if there is any reduction in wages it is due to this other cause—namely to the whole position of this country in the economic framework of the world which leads to our foreign investments being at a certain level. Therefore, you must not accuse the Bank rate method of having brought that about. All the Bank rate method has done is to set in movement this series of events, which, assuming fluidity in the economic system, eventually leads to the right distribution of labour between different purposes, the right distribution of investment between at home and abroad, and does not have any adverse effect, when equilibrium has been brought about, on labour and real wages.

(MR TULLOCH) *Do I understand you to say that when we invest abroad we necessarily force our specialities on the foreigner, perhaps at a lower price?* Yes.

And, therefore, to the detriment of the working classes? Yes. It may be slight, it may be large, but that is the tendency. This is not a doctrine peculiar to myself, it is the historic theory of international trade as it is always expounded. The person who has put this most clearly is Professor Taussig. What I have been trying to set forth is the historic doctrine of Bank rate policy as it was evolved during the nineteenth century as a means of maintaining monetary equilibrium. You see what a very good doctrine it is, because the completely harmonious disposition of the economic forces of the world is preserved merely by the Bank of England changing the Bank rate from time to time in an appropriate way and leaving all the rest to the operation of *laissez faire*. And not only so; the Bank of England is set, in a sense, a very easy task, because movements of gold will always operate as a barometer to tell the Bank of England exactly when a change of Bank rate has become necessary, so that the method, assuming that it works according to the way in which it is supposed to work, is as simple as possible. All you have to do is to watch those movements, change the Bank rate accordingly and the economic system will then automatically grind out the proper levels of price and of wages at which everyone can be employed, at which business men can get normal profits and which furnishes the most advantageous division of the country's savings between investment at home and investment abroad, all owing to the fact that the Bank rate has this double influence. While it is not always analysed down to its bottom I think it is true to say that adherence to this system is the beginning and the end of traditional sound finance in this country. I have told you the whole story of how the traditionally sound financier thinks that he can make the adjustments required from time to time in our economic system, and I think—when one sees the way in which one part dovetails into another—there is no need to wonder why two generations, both of theorists and of practical men, should have been entranced by it.

I do not know if there is anything on that point that anybody would like to ask?

(MR MCKENNA) *Personally, I agree with everything you have said. I think it explains the effectiveness of the Bank of England rate.*

(CHAIRMAN) *An extraordinarily clear exposition.*

(MR MCKENNA) *An extraordinarily clear exposition, and thoroughly understood by us.*

(MR NEWBOLD) *So far I am thoroughly satisfied. Now I want to know what to do.*

(MR MCKENNA) *Is it that you and I are doubtful about the assumptions?*

(MR NEWBOLD) *I am satisfied with the analysis; now I want the alternative.*

(CHAIRMAN) *Mr Newbold's attitude is, the laws of nature may be beautiful to watch but they are damnably cruel!*

(MR NEWBOLD) *I am not concerned with whether they are cruel. I am perfectly satisfied with the way things are going.*

(PROFESSOR GREGORY) *It may be a very beautiful and perfect series of assumptions—but they were in fact assumptions which worked.*

(MR MCKENNA) *Oh, yes.*

(PROFESSOR GREGORY) *I thought you rather threw doubt on the fact that they worked?*

(MR MCKENNA) *Oh, no. Pre-War they worked.*

(PROFESSOR GREGORY) *We must not throw the whole thing out of the window.*

(MR MCKENNA) *Oh, no; on the contrary, they worked.*

(CHAIRMAN) *Mr Keynes has given us a structural analysis of the whole thing and laid before us the subsidiary causes which may have an accelerating or retarding effect.*

(PROFESSOR GREGORY) *I accept everything that Mr Keynes has said, but I should like to emphasise that this is not only a beautiful series of assumptions, but assumptions which translated into action have worked.*

(CHAIRMAN) *He said that practical men had worked this scheme.*

(MR MCKENNA) *It worked, and worked effectively.* I am coming to the limitations and imperfections of the operation of this method in present-day conditions, but before I come to that I should like in parenthesis to digress for a moment to distinguish the three possible types of international dis-equilibrium which Bank rate policy may be called in to cure. Bank rate may be raised to meet a purely temporary disturbance in the outside world, something that does not mean that we have got to have any new equilibrium level of wages and prices in this country. In this country we may be able to tide over the difficulty without its affecting or tending to affect any readjustment in the level of income at home, and without pushing it to the point where any important degree of unemployment of a more than quite transitory kind is involved. There may be a slight effect in retarding home enterprise for the time being and some transitory unemployment, but it will not be necessary to prolong the unemployment to a point where there is any sensible effect on the level of wages. The use of Bank rate to tide over a mere temporary disturbance is, I think, an example of Bank rate operation at its best. I should have been inclined to guess, perhaps rashly, that before the War probably four out of five changes of Bank rate would be of this character. The demand on us to lend abroad must be rather irregular in order to fit in with all sorts of irregularities which are happening in the world at large, and movements in the Bank rate have to occur in order to preserve a proper regularity. Savings are very regular; they come month by month, but we would not naturally lend the same amount abroad month by month, and the Bank rate has to be adjusted to avoid disturbance. Bank rate cannot help, on these occasions, causing transitory unemployment, but it is not intended to establish any new wage level or anything of that kind.

The second occasion of Bank rate policy is to meet a permanent change in the value of gold in the outside world. I do not include cyclical fluctuations in the price level which are to be reckoned among the temporary influences which I have been speaking about, for though they may last a little longer than the word 'temporary' would strictly imply, they are things which will pass and which need not be met by a change of wage level. Changes in the value of gold had been for many years before the War very slow, and, apart from the slowness, for 60 years prior to the War the long-period movement of prices was always upward, with the exception of some 10 or 12 years from the middle 80's to the middle 90's. Apart from that, as long as we have had anything resembling our modern system, the long-period movement of prices has been continuously upward. During the decade from the middle 80's to the middle 90's great difficulties were in fact experienced. Unemployment reached a point which, up to then, was unprecedented, and a Royal Commission, very similar to this body, was appointed to look into the matter.

(MR BEVIN) *The percentage was as high, was it not?* Well, as you know, the statistics are so lacking in comparability it is difficult to say. The trade union percentage was for a short time as high as it is now, but I do not think it was for more than 6 months, in 1892 or 1893.

(PROFESSOR GREGORY) *That was complicated, I think, by the American crisis of 1893. I think you have to allow for cyclical movements.*

(MR BEVIN) *There was a very high percentage in 1886.* That was the very start. It was also high in the 90's.

You had another very high percentage of unemployment in 1905? That was a cyclical fluctuation.

(MR MCKENNA) *Very short.* Very short.

The long period of unemployment was about from 1885 to 1895. However that may be, the position was, as Professor Gregory points out, complicated by other circumstances outside this country, but the character of those circumstances was to mitigate the effect of the price level on wages, whereas today the effect of what is happening in the outside world is to aggravate them. During the 90's the English investor suddenly found foreign investments extraordinarily unattractive. A whole series of events conspired to that end. During the 80's he had been investing abroad on a colossal scale and then in 1890 came the Baring crisis which put him off South America; there was the silver campaign on in the United States and that put him off his American investments; there was the agitation which led to the closing of the Mints in India, which made him nervous of India; there was the bank crash in Australia, which disturbed him; there was a series of troubles in the investment trusts in the late 80's; many of them having got into low water, which made him distrust investment trusts. The result was that foreign investment sank almost to nothing and all the rest of the world consequently owed us gold, and gold flowed into this country until the stock of the Bank of England had increased 50 per cent, and just as now the situation of wages is aggravated by the fact that people are wanting to invest abroad—so then the world situation was very much aggravated by the fact that we were deflators, and it took a tremendous effort to get foreign investment going again and get our investment up to the level of our savings. The Bank rate stood at 2 per cent for two years before the business world lifted its head again. That was the only experience of a downward movement of prices, apart from cyclical fluctuations, which any recent generation has had. All the rest of the time prices were on the whole tending upwards, and allowing for the very sharp increase of efficiency which was going on all the time there was never any occasion to use Bank rate to bring about a downward adjustment of wages. It was sufficient to use it as the regulator of the rate of the upward movement. Efficiency itself was enough to allow wages to rise quite materially year by year, and all the Bank rate did was to regulate the rate at which we could afford to pay higher wages. The position in the last four years has been entirely different. The return to the pre-War gold parity in 1925 committed us to use Bank rate policy to force wages down 10 per cent, except insofar as increased efficiency could diminish the amount by which we had to reduce them. That was setting Bank rate policy a task it had never been asked to do before in the economic history of this country. Supposing prices in the outside world had gone up, supposing efficiency in this country is increasing one or one and a half per cent per annum, we could reasonably have hoped to have swallowed that 10 per cent in the course of 5 years, but as it happened on top of this the world price level has been falling, and the rate of the recent fall in the world price level is, I think, unprecedented in the economic history of the world. I do not think there has ever been such a heavy fall of prices as has taken place lately except during reaction after a boom. If you take a period during which the cost of production has had time to adjust itself, we have never been in such a position before as that in which our wholesale index number has in four years fallen 20 per cent. Besides this we have the fall in the price of silver, and the fall in freights of 30 per cent in a year is a catastrophe in perhaps one of our largest industries of gigantic dimensions.

(SIR T. ALLEN) *Would you draw a line of demarcation provided it could have been cleared in 5 years?* It might have been cleared in 5 years if luck had been with us. Luck has been against us; we have failed.

(MR BEVIN) *Relatively we are worse than in 1925?* I should say we are further off equilibrium than we were then. The reason for this fall in price level is another story. I should say that we ourselves played a very considerable part in causing it and that the efforts we made to tighten up caused deflation in all the rest of the world. I would not put forward the United States as the main criminal, except for very short periods. It was, really, the return to the gold standard in many other countries which caused them to behave just as we have; they were struggling to deflate. That is the root cause of the situation. This is much more controversial, much more dependent on a judgement of the strength of forces, than what I have been saying previously. All the same I should like to interpolate that this what I began by describing as a piece of bad luck, is not entirely a matter of chance. The phenomenon has occurred and we are not entirely innocent of having caused it.

(PROFESSOR GREGORY) *When you say you think we are primarily responsible, on what do you base that opinion?* Because we led the way at the beginning of 1925. I think the world was running on more or less an even keel then and everything was set for better times, and then we started our return to the gold standard.

Do you ascribe the very rapid fall of prices in recent years primarily to the return to the gold standard, or more directly to the banking policy which has been pursued? I think that policies which would have been innocent, given certain methods, are less innocent given other methods.

(MR BEVIN) *It was almost inevitable, with 10 per cent jump at one go.* I think it was almost inevitable. We put a strain on Bank rate policy which had never been put upon it during the 100 years or less that it had been a method in use. We never expected Bank rate to put wages down 10 per cent or anything of that order. One or two per cent if you estimated for increase of efficiency was all that we asked it to do.

(MR BEVIN) *May I interrupt there? Have you made any attempt to estimate what the cost of capital reconstruction at home would be to meet that 10 per cent?* I do not think the capital cost of useful reconstruction at home would be at all heavy. The question is, can you reach the necessary degree of efficiency at all except slowly? I do not believe we are as inefficient as is alleged. I think the business man is suffering from general forces outside his control, that his efficiency is much greater than is believed.

57

I am not assuming that we are inefficient. I believe that we are not so inefficient as people say. I have seen American production and I have seen German and British, and the only difference I have seen is that America goes in for a period of 5, 6, or 7 years of wholesale slaughter and makes the tremendous change which she did in 1921, and in this country progress is steady; efficiency is steady.

(CHAIRMAN) *Fits and starts?*

(MR BEVIN) *Fits and starts in the States, as I saw it. I think those who have been there will probably agree with me. They get into a crisis and then they go very ruthlessly and spend an enormous amount of capital, and then they run easy for a considerable period. That is what struck me at any rate. In this country the change is steadier, it is constant. If you accept the principle that there is constant change, as we know there is because we are following these things every day, you take the view that to jump 10 per cent to meet the change by efficiency of 10 per cent is giving industry an impossible task.* Yes, that is my feeling. I have made the guess—it has not very much behind it; it is just a statistical judgement—that we are increasing efficiency about $1\frac{1}{2}$ per cent per annum. Over 50 years that is a terrific rate.

Has it been rather more rapid in the last 5 years? I think putting it at $1\frac{1}{2}$ per cent per year is fairly generous. In 5 years that is $7\frac{1}{2}$ per cent, therefore, if prices had not fallen abroad we should have got a very long way towards the 10 per cent task which we have set ourselves. To get back to equilibrium with the gold standard would have meant 10 per cent, but with the subsequent fall of world prices it has meant 20 per cent so while we were 10 per cent out in 1925 we are $12\frac{1}{2}$ per cent out now. That is just a guess but it gives you an idea of the order of magnitude, and to cure that would take 8 years more assuming there is no further misfortune.

In analysing this, have you any idea as to what led those responsible for jumping that 10 per cent to give industry such an impossible task? I will come to that. I have an hypothesis, but, as Lord Bradbury was one of the principal signatories, perhaps he can tell us.[2]

We were all given an absolutely impossible task. I am sure from the wording of the relevant report there was a complete failure to distinguish between spurious equilibrium and real equilibrium; that is to say, equilibrium brought about by selling at cut prices and equilibrium brought about by lower costs of production. The report of 1925, incredible as it may appear, alleged that at that moment equilibrium was for all practical purposes restored, and what that meant was that prices had fallen to the correct amount, without consideration being given to whether costs of production had fallen.

[2]   Of the Chamberlain Bradbury Committee. See *JMK*, vol. XIX, pp. 238–61 and 371–8.

(MR BRAND) *Out of profit.* The fall of prices was at the expense of profit; and it was then thought that the very big fall both of prices and wages which took place in 1921 was a good precedent.

(LORD BRADBURY) *Yes, of course, we did not know that wages were going to prove anything like as stubborn as they have proved—I mean money wages; I am not talking about real wages at all. The previous history was that adjustments of money wages were comparatively easy both before the War and after.* You cannot quote any case in which they had gone down.

We had very considerable reductions in the export industry. Apart from the fall in 1921 during the reaction from the boom, if you go back to pre-War history there was no case in which it ever occurred.

Actual reduction? Yes.

No, but we had the post-War reductions. You were thinking that 1920–1 was a good precedent, and you had not analysed to see why it was not.

There was no reason, I think, why it should not have been a good precedent as to rates of money wages. As you know, I took this view very strongly at the time, that we were setting ourselves the task of reducing wages and that it was an impossible task, and I published a pamphlet[3] in which I put forward an appeal. Before it was done I said 'You will never get wages down by the instrument of Bank rate'; after it was done, I urged that the only possible chance was to have a sort of national conference between the Prime Minister and the trade union leaders in which he would try to persuade them to reduce money wages, pointing out that the fall in real wages will not be corresponding, at the same time putting burdens on various classes of income tax payers so that everybody would share. I put forward this scheme in 1925, but it was repudiated.

That is always on the assumption that the reductions of money wages correspond with the fall in prices. The general fall in money wages put the working classes in a worse position. My argument was that it need not put them in a worse position. Therefore the great thing was to have a national appeal. That was the general basis of my pamphlet. I said 'Do not attempt to do that by Bank rate; you cannot do it by Bank rate method.'

(MR BEVIN) *Has it occurred to you what is the cost of taxation on the other side, as compared with this Bank rate method of cutting wages 10 per cent? You talk of the insurance charges on the other side, but what is there to set off even if you have 10 per cent on the other side.* What was done in 1925 was done at a cost to the country of—I think it is of the order of £1,000,000,000.

I think that is a low estimate. You had no coal production for six months.

(SIR T. ALLEN) *Markets have never recovered.*

---

[3] *The Economic Consequences of Mr Churchill, JMK,* vol. IX, pp. 207–30.

(SIR W. RAINE) *Can you tell me how it is that the fall in world prices has added to the burden?* Because it means that in order to be in equilibrium with prices outside this country, we have to have a still larger cut in money wages here than we had to have merely as the result of returning to the gold standard. The value of money has gone up, therefore we can no longer afford to pay as high money wages as we could otherwise.

(LORD BRADBURY) *Why do you think that that last 10 per cent was more difficult than the preceding 20?* Because the whole economic body was adjusted to this new level, whereas before it had not been. During the boom there were all kinds of advantages which had been enjoyed only for a matter of days or weeks or months which were quite easily swept away. When you got to the level of 1924 you practically got to the level which people had enjoyed continuously for 10 years or so—not quite 10 years; I should say from about 1916 to 1925.

From 1921 or 1922 you had had a perpetual fall in prices, up to the time of the Committee of 1924. Yes, but you had this sharp peak for the two-year period and you got back to something like equilibrium level, and after that everything got sticky.

When we returned to the gold standard you thought we were on the threshold of the millennium. That is what I thought in 1924. We had got through the adjustment following the post-War boom. The United States were about six months ahead of us, and the millennium which they have enjoyed since is one which we could have enjoyed.

But even assuming that, why should that 10 per cent itself cause further disturbance than the previous fall in prices before we got that disturbance? I agree it put off the millennium, but why did it not put it off for a shorter period? They were cyclical fluctuations of a different type. We had the famous post-War boom and depression, for which there were many precedents. There were a good many precedents in the nineteenth century for being able to deal with that satisfactorily, but when you get down to the level at which you have had it for some time then I say there is no evidence that you can shift people from that.

(MR BRAND) *Have you the price levels from 1918? In that boom it was 360.*

(LORD BRADBURY) *There was a considerable fall. The discrepancy between the level of prices seemed consistent with the return of a free gold market. It altered very considerably while the Committee were sitting.* (PROFESSOR GREGORY) *Yes. Because you had the depression in America in the first half of 1924.* That was what took you in. In 1924 you begin a deflationary policy leading up to the gold standard.

(LORD BRADBURY) *That was after the Committee.*

(PROFESSOR GREGORY) *You reported in February 1925, did you not?*

(LORD BRADBURY) *I do not think we had a high Bank rate while the Committee were sitting.* The deflationary policy of the Bank of England had being going on for quite a number of months.

The policy of the Bank of England goes back a good deal further than that. You took the wholesale index number, which had fallen; when the first Labour Government came in the exchange weakened, and consequently we enjoyed considerable prosperity. When the Labour Government went out— what was the date of the Labour Government going out?—

(CHAIRMAN) *1924.* From that moment—I think it began a little before that—you had the exchange improving; as the exchange improved it would tend to put the wholesale index number down.

(LORD BRADBURY) *But the Committee we are talking about was before the Labour Government came into office.* I am not talking about the Cunliffe Committee.

No; the Committee of which Sir Austen Chamberlain was originally Chairman and I succeeded him. That was in 1924, before the advent of the Labour Government. Its Report was published in 1925.

And the gold standard was introduced by the Conservative Government that succeeded the Labour Government. That document refers to the fall in the price level which took place after the recovery of the exchange.

(MR BEVIN) *Of course there is a very important point to remember about the adjustment of labour after the boom and the depression. Over 8,000,000 workers then were on sliding scales; automatically as prices dropped their money wages came down. They had come to the stop point before 1924; long before that you had got to the stop point. The stop point was the pre-War wages that a man had to meet the difference of post-War values, and when you took the 10 per cent jump you had to attack the standard of real wages.*

(MR BRAND) *The stop point being the standard whatever the cost of living.*

(MR BEVIN) *Yes. In the 1921 period, apart from the big mining trouble, you had railwaymen, distributive workers, practically everybody, on what was called 'War bonus', and there were automatic adjustments over a considerable field of industry. Every five points meant 1s. on or off wages, or something of that kind, according to the Board of Trade figures, and your cost of living fell almost automatically; but has your cost of living fallen with that 10 per cent since 1925? It stands at 165 as against 169; almost precisely where it was.* It is six points down.

And then it is only temporary. You made that difference of ten per cent, but only four per cent difference in the cost of living.

(PROFESSOR GREGORY) *There is one question which I should like to ask Lord Bradbury. I agree with Mr Keynes that the drop in 1921 was partly cyclical; I think it was also partly deliberate. I think when the Cunliffe Committee was put on it was partly deliberate. Why did you not drop it more to get down to parity with the dollar in 1921? I cannot understand why the Treasury, together with the Bank of England, at that time, when prices and wages were falling together, did not take action. It seems to me that that would have been the proper time to get back to pre-War parity with the United States.*

(LORD BRADBURY) *I was not in touch with what was happening. I was in Paris.* Our prices followed the world movement downwards. If they had gone against the world movement it would have been as difficult to reduce them to parity as in 1924.

The Committee was appointed in June 1924. That was after the first Labour Government.

(CHAIRMAN) *During the Labour Government.*

(LORD BRADBURY) *We were appointed when the Labour Government was in office.* Yes. And you did not sign your Report till February 1925, and the fall of prices which made you so optimistic took place in late autumn or early spring.

(CHAIRMAN) *Lord Bradbury says we were in a period of declining prices, and we thought we might safely risk a further decline. You say the decline had been going on before that, and was more or less a correction on the normal line of abnormality.* Yes.

And the additional 10 per cent was of a different order, different in kind from those alterations that had been taking place before. I am merely putting the argument; that is really what happened?

(LORD BRADBURY) *Yes, that is so, and I think probably we did not realise that, assuming Mr Keynes is right.—*

(CHAIRMAN) *You might well have inferred from the fact that you were on a period of declining price levels.*

(LORD BRADBURY) *I remember the decline was going on when the Committee was sitting. When we discussed the question one of the policies we had under consideration was the return to gold standard at a new parity.*

(PROFESSOR GREGORY) *You discussed that?*

(LORD BRADBURY) *We discussed that amongst ourselves, and there were arguments against it which were quite obvious, which I need not develop now, and the question was whether the inconveniences of a further adjustment were sufficient to outweigh the advantages of getting back to the old parity, and we thought the arguments in favour of getting back to the old parity were the stronger.*

(CHAIRMAN) *I think Mr Keynes's conclusion upon that is that the operation of that view is largely responsible for the present disturbance.* I am afraid I have rather broken the logical order of my remarks. I was saying there were three causes of disequilibrium which the Bank rate might be called in to cure—first a temporary situation, secondly a long-period change in the value of gold.

The third one which Bank rate might be called upon to cure if investment abroad is more attractive than it was before relative to investment at home. We have to export more corresponding to the greater proportion of our savings that we wish to invest abroad. That requires a lower level of wages and that also has to be brought about by a higher Bank rate *via* unemployment. In the 90's when there was a fall in the world value of gold, this factor operated in the opposite direction from what it does today because we were then reluctant to invest abroad; whereas today I believe there is a rather strong attraction towards foreign investment, which is due not so much to special attractions abroad such as there was in the case of railway investment in the nineteenth century, but to a feeling of discouragement at home. That discouragement works in a vicious circle. The falling off in profit because of the Bank rate makes people less eager to invest at home. Then we have to put the Bank rate higher to prevent them investing abroad and that causes still further discouragement at home and sets up a vicious circle. Our investors cannot lend money abroad on a larger scale than the amount of our income balance, so when there is a desire to invest abroad that desire has to be thwarted by a high Bank rate, and that high Bank rate by causing further discouragement at home may still further increase the tendency to invest abroad. The high Bank rate ought by making interest higher at home to make home investment more attractive than it was before, but if there is an atmosphere in which everybody is losing money the higher rate of interest is outweighed by that, so the higher Bank rate operates to make them still more anxious to get their money abroad.

(MR MCKENNA) *Do not you always acquire the means for investing abroad by a high Bank rate?* Not on balance.

A high Bank rate induces the foreigner to lend us short? Yes. But I am speaking of the *net* balance of foreign investment.

And, therefore counteracts the otherwise unfavourable balance that we should have through lack of exports. Therefore, we have the means of lending long abroad, and that is what we have been doing. We have been lending long abroad and borrowing short at home.

(MR BRAND) *By investment abroad, you did not mean public issues only, but an investment abroad through private channels?* Yes. All this means that we are under three simultaneous embarrassments today. We first of all have to balance the return to gold. Then we have to balance the world fall in gold prices and, thirdly, we have to effect an increased volume of exports to balance the increased volume of our savings which is trying to find its way abroad. If we can increase our efficiency enough to bridge the difference, well and good; the problem will be solved. If not, the choice lies between reducing wages, the continuance of a spurious equilibrium, that is to say, with prices at an unremunerative level compared with the cost of production, or some other alternative, the discussion of which I should like to postpone. I think I have already said enough about this distinction between a spurious equilibrium and a real equilibrium, the confusion in regard to which has led to a great many troubles,—the spurious equilibrium which a Bank rate brings about immediately, but which does not last, and is brought about without materially affecting the cost of production, and the true equilibrium which only comes at long last.

I should like to return to what we were previously discussing, namely, that the use of Bank rate to bring us to the true equilibrium rests on the assumption that money wages are not fixed, that they are reasonably fluid and responsive to unemployment. Since 1924 money wages have remained for all practical purposes fixed. Some industries have gone up, some down, but on balance the position has remained unchanged.

(CHAIRMAN) *Why has there not been a response?* It is alleged to be due to characteristic features of post-War conditions,—for example, the dole, the electoral power of the working classes, which makes our political parties afraid of the pressure that would be brought to bear upon them if they attempted a reduction of money wages, also the growth of the social conscience which sympathises with the working classes in their resistance to what appears to the vast mass of the public an attempt to depress their standard of life. There is a general public sympathy with the working classes in their resistance.

(MR BEVIN) *And the greater power of their organisations to resist that?* And the trade unions. But I believe that the influence of these factors is exaggerated. My reading of history is that for centuries there has existed an intense social resistance to any matters of reduction in the level of money incomes. I believe that, apart from the adjustments due to cyclical fluctuations, there has never been in modern or ancient history a community that has been prepared to accept without immense struggle a reduction in the general level of money income. Throughout history I can only recall two occasions at all comparable to the present one. One was the highly analogous deflation which followed the Napoleonic Wars, the first period of which was similar to the deflation following 1920-1, and was carried through without very great difficulty. The second deflation, very much like the one we are going through now, was one which brought this country to the verge of revolution, and if you read the economic literature of the period you will find many people thought it would involve revolution, and the troubles of the 20's and 30's are largely traceable to that. The other analogous case was the price fall in the middle ages prior to the discovery of America and the influx of precious metals to Europe. The fall of prices was, then, an appalling problem, and it was only mitigated by monetary readjustments. Many of our monarchs rest under unjust imputations of depreciating the currency for their own personal advantage, I am sure they only did it to avoid what they regarded as intolerable wage adjustments. There is no question as to the impoverishment of the world that occurred; and subsequently the High Renaissance and the general process of recovery were based on the accumulation of profit which took place during the period of the rise in prices, lasting about 100 years, which followed on the influx of gold from America. But apart from those two periods I do not think there is anything to prove that it was ever easy to bring about material fall in the level of money incomes.

When you get a war like we have gone through everybody expects some readjustment, which accounts for the comparative ease of the first readjustment following the War.

(CHAIRMAN) *There is a moral factor.* Yes—whatever the cause was, it was to be expected.

(MR BEVIN) *Once that has been accepted then the stubborn resistance begins. The phrase we often used when we were appealing to employers and big interests— and I think one of the great tragedies in this post-War readjustment is that those who have been responsible for handling our finance have done it in an exclusive way, without consulting the more modern views of trade unionists and other people who had handled this side of the problem—When the last 16s. 6d. was forced on the engineers the phrase used by Mr Brownlie, I think, was 'You are turning the screw once too far.' I think that sums up exactly what has happened in regard to the wage position, that that is what has caused our troubles since.*

(CHAIRMAN) *Do you think if there had been more steps taken to explain the meaning of what was pending there would have been less trouble?*

(MR BEVIN) *Not only to explain what they wanted to do but to understand from us—and when I say 'us' I mean employers and workpeople—the difficulty of doing it. Then there would have been a better balanced judgement, and probably a longer period would have been taken before they did it. For instance, I think you have gone faster than you should; Five per cent per annum, beginning about 1920, would have taken you beyond this period at least, and that would have been a steady, rational thing to do.*

(CHAIRMAN) *It was the jolt that you objected to?*

(MR BEVIN) *It is not the jolt. You cannot alter industry to make a 10 per cent difference. You cannot do it so fast.*

(CHAIRMAN) *We must show some consideration for you, Mr Keynes. You have been good enough to discuss these matters with us rather intensively for two hours. What do you think?* I have reached a rather convenient stopping place. If you want me to go on I have a great deal more.

I do not think you need. It is extraordinarily useful, probably a great deal more than some of the evidence we shall have to listen to. There is a further subject which you might want to hear about—a classification of the possibilities of remedy. After all, we have got to come to the remedies. I think that all the possible remedies that anybody has proposed so far as I remember can be classified under certain headings, which fall into line with my general diagnosis of the situation.

It would be preparatory to the process that we are going to embark upon in examining witnesses if we had a classification of the remedies suggested; we would be able to put questions to the witnesses—those of them to whom it would be suitable to put them. Personally, I do not think we are wasting a moment; on the contrary I think this is probably the most profitable thing we could do, and it is an excellent preface to the next stage of our inquiry. I thought of classifying the remedies. One is naturally drawn into praise or dispraise of them, but that would not be my primary purpose.

Rather praise than criticism. We could do that tomorrow. Then I think we should arrange a week ahead. The National Union of Manufacturers are coming on Thursday next week. We will resume this discussion on Friday, and not ask any witness for that date.

(Adjourned till tomorrow, Friday,
21 February, at 4.30 p.m.)

COMMITTEE ON FINANCE AND INDUSTRY

Friday 21 February 1930

Present:

The Rt Hon. Lord Macmillan (*Chairman*)

Sir Thomas Allen	Mr Cecil Lubbock
Mr Ernest Bevin	The Rt Hon. Reginald McKenna
The Rt Hon. Lord Bradbury, G.C.B.	Mr J. T. Walton Newbold
The Hon. R. H. Brand, C.M.G.	Sir Walter Raine
Professor T. E. Gregory, D.SC.	Mr. J. Frater Taylor
Mr J. M. Keynes, C.B.	Mr A. A. G. Tulloch
Mr Lennox B. Lee	Mr G. Ismay (*Secretary*)

(CHAIRMAN) *We shall be very glad to resume the discussion.* There are certain figures that the Ministry of Labour published yesterday which are rather interesting in connection with a certain part of our discussion—that is, the movement of wages downward. They do not publish an index, as Professor Bowley does. They publish a range. The upshot is that since the last quarter of 1922 wages have been stationary—going as far back as that.

I think I may say without any breach of confidence that in the inquiry I was

66

recently carrying on into the wool industry I discovered that there had been no fall of wages since 1922. Both sides agreed that the prices [wages?] had been stabilised since 1922.

(MR BEVIN) *That would not apply to mining, would it?* Some have gone up; some have gone down. It is the average.

Do you think the average is stable? Stable. Professor Bowley has produced an index for the London and Cambridge Economic Service, and month after month I feel it must have gone down, and I badger him to tell me that it has, but what he tells me is that at present the index as compared with 1924 is 98·5. When the railwaymen's wages go up again in May it will return to 99.

(CHAIRMAN) *It was agreed in the wool industry.*

(MR BEVIN) *Yes. I know in some industries.* Agricultural labourers have gone up slightly. I think bricklayers have gone up slightly.

They have gone down this week. That is what moved the Bowley index from 99 to 98·5. I do not think it brings them to the level of 1924.

(CHAIRMAN) *Those that have a sliding scale will be affected. Has the building trade a sliding scale?*

(MR BEVIN) *Yes; it is $\frac{1}{2}$d an hour over the whole industry.*

(MR LEE) *And the finishing trades in cotton.*

(MR BEVIN) *Cotton has gone down.*

(CHAIRMAN) *The stickiness goes back longer than 1925.* Yes.

Does that show generally that there is a failure on the part of wages to respond to the monetary position? It is a rather more definite statistical indication of the extreme stickiness of wages; I mean what has happened since 1922.

That has remained constant throughout? That has remained constant throughout.

(SIR THOMAS ALLEN) *Can we also conclude that we can have acute and widespread unemployment with a reasonably stable wage?* Yes.

(CHAIRMAN) *That is another inference that can well be drawn.*

(MR BEVIN) *Is there any figure of earnings?*

(PROFESSOR GREGORY) Yes, the Ministry of Labour Gazette. Mr Rockeling makes an index of the volume of employment in which he allows for sickness but not for short time.

You can get an index by multiplying the population by the Bowley rate and dividing by the cost of living. That is wage rates, and does not indicate the cost of living. In America they have what they call the 'pay-roll', which I think is fairly accurate; practically all the big businesses return their pay-roll. It would be an excellent thing if we did that.

(MR BEVIN) *Who does that?*

(PROFESSOR GREGORY) *There is a census of manufacturers every four years. I was to ask whether it would be possible to ask the Ministry of Labour for an estimate of the total number of wage earners whose wages are covered by cost-of-living agreements. It is a rather important figure; I think we ought to have it.*

(MR BEVIN) *You may get a wide number on a cost-of-living agreement, but if you take the cost-of-living operative figures, where the scale is actually moving, and not on paper, I should not imagine there are much over a million now. There has been a gradual conversion into a stabilised wage.*

(PROFESSOR GREGORY) *We might know what the facts are.*

(MR BEVIN) *It is very interesting, but I should ask them as well to what extent the sliding scale is operative. They might give you the pigeon-holed statistics of people on the cost-of-living scale, which the sliding scale may not represent.* If I may pick up the argument from yesterday, my conclusion broadly was that in 1925 we put on the Bank rate policy a task of greater magnitude than it had ever been asked to perform before and which it proved to be incapable of performing. If we make the usual assumptions about perfect markets and absence of friction, Bank rate policy must always be capable of doing the work asked of it; but humanly and politically it was impossible. The result is that we are left jammed in a position of what I described as spurious equilibrium without applying any alternative policy to Bank rate policy; and that spurious equilibrium may be gradually ruining us.

One can put it another way by saying that we have a currency policy and a wages policy which are incompatible with one another. We have, as I have heard Mr Brand put it, two fixed points in our system, two fixed millstones between which we are being ground; whereas, the system assumes that there is only one fixed point, namely, the currency policy, that wages will always sooner or later follow business receipts. In effect our currency policy fixes the total monetary receipts that we get from the sale of our goods. It also fixes at a very high level the money incomes of owners of War debts and other rentiers. Our wages policy fixes the rate of money wages, and the result is to leave no adequate profits to business men. The total money receipts from the sale of our produce as determined by currency policy after the fixed deductions have to provide the wages payment, and wages payments are influenced by wages policy. When those two have been deducted there is not the normal margin of profit for the business man and his only course today is gradually to withdraw, first by reducing the employment he offers and, secondly—which is much slower in effect—by not investing in new enterprises. Where he is in an enterprise from which he cannot withdraw he may continue for quite a number of years offering not full employment, but fairly good employment, at the expense of not paying interest or depreciation. He will not go on doing that indefinitely. Experience has shown in different industries that for various reasons business men will go on much longer than was previously supposed, so that the full effect in unemployment is only realised very gradually. In many instances where there is now a tendency for unemployment to increase, the actual margin of profit is not much lower than it has been for a long time. A secondary result of this is the embarrassment of the Budget. A large part of the Budget disbursements goes to rentiers and pensioners, and those are fixed high by our currency policy. Much of the rest goes directly or indirectly in wages, which are also fixed high by our wages policy. But the revenue very largely comes directly or indirectly out of profits and naturally fails, therefore, to show its ordinary resilience if the margin of profit is considerably reduced. That sets going one more vicious circle, because taxes have to be raised, particularly on income and profits, which further increases the discouragement of industry and makes the investor more and more unwilling to embark his money on enterprises at home.

(CHAIRMAN) *There is one factor that I have been rather impressed with—I do not know whether it is of the order of magnitude of the factors you have been speaking of. The large amount of what we may call social legislation which has been passed and which is met to a considerable extent by taxes is constant again now?* Yes, that is true.

I do not know what percentage factor it is in the cost of production, but it is quite considerable. It is 5 per cent to $7\frac{1}{2}$ per cent of the wages bill. Professor Clay has worked it out; it is about that. Perhaps that is high.

And in turn does not that enhance the value of wages? These contributions are made partly by employees, partly by employers and the state; the burden of years is lightened, the individual is relieved of the responsibility of providing for certain of the contingencies of life for which he had previously to provide. It is part of the wages problem.

But with this difference, that whereas wages may be subject to alteration these things are not subject to alteration. They are constant, they are imposed by the legislature or are the result of contract between parties.

(PROFESSOR GREGORY) *Of course, the magnitude of the expenditure on unemployment is part of the backwash of unemployment.*

(CHAIRMAN) *There are many other things which go to make up the standard of life now. If a person is relieved of the responsibility of providing for a number of the contingencies of life then you can spend more freely for you do not require so much money to provide for those contingencies. But I do not think that those constants in the cost of production are of sufficient magnitude to tell.* They are, in the aggregate.

(PROFESSOR GREGORY) *I think Professor Clay in his last book puts the deterrent effect of these social services high—not in money, but psychologically.* They are a tax on the employer in proportion to the amount of labour he uses.

(CHAIRMAN) *They may have a psychological effect in this way, that they remove a certain amount of the responsibility of life?* No, I do not think I should attach too much importance to that.

(MR BEVIN) *One would put it rather this way: The social services may be*

69

carrying a portion of what might be otherwise a developing responsibility; that is to say, if you take the ordinary big city today the cost of transport and many other things which have entered into the standard of life of the worker is 200 per cent or 300 per cent more than it was a few years ago, but there are so many other factors which have entered into the standard of life that the social services are a compensation against what otherwise might have to be met by higher wages.

(CHAIRMAN) *The cost that a man has to pay to get to his work is a charge, but the relief that he gets to his mind by not having to provide for certain things out of his wages which he had to provide before, has a psychological effect.*

(MR BEVIN) *I would like to press that, because I think as an actual fact the amount of provision for contingencies that were not previously provided for is greater for the individual now. For instance, payments for old age, payments for superannuation schemes, that did not exist before the War, cover several millions of workers. Notwithstanding the state contribution of a proportion you have a very wide individual responsibility for providing for old age pensions, and things of that character, which were not in existence with the masses before the War.*

(PROFESSOR GREGORY) *The money for these services represents a greater proportion of the fixed national income.*

(SIR THOMAS ALLEN) *I would like to supplement what Mr Bevin said. Not only does it apply to the transport cost of getting to work, but the extra payment that the worker has to make when he is at work by reason of having to buy food away from home; that enters very largely into the reduction of the actual wage earned.*

(CHAIRMAN) *I did not mean to divert you, Mr Keynes.* I am nearly at the end of the first section of the argument which I wanted to develop. There is another reason why Bank rate policy is a very costly and inefficient instrument for bringing down levels of income at home to parity with those in the outside world. Some industries, those we speak of as sheltered industries, are in a much stronger position for maintaining their level of profit and income than others which we call unsheltered industries; consequently the pressure which Bank rate puts on towards a lower wage level is unequal, and puts an intolerable burden on the weaker industries—weaker from the point of view of bargaining power and weaker from the point of view of making profits. Reduction of wages which is an all-round reduction does not alter the real wage. But it never is an all-round reduction. If you use this particular method it always means a reduction which falls heavily on certain industries and leaves other industries as they were, and in those industries on which it falls heavily it will always tend to reduce the standard of life. If the wages in the sheltered industries do not fall then the amount of fall which there must be in the unsheltered industries to restore equilibrium becomes not 10 per cent, but something very much higher, because the costs of the sheltered industries will enter into the costs of production f.o.b. almost as much as in the industries that are producing directly for export.

(MR BEVIN) *Would that apply to costs, taking wages as expressed in costs, in the sheltered industries?* It would mean that the f.o.b. costs would not have fallen more than the required amount, but in order to bring that about the wages of the individuals in the unsheltered industries may have fallen more than ten per cent.

(CHAIRMAN) *The railways are a sheltered industry. They have wages settled by a system of their own, and if you are going to take a ton of steel for export it has to carry freight charges which are on a level with the wages in those industries, and therefore every ton of steel has to carry wages. If you take the cost of production in such an industry as mining there is not merely the manufacturing cost but the cost of transport as well. A ton of steel is no use unless it can be sent to the purchaser.* In some industries their own wages bill would be a very large part, as it is in the case of coal; but in the case of cotton, for example, that would not be so. I conclude, for these various reasons, that Bank rate policy, whilst theoretically intact, has broken down as a practical instrument for restoring true equilibrium. It leaves us in a chronic position of spurious equilibrium, and in that spurious equilibrium the brunt falls on profits. As long as we have a form of society in which profit is the driving force of enterprise you will have a gradual decay if you have a situation in which it is impossible to earn profit. The choice then is between accentuating Bank rate policy until it does do its work or falling back on some alternative method. The worst thing is to have a Bank rate policy which is not severe enough to bring about equilibrium by that method, and yet diverts our minds from any alternative policy. If we are going to depend on Bank rate policy then I think the state of mind of the Governor of the Bank of England ought to be one of enthusiasm when he sees the unemployment figures rising after he has raised the Bank rate, and he ought to say to his Committee of Treasury 'Do you think six per cent will raise the unemployment to 2,000,000, or to what higher rate ought we to put it to be able to rely on 2,000,000 unemployed, to bring wages down.' If he thinks, humanely, that that is the wrong line to take, then he ought not to use this instrument, though it is his sole one, because he is only prepared to hamper without hitting, to injure without killing, and so to get the worst of both worlds.

(MR BEVIN) *The public might get to understand the gold standard then, might it not?* It might do. I think there are a great many alternatives, which would not, by any means, mean scrapping Bank rate policy. I am absolutely convinced that a Bank rate policy for certain purposes and within certain limits is essential, but there are alternatives that can be discussed and with the leave of the Committee I will deal with them next week, classifying them under the headings into which they fall.

I want today to go on to something different, to which I personally attach enormous importance, perhaps too much, but which is likely to be relatively unfamiliar to all members of the Committee. You will remember that we agreed yesterday that the effect of a high Bank rate is to reduce profits,—that, I think, is a commonplace, but it is not a commonplace as to exactly how it does it. Economists spend most of their time describing and discussing what happens in a position of equilibrium, and they usually affirm that a position of disequilibrium is merely transitory. I want to study what happens during the process of disequilibrium,—one which lasts long enough to observe it.

I should like, first of all, to go back to one point which was raised by Mr Lubbock as to what I mean by a high Bank rate. I do not mean by a high Bank rate five, or six, or seven per cent. I mean a Bank rate which is relatively high in the sense that it is deterrent to investment and business enterprise. If the business world believes that they can use borrowed money to advantage to get six per cent or more, then five per cent is not a high Bank rate, but if they do not believe that they can make more than four per cent then five per cent is a high Bank rate. The beliefs and expectations of the business world are the result of many factors, particularly the actual margin of profit they are getting on current business, and whether they think prices are going up or down. When prices are expected to go up business will willingly pay a much higher rate than when prices are expected to go down. So $4\frac{1}{2}$ per cent might have been a very low Bank rate in 1919–20 and yet high today. When I say a high rate I do not mean an absolutely high rate, but one which is high relatively to the feelings of the business world.

What happens when Bank rate is high in the sense that it is a deterrent to enterprise? Let me begin by posing the problem in this way: The amount which we can invest abroad *net* depends on our favourable balance on income account. It is impossible that we should invest abroad more than that, except to the extent that we are prepared to export gold. We can, as Mr McKenna said, making long investments and finance them by borrowing short from foreigners, but that is not *net* foreign investment; you can have no *net* foreign investment except to the extent that you have a favourable balance on income account plus exports of gold. If we try to lend more than the amount of that balance so that gold is flowing out, the Bank of England has to stop us from doing so by raising its rate. That will right the situation partly directly by stopping us making loans, and partly indirectly by causing us to borrow back short what we have already lent long. Independently of this there is a certain amount of saving going on in the country. I mean by saving that individuals spend less than their income on current consumption. Any individual whose income is larger than his personal expenditure on current consumption is saving. There is a certain sum of money which is the difference between his income and his expenditure on current consumption, and the savings of the community are the aggregate of those moneys. Part of this money is used in home investment which is represented by the net increment of material capital wealth, the building of houses, the building of factories, the building up of working capital and stocks, all the accumulation of finished and half-finished goods, raw material, plant and so on. There is a certain amount of material investment going on and a certain amount of saving representing the cost of production of that material capital in the country. The amount of investment which is thus going on in the country depends on the actions of business men,—whether they think it is worth while to go in for such enterprise or not. It depends to a very important extent on the banking system, how ready the banking system is to finance people who are willing to make real investment if they can get the finance to do it with.

(MR BRAND) *By investment you mean not simply buying securities, but investment in bricks and mortar?* Investment in bricks and mortar, which is the best way of typifying a large group of things. Therefore, the *total* investment is the amount of bricks and mortar put up by the business men at home, plus the amount of our foreign investment which depends on the amount of our surplus on income account. There is no reason in the world why those two things, the net amount of our export balance, plus the cost of production of bricks and mortar at home, should add up to the amount which individuals have saved.

Individuals and companies? Individuals and companies. The decisions are made by quite different sets of people. They are made to a great extent at different moments of time. So that it is not true that all the savings which are not used at home in home investment are necessarily used for foreign investment; only those amounts of it can be used for foreign investment which can be got out on to international markets in the shape of exports. Therefore, that brings us to the question, when the available savings are greater than the total amount of home and foreign investment, what happens to the difference? And, equally, when the amount of investment is greater than the available savings, i.e. the cost of production of bricks and mortar, plus the foreign investment, is greater than those money savings—how on earth, from what source is the excess provided? The explanation is not paradoxical at all, it is plain common sense, but it is extremely difficult to state it so as not to seem paradoxical. I had better begin by giving the answer. When investment is exceeding savings, the difference is represented by abnormal windfall profits. When investment exceeds savings, the business world makes an amount of abnormal profit equal to the difference, and that abnormal profit finances the extra investment.

(PROFESSOR GREGORY) *When the investment exceeds the savings, the excess is represented by abnormal windfall profits of the business world out of which the excess investment is financed.*

(MR FRATER TAYLOR) *Could you illustrate that?*

(MR MCKENNA) *It is included in savings. It does not matter how the savings are obtained, whether by normal or abnormal profits. You define savings as not including abnormal profits?*

(CHAIRMAN) *Where my difficulty arises is in the application of savings.* You had better let me develop this, if I may.

Certainly. And equally, when savings are in excess of investment, there are abnormal business losses, and the extra amount which the public has saved is used to finance the losses of the business man. In the most straightforward case the public deposit extra savings with their bank, and the bank lends those extra savings to the business man who has lost money; so the savings either materialise in additional wealth or they may take the form of balancing losses by the business world.

Let me go back. I think it is easier in the first place to take the case where investment is in excess of savings. That means that the incomes which are being paid out to producers, both those who are producing capital goods and those who are producing consumption goods, minus what they are saving, are greater than the cost of that part of their output which takes the form of consumption goods. You are increasing expenditure out of incomes faster than you are increasing the supply of consumption goods. For total income is governed by the cost of production of investment goods plus that of consumption goods. To get the expenditure on consumption goods, you take off from the total of incomes the amount which is being saved. If the amount you so take off is less than the amount of investment, the sum which is left to the public to spend on consumption goods is greater than the cost of production of those goods; so that their prices go up to a figure in excess of what they have cost to produce.

(MR BRAND) *For me you will have to say that again.* Incomes are divided into two parts, that part which is saved and that part which is spent on consumption goods. If income is divided between consumption goods and saving in a different proportion from that in which production is divided between consumption goods and investment goods, you get a fluctuation up or down as the case may be in the price level of consumption goods. In the one case the amount of money which people are spending on consumption goods is greater than the cost of production of those goods; in the other case it is less. The entrepreneur therefore gets in the first case an abnormal profit because he is selling what he has produced for more than it has cost him to produce, and with that excess he can finance the additional investment; in other words, incomes are worth less than people expected in terms of consumption goods. They cannot get as much for their money as they hoped; therefore, there is a transfer of wealth from the general public to the entrepreneur.

(CHAIRMAN) *They are saving in turn?* If you like, but I am not including the entrepreneur's windfall gains as part of his normal income; they are not in his normal cost of production.

So the excess investment is really financed by the profits the entrepreneur makes? In the case of excess investments. But if you take the opposite case where incomes are more valuable than they were expected to be, that is, where prices are falling, then the positive savings of the public are balanced by the negative savings of the entrepreneur, the windfall losses—and if the public is saving more than the sum of what the entrepreneur is putting into bricks and mortar and of what we can get out over the frontier in the shape of exports, then by reason of the excess of saving some business man or other must make a loss. And correspondingly he must make a profit in the other case. The public who save are saving without any cost to themselves, because, owing to their savings, prices fall, so that they can consume just as much as they did before. Yet they have increased wealth corresponding to their savings, but owing to lower prices those savings are balanced by the losses of business men. The way the whole monetary system works is this, that the Bank of England regulates the rate of investment; it is on the Bank rate largely that the rate of investment depends; therefore, if the Bank rate is such that investment is greater than the savings, prices rise. In the first instance they rise because profits are abnormal, business men then bid against one another for the services of factors of production; naturally, wages rise, and then if the policy is not reversed you have prices at a higher level. On the other hand, the way prices are forced downward is this. You put the Bank rate at a level at which savings are in excess of investments. Business men make losses, prices fall, and then at long last the business man forces down the remuneration of the factors of production and prices are then lower. But if you jam the machine halfway through so that you have a chronic condition in which business men make losses, you also have a chronic condition of unemployment, a chronic condition of waste; and the excess savings are spilled on the ground.

(MR BRAND) *I do not quite follow, in your first part, how it is that the price of the consumption goods rises. There is more money being spent on capital goods?* No, there is not more *income* being spent on capital goods, but more *wages* are being paid out for the production of capital goods. In equilibrium you ought to have an amount of expenditure on consumption equal to the wages of the people who are making consumption goods and an amount of saving equal to the wages of the people who are making capital goods.

If you get more spent on consumption goods than the wages of those making the consumption goods, prices go up.

(MR MCKENNA) *It becomes intelligible to me if I think of positive savings or losses and negative savings.* You naturally start that way.

Then I think of the negative savings not appearing as negative to the equation until after a time lag, and consequently while your balance of exports is governed by your positive saving, the negative saving does not appear till afterwards. It is not a question of a time lag, but I can express it in the form of negative saving, namely, that if you have positive saving by the public—leaving out the business man—in excess of investment, then the business man will have to have negative savings corresponding to his loss on production.

Subsequent. Well, a week subsequent.

That will bring an equation whenever the line is drawn, there must be equality. Yes, his negative savings take place at the same moment as the positive savings of the public.

(PROFESSOR GREGORY) *I can perfectly easily see that when the volume of money savings exceeds the volume of money investments—* Cost of production of investments.

—exceeds the money investments because of the actual capital cost of the goods produced, you then have a fall in prices because everybody is holding back goods. It is much more complicated. Let me give it to you in a parable which I have found, with some people, is helpful in getting it down absolutely to its simplest terms. Let us suppose a community which owns nothing but banana plantations which they labour to cultivate. They collect bananas and they consume bananas and nothing else, and we will suppose that there has been equilibrium between saving and investment in the sense that the money income of the community not spent on the consumption of bananas, but saved, is exactly equal to the cost of production and new investment in the further development of banana plantations. You see that that part of their incomes which the community do not spend on bananas is exactly equal to the cost of new investment. Let us suppose that the selling price of bananas is equal to the cost of production, and that ripe bananas will not keep for more than a week or two. Into this Eden there enters a thrift campaign urging the members of the public to abate their improvident practice of spending nearly all their current incomes on buying bananas for food. 'You have no provision for your old age; save more money.' But at the same time there is no corresponding increase in the development of new plantations—which may be the case for one or other of many reasons. It may be that counsels of prudence are influencing the entrepreneurs, also, that they feel no confidence in the future price of bananas, they fear overproduction of bananas and are not disposed to enter on new development; or it may be there are technical reasons which prevent banana plantations from maturing until long after the laying of the plans; or it may be that the labour required for the making of new plantations is a highly specialised form of labour which cannot be trained except after a generation, so that you cannot divert men from the

harvesting of bananas to the preparation of banana plantations. What in that case will happen? The same quantity of bananas as before will continue to be marketed; they will not keep, so that they must be sold. But the amount of current income devoted to the purchase of bananas will be reduced in proportion to the success of the thrift campaign. Since bananas will not keep and people are spending less on them than before, their price must fall, and it will fall exactly in proportion to the amount by which the savings have increased. The consequence will be that as before, the public will consume the whole stock of bananas, but at a reduced price level. Well, that is splendid, or seems so. The thrift campaign will not only have increased saving, it will have reduced the cost of living. The public will have saved money without denying themselves anything, because owing to the reduction in the price of bananas they will be consuming exactly the same quantity of bananas that they were consuming before the thrift campaign; and however much they save, since the price of bananas will fall correspondingly because all the bananas must be marketed, there will never by any change whatever in the amount of bananas they consume. But unfortunately that is not the end of the story; because, since wages are still unchanged—and I assume for the moment that the selling price of bananas will have fallen, but not their cost of production—the entrepreneurs who run the banana plantations will suffer an enormous loss. What will happen is that you have just as many bananas consumed as before, but the entrepreneurs will lose an amount equal to the new savings of those people who have saved.

(CHAIRMAN) *The savings will be in the hands of the banks, and the unhappy* entrepreneur *will have financed the bananas through the banks.* Yes; the public will provide the deposit and the whole of the deposit will be lent out to business men to make up their losses. So that the aggregate savings have not increased the wealth of the community. The only way to increase the wealth of the community would be to have more banana plantations. The only effect has been to transfer the wealth of the entrepreneurs out of their pockets into the pockets of the public.

So all this financial jugglery does not increase the actual wealth of the world. The only thing that increases the actual wealth of the world is actual investment. But that is not the end of the story. The continuance of this will cause entrepreneurs to try and reduce wages, and if they cannot reduce wages they will try to protect themselves by putting their employees out of work.

Now I come to disclose the full horror of the situation. However much they do that it will not help them at all, because as they reduce wages and throw men out of work the buying power to purchase bananas will be reduced by that amount; and so long as the community goes on saving, the business men will always get back from the sale less than their cost of production, and however many men they throw out of work they will still be making a loss.

(PROFFESSOR GREGORY) *I do not agree with this; but go on,—on your assumption that they are only bananas.* It does not really make any difference. The result is that no position of equilibrium can be reached until one of four things has happened. Either finally everybody is out of work and production ceases, and the population starve to death, or the *entrepreneurs* combine to keep up prices on the basis of organised withholding of bananas by means of a combine or cartel; because if they all combine then they can sell their bananas for their cost of production, though even this will not help if the public distinctly save.

(MR BRAND) *Will they sell all the bananas that are over the cost of production?* No; they will not sell all. They will throw part of them away. The rest will rot. Or the thrift campaign falls off, or peters out. Or investment is increased. If some way is found of using these savings then the balance will be again restored. But there is no cure for the reduction of wages and unemployment, except universal starvation, the cartel, the calling off of the thrift campaign for these or other reasons, or the finding of some new outlet for investment. Does that help you, Professor Gregory?

(PROFESSOR GREGORY) *I think your fourth point, namely, that you have got to find an alternative, saves your illustration.*

(MR MCKENNA) *You must balance your savings spent on production by an increase of spending power, which means demand. If you save, and thereby reduce the consumption demand, you must have a corresponding increase of demand coming from some other source, and the banking system supplies that demand by creating more money.* The banking system is a balancing factor because the banking system decides what the aggregate amount of investment is. Therefore you can always cure this trouble by allowing the banking system to operate if you belong to a closed system, as in the banana world. But if the Bank of England were to put the Bank rate at a figure at which current savings could be absorbed by home investment we should try to lend so much abroad, that we should lose gold; therefore the Bank of England, in order to keep our foreign lending on an appropriate level with our balance of trade, has to keep the Bank rate at a higher level than will enable home investment to absorb the quantity of savings; and as long as one is in that dilemma it is necessary that the business world should be losing a sum of money equal to the difference between the aggregate savings of the community and that part which either goes abroad in the form of surplus exports or is embodied in railways or similar things at home. When people call for more savings what they ought to do is to call for more investment. What men get rich by is not by their money savings, but by having more railways, roads and similar investments. There is no other way of getting rich. When these investment processes are not going on *pari passu* with savings, then somebody has to lose; and in our economic system the loser is the business man; and as he is the driving force of the machine, as soon as you put him in that position unemployment must result. It is very easy to overlook all this, because the business man who will in fact suffer most will be the one who for other reasons is in the weakest position. Some classes of business either do not find the demand for their particular goods falling off or they are for some reason in a stronger position. The actual people who suffer losses are people who are anyhow rather near the edge. If it is our textile people who are making losses people say it is not due to general causes, it is due to the fact that we have not any reasonable hope of keeping the proportion of the world trade we had before the War. There are always trades which have difficulties to contend with, and those are the ones who will be pushed over the edge by the operation of general causes.

(CHAIRMAN) *One of your correctives is investment, and it must be investment of something which is of value to the community to increase the wealth generally. Can you always get that investment; is there always a demand for an additional banana plantation? There is no use starting another banana plantation unless you have some means of developing it.* If that is the case, then the only thing is not to be so foolish as to save. But the position is that there are always plenty of useful things to do at a price if you can borrow cheap enough.

If the object is to create banana plantations for the fun of the thing that is not really desirable. If you have more banana plantations than you want, for Heaven's sake stop saving. That is the remedy if we reach that situation, but we have not reached it.

Some things would naturally be of the nature of investment, as you have described—works employing labour and resulting in structures of bricks and mortar, but, having been constructed, would not be of economic value to the country. It all depends what rate of interest you are looking to. At present it may be that the amount you can get for a house will not yield you 6 per cent on its cost of production, but half the amount will yield you 3 per cent. If we were an isolated community the rate of interest would always tend to fall to the yield of the next thing which was worth doing. If new investments could afford to pay a rate which was 3 per cent on the cost of production, then 3 per cent would become the prevailing rate for money; but if we are not in the closed system, then we are in a dilemma because we must keep our rate of interest at a figure which prevents our foreign lending from exceeding our available balance of exports. In a fluid system we should always have enough customers, because if the rate of interest is higher abroad than it is at home, there is a certain eagerness for our goods, at a price, and our wages have to come down to a level at which our exports are large enough to finance our surplus balance of lending. If you had complete fluidity there would always be a point where our wage system would allow our foreign investment to be equal to the surplus of our savings over home investment; but if our wage system is rigid the amount of our foreign investment is rigid also.

(MR BRAND) *You say for Heaven's sake stop saving in bananas, but is that equivalent to saying go on consuming bananas?* If we have eaten all the bananas that are good for us and we should merely have indigestion if we ate more, we can have a slacker time.

The other point I do not quite follow is this; I have always assumed that if I save money those savings go in some form, either by my own investment or by the banker's investment, back into industry. In a fluid system they always would, because the rate of interest as a result of your savings would fall, and, therefore, there would be more demand for investment; but as the rate of interest cannot fall for foreign reasons, your savings can only flow into investments if it takes the form of increased exports.

What happens to my savings? The fact that you do not spend that money means that some business man fails to sell you something he hoped to sell you and has to accept a lower price, and is, therefore, poorer by the exact amount that you are richer.

(PROFESSOR GREGORY) *By the fall of prices.* And very likely, without your knowing it, you yourself as a shareholder find that you are that much poorer. One of the remedies that eventually comes, is that this process so impoverishes the community that in the end it cannot save at all and so you reach equilibrium.

(CHAIRMAN) *That is a strange doctrine to a Scotsman.* What increases the wealth of the world [or] of the country is material things.

(MR BEVIN) *You might have taken oatmeal instead of bananas.*

(MR FRATER TAYLOR) *Really in brief we might say that savings travel by a by-pass road avoiding the route travelled by investment.* Yes, that is what it amounts to. The Bank rate is the balancing factor which determines how much is invested and whether this amount is larger or less than the amount of savings.

(CHAIRMAN) *And it is that amount of investment that is really the governor of the machine?* Yes, if the effect of Bank rate is that investment exceeds saving you have an inflation. If people are able to borrow more [than] the equivalent of saving, prices rise above costs of production and the *entrepreneur* makes windfall profits and the extra investment that is created becomes the property of the *entrepreneur*. Owing to the rise of prices the consumer finds his money income worth less than he anticipated, the profiteer makes the profit and the extra quantity of goods represented by the extra investment—which belongs to the profiteer—is created by the abstemiousness forced on the consumer.

(MR LUBBOCK) *How can you invest more than you save?* You can build material objects in the country which have a cost of production greater than the amount of money saving of the public, apart from the windfall profits of the business man.

(PROFESSOR GREGORY) *You can provide the excess cost of the structure by diminishing the consuming power of the population more than they intended it to be diminished.* The important point is that in periods during which prices are rising for any reason, if you continue the process of investing in excess of saving the excess cost of the extra investment in terms of human effort is met by the reduction in the real income of people who are consuming goods. If prices rise 10 per cent, and a man has an income of a thousand pounds of which he intends to spend £500 and save £500; then when prices have risen the £500 he spends is worth only £450.

(MR MCKENNA) *Mr Lubbock's point was, admitted prices have risen, he saves £450 instead of £500.* No. He saves £500, but the £500 he spends is worth less to him.

But the investment is more than the aggregate of the £500; the difference is found by the— There is one thing which I will not bother you with now in detail. Supposing that the profiteer does not want to save his profits but decides that he is going to live luxuriously. However much extra he spends on consumption his profits (as a class) will be increased by that same amount. Nothing diminishes his profits; his profits are always equal to the difference between the cost of production of investment goods and the amount of saving by the public however luxuriously as a class profiteers live.

You start at any given moment with a certain condition of quantity of money and quantity of production. If you save more at that moment your quantity of bank credit is in excess of your consumption requirements.

(MR LUBBOCK) *What happens then?*

(MR MCKENNA) *Inflation.* The other way round.

(MR LUBBOCK) *Deflation.*

(MR MCKENNA) *Inflation in relation to production; deflation in relation to consumption. You have either a deficiency of bank credit or an excess of bank credit according to the quantity of saving.* Yes, it is very difficult to make it really precise in terms of language.

The saving must be regulated by the quantity of bank credit in existence at any given moment. There are other conditions that happen, because the bank credit is also used for financial transactions; therefore, the most convenient way is to say there is at any given time a certain level of Bank rate which causes the business world to embark on an amount of real investment the cost of production of which is exactly equal to the amount of saving. Any Bank rate which is higher than that is deflation; any Bank rate which is lower is inflation; and you can only tell which the Bank rate is by watching prices.

I agree. So that the price level at any time is made up of two factors; the first factor is cost of production, which is the same thing to the community as a whole as its money income. In equilibrium the prices may rise above or fall below this level and you have an oscillation up or down according to [whether] investment is exceeding saving or saving is exceeding investment, and the difference is profit to the business man.

(CHAIRMAN) *What in turn makes the price level vary?* The oscillation of the price level round the cost of production is brought about by changes in Bank rate; and eventually an oscillation in the cost of production is brought about by the profits or losses stimulating the business world to offer the factors of production a higher or a lower level of income. If there is more gold in the world the way it would work would be the abundance of gold would cause the Bank rate to be low, which would cause investment to increase, which would cause the business men to compete against one another to secure the service of the factors of production to get for themselves the profits resulting from this, and in the long run both prices and the level of income would be raised.

This is all related to the supply of gold? Yes.

Is it not related to the natural phenomena of the world, good harvests and bad harvests? No, that relates to the price of commodities.

If the Bank rate is the panacea, why is it not easy? When you use it for regulating income downward then comes the hitch; and you get into a chronic state of underinvestment, bad profits, unemployment and so forth.

That is to say, you may get into a state of matters which the Bank rate cannot control. It jams; the process does not follow through to its final conclusion.

It comes up against something it cannot surmount? Yes, and that is the worst possible condition, to be left in this jammed state.

It is like a law of nature in that sense; it is ruthless, but it is supposed to be a healthy state. If you are out of equilibrium in the sense in which we are now, there are only three things to get you back to equilibrium, either you must reduce the level of efficiency wages so that foreign investment can increase, or you must diminish saving, or you must increase home investments.

May I put to you quite a general consideration that I think I once put to you when we were talking about these things. Of course, if you are in a realm in which natural law functions nature carries its processes out ruthlessly. If you are in a region in which economic law is allowed to operate then you will not get the results which natural law produces—I mean absolute results. But just as in our civilisation we do not allow natural law to operate, that is to say, we do not allow the weakest to go to the wall, we do not allow a person who is an invalid to be beaten by the rest, we put him in an hospital and try to cure him—in short, civilisation largely consists of trying to prevent the operation of natural law— have we not got into a condition where we have been trying to prevent the consequences of economic laws and prevent their operating by various expedients? We do not allow populations to starve and we have all sorts of expedients. If you get into an artificial condition of affairs, either economic or natural, having to devise expedients to deal with the economic conditions which we have produced, just as we are constantly saving from reasons of humanity lives which are perhaps not worth saving, by providing hospitals for them, so may we not be in a position in which we have to have recourse to expedients which are not economically sound but which those who have been expounding the economic law have allowed to operate.

Yes; and these are the consequences which ensue if you rely on that economic law but do not allow it to operate.

If you impede the action of the law of economics you produce an artificial condition of affairs.

(MR MCKENNA) *I do not think I should accept that view. I should regard the hospital as just as much the outcome of natural law as anything else. The natural law for us does not only include eating and drinking; it is keeping ourselves healthy under conditions of competition. Natural law today includes moral development and the hospital has become a part of the natural law as much as anything else.*

(MR BRAND) *Yes, but it is necessary to see what is happening.*

(CHAIRMAN) *It is not nature red in tooth and claw. I was thinking of nature in the lower creation.*

(MR MCKENNA) *You have to take human nature as it is, and that is part of the natural law.*

(CHAIRMAN) *In that sense it is.* I do not think it is a question of the alternatives being more or less artificial. We have been employing a method which makes a series of assumptions as to the nature of natural law, which are, in fact, invalid.

(MR BEVIN) *So we have got to provide the economic hospital now.* We have to get other instruments of policy, and that is extremely difficult.

(CHAIRMAN) *Just as we have to provide the hospital to satisfy that higher law of our nature, so may we not also have to provide the economic hospital?* I think that is the wrong analogy. I think we are forced by the use of the wrong weapon to have a hospital because it has resulted in there being so many wounded.

(MR BEVIN) *Do you propose to take the economic basis?* I want to use a new weapon of policy so that I have no need for hospitals.

(CHAIRMAN) *The analogy is not so incomplete because the real object is not to provide the hospitals in the natural world, but to have preventive medicine. The other is merely dealing with the products of imperfect prevention.* At present we have been dosing with cascara a patient who has a stoppage.

As I see it—I generally see pictures in my own mind; as you have very properly said, the parable instructs the less instructed mind—in the economic world we have been resorting to things like unemployment insurance and those sort of things which are palliatives to deal with a situation which may be a result of our sins against economic law. I do not think they are sins against economic law. I do not think it is any more economic law that wages should go down easily than that they should not. It is a question of facts. Economic law does not lay down the facts, it tells you what the consequences are.

It does not tell you the right method of doing it, it tells you the circumstances. Yes.

What we are after is not the person who will describe to us what the trouble is in scientific language, but the person who will tell us some method of curing rather than palliating a state of matters which is unhappy. That is our object.

Preventive medicine has achieved a large measure of success; the expectation of life has been improved by several years. Has the economic side any aspect? You are keeping us in suspense; you are a complete dramatist. At the moment the remedies have not been unfolded; I suppose they will be on Friday next? There are so many; yet they all seem imperfect.

Have I gripped more or less the idea of your exposition? Yes; I have been trying to give a diagnosis of what the existing situation is, and what the diagnosis amounts to is, that we are using a weapon as being calculated to bring about economic equilibrium which is in fact not so calculated.

Therefore, it is the Bank rate to which you ultimately attribute everything; you bring it back to the Bank rate? Bank rate I use as shorthand for the terms of lending as a whole.

(MR MCKENNA) *Including the restriction of credit. In what you are going to tell us later you are not leaving out of account, I trust, the effect of an increase or diminution of the quantity of credit apart from the [Bank] rate?* I am not going to say a great deal about that; I could say a great deal about that, but that is a little off what I was going to say.

That is a very important factor.

(CHAIRMAN) *Taking Bank rate in the large term which we understand.*

(MR MCKENNA) *That is the regulator of the rate of investment.* The Bank rate is determined within certain limits by the demand and the supply of lending. There is this terrific complication which I tried to get out of the way yesterday: That we belong to an international system; if we did not belong to an international system I should have said there was no difficulty whatever; one could simply reduce the Bank rate to that level where savings and investments were equal.

(CHAIRMAN) *In a self-contained state Bank rate would function perfectly?* Yes; because in the self-contained state you could keep wages fixed; you could reconcile yourself to that fact and keep your investments always equal to the savings, and let the price level adjust itself to the level of income.

(PROFESSOR GREGORY) *I think it all boils down to the fact that the Bank rate at the present time is primarily fixed with reference to a certain international standard and that does not coincide with the effects of economic policy in other directions.*

(CHAIRMAN) *I think that is a very useful summary, that because we live in a world in which there are other people than ourselves we cannot have regard only to ourselves; we have to have regard to those other people.*

(PROFESSOR GREGORY) *I would like to express a little scepticism about the ease with which Bank rate can always be adjusted to the marginal rate of enterprise.*

(MR BRAND) *In the closed system do you mean it does not matter whether the rate is two per cent or six per cent?* No; I say you can always maintain an equilibrium in which investment is equal to saving. In that closed system you can always allow enough investment to make sure that the whole of the saving is being absorbed.

(MR BRAND) *But the saving is very small. Can you have a very low Bank rate?* You will then have to have a high one.

(MR LUBBOCK) *You would look at the prices?* I should look at the price level primarily.

(CHAIRMAN) *Does it come to this—that because we are not a closed nation the Bank rate cannot achieve the results?* There is also another reason. It could if we were in a *fluid* system. For in that case, when we had a surplus of home investments over savings, the Bank rate could always force wages down to a level where the exports would be adequate.

It would be the principle of hydraulics. Yes; that is the beauty of the Bank rate.

Why is it not fluid now? Well, as I say, I do not think we have ever asked Bank rate to do as much as we are asking now. There are also a great many other reasons. One of them is that it is much harder for us to expand our exports than it used to be. In the glories of the nineteenth century, when we had money that we were prepared to lend abroad, railway systems were developing abroad, and this often materialised in a greater eagerness to take our exports. We were practically the only suppliers of the kind of things that people wanted to put their money into.

(MR MCKENNA) *We built the American and Argentine railways on that basis.*

(CHAIRMAN) *Has the field of world enterprise become exhausted?* No; what happens now is that when we lend £1,000,000 to a foreign country for them to make investments, a comparatively small proportion of that £1,000,000 comes back to us in the form of orders. At one time a very considerable part would come back. So we would quickly stimulate our exports. At present it is very difficult for us greatly to expand our exports, even if we do cut wages. Tariffs in foreign countries are on a sliding scale. As soon as we begin to get in, the tariffs are raised. In other cases where there is an all round surplus capacity, as in the case of coal, our competitors cut their prices. I think, in the case of coal, by reducing wages we may have worsened our situation, because we have put the price of coal down more than we have increased the quantity. If by cutting our prices ten per cent, we increase our exports by less than ten per cent, we have not made our position any better. Cutting prices only helps the situation if trade increases a great deal more in proportion. In the nineteenth century conditions, when we had not a great many competitors, we could quickly stimulate a very considerable increase of trade by being prepared to meet them on terms.

Would it increase employment? Yes; but it would increase employment at the expense of the standard of life.

(MR MCKENNA) *In other words, it can only increase employment if it lowers real wages.*

(PROFESSOR GREGORY) *If a larger output enables you to cut costs.*

(MR MCKENNA) *If you reduce wages there is an end of it?*

(PROFESSOR GREGORY) *A larger output does enable you, among other things, to produce at a reduced overhead cost.*

(SIR WALTER RAINE) *Take the ascertainment in the coalfields for last year— the different quarters. As the production became larger and work was more constant day by day, particularly in Durham and Northumberland, so did the loss fall, and what caused great consternation among the mining community in particular was the paradox of what happened in December. The explanation came out that it was owing to the holidays and the less number of days worked ; you did not get such a good price because there was not so much coal.* Not so much margin of profit?

(SIR WALTER RAINE) *No ; the overhead charges were high.* I think that is all I have to say about that particular aspect of things.

(CHAIRMAN) *Well, you have given us much food for thought. We can only give you an interim dividend of thanks today, because we are still awaiting breathlessly your remedies.*

(MR BRAND) *Would it be possible to have a part in writing about investments and savings?* I have written this out at great length in technical language. It is the only accurate way. But it is enormously complex.

(CHAIRMAN) *We quite realise we are getting the fruits of your research presented to us in a form in which we can understand it. Behind it there is the technical mind.* This has been read now by some of the principal economists of Cambridge, who did not all start sympathetic to it, but they are now satisfied, I think, that it is accurate.

Of course for our purpose we are really not engaged in writing a treatise on political economy. At the same time it is exceedingly important that anything that we say or recommend should not be unsound economically. The only difficulty—I will be quite frank with you—is this: Looking at it, as I say, from the point of view of a purely practical person who has got to make a report, the theories of political economy, as of any other science, are progressive, and vary from time to time. Could we be certain, if we found ourselves in the position in which we could make recommendations in which that doctrine was implicit—could we have any assurance that that was absolutely sound? I think it is very probable that my complete treatment of this will be published before we report. Therefore it will be exposed to the hostile criticism of the world for an appreciable time.

I cannot believe that finality has been reached, even in an exposition by you.

(PROFESSOR GREGORY) *Although I have not seen Mr Keynes's full* exposé *there is not a very wide margin of difference between him and myself on some of the analytical points he has raised.*

(CHAIRMAN) *I rather gathered from those round the table that yesterday's exposition had achieved practically universal consent, but today we have been hearing something rather in the region of new doctrine.* I shall have the proof sheets in a few weeks, which will be at the disposal of any member.

(PROFESSOR GREGORY) *I think the main difference will come over points of policy rather than over theoretical points.* I think it makes a revolution in the mind when you think clearly of the distinction between saving and investment. In pre-War days everybody thought that we were in a state of fluidity, and the whole assumption of orthodox economics and orthodox financial practice is that you have a state of equilibrium.

(CHAIRMAN) *How far have we got to disabuse our minds of that? Have we got to recast the doctrine and instruct the public in a new view?* I think we have.

It is a case of respice finem. *We are not here to traverse the whole subject of political economy; that is not our problem. On the other hand we have to bring our collective wisdom to bear on certain practical problems of the day, and to make recommendations if we can, but the object of all we are hearing is to prevent us making a shocking gaff in the recommendations we make.*

(MR MCKENNA) *Supposing I go to a bank and borrow £100,000; I have saved nothing; the aggregate savings of the community are exactly as they were before; and if I use that £100,000 in bricks and mortar I have increased the amount of investment, but without any relation to any increase in savings.*

(CHAIRMAN) *But is it not true, from what I have learned at this table, that you will not lend me that £100,000 unless Mr Keynes has saved £50,000 and put it in your bank?*

(MR MCKENNA) *No.*

(CHAIRMAN) *I thought the amount you advanced to me was dependent on the amount that other people deposited.*

(MR MCKENNA) *No; it is the other way round. The amount that other people deposit with me depends on what I lend. I do not lend what they deposit with me. What I lend they deposit.*

(PROFESSOR GREGORY) *It is both ways round.*

(MR MCKENNA) *I have got to make the first move.*

(PROFESSOR GREGORY) *I do not agree.*

(MR LUBBOCK) *When you use your £100,000 what do you do? You are investing more than you have saved.*

(MR MCKENNA) *I have saved nothing, but I have invested £100,000. Then you can follow out what happens as the result of that.*

(MR LUBBOCK) *Prices rise.*

(MR MCKENNA) *Prices rise, or may rise.* It may prevent them from falling. *It may prevent them from falling.*

(PROFESSOR GREGORY) *If Mr McKenna lends £100,000 to a builder at a time when I am deliberately abstaining from doing anything else but putting £100,000 in the bank there is no effect on prices. If I spend and you lend £100,000 it cancels out.*

(MR MCKENNA) *I speak as an individual. I go to a bank and I borrow, saving nothing, £100,000, and I put that into bricks and mortar. I produce to my banker a very profitable plan for the use of £100,000 in a building which is required.*

(MR BEVIN) *Where did the bank get the £100,000?*

(MR MCKENNA) *The bank has always got a margin.*

(MR NEWBOLD) *Someone must have put it there already.*

(MR MCKENNA) *It is there. Starting at any given moment the bank I go to has £100,000 in its tills. I go to that bank and say 'Lend it me.' I have saved nothing. I use that £100,000 in bricks and mortar. I have then created a new investment of £100,000 and that comes back to the bank as a deposit.*

(MR NEWBOLD) *Supposing your average depositors went to the bank and withdrew their deposits and took them home.*

(MR MCKENNA) *The Bank of England would not let them have the money.* Then the Bank of England, owing to the enormous increase in the note issue, would have to buy a greater quantity of Treasury bills from somebody or other in order to balance the other side of the account, and they would buy them from Mr McKenna, who would be parting with them at the same time; you would simply be parting with deposits at the bank in exchange for deposits at the Treasury.

(CHAIRMAN) *I cannot see why Mr McKenna and other bankers should plume themselves on the amount of their deposits.* The aggregate of all the deposits depends on the action of the Bank of England. What proportion of them he gets depends on how much he 'does down' the other banks.

(MR LUBBOCK) *Mr McKenna in the bank from whom he has borrowed has £100,000 on one side for deposits and on the other side £100,000 for advances. Each side has increased £100,000 and he has created £100,000 purchasing power.*

(MR MCKENNA) *I have got, say, £40,000,000 of money; that gives me a ratio of 11 per cent to my liabilities. I choose to reduce my ratio to 10 per cent. I can then lend four millions of money to anybody.*

(CHAIRMAN) *You possess a credit at the moment which enables you to make an advance of that sort, but that credit in turn surely depends upon the extent to which the public have confided their money to you.*

(MR MCKENNA) *Yes, they have confided it to the extent to which I have lent them.*

(MR BRAND) *If I come to you today and your percentages are quite right, you can lend me £100,000 merely by writing in a book?*

(MR MCKENNA) *Yes, and whatever I lend comes back to me.* At the same time he lends Mr Brand £100,000, Mr Brand must deposit this sum or pay it out to others who deposit it.

(CHAIRMAN) *I do not understand how Mr McKenna can do that. It is no use my going to a book and putting £1,000,000 in it. How is that Mr McKenna can do that?*

(MR LUBBOCK) *He is making himself liable to pay out £100,000 in notes.*

(MR BEVIN) *Is this the real explanation of bank profits?*

(MR MCKENNA) *No; unfortunately the gentleman who places the deposit with me demands payment of interest on the deposit.* One might suppose that our banking system would be such that it would always try to lend an amount equal to the amount of savings entrusted to it. As a matter of fact it never troubles about that. The individual bank never considers how much is being saved, it simply thinks of its balance at the Bank of England, and the Bank of England in lending them that never thinks about the amount the public is saving, but about the gold position. Under the system that I have outlined, they are seeking to grind out equality between saving and investment by the economic machine which by a series of manoeuvres, brings wages and prices to a level at which these two things are equal—that is, assuming that the machine is working without grit in it.

The machine has not worked for the last 10 years.

(MR BEVIN) *I do not think it can again; can it?* If once we get back to equilibrium, it might.

(MR MCKENNA) *If you get another Rand.* If the Rand Mines produced [sufficient gold to raise prices] and they do, we might be all right.

(PROFESSOR GREGORY) *In order to get equilibrium you will have to keep your prices down whilst in the rest of the world prices are rising.*

(MR MCKENNA) *If there were more gold, prices would rise all over the world.*

(PROFESSOR GREGORY) *And our wages would not.*

(MR MCKENNA) *Our wages would not. We can raise them but we cannot force them down.*

(CHAIRMAN) *What is the purpose of the witnesses coming here and telling us that they always keep their advances to a certain ratio of deposits if their advances are not dependent on their deposits? Yes, they are; they are interdependent.*

(MR MCKENNA) *If I lend £100,000, when it comes back to me I have the same cash but more liabilities, therefore, my ratio has fallen; therefore, I do not lend.*

(MR BRAND) *It depends on his power to get notes.*

(MR MCKENNA) *My power to get cash depends on the Bank of England.*

(MR BEVIN) *If £40,000,000 taken out of the Rand means that amount of credit issued, would not the alteration of the ratio produce the same result?*

(MR MCKENNA) *If all the world did it you would probably need another £40,000,000 today to keep the ratio stationary; if France and all the other banks of the world go on absorbing gold as they have you will want another £40,000,000. Last year France absorbed £80,000,000; trade and India absorbed £40,000,000, so last year there was a useless consumption from the point of view of credit of £120,000,000 of gold. The total production was £80,000,000, so prices went down.*

(MR BEVIN) *Do you take the view that we must inevitably go off the gold standard?*

(MR MCKENNA) *You might have a gold standard differently worked, but that is another point. I am not suggesting a remedy at the moment; we are only dealing with the situation as we see it.*

(CHAIRMAN) *We have to look ahead at our Report. The first part will be a more or less non-controversial* exposé *of the present position in which we shall be able to use much of the material that Mr Keynes and other people have given us. We have a description of the working of the Bank of England system which Sir Ernest Harvey has given us, and other banks have given us a description of the working of their system. Then we should have an account of the economic presuppositions, what is the principle behind that structure and how it is working. Having got that, we should probably then discuss the relation of the present difficulties, unemployment, industrial unrest and so on to that system, with a view of seeing if an explanation can be found of those phenomena in that system which we have just described. It may be we shall find in the imperfections of the existing system some at least of the causes of the present phenomena. On the other hand, we may not. I do not know what we shall find. I have no doubt that we shall have witnesses come and ascribe much of our misfortune to the present system. How far they will persuade us remains to be seen. It may be that in part or in whole the present phenomena that we are desirous of curing have their origin or are associated with the monetary system. That may be our conclusion. On the other hand, it may be that we shall find that the monetary system has practically nothing to do with it. Mr Keynes says 'whatever may be my criticism as to the wisdom of our method of reversion to the gold standard, or a gold standard system in one shape or another, I accept'—that is what I understand—'the present system'*. I am prepared to do my best to suggest alternative remedies; whether they will work is another matter.

On the hypothesis that the present system is to go on, what is the best that you can do within the present situation to alleviate the distress? I think if we decide that one of our pre-suppositions is to leave the existing system as it is, we have to give reasons for that. We must try to find reasons.

(MR BEVIN) *And that is difficult.* Oh, no. There are some quite good reasons. I would not acquiesce in that if there were no good reasons.

(CHAIRMAN) *It may be that the reasons for adhering to that system are more potent than the reasons for departing from it. It may be that if you were in an ideal world you would not wish to depart from it, but in a practical world the consequences of departing from the present regime might be such as to cause greater distress.*

(PROFESSOR GREGORY) *It is perfectly obvious if we recommended getting off the gold standard for any reason, because we accepted Mr Keynes's views or any other, we should be simply adding to the dislocation and confusion of the City.*

(CHAIRMAN) *The existing regime furnishes for us the primary data, and what we are entitled to see is whether within these presuppositions we can do anything to make that system work better.* If I were the drafter of the Report I should not recommend going off the gold standard at this moment; not until I had tried other expedients, but I should not have complete confidence in the efficacy of these alternatives. Meanwhile I think the dangers of going off are such, that I would not even talk about it.

(MR MCKENNA) *I would not discuss the gold standard if it is possible to avoid it, but I do think we might reasonably discuss certain remedies in the working of the gold standard.* One need not be supposed to have complete confidence in the remedies that one is recommending.

(MR BEVIN) *On the other hand, while you may express your fears of dislocation, the effects of the operation of the monetary system in the last four years on poor people have been very terrible, and have certainly been serious in this country and other parts of the world. Assuming having discussed all the expedients for making the system work, having regard not only to the well-being of the City of London, but the needs of the community, you come to the conclusion that your expedients are not workable or you have grave doubts as to their wisdom, surely the Committee would not refuse to go to the root of the trouble and even revert to the former position?*

(CHAIRMAN) *If we were in that position, if we had reached the position that we were satisfied that nothing but a radical operation would cure the disease, the radical operation being departing from the gold standard, and adopting some new system.*

(MR BEVIN) *Demonetising gold, for instance?* I do not think it will come to be as bad as that. There is something to be said for each of the different remedies that people have been proposing, and one might make a concoction which in the aggregate might be of value.

One is rather reluctant at this stage of the proceedings to make up one's mind that under no circumstances are you to tackle the gold standard.

(CHAIRMAN) *If we were at the stage that we were at years ago when the matter was still open, we might do very good service in discussing the pros and cons of that question, but it seems to me, the plunge having been taken and already everything having adjusted itself to that, we should be in grave difficulties if we were to try and retrace our steps now, because the consequences of that might be too appalling to contemplate; and the trouble in these financial things I think is this, that it is almost as dangerous to talk about them as to do them.*

(MR LUBBOCK) *Is not this rather premature?*

(MR BEVIN) *It is my fault. I was not here, I was away in the country; I read the Minutes and I thought you ruled out the gold standard.*

(CHAIRMAN) *We did come to a conclusion.*

(MR BEVIN) *I am taking this opportunity, not so much to say that we should go back on it, but to make that observation, that one would like to see whether any expedients are workable before we come to a conclusion on anything.*

(CHAIRMAN) *I think the public would like to have from us something about the gold standard, but, frankly, I should be very cautious indeed in saying anything unless I was very sure of my ground. I should be very much afraid of hesitating doubts.*

(MR BEVIN) *There are two things to accomplish: One is to maintain the standard of living and even to see it progress—that is the object of industry, is it not?—and I want to test every expedient by that standard.* I agree with Mr Bevin we must be in a position ourselves to enter into the whole thing. I have given a great deal of thought to what one could do if we were to go off the gold standard. I do not like the look of it.

(CHAIRMAN) *It is not ourselves alone; the world is involved in this. We are not masters; we cannot afford to experiment and act as if we were the only people concerned.* But I do not think that the evils would be so great that you could not suffer greater evils.

(MR BEVIN) *I agree.*

(MR LUBBOCK) *The trouble is, we are going to pay our debts in gold.*

(MR MCKENNA) *The French took £80,000,000 last year; they have the capacity to take another £300,000,000.* Other people have contracted to pay debts to us.

In sterling. We have not yet contracted to pay in gold.

(MR LUBBOCK) *No, but we have passed a law that any government can get gold.*

(MR MCKENNA) *Our contract is sterling. The American contract is gold.*

(MR LUBBOCK) *Technically I am down.* The great trouble is that if we do something to depreciate sterling we lose a very great deal of interest earnings in sterling. If we owed the world a lot of money I think you would find we should have got off the gold standard by now.

We should have remained off.

(MR BRAND) *If we owed them in sterling.* Yes, if we owed them in sterling.

(MR LUBBOCK) *The Committee is not presumed to have accepted entirely everything that Mr Keynes has said.*

(CHAIRMAN) *Nobody has accepted everything.*

(MR LUBBOCK) *I do not mean to say we do not accept it.*

(CHAIRMAN) *No judge ever pronounces his judgement until he has heard the whole case.*

(Adjourned until Thursday next,
27 February 1930, at 4.30 p.m.)

After the second day of his presentation, Keynes reported to Lydia.

From a letter to LYDIA KEYNES, *23 February 1930*

On Friday they found my speech much more perplexing as I thought they would. I think I did it all right. But it was unfamiliar and paradoxical, and whilst they couldn't confute me, they did not know whether or not to believe. However, it was real progress, I think.

The next Friday Keynes continued his presentation.

COMMITTEE ON FINANCE AND INDUSTRY

Note of discussion on
Friday, 28 February 1930

Present:

The Rt Hon. Lord Macmillan (*Chairman*)

Sir Thomas Allen	Mr Cecil Lubbock
Mr Ernest Bevin	The Rt Hon. Reginald McKenna
The Rt Hon. Lord Bradbury, G.C.B.	Mr J. T. Walton Newbold
The Hon. R. H. Brand, C.M.G.	Sir Walter Raine
Professor T. E. Gregory, D.SC.	Mr J. Frater Taylor
Mr J. M. Keynes, C.B.	Mr A. A. G. Tulloch
Mr G. Ismay (*Secretary*)	

(CHAIRMAN) *Mr Keynes, I see that last time, pointing out the difficulties of Bank rate policy in its adaptation to the present emergency, you said that 'Bank rate policy, whilst theoretically intact, has broken down as a practical instrument for restoring true equilibrium.' Then you add 'I am absolutely convinced that a Bank rate policy for certain purposes, and within certain limits, is essential, but there are alternatives that can be discussed, and with the leave of the Committee I will deal with them next week, classifying them under the headings into which they fall.' May we take it that we have got your exposition of the disequilibrium in which we are living, and of the inadequacy of existing Bank rate policy to meet it, and are we to have from you today some of your suggestions as to those alternatives which would make the Bank rate policy to operate?* Yes. I should like just to link up the argument by a very brief summary of the broad conclusions of the previous discussions. I think that the condition of trouble in the country is primarily due to general causes, though in each specially afflicted case special causes naturally appear, because when general causes operate it is those industries or individuals who are not in a condition to stand any trouble that suffer most, and then you can always attribute what has happened to that element in their condition which made them vulnerable rather than to the general cause. The general causes seem to me to be two; though they both arise out of what is essentially one situation, they are two factors of that situation. The first general cause, as I see it, is that relative costs of production at home and abroad, taken in conjunction with the relative demand for loans at home and abroad for investment purposes, are such that a Bank rate which is high enough to prevent us from lending too much abroad is too high to enable us to have the right amount of enterprise at home; so that our savings can neither get out over the frontier in the shape of exports, because our costs of production are relatively too high, nor can they be employed at home in domestic enterprise, because the rate of interest which the Bank of England has to maintain is deterrent to domestic enterprise. That works in a vicious circle in which the initial effect is aggravated by the subsequent reactions. That means that a certain amount of our savings is spilled on the ground, and becomes business men's losses. The savings of the public, plus the profits or minus the losses of the business world, are actually equal to the total amount of our investment. Our investment abroad is fixed by the cost of production, our investment at home is fixed by the rate of interest, and the two together fall short of our savings, and the difference is accounted for by the loss to the business world. If I wanted to get at the magnitude of it, I should say the loss to the business world due to those causes is now of the order of £80,000,000 a year. Of course, that is a very rash guess, but I feel pretty confident it is more than £50,000,000 and less than £100,000,000, and I put it at £80,000,000. Business men are making losses. I mean by losses not necessarily absolute losses but less than normal profit—less than they expect to get. This wastage of savings having emerged in the shape of losses, the losses discourage the business man and investor, and are an additional deterrent to new enterprise. This discouragement comes on top of the high Bank rate to which I have previously alluded. But the latter is also aggravated by it because investors become still more anxious to invest abroad, owing to business at home being unprofitable, and in order to prevent that you have to have a still higher Bank rate, so that again the business losses tend to increase.

(MR BRAND) *May I ask one question? Did you say to start with that it is because our relative costs are higher that a Bank rate such as we have now is a deterrent?* I do not say that. I say that our relative costs are too high to enable us to have more exports than we have got; those exports are not large enough to finance all the lending abroad that we should like to do; the Bank rate has to be raised to prevent us from lending abroad a sum in excess of that which can be financed by exports. But if our costs of production were lower we should have more exports; we could therefore finance more foreign lending, and therefore the Bank of England would not have to have such a high rate.

Is it the height of the relative costs? Taken in conjunction with our wanting to invest so much abroad. If we were wanting to invest more at home and not to invest so much abroad, then the demand at home would be keener, and it would not be necessary to force out our exports. For various reasons the investor is discouraged. We are an old country, and it is always more difficult to pay a high rate in an old country than in a new. Apart from that you have a vicious circle, business men and investors are discouraged by their experience so that they will not invest except on very attractive terms.

95

We have got now a five per cent Bank rate. A five per cent Bank rate here might be a deterrent; a five per cent Bank rate in Germany might not be a deterrent at all. Yes.

What is the difference between the conditions in Germany and here that makes it a deterrent in one case and not in another? Business men do not see enterprise at home sufficiently attractive to justify their borrowing at the current rate of interest.

Why is it not attractive? Is it because our costs of production are too high? If we were a closed system the costs of production at home would not matter, because you get it all back, as Mr Ford would say; if you are paying high wages you are getting a better market; therefore if you were thinking of a closed situation the costs of production would not matter. It is not the absolute cost of production, it is the relative cost of production here and abroad as exhibited in the diminished exports.

(MR LUBBOCK) *I cannot quite see why a reduction in the cost of production would not help home industry.*

(CHAIRMAN) *Mr Keynes is only referring to the position there would be if we were a closed system.* As far as the home situation is concerned, if you reduced wages you would be reducing buying power on the other side.

(MR BRAND) *Supposing costs were lower now there would be greater exports with the same Bank rate?* Yes, there would be greater exports.

(PROFESSOR GREGORY) *And you would not have to pay such a high rate.*

(MR BRAND) *You have got to find an equilibrium.* I had got to the point that owing to this disequilibrium there are business losses. As a result of the business losses unemployment ensues, so that we have a second loss. First of all there is a loss of current business, which I guess at £80,000,000 a year, which is money being lost by business men who are carrying on. Then in addition to that you have the loss in the national income caused through those business men who do not carry on.

(CHAIRMAN) *Who give up.* Yes. And the unemployment which results from that. If we were to guess the unemployment through this source as equivalent to the labour of 600,000 men—part of it is female labour and part of it you certainly cannot attribute to this cause—then the reduction of the national income through labour idleness—allowing for the fact that we also have the plant and the instruments which they have been using lying idle,— can be taken at £120,000,000. A man with his equipment is worth about £200 a year. Therefore the total impoverishment directly attributable to the disequilibrium, I should guess as being of the order of about £200,000,000 annually, of which £80,000,000 would be savings which have to go to balance the losses of business men, in order to keep the national wealth stationary, instead of actually increasing the national wealth as they ought.

96

Would that £200,000,000 be cumulative? Cumulative each year.

(MR MCKENNA) *That supplies the answer to the question you put yesterday, Mr Chairman: Where is the market for the additional goods supplied by the labour of those additional 600,000 men?* If one puts it that way it emphasises what a large problem it is—£200,000,000 a year is an enormous sum by which to reduce the national income. On the other hand it is only about five per cent of the total national income, so that looked at in that way, one sees that it is not a thing so large that it cannot come about by the rather intricate working of actions and reactions.

(SIR T. ALLEN) *At what figure would you put the national income?* At £4,000,000,000 from all sources.

Have you an idea how much is represented by wages? The usual guess is half. It depends upon where one draws the line between wages and salaries. All the recipients of this income are potential consumers. If these figures are right the loss is something very substantial, and quite enough to account for what we have experienced. At the same time it is not absolutely devastating; it is compatible with the maintenance of a high level of living for the bulk of the population. Five per cent of the national income probably does not represent the increased efficiency of the last ten years. The increased efficiency may easily have been ten per cent in the last ten years; therefore we may have a loss of the national income of the order of five per cent and still be five per cent better off than we were ten years ago. But the way in which this loss falls is such as to make it much worse than if it were an all-round reduction of income of five per cent. So far as unemployment is concerned it is on the backs of a comparatively small part of the working population, who suffer the misery and deterioration of character that follows, and so far as the business losses are concerned, so long as we have a society in which business profit is the mainspring of enterprise, it has a very disastrous psychological and human effect because those people on whom we depend for setting everything in motion are not getting their proper reward.

(CHAIRMAN) *They are discouraged.* Yes. So the evil effects are very much greater on the general progress of the community than they would be if everybody's income were five per cent less than it is.

(SIR W. RAINE) *Do you mean that certain trades or sections of a trade, have their cycles of depression, and whilst they may be having a very bad time other sections may be having a good time, which compensates them in one particular year?* I say that at the present time this is not in the nature of an oscillation between one industry and another. It is a general cause affecting all industries; the weaker ones bear the brunt of it, but most industries are making less than normal profits.

Is this loss of £200,000,000 being made in the weaker trades, or is it being lost

97

in particular trades in particular years, while other trades may be prosperous, so that the upshot of it may be that in the course of years the weaker people will be squeezed out? I think if this was to go on for another ten years we would have large branches of industry extinguished.

During the last few years the north-east coast, where I come from, has suffered terribly, whereas they have had a great amount of continued prosperity in Birmingham and the Midlands. Then the position has slightly turned, and through fortuitous circumstances the north-east coast has been very busy. What I should like to know is, have all the trades suffered or is it in cycles? I should say that the particular trades which bear the brunt of the £80,000,000—if that is the right figure—vary from year to year; it is sometimes one, sometimes the other.

(MR McKENNA) *Would you say that the loss is nearly all in the unsheltered trades, and the trades that have got the benefit are the sheltered?* The railways are often thought of as sheltered trades, but the railways are bearing quite a large share of the loss.

(CHAIRMAN) *I was very much struck by what you said last time, that the unsheltered industries are actually carrying the sheltered industries on their back.*

(MR McKENNA) *If you take the men in the railways, they are anything but suffering; they are doing very well. The rate of wages on the railways is very high.* MR BEVIN: *No.* SIR W. RAINE: *Compared to shipbuilding.* MR BEVIN: *It all depends on what you call high.* MR McKENNA: *Relatively.* MR BEVIN: *No, not relatively. You have 50 per cent of the people on the railway who are getting 50s. per week.* MR McKENNA: *But if you compare that 50s. with what other and more skilled men get for longer hours, or at any rate, for harder work, relatively they are doing very well.*

(MR TULLOCH) *On the subject of business efficiency, I think you mentioned an increase of 1½ per cent per annum. If you have a very bad time, such as we have been having during the last two or three years, that ratio would not be the same?* Certainly not, It is irregular. I am trying to get an average figure. I think it is one per cent; I think the Census of Production and various other checks that one has would justify one in saying it may be even more than one. I do not mean an increase of profit.

No; I know what you mean exactly, you mean business efficiency; so that when trade is there we can produce more efficiently. Yes, that is what I mean.

(MR BRAND) *You start from the assumption that in a closed system there is no reason why anybody should be unemployed?* Yes.

(MR TULLOCH) *That would depend on the amount of production. You would not get overproduction?* No; you would always let the rate of interest fall to the point at which new enterprise could be stimulated, and if you got to a point where everybody had what they wanted then it would be time to stop saving and enjoy increased leisure.

(CHAIRMAN) *This ideal state does not exist.* I look on the task of this Committee as being to save that £200,000,000 a year, as near as may be.

(CHAIRMAN) *You are helping us by going right down to the fundamental causes that are not realised by ordinary people. The trouble with most practical people is that they address themselves to the symptoms rather than the causes. We want to treat the disease as we see it, and most of the expedients strike me as being addressed to the symptoms rather than to the causes. You are unveiling to us the causes which in your mind are behind the whole thing.* Yes. On the other hand I think you will see when I come to my suggestions that the remedies which are being suggested have nearly all of them something in them; that whilst the empirical method is not by any means successful for the diagnosis it is not by any means valueless for seeking the cure. While I have my preferences, practically all the remedies seem to have something in them.

Of course, a palliative may do a great deal of good; it may remove the symptoms for the time being; on the other hand you may break up your general health in trying to oust the disease.

(PROFESSOR GREGORY) *Assuming that there are classes of business losses of any order of magnitude, that does reduce the flow of savings?* Yes, probably.

But you have not got a constant stream of savings dammed up. As long as the actual material wealth of the country remains stationary, if particular individuals are losing £80,000,000 other individuals are saving £80,000,000 and we should be level. What I am saying is that £80,000,000 of normal savings are being used up in making good losses; and while those £80,000,000 savings may appear to be used in giving employment in industry, it is balanced by the £80,000,000 losses. The material wealth of the country is not increased to the extent it should be.

I shall now be classifying the suggested remedies in such a manner as to fit in neatly with this general analysis and diagnosis. I hope the Committee will excuse me if in doing this I show no delicacy of mind whatever.

(CHAIRMAN) *You mean susceptibilities must for the time being be laid aside?* I propose, as a scientist, to be—

Remorseless. The first class of remedy consists in the revaluation of the gold value of sterling. That is often described as 'going off the gold standard', but it is not really so; it is a change in gold parity. Going off the gold standard would be to take up some alternative standard such as the tabular standard, silver or wheat. But revaluation would be doing what might have been done in 1925, that is, fixing the gold parity at a different level from that at which it was fixed. It would be doing something which we should very likely have done in 1925 if we had foreseen all that has happened since, and which we could have done at that date without any untoward consequences worth bothering about. That is a controversial statement.

And it has been done elsewhere? It has been done in almost every important country which suffered a severe depreciation during the War.

(PROFESSOR GREGORY) *Is there not an exception—Sweden?* They had no war debt. Every other country had. If we did such a thing, of course, the preparations would have to be made with the utmost secrecy and the blow struck suddenly, and if it were done I think it would be essential to our credit that the Bank of England should be provided with a large fund to compensate all *bona fide* holders of short funds in London, so that no one who trusted to our credit would be a loser. We should also lose in respect of sterling debts due to us because we should be paid the interest and repayment of capital on those loans with proportionately less goods. Supposing the change were 10 per cent, supposing the revaluation were of the order of 10 per cent and supposing the compensation on short funds amounted to the order of £50,000,000; if the sums due to us in sterling were of the order of £2,500,000,000 we should lose on that score also a lump sum of £250,000,000—

(MR BRAND) *I thought our total foreign investments were larger.* Our total foreign investments are larger, but a considerable amount is not fixed in sterling. I am simply using these figures as an illustration, not as a scientific estimate of the actual figure. You get a loss of something like £300,000,000. Such a loss is not so large that we should refuse to contemplate it in any circumstances. It is only a year and a half of what I suggest the present loss of equilibrium may be costing us. But taken in conjunction with the extraordinary disturbance of credit which a thing of that sort would set up in people's minds, I think these factors in themselves constitute a weighty argument against this remedy. If it had been done in 1925 the compensation would not have been necessary, and the general disturbance and so on would not have existed. In 1925 there would only have been one of the three factors of loss, and it certainly would have paid us to have made the loss of £250,000,000 in 1925 rather than suffer £200,000,000 loss each year subsequently.

(MR FRATER TAYLOR) *An opportunity was lost.* I think so. But whether or not one thinks that these various considerations are weighty arguments, I feel pretty confident, and I expect other members of the Committee do, that it is a remedy which in fact the powers that be would refuse to adopt except, so to speak, under duress, and by that I mean only if all other remedies had failed us and in consequence of that the state of affairs had got very much worse than it is now. There is no likelihood of such a remedy being adopted in present circumstances. Therefore, the country, and this Committee as representing the country, will do well first of all to explore all the other exits that offer themselves, because one can be sure that the powers that be will only fall back on this one as the very last resort. Therefore, I propose to say no more about it. It ought not to be regarded as an unthinkable expedient and I think we could, at sufficient cost, take measures that would go a very long way towards protecting our credit. We could protect ourselves from the charge of in any way defaulting.

(CHAIRMAN) *You would be giving more for your purchases.* We should be getting more for our exports. In current trading there is nothing in it on balance, but only in respect of debt. It would not really cost us £250,000,000 at once; it would cost us five per cent on that per annum; what we should have to find would be the £50,000,000 of compensation to write off at once and a loss for a long period of years hereafter of £12,500,000. That makes it still less formidable. In putting the figure of £250,000,000 I am capitalising the £12,500,000.

(LORD BRADBURY) *Your American debt would cost you more in sterling.* That would not matter, because sterling would be worth less.

(MR BRAND) *Every foreign holder of sterling securities would suffer, whether he was a holder of short or long securities.* Every holder of sterling securities would lose and one would have to draw a line between those who had an equitable claim to compensation and those who had not.

(MR FRATER TAYLOR) *As regards bargaining, you would be on a more competitive basis.* We should be.

I do not follow why we should not have to pay more for the raw cotton. It would cost more in terms of sterling but we should get more for our exports. Regarded as barter we should be sending out the same value of British goods for raw cotton.

(MR BEVIN) *How would it affect services?* It would not affect those at all. Freights we should in effect get gold prices for, which would be turned into ten per cent more sterling.

(MR LUBBOCK) *Prices would rise.* Prices in sterling would rise all round.

(SIR T. ALLEN) *When we have examined the other remedies that you propose putting up, if we find we have to come back to a proposition of this character, would it be possible to forward some Minute to the Treasury that need not be put into our Report at all, but that would draw the attention of any Government to such an alternative?* I should prefer not to dwell upon or contemplate this expedient any further.

(CHAIRMAN) *The mere fact that we had discussed it as within the range of possibility—*

(PROFESSOR GREGORY) *Oh, if we discussed it in the Report you may be certain there would be a drop of ten points in sterling the day after.*

(MR BRAND) *Not ten points.*

(CHAIRMAN) *Then we would be far from being a blessing to our country!*

(PROFESSOR GREGORY) *Mr Keynes is right; if it were done it would have to be done with great secrecy.*

(CHAIRMAN) *Only reasons of high state policy would justify it.* I think it is useful to have had it before us in this limited way.

(MR BEVIN) *Assuming that one did revalue, would the disturbance be any greater than it was to the work-people of this country with all the starvation that was involved in 1926?* I think we should forget about the effects of it in a very short time if we did it. But that does not affect its practicability.

(LORD BRADBURY) *It is just possible that the beneficial results would be just as short-lived.* That remains to be seen. May I pass on to the second class of remedy? The second class of remedy is an agreed reduction of the level of money incomes in this country. This is the remedy that I advocated in 1925, immediately after the return to gold. I do not suppose it is practicable now, but I still believe it is in some respects the ideal remedy, and I think it is one that this Committee ought to ponder to a certain extent before they reject it. Its feasibility is almost entirely a matter of psychological and political, and not economic factors, and I shall be particularly interested to hear Mr Bevin's reaction.

(CHAIRMAN) *What is the principle?* It would consist of a great national treaty among ourselves. I conceive of the Prime Minister calling together representatives of all the economic elements in the country, and proposing to them a national resettlement of the level of money incomes of every description whatsoever.

(PROFESSOR GREGORY) *Including War debts?* It would be agreed first of all that all wages, salaries, and emoluments of every kind whatsoever expressed in money should be reduced by ten per cent as from an agreed date—everything which income tax regards as earned income should be reduced ten per cent. It would be possible to point out, of course, that the cost of living would fall to a considerable extent as the result of that, so as to balance that to a considerable extent.

(MR BEVIN) *What guarantee of that is there?* How much it would fall would depend on circumstances. You could not guarantee that it would fall to a full extent, at any rate, quickly.

(MR BRAND) *Is that for one year?* You start from a new base. You do not fix the new level any more than it is fixed now. You start on a new level, and any improvement would take place from that level upwards. There are three classes of income. There are wages, salaries, and emoluments, which I have just dealt with. I do not think it would be practicable to deal with the second class in the same way, namely, fixed payments in terms of money,—rent, interest, and debentures—it would lead to endless difficulties and complications if you tried to write them down in any way. I should deal with them by a special tax of 2s. in the pound on all unearned income.

(MR BEVIN) *That would be very popular with the country.* So that all earned income would be reduced 2s. in the pound and all unearned incomes would be taxed to the same extent. It would be better if that tax were regarded as a special tax, and were entirely devoted to reducing the cost of production in other ways; for instance it might be used to meet the employers' contribution towards social insurance, which is beginning to work very much as a tax on industry—being based on the number of men employed; and the balance might be used for relief of rates. As regards the merchant, who neither has a fixed salary, nor is a recipient of unearned income, I think it would be difficult to put any definite reduction on him. He lives mainly by percentages; if he is a broker or a middleman he definitely gets percentages, therefore if all the other things are cut down his income falls with them, and I do not believe there is any way of taxing otherwise the recipient of that class of income.

(MR FRATER TAYLOR) *Could you not deal with his profits?* Well, you might, but I should shrink from the proposal. It would be extremely impracticable.

(SIR W. RAINE) *I think you would have to deal with it on the lines you have mentioned—by a fixed income tax.* That might be possible.

A merchant does a certain amount of business on a small percentage and his income varies widely. In one year his business might be very large, and you might have a profit; in another year you might have a loss; therefore you could only do it on the lines you have mentioned. It depends how particular you want to be. My own preference would be for something as simple as possible, namely, to keep the existing income categories of earned and unearned. That would, as you correctly point out, lead to anomalies, and undue preference in particular cases.

(MR BEVIN) *Have you considered in your ten per cent reduction all-round the position of the people who have already suffered 20 per cent reduction as the result of 1925?* That would be one of the difficulties, and it would have to be considered whether there were any exceptions to be made. That would be precisely the kind of difficulty encountered; I think it is very great.

How would you take into consideration a case like this: this morning I dealt with a wage problem which does not reduce the money income, but gives a 25 per cent addition on the output. Would you come along and take ten per cent off? Not if there were any new settlement made.

You must remember that since 1925—you mentioned railways—the amount handled per unit is up 25 per cent on the average. I am assuming that the increase of efficiency has not been enough to balance the extra buying power.

Take shipbuilding now and compare the output per unit with the modern plant with what it was before. That is a separate problem; the fact that the wages in different trades have got out of gear is a different problem from the general forces I am talking about.

If, as you argued just now, the sheltered industries have been maintained all this time and the unsheltered industries, either by increased output or lower wages or some other factor, have had their wages altered already by 20 per cent and you say you are not to upset the relative positions by taking 10 per cent off, how would you expect to get any settlement? I would take 10 per cent off now and I should expect that the unsheltered industries would benefit more than the others, and they would, after this reduction had been in force a few years, be in a position to work their wages up as compared with the sheltered industries. I think the net effect of this on the unsheltered industries would be enormously advantageous, and that with its aid it is much more likely that they would rehabilitate themselves. But I could not hope by this means to cure the individual discrepancies.

Would you not get a further loss of production owing to the increased cost? Why should I? It might be that this would influence people's minds in that way.

When you said that you would not contemplate the first proposal because of the disturbance, would not the disturbance of the second proposal be so great psychologically that it would not be wise to contemplate it? It depends on the spirit in which it is done.

(PROFESSOR GREGORY) *Is not the answer to Mr Bevin this? Supposing you could get it through, Mr Keynes's point is that it would lead to a very rapid diminution in the volume of unemployment; you would get a comparative [competitive?] wage level and you would then start to bargain up to the improved conditions of employment.*

(MR BEVIN) *That is assuming that you did not have unemployment before the War, and that you had your equilibrium before the War as perfect as you could get it. Yet, taking the insured population, except for the short period when we were busy making war material, when you were carrying nearly 33 per cent of your population in the provision of warships and other direct and indirect implements of war, apart from that period, from 1911 to 1914 we carried in proportion to our total output almost the same percentage of unemployment as we carry now.*

(MR MCKENNA) *Surely not.*

(MR BEVIN) *Yes, we did proportionately. You did not have the same register: do not forget that. Do not forget that Campbell-Bannerman had to declare that there were 12,000,000 people below the poverty line in 1906 when you had a perfect equilibrium but a smaller population.*

(PROFESSOR GREGORY) *In spite of all these disadvantages the trade union movement has been in the position in the last 50 years to raise the standard of wages considerably, and to force indirect economies on the employers. Do you not think that would operate to a larger extent on half a million unemployed than on a million and a half?* I think there is real force in Mr Bevin's objection. And there are other objections. For one thing, I should not expect the effect of the proposal on unemployment or on the cost of living to be immediate. On the other hand, in time, I think, this measure would do an enormous amount.

(MR BEVIN) *How long would it be before the cost of living came down?* It would come down somewhat almost at once, but I would not expect to get the full benefit of it for a year or so.

You would reduce the earning power of the population. You might temporarily reduce the purchasing power of wages five per cent; I should not expect it to be more.

If you reduce their purchasing power five per cent would you not create another psychological effect by the lack of business and lack of enterprise? I do not think so, because you would be cutting costs. If it were done in the spirit of a great patriotic movement, and everyone agreed to get prices down to a new equilibrium, you might get the benefit very rapidly.

(MR FRATER TAYLOR) *I suppose that the percentage would be graded over certain incomes? It would not be a level ten per cent over all?* I think it would need to be a level ten per cent over all.

That is a point where we would differ. From many points of view, I should not differ on the desirability of increasing the level of the income of the most poorly paid, but I think it is undesirable to give an outlet to our philanthropic feelings by forcing the economic machine and trying to make the employers give more to the poorer paid workers irrespective of the work they do; I think that would work injuriously. We are trying to give the increased share of the national income which we should like the working classes to have through the existing wage machinery. But you cannot do it through that machinery.

Salaries seem to bear very heavily on overheads. Coming from Canada and the States, as I did four or five years ago, I was rather impressed by the high level of salaries which ruled on this side. I should have no objection to saying that salaries above a certain level should be cut more than ten per cent.

That is my point.

(SIR T. ALLEN) *What guarantee have you that a ten per cent reduction of income all round would not be loaded on the consumer, or an attempt made in that direction?* I cannot guarantee it. I should only rely on economic forces and public opinion.

Would not there have to be some means of preventing that? I think if there were a great national effort of this kind the pressure of public opinion on anybody who tried to profiteer would be enormously strong.

When I was in Australia some years ago I made an analysis of the movement of prices over a period of years, and I gathered from state statistics that every movement in wages had resulted in a corresponding increase in the price of essential commodities, and that prices always moved faster than wages. Whatever movement has been made in wages over a period of fifteen years there was a corresponding increase in the price of commodities at every stage. It may be so, but I do not think it need be so. I have no doubt that this remedy is chimerical but in order to make a complete list of remedies it was necessary to bring this proposal in.

(MR BEVIN) *When you take the commodities, clothing and so on, that the workers have to buy, do you think the price varies in accordance with the cost of production?* Yes.

Do you think so? I think Sir Marcus Samuel was right when, speaking of oil, he said the price was determined by the price they could screw out of the public. It is pretty general in everything.

(PROFESSOR GREGORY) *Supposing that all incomes were cut by ten per cent, that in itself would be a considerable factor in bringing your prices down.*

(MR BEVIN) *That has not been our experience. We have had some heavy cuts— 20, 30, 40 per cent. Our experience is that prices do not fall until long afterwards, and they never fall to the extent that wages have been cut.*

(SIR T. ALLEN) *You do not actually touch the distributor's earning power unless he gets less profit on his goods. If you reduce the industrial wages by, say, ten per cent, and allow the distributor still to make the same ratio of profit, he is in exactly the same position.* If it is the mere ratio of profit which is unchanged all is well, but if it is the absolute profit my scheme is defeated.

My theory is that he would adjust the price of the commodity in order not to suffer the ten per cent, and the reaction would be on the man who could not help himself.

(LORD BRADBURY) *Leaving the export trade out of account, you would only benefit by your scheme, I take it, if the fall in prices were somewhat less than the reduction in income. If your fall in prices were exactly equal to the reduction in income your new equilibrium as regards profit, or disequilibrium, would be the same, and profits would not be improved.* No; I should rely on the improvement of profit if we had more exports.

We would have to work through exports? Yes. There would no longer be this difference between money costs of production at home and abroad. If our savings can get out in the form of exports there is no reason why there should be any business losses. I do not think it is the high cost of production at home that is making business losses, but the effect of that in making a certain proportion of our savings abortive.

(CHAIRMAN) *The diminution in exports.* Yes. The next remedy,—and theoretically there is a great deal to be said for it, though practically it has not very much, and I doubt if we need consider it very seriously—is the system of bounties to industry in general or to particular industries. The cost would be provided out of a central fund which would have to be raised by taxation. You could give a bounty to industry in general by paying out of taxation, say, the whole of the employers' contribution to insurance, or a portion of rates—the de-rating measure of the last Government falls under this head. In the case of particular industries you might either have a state form of bounty or you could have certain privileges given to the industry such as have been given to the heavy industries by making concessions to the railways on condition that they make reductions in certain rates. We have given that to the heavy industries.

(MR BEVIN) *Is that showing any effect?* I think so. Of course, the order of magnitude was small.

Would you not achieve the same result if you took charges off the local rates and put them on to the national exchequer? I think the effect of those bounties on those industries has been so far a diminution of their losses; it has not brought them to the point of making profits, therefore it has not led to their employing much more labour. I think the rate concessions, especially to the heavy industries, have gone more or less into the pockets of the employers; but you have to fill up the pockets of the employers before you can get their industries moving forward. That is one of the awkward features of the situation.

So that as regards the working people you would give the spur to harder work by reducing the standard of living, whereas the spur to the employers would be by filling their pockets up. My object would not be to reduce the standard of living. All these remedies would have to have the effect of bringing profits to the ordinary level. As long as you have a form of society in which profits are the driving force of enterprise you cannot drive profits below the level which will attract investment.

Does that mean that so long as we go on making profits and that is the sole drive to industry, there is no real solution without adopting one or other of these expedients? Yes, I think so. You can also give bounties to particular industries by machinery which compels the consumer of those articles to pay. The clauses of the Coal Bill which were carried yesterday were of that character.[4] We have, therefore, tried the bounty method on a small scale in a good many ways.

Does it follow that the clauses carried yesterday make the consumer pay? That seems to me to be the main object of them, and I should think, probably, it is a desirable object.

But you get a position that the price of a thing bears no relation to the cost of production. Surely you can have no more striking case. At the present moment if I want a ton of coke in London I am charged £2 for it, after more than the original value of the coal has already been extracted in the way of by-products and gas. Might not the clauses of the Bill passed yesterday result in preventing that tremendous extraction of profit from the commodity? Yes it might. I agree that

4 See below p. 343.

you might get your bounty not out of the consumer but out of the other factors of the industry.

Those factors of the industry of a monopolistic kind are extracting those large profits and therefore preventing the other factors from getting normal profits. I quite agree; assuming that that is true, that is another possible source of bounty.

Well, is it a bounty? No, I think bounty is the wrong word in that case. It is strengthening one of the factors in the industry against the others.

In the Welsh tin trade we have had a quota ever since the days of the McKinley Tariff, when it went smash. Then John Hodge and Ben Tillett, and leading employers got together and formed the South Wales Board, and from then they have operated their quota. It was one of the quickest trades to revive up to the time of the War. I agree. Coal was a very controversial example to give. Take the cotton industry. If the Lancashire Cotton Corporation results in enabling the spinners to get better prices, that may quite easily come out of the other factors in the industry—the finishers and merchants. I quite agree as regards coal, it is a bad example of the working of bounty.

May it not be that when you get organisation behind coal, as you are likely to get now, you may prevent an unnecessary waste of the product even on the foreign market? Certainly. I must not be taken as criticising; I should have voted for the Government last night if I had been in the House of Commons. Theoretically there is much to be said for the method of bounty; because if on the ground of humanity, or social policy, or justice in the distribution of income, we decide that the working classes ought to have larger incomes than the economic machine grinds out for them, then we ought to be prepared to subscribe to a fund to meet the excess due to them over what the economic machine grinds out for them, or else not use the present machine. It is erroneous to use the economic machine and then fix wages, not at the level which the economic machine grinds out, but at what our feelings lead us to think is a satisfactory income for a man and his family. It may be that our social feelings have caused us to fix wages at a higher level than the economic machine grinds out. If we were to balance that by a bounty that would be the public subscribing to meet the difference out of the common purse.

(CHAIRMAN) *A compulsory tariff?* Yes. And it would be a much better way to do it. On the other hand, the adoption of a bounty is very unlikely, because we refuse to accept the logical position.

But if you postulate profit as the sole motive of an employer, does not every increase in taxation accentuate the disinclination to make profit? I believe very much less so than imposing a poll tax on the number of men employed. The taxes fall on him in a different way. They only fall on him after he had made his profit, and they fall on a much wider area. I feel that while there is a deterrent effect in taxation, if you want to give the poorer part of the community £100,000,000 more income you would be wiser to do that out of taxation than by fixing the wages of individuals at a higher figure than it pays their employers to give them.

(MR BEVIN) *So far as social charges are concerned, if you say that insurance and that kind of thing is better met out of direct taxation than by a direct charge on the workman and employer we would be on common ground there.* Yes, that is what I say.

The more people the man employs the higher the taxation, and the direct taxation of wages is also a deterrent; therefore we are on common ground that industry ought to be relieved of the charges on unemployment insurance, national health and that kind of thing, and that it ought to be put direct on to the income tax.

(LORD BRADBURY) *The first old age pensions bill then was the right one?*

(MR BEVIN) *Yes, from the point of view of industry. I am certain of that. The man who is employing 10,000 people pays a heavy tax, whereas the broker or merchant, who may be employing fewer people and making larger profit, pays very little, and it means an unequal distribution.* My fourth remedy consists of an increase of productive efficiency. This is the remedy which it is now orthodox and conventional to contemplate, to the exclusion of all others. It is commonly called 'rationalisation'. It is, in effect, the one remedy which our witnesses from the Big Five suggest to us. Obviously we ought to seek this remedy as much as possible just as much when there is no unemployment as when there is. The doubt in my mind is whether it is practicable to increase efficiency sufficiently to bring about equilibrium, except after the lapse of more time than we care to contemplate. I believe it to be a slow remedy, though a very real one in the long run. I think it would be a very good thing if there were sufficient margin of immediate remediable efficiency to bridge the gap. But we have to take human nature as it is, and when we are talking about an increase of human efficiency we must not imagine that we can obtain what would be in fact attainable if the average man were equal to the superior man. I do not see why it should be practicable, by adjuring people to get much more efficient, to get them more efficient than they would be anyhow. Moreover there is a very clear distinction to be made between the various measures which are offered to us. The distinction is between measures to bring about increase of efficiency in the sense of ability to produce more real goods, and measures which are necessary to mitigate and deal with the worst consequences of the existing situation. A great deal of what is now going on in the name of rationalisation belongs to the latter category and does not really involve any material increase in efficiency at all. The reason for this is that the existing regime of unemployment and low profits has caused, in the first place, an accumulation of losses in companies' balance sheets, which need writing off, and secondly the existence of redundant manufacturing capacity. Now the writing off of assets is often necessary and desirable, but it does not always increase efficiency in the sense of reducing real costs.

(MR TULLOCH) *In the cotton industry the various schemes which have been framed do involve a great deal of writing down, particularly banking charges.* It does not affect your cost of production in the real sense. Take a spindle. Its replacement cost is 30s.; write down that spindle to 2s. 6d., establish your industry on a basis in which it cannot earn interest and depreciation on 30s. but can earn interest and depreciation on 2s. 6d.; that is not the same thing as increasing the efficiency of the spindles eightfold.

That is not my point. In this particular case the mills have a great deal of dead weight debt. It is not part of their costs of production.

No, not in that sense—not costs of immediate production. The interest tends to pile up. Yes, but you do not increase the efficiency of the spinning industry, except that you remove business worry.

You are saying that such profits should be devoted to new machinery instead of paying banking charges. My point is, you might get a redistribution of certain receipts, but that is not the same thing as increasing the efficiency of your unit cost of production. If we sit down to spin cotton on terms which yield interest and depreciation on spindles which are written down to 2s. 6d., what is going to happen when the spindles wear out? It merely means that our spinning industry then vanishes.

(MR FRATER TAYLOR) *I have had occasion to write down the capital of a company, but it has had no effect beyond simply letting the company live; it has not increased efficiency, it has merely removed the strangling influence of debts.* Yes; it may be desirable to do that; but it does not follow because we call both this and a real increase of efficiency 'rationalisation' that they are the same thing.

(PROFESSOR GREGORY) *A good deal of what goes by the name of 'rationalisation' is simply the exploiting of monopolistic action.* Yes. When there is redundant capacity as the result of loss of trade and unemployment, the organised ways of eliminating redundant plant and forming cartels for the avoidance of overproduction are really ways not of producing cheaper but of selling dearer. Those methods are very necessary; they are required primarily because the methods of individualistic production, with small units, which were characteristic of British industrial organisation in the nineteenth century, are utterly unsuitable for taking a step backward. We had not a business organisation which was biologically constructed so that it could walk backward; the consequence is that even a small surplus capacity leads to difficulties. When you get a certain surplus capacity developing, our way of running business does not work at all, and one has to try and evolve new forms. Of course, that will only be necessary during a certain period, and rationalisation of this nature, however necessary and desirable, is not a means of producing more cheaply, it is a way of dealing with the present situation without employers being made bankrupt.

(MR FRATER TAYLOR) *Take the shipbuilding industry. If you shut down one department which is working to half capacity and concentrate production in another department does not that mean you will have more efficiency?* It is possible that by concentration economies may ensue. It is also possible that it may be the other way round. It may be that the present pressure towards concentration because of surplus capacity causes them to decrease costs of production because it makes business men do what they would not do otherwise. It may on other occasions bring into being unwieldy combines.

(MR BRAND) *It is said that the Mond Anthracite Combine in Wales has considerably increased its overhead charges. Whether that is so I do not know.*

(MR BEVIN) *They do not add to efficiency; it was merely a case of a company promoter taking a huge profit out of an industry which was fairly well run, with the result that it broke contact with a good many markets which were held, and nearly destroyed it.* In Lancashire I would hope for real economies by concentration. I believe in Lancashire there is a tremendously strong case for concentration, and therefore surplus capacity may in the long run prove to be a blessing in disguise. It may be the only thing to overcome the individualistic tendencies of Lancashire enterprise. I think it differs from one industry to another. But from those economies I do not think one can expect enough help to bridge the gap.

(CHAIRMAN) *They would not help employment.* They would not help employment. It is very important to realise that of the rationalisation with which we are now so busy, only a comparatively small part is directed to the solution of our problem, and that the rest consists in making the best of the present situation much more than in remedying it.

(MR BRAND) *Does it follow that if we had equilibrium and yet had rationalisation, that, in itself would produce unemployment temporarily?* Only if it were true economy, and that would cause very slight unemployment. It is dealing with redundant capacity that causes unemployment and redundant capacity is because of loss of trade.

I remember Owen Young telling me that in the General Electric shops he had had to tell his officials not to put in new machinery and labour-saving appliances for some time, but to do it gradually. Yes. This is a very important remedy because we are all in favour of it and everybody is talking about it. I think it is filling the picture much too much. It is very harmless as compared with my other proposals. It is terribly harmless. I think there is a good and bad side to it; most of it is good but it is easy to over-estimate the practical value. That is the danger of it.

(PROFESSOR GREGORY) *If you start even good rationalisation schemes at a time of existing unemployment you do make existing unemployment temporarily worse.* Yes.

(MR BEVIN) *Can you have rationalisation unless you get down to the root causes of wage agreements?* No, I should think that is most important.

In the coal trade, for instance, there are percentage proportions for the division of the products of industry. There is very little product to divide except the piling up of debts, as far as I can see. That is under the present agreement. That has been, I think, the biggest handicap to rationalising the coal trade, in relation to by-products, because it has compelled the calculation of the wage base at the pit head. Instead of being able to develop, as you would in gas, so that every kind of by-product is brought into the common pool—new changes, new scientific development go on and all that is an inducement to link it up and connect it with the basic trade—it has had the direct opposite effect; it has caused the formation of new companies in order to avoid wages coming into the pool. I think what Mr Bevin says is of first-class importance.

You will never get rationalisation in your basic trades unless you alter the whole concept of your consultations on wages agreements. Renegotiations on wage contracts as distinct from altering the average wage earnings of a man; readjustment in regard to the basis of the ascertainment.

I do not think there ought to be an ascertainment. I have never believed in trying to ascertain the profits of industry; I have always gone for the wages of industry and let the employer get them where he will. That may sound very brutal, but what he says is this: 'If I am to pay these wages I have got to get the coal.' But, also, he is on the look out for something else to bring into the common pool. Take the Consett Iron Company. I understand they are making £30,000 a year out of waste [from the] gas plant. They have formed a new company. If the wages of the miners had been on a fixed standard irrespective of profits, the probability is that the Consett Iron Company would have so organised their company that the whole thing would have been in one concern and it would not have been segregated in different departments, which is what it amounts to at the moment.

(CHAIRMAN) *What you mean is that all these by-products ought to be brought into the miner's ascertainment.* Your quarrel is with the method.

(MR BEVIN) *Yes, I am quarrelling with the method. Take soap. We do not sit down with the Lever Combine and say, 'We will fix so much for the man who makes soap, and the man who makes glycerine, and the man who makes scents'; the whole wage bill of the Lever Combine is taken into account in making the wage and it ranges from margarine to soap. It is an inducement to be in the pool. Take the buses of the London General; they have been contributing £300,000 to the*

Underground for about five years. We have never worried about that, as representing the busmen. The busmen might say, 'We ought to get higher wages because the buses are contributing to the Underground', but as a trade union official I know that, if I interfered with that, that would mean a disturbance on the Underground, a cutting of fares, a disturbance of the rationalisation of industry. That £300,000 which has been contributed by one part of the industry to the other has really been an insurance to keep up my own wages. Now, the reverse position has happened. Owing to the fact that you cannot move about the streets very fast on a bus people have started going underground, and the Underground receipts are up this year while the buses have slowed down. You get it into the common pool and you maintain the wage bill over the whole area and I regard that, representing the men, as a proper thing to do. I have never gone to Lord Ashfield and said, 'Give me 6d. out of the 1s.'

(CHAIRMAN) *That form of rationalisation broadens the industry.*

(MR BEVIN) *It broadens the industry, and you cannot get rationalisation in your basic trades unless you do it.* I meant my remarks to include also renegotiation of wage agreements on other points which would not lead to a reduction in the average earnings.

The four remedies we have discussed so far resemble one another in that they are all ways of being able to produce at lower costs in terms of gold, so they are all ways of restoring equilibrium by enabling us to produce more and find an outlet in foreign investment for a portion of our savings which is going to waste. They are all variations of the same tune, though they are often regarded as quite different.

I now turn to three remedies of a different class. The next remedy is the system of protection. Now several of the traditional free trade arguments have now become, in part, arguments for protection. For example, free traders like myself have been accustomed to say that protection is a way of increasing the profits of a particular class of *entrepreneurs* at the expense of the rest of the community. That is precisely what we want, provided you choose the particular class of *entrepreneurs* from amongst those who require to have their profits increased as any ordinary protectionist programme would. The first people you would naturally protect are those among the unsheltered industries. Another thing I used to say was that protection was a surreptitious way of decreasing real wages. That, again, is something that we want; and again it would mean the raising of prices, which also is something we want. But let me go rather deeper than that. The free trade argument is largely a branch of the Bank rate policy argument, which we went through the other day.

What about your first point? Are you going to prove that it does raise prices? Being a transport worker I am naturally a free trader, but you have got to meet the points made by the steel trade, I think, when you say that. If you are going to take action purely on the unsheltered industries you have got to meet that point, which I think is a very strong one. If you have your works running full time, making 15,000,000 tons, you would reduce your overheads etc. to such a point that in fact you would not increase your cost of steel. I did not mean to beg that question; I was only rehearsing the things that free traders were wont to say.

I thought the rehearsal was the play. Let me come back to the point. The free trade argument is very similar to the Bank rate policy argument. Take the case of the McKenna Duties: What would happen if they were to be taken off— saving Mr McKenna's presence. We should presumably buy more foreign cars. From that point onwards the free trade argument would be, that would lead to a loss of gold, the loss of gold would lead to an increase of Bank rate, the increase of Bank rate would lead to unemployment, the increase of unemployment would lead to pressure for a reduction of wages; when wages had been reduced we should be able to produce cars in competition or to make some other article which we now import. When the final position had been reached, while money wages would be lower than before, real wages would not be lower, in fact they would be higher than under protection, because we should be producing those articles for which we are distinctly better suited.

(SIR W. RAINE) *Is there not another important factor in the action which the foreigner would take? He would put his tariff up.* He might put obstacles in our way, but the free trade argument is that we should end up in a better position. But the object of taking off the McKenna Duties would be to cause more unemployment. It is absurd for a free trader to say he is a free trader and not wish that result to ensue. That is the whole point.

(PROFESSOR GREGORY) *Only if you start with the assumption that your wages rates and your production costs generally are so high that you cannot export.* The fundamental ground of the free trade argument is that we ought to take the McKenna Duties off in order that we should stop the making of cars and make something else for which we are better suited. And the logical link between one and the other is through this chain, and no other. Just like the Bank rate argument, it works beautifully in a fluid system. But supposing we get jammed at the point of unemployment, the alternative for a time may be between producing motor cars or producing nothing.

(CHAIRMAN) *Take Sir Walter Raine's point. Supposing the steel industry, which is so vital to our export trade, were stopped by tariffs in foreign countries.* On the free trade argument, that merely means that the fall of money costs of production in this country would have to be greater. If it goes on to the bitter end, if every country has a tariff of one-thousand per cent *ad valorem*, we can nevertheless get to a position of complete equilibrium, provided our money wage is sufficiently low. We inflate their prices and deflate our own, until we get over their tariffs, and our real wages will not fall at all, always assuming that this process works through to its logical conclusion. If we get jammed, it may be that the free trade method leaves us for the moment in a worse position, because the choice is not between making one article and something else for which we are not so well suited, the choice is between making something for which we are not so well suited and making nothing. But in a sense free trade and protection are both ways of restoring equilibrium by bringing wages down.

The virtue of free trade is that it does bring money wages down and it does not bring real wages down, whereas protection is not so likely to bring down money wages, it is much more likely to bring down real wages. But the virtue of protection is that it does the trick, whereas in present conditions free trade does not. Therefore the question is, how far one is prepared to be governed by short [period] considerations, and it seems to me, when one has by virtue of Mr McKenna got some duties, it would be a very strange act to aggravate the position by removing them. When it is a question of putting on new duties it is a much more difficult question, and it also depends on what alternative remedies there are and how long the present situation is to last. If we are jammed for some time I think we should get some immediate relief by well-adjusted tariffs.

(MR BEVIN) *Take steel. Supposing you could get as a first condition, rationalisation of the steel trade in the proper sense.* You could make a bargain to get this in return for tariff.

Supposing you could get a real bargain. First of all, it would be rationalisation of the steel trade; the Bank of England or somebody else would find the necessary capital; there is a lag even then in that process of rationalisation between that point and when you have brought it to fruition, and you would be open to at once to the blast of every possible attempt to prevent rationalisation being a success. Yes.

Under such conditions might it be a relief to give steel safeguarding for, say, five years if you like? They are trying to bring about a lot of these things now by giving them another name—subsidy, lending money free of interest, and all that kind of thing. But they do not get the volume of capital sufficient to carry out rationalisation; consequently they cannot carry out the job. £100,000 might be wasted, but £1,000,000 might be wise expenditure. Thirdly, there is no method open to us except safeguarding, as far as I can see, in a trade of that character, given the two other conditions, to tide over the period. I think it is arguable,—I would not say it is a remedy because I have not reached a conclusion but I think there is a case on the argument you are stating for iron and steel.

And subject to a further safeguarding in the secondary use of steel, like bars for export trade, or plate, a definite regulated system to prevent abuse of the tariff. Yes. It ought to be recognised that from the long-period point of view it may be thoroughly undesirable. Once you put tariffs on you will never get them off again, and the question is, how much is one prepared to pay for an immediate benefit.

(MR FRATER TAYLOR) *If we tackle the steel industry as a whole and the period of new construction sets in it will take from two to three years to modernise the plant; during that time we are going to have intense difficulty in working even up to the present level, because peculiar considerations operate to prevent blast furnaces and other things from being shut down. When I gave evidence before the Civil Research Committee I suggested taking a leaf out of the Canadian book, and I said 'Could we have bounties on steel during that period at least?' I also suggested that the Government might take some ordinary shares to cover interest on reconstruction during that period.* I believe that we can produce steel competitively with any part of the world; if I believed that we could give iron and steel five years' safeguarding and get rid of it at the end of that period I would undoubtedly agree to it.

(MR MCKENNA) *I take a rather different view. I am a free trader, like Mr Keynes. I take the view that unless you have an unrestricted protection for the steel industry without any period of time you cannot provide it with the necessary capital. Nobody is going to invest money in the steel industry of this country unless he is sure of a market for a certain quantity, and it is only on that condition that money and enterprise will go into steel. If money and enterprise do go into steel, we can produce as cheaply as anybody in the world. If you fix a period and say, 'At the end of five years we will throw the market open again', I doubt whether money and enterprise would go into steel. You have got to have a closed market and then you will get all the money and enterprise in the steel industry that Great Britain wants and you will get the industry revived. I go further and say that the only condition in which I can foresee any rational agreement throughout the world to get back to something like free trade is, if we protect. As we stand at the present moment we are encouraging every other nation in the world to put up tariffs against us. I speak as a life-long free trader. I see Lord Bradbury looking at me with disdain, but it is true.*

(CHAIRMAN) *It would be a surprising result if our Report were a Report in favour of tariff reform.*

(SIR W. RAINE) *I certainly expect the draft Report to be on those lines.*

(MR MCKENNA) *If our Report contains anything of that kind I for one should very much want to see in it a clear statement of the free trade case, which I still uphold, and I would like it to be stated that the theory breaks down here and there because of the particular conditions.*

(PROFESSOR GREGORY) *I do not think it has ever been part of the free trade theory that you cannot protect one industry independently. My difficulty is, in this interim process of safeguarding or protection what is to happen to such dependent exports as we still retain.*

(MR MCKENNA) *The main trades which depend on steel are shipbuilding, tin plate and galvanised, but you can always give a rebate on export; there is no difficulty in that. It may be a bounty system, if you like, but I see no other method of regaining trade that has gone.*

(MR BRAND) *I agree with Mr McKenna that it should not be less than five years.*

(MR MCKENNA) *You must not give them notice that you are going to give it for a short period. That is why I think safeguarding is a thoroughly bad policy.* We could, no doubt, usefully discuss protection for a good many meetings.

(CHAIRMAN) *I do not quite see how far that is within our reference.* I want to link up what I have said about protection to my general analysis. We have seen that protection is another way of increasing the amount of our foreign investment and that is how it profoundly works in with my argument. The other way is by increasing our exports. We can increase our favourable foreign balance on income account by diminishing our imports, and the real contribution that protection makes is that, by diminishing our imports, it increases the amount of our foreign investment and brings exactly the same sort of relief as the first four remedies that I was discussing. Free trade tries to do it by increasing our exports. Protection tries to do it by diminishing our imports. If it is essential for equilibrium that we should invest abroad on a larger scale than at present, the protectionist way of doing it may be the method of least resistance, because it does not require reduction of money wages and it has less effect, for reasons that some of the members have been suggesting, in turning the terms of trade against us. It is easier to produce things ourselves than to reduce wages to a point where we can get over the foreign tariffs! It may be that the free trade method of increasing our foreign investment has broken down; if so, there may be something to be said for the protectionist method of attaining the same result. The upshot would be that with protection we should have lower real wages but less unemployment; with free trade, if it works, we should have no unemployment. But free trade assumes that unemployment is an abnormal break in prosperity of which one should not take account. It assumes that if you throw men out of work in one direction you re-employ them in another. As soon as that link in the chain is broken the whole of the free trade argument breaks down. The protectionist method serves to restore equilibrium by seeking some way of increasing the volume of foreign investment without reducing money wages. In my next remedy I shall disclose a different way.

(Adjourned till Thursday next,
6 March 1930, at 4.30 p.m.)

COMMITTEE ON FINANCE AND INDUSTRY

Note by Mr Keynes amending Discussion of 28 February 1930

On page 4 [above p. 96] of our discussion of 28 February I estimated business losses due to excess of saving over investment at £80,000,000, and the waste through the unemployment of men and plant resulting from business discouragement arising out of the experience of these losses at £120,000,000. I then added these two sums together as representing the loss. This was a muddle. The right way of putting it is as follows.

As compared with what would happen in equilibrium, the loss to the accumulated wealth of the country is £80,000,000, i.e. an amount exactly equal to the amount of the business losses. But there is in this an offset to the consumer, who is able to buy things cheaper because they are being sold at a loss. Therefore it is not right to add this sum to the £120,000,000, the two sums being not totally *in pari materia*. On balance consumption is reduced by £40,000,000 and capital accumulation by £80,000,000; and the £120,000,000, namely the sum of those two, represents the total loss to the community.

I think that in some other pages I speak correctly of £200,000,000 as representing the total estimated loss to the country, since I am there calculating the loss on the basis of there being one million men unemployed, whereas in the passage discussed above I am only dealing with the loss through the unemployment of 600,000 men.

11 April 1930   J.M.K.

After the meeting Keynes again reported to Lydia.

From a letter to LYDIA KEYNES, 2 March 1930

My speech at the Currency Com^{ee} on Friday went off very well and the atmosphere was good. But I didn't finish it and will be going on again next Thursday—that ought to be the end. I have been speaking now for $6\frac{1}{2}$ hours!

THE MACMILLAN COMMITTEE

COMMITTEE ON FINANCE AND INDUSTRY

Note of Discussion on
Thursday 6 March 1930

Present:

The Rt Hon. Lord Macmillan (*Chairman*)

Sir Thomas Allen	Mr Cecil Lubbock
Mr Ernest Bevin	The Rt Hon. Reginald McKenna
The Rt Hon. Lord Bradbury, G.C.B.	Mr J. T. Walton Newbold
The Hon. R. H. Brand, C.M.G.	Sir Walter Raine
Professor T. E. Gregory, D.SC.	Mr J. Frater Taylor
Mr J. M. Keynes, C.B.	Mr A. A. G. Tulloch
Mr Lennox B. Lee	Mr G. Ismay (*Secretary*)

Sir Frederick Leith-Ross, K.C.M.G., C.B.
(*Deputy Controller of Finance in the Treasury*)

(CHAIRMAN) *Mr Keynes, you first of all discussed with us four remedies which were of the same class in the sense that their object was to enable us to produce at lower costs in terms of gold; then you passed on to deal with three remedies of a different class. You had dealt with the first of those remedies, that of protection, at the time we adjourned. That leaves two remedies which you have not yet disclosed to us.* There was one small point in my argument last week, at the bottom of page 23 of the Evidence [above p. 114], which I should like to correct in the interests of formal accuracy. I there overstated the force of the free trade argument in the case where other countries put on a tariff against us; I said that even in that event there would be no fall in real wages provided that money wages were allowed to adjust themselves freely. That is not correct. The effect of foreign tariffs, I think, tends in any case in the direction of lowering real wages here, because it is practically certain to turn the terms of trade against us. It need not necessarily have a very adverse effect on real wages— though if it were a very high tariff it would probably have a very bad effect— but the tendency would be in that direction. Therefore what I said last week was not sound.

(MR BRAND) *Where is that?*

(CHAIRMAN) *In the last paragraph on page 23.* I agreed that on the free trade assumption of a fluid system, even hostile tariffs abroad do not hurt us. That is not true. Would you not agree, Professor Gregory?

(PROFESSOR GREGORY) *Yes, I would agree.*

(SIR W. RAINE) *Is Mr Keynes going to say anything more about protection before passing on? I raised with him quite a serious point at the end of the*

119

discussion as to how far he thinks that the views of free traders may have to be modified in this country in view of the persistency with which the foreigner is putting up tariffs; that is to say, how far it may be necessary for us to alter our ideas with the view of ultimately trying to get back to the free trade position which we have adopted for the last 50 years. The correction I have just made is a concession to Sir Walter Raine's point of view.

What I mean is this. How far do you say it will be necessary—I will put it personally—to modify your free trade view, looking at it from the other end of the stick, seeing that the foreigner is so persistent in putting up his tariffs? For instance, it came out in the debate in the House of Commons in connection with the Tariff Truce at Geneva that 14 out of 27 countries have put up their tariffs during the past six months, and seven out of the other 13 intend to put theirs up. The point I am putting, quite seriously, is how far, in your opinion, it will be necessary for this country to alter its views on that question in order ultimately to try and get back to our previous position. I think it certainly makes a difference, but I have not reached a clear-cut opinion as to where the balance of advantage lies. I am frightfully afraid of protection as a long-term policy; I am sure it is radically unsound, if you take a long enough view, but we cannot afford always to take long views, and I am almost equally clear that there are certain short-run advantages in protection; the question, in my opinion, is how far I am prepared to risk long-period disadvantages in order to get some help to the immediate position. It is a very difficult position to meet. Perhaps a further consideration is biassing me unduly. It is extremely difficult for anyone of free trade origin, so to speak, at this juncture to speak in a way that he himself believes to be quite truthful and candid without laying himself open to misrepresentation and to being supposed to advocate very much more than he really does. It is very difficult, I think, to be quite candid and at the same time not to give a false impression.

(PROFESSOR GREGORY) *I think the answer to Sir Walter Raine would be that there is no guarantee, if this country started putting on a tariff, that the relative position of the tariff level would be changed by that fact. If you are trying to force exports on foreign countries, and trying to get a better bargaining position by putting duties on their imports, you simply set going a renewed wave of tariff legislation, which may make your ultimate position worse than it is now, because you have added to the dislocation of world trade.*

(SIR W. RAINE) *Mr Keynes has been giving us some very interesting addresses which I have followed with great appreciation. One of the remedies he mentioned was protection, and I was hoping he was going to follow the thing out. I am trying to get at a practical solution; I am not a theorist, and therefore I was hoping that Mr Keynes would tell us quite seriously what his views were. Can he advocate—I call it protection; I do not use the word safeguarding—as the remedy for our present troubles, having regard to the way in which the foreigner is treating us at the present time?* I think it would help the immediate situation. I think to leave the existing tariffs as they are and add one or two more to them, as in the case of iron and steel, would almost inevitably relieve the present situation. But I am afraid of the general protectionist atmosphere. I say if we were to advocate protection in order to help the immediate situation, there would certainly be offsets to the advantages we could get in that this would promote the protectionist atmosphere as against the free trade atmosphere. You see the difficulty of choice.

Mr McKenna, I understood, last Friday, when he was commenting upon what you had said, remarked that whilst he was a free trader he was afraid—I hope I am quoting him correctly—that it might be necessary to go in wholeheartedly for this remedy—and he would not put any time limit on it—in order to get back to our free trade position. I think he was talking about iron and steel.

(MR MCKENNA) *Yes, iron and steel.*

(SIR W. RAINE) *Was it iron and steel only?*

(MR MCKENNA) *There may be other cases, but I was at that time speaking of iron and steel. Five years protection would be no use for iron and steel. You must have definite protection.*

(CHAIRMAN) *This topic of economics has been mixed up with political considerations and then people indulge in gibes about inconsistency. The scientific person is never inconsistent; he merely progresses by changing his views; but in the political world you lay yourself open to the charge of inconsistency.* And also it makes one hesitate to express one's views.

Yes, they are so liable to misinterpretation that one hesitates.

(MR MCKENNA) *If I go back to the position in 1914, unhesitatingly I should have voted against the protection of iron and steel under the conditions of 1914. Under the conditions which exist today, and which are likely, as I see them, to continue to exist, I should favour the protection of iron and steel. There is no change in theory in my case; it is a change in conditions.*

(MR BRAND) *Sir Walter Raine talks about a solution. I do not imagine Mr Keynes would talk of protection as a solution. It would alleviate certain evils, but I do not think any country has found it a solution.* No; I should put it as an alleviation.

(SIR W. RAINE) *I ought to have said* one *of the methods, because I do not think the evil can be attributed to any one thing. The point is to find out what are the causes. I have it in my mind that this is one of them. I wanted confirmation of that.* There is one other argument in my mind; I have not mentioned it; I believe that a well-designed measure of protection at the moment would do a great deal to revive business confidence. I think it is getting a matter of absolute first-rate business importance to revive confidence in investment in this country. That is a psychological argument; it is making a concession to meet temporary situation. I regard it as drug taking.

(CHAIRMAN) *Then the result of that is that you are going to leave us worse than ever; we become drug addicts.* We may or may not. In some cases, where it is a case of protecting an industry for which we do not believe ourselves to be in any way unsuited, the amount of permanent harm may be comparatively small.

In a world which is building tariff walls against us at every turn how is it possible to capture a reasonable volume of exports which you told us last time is very necessary? It is very difficult.

(MR MCKENNA) *Regarding what Professor Gregory said, I am not at all sure that under existing conditions the effect of Great Britain adopting a tariff policy would not be a real factor in influencing the policy of foreign countries. We are the biggest buyers in the world, and so long as other countries had the biggest buyers open to them they would never be willing to consider arrangements with us.*

(PROFESSOR GREGORY) *I should dispute both those propositions.*

(MR MCKENNA) *Which one would you dispute?*

(PROFESSOR GREGORY) *I should dispute the proposition that if Great Britain went in for a formal protectionist policy it would cause the attitude of other countries to alter. I think that has been the great fallacy behind the protectionist policy. There has been no sign of any alteration of policy on the part of the leading protectionist countries in the direction of producing a favourable effect on English public opinion by reducing their tariffs. They have always put them up, so as to have something to bargain with in case we went in for protection.*

(MR MCKENNA) *But here it is a case of the biggest buyer in the world changing his policy.*

(PROFESSOR GREGORY) *I think the attitude of most countries would be 'We have to protect ourselves and our own home market by putting a tariff on imports.' It must be remembered that, if we are the biggest buyers, we are also large sellers.*

(MR MCKENNA) *They have to negotiate tariffs with the biggest potential buyer in the world.*

(SIR T. ALLEN) *And I take it when the point has been reached that has been foreshadowed by Professor Gregory we shall be in the position indicated by Mr McKenna last week, namely, to bargain.*

(MR MCKENNA) *Our power to negotiate is far greater than that of any other nation. So long as we—and I think rightly—in the past did not adopt a policy of tariffs, we did abandon frankly the power to negotiate. I think it is rather a big assumption, to assume that we should have no power to negotiate if we, the biggest buyers in the world, adopted a tariff policy.*

(PROFESSOR GREGORY) *If I were the Finance Minister of a foreign country, seeing that Great Britain was going to put a tariff on my exports to Great Britain,*

I should proceed to place myself in a position to bargain effectively by putting up my tariffs straight away. That has been the position of Germany and France vis-à-vis one another, throughout the nineteenth century. These tariff 'bargains' have never really been bargains, because both sides have raised them as a preliminary to the lowering of the tariffs.

(MR MCKENNA) *Are you not giving away your case? We should raise our tariffs in order to bargain for a lowering. It would be a mutual lowering.*

(PROFESSOR GREGORY) *The end would be that we should be left with a tariff which might be good or might be bad, but so far as the effective Continental protection against our policy was concerned we would be exactly where we were before. May I put one other point. I think the argument that we have never been in a position to bargain has been, if I may venture to say so, somewhat overstated. We do enjoy most-favoured-nation treatment by the majority of countries, and the degree of international specialisation has never been so great that we have not benefited by the advantage that other countries have tried to obtain.*

(CHAIRMAN) *I would like you, before you leave this topic, Mr Keynes, to indicate to us precisely how it works into our actual terms of reference. I am frankly rather concerned about that, because I think one of the results of our appointment may be a report dealing with tariff reform. Following your argument it seems to me, as you put it, it does have a quite intimate relation to the question of credit, banking, and finance generally, from the international point of view, because according to you we cannot get the international financial position straight until we get the price position right, and that seems to depend among other things upon this form of remedy. I am a little concerned as to how it fits into the scheme of our reference. It would be an unexpected result of our appointment, I think, if we found ourselves dealing with this topic.* I think it fits in just as you have indicated. If it is true that money values in this country make trouble in regard to the balance of trade, we have to consider all ways in which the balance of trade can be improved.

(MR LUBBOCK) *Checking imports.* Checking imports is one of them.

By checking imports the balance on income account is improved in our favour. If such a thing as increasing exports by reducing costs of production by having greater efficiency is within our terms of reference I should have thought companion measures for reducing imports would equally be within our terms of reference.

(CHAIRMAN) *Do you think that our Report would be necessarily incomplete unless this topic were gone into; in other words, that it is an inevitable topic for our consideration, or do you put it into the category of your first remedy, where you said that it would be most inexpedient to raise the revaluation remedy because of the perils attendant upon it?* I think it is just a question of degrees of indiscretion.

I gather that you would regard this as probably the least indiscreet. Yes. For it would be a different kind of indiscretion. It would do no harm to the country.

(MR LUBBOCK) *I understood you to say that the connection was the checking of imports following what you said to us about the favourable balance on income account and adverse balance on capital account. That is one of our troubles; we had to have a high Bank rate on account of our balances.*

(MR BRAND) *Through rising prices as well.* Through bringing prices more into adjustment with costs of production.

Readjusting wages. It makes it less necessary to reduce money wages.

(MR MCKENNA) *And levelling the disparity between the [sheltered and] unsheltered trades.* Yes.

That is one of the troubles that we have to face, the unsheltered trades buy what they need in the home market at a level of 166–167, and they sell their products at a level of 129, and they cannot live by it.

(PROFESSOR GREGORY) *I think it ought to be pointed out—I am not going to press either for the inclusion or exclusion of this subject as a topic for discussion— that if we are going to discuss it, some of our leading unsheltered trades could not possibly be affected by a tariff for some time—for instance, coal.* No industry would gain more from a tariff on iron and steel. I think coal might even gain more than iron and steel would.

(CHAIRMAN) *We have not invited evidence from people who would like to give evidence on tariff reform. I think it would be a mistake to open the flood gates.* Quite; I think it would be a mistake to go into it in great detail. We shall have to say a great deal about the failure of wages to adjust themselves easily as a prime factor in the situation—I think everybody agrees about that. That fact reacts on the validity of a good many orthodox maxims,—it reacts on the validity of Bank rate policy and also on the free trade argument. It is essentially the same story that I am telling in both cases.

(MR BRAND) *They both depend on fluidity—readjustment.* Yes. If you could rely upon wages to adjust themselves then I still believe that free trade would probably be in the interests of the working classes, as much as anybody else, but if there is a difficulty in getting money wages down you have to look round and see what you can do about it, and this is one of the things on which one's glance is bound to rest.

(SIR T. ALLEN) *Without committing Mr Keynes to any conclusion in the development of his argument or thesis I am rather inclined to the view that we ought as a Committee, perhaps, to look at this problem in the collective sense. Undoubtedly we cannot escape; we are charged to report on the development of trade and industry and how we can best promote employment while at the same time maintaining the gold standard. There is the possibility that some modification of our fiscal system—our tariff system—may be of some value, if it only be of a temporary character, and I really think that we have got to get down to it as a Committee before we can report, and we have to report as early as possible, with a view to getting things moving. I would not like Mr Keynes in developing his evidence to commit himself unless we were generally committed. To ask him at the present juncture to develop further the arguments advanced in concluding his evidence last week might be asking him too much at the moment.*

(CHAIRMAN) *Yes. I was more concerned to see how far it had a bearing on the practical problem; because we have to make recommendations, and if some of us round the table feel that a recommendation in that direction is an appropriate recommendation to make we ought to make it, whatever be the consequence.* We could explain its bearing on the whole situation, even though we did not make a recommendation.

It might have this effect, that our Report might become a document of first-rate political importance. It would be a rather unexpected result; I do not know that it would necessarily be undesirable.

(SIR W. RAINE) *I was not attempting to get Mr Keynes to commit himself. First of all he gave us four remedies and set out the arguments why they were not feasible, or why they were only partially feasible; then he mentioned protection, and we had a very interesting discussion on it, and I raise the point today again because I feel we are leaving it in the air. He has not satisfied me; I am not asking him to commit himself; it is not going to get into the press, or anything like that; but he has given us his ideas as to how this question might be dealt with. Protection was the fifth remedy and I venture to think it was left in an unsatisfactory situation.*

(CHAIRMAN) *Mr Keynes, do you regard the three remedies we are now dealing with, the one you have already spoken of, and the two which are to come, as being in a different category from the four you dealt with at first?* I have not come to my favourite remedy. What I am trying to do is to do justice to all the remedies that have been put forward. I think I said at the beginning that there was something to be said for all of them.

You are really putting the pros and cons? Yes.

But in the end we shall have to make a selection between the pros and the cons. I think it would be a great mistake to think that the benefits, if any, to be obtained from protection would be anything like adequate to the situation. I do not think they would. Shall I come to my next remedy?

Yes, please. All five remedies that we have so far discussed have been seeking to restore equilibrium by increasing foreign investment so as to absorb the excess of home saving over home investment, four of them by increasing exports and the fifth by diminishing imports. The sixth remedy tackles the problem from the opposite side. That is to say, it attempts to restore equilibrium not by increasing foreign investment but by increasing home investment. As I have already indicated, this is my own favourite remedy—the one to which I attach much the greatest importance. We shall find that the various plans for the increase of home investment fall into two groups according as they do or do not require Government intervention of a direct kind. But before I come to these I should like to remind the Committee why an increase of investment would help the situation, and to deal with one or two objections of principle which have been raised against it as a remedy.

(MR MCKENNA) *Foreign or domestic?* Domestic; home investment. Let me put it this way: The following is substantially the same thing that we have been saying at previous meetings, but by being put differently it may be helpful. If we are to employ more men—that is to say, if there is to be a net increase of employment—let us consider what forms this employment can possibly take. I do not mean that the actual individual men now unemployed would necessarily have to be employed in the ways that I am going to outline. But to get a *net* increase of employment, what is the complete list of ways in which it can happen? First, they might be employed in making more exports. The possibilities of that we have already discussed. At present, at least, the high level of money wages appears to stand in the way of an adequate remedy in this direction. Secondly they might be employed in making goods which we now import. That is the protectionist solution, which also we have discussed already. Thirdly, the men might be employed in making goods for additional consumption at home. Now the possibility of such additional consumption can only come out of one or other of two sources. Either it must come out of the increased earnings of men who are now unemployed or it must come by our saving less of our present income and spending more of it on consumption. As regards the first, it is more in the nature of a repercussion than of a cure for unemployment. If we have a cure for unemployment of a different kind then the ultimate effect of that may be indirectly greater than it will be by reason of its initial effect, because the consumption of the men thus employed will lead to more employment. But you cannot start the ball rolling in this way. Therefore, it is a repercussion which should later on accentuate the benefit of other remedies, rather than an independent remedy. On the other hand saving less of our income would—though it may astonish the Committee,—really help the situation; and that would be better than nothing. If we were to save less and to spend more on current consumption that would truly increase employment provided the things we bought were things produced at home. And, as I say, it would be better that the unemployed should be employed making things for additional consumption than that they should be unemployed and that we should go without the additional consumption. Therefore, a reduction of savings, a spendthrift campaign, would do good. But, clearly, from the long-period point of view it is not one of the preferable alternatives, because it would mean that the rate of increase of the wealth of the community would be retarded. In actual fact, it is worth pointing out that we do get some relief from this remedy insofar as the growing impoverishment of the community is leading to diminished savings; it is the route by which in the long run you would—failing any other—bring about equilibrium. The continuation of the present state of affairs would in the end so impoverish the community that they would not have a sufficient margin of income to save, and when that had gone far enough we should find unemployment disappear. But at the same time, of course, the normal increment of the wealth of the community would cease.

(MR LUBBOCK) *Is this argument based on the assumption that we are not investing all our savings?* Yes. The diminution of savings is therefore a remedy which I ought to mention in justice to present policy, because it is the remedy which the present policy is seeking to invoke.

(MR BRAND) *That means that if we had no savings at all you could employ all the unemployed.* One would not have to go so far as that. One would only have to diminish savings to the extent of preventing excess of savings over investment. I should say that a reduction of 20 per cent in the present volume of savings would probably bring about equilibrium; in fact, if there were not some reduction of savings going on I think the position would be very much worse than it is from the point of view of employment.

(CHAIRMAN) *But what are we to spend more on?* Consumable goods produced at home.

(MR LUBBOCK) *If we invested all our savings you would not be talking of this remedy being necessary.* No, but as long as the Bank of England has to prevent us from investing all our savings it is better that we should employ gardeners and chauffeurs than that the men should be unemployed.

(MR BRAND) *But it would be better that they should be employed more productively than as gardeners and chauffeurs, if we are able to do it.* Yes. I should put this very low in my category of remedies, but it is a remedy.

(SIR W. RAINE) *Does not that employment of more people take place naturally when you get a revival of trade? People put off buying houses and so on when times are bad, they cannot afford it; and then, when there is a revival of trade—* Yes, I agree.

—that is what makes a boom. Yes, but if we were saving today as much as we do in good times the position might be appalling.

(CHAIRMAN) *Do you think that our Report would be necessarily incomplete depression people are so frightened that instead of launching out and employing additional chauffeurs and gardeners, or people on even more productive forms of employment, they shrink from it and begin to retrench. Therefore, psychologically, it seems to me the remedy would be very difficult to enforce.* I should say, on balance, there is much less saving by the very rich than there would be if we were in bumper times.

(MR BRAND) *Undoubtedly. They do not cut down their expenditure proportionately to the loss of their profits.* No. I have now mentioned three alternatives. That the unemployed should make more exports, that they should make goods that we now import, that they should make more goods for us to consume. Then, there remains the fourth alternative, that the unemployed might be employed making goods for additional home investment. I think that is an absolutely comprehensive list; I can conceive of no way in which a man now unemployed could be employed except for one or other of those purposes.

(CHAIRMAN) *I do not follow the last one.* The last one is making goods for additional home investment.

Creating new capital assets. Creating new capital assets at home.

(MR LUBBOCK) *Investing all our savings.* Yes; and that is the remedy which I am now going to elaborate. It is the only remedy left, if one holds that the other three remedies are either impracticable in the position today or are inadequate, or are in themselves undesirable.

(MR BRAND) *That is the remedy that Dr Schacht has accused the German municipalities of employing—that they have spent large sums of money on what they term 'investment'.* The problem in Germany is rather different from ours, because they are under obligation by treaty to maintain what is the equivalent of foreign investment at a given figure. We have no treaty obligations at all costs to raise foreign investment to a certain figure. We have a choice as to whether our savings shall be invested at home or abroad. If we were in the position of Germany, unless we were to run the risk of defaulting we should have at all costs to pursue the remedy of having a more favourable foreign balance.

(CHAIRMAN) *Would this remedy of increasing home investment be in the nature of a mortgage of future development, a method of overtaking that which in the normal course would be spread over a period of time?* I do not think that the limit of improvement is yet in sight, but if it is in sight the sooner we reach it the better. No doubt the time will come when we shall have all the capital which is good for us. There will then no longer be any particular reason to save, and we can fall back on the non-saving remedy. But as it is we are a good long way off the millennium in that respect. It is not a criticism of my policy that it brings the millennium nearer?

No. I see no reason whatever for supposing that additional home investment, assuming that it really is additional, will not increase employment, to the full extent that it requires home-produced goods. The only deduction that we shall have to make will be in respect of additional imports which it may require. It always seems to me that this argument is quite agreeable to common sense. It is agreeable to common sense to suppose that if you erect a house that would not otherwise be erected, and there are unemployed men in the building industry, you really will help unemployment. But there are two important arguments which are commonly adduced against this policy. The first one is, in effect, that any additional home investment which we could artificially stimulate would not in fact be any net addition at all, that it would be in fact diverted from other existing investments either at home or abroad. I hope I am not misrepresenting the Treasury Memorandum if I say that that is substantially the attitude taken up by the so-called 'Treasury view'. I fancy that the belief that something of this kind is true, or the suspicion that it may be true, has very largely influenced the actual policy, both of the late Chancellor of the Exchequer and of the present Chancellor of the Exchequer. I believe all the same that it is a pure logical delusion, without any foundation at all in sound thinking. But whether I am right or wrong, it is one of the most important tasks of this Committee, I think, to endeavour to arrive at a clear-cut final opinion on the matter. It is an issue which we ought to put in our questionnaire to all the expert economic witnesses we are to hear, in order to see what their views are in the matter. I believe that this doctrine is fundamentally based on a failure to make the distinction which I have been trying to make between savings and investment, or, if you like to use the language which Mr McKenna prefers, the distinction between gross savings and net savings, where gross savings represent what is saved out of normal income and net savings are the same thing after deduction of business losses or after adding abnormal business profits. It may be more in accordance with usual language not to say that savings and investment are unequal, though that is the way in which I prefer to use language, but to say that investment is equal to savings *minus* business losses, so that you *can* get more investment if you diminish business losses. But it is more than that, because I think that there are unanswerable theoretical reasons for saying that, if you increase investment and leave savings the same, you *must* increase business profits and diminish business losses. That is to say—returning to *my* definition of savings—that abnormal business profits are *necessarily* equal to the excess of investment over savings, and business losses are equal to the excess of savings over investment. So whenever you increase investment over savings you are necessarily increasing business profits by that amount. When you raise business profits beyond a normal level you have an inflationary process which brings windfall profits to business men; but so long as they are not making normal profits any increase of investment merely restores them to the position in which they ought to be, and it is out of that benefit to the business world that your additional investment is partly financed. In fact there is never any difficulty whatever in financing investment; the line is between whether you finance it by avoiding deflation or whether you finance it by creating inflation. At the present time you would finance it by avoiding deflation. The contrary view, like too many things we have been discussing, results from following too obediently the teaching of the doctrine of the economics of equilibrium. The assumptions from which the Treasury view follows also prove that there is and can be no unemployment. The Treasury view only demonstrates that home investment is not a cure for unemployment, by first of all assuming—in effect—that there is no unemployment to cure. It is not at all surprising that anyone should hold that view, because practically all economic treatises do assume in most of their chapters that unemployment, except of a merely transitory character of which one need take no serious account, is an impossibility. Most economic doctrine teaches what happens when you have reached the new equilibrium. It is always assumed that unemployment is a transitory phenomenon to which it would be very unwise to attach too much importance, that it would lead you into unsound ways if you admitted the possibility of continuing unemployment. One might say, perhaps, that the view in question is the natural result of standing half-way between common sense and sound theory; it is the result of having abandoned the one without having reached the other.

Looking at it from another point of view, from what physical resources, so to speak, would additional home investment be financed? Let us come to details as to how it is possible to have home investment which really is a net increase. First of all, it would be financed out of what is now spent from the 'dole', and from relief, etc., and from the working classes using up their savings. An unemployed man does not starve; he and his family spend and consume through one source or another when he is unemployed at least one-third, perhaps one-half, as much as when he is employed. Moreover money would be saved on the 'dole' in respect of far more men than are directly employed by the new investment;—because insofar as the additional consumption of the additional men directly employed is directed to home-produced goods more men are employed producing such goods; this time it is a miscellaneous consumption of goods, and so there is a cumulative snowball effect. I believe it can be shown that including these repercussions at least one-half of the new investment would be found out of the unproductive expenditure of the men now unemployed who would be brought into employment. What you really have to look at is the half of the money paid out to the newly employed which would represent new expenditure to them. Insofar as the 'dole' is concerned, it is quite easy to translate this into terms of finance. If the Treasury is not having to pay out as much unemployment benefit they are actually in receipt of funds available for alternative purposes, funds equal in amount to the 'dole' that they would otherwise pay. Part of the present expenditure of the unemployed comes from other sources, partly local relief, partly the resources of themselves and their friends. Insofar as they no longer have to draw on those resources, those resources are available alternatively to finance investment. So I do not believe it is an exaggeration to say that *pari passu* with the increase of employment you automatically get the resources for at least half of what you are doing out of the 'dole' and analogous resources.

Secondly, as we increase the amount of additional home investment—this applies only to the investment, and not to repercussions—we diminish the gap between total savings and total investment, and to the extent that we do this we necessarily diminish businessmen's losses, so that the savings which are now used up as an offset to those losses become available for the new investment, bank loans which are at present advanced to firms to meet their losses become available for the new investment, firms which are making profits are able to write down by depreciation to an appropriate extent, pay off bank loans, liquidate their position, and all these additional profits they make are directly available as a method of financing the new investment. As I have said, if businessmen's profits were already normal this would represent something which could properly be described as inflation, but in actual conditions it only means the avoidance of the deflation of profit. And the cure for unemployment, whatever it is, absolutely requires that the process of deflating profits should be reversed, because no remedy can be lasting which does not restore business profits to a normal level. It seems to me very important to realise, that that is the preliminary to any cure whatever. Because as long as the making of profit is the spur to enterprise, until you have restored profit to a normal level you cannot get equilibrium. Therefore it is very short sighted to use words which are supposed to have an abusive flavour, like 'inflation', for something which is the remedy for deflation—you can only begin to use the word 'inflation' in an opprobrious sense when you have got back to equilibrium and are thinking of financing an artificial boom by giving business men abnormal profits at the expense of the consumers, and financing your boom out of those abnormal profits. The only qualification to a claim that we can get the *whole* of what we require from the two sources I have mentioned is that the additional home investment will partly decrease foreign investment. To the extent that the new home investment worsens the balance of trade it will decrease foreign investment; therefore, there will be an offset. It only does that to the extent that the new investment and the new consumption are utilised in the purchase of imports or goods which would otherwise have been exported. The employed men and their families, being no longer unemployed, would consume more food, a large part of which would have to be imported and the new home investment would almost certainly require a certain amount of imported raw materials. I have rashly ventured to guess the proportion of the new investment that would directly or indirectly go to swell imports as being of the order of 20 per cent at the outside, but whatever that figure is it merely means that the *gross* amount of new home investment has to be a sum in excess of the *net* additional total investment. When you increase home investment I think you cannot help slightly diminishing foreign investment, therefore you will not increase total investment as much as you increase home investment. My point would be that in order to increase the total investment by £100,000,000 you might have to increase the home investment by £125,000,000, I think that would be the kind of proportion. If these figures of mine are right, an additional home investment amounting to £100,000,000 per annum, which is only $2\frac{1}{2}$ per cent of the national income, would cure nearly half of the existing unemployment and would increase the national capital wealth by £80,000,000 a year. I am assuming that the £100,000,000 will decrease the foreign investment by £20,000,000, so that the national wealth would be increased by £80,000,000, of which a certain proportion would be at the expense of consumers who are now enjoying the benefit of getting certain articles too cheap—that is to say below their cost of production. But I would not admit that that is a disadvantage to the scheme. It is an advantage, because any remedy which is sound must have that effect, any remedy which is sound must aim at getting prices and costs of production nearer together. On some kinds of articles the consumer is getting an illegitimate benefit which he cannot possibly hope to maintain; that is to say getting things for less than they truly cost. As I say, you would have a real increase of national wealth by £80,000,000, some of which would come out of the labour of people now unemployed, because their increased labour production would be more than their increased consumption; you would get part of it out of business profits which would accrue from the more adequate use of plant; and the remainder because in some directions consumers' incomes would be worth less as a result of their having to pay more nearly what the articles cost to produce. Out of those three sources together you would be curing something like half the existing unemployment and you would be increasing the national wealth at the rate of £80,000,000 per annum.

I do not know whether the Committee want me to pause at this point. That is all I have to say about this particular argument, namely, the argument that it is intrinsic and in the nature of things that you cannot increase home production without setting up repercussions which will diminish investment in other directions by an approximately equal amount.

Of course, our recommendations are to be designed to be carried into practical execution. I can conceive that various expedients which you have discussed theoretically might have the consequences you indicate, but how are you to bring them about? That I am coming to. I am only dealing now with the *prima facie* objection that this whole class of remedies, whether feasible or not feasible, is unsound.

You are discussing remedies, so to speak, in vacuo *at the present time as if you were in the position of saying, as a Mussolini might, 'This is how we shall conduct our affairs in future'; but we are living in a practical world, the remedy of protection may be a practical thing or not, I do not know what the political complexion of the country may be in a few years. Equally in regard to the increase of home investment, how is that sort of thing to be brought about?* That is what I am coming to. If there is anybody who shares the view that there is a *prima facie* objection to this class of remedies I shall be glad to deal with it.

(MR BRAND) *I suppose you would agree that the whole of your case depends upon whether this relationship that you said existed between savings and investment is actually true, that the losses and profits do occur according to your theory?* Yes.

That is the point which I should like to get clear. That is the point that I do not feel I have accepted yet. I have tried to understand your case.

(MR MCKENNA) *Although I am not in entire agreement with the Treasury view on this subject, may I put one or two questions to you?* Yes.

Supposing you imagine a zero hour in trade and finance at which you accept things as they are at that moment. At that moment, making a new start from zero hour, with everybody's engagements exactly as they are, you introduce a new factor; you say, 'The state is now determined to spend an additional £1,000,000 upon, say, building. Nothing else is changed at that moment; we are going on with everything else as it is.' When the state makes that declaration to spend £1,000,000 it must obtain, not the whole £1,000,000, but at least £100,000 of it for immediate expenditure. Yes.

Where does it get it from? Only out of the banking system. The banking system can either make this possible or prevent it. It may be by the acquiescence of the banking system. It may be, on the other hand, that the banking system is in effect bottling up savings.

I am trying to imagine there is a conflict between you and the Treasury. £100,000 has to be found from somewhere immediately— £1,000,000.

I am starting with £100,000. £100,000 has to be found immediately. It is assumed that at that moment so far as the banks are concerned they are all lent up to what they regard as their maximum power having regard to the ratio of cash and deposits. They cannot provide the £100,000 unless one of two things happen; either they are given power to lend more by having a slightly increased cash basis given them by the Bank of England, or else they reduce their cash ratio. Yes.

Which do you say they should do? I should say it does not lie in their power. If the Bank of England is determined that the new investment shall be a substitute for the existing investment and not a net addition, they can as long as they have a stranglehold on the money market make sure that the Treasury view is right.

That is my view, that the Bank of England can make the Treasury right. Yes.

You also say the Bank of England can make the Treasury wrong. Yes.

(MR FRATER TAYLOR) *To a certain extent the state is creating through the 'dole', not employment, but spending power. Would it not pay the state to spend more? If we say, for instance, that the 'dole' costs £50,000,000, could we not provide from that the interest and sinking fund on a capital sum which might be spent on national enterprise?* Certainly, if you are quite sure that you will save on the 'dole' what you are spending in this direction. I am trying to answer the argument that in fact you will not save on the 'dole' what you would in fact have to spend otherwise. That is the argument I have to meet. I am trying to get away from the monetary veil, which is so confusing. Here are people to be employed. They will use their wages in a certain way.

(MR MCKENNA) *I think, Mr Chairman, it is rather important for us, a committee appointed to consider credit and trade, finance and industry, to see where the relation between the two ceases.*

(CHAIRMAN) *Exactly.*

(MR MCKENNA) *I agree with Mr Keynes, if his policy is adopted, and the Bank of England acquiesces, he is right; but if the Bank of England does not acquiesce, then I think the Treasury view is right.* That is not the end of the story. It would be possible for the new investment to take place without the Bank of England making a change in its present policy if the public made a change in their habits. Supposing the public became high-spirited, and began taking up new issues with money which at present they are rather inclined to put on fixed deposit with their banks, you would then get what I should wish to see, without there being any change in the volume of advances or deposits with the Big Five or any change in the assets of the Bank of England. But the monetary machine is such that you cannot get fresh investment unless there is a change of policy on the part either of the public or of the Bank of England.

(MR MCKENNA) *We cannot deal with the public; they are not an entity; the Bank of England is a single entity, and the Bank of England can vary its policy according to whether the public do or do not act. If the public act as you say they should, then the Bank of England need not increase the basis, but if the public do not so act, and do not increase investment, then the Bank of England must act.*

(MR BRAND) *The public can act by subscribing to £1,000,000 Government loan.*

(MR MCKENNA) *It must be an additional investment by them; if they merely substitute one for the other—* If they subscribe money which they have on deposit.

—if they subscribe money which they have on deposit, or which they were going to leave on deposit, yes; if they only subscribe money to a Government loan in preference to an issue which they do not subscribe to, you are correct. The Bank of England, if they are willing, can determine their policy according to whether the public are or are not investing in new issues. You cannot control the public but you can control the Bank of England—or rather, the Bank of England can exercise a controlling influence; they can control their policy, but we cannot control the policy of the public.

(MR BRAND) *My difficulty is to understand what Mr Keynes calls savings. I can understand investment, that is, bricks and mortar; when I come to savings I admit, frankly, I do not know what savings are. The great difficulty I have is to see what happens to savings that are not invested. Mr Keynes says they really go in by the banks advancing to meet business losses.* You save with one hand what you lose as a business man with the other.

But the amounts the banks advance to meet business losses are small. If you lose £1,000 in your business and you save £1,000 out of your salary the wealth of the country is as it was.

(PROFESSOR GREGORY) *There is a difference between savings and investment in one sense,—I deposit £1,000 with Mr McKenna's bank and I can stimulate a demand for goods by spending, and reducing my balance. Let us take the other explanation of the difference between savings and investment, in which a certain part of what is saved and invested by the individual is offset by losses by business men. That is another side, is it not?* No; I say one necessarily leads to the other, that if the banking system acts in such a way that not the whole of the current savings is invested it logically follows not merely that business men lose, but that they lose the exact amount of the difference between savings and investment.

(MR MCKENNA) *I am beginning to understand.*

(MR BRAND) *Everything seems to me to rest on that. If that is true, all the rest of your argument follows.*

(MR LUBBOCK) *When the man who has saved money leaves it on deposit with his bank does the banker not employ it?* He employs it in a sense, but it does not follow that there is a net addition to the banker's deposits. If the public are using their deposits more sluggishly you have less investment, but the aggregate deposits may be the same.

(MR MCKENNA) *I think Mr Keynes is right as regards what happens in practice when the money is left on deposit with us and we use the money, we lend it in trade. We have had very large losses in the last ten years. That has been the fact*. I should hope to have a strict logical treatment of the theory ready before long for any member of the Committee who cares to examine it,—a much more rigorous treatment of the subject from the logical side. I have already submitted it to some high academic authorities, who have accepted it as broadly correct.

(PROFESSOR GREGORY) *Is this the sequence of the difference between savings and investment, that it is not a question of the public being unable to invest, but of the action of the monetary machine; that if the Bank of England, or any other monetary authority, keeps the Bank rate above the equilibrium level, then there will be losses to the business world?* Yes.

And that then any savings by the public will in fact only offset the losses caused by monetary policy. If the monetary machine holds the rate of interest at such a level that the cost of production of the bricks and mortar etc. which the business men chose to erect at that rate of interest is less than that part of their income which the public do not spend on their own current consumption, then the difference must emerge in business losses, because business men must necessarily find that the buying power which is coming forward to relieve them of their goods falls short of the wages etc. which they have paid out by precisely that amount.

(MR BRAND) *Supposing wages were in equilibrium?* In equilibrium with what?

Supposing wages were at the proper level in relation to prices. No, because as soon as savings exceed investment, whatever is the level of wages, prices must fall below the equilibrium, because business men can only get rid of the goods they have made by making concessions in price. Moreover this may be a world-wide phenomenon, and during international credit cycles it is; every few years you get a situation in which in the world as a whole savings exceed investment, enterprise is diminished, and producers throughout the world are unable to sell their produce. At other times you get an orgy of investment far beyond the volume of saving; and if the business world is allowed to do this by the banking system, the business men will be able to sell their goods for more than it has cost them to produce; and they can finance the cost of the additional investment out of this excess. The oscillation between deflation and inflation is the same thing as an oscillation between saving exceeding investment and investment exceeding saving.

At the present time if a man wants to build a house what deters him and what makes him save is the enormous cost of building, not the Bank rate. Oh! yes; because he is thinking of it in relation to the rents he can get. If the rate for borrowing is six per cent the rents he expects to get must be six per cent on what it has cost him to build the house; but if the rate for lending were three per cent, and rents represented five per cent on the cost of production you would have a tremendous boom. The question whether you shall build the house depends on the rate of interest on the cost of production in relation to the rents you can expect to get.

I cannot expect the Committee to accept all this, or follow it closely, because it is a very intricate idea. It is very difficult to avoid using unfamiliar language. I think it is extraordinarily comfortable to commonsense once you have got hold of it. It is not a paradox. My experience of it is that people first of all think it is a paradox, but ultimately they find it comfortable to common sense. You can use it to explain what happens in a remarkable way. You can interpret the main crisis and economic events of the past in the light of time; and it works.

May I come to the second argument? The second argument against proposals of this character does not base itself on any high theoretical ground, but contends that it is in fact impracticable to find objects of an economic character which are, as it is sometimes expressed, sufficiently productive to justify the expense. This argument involves, I think, a fallacy no less serious than the first. It all depends upon what we mean by 'sufficiently productive'. Supposing the current rate of interest as fixed by banking policy is five per cent. If there are alternative investments available, whether at home or abroad, which will yield that return, then money invested at four per cent is, I agree, in a sense economically unproductive; you are choosing the worse of two alternative investments. But the mere fact that the policy of the Bank of England is maintaining the current rate of interest at five per cent does not prove that that is a true picture of the choice before us, because it will be evident to anyone who has entered fully into the inward parts of the preceding argument that the choice may be between investing at four per cent and not investing at all; between getting a four per cent return and getting nothing with the savings balanced by business losses instead of by an increase in the material wealth of the country. The five per cent rate enforced by the Bank of England might have been intended to prevent foreign lending in excess of our foreign balance, and it might have had the effect of deterring home investment. So that if we say in such circumstances that we will not invest at home unless we can get five per cent we are really saying that unless we can get five per cent we prefer to spill our savings on the ground and get nothing; rather than get less than five per cent on £100, we would prefer that someone should lose £100.

Then the spending must be done by the Government, and not by any individual. No, that does not follow.

(MR MCKENNA) *You are speaking of the aggregate.* As long as the Bank of England is paying [charging?] five per cent it cannot pay an individual to invest at four per cent. It is another example of how deeply embedded in our minds are these assumptions in regard to equilibrium. If we were in a state of equilibrium it would always be wasteful to invest at four per cent if the market rate of interest were five per cent. But if we are in a state of disequilibrium the assumptions on which that is based are not correct. If the argument is pursued to its logical conclusion any investment which produces more than one per cent would be economical to the nation;—for if for every £100 you invest at home you fail to invest £20 abroad which would yield five per cent, the other £80 being wasted, if your home investment yields you anything more than one per cent the nation as a whole will be richer than if you had not done it. But I should like to allow for a wide margin of error, and also for waste, for various psychological factors, and also, as in the case of protection, for the risk of forming habits during disequilibrium which will continue to prevail, to our great disadvantage, after we have returned to equilibrium—which must be sooner or later our goal, unless we are prepared to change altogether our present economic system. So let us say no more for the moment than that new investment yielding four per cent or in special cases three per cent would be nationally preferable to unemployment and business losses. It is better that we should have a man employed in using plant which will produce an investment to yield four per cent in perpetuity than that the man and the plant should be unemployed. It is not a choice between investing at four per cent or five per cent; it is a choice between investing at four per cent and having 80 per cent of the savings wasted and spilled on the ground. If that is true, then to insist from the national point of view on an assured yield of five per cent is surely misguided. So that it is not sufficient to argue that five per cent propositions are getting scarce; you have got to take some lower figure than that and prove that those propositions are getting scarce too.

With that preamble, I should like to consider the various means that are open to us for stimulating home investment, accepting for the moment the proposition that if it could be done it would help the situation. I should like to take, first of all, plans for stimulating home investment by means of perfectly normal private enterprise.

The first class of remedy consists of means for enabling the banking system to meet a larger proportion of the at present unsatisfied demands which come its way, and at present fail to materialise in actual enterprise, either because the lending power of the bank is insufficient or because the present rate of interest is a deterrent. Some of our witnesses have laid more stress on the former, the lack of lending power on the part of the bank, and some on the latter, that is, the failure of borrowers to come forward at the present rate of interest. I think that both operate, and as the two are part of the same problem I might take them together for practical purposes. The difficulty in the way of enabling the banking system to act in this direction is that the international loan market is so closely intertwined with our domestic loan market that it is almost impossible to relax your lending in regard to the latter without relaxing it in regard to the former, and so leading to a reversal of policy in order to regain our gold. But I think there may be various gadgets, as I have called them, by which the two markets for home lending and foreign lending can be, within limits, separated from one another a little more than they are now. The degree of interconnection which exists in this country exists in hardly any other country; our conditions are abnormal in that respect. If one could invent a device of this kind, it would be possible for the Bank of England to enforce a rate which would prevent excessive foreign lending without necessarily applying that rate in its full rigour to home transactions. Something of that kind I think Mr Payton[5] had in mind last week. The devices aiming at this are highly technical. I have several suggestions to make—I rather think Mr McKenna has a good many to make—bearing on that point, but they are of a too detailed character to find place in a general discussion of this kind. Let me put it down as one of the things we have to consider, namely, whether we should not make certain technical changes in the banking system whereby it would be easier for the Bank of England to relax the terms of home lending without relaxing to an equal degree those for foreign lending. I think it is enormously difficult. I think we should do well to try experiments in this direction, and I should hope for something from them. But I think it would be unwise to expect too much. I am not sure that Mr McKenna would not expect a little more than I should. I am thoroughly in favour of them, but I am very much impressed with their difficulty, particularly at the moment. The pressure to lend abroad is now so great, and the discouragement to home investment is now so general, as a result of the long period of business losses, that the intrinsic difficulties in front of the Bank of England, if it were to try and move very far in the direction I am indicating, seem to me hard to overcome. Provided the Bank of England keeps its rate high enough in relation to the rest of the world and restricts credit to an appropriate degree, I think its strength is beyond dispute. I do not think that the Bank of England need ever be afraid of being weak, provided it is allowed to use the Bank rate weapon to the full internationally. But if it relaxes its rate without extreme care my opinion is that the intrinsic weakness of its position today would soon become apparent. I should hope it would try experiments to the utmost, and not draw in unless it was forced to, but if I had influence with the Bank of England I would advise them to exercise a very considerable degree of caution. I should be nervous as to the possibilities of relaxation, and I should only be prepared to undertake them to any great extent, apart from other

[5] See Committee on Finance and Industry *Minutes of Evidence*, (London, 1931), Questions 2498–2521.

remedies being applied simultaneously, in the event of something like international agreement. If everybody comes down together then the risks of reductions are nil, but anything beyond that I should feel was rather dangerous.

The next type of remedy would consist of encouraging home investment by various ways relative to foreign lending, not so much by the banking system as by bringing about a changed demeanour on the part of the public. We might have, for example, a special coupon tax on foreign bonds, such as exists in France, and has, according to the witnesses we have heard, been extraordinarily successful in curtailing foreign lending in France, in fact so successful that it has gone much too far; it was put on at the time when the flight of the franc was causing a very dangerous situation in France.

(MR BRAND) *Coupon tax plus stamp tax.* Coupon tax plus stamp tax. If I were the Chancellor of the Exchequer I should examine very carefully the possibilities of that. But of course, it is contrary to our traditions.

It has been done. The two per cent stamp tax is a great handicap to issuing here as compared with New York. Yes. But it has not been done here in the shape of a diminishing tax in favour of home investment.

(CHAIRMAN) *This is for the purpose of influencing money towards home investment.* To make the relative advantages to the investor greater in regard to domestic lending than in regard to foreign lending.

That is by a form of taxation. It would bring in a revenue, but its object would be to encourage home investment.

(MR BRAND) *On the other hand, you would not get the man who says 'I am going to invest abroad; if you do not want me to invest in foreign bond issues I am going to invest in market shares'.* You would not get him. It would probably be incomplete unless it were combined with other measures, such as an appeal to the big issuing houses not merely to discourage foreign issues but to bring home issues to the attention of investors in every possible way whenever they could find a home borrower who could make out a reasonably good case.

(MR BEVIN) *That is the opposite of what we saw yesterday.* Yes. I do not believe that the influence of publicity in this case is by any means negligible. I should have thought that the enormous advertising expenditure in connection with new issues must have a very considerable effect on the investor, that he does not go out of his way to buy bonds which are not issued in London and quoted on the London Stock Exchange. I think issuing houses could do an immense amount towards increasing home investment relative to foreign if they definitely took up a policy.

(MR BRAND) *I agree, if they found good home investments which looked profitable, but Mr Keynes's whole point, which I think is true, is that profits are too low.* Quite apart from that, I think that there is reason to suppose that they have not pursued a passionate policy of trying to find everything they could at home in preference to abroad.

Quite, but it is a mistake to think that the issuing houses can do as much as stockbrokers. Yes, I think that is so.

(MR BEVIN) *Could you adjust this by means of the French method of taxation? Would the taxation method be adjustable enough?* You could make it so. You could give a certain discretion to the Treasury and the Bank of England acting separately or jointly. I believe that some abandonment of *laissez-faire* towards foreign investments will be necessary to this country as a permanency, and that the Treasury and the Bank of England will have to take a view at any given time as to how far they want foreign lending to go on and how far they do not. A tax weapon might be used for that. By the way, I should correct one thing I said. This would also operate, except in so far as the investor is prepared to commit perjury, in regard to people who bought bonds elsewhere; the stamp tax would not, but the additional tax on coupons would apply to bonds issued in New York, and it would only be possible to avoid it by making a false declaration, which investment trusts and insurance houses would not do.

(LORD BRADBURY) *Is there not a danger, if you have protection, or provisions of a fiscal nature, which are capable of being defeated, of setting up a psychological reaction? The investor, seeing all the obstacles put in the way of foreign investment, might think that foreign investment for that reason had become more desirable.* That has not happened in France.

France has bought a lot of American securities. Like other remedies, it has a psychological effect. I believe the yield on investments is a very important factor; it has proved to be so in France; I believe that an investment trust or insurance company will be influenced by there being a larger tax on the dividend from one source than from another source.

(CHAIRMAN) *Is there not a diminution in the foreign investment?* It is not necessarily a diminution of foreign investment. We must always invest abroad to the extent of our favourable balance, and I do not want to do anything to diminish our favourable balance. This is an alternative way of checking foreign lending from becoming excessive. One way is to raise Bank rate and borrow back short what you are lending long. Another way is to check the amount of lending long. But I should not expect the amount of foreign investment under my system to be a penny less than it is under the present system. In both cases it is exactly equal to our favourable balance.

If you have a policy of discouraging foreign investment— Foreign lending.

What is the difference? There is not a difference in common parlance, but in the language I have been using there is a difference. Foreign investment is the extent to which we succeed in increasing our aggregate assets abroad by a favourable balance on income account. If we lend more than that we have to meet the difference in gold; therefore, we have to be prevented from lending more than that. If we send out a certain quantity of exports in excess of what we buy—meaning by exports visible and invisible exports—we shall have increased our assets abroad by that amount and will therefore have invested abroad to that extent. But if we lend abroad more than is desirable we have to be stopped. One way is the Bank rate.

(MR LUBBOCK) *Can you stop it exactly at the point?* We must do so, because to the extent that we do not do so we lose gold.

(MR BEVIN) *This is to be a tax that could be put on by the Treasury or the Bank of England at any moment; it is a fiscal weapon as against the Bank rate weapon?* Yes. I think it would be important not to change it often. I should not change it as often as I would Bank rate; but when there was a fairly large-scale change in the situation I should modify it. It is not a thing that I should consider whether I would modify it or not every Thursday.

Would it be possible, or do you think it is likely, that Parliament would hand over power to the Treasury or the Bank of England to conduct fiscal operations in that way? I do not see why not. It is a thing that would have to be done suddenly. It would be analogous to the existing power to alter the fiduciary issue.

(MR LUBBOCK) *A man with foreign bonds would never know what his income was likely to be.* Within the limits of the tax he would not, just as now he does not know within the limits of the income tax. It would be an extra reason that you would have to take into account when you bought a foreign bond, that you might be subject to this additional tax. Even if the tax were not in force at the moment it would be one of the things that you would have to take into account.

(MR BEVIN) *What effect would that have on the issue of credit at home?* It would mean that the investor would be satisfied with a rather lower rate of interest from home investment than he is satisfied with now. The discrimination in the case of France is of the order of eight per cent.

(MR BRAND) *On coupons for home investment it is 18 per cent and foreign 25.* If you take it at ten per cent for convenience of calculation, and assume the rate of interest at five per cent, this would amount to a discrimination of half per cent per annum. It is of the character of a special income tax on the fruits of foreign investment.

(MR MCKENNA) *Such as we had in the War.*

(MR LUBBOCK) *To make people sell their foreign bonds.*

(MR MCKENNA) *I imposed a tax for the very same purpose.*

(MR LUBBOCK) *In order to make people sell their foreign bonds?*

(MR MCKENNA) *To make people sell their foreign bonds.*

(MR LUBBOCK) *And put them into home investment?*

(MR MCKENNA) *Yes.* That was to meet an acute difficulty. It would be necessary to combine this with a general stimulating influence, a sort of patriotic movement, towards the fostering of home investment; but I believe that if the issuing houses, the insurance companies, the investment trusts understood the situation and agreed with the diagnosis, and were appealed to in the right way, it would not be difficult to get a very considerable change-over of sentiment in the direction I am suggesting. As regards the private investor, he would be, I think, very much influenced by the tax and by the publicity policy of the issuing houses. Of course, one must not expect too much. The margin within which investment habits can be affected by measures of this kind is limited, but I am sure there is always a lot of investment that is on the margin; and it is not an enormous change-over that I want to make, for it is not so much a question of diminishing the amount of foreign investment as of diminishing the pressure towards foreign investment by encouraging home investment; the point of it is much more to encourage home investment than to discourage foreign investment. I do not want to make foreign investment fall in the least degree below its present level; the object of these measures would be much more to give a fillip to home investment than hold back foreign investment.

(CHAIRMAN) *And what is to be the nature of the home investment?* They would be very various; it would depend on what were the go-ahead things. It would be a matter of great detail to predict what will be the go-ahead industries of the next few years.

(MR BRAND) *If you take insurance companies or investment trusts, their attitude is determined entirely by the yield; the risk being the same they refuse an absolutely good home investment unless it has a certain yield which they feel is necessary—particularly all the new investment trusts. Do you not think so?* I think that is a primary consideration, but a half per cent would make a good deal of difference, would it not?

Oh yes, it would make a difference. There is a third branch of this class of remedy, namely new machinery for providing long-period lending to relatively small borrowers. The necessity for what the French would call a 'crédit mobilier' has, I think, been borne in upon all of us by the evidence we have received. I am sure that proposals for the creation of machinery of this kind should figure in our Report. How large the sum to be borrowed in this way would be, it is hard to say, but it would certainly do a little in making possible some forms of investment which at present do not materialise. It is one way of increasing home investment.

These are the chief ways which have occurred to me for increasing home investment without direct Government assistance. I come now to the class of cases where the Government would come in to a greater or lesser degree. There is, first of all, direct capital expenditure by the Central Government on capital expansion within their normal sphere of operation—for example, the telephones or the roads. This is important, but I do not think that too much stress ought to be laid on it quantitatively; it should be kept in its place in proper proportion as one item amongst many, but I should think you could certainly get a contribution of something approaching £20,000,000 out of over £100,000,000—which is the total that I was thinking of—from that source. It may be less. It is something about which nobody who is outside the appropriate Government Departments could give a good opinion. Then there is the encouragement by the Treasury, and other Whitehall Departments, of expenditure by local authorities and public boards. I believe that this might be on a very large scale, as soon as one admits that it is legitimate to let them have money at a lower rate of interest than that which is fixed by conditions abroad. In actual fact, when Bank rate was put up last year the Treasury raised the rate of interest on Local Loans, i.e. on borrowing by local authorities; that is to say, they acted on the traditional principle that the rate which it is proper to charge must be fixed by external conditions. I think that was misguided. It was very important to encourage local authorities to the utmost extent; much better to say to local authorities 'If you will anticipate your expenditure, or produce anything that is at all reasonable we will let you have money out of the Local Loans Fund below the standard rate of $5\frac{1}{4}$ per cent, or whatever it is now, going down to 4 per cent or even 3 per cent as a temporary expedient to be employed only so long as there is a serious difficulty in home investment.'

An actual loss to the Treasury. An actual loss to the Treasury; they would have to find the difference from some source, but in so far as it actually increased the wealth of the community the Treasury would get part of it back. In so far as business men began making profits again the Treasury would get the income tax, and in so far as men became employed they would save the 'dole'. It seems to me we have got into quite a desperate habit of thinking in separate compartments; the Treasury will reject something on the ground that it will cost money regardless of what they could hope to save on the 'dole' or from increased revenue. We get into a vicious circle, we do nothing because we have not the money; but it is precisely because we do not do anything that we have not the money. The buoyancy of the revenue gets less and less. There is also the idea of keeping down home investment with a view to getting the interest on the national debt down as low as possible. That is one of the most desperate muddles the human mind has ever entertained. If you were to push it to its logical conclusion, the right thing would be to prohibit house building, for example, altogether. If you absolutely prohibited any outlet for investment and if you could control the foreign situation, we might all be dead, but at any rate the rate of interest which it would be necessary to pay on consols would have fallen to zero. The whole object of having a low rate of interest is in order to do things. But if you begin thinking that it is wise to stop doing things in order to lower the rate of interest, you are standing upside down. I think it ought to be sufficient to prove that the national wealth and the national income and the national employment will be increased by a certain measure, and if you can demonstrate those three things it ought to be irrelevant to reply that the Local Loans Fund will have to pay five per cent on one side, and only get back four per cent on the other.

(PROFESSOR GREGORY) *If that is the lesser of two national losses.* If that is the lesser of two national losses, yes. The calculation is whether the indirect benefits are greater than one per cent or not.

The character of investment under this head is a matter into which it would not be proper to enter into detail now, but I should expect much more from this than from any direct government expenditure, because it covers a miscellaneous field. What we want to do is to get a variety of things going, which will increase the national income.

(MR BEVIN) *Of course the amount of interest on Local Loans is indirectly expressed in the rates, and then directly it goes on to the cost of production.* If you have a high rate of interest for Local Loans?

Yes. Yes. Similarly, you can give encouragement to railways and industry generally. There are bodies like tube railways, which depend very closely upon a narrow calculation of interest. Whether an underground system does or does not make expansion depends upon a rather nice calculation of interest, and if it is to the national advantage that the investment should be made now I believe you can find very valuable outlets in that direction. I have always been in favour of the principle of the Trade Facilities Act, by which a great variety of enterprises, if they make out a good case, could be allowed to borrow at less than the market rate in return for immediate investment of the right kind.

Would you apply that purely to local effort, or competitive effort, as well as to commercial effort? When you get into the world of private enterprise you raise a great many difficult questions for consideration, as to the desirability of helping one man and not helping his competitors. Therefore I think there would be much greater scope in things like railways.

May you not, in fact, at a critical time increase indirectly your foreign investment by a low rate of interest? You may. You would have to be very careful about it.

Is not that what actually happens? No, I do not think it need. Supposing the new body formed under the auspices of the Bank of England feels it is wise and right to make new rationalisation loans, it ought not to be too closely governed by whether a reasonable rate of interest that a purely cold-blooded investor would expect to get is exactly the market rate at the moment. Supposing the yield ought to be six per cent if the issue is to be a success, but a really truthful accountant would not assess it at more than four per cent, it would be wrong for the Bank of England to be prevented from bringing out the issue for that reason. The argument is the same as I have been meeting in other cases. If investment in a four per cent proposition of this kind were to prevent money from going into another six per cent investment, this would be a very foolish thing to do. We have to meet the argument that that is the situation. I am arguing that that is not the situation. It is not true that the money going into the four per cent investment is going otherwise into a six per cent investment; for six per cent does not represent what an alternative investment is yielding, it represents the rate that has to be enforced by the banking system to prevent us from lending abroad more than we can finance by our balance of trade.

Would you limit Trade Facilities to reconstruction or, so to speak, putting our house in order? I do not know enough about it. I should rely on wise administration, I think, more than on formal rules.

(MR BRAND) *A Government Department on that has to lend at less good security. I remember the Secretary of the Trade Facilities Committee coming round and saying 'For goodness sake, can't you find something for us to lend on?'* They were always applying such ridiculous criteria. They were trying only to embark upon investments which were six per cent investments. If you work the Trade Facilities Act on the theory of investing only at six per cent without appreciable risk, what you describe is the result you will get.

I think you must limit it to competitive enterprise, because it is extraordinarily difficult for a Government Department to take risks for private enterprise. There would be some cases where assistance would cover an industry as a whole, where you could offer terms to all persons in an industry of a responsible character.

(SIR W. RAINE) *Yes, but you get a limit to that. When the Trade Facilities Act was in operation so many shipbuilders came in and got facilities, then others came in, and the Trade Facilities people said 'We cannot let you have any more money.'* That is an objection. I dare say it might be wise to limit it. It would depend upon the demand you found from other sources.

(MR BEVIN) *It is a question of balancing requirements.* Yes. In conclusion I should like to say about Government action of this kind, that obviously it cannot be a permanency. You cannot be permanently stimulating local authorities to anticipate their programme, and you cannot permanently be going ahead at a great pace with public developments. Nevertheless I think the first impetus forward must come from action of this kind, that it must be

Government investment which will break the vicious circle. If you can do that for a couple of years, it will have the effect, if my diagnosis is right, of restoring business profits more nearly to normal, and if that can be achieved then private enterprise will be revived. I believe you have first of all to do something to restore profits and then rely on private enterprise to carry the thing along. Assuming that there are a number of forms of capital investment which are, for good or for evil, definitely in the hands of public boards and local authorities today, we must look to a bold Government programme to lift us out of the rut; and if that is done, if it has the effect of restoring business profits, then the machine of private enterprise might enable the economic system to proceed once more under its own steam; and since I should look forward to that, I also look forward to being able gradually to diminish the amount of Government intervention.

I should, however, like to say this, that I do very greatly doubt whether we shall ever be free in this country to return to unbridled *laissez-faire* in the matter of foreign lending. For this reason, that I believe that *laissez-faire* in foreign lending is utterly incompatible with our existing wages policy. For if individuals are entirely free to lend their savings without discrimination in whatever quarter of the world they obtain the greatest reward, this means, broadly speaking, that the proportion of the joint product which we award to labour as compared with the proportion which we award to capital cannot be greater here than it is in other parts of the world. If we have complete liberty of foreign investment, that must necessarily mean that we cannot run more than a very little ahead of the rest of the world in our treatment of labour—I mean by that, the way in which we treat labour relatively to its efficiency. Assuming that labour and capital are equally efficient in Germany and England, and in England our wages policy awards three-fifths of the value of the product produced to labour and two-fifths to capital, and in Germany it awards three-fifths to capital and two-fifths to labour the rate of profit must be 50 per cent higher in Germany than it is in England and they will be able to offer $7\frac{1}{2}$ per cent when the English borrowers only offer 5 per cent. If that is allowed to go on freely we are bound to get back into the position we are now in, that is to say, either we shall be in a state of chronic disequilibrium between the pressure to lend abroad or we shall have to force down wages in England until capital gets the same proportion of the product as in Germany. I am taking Germany merely as an illustration.

We have now reached this point, that our wages policy is definitely set to a more liberal remuneration of the worker relatively to his efficiency than prevails in a good many other countries. The comparison with the United States is exceedingly difficult, owing to difficulties in comparing costs of living and also owing to vital differences made by their size, their protective system, and the fact that they approximate very closely to a closed system, and are therefore able to go in for all kinds of things that we are absolutely cut off from.

A higher standard of living. That may be due to an increased efficiency which we might conceivably imitate some day; but if it be the case that there is any important part of the world which is going to treat the worker less favourably than we, then this wages policy of ours, I think, is definitely incompatible with the policy of *laissez-faire* towards foreign investment.

I am afraid that the discussion of this sixth class of remedy has led me over a somewhat wide field. I still have my seventh class, which I have not reached, but it might be well to break off what I have to say to you at this point.

(CHAIRMAN) *We hardly notice the lapse of time when you are speaking.*
(MR MCKENNA) *Extraordinarily interesting!*
(CHAIRMAN) *We must not put too much strain upon you.*

(Adjourned till tomorrow, Friday
7 March 1930 at 4.30 p.m.)

COMMITTEE ON FINANCE AND INDUSTRY

Note of Discussion on
Friday 7 March 1930

Present:

The Rt Hon. Lord Macmillan (*Chairman*)

Sir Thomas Allen	Mr Cecil Lubbock
Mr Ernest Bevin	The Rt Hon. Reginald McKenna
The Rt Hon. Lord Bradbury, G.C.B.	Mr J. T. Walton Newbold
The Hon. R. H. Brand, C.M.G.	Sir Walter Raine
Professor T. E. Gregory, D.SC.	Mr J. Frater Taylor
Mr J. M. Keynes, C.B.	Mr A. A. G. Tulloch
Mr Lennox B. Lee	Mr G. Ismay (*Secretary*)

Sir Frederick Leith-Ross, K.C.M.G., C.B.

(MR KEYNES) Mr Chairman, may I begin by repeating two important qualifications which were brought to my mind by yesterday's reduction of Bank rate? In my foregoing remarks I have been using 'Bank rate' to mean terms of lending generally, not merely the Bank of England official rate. If the existing level of Bank rate is expected to last, the two would come to much the same thing, terms of lending generally and Bank rate, but not otherwise. Over a short period you do not necessarily get the corresponding relief in other forms of lending that you do in the form of lending through bills. The other point is also one I have mentioned before, namely, that the acute trouble, as I see it at present, is the failure of home borrowers to come forward. The danger of reducing Bank rate without taking any other step simultaneously seems to me to be, that it may stimulate foreign borrowers more than it stimulates home borrowers. That is the dilemma in which the Bank of England stands. If this is the effect, a reduction of Bank rate only means that it will have to be raised again after a not very long interval; and the cheap money policy might then be declared a failure and the Bank of England accused of having made a mistake. It seems to me, therefore, frightfully important that home borrowers, whether official or semi-official, should somehow be induced to come forward ahead of foreign borrowers. If only great plans for capital expansion had been maturing during the last six months, the fall of Bank rate would provide an ideal opportunity for bringing them to fruition. But if there are no home borrowers ready to come forward at the moment when Bank rate is reduced, then it may very easily prove a bit of a fiasco and stimulate foreign borrowing.

(CHAIRMAN) *'Home borrowing' connotes home enterprise. The borrowing itself is of no value; it is borrowing for some enterprise.* Yes. The home borrower is discouraged and large scale borrowing by public authorities is not very great. The greater the extent to which Government or semi-official authorities are using up borrowed funds for new enterprises the easier will the task of the Bank of England be. Very often the opposite is believed to be the case. It is often supposed that the less these activities are, the easier the task of the Bank of England will be. If there were now very large demands for borrowing in the London market for home purposes the risks which the Bank of England is running in reducing the Bank rate would be far less than they are at the moment.

(MR BRAND) *Would you develop that?* Because there would be an outlet for funds of home borrowers and, therefore, there would be much less temptation, much less likelihood of available funds being lent abroad.

(MR TULLOCH) *The question of rate comes in, does it not? If the home rate is a low rate and the rate abroad a bigger rate, how would you prevent your money being lent abroad?* There would be a slight difference in rate but the more outlets there are for money at home, I think you may conclude generally speaking, the less likely are funds to be lent abroad and, therefore, the less likely is a low rate to put intolerable pressure on the Bank of England. I emphasise it, because it is often believed that the opposite is true. Furthermore, the conversion loans that the Treasury have brought out in recent months have very much aggravated the difficulties of the Bank of England and have, by diminishing the supply of Treasury bills made it much more dangerous to lower the Bank of England rate. If the policy of the

Treasury was to fit in with the Bank of England, they ought to do exactly the opposite.

(MR MCKENNA) *Is your point really that if there is domestic borrowing the Bank of England rate will be effective?* Yes.

That will keep up the market borrowing rate. Yes. Consequently the market borrowing rate will be less attractive to the foreigner. The trouble is, if there is no domestic borrowing, even when the Bank of England does lower Bank rate it still remains an ineffective rate and the foreigner is tempted to borrow at a rate which may be under 4 per cent.

(MR BRAND) *The rate for long money is not very much affected.* No, the rate for long money is not very much affected, but the bill rate will remain so far below the Bank rate, that the Bank rate will be ineffective even at four per cent unless there is domestic borrowing. Domestic borrowing would absorb sufficient funds to make the Bank rate effective.

But unless it is borrowing by the Government, domestic borrowing must be shown to be profitable; if you produce a prospectus and bring it to the notice of the investor it must show that he is to have a run for his money. That is why I believe the first step has to be taken by official or semi-official authorities. Then, when profits have been restored to normal, private enterprise can return.

One has got to accept your doctrine that large Government borrowing will bring profits back to ordinary enterprise? Yes.

(PROFESSOR GREGORY) *I do not think anybody disputes that if the Electricity Board can get their money taken up with the underwriters they could have stimulated the electrical industry.*

(MR BRAND) *If industrial profits had been enlarged by the action of the municipal bodies, that might be regarded as true. I do not think it is true in Germany.*

(MR MCKENNA) *I think it must be so. Corporation borrowing means more labour employed, more labour employed means more consumption by those employed. It will necessarily entail a greater degree of prosperity in all the supplying trades.*

(MR BRAND) *And a higher rate of interest for borrowing.*

(MR MCKENNA) *Not necessarily higher.*

(MR BRAND) *My experience in issuing is that if a certain number of issues has taken place you know quite well that unless you get your issue in quickly the supply of money will be swallowed up except at a higher rate; then you have to wait a bit.* Your conclusion would follow in the event of its being foreign lending and also in the event of its being home lending, if we were in a condition of equilibrium; but if we are below equilibrium then I do not think it applies to home lending.

Now, Mr Chairman, may I come to my seventh and last category of remedy. The first six classes have all sought to bring us into equilibrium with the outside world by making changes here. Our situation might also be helped if we could bring about changes abroad. Therefore in our list of remedies we must include the adoption of a concerted policy between the leading central banks of the world not only to prevent a further fall in international prices, but I should say also to raise prices to a parity with the international level of money incomes and with the international level of money costs of production, so as to avoid the appalling waste and loss and dislocation which would result from having to force down money incomes throughout the world to a parity with present prices. I think it is clear that in nearly all parts of the world money incomes are too high in relation to the international raw commodity index numbers at the moment.

(CHAIRMAN) *Would the fact that central banks have now been established in most of the countries of the world assist in that process of co-operation.* Oh, certainly; it is very much easier than it would have been prior to the creation of the Federal Reserve System in the United States.

And the central banks on the Continent and in the Dominions. Yes; but, of course, the central banks on the Continent existed previously in the larger countries. The new ones are mostly in the smaller countries and are not so relevant.

Could such a convention as you contemplate be represented to other countries as being so much in their interest as to render it highly desirable? I think if we had approached them two years ago to do something to alleviate our own domestic problems, it might have been difficult to represent that it was in their interest, because at that time international prices had been running on an even keel, especially in the United States.

We cannot expect them to do it from mere altruism. No, but now that the fall of prices in the rest of the world is affecting them hardly less than it is affecting us, there would be more possibility of getting collective action, and more reasonable indeed to ask for it on the ground that it is now an international problem.

What direction do you think this co-operation should take? I think effective results could be reached primarily by agreement between three countries—ourselves, the United States and France—but it would certainly be wise to bring in a number of others at some stage—Germany, Holland, Sweden, Switzerland, Spain, Italy, the Argentine, and Japan. The measures which could be proposed for the collectivity of the central banks would be as follows. First of all, the policy of a concerted lowering of Bank rates. Bank rates have two purposes. One is to maintain equilibrium with your neighbours, the other is to avoid world-wide underinvestment or overinvestment, as the case may be, to avoid slumps and booms. Insofar as it is necessary to maintain Bank rate for the first purpose agreement is completely adequate to the case; if everyone comes down together no one is worse off from the point of view of losing gold to his neighbours. The policy would only be dangerous if it were tending to stimulate world-wide overinvestment, which would be followed in due course by world-wide inflation. I think it could be represented today as very greatly in the interest of all quarters of the world if Bank rates were lowered in a concerted manner until the price level had risen quite materially from its present figure.

(SIR T. ALLEN) *How far could you limit a political theory?* I do not believe that would come in if everybody worked together. I think that might be a factor in any individual country, but it is one of the advantages of international action that that factor would be almost negligible.

I was reading yesterday a speech by the Federal Prime Minister of Australia. He said that there is overproduction of wheat throughout the world, which has depreciated prices, and his theory is, produce still more wheat and let it be further subsidised by the state. Let him do whatever he likes in that respect. I would not bring in difficult local problems of that kind.

Would it not enter into it? No, I do not think so. I would bring to bear general forces. In addition to these there would be all kinds of particular forces affecting particular commodities in particular countries. But if I could get my general forces operating I should rely on their average effect being what I wanted.

The second proposal that might be made would be a concerted reduction of legal reserve proportions. I think it is widely agreed now that it was a pity when the central banks were fixing their legal regulations on the return to the gold standard that so many of them fixed rather a high ratio. That is a matter where what your neighbours do is considered important; it is largely a standard of respectability, and if we were all agreed that a minimum ratio of ten per cent less than that which is now generally prevailing was respectable, it would become so.

(PROFESSOR GREGORY) *Yes. The standard of respectability was fixed by the Federal Reserve System on purely empirical grounds before the War at 40 per cent.* Yes, they were the first to use this figure. A third factor to be considered would be a concerted blessing of gold exchange methods. Another possibility—though possibly this is premature—would be an attempt at an early development of some of the potentialities of the International Bank [Bank for International Settlements] as a means of economising in the use of gold. The potentialities are very indefinite, but I think some of the drafters of the International Bank had in view a further development of gold exchange methods which would function rather in the same way, but would go further than anything that was thought of at Genoa. Then lastly, I believe it would help very much—though that, perhaps, is attributing too much virtue to my own particular doctrine—if all the banking authorities of the world were to agree that a world-wide encouragement of investment and of capital development generally would help. Sir Thomas Allen has called attention to there being an overproduction of wheat. It is alleged in the case of all kinds of commodities that there is overproduction. I think that is a wrong way of putting it; it is under-demand, and the lack of demand is due to the lack of investment.

(MR BRAND) *Not always under-demand.* Well, it differs with particular commodities. For instance, in the case of wheat I think it is hard to put it down to overproduction. Over more than half the world the harvests of 1929 were the worst for many years.

(MR BEVIN) *Of course, there is a great reduction in the consumption of flour. Lancashire and Yorkshire used to consume about 1,000,000 sacks a year for dressing of certain cotton stuffs. Artificial silk has come in, mixed with cotton, and there is not the demand for flour; it has obviously gone down because it is not used to the same extent. That has a very big effect on wheat.* I am not thinking of a particular cause. If throughout the world one had a general cause operating which was making everybody more prosperous, and making the earning power of the working classes throughout the world larger, you would certainly have an increased consumption of wheat.

I do not think you are right there, because experience shows that the higher the standard of living the less the consumption of flour. Wheat is not a good example to take. I do not agree with you on this. I am taking the whole world; I am not taking this country. I believe the whole world is very susceptible to such an influence as this. But I am only taking wheat as an example of a general case. The working classes are capable, you agree, of consuming more of something.

Yes, consuming more of something. Therefore there would be some range of articles which would get a stimulus; if wheat is becoming an obsolete article, labour will have to change over and produce something else.

(CHAIRMAN) *More meat.*

(MR BEVIN) *So far as industrial countries are concerned—I have been connected with the trade for years, and have had to follow it very closely—when you get depression the consumption of flour is inclined to increase because bread is still the cheapest cooked food.* I do not want to be led into the discussion of particular cases.

If you take wheat, prosperity does not mean a bigger consumption on the whole, except insofar as this, that if you increase the prosperity of the industrialists of the east, as of the industrialists of this country, they take to wheat as against rice.

(CHAIRMAN) *Yes, that is one of the causes of the Canadian wheat development, that you may get the Chinaman to take to wheat instead of rice.* I

153

am dealing to-day with general causes. If, besides all this, the United States and France were to declare that they would do everything reasonably in their power not to take more gold for a year or two, and, if practicable to lose ten per cent of their present holding, one would say that, in addition to the other expedients, would make the position almost safe. I am absolutely confident that we could bring back the level of prices to what it was a couple of years ago.

(MR BRAND) *But they could only do that by reducing their rate. They could not say ' We will not take more gold'. They would have to take the appropriate step.* Yes, by all the various actions associated with a reduction of rate. I fancy—though it is not a point on which my opinion is worth anything—that the obstacles to this policy are really only two. The first one is lack of familiarity in France with the whole order of ideas which lie behind the sort of thing we have been discussing. It is very doubtful how far the Bank of France is aware either of the existence of the problem or of the nature of the solution.

I might, perhaps, give you a small instance. In the last few days the German–French exchange has demanded that gold should go from France to Germany but no French banking house has been willing to brave public opinion up to the present by sending gold to Germany. Public opinion in France thinks that it is unpatriotic to export gold. Both in official and academic circles in France it is hardly an exaggeration to say that economic science is non-existent. French thought on these matters is two generations out-of-date. This is a very serious matter. I think if this Committee were to invite evidence from some people who have been in touch with the Bank of France—I have talked with some of them—they would find them shocked by the state of mind that they find prevailing there. That is one obstacle. The second obstacle lies in the tendency of the Federal Reserve System to be dominated by domestic rather than by international considerations. American domestic considerations take different forms at different times. At present they still take the form primarily of fear lest if there were easy credit Wall Street speculators might again take the bit between their teeth.

The fact that the fall in commodity prices is attacking the American price level is undoubtedly tending at the moment to make them more internationally minded. A great many American interests are being very much hit by the fall in international prices. I should not therefore despair of bringing America into collaboration on these lines if the situation gets any worse than it is now. Of course, international co-operation on these lines has been talked about widely ever since the Genoa Conference of 1922. But it has been greatly interfered with, first of all by preoccupation with reparations, and then by preoccupation with the restoration of the gold standard. But it may be that the time has now come when there is more chance of making progress. The worst of it is that in the meantime, as I have mentioned, the restoration of the gold standard was effected in such a way as to establish too high a standard of gold reserve, and, for various reasons which I must not stop to go into, gold [exchange] standard methods have been losing rather than gaining in popularity. A great many people who at the time of the Genoa Confeence were advocating gold [exchange] standard methods are now more dubious, and central banks which were willing to keep their resources abroad, are less willing to do so now. Then on top of this we have the gold hoarding propensities of the Bank of France freely indulged in. I should rather expect that we can all agree about the extreme desirability of international collaboration. I think we ought to seek detailed evidence from witnesses as to what is practicable, and this matter should, I suggest, receive attention in our Report.

(CHAIRMAN) *Who would be the class of person to assist us in this inquiry?* Sir Josiah Stamp, I think, would be a very important witness. The Governor of the Bank of England would be a very important witness. I do not think it is a matter on which there is any difference of opinion between high authorities in this country. What is actually feasible it is hard to say. It is not only a less controversial remedy than many that I have discussed, but it is all of first-rate importance, particularly if one is looking further forward. A great deal of what we have been discussing is in the nature of a short-period problem; sooner or later we shall get out of our present disequilibrium; for this is essentially a temporary problem, it is not a thing which is to be with us for ever and ever; but this international problem, unless it is solved by co-operation, will be with us for ever.

While I think there would be agreement on the desirability of such co-operation the divergence of view would be on the method.

(PROFESSOR GREGORY) *I agree with everything that Mr Keynes has said. I think the ranges of possible solution as far as international action is concerned is perfectly clearly defined, and is agreed to by any economist who has occupied himself with these matters. The only question is the probability or the improbability of agreement on method.*

(SIR T. ALLEN) *I would like Mr Keynes to tell us whether there is any sequence of thought in regard to what he is aiming at. I quite appreciate the possibilities of what he has advanced in relation to what might be termed the central bank policy, and the general fall in commodity prices as they exist today, but my trouble is, how is that going to be followed through? Coming back to wheat for the moment, we have wheat, say at 5d a bushel over what it was in 1913, about three per cent, but when we come to the price to the consumer there is an increased spread of 55 per cent. How are you going to deal with the wage problem?* It is a very intricate question. I should put it like this: That international collaboration would permit the relaxation of credit, the relaxation of credit would permit world-wide development of investment; that would increase the consumers' purchasing power relative to the amount of goods available, partly by employing people and giving them more wages to spend, partly by diverting labour from the production of consumption goods to the production of investment goods. Therefore one can say that over a whole class of goods prices would tend to rise up to their cost of production. One cannot particularise and say that a particular group of consumption goods will benefit, because they may be affected by special considerations which are not susceptible to remedies of this kind, but over the whole field on the average I should predict that the result would be an upward tendency in prices.

There is one other thing I want to say about international collaboration, and that is that it has become increasingly important in the course of the last few months because it is now fairly obvious that we are on the downward slope of an international credit cycle; we had begun to think that we were going to avoid such things without having any very definite collaboration, that each central bank behaving fairly reasonably within the limits of its own discretion would avoid that. It has now been proved to us that that is not so, and that we are liable to the same kind of world-wide disturbance that has afflicted the world on many previous occasions. The intensity of our own problem today is due to the fact that we now have the influence of this international depression superimposed on our own pre-existing domestic troubles. I should attribute a much greater proportion of our perplexity to international conditions today than I should have done a year or two ago. A year or two ago our troubles were primarily domestic; now the international problem is at least equally important.

I have now finished what has turned out to be rather a long story in spite of my having tried to avoid details and to limit myself to blocking in the main outline of our problem as I see it. I am afraid I have now spoken for something like nine hours, and I must thank the Committee for the patience and sympathy with which they have heard me.

(MR LUBBOCK) *Thank you. (Hear, hear).*

(CHAIRMAN) *I am sure I say what all my colleagues would wish to say, that we are greatly indebted to you for your exposition, not only of the orthodox view, with which you started, but also the more startling views, if I may say so, with which you developed your argument. I think it has been extremely interesting because it has enabled us to think more fundamentally about these problems than we had been able to do. I feel myself personally very much indebted to you. It does strike one that when we come to frame our Report there will be two main topics. There are those large questions which are behind the whole system of credit, which go down to the fundamental principles, the organisation behind the scenes. We may have to touch upon the fundamental principles of the economy, of finance and banking. The other kind of things we have been listening to, through our witnesses, has been the practical side—the clinical side—what is done by the banks without regard to the general causes that are at work. We shall have to deal with both those aspects, both the fundamental causes and the action of those who, perhaps without knowledge of the causes, are empirical persons who are in fact working the system; but their actions, I suppose, are ultimately, although they may not even know its controlled by causes which you have been unfolding or suggesting to us as fundamental. Yes.*

That strikes me as very important. We have these two topics of what is going on behind the scenes which men do not realise, just as men engaged in a craft work at it empirically without understanding the principles. Here we may be of some value if we can bring to the surface these fundamental conceptions, and possibly we may find in those fundamental conceptions some means of altering the system and bringing it into line with the sort of thing you have in mind. Yes.

(Adjourned till Thursday next,
13 March 1930 at 4.30 p.m.)

The only other 'private evidence' given at this stage was that of Reginald McKenna. The Committee devoted its meeting of 21 March to this purpose.

Keynes's membership of the Macmillan Committee at this stage had one unexpected consequence. In his personal papers in the Library of King's College, Cambridge the editor found an envelope marked as follows:

Not to be opened

New Process

To be delivered to The   JMK
Rt Hon. T. McKenna   April 1930

As McKenna had died before Keynes, the envelope remained unopened in Keynes's papers until November 1979. Inside the envelope was a 19 page manuscript in Keynes's hand.

New Process

In case anything comes of this, it may be interesting to record one's first impressions on hearing of it.

During recent meetings of the Macmillan Committee on

157

Currency Reggie McKenna, who sits next to me, has often produced out of his pocket a small bar of gold and has asked me how much more such gold would be needed in my opinion to put right the monetary management of the world. I forget my precise answer, but it was something like this: 'a lump sum addition of £200,000,000 to the world's monetary stocks of gold and thereafter an annual supply £40,000,000 greater than the present supply ought to be enough to make all the central banks of the world quite easy'.

On Wednesday April 9, 1930, after a dinner at the Tuesday Club at which I had opened a discussion on the presupposition of free trade, he took my arm and walked away with me, in a state of much excitement. He had heard that morning, it turned out, that the attempt to apply New Process on a commercial side had proved successful.

He had, he said, a great secret to tell me. Would I agree to be sworn to complete and absolute secrecy. I swore; though later in the evening he released me from my oath so far as Lydia was concerned.

This was the secret. A German chemist of the name of Gladitz had found a way to produce in unlimited quantities at a cost of 1^{s}/– per oz! A syndicate existed to exploit the business (1,500,000 shares of 1^{s}/– each), in which he, Reggie, was substantially interested; he would give me 500 shares for the benefit of my advice and conversation about it: (and next day at the Macmillan Committee he handed me a paper assigning me to his interest in 500 shares, saying 'this is worth either nothing or £50,000'.)[6]

Meanwhile he walked from the Cafe Royale arm in arm down Regent Street, across Piccadilly towards Pall Mall, I trying to grasp out intelligent questions, wondering whether he was balmy, a practical joker, or whether (as I had written seven years before in my *Tract on Monetary Reform*[7]) 'Years may elapse without great improvement in the methods of extracting gold;

[6] See below p. 165.
[7] JMK, vol. IV, p. 133.

and then the genius of a chemist may realise past dreams and forgotten hoaxes, transmuting base into precious like subtle, or extracting gold from sea-water as in the Bubble'. For he was much excited and the story came out very gradually. We walked to his flat in Pall Mall, he opened the bottom drawer of the little cabinet where he keeps his cigars to take out two or three of the famous 'sticks' to show me, we talked disjointedly sitting on the arms of the chairs and the sofa, when I said it was time to go he came down with me and walked back to Piccadilly until I got into a taxi. That weekend Lydia and I went down to stay at Mells and I heard more about it. This is the story, to the best of my recollection, as it gradually came out.

This German chemist of high technical reputation, married to an English wife, happened to be in England at the outbreak of war and was interned. Since his technical knowledge would have been useful to his country, we refused to exchange him, and it happened to be McKenna himself, who, as Home Secretary, signed the order to keep him in the Isle of Man for the whole duration of the War. In this enforced leisure he thought out his plan. Subsequently he became naturalised and has now, with his son who is associated with him in the work and his wife, made England his permanent home. McKenna came into it through Hugo Cunliffe-Owen who saw that the association of the Midland Bank with the plan might be invaluable. Cunliffe-Owen had got mixed up with it a year or two ago entirely by accident, through having overheard an incautious lady saying at a dinner party something about a new gold process someone was discovering. Cunliffe-Owen who is 'a speculative sort of fellow' had taken it up on a big scale at a very early stage before anything was proved, and had helped to find the money for the initial experiments which had cost (I think I was told) more than £100,000. But the inventor held the control and much the greater proportion of the shares. Hyde of the Midland Bank was also in the secret and hardly anyone else insofar as I was told by Reggie.

The inventor's conception was this. In the core of the earth all the elements are present together in minute particles. Thus one would expect lava to have a high metallic content. As a matter of fact lava yields to the ordinary analyst practically nothing but carbon. This must be due, the inventor conceived, to the metals being dispersed into minute quantities, which he called (I think) 'telemons', each particle being encased with a coating of carbon through which ordinary chemical analysis could not pierce. His idea was that by reversing the process these telamons could be released and brought to the surface; that is to say, just as the lava has been slowly cooled down from a great heat, so he would slowly heat it up again to its original temperature.

The experiment was performed and on a minute laboratory scale it appeared to be successful. The powdered lava was re-formed into what on being re-cooled became a black vitreous stick very thinly coated with various metals, particularly gold, platinum and iridium, of which the gold could then be isolated very easily by the ordinary processes, each stick (about half the size of a stick of sealing-wax) having perhaps 3ˢ/– worth of hold on it.

Well, it is useless for me to try to describe technical processes which I do not understand and which were explained by someone who also did not understand. But it helped my unbelief very considerably to know at any rate that it did not purport to be synthetic gold but was just a new and very cheap method of extraction.

I will only add this much. Some kinds of lava proved to have a larger gold content than others. The particular lava which they are now importing is particularly rich in gold and iridium, also platinum, yielding about £5,000 worth of gold per ton. Thus the amount of lava which has to be imported is not a formidable tonnage. A concession for obtaining the lava, alleged to be required for brick-making, has been secured.

After the laboratory experiments had been successful, attempts were made to design a large furnace capable of dealing with substantial amounts of powdered lava at a single heating.

But this proved difficult and recourse has now been had to a multitude of small furnaces. The workmen who serve them see only the powdered lava which they put in at one end. The gilded 'sticks' which emerge are taken out by Mr Gladitz and his son and the gold is separated and refined by them.

When McKenna spoke to me gold was being produced, so he believed, at the rate of £300 a day. The additional furnaces under order were expected to raise the output to an annual rate of £10,000,000 a year by the end of 1930; and there seemed no reason why there should not be an annual output of £30,000,000 or indeed any other figure later on. McKenna had already sold a small quantity of the gold to the Bank of England, whose assayers had accepted it as being what it pretended to be.

I raised, of course, the natural doubt whether the inventor was not mixing in at the start the gold which he purported to extract. But McKenna declared that the financial arrangements were such that he could have no *financial* motive for the deception, whilst the amounts of gold were now becoming greater than what he could get hold of for such a purpose.

What were one's first reactions to such a story, when a little of the first incredulity had begun to evaporate? What, did one feel, would be the right way to exploit and to utilise such an extraordinary situation? For this is what Reggie and I chiefly talked about.

First of all an immense *schadenfreude* towards the gold standard and its advocates and a feeling that this, at any rate, was the end of the 'barbarous relic'. We reminded one another that our debt to America was unequivocally payable in gold, that our foreign loans on the other hand (unlike those of any other country) were payable not in gold but in *sterling*, the German reparations, which the Dawes Plan had fixed in terms of an index number, had been re-settled by the Young Plan in terms of gold. Thus the collapse of gold would wipe out German reparations and our own debt to America. Incidentally the Rand would be ruined.

But on second thoughts all this seemed superficial. At any rate it would not suit those who wanted to make money (very much money) out of the invention. Besides would it really be practically or morally possible to enforce contracts expressed in gold, once the gold standard had collapsed? Obviously the maximum individual and national advantage, probably the greatest international advantage also, could be won by using the invention to control and regulate the gold situation. Why should it not be operated just as if an incredibly rich gold mine had happened to be discovered on the Horse Guards Parade? If the output was controlled and kept at the level which was most in the interest of stability in the value of gold by producing, let us say, £30,000,000 to £40,000,000 a year, we could pay for the American debt out of the proceeds, London could seize the leadership from New York and maintain with impunity a level of Bank rate which would cause the international price and credit situation to develop in the way in which we thought it ought to develop;—in fact there would be a managed international currency run from London, and if Paris or Washington or any other place showed an inclination to absorb a quantity of gold, there would be no difficulty in obliging them.

But there was a necessary, inevitable condition of such a plan, yet extraordinarily difficult to secure. Namely secrecy. This was obviously the kernel of the problem. It would be no good to patent the process; for once the general idea was known, it would be so easy to reconstruct the whole process and to produce 'bootleg' gold in every quarter of the world, that the game would assuredly be up. Nor would the rest of the world readily acquiesce in the situation if it were to become known that England had a recipe to make gold for nothing. Yet once the secret was out, the gold standard would be doomed and—the fat would be in the fire.

About the possibility of maintaining for any length of time the absolute secrecy, which is required, in face of any really large output, I was and remain sceptical. But the following is the plan which McKenna had very carefully thought out; and after much cogitation I cannot devise a better one.

He believed that the facilities of the Midland Bank would enable him to market up to (say) £5,000,000 a year without exciting remark. Sums of this order of magnitude coming on to the market through this channel could appear for some time to be in the ordinary course of business. But if all goes well, this would only look after the position during 1930. In the course of 1931 two difficulties, one minor the other major, would arise. The minor difficulty would be the large profits of the company which within a short period after the end of their financial year would have to be disclosed to the Inland Revenue and could not but excite their persistent curiosity as to how such profits had been made. The date of the Company's financial year had been altered to put this off as long as was legally possible. But, in the event of success, this question was bound to arise before the end of 1931.

The major difficulty, however would be the disposal of really large quantities of gold without arousing suspicion as to its origin. If the Bank of England were to be brought into the secret, they could probably dispose of large quantities of gold for a considerable time without exciting anything more than perplexity in the outside world; and even if suspicions were aroused, it is difficult to see what the outside world could do about it—so long as the main secret was kept.

McKenna had, therefore, decided that he must at an early age bring the Chancellor of the Exchequer into the secret. His plan was as follows:

Under the binding pledge of secrecy he would divulge to the Chancellor the broad outlines of the business and would offer to sell him the results of the process for the sum of (say) £150,000,000, the purchase price to be paid over only against, and *pari passu* with, deliveries of gold;* that is to say it would amount to an arrangement by which the Chancellor bought this amount of gold at its usual price and was then entitled, free of

---

* An indirect advantage of this method of sale would be that the owners of the invention would save income tax and supertax.

charge, to all deliveries in excess of £150,000,000; or alternatively £75 of the purchase price might be paid against each £100 of gold delivered, so that the Chancellor would make a profit from the outset.

If the Chancellor were to be disinclined for the deal, then he would then threaten—this is very shocking—to offer the secret to America.

If a deal on any such lines were to go through, the business of disposing of the gold would become the job of the Bank of England acting as agent of the Treasury. It would mean in practice that the Bank of England would be able to dominate the monetary policy of the world, and hence the international price-level, owing to its ability to part with very large quantities of gold without embarrassment. For example it could keep the new gold as a concealed reserve and so feel free to part with a large quantity of its published gold.

The practical problems which would arise would be fascinating to solve. But the main point is the preservation of secrecy. Essential and yet, does not one feel, almost impossible. And the peculiar feature is that not only would the syndicate and the British Treasury and England fasten most on the rest of the world by keeping the secret, but the rest of the world too would probably be the better off for the secret being kept! For consider the chaos which would follow on sudden or premature disclosure.

In the long run, one must assume that secrecy would be impossible. In the long run, the international bank must function and plans must be completed for the substitution of an international managed currency before the gaff is blown.

Is it all true? Is it the greatest hoax in the world? God knows. But I keep my mind open to the possibility of its being at least a part of what it pretends to be.

It will be a wonderful last chapter to the long history of gold's dominion over our greedy minds. I look forward with every emotion of satisfaction to the prospect that the world may be forced in my lifetime to the substitution of a scientific control of the lever which works the balancing factor in our economic life.

J. M. KEYNES

April 22·26, 1930

Nor did the story end with the note, for in the Keynes Papers in the Marshall Library of Economics was the letter from McKenna referred to above (p. 158).

From Reginald McKenna, 10 April 1930.

Dear Maynard,

In consideration of your payment to me of one shilling, I hereby undertake to pay or transfer to you all the dividends and cash bonus accruing on 500 Ordinary shares of 1/– each, fully paid and fully participating, in New Process Company Limited, and in the event of your consent to the sale of these shares or part thereof to pay to you the proceeds of such sale.

Yours ever,

R. MCKENNA

Further enquiries to Mr David McKenna have brought back childhood memories of the 'gold sticks', but a search of the family papers has revealed no more. Nor were enquiries to the Midland Bank successful. Scientific enquiries in Cambridge lead us to believe that the scheme was a hoax.

As noted above, Keynes played a considerable part in the Committee's examination of witnesses. In fact, he was absent on only two occasions when witnesses were examined, both in June 1930. Of Keynes's encounters with witnesses two stand out; the first examination of Governor Norman on 26 March 1930, especially on the Bank rate mechanism; and the second examination of Sir Richard Hopkins on the Treasury view. As the evidence of the Governor has been recently republished and is thus fairly generally available,[8] we do not reprint it here. However, we do reprint the exchanges between Keynes and Hopkins on 22 May 1930, opening with the latter's general statement on the matter and then picking up the discussion with Keynes's questioning.

From Committee on Finance and Industry, Minutes of Evidence, *22 May 1930*

5561 (CHAIRMAN) *I think the next matter on which you were going to offer some observations was on the question whether industry might be set going by the initiation, with Government aid, of a large programme of public works?—Yes. Perhaps you will allow me, Mr Chairman, to try and express my view at some little length with regard to this. It is a topic which is associated with a document which has come to be known as 'The Treasury View'.*

5562 *I have the document[9] in front of me?* I think the Treasury view has sometimes been rather compendiously and not very accurately stated.

5563 *Now is your chance, Sir Richard?—If I may say so, officials, if their views are published, start a controversy, and they are not able to intervene in its progress, and sometimes the exact form of their view—*

5564 *Is a little misunderstood?—is a little misunderstood.*

5565 *I have in front of me the document in question. To start the discussion, I find at page 45 it is stated: 'Their root proposition is that the state should deliberately expedite and put in hand large additional development schemes which are not yet economically justified in order to bring about a reduction in unemployment. This involves a question of fact (not dealt with in this Memorandum) whether these particular schemes would give the amount of employment claimed. It involves the further question whether the financial reactions of the scheme would diminish employment in other directions'. That is a summary of the question?—Yes, that is quite so. Of course, it was directed to a particular plan which had at that time been recently put forward and which contemplated an expenditure of a minimum of £125,000,000 per annum raised by direct Government borrowing over a period of two years, followed by further expenditure afterwards. I think this Memorandum has sometimes been taken as though it were a general statement of the view of the Treasury in regard to all development expenditure, whereas it was directed to that particular scheme. In*

---

[8] It originally appeared in the Committee's published *Minutes of Evidence* (London, 1931), especially Questions 3378–99. It appears also in R. S. Sayers, *The Bank of England 1891–1944* (Cambridge, 1976), vol. 3, Appendix 21, especially pp. 178–80. The Sayers volume reprints the evidence of Norman, Sir Ernest Harvey and Sir Richard Hopkins as it affected the position, principal arrangements and activities of the Bank of England.

[9] *Memoranda to Ministers on Certain Proposals Relating to Unemployment*, Cmd. 3331 (1929). This was the official reply to *We Can Conquer Unemployment*, the Liberal platform for the 1929 general election. See *JMK*, vol. XIX, pp. 000–0.

paragraph 3 the Memorandum dealt with what I should call the Treasury view in its more general aspects. It there stated that 'It is common ground between all parties that the state is responsible for ensuring that public services such as roads, telephones, housing, &c., are maintained and developed to the fullest extent that can be justified by our economic needs without extravagance'. Then there followed a passage in regard to the actual amount of expenditure in recent years. 'The scale of state capital expenditure is therefore not a question of principle, but of degree. The view hitherto followed has been that state expenditure should be framed with due regard to other competing calls on our national capital resources, and that, as the natural test of profit-making capacity was absent, the economic justification of all schemes ought to be very thoroughly examined before they are put in hand'. That was a statement of our approach to development expenditure in general. The rest of the Memorandum dealt with two particular sources which were stated in the original pamphlet as sources from which the necessary money could be obtained, namely, diversion of investment from abroad to home and the mobilisation of idle balances. It examined those arguments in relation to a scheme of this kind and width, and went on to say that in our view the solution for our troubles must be found in another direction, the reduction of cost of production in its widest sense and the reform of business organisation. Shortly afterwards there appeared an exceedingly able and lively pamphlet under the names of Mr Keynes and Mr Henderson,[10] in which Mr Keynes rather severely, though not unkindly, beat the Treasury about the head for views which he ascribed to them. It indicated, I think, a rather wider range of sources from which the money for a development loan might come, namely, those I have referred to and also savings on the money borrowed for payment of the unemployment benefit, and also the general results of, shall I say, a cycle of prosperity that the scheme would be likely to initiate. Now, I should be the first to agree that a large scheme of this kind, seriously put forward as a means of escaping from perplexities which were serious then and are far graver now, deserves the most unprejudiced consideration, and I should be the last to endeavour to place any obstacle in its way from the point of view of mere Treasury dogma or anything of the kind if I believed in it. From the economic point of view, with which I should join issue with Mr Keynes under a heavy handicap, I may be allowed to say a word or two later, but it is from a practical aspect that the difficulties of the scheme seem to me to emerge. When I speak of 'the scheme', I mean any scheme of a really great and far-reaching size based upon direct Government borrowing and direct Government action.

It was of the essence that the scheme should be started swiftly and simultaneously, and in trying to picture what is in my mind I would like to take the example of a road, because a very large proportion of the expenditure was to be

---

[10] *Can Lloyd George Do It?* (*JMK*, vol. IX, pp. 86–125).

expended upon roads. A road, of course, must run fairly straight between different points and with reasonable gradients, and it runs over land which previously was in private ownership. It cuts across people's gardens, it sometimes runs through a row of cottages, in certain parts of the country it runs through beauty spots and arouses intense passion in the minds of people who are associated with societies for the preservation of the beauty of rural England and so on. Moreover, the business of the construction of a road is the business of the larger local authorities, who in turn have to satisfy the feelings of the minor local authorities. I think the residents in a district where a by-pass is under consideration will know the extraordinary amount of local feeling which can be engendered about the proper route for a road, in other words, who are the proper persons to suffer the damage which the road will entail, and that a good deal of time is necessarily involved, in ordinary conditions, in assuaging feelings of that kind. There is, beyond that, the time that has to be spent by engineers familiar with the locality in making plans, and when one is considering any really large project there are questions of the proper recruitment of labour and the proper accommodation for labour employed on the road. You may say that these are difficulties which are day by day overcome, and, of course, that is perfectly true, subject only to this, that even when those projects are taken up on a small scale, ordinarily speaking, a great deal of time must be previously devoted to their preparation, and, as I have said, to getting rid of the difficulties which arise in connection with a project of this kind. But if you take a very large scheme of this kind it seems to me you may get an altogether different public sentiment attaching to it. There may be very many people who think the scheme a good scheme; I am quite sure there would be larger numbers of people taking the contrary view. There would be those who say, for example, that this country is the country with the best roads of any in the world, that the construction of more roads in very large quantities would be liable to interfere, it may be, with railways, and to have other unfortunate repercussions. It seems to me that a feeling might widely arise that this was a project of extravagance and waste. Nor do I see how it could be carried out on this scale, and swiftly, without a very wide increase in the powers given to the officials who are to carry it out. I think you would have to have powers of entering upon land summarily in advance of the settlement of claims, in regard to which certain people's interests might have to be interfered with, it might seem in a very arbitrary way, and so on. Those practical considerations seem to me to be very important. Whether the view would be a right one, that this would be wasteful and uneconomical, is really apart from what I have in mind. I should have thought that a scheme of this kind so far from setting up a cycle of prosperity would produce a great cry against bureaucracy. After all, people are very jealous, and rightly jealous, of any tremendous and hasty Government activity, and so far from it producing a general willingness to invest in these vast Government loans I should have thought that the loans would have to be put out at a very high price, and that the process might be accompanied by despondency on the part of general business, rather than otherwise. There are two other points that I would like to mention. In the first place, the scheme seems to me—assuming that those difficulties were imaginary, and did not occur—to contemplate an enormous access of work and activity for a certain number of trades, such as quarry making, already very prosperous, the road contractor, and, in some other aspects of the scheme, the manufacturer of telephone apparatus and other things of that kind, while it does something, but not much, to assist iron and steel, nothing to assist cotton, or textiles, or shipbuilding, or shipping. Generally it seems to me it would produce a singularly lopsided form of prosperity, and one which could not possibly be permanent. Clearly it must be contemplated, and I understand it is, that the scheme would be accompanied by such increase of credit as was necessary to finance the larger volume of activity which it contemplates. Whether it was an idea of the authors that prices should rise I have never exactly been able to follow, but it seems to me that in practice it would hardly be avoidable, but that such a thing would happen. It might well be necessary to protect our position in the world by a high interest rate in the meanwhile, and on the whole it would tend in a direction the opposite from that in which we need to tend, namely, a rise in prices elsewhere, in the wake of which we could follow and allow our own external trade to develop.

I hope I have not put it too high; I am very anxious not to be an unfair critic; at the same time I wanted to put this aspect quite clearly. I am not speaking, of course, of all development schemes. The best form seems to me to be one in which the Government may secure in one way or other the undertaking of a very considerable volume of development work by public authorities or the like, giving such financial assistance as may be necessary, the capital being raised by those authorities in the ordinary way upon the market, and the state being the background—indeed, the type of increased development work which has been secured in recent years in part by the St Davids Committee and in part by the Act of last year, the Home Development Act. I am sorry to have been so long. . . .

5600 (MR KEYNES) There are two separate propositions. There is the proposition that schemes of capital development are of no use for reducing unemployment? *Yes.*

5601 And there is the proposition that it is difficult to find good schemes? *Yes.*

5602 Would it be a misunderstanding of the Treasury view to say that they hold to the first proposition? *The first proposition goes much too far. The first proposition would ascribe to us an absolute and rigid dogma, would it not?*

5603 Well, there might be various reasons. One reason which, when I misunderstood the Treasury view, I thought would be advanced was, that quite apart from the utility of the schemes they would not help on balance because it was the nature of the economic machine that any capital that could be found for those schemes would be diverted from other uses. That is a misunderstanding? *Yes. That is much too rigid an expression of any views that have come from us.*

5604 You do not express in your evidence today any view remotely resembling that? *No. I would not say that. As I see the position it is this, that we should pay regard to the economic justification of schemes wherever it be possible.*

5605 My difficulty is this: I can quite see that the decision as to whether one should adopt a scheme must be taken on a balance of considerations and a scheme might be so bad from other points of view that it ought not to be adopted, even though it did cure unemployment. But do you hold that the schemes that you like create more employment than the schemes that you do not like? *No.*

5606 So that those schemes do not differ in respect of the employment they create, they only differ in respect of their ulterior consequences? *I think the atmosphere in which schemes may be undertaken will itself condition the immediate consequences which they produce.*

5607 You mean, if the schemes are very unpopular, they may have other reactions of an adverse kind? *Yes.*

5608 But that would not affect the amount of employment which that scheme would create? *Not the amount which the particular scheme will create at the time while it is in being, but it immediately alters its dynamic effect.*

5609 So your criterion is really, whether a good scheme seems rather silly to public opinion or not? *Well, if you like to put it like that.*

5610 (MR BRAND) *Would it not come to the same thing as this—to give an illustration which is often quoted—that we could break all the windows in London to-morrow and mend them and that would give the same amount of immediate employment as the building of a factory?—Yes.*

5611 (MR KEYNES) So the issue between those who are in favour of these schemes and those who are against them is not whether they cure unemployment. . . .? *Do you wish me to agree?* (CHAIRMAN) *I do not think you must take it that Sir Richard agrees.*

5612 (MR KEYNES). What is the point where we differ? *The capital for these schemes has got to come from somewhere.*

5613 That is equally true of good and bad schemes? *Yes. The contention which was advanced against the Treasury Memorandum was to the effect that these schemes would pay for themselves in part by diverting capital from abroad, in part by mobilising idle balances, in part by diminishing unemployment, and in part by setting up a cycle of prosperity. Given all the assumptions underlying the scheme, I do not know but that I would be prepared to give you that argument; but if in fact a scheme of this type of work is undertaken under different conditions and is not itself a dynamic force towards a great renewal of activity and prosperity, the capital has got to come from somewhere. I agree that some of it, a little of it at any rate, is provided out of savings upon the Unemployment Fund, some of it from other sources, but it does make a hole in the capital which is available for the purposes of the community.*

5614 But do bad schemes make a larger hole than good schemes? *Not intrinsically, of course; they may in their consequences.*

5615 How can they in their consequences? I can conceive that they may have other bad consequences. I fail to see the logic of what you are saying? *Well, it may divert capital from more useful schemes.*

5616 That is equally true of good and bad schemes? *In addition to that, it seems to me that the general effect upon the public mind of what you are doing is very largely going to influence the amount of capital which is going abroad.*

5617 In what way would it affect the amount going abroad; would it increase it or diminish it? *It might lead people to think that this country was a much better place in which to invest, or it might lead them to think it was a worse place in which to invest. When you were speaking of bad schemes, I was thinking of the latter.*

5618 Our foreign investments cannot increase unless our exports increase? *No, but the burden on the exchange can increase.*

5619 (MR NEWBOLD) *How would the building of a road help us to increase our export trade permanently?* (WITNESS) *That is exactly the difficulty I have.* (MR NEWBOLD) *It is mine too.*

5620 (MR KEYNES) Coming back to the effect on public opinion, you were saying that one of the indirect consequences of this might be the effect on public opinion; it might create a frightful disturbance? *Yes.*

5621 I am trying to separate these two issues and to find out what are your views, but you did not in your evidence-in-chief give us any reason for supposing that schemes of capital development would necessarily absorb money that would otherwise be used in other directions? *No. Let me take an illustration—a scheme which is not a bad scheme, nor yet a good scheme, but is an intermediate scheme, and is regarded by the Treasury as an intermediate scheme. A loan is placed for £5,000,000 and it employs men at the rate of 4,000 for each £1,000,000 for a year. Some of the capital for that sum is undoubtedly provided for out of the saving which I mentioned, what is now being borrowed for unemployment benefit. In some cases the balance, or part of it, might be replaced out of a greater willingness on the part of people to invest money which they keep idle—it might or it might not. But beyond that, as far as I can see, it is a drain upon the sum of capital, whatever it may be at the moment, which is available for investment.*

5622 Is it your view that all the capital which is available is used? *No, I should say very likely that may not be so now.*

5623 So that as long as we did not push it so far that we took up more than the slack, that position would not arise. I am simply trying to get at the logical consequence. Nearly all of what you have been saying today comes to this, that it is difficult to find good schemes? *Yes.*

5624 And that bad schemes are open to indirect objections. That is quite different from what I previously thought to be the Treasury view. It was not a view of that kind but a theoretical view, that the objection to these schemes was that they caused diversion on theoretical grounds. That was a misunderstanding on my part of what the Treasury intended, was it? *Yes. Certainly in the case which we have been discussing, the main case, the Treasury view does come back to that. It is not a rigid dogma. It is the result of the views that we take as to the practical reactions of the scheme.*

5625 It bends so much that I find difficulty in getting hold of it? *Yes; I do not think these views are capable of being put in the rigid form of a theoretical doctrine. I do not know how to define the thing better than it was defined in the extract which I read at the outset.*

5626 The schemes which in your mind, or in the mind of the public, are for good purpose, do cure unemployment, in your opinion? *Yes.*

5627 (MR NEWBOLD) *What do you consider 'good purposes', translated into economic language?—Well, it is all here, you know. We suggest that the public services, such as roads, telephones, housing, etc. should be maintained and developed to the fullest extent that can be justified by our economic needs without extravagance. Once you begin to apply a theory like that, personal judgement comes in.*

5628 (MR KEYNES) It is not apparently so much a question of personal judgement, it is a question of the effect on public opinion; when you are considering whether or not a scheme will cure unemployment you are forecasting the effect on the public mind? *It is very important to do so.*

5629 That is your main criterion? *It is the criterion which more than any other leads me to think that the particular scheme which we were discussing at the outset has a very practical drawback, but when I come to discuss a desirable scheme in a much narrower ambit, knowing no better, I prefer to take the test whether it seems to be economically justified.*

5630 If Mr Bevin could assure you that the schemes would be popular, then you would say they would cure unemployment? *No. You are asking me to say that if I thought that the public sentiment would endorse the large plan to which we were referring, then it would cure our situation?*

5631 Yes? *But I went on to say that I felt there were other difficulties. I do not want to lose your argument. I went on to say that I thought there were other difficulties, inasmuch as if it could be compassed it would concentrate employment in certain industries to the detriment of others, and would lead to a rise in prices.*

5632 That contemplates a scheme of a particular kind. Let us come to the question of prices. So far as prices are below the cost of production, and business men are selling at a loss, is it not characteristic of any cure of the situation that it must raise prices? *I am not quite sure that that is so ; at any rate I am not perfectly certain of what is moving in your mind. I do not think it is true in all cases. For example, there surely are many businesses in this country which are working at a loss at the existing cost of production because their works are only 70 per cent full. If you could find a policy which would make them 100 per cent full, I should think they could turn their loss into a profit without any alteration of price except a downward alteration.*

5633 I agree with you. Why should one cure of unemployment have more effect than the other in the direction of raising prices? *The difficulty I feel on that side is, that while endeavouring to cure unemployment you are creating an excess of not only temporary employment in certain industries, you are almost going to have to reintroduce the Excess Profits Duty for the purpose of justifying the existence of road contractors.*

5634 Whatever you do, you increase the existing employment in some particular direction, do you not? *Yes. And the type of remedy which I would like to find, if only I could find it, is a remedy which would increase the volume of work which was available for the depressed industries, or alternatively reduce the total installations of those industries to the existing volume of work, and scrap the redundant.*

5635 If you increased unemployment still further would you not expect prices to fall still more? Whenever you increase unemployment you reduce the demand for goods, and therefore lessen their prices? *Yes, that would be so.*

5636 Why are you so pleased with the reduction of prices which the present crisis has brought about so far? *Of course you only say that because you know quite well that I am not pleased. I am, on the contrary, no more pleased than you are.*

5637 You take objection to the cure of unemployment on the ground that it might have some effect on the raising of prices. That is what I understood? *I am sorry, but my diagnosis is different. I should have thought what we want is some tendency which will create a rise of prices throughout the world to begin with, excepting here, so that we may follow in its wake.*

5638 (MR BEVIN) *How can you do that?—Not by a scheme of this kind.*

5639 *How?—I have suggested that a certain contribution has been made by the recent Government debt operations.*

5640 (MR KEYNES) You want all other countries to adopt plans which you wish to reject for your own? *Yes, that might serve.*

5641 Coming back to the main question: the Lord Privy Seal claimed the other day that he had set on foot capital development schemes to the amount of, I think, £92,000,000, or £96,000,000, was it? *Somewhere near £100,000,000.*

5642 Can you classify those for us, as to which of them will help unemployment and which will not? *In my judgement all of them will. I see no reason why they should not.*

5643 All of them will? *All of them are in a natural development of a programme of economic development of the country. There is included in them a natural expansion of road making, there is included in them an expansion, at a somewhat accelerated rate, of telephones, there is included a great deal of development of railways and the like. There is no sort of public feeling, as far as I know, that they are otherwise than desirable things.*

5644 So that if one could think of other things of a desirable character, you would think it would help unemployment? *Yes. This is a question of degree and reason. I expect you will most violently dissent from this, but I would say that the ultimate test that I would adopt of whether this was a good scheme is this: Is it on a reasonable view economically justified or not?*

5645 You have a certain test of a good scheme? *Yes.*

5646 If a scheme would yield five per cent from the start and continue, you would say it was a good scheme? *Yes.*

5647 If it would yield only four per cent would you say it was a bad scheme? *No, not necessarily, because, then comes the question of the existing rate of interest as compared with the future rate of interest.*

5648 What would be the point where you would say it was a bad scheme? *If you are speaking of the development of private business, then I think a set of different questions arises, but if you are speaking of public utility companies, the test we have taken is, would the scheme become satisfactorily productive at any time within, say, the next seven to eight or ten years.*

5649 What does that work out at in terms of the rate of interest of a loan for 30 years, say? It comes to round about four per cent, does it not? *Yes, probably so. It is done in the form of giving grant by Government towards the interest charges for, it may be, 15 years.*

5650 Is it your view that schemes which yield four per cent reduce unemployment while schemes which yield three per cent do not reduce unemployment? (WITNESS) *Oh! no. I see the logical dilemma into which you are endeavouring to drive me. I shall, of course, naturally come into it slowly and diffidently.* (CHAIRMAN) *You are not obliged to answer, Sir Richard.*

5651 (MR KEYNES) Might I repeat that question: Whether you consider that schemes which yield four per cent cure unemployment whereas schemes which yield three per cent do not cure unemployment? *The Chairman has made an observation in regard to that question, so perhaps I may be permitted to add that there must be some point in this discussion at which I shall claim the right of a layman not to follow the argument of the economist.*

5652 This is not an argument but an attempt to elicit your opinion? *I gave my opinion. Frankly, it has not moved from the time the Treasury Memorandum was issued.*

5653 What is your opinion? You say that schemes that yield four per cent do help unemployment. That is what you told me? *Yes.*

5654 I ask, do you consider that schemes which yield three per cent do not help unemployment? *We have already agreed before that both good schemes and bad schemes benefit unemployment.*

5655 Then you do agree that schemes which yield three per cent help unemployment? *Yes. I suppose schemes which yield a minus per cent, for example, reduce unemployment.*

5656 That is what I expected you to say. What price in the rate of interest is it advisable to pay to cure unemployment? (MR NEWBOLD) *Is it to alleviate unemployment for two years or to cure it permanently?—That is profoundly difficult to say. The one thing which of all other things would be wrong, I think, is, at the time when we are at the bottom of the wave, to assume that we are to remain there, just as it would be wrong to assume that at the time when we are at the top of the wave we are to remain there. What alleviation of our conditions may come— either through world conditions or otherwise—after two years, no man can say.*

5657 (MR KEYNES) It seems to me we are getting near the point where we can agree? *I am sure not!*

5658 We have now got to a point where all these schemes, whatever rate of interest they yield, help unemployment, and the question is what price it is worth paying. In calculating that, you have first of all to allow for the saving on the 'dole'? *Yes.*

5659 Have you calculated what that would be on a good scheme? *I have seen figures which suggested that it would be [not] much in excess of 25 per cent. I myself would put it below that figure.*

5660 You would put it below 25 per cent? *Yes.*

5661 Then there is a certain improvement to the revenue through economic activities, is there not? *Yes; that I think is small and speculative.*

5662 Then there is the increment to the wealth of the community through employing men instead of not employing them at all? *Yes.*

5663 So that the issue really depends upon making an estimate under this, and possibly under other heads, and then seeing how far it is worth while to abate the rate of interest in order to get those advantages? *I do not follow quite what is in your mind when you speak of abating the rate of interest.*

5664 Supposing a moderate rate of interest is five per cent at the present time; to embark on a scheme which yields three per cent requires a certain justification? *Yes.*

5665 I was trying to make a list of the sources from which that justification might be found. I am not saying three per cent is a figure which would be justified, but evidently some figure below five per cent would be justified? *Yes.*

5666 (MR BRAND) *The loss being borne by the taxpayer?—Yes.*

5667 (MR KEYNES) The loss being borne by the taxpayer. There would be an increment to the wealth of the community through men being employed; there would be a saving to the Exchequer through less being required for the 'dole'; there would be a gain to the Exchequer through increased taxation; and the right criterion would be reached by summing up all those elements? *Supposing it were possible to sum them up.*

5668 Supposing you could perform some work entirely by the labour of unemployed men, would you rather have them unemployed, or that they should make something which would yield three per cent? *Well, possibly you could tell me rather more clearly what you mean when you say 'make something which would yield three per cent'?*

5669 If they could build a house which could be let at a sum to yield three per cent on the wages of the men you were paying to erect it? *Well, it may be so, but already a very large sum of Government money is engaged in the building of houses, and I would hesitate to say that that was a form of activity which should be pushed beyond what it has been pushed to at the present time. If you are thinking of a development by some public utility company—*

5670 Are you saying that there are enough houses built? *I am saying this, that there has been an immense sum of money which has been placed by the Government into the building of houses in this country within recent times. While I myself have made very little study of this matter—other Government officials could give you better evidence—one of the results, as it seems to me, has been to keep up the price of houses, to render subsidies which we commenced exceedingly difficult to take off, and to render that industry a very long way from being an ordinary economic industry at the present time; and when you are asking whether I think there are enough houses I merely want to say this, that I am sure there are considerations to be borne in mind outside any that I am sufficiently familiar with. If you are thinking of schemes which are worth three per cent in the region of public utility companies, or which are worth three per cent in the region of private industries, in that first class of case surely it is the type of case in which Government assistance is already recognised, and in regard to which neither myself nor any of my colleagues has raised any question. When you pass on to the question of giving such grants of money to ordinary private industries which are quite free from Government control then a great number of new questions arise. I should be exceedingly slow to agree that that bounty in a great number of cases would mean an increase of activity, it might be a mere gift to the existing shareholders of the company.*

5671 You would approve public utility schemes which would yield three per cent? *I am not pinning myself to any percentage; I am a little suspicious of where I am being led if I agree to a particular percentage; but it is certainly the case that many grants have been made, and it seems to me rightly made, in respect of undertakings which cannot expect to be remunerative for some considerable time, and may not be remunerative, according to the existing rate of interest, ever.*

5672 (PROFESSOR GREGORY) *Your point is this: if you start by taking a good scheme, bringing in roughly three per cent, that scheme becomes good or bad according as the rate increases or diminishes. In addition, I take it, you would hold the view that even good schemes become bad schemes if they upset public opinion?—Yes.*

5673 *You think public opinion is becoming increasingly suspicious of housing schemes?—No; that is not what I meant to convey. I am sure there are, with regard to the housing question, a number of economic considerations with which I am not familiar, and I am going to shirk the business of defending my view with regard to that.*

5674 *In any case, your view is that schemes are good or bad, partly because of the yield which they give, and partly because of the effect they have on public opinion?—Yes.*

5675 *And partly because of their repercussions on trade and industry?—Yes.*

5676 (MR BRAND) *Might not the difference which exists between you and Mr Keynes be found in practice to be a small one? I do not know whether Mr Keynes would agree, but supposing he ruled out, so far as public assistance is concerned, all competitive industry, all merchanting business and everything of that kind, then you have two spheres left—you have schemes and projects on which, perhaps, a return of interest can be calculated, which is more or less limited to the public utility sphere, and you have schemes on which it is impossible to calculate interest, such as road-making and so forth. On that side, you have got to build on certain other criteria which are fairly simple; you build up a big programme, but not an exaggerated programme, you do not want to put up the price of materials beyond a certain point; but apart from this you come down to the question how many public utility schemes it is reasonable for the public to assist at any particular moment. Is not that, more or less, the real problem? (WITNESS) Yes, I think so. What divides me, I think, very much more from Mr Keynes than you are suggesting is the question of degree. (MR KEYNES) How far down the scale would you go with good schemes to kill unemployment? (MR BRAND) 'Kill' is a large term. I think the amount of schemes of this kind is rather limited.*

5677 (CHAIRMAN) *I would like to ask you a question or two, Sir Richard, about the possible diversion of capital. Let us assume that there is money that is not being employed at present, and that could be employed on large works of public utility, and that people are induced, by interest attractions and perhaps by public spirit to put their money in those schemes. The ultimate object, I suppose, of the whole thing is to create a revival of enterprise?—Yes.*

5678 *May you not exhaust your capital in enterprise in a time of trade depression and be in short shrift when there is a trade revival and you want your capital for development?—As I understand, it does follow on Mr Keynes's view that there is a great deal of investible money which is lying in the banks at the present time and is represented by a low velocity of circulation.*

5679 *Is it wasted really?* (MR KEYNES) I would have said that savings cannot keep. (CHAIRMAN) *Honestly, I do not understand that?—I must put it a different way, that at this particular moment there is money in balances which, according to Mr Keynes's view, might be lost if it remained there, but is not being pulled out by the ordinary competition.*

5680 (MR KEYNES) You cannot keep it there and use it for rationalisation schemes two years hence? *It will not be pulled out in my judgement by big Government loans of large size for the purpose of ambitious schemes. Very likely it might be pulled out by issues on the part of public utility companies and the like for schemes of an economic character with Government assistance.*

5681 Do you mean that the Government loans would not be taken up? *I am speaking of big Government loans.*

5682 If two loans are taken up, how can they operate differently? *If you are speaking of a small loan—*

5683 I am thinking of how it would operate differently if it is taken up at the same time? *I think you will find it very difficult to take up except at a very high rate.*

5684 If it were taken up, whatever the rate, it would be all right? *Yes, but I think that if you had to get it taken up at a very high rate and accompanied by an adverse public sentiment you would very quickly lose what you gained by that from the number of people who would think it better to invest the next lot of money that they had to invest in America.*

5685 Supposing the loan were not taken up but were borrowed on Ways and Means, it would not make the slightest difference to its economic effect? *Is not that fantastic?*

5686 (MR NEWBOLD) *Would you regard that as an immoral transaction—If I am right in thinking that a great loan directly raised in the ordinary way would carry with it a bad public sentiment, and carry with it adverse repercussions, what would happen if it were raised by what is ordinarily called plain inflation I cannot imagine.*

5687 (MR KEYNES) I was trying to discuss the technical monetary problem. I want to know, assuming you are given an amount of real investment, whether the precise way you raise the money makes any difference? *Discussing it from the point of view of economics, I do not think it would. I think the practical aspect would altogether outweigh the economic aspect, in the suggestion that we should raise £100,000,000 on Ways and Means. True it happens in a critical time, in time of war, but it does not happen in peacetime.*

5688 I am not suggesting that it is a reasonable thing to do. I am asking whether the precise technical means of raising the money makes any difference? *I could not pretend to say, at the end of this lengthy discussion, at a moment's notice what the whole of the repercussions would be.*

5689 I have not any more questions on this point. I find, as a result of your evidence, Sir Richard, that the Treasury view has been gravely misjudged? *But I should be very sorry if Mr Keynes thought that all his strictures on the Treasury were quite unjustified. Many of them were very fully earned!*

5690 (CHAIRMAN) *I think we may characterise it as a drawn battle!*

After Hopkins's evidence, the Committee continued hearing witnesses until the end of July 1930. By that stage it had met 48 witnesses and held 46 days of 'public' hearings. The Committee then recessed until October.

When the Committee met again on 16 October it began to consider the shape of its report. As a part of these often wide-ranging discussions, individual members often took the lead for a meeting or more. Thus, for example, J. Walton Newbold had the floor on 31 October and 7 November, R. H. Brand on 6 November and T. E. Gregory on 20 and 21 November. It was after almost six weeks of such discussions that Keynes took the lead in the discussions of 27 and 28 November and 6 December.

COMMITTEE ON FINANCE AND INDUSTRY

Thursday 27 November 1930

Present:

The Rt Hon. Lord Macmillan (*Chairman*)

Mr Ernest Bevin   The Rt Hon. Reginald McKenna
The Rt Hon. Lord Bradbury, G.C.B.   Mr J. T. Walton Newbold
The Hon. R. H. Brand, C.M.G.   Sir Walter Raine
Professor T. E. Gregory, D.SC.   Mr J. Frater Taylor
Mr J. M. Keynes, C.B.   Mr A. A. G. Tulloch
Mr Lennox B. Lee   Mr G. Ismay (*Secretary*)
Mr Cecil Lubbock

Sir Frederick Leith-Ross, K.C.M.G., C.B.

(MR KEYNES) Mr Chairman, the task of the Bank of England as managing the monetary system of this country falls into two fairly sharply divided parts. There is, first of all, the duty of joining with other central banks to regulate international prices. That part of their duties I shall only deal with today indirectly. So long as we are on an international standard it is clear that we must be tied, so far as our long-period movements are concerned, to what is going on in the world at large, and, therefore, the Bank of England can only protect us from misfortune by influencing the international situation in the right way. The methods that are open to them for that purpose are not my subject in what follows. But assuming that we are on an international standard and that the Bank of England is doing what it can by international co-operation, there remains the further object of reconciling the interests of London as a centre of international finance with the interests of domestic industry and trade. That is primarily a question of avoiding unnecessary short period fluctuations. Any long-period change in the world outside we must follow so long as we are on an international standard, but we do not want to have our domestic trade and industry blown about by the fact that some aspects of our functions must conform to short-period international fluctuations. We want to combine with adherence to an international standard the maximum of domestic autonomy that is compatible with that. I can put it more generally perhaps by saying that it must be our object to reconcile the fluctuating character of capital movements in the international loan market with the relatively steady character of our income surplus available for foreign investment. Our income surplus may change from one year to another, but it does not change greatly from week to week or from month to month; it is dependent upon our invisible exports together with the surplus of our visible foreign trade. Both of these are subject to relatively long-period influences. We do not suddenly find ourselves in a much better or a much worse position for selling our exports abroad. On the other hand, it is the nature of the international loan market that very large fluctuations may take place in a period of a few weeks unless something is done to prevent them.

Well, now, since our net outward capital movements must at all times, every week, every day equal our income surplus, except insofar as we are prepared to allow gold to move, the Bank must either allow large fluctuations of its gold reserve or it must govern credit policy mainly with an eye on influencing the net outward capital movement, balancing a movement in one direction of a character which is outside its control with a movement in any other direction of a character which is inside its control. Therefore, it is obvious, *prima facie*, that the duty of the Bank of England to keep the net capital movements at all times within narrow limits may force it to take steps which are not what it would wish to take if it were only looking to the domestic situation. I repeat, that if the outward or inward movements of capital are symptomatic of a long-period change in the world at large, then the Bank ought to use its influence on the internal position, but if they do not reflect a long-period change then it would not wish to influence the domestic situation.

So a very difficult task lies before it in endeavouring to reconcile these two interests, and my object in what follows is to make suggestions for increasing the power of the Bank of England to reconcile these two possibly divergent sets of interest.

(PROFESSOR GREGORY) *May I ask a question? You say for completeness you would add to the problem of managing the gold movements the problem of adjusting the temporary income by a movement of short balances?* Yes. I am including movements of short balances in the net capital movement, which include loans both on short and on long term. There is one point which I should like to mention in passing before I get on to my main argument. It is, at first sight, a matter of wonder that there are not more frequent movements of gold. The Bank of England moves its Bank rate comparatively seldom and even the market rate for bills is not being altered to any great extent perpetually; yet the net result of all the innumerable transactions which pass through London would, one would suppose, be constantly in excess by (say) ten millions in one week compared with what they would be another week. It is rather odd at first sight that we have not a large amount of gold perpetually coming in and out as a balancing factor. One would expect more short-period movements of gold than actually take place. The comparative infrequency of movement is due to a very beautiful piece of mechanism of an automatic character which tends to prevent that. That arises out of the fact that the attractiveness of London for arbitrage loans—I mean, by 'arbitrage loans', short-term loans made by professionals in order to take advantage of small differences in the international markets—is a function not only of the bill rate but also of the precise position of the foreign exchanges between the gold points. For example, if the bill rate is 3 per cent and the sterling exchange for dollars is 4.86, London is a more attractive centre for American money than if the bill rate is 3 per cent as before and the dollar exchange is 4.87. Thus, every movement of the exchange against a country within the gold points makes it a more attractive centre for arbitrage loans; that is to say, every adverse movement in the exchange brings in a corrective force tending to check the movement, even though there is no change at all in the bill rate. So it is only necessary to alter bill rate when the adverse force is stronger than the corrective force. That happens not infrequently because the range within which the corrective force can operate is comparatively narrow; but nevertheless that corrective force is sufficient to prevent perpetual daily oscillations. If there were no difference between the gold points, if the exchange were absolutely pegged at an identical figure, then this corrective force could not function. It is the distance between the gold points which makes this corrective force possible, and that is what preserves London from more violent very short-period oscillations. So that the difference between the gold points is a very fundamental part of London's mechanism and one which is not always noticed as much as it deserves. One could illustrate that by pointing out one of the most tiresome features of the present French drain, that it is not subject to this corrective force, because, owing to the inelasticity of the French system, when the French banks want to turn from sterling into francs they must do it at any reasonable rate. They cannot be induced to leave their funds in London by changes in the franc/sterling rate, which, if the corrective force were operating properly would certainly deter some of them.

(MR BRAND) *You mean it does not act in France?* There is no adequate amount of funds available between Paris and London for arbitrage loans. When the French banks are wanting to draw money they definitely want the money and they cannot be induced by small advantages to leave it where it was previously. On the other hand, between this country and New York the corrective factor operates admirably at the present time, because there probably is a large trade in arbitrage loans; they can be induced to change their mind by changes in the rate of exchange without any change in bill rate.

It follows then that the Bank of England's first line of defence against excessive domestic fluctuations to meet the external position is this automatic corrective. If the automatic corrective is insufficient to keep gold movements within sufficiently narrow points the Bank's choice then lies between losing a substantial quantity of gold or, it may be, gaining a substantial quantity of gold. (In order to fix the argument it is better to assume that we are dealing with a case of avoiding the loss of gold, and not complicate it by making it work both ways.) The Bank's choice lies between losing a substantial quantity of gold or curtailing credit so as to raise the market bill rate, and, finally, if they have raised the market bill rate as much as is compatible with the existing Bank rate, of, supplementing the curtailment of credit by a movement of the official Bank rate also. The criticism of this method is, not that it is ineffective for its purpose; indeed it is extraordinarily effective, as long experience shows; in fact even in the most extraordinary circumstances the Bank of England has avoided really large gold movements quite successfully over a very long period of time—the criticism is, not that it is ineffective, but that the desired result is only brought about as a sort of by-product, so to speak, of a process which affects credit facilities for all sorts of internal purposes. In order to bring about the necessary change in bill rate to supplement the automatic corrective, the Bank has to do something which has far wider effects than those which it has asked for, and those which it deliberately wants.

The peculiarity of the London market consists in two things—first of all the tendency to large short-period fluctuations in capital transactions, because of our importance as an international financial centre, and, secondly, the degree of the Bank of England's reliance on the method, which I have just described, for evening things out. There is no other country where the international transactions bear so high a proportion to domestic transactions, and no country where the instrument of bill rate plays such a vitally important part as it has played for many decades in the London system.

Now I come to my proposals, which, as I say, are directed to the object of strengthening and supplementing the Bank of England's powers for evening out fluctuations in overseas capital transactions without upsetting the domestic situation. But I should like to repeat that, if the pressure on the exchange is of a long-period character, then it is necessary to take steps to produce a new domestic equilibrium. Sometimes the international disequilibrium would be of such a character that the Bank would welcome both the effect on the shortloan market and the other effect on the domestic situation, but very often the pressure on the exchanges will be, quite obviously, of a short-period character, and then it would be much better if the Bank of England were in a stronger position for handling it by means which do not upset domestic equilibrium.

(PROFESSOR GREGORY) *When you say that the Bank must adjust the British situation to the international situation as far as long-period movements are concerned what do you mean—long-period movements of prices or long-period movements in the distribution of capital as between British and foreign investment?* I mean the level of incomes,—that money incomes relatively to efficiency in this country must over the long period be much the same as they are elsewhere; therefore, if there is a change in the level of money incomes relatively to efficiency elsewhere we cannot permanently resist a similar change in this country without going off the international standard. So if the nature of the external disequilibrium is what looks like a lasting change in the level of money incomes, then the Bank of England must do something about the domestic situation. But, of course, there are all kinds of things happening from week to week and from month to month in the international loan market which are not at all of that character.

There is one other preliminary remark which I would make, and that is, that I agree with the view that in making any changes at the present time we must have great regard to appearances. In recent times foreigners have abused our good nature and misinterpreted our good intentions, and they will undoubtedly continue to do so in future. We are not in the impregnable position in which we used to be, and therefore we have to pay regard to appearances which would not have been necessary at other dates. I shall try to bear that in mind in what I suggest.

(MR BRAND) *When you said that money incomes relative to efficiency in this country must be the same as they are abroad, that is because if they are on a wrong basis they affect our exports in the main?* Yes, because they affect our foreign trade balance. If we had no freedom of foreign lending then it would be possible to have a much wider discrepancy in the level of money incomes. But that takes one on to much wider topics. If we wish to have our money incomes move differently from the rest of the world, but nevertheless remain on an international standard, we may be able to do it by handling our foreign trade on the Russian model. The Russian model has immense theoretical interest for me from that point of view, and it may be that some day we shall come much nearer to the Russian model than we think probable at this moment.

Exporting things below cost? Well, to go into that would lead me rather away from my argument; it is an interesting subject, but I wanted to keep much more on the earth today, if I may. We have to begin by making some sort of estimate of the magnitude of the fluctuations of the international loan market which we have to deal with. Those fluctuations are made up of a number of items, all of which are capable of fluctuating substantially. There is, first of all, the short-term foreign borrowing in London, which can be increased or withdrawn. Secondly, there are the corresponding British balances abroad, and perhaps from some points of view one can add to them the volume of our acceptances on foreign account. Those acceptances have to be met at their maturity by the foreign exporters on behalf of whom we have accepted, so that they represent a short-period asset very similar to the short-period asset which we have in the shape of balances abroad. Thirdly, there are the new foreign issues on long term in the London market. Fourthly, there are foreign purchases and sales on the London Stock Exchange, a very large item today, owing to the large number of securities which now are of an international character. Finally, there are the British purchases and sales on foreign stock exchanges, which for this purpose means mainly Wall Street. There are no satisfactory statistics for estimating the magnitude of these purchases and sales.

The statistics as to the magnitude of these various elements are very unsatisfactory. Mr Hawtrey has claimed that the movements are small. In a sense I think that is obviously true, but that is not quite the point. The fact that movements of gold are small proves that the net fluctuation of capital movements, under all my five heads taken together, round the income surplus must also be small. It necessarily follows that if there were any large fluctuation on balance we should have large movements of gold, and as we know the movements of gold are not large we know that somehow or other the changes in one or other of the five heads must in practice balance the others. That is not the point. What we want to measure is the strength of the tendency to fluctuate if we do not take steps to control it; and hence the amount of strain that is set up in our system by the necessity of counteracting the tendency. We never in fact allow very large movements of gold without taking steps to control them. If one of the above items moves largely, we have to do something to make the other items move in the opposite direction. So that the fact that the net result is always fairly well balanced is no secure indication as to the strain we have suffered, and as to what we have done in order to preserve the equilibrium. One might get a little light on the amount of tension that is set up by considering the magnitude and, if possible, the fluctuation, of the separate items which I analyse.

(MR LUBBOCK) *I suppose we start with the bedrock fact that we have £150,000,000 favourable balance which we can invest in the course of the year.* And *must* invest. It is the tendency of the aggregate capital movements to oscillate around that; if you regard them as growing at the rate of £12,000,000 a month.

If we invested £3,000,000 a week and anything happened we should be all right? Yes.

(PROFESSOR GREGORY) *But that is not all that has to be taken into account.* Oh! no.

(MR LUBBOCK) *That is the bedrock figure at which we have to come to rest.* I want to get at the scale of the whole thing, because the amount of the resources that the Bank of England ought to hold is determined by the scale of the factors that it is providing against. There are, first of all, the short-period foreign balances in London. We have obtained from the Bank of England and the joint stock banks some very valuable figures, which are now available for the first time in the history of this country, I think. They show that at the end of 1929—I have not yet seen the June 1930 figures—

(THE SECRETARY) *They have not reached me yet.* At the end of last year in these particular banks the deposits, and sterling bills held on foreign account, amounted to about £310,000,000. That excludes the exchange banks, the foreign banks with their offices in London, and the merchant bankers. I find it very difficult to guess how much difference it would make if we had those figures. I think it would be useful if we could ask the merchant bankers when they supply us with their total of acceptances to let us know also their foreign balances and holding of sterling bills for foreign clients. I should think they would bring the £310,000,000 to £350,000,000, would they not, Mr Brand?

(MR BRAND) *Much more.* They might bring it up to £400,000,000.

Over £400,000,000 if your £310,000,000 is correct. My £310,000,000 is for the Bank of England and the clearing banks. The total, then, may be of the order of magnitude of £400,000,000; it may be larger. It is very important, I think, for us to have an accurate figure of that. That would be the absolute amount at the present time. What is the order of the fluctuation in that? We have got statistics covering three years for the Bank of England and the clearing banks. That is not a very long period on which to base any calculation, but in two years during a period of 18 months—that is to say from June 1927 to December 1928—the short-term balances and bills increased by £79,000,000. Then in the next six months they fell by £19,000,000, and in the next six months they were substantially stable. If this part of the balances can fluctuate by as much as £79,000,000,then, unless there was a transference of balances from one class of institution to another, it looks as though the aggregate can vary by as much as £100,000,000 within 18 months. This actual case was one of a favourable variation; that is to say, an increase of our balances. But if our balances can increase, they can also decrease, and if we hold £400,000,000 it is easy to imagine a combination of circumstances which might lead us to lose one-fourth of them. A movement of £100,000,000 within a year or two would be nothing particularly exceptional; it is something which could happen without our credit being in question, or anything of that sort.

The second item is the amount of British balances abroad. I have really no idea of the amount of these; I should imagine they are probably not very large.

(MR MCKENNA) *Very small.*

(MR BRAND) *Of course the joint stock banks do not keep much, but the private banks keep a good deal more, I should say.* It would be useful if we could have any guess. I have thought about it but I have no basis for a guess in any published figure.

(MR MCKENNA) *The total is not commensurate with these figures.* No. The total of the balances in New York for all foreign countries is large, but I have no means of knowing what the British proportion is.

(MR BRAND) *There would be quite a lot of balances lent to German banks. You mean British deposits?* British deposits with German banks.

With German or American or other banks? Yes.

A quite considerable amount. What would you guess? £50,000,000?

I could not possibly guess. It might be. It is an extraordinarily difficult situation because there are so many unknown factors, but I should add to this, as I have mentioned, the acceptances on foreign account.

It is very difficult to say. Every bank that does exchange will keep certain balances abroad for that purpose; they will keep balances with all their foreign correspondents, of a greater or less amount.

(MR MCKENNA) *I should doubt whether the joint stock banks keep more than £10,000,000 abroad all told.*

(MR BRAND) *Some of the banks keep bigger balances. Then they have acceptances which they have to meet here.*

(MR MCKENNA) *I mean in Germany, they have to have acceptances.*

(MR BRAND) *I should think it is a considerable sum.*

(CHAIRMAN) *Is there not a set-off in liabilities the other way?* Oh yes, to all these things there are offsets. I am considering the gross amount. There are liabilities against which they must be held. That is also true of some part of the balances here which are held to meet acceptances which are maturing.

(MR MCKENNA) *The major part.* That is one of the reasons why I estimate the reasonable fluctuation as low as 25 per cent. If it were not that many of the balances are kept here for a reason, the fluctuation would be more than that. A lot of balances here are held for other motives than which is the most advantageous centre from the point of view of arbitrage loans. Then there is the possible variation in our acceptances on foreign account, and that I should estimate is fairly large; it might be as much as £40,000,000 to £50,000,000. That is to say, the extent to which the international market would depend on dollar or sterling acceptances might vary from one period to another by as much as £40,000,000 to £50,000,000.

Now the effect on that is one of the most important functions of Bank rate. It is not the effect which is produced instantaneously, but over a period of 3 months the bill rate operates very powerfully in its relation to the market rate by causing borrowers to move over between sterling and dollar acceptances.

(MR BRAND) *Or between London and Amsterdam.* Or Amsterdam. That is certainly one of the most important functions of Bank rate, and I should have thought it would have been possible over a period of two or three months to get a relief of £50,000,000 in that way. I think that order of magnitude would not be far out.

It would not be more than that, I should say, over six months or nine months. If you take the sort of institution that I know best, the acceptance houses, the liabilities of foreigners to all of them would be much bigger; therefore, if you take them as a branch, certainly London is a creditor centre, not a debtor. Yes, but if you take the whole aggregate that is not so; London is today, I should say, a debtor centre on balance.

(MR MCKENNA) *A short-term debtor.* A short-term debtor; which, of course, is natural for a country which sits [acts?] as an international bank; a bank is always a debtor on short terms.

The third item is that of new foreign issues, on the London market. We have figures which enable one to estimate that much more accurately. It would certainly vary from £100,000,000 to £200,000,000 per annum. That is an element which is controlled to a considerable degree by the wishes of the Bank of England; it is one of the items which is under a certain amount of control, because issuing houses will pay great respect to the opinion of the Bank of England as to the pace at which they bring out new foreign issues.

(PROFESSOR GREGORY) *Does the control of the Bank of England really affect the time of issue rather than the aggregate amount, if you take more than very short-term issues?* Foreign borrowers could anticipate by offers of bills, as the Australian Government did—or the Chilean Government this week—but the extent to which they would anticipate would always bear a not very large proportion to the size of the loan. Also I should think the Bank of England has considerable control over the amount of short-term credits that are given to governments, has it not, Mr Brand?

(MR BRAND) *Yes, I should say so.* That is one of the elements of the situation that is more definitely controlled than some others.

Of course, much the biggest control is that of the public. At one moment you find you can easily place a foreign loan, then one or two are placed and you cannot place any more. They will be influenced partly by sentiment and partly by the volume of bank credit. The fourth possible occasion of fluctuation is foreign purchases and sales on the London Stock Exchange. I have never heard any close guess as to that. I should say the amount is not very great over quite a short period, because if Paris or New York or Amsterdam start selling their favourite internationals in London the jobbers will not take much and the price goes against them very fast. So it is limited over a period of a few weeks, but it might easily mount up over a longer period. I should have thought that in the course of a year the net amount of international securities, of new issues between different centres, is sometimes enormous. I remember being in a position to make some calculations as to how much we had sold the Americans in, I think it was, the year 1928, of a few securities—Columbia Gramophones, General Electric, and some other securities which Americans happened to be swallowing wholesale at that time. I ought not to quote figures, as it is a rather vague estimate—but the value of the Columbia Gramophone shares sold to Americans within the year was perhaps as much as £20,000,000 to £30,000,000, in that single security; and when the Americans are buying that class of security the movement in our favour as compared with when they are selling a similar class of thing can be enormous.

Are you including the sale of British issues? I know two businesses which were sold for something like £20,000,000 to Americans. I ought to include that. That comes under this head. In the aggregate, the fluctuations in this item are of an order of which account has to be taken. I am sure they can easily be £50,000,000—that is half our favourable balance available for investment. It is very big in comparison with the balance we have. Then there are British purchases and sales on foreign stock exchanges, mainly Wall Street. I suppose they are not so big as they were in pre-War times. That might be one of the items which is less fluctuating.

In 1928–9 they were bigger than they had ever been. Perhaps they were. If the investment trusts are favouring American securities the movement as compared with the situation when they are not favouring them may be very large. I should have thought this was easily capable of varying from plus £50,000,000 to minus £50,000,000, that sometimes we increase our purchases on Wall Street by £50,000,000 and sometimes decrease them. I do not know whether that would appeal to the members as being correct. It is pure guess.

(MR MCKENNA) *The figures are not too large.* Finally, the net result of all these things which are not due to any one cause,—speculation comes a great deal into this—has to be equated to our surplus available for foreign investment on income account, or if it is not so equated, gold movements ensue. That surplus available for foreign investment has varied in recent years according to the estimates of the Board of Trade from nought to £200,000,000. It will be obvious to the Committee what a delicate and indeed appalling task the Bank of England has so to operate to make all these add up almost to equality. Gold movements in excess of £10,000,000 are considered large, and I do not think there have been gold movements in excess of £30,000,000 at any time in the course of a year. I mean movements of balances over an annual period.

(MR LUBBOCK) *£45,000,000.* Inwards or outwards?

Outwards. £175,000,000 to £130,000,000. I think it is a miracle in a way that it is possible to bring various influences to bear upon these very refractory elements to cause the net result to be so favourable, but it has to be done almost entirely by influencing the first three items, that is to say, the short-term funds by fluctuations in bill rate, and some of the other items by fluctuations in the volume of credit, and so far as new foreign issues are concerned, by bringing influence to bear on issuing houses. Those are the only weapons the Bank has, and I am not surprised that their work is cut out to achieve the result, and it means that the Bank is very seldom in a position to be able to risk very much for the sake of the home position. They have got a tremendous task in bringing about this difficult equation and, therefore, they have been driven by necessity into the habit of keeping their eyes mainly upon bill rate and foreign exchange in the way that Sir Ernest Harvey described to us. They simply dare not take their eyes off those two factors because they are faced with a position of such difficulty that it could get out of hand very easily if they began averting their eyes from the essential elements in the international equilibrium position.

We have had an example of that given us more than once by Mr McKenna, how sometimes when the Bank of England is in a mood to expand credit the first effect of that has been to weaken the bill rate. With our present technique it almost must be so because the purchase of bills is the first thing the joint stock banks do with any additional funds, and reaction of that on bill rate has frightened the Bank of England—quite rightly—so that they have had to retrace their steps rather hurriedly.

Do you regard that as an inevitable result of a further creation of credit by the Bank of England? I want to come to ways of avoiding it. What has happened in the past is that whenever the Bank of England has tried to pay attention to the domestic situation it has very quickly had its attention pulled very sharply back to the international situation by the weakening of the bill rate, and it has been confirmed in its traditional opinion that it is very dangerous to take its eyes off the bill rate and the foreign exchanges. It has felt itself confirmed in regarding attention to those as its main task, and I do not wonder. When one thinks of the size of these possible fluctuating items in relation to the Bank's resources, it is natural that they dare not take their eyes off that particular ball.

Quite correct! I think it is also very important to understand that the problem is probably much more difficult than it used to be prior to the War; for several reasons. There is, first of all, the much greater size of the foreign balances. Unluckily we have no pre-War statistics, but I should suppose that to-day's figure of £400,000,000 of foreign balances is far and away beyond anything that existed in pre-War days. Nothing of that order of magnitude existed.

(MR MCKENNA) *Foreign balances and bills?* Foreign balances and bills.

You said 'balances'. I meant to include bills. Then there is another item which to a certain extent cuts both ways, that is the existence of competitive centres for foreign balances. I say it cuts both ways because it means there are international short-term loans which we can draw to London for our protection to balance other items, but it also aggravates our difficulties because in pre-War days the vast bulk of international short loan funds was kept in London, and there was not much chance of that diminishing unless it was being turned into long-term assets, which would be a slow process and one which would be very definitely correlated with foreign issues in London. We had not got the risk of tens of millions of money being attracted elsewhere to an equally good international financial centre by a slight change in relative terms. There would not be in practice anywhere else where money could go on a large scale; I should say Amsterdam was the only other serious centre; New York perhaps to a slight extent. For short-term money they had, therefore, mainly to accept the terms which London offered, consequently the task was much more one of keeping equilibrium between the long and short position. It was not a question of quoting competitive terms for short-term balances as it is today.

Thirdly, there is the growth of the inter-bourse dealings on a large scale. Of course, there was a great volume of American holdings in pre-War times, or, rather, holdings by Englishmen in American securities, but there was nothing like the international ordinary shares of which today there are several hundreds of millions of pounds' worth which can move in very large volume between international centres. I think that is a post-War phenomenon, so that that particular item of fluctuation is a new one, and also it is a particularly dangerous one because it is not susceptible to the ordinary methods of control. If Amsterdam and Paris feel inclined to sell Shell to London movements in bill rate or fluctuations in the volume of credit are not going to have any influence on the situation. London's only protection, therefore, is her power to put down the prices. But if London, which very often is the case, has rather steadier nerves than certain other foreign centres, London may be prepared to buy at what appears to London to be a bargain price a tremendous volume of international securities. So that, I think, is an aggravating circumstance.

Then finally there is the new feature of the tendency of our foreign lending on long term to exceed over a period our income surplus. In pre-War times I think there was much less of a struggle to keep our foreign lending equal to our income surplus than there is today.

(MR LUBBOCK) *How are you to know when it exceeds our income surplus?* That is another question. Excuse me, I would rather not embark upon that.

It is rather important, is it not? It is, but it takes me back to the subject of savings and investment. What are the resources of the Bank of England to deal with these potential fluctuations in the international position? The Bank of England has a total quantity of gold which has fluctuated in recent times, I think, between £130,000,000 and £175,000,000. I put in my notes £160,000,000, but Mr Lubbock reminds me that it is £175,000,000, and I think £100,000,000 to £110,000,000 is locked up against the notes.

Unless the Bank of England chooses to ask the Treasury to deal with it. Yes, apart from that contingency. The free gold has amounted to something between £65,000,000 and £70,000,000. In addition to that, the Bank of England has certain dollar balances, as to which Sir Ernest Harvey gave us certain glimpses; but he was on the whole reticent; therefore I am not certain what they amount to. The impression I derived from his evidence was that perhaps they were less than £10,000,000 sterling and that they were probably not greater than £20,000,000 sterling, but I cannot say more than that, and for the purpose of my argument I am going to assume that they are £10,000,000 sterling.

(MR MCKENNA) *Do they not vary in the course of a year?* No doubt they vary, but I am taking a normal figure around which they vary. Not all the free gold is really available in ordinary circumstances. The Bank of England cannot allow its reserves to fall towards zero unless it be for exceptional reasons; so that the actual fluctuation that the Bank of England can suffer with a light heart in ordinary circumstances is much more of the order of £30,000,000, and sometimes not as much as that, and whatever the Bank itself may feel, however free the Bank itself may be to go to the Treasury, a movement of anything like £20,000,000 of gold seriously upsets the market, and, this is more important from many points of view, even if it does not upset the inner circle of the Bank of England. If the market becomes upset results may ensue which the Bank of England has not wished or intended, because the market will act as though the Bank of England would soon be forced to take restrictive measures, even though the Bank itself knows that it is far from being in need of resort to such measures as the market believes. The result is that there is really a very trifling proportion of uncontrolled movements possible. I do not think that the Bank itself, judging from the evidence we have received in this Committee, has faced sufficiently frankly what seems to me the indubitable fact, that in modern post-War conditions the resources of the Bank of England for meeting short-period fluctuations are hopelessly inadequate. They are relying on pre-War practices, and while they have managed to use them, in a way, with remarkable success, it has been, in my judgement, at the cost of a great deal of interference with the domestic market, which everyone would have wished to have avoided if possible. I do not say the resources are inadequate for the safety of the Bank. I think the power of the traditional method is so great, provided you do not mind upsetting the domestic situation, that the Bank of England probably has been at all dates since the War essentially secure. But I think that its reserves are inadequate to allow the Bank to attend as much as it ought to the internal position with an unpreoccupied mind. It leads to the Bank having to concentrate on the external position to a greater degree than is to the general advantage. The maintenance of its reserves keeps its hands full and no wonder. I think there is another point. Nothing is worse for our credit in the world at large than this constant appearance, and indeed reality, of some measure of anxiety. For some years past there has been a reason for anxiety to all appearances. There have been constant discussions whether the Bank could not do a little more for the domestic situation and the reply was that the international situation rather ties its hands. All that suggests that it is working on a narrow margin of safety. I believe that is becoming increasingly dangerous from the point of view of our international credit. We are getting the name of being very nearly on our beam ends—a name I do not think we really deserve—owing to these constant apprehensions.

(MR LUBBOCK) *Not for that reason are we getting a bad name.* Is not it partly so?

I do not want to interrupt your argument, but we must not be taken to agree with Mr Keynes in everything. Our worrying so much about our gold situation leads foreign countries to think that we are working on a narrow margin of strength, and indeed that is true. Anybody who looks at our figures must see that it is true. Whatever happens in the outside world makes us feel nervous. If there is a boom in Wall Street, or nervousness in Paris, as well as trifling events at home, all become occasions of nervousness in the market, whereas there is not really any reason why we should upset the domestic credit situation in such circumstances, and nobody ought to feel that there is. At present any event of the kind which I have described causes the market to feel want of confidence that the Bank of England will be able to maintain a discount policy which is most in the interests of the domestic situation. They feel that events may be too strong for the Bank and that it will not be many weeks before they begin to curtail credit in order to handle the international market in accordance with their traditional methods. I suggest, therefore, to the Committee that we ought to consider, with as much care as perhaps anything, whether the Bank of England has a large enough margin, not so much for safety as for the avoidance of anxiety and trepidation—which is rather a different thing.

(CHAIRMAN) *Does it mean this, in a simple form, that the Bank ought to be able to see a diminution in its gold reserve with greater equanimity?* Or that it should have a technique for dealing with the international situation which reacts less on the domestic situation. This is quite a convenient moment for me to break off if the Committee would like to interrupt and put any questions.

(MR BRAND) *Might I ask one thing. Of course, the situation would be far worse if we were not still a big creditor nation?* Yes.

It would practically be impossible, but I suppose theoretically it would be possible, for the Government to decree that there should be no foreign investments for a certain number of months, and that the Bank of England instead should invest our surplus in dollar securities or in gold. I suppose theoretically, but I agree with the suggestion of your remark that the fact that we have a certain amount of surplus all the time is an essential element in the situation which makes our position possible.

Otherwise it would be impossible. The proportion of that margin to our liabilities is falling compared with what it used to be.

(CHAIRMAN) *I was going to ask you about that credit balance historically. It has diminished, has not it?* The estimates are open to a great deal of controversy. In the pre-war days the figure used to be put at 200 to 250 millions.

It is not constant. No, not in any sense—it is not constant in any sense. It is now at round about £100 millions.

Is it diminishing? It fluctuates very rapidly. I should say it is diminishing.

This year it will diminish a great deal. In the year of the General Strike it sank to nothing. But the statistics are not very reliable.

(MR MCKENNA) *May I make the point in a slightly different way. The balance against us on other accounts is increasing. We do not diminish the balance in our favour as much as it would otherwise diminish because we are every year increasing the total indebtedness of figures [foreigners] to us.*

(CHAIRMAN) *The set off.*

(MR MCKENNA) *The set off. We are increasing the total capital account on which we draw interest. If we had a surplus of 100 millions next year we should have the increased interest of 5 per cent on that, namely 5 millions. The whole of that £5 millions and something more is being used up in the successive years in order to meet the adverse balance.* But the adverse balance may be increasing.

The adverse balance is always increasing against us. We are not increasing the amount of our credit balance on investment account on which we could draw annual interest as fast as we are increasing the adverse balance on other accounts.

(PROFESSOR GREGORY) *Is that so as a matter of fact, or of necessity?*

(MR MCKENNA) *The figures I think, show it.*

(PROFESSOR GREGORY) *As a matter of fact?*

(MR MCKENNA) *As a matter of fact. I agree with Mr Keynes's figures. The figures pre-War showed there was a balance in our favour of from 200 to 250 millions. That was the annual balance in our favour of all kinds. Today the annual balance is somewhere between 100 millions and 150 millions. We have to our credit all the accumulations since the War because every year since the War with a single exception we had a balance in our favour and upon that today we are drawing interest, but that interest is more than taken up by the adverse balance on other accounts.*

(LORD BRADBURY) *But the increase of the adverse balance on other accounts leads to an interest liability against us, and there is a set-off against the increase of interest.*

(MR BRAND) *You mean on export of goods?*

(LORD BRADBURY) *The falling off of our exports.*

(MR MCKENNA) *It is leaving a balance on our other accounts against us.*

(LORD BRADBURY) *I thought you meant the accumulation of foreign balances on investment.*

(MR MCKENNA) *It is so much against us, it not only absorbs the increased interest from the previous total balances in our favour, but is actually eating into the balance itself. I think the figures show that.* I can illustrate the case thus. Before the War our foreign surplus on income account would have paid off what we owed the world on short term in six months—today it would take four years.

(CHAIRMAN) *That shows a progressive deterioration of our position, does not it?* It means that we are operating as bankers on a wider scale internationally relatively to our annual surplus than we used to. It is not necessarily a deterioration that we are acting as bankers on such a large scale, but it is an increase of the element of precariousness.

If it is the credit balance which is enabling us to maintain the situation, if that credit balance is diminishing, then the margin of security is deteriorating. Yes.

(MR MCKENNA) *It would mean ultimately that the balance in our favour on all accounts would disappear.*

(CHAIRMAN) *In that case we would be in an awkward position.*

(MR LUBBOCK) *We should have to go and borrow abroad if that went further.*

(MR MCKENNA) *Our whole system would break down.* Apart from that there are these huge fluctuating items which have to be kept in aggregate equality with one another.

(PROFESSOR GREGORY) *There are two questions. There is the question of the degree of fluctuation which is possible at the moment. You have dealt with that; but I could not accept the view that the adverse balance against us on short-term account is increasing every year. I should have thought that we had reached a maximum which is like to decline.* I did not assert that. I asserted it was very much greater than pre-War.

I agree with that. It goes up and down. Some years it decreases, and some years it increases.

I should have thought the trend of the international trade [short?] loan fund that balances us on short account is to decline rather than to go on increasing. We have not the figures for a long enough period to detect the trend, but for the period we have it has been upwards and since then a little bit downwards, but as New York has 600 millions against 400 millions, if we were to become relatively better for short loans than New York we might have a large increase.

(MR BRAND) *The result is shown on public opinion. I remember M. Moret, of the Bank of France, saying he was certain he could get his money from New York, but he was not quite certain with regard to London.*

(MR LUBBOCK) *My Keynes suggested there should be more flexibility of the banking account by which I understand him to mean whereas we have seen the gold stock fall from 170 millions to 130 millions, we ought to be prepared to see it fall to 100 millions or 70 millions.* I did not mean to have indicated that the Bank could have done anything more in the past, subject to its present practices and conventions. But what it could do I am coming to.

(CHAIRMAN) *You are going to suggest a method?* Yes.

I am much impressed by what you point out about the diminishing balances. That must be symptomatic of some cause at work.

(MR LUBBOCK) *Too high costs.*

(CHAIRMAN) *Is it really the invisible exports which are diminishing?* No, it is mainly the visible exports which are diminishing.

(MR LUBBOCK) *The manufactures.*

(CHAIRMAN) *Not freights.* The invisible exports have kept up pretty well. If you take this particular year freights are very low; but though freights are bad, we have maintained our proportion of the world's shipping remarkably well. Over the whole post-War period the invisible exports have been upwards.

Then it is the visible ones—that is bad trade. Yes.

(MR MCKENNA) *Imports increasing.*

(CHAIRMAN) *Imports increasing and exports decreasing.*

(MR MCKENNA) *Yes. The real balance against us has been very much obscured because we have been getting in relation to the price we paid for our imports an abnormally high price for our exports.*

(CHAIRMAN) *The position might be reached ultimately when it would be the worse for us.*

(MR MCKENNA) *It would be worse for us if we got a true relation between the export and the import prices.*

(CHAIRMAN) *The position might become ultimately such that the balance would disappear?*

(MR MCKENNA) *Not for a long time.*

(MR LUBBOCK) *If the costs remained high.*

(CHAIRMAN) *It is the visible exports that are losing ground and if trade continues to go back, then ultimately you will be left with the invisible exports to balance with.*

(MR MCKENNA) *I think Professor Gregory takes a different view.*

(PROFESSOR GREGORY) *No, I entirely agree.*

(MR MCKENNA) *I thought you disagreed.*

(PROFESSOR GREGORY) *I expressed a doubt on this point that the adverse balance represented by items like deposits of foreigners were going to increase in the future as they have been increasing since the War. I agree that our exports have been falling off.*

(MR MCKENNA) *I am dealing with the total balances.*

(PROFESSOR GREGORY) *I say that broadly it is the international funds which are creating the adverse balance.*

(SIR WALTER RAINE) *Did you see the figures in one of the banking magazines. I cannot give them exactly, but in pre-War days we required about 12 or 13 per cent of our invisible exports to make up our trade balances, and now it is something like 27 per cent.* I can well believe that.

The actual sum of money is £127 millions more than we have got to pay out of our invisible exports to balance the account as compared with 1913. We are depending on them much more than we were but they have kept up whereas the visible exports have not kept up. Shall I go on with my statement?

(CHAIRMAN) *Please do.* If the Committee would like a programme of what

196

I have to say, it falls under these six heads as measures which I think might be worth considering. First of all, means of increasing the effective reserve of the Bank; secondly, the development of techniques which have comparatively a large effect on the foreign position and a small effect on the home position; thirdly, the development of more intimate relations between the Bank of England and the joint stock banks for joint action, so that the desired part of the market is affected; fourthly, the regulation of foreign investment; fifthly, any measures of a general character to increase the strength and resources of the Bank of England; sixthly, the increase of the information at the disposal of the Bank—both the information at its disposal and the giving of that information by it to the rest of the world.

First of all, as to the increase of the effective reserves of the Bank, my feeling is, though, of course, it is not a figure one can justify logically, that the Bank of England ought, when things are in our favour, to hold not less than say 200 millions in liquid international assets—liquid foreign reserves including gold,—and that ought not to be allowed to fall below 100 millions in any ordinary circumstances, but we ought to get the world accustomed to seeing fluctuations between 120 millions and 180 millions as almost a common event, or, at any rate, a frequent event, and in that way in effect really restore a free gold market, allowing anybody who wants a bit of gold to have it on quite a large scale if he wants it, without taking any particular steps to stop it.

(MR LUBBOCK) *On the assumption that it will come back in the normal course later on?* Yes. Whilst seeing fluctuations between 120 millions and 180 millions as very ordinary affairs, also to allow a fluctuation between 100 millions and 200 millions without too much reluctance.

(MR TULLOCH) *Are you speaking of gold alone, or gold and foreign reserves?* Gold and foreign reserves. A fluctuation between 100 millions and 200 millions should be considered nothing wonderful. Outside those limits, there would be an abnormal situation. If that be the case, the obligatory minimum holding of the Bank ought not to be so large as the 100 to 110 to 120 millions that it is at present. It depends upon the season of the year how great it is, when the note issue is at its maximum. When trade is good I suppose that something like 120 millions is locked up in present circumstances. It would be better if the amount of gold which was not available and which the world knew was not available except by application to the Treasury was not so large as it is now.

(LORD BRADBURY) *That is really an increase of the fiduciary issue.* Wait a moment. There are two ways in which you can strengthen the Bank of England. One is by making a larger amount of its present reserves available and the other is by increasing its present resources. It would be a bad example to the rest of the world and it would aggravate the shortage of gold, if we were substantially to increase our holdings of gold. On the other hand, it would be a good example to the rest of the world and also useful for reasons that I shall come to later, if we got into the habit of holding substantial, but highly fluctuating foreign balances. I think it is wrong for us to go on pretending that we are the only financial centre in the world. It is much more important for us than it used to be to keep liquid reserves at other financial centres. Apart from that, if the B.I.S. develops along the lines we might hope, I think we ought to keep substantial balances with them, but of a highly fluctuating character, with the rest, perhaps, in New York. I should like to see our foreign balances with the B.I.S. and New York fluctuate between nought and 50 millions, as quite a normal procedure. That would be mainly additional to the present reserve.

(MR BRAND) *Do you mean have them published?*

(MR LUBBOCK) *Do you require that to be shown?* I should prefer that it is shown. I think the more publicity you get people into the habit of expecting the better it is in the long run, and the less occasion for alarms based on misleading so called inside information. There are no secrets—everything is known. Therefore, you only lose by mystery in these matters. But that was not my main point at the moment. My main point at the moment is that there should be a fairly large increase in the Bank's resources when things were going well, and that that increase should take the form of foreign balances rather than of more gold. The advantages of that would be several, apart from its effect on world practice. I think there would be greater delicacy of operation open to the Bank of England if it was regularly dealing on the exchanges. It could meet the short-term movements without allowing any appreciable reactions on any of the internal factors. Moreover, even if the figures are published, the movements of foreign balances are much less ostentatious than gold movements, and I think it would be useful for the Bank to have a choice between an ostentatious method and a less ostentatious method. Sometimes the movements of gold can have a valuable effect on sentiment in the desired direction. Sometimes they have an effect you do not want at all. I think it would be useful for the Bank authority to choose whether the Bank should lose gold, or lose foreign balances. Finally, there is the possibility of forward dealings on the exchange which I shall come to later, as part of a new technique.

Whatever we do about increasing the resources of the Bank of England, I think that we still ought to consider the necessity of increasing the available portion of existing gold resources by say £40 to £60 million. As Professor Gregory told us last week there are two ways of doing this. One way is by increasing the fiduciary portion of the note issue. The other way is by decreasing the joint stock banks' holdings of notes;—which would require no legislative change. I have been looking into that. I have for a long time past been thinking about that a good deal and you will find the result interesting. I should like to take the possibilities of that first before I come to the question of the fiduciary issue.

The peculiarity of our system is that a very large part of our so-called active circulation is, in fact, held by the joint stock banks. Apart from window dressing the banks appear to hold about one-third of their reserves at the Bank of England, and about two-thirds in notes. Moreover, it is the part at the Bank of England which bears most of the short-period fluctuations. The return which Mr Ismay has got out for us shows that the holdings of notes by the banks were quite extraordinarily stable. I would like to dwell on those statistics. It might be useful if the Committee would be so good as to take notes of the figures so that I have not to keep on repeating them. The balances of the clearing banks at the Bank of England seems to have averaged in recent times, though there is some guessing about this, about 55 millions, as against total deposits of about 1,750 millions. That is to say, their balances at the Bank of England represent about 3 per cent of their deposits. On the other hand, the banks show in their returns of balances at the Bank of England, apart from the half years when they get much larger, about 75 millions; that is to say, at least 20 millions of their alleged reserves are window dressing.

(MR BRAND) *The 75 millions is at the window dressing period?* No, in their monthly balance sheets. In their monthly balance sheets, apart from the half year, they show balances at the Bank of England of about 75 millions.

(SIR WALTER RAINE) *Where does the 55 millions come from?* The actual balances at the Bank of England as shown by the Bank of England itself are 55 millions.

(MR LUBBOCK) *It is the different days of the week added up.* Yes, so that about 20 millions is fudge. I should be interested to have these figures criticised.

(MR MCKENNA) *The Bank of England must know.*

(MR LUBBOCK) *What Mr Keynes means is that if you add up on one single day you get 55 millions, but if you add up Monday, Tuesday or Wednesday at different banks you get 75 millions.*

(CHAIRMAN) *Sir Ernest Harvey gave us a figure of about 20 millions.* I do not think he actually gave us any figure.

(MR LUBBOCK) *There are 5 millions which go round on the four different days. There are 5 millions going round during the week. It appears on Monday in one bank and on Tuesday in another.* It is worse than that.

(MR MCKENNA) *May I ask if I should be allowed to use this figure? Is it a public figure?* It is not public yet.

The Bank of England show a figure at 75 millions. You have published that figure of 55 millions. You show it, I suppose Yes, but it is only obtainable by the confidential information at our disposal.

I cannot use it.

(MR LUBBOCK) *But you knew it.*

(MR MCKENNA) *I did not know it was anything like that.*

(MR LUBBOCK) *It is the same 5 millions taken four times over.*

(LORD BRADBURY) *It is 5 millions multiplied by four, not by five.* It is larger than that, because the original 5 millions is in the 55 millions. Therefore, if there are four banks doing it that makes four banks making 5 millions into 25 millions.

(MR BRAND) *Is not it 6?*

(MR MCKENNA) *No, there are the original 5 millions which are genuine, but they show 25 millions, when they ought to show 5 millions, so that it has been multiplied six times.*

(MR MCKENNA) *You take off 10 millions for the one bank. That will leave the others 45 millions, and they show 65 millions. It is only 10 millions. It is 20 millions into four banks.* The reserves shown by the four banks are some 50 per cent greater than their true reserves.

(MR LUBBOCK) *I do not give the figures, but there is a fluctuating amount which goes round, and you multiply that.*

(MR MCKENNA) *I had no notion it was of that magnitude.* That means that the window-dressing for the totality of the banks is from 1 to $1\frac{1}{2}$ per cent of their deposits. I think we should make a strong recommendation for the abolition of this practice.

Please. I do not know how the Bank of England gets on with it. I will come to that later on. It is connected with one of my suggestions for strengthening the Bank.

The reserve held by the banks in notes is about 104 millions. That figure, as I have said, is very stable. That represents about 6 per cent of their deposits.

Is that all it is? Their holding of notes, so that the total reserve will be made up in this way: Notes 6 per cent, Bank of England deposits 3 per cent, and window-dressing nearly $1\frac{1}{2}$ per cent; making a total of $10\frac{1}{2}$ per cent as shown.

(SIR WALTER RAINE) *On which day of the week is this 104 millions taken?* That is on window-dressing days; but I do not think they window-dress their notes—I have never heard that they did.

(MR MCKENNA) *They call on the market 5 millions.*

(SIR WALTER RAINE) *Do not the notes vary, as you pay out the wages towards the end of the week?* I do not think they take the weekend dates. It is Monday, Tuesday, Wednesday, Thursday; so that it is the average of those four days.

Thank you. I do not think there is much reason to quarrel with that figure. That is one of the more reliable ones. I do not know for certain how much of the notes they hold are really required as till money; but I should think 3 per cent of their deposits would be a liberal allowance for what they require to have in their till; or at any rate 3 per cent could be made liberal, if the Bank of England had depots of unissued notes available at provincial centres where there is a clearing house.

(MR MCKENNA) *3 per cent is right.* I think at present you have to get notes either from Threadneedle Street or from one of the branches of the Bank of England.

(MR LUBBOCK) *Yes.* It would be quite consistent with a policy of curtailing the Bank of England branches for commercial purposes, if the Bank of England was very greatly to increase the number of its depots.

(MR MCKENNA) *The banks keep the 3 per cent notes for till money.* I should have thought that by increasing facilities for obtaining notes at short notice from the Bank of England round the corner, 3 per cent would be quite a large enough allowance for till money.

We do not require it from the Bank of England. All the banks have their own centres.

(MR LUBBOCK) *3 per cent covers it.*

(MR MCKENNA) *3 per cent covers it. The 3 per cent covers us. We have 3 per cent till money; and any particular branch that has a special drain on it will get what it requires from our own note centre in the district.* I am rather glad to have that confirmation. It was a guess on my part. What Mr McKenna says confirms the suggestion I was going to make that in future the bank[s] should hold as a reserve 3 per cent in notes.

(CHAIRMAN) *Instead of 6 per cent?* Yes; and 7 to 8 per cent at the Bank of England, window-dressing being abolished, shewing a reserve somewhere between 10 and 11 per cent altogether.

(MR LUBBOCK) *The Banking Department's reserve would be something like 100 millions.* I am coming to that. I should like it to be laid down that the Bank of England deposits of 7 to 8 per cent should be required as a daily average over monthly periods?

(MR MCKENNA) *Yes.*

(MR BRAND) *And exclude window dressing.* In order to exclude window dressing, I would allow the banks' reserves to fluctuate for short periods. I would not make it weekly for them even, but I would make it a monthly average, so that the banks could go substantially below even 7 or 8 per cent for periods of the week, provided it would not be for a long period.

It would be a daily average. Yes, provided it was made up to the requisite figure over the month.

New York works on a weekly average. My impression was that it was average monthly.

(CHAIRMAN) *You say actual sterling average?* Yes.

(LORD BRADBURY) *What is the reason for the present practice of holding this 6 per cent in legal tender money rather than 3 per cent, which, according to Mr McKenna, is all that is necessary?* I have no idea.

It makes financially no difference to the bank. The balances of notes are equally non-interest bearing. Is it only custom that has induced them to hold these unnecessary notes?

(MR TULLOCH) *If you had depots about, as is proposed, of the Bank of England, there would be no real necessity for it. So far as I know, these notes held in reserve in the till do not vary. Ours never vary from year to year; but we feel we must have them for emergencies. If you once had—as in point of fact we had—a Bank of England branch with every available note, so that you could have these notes at any time, there is no earthly reason for holding all these notes in reserve.*

(LORD BRADBURY) *There is in point of fact something like 52 millions in the hands of the joint stock banks, which are not required for the machinery of the banks.*

(MR TULLOCH) *On this figure of 104 millions, yes.*

(CHAIRMAN) *The position of the Scottish banks is quite different.* I am coming to them in a moment. They are even more peculiar. If the banks would keep 7 to 8 per cent in balances at the Bank of England, and reduce their notes more or less to the extent that Lord Bradbury says, that would have the effect of reducing the note issue by a little more than 50 millions, and increasing the Bank of England reserve by the same large figure, without any change in the fiduciary issue, or any change in the relation between the profits of the Bank and the Treasury.

(MR BRAND) *Really the effect is to enable you to increase by 50 millions of gold—it is really increasing the fiduciary issue.* Yes, if you assume there is any sense in the existing fiduciary issue; but if that is a sort of traditional figure, then you would have 50 millions more to play with. If we thought the Bank ought to have more gold, this gives us a way of doing it without upsetting any traditions.

(MR TULLOCH) *You are not going to recommend the amalgamation of the Issue Department and the Banking Department?* Yes, I was going to suggest that. It has not any very great bearing on this, because whether you amalgamate them or not, you are increasing the reserves of the Bank of England by 50 millions. Then there is the question of the Scottish banks, which Lord Macmillan raises. Their position is still more extreme.

(LORD BRADBURY) *I am not quite clear about this yet. This alteration in banking practice, the transfer of notes or exchange of notes without increasing the balances at the Bank of England, would in substance be exactly the same as an increase in the fiduciary issue.* Exactly.

But it is a question whether that would not involve some kind of prejudice in the world. That is a point.

(MR BRAND) *It means if this 52 millions had been in the Bank of England when the fiduciary issue was fixed, it would have been fixed at 210 millions instead of 260 millions.*

(MR LUBBOCK) *No.* I do not think so, because the history of the fiduciary issue goes back far beyond that.

(MR BRAND) *I meant when it was fixed at 260 millions.* It was fixed at 260 millions because that was stabilising it at the figure which it had been prior to that.

(LORD BRADBURY) *But stabilising it at a figure at which it had stood, this practice of the joint stock banks being one of the elements.* If the 260 millions was the result of a considered decision that we ought to lock up out of use 100 to 120 millions, then the fiduciary issue ought to be altered as a result; but if it was not a considered decision that 100 to 120 millions was the figure we ought to lock up—

(MR LUBBOCK) *Gold, you mean?.* Yes; but was done out of a desire not to break with tradition at that particular moment, that gives us an opportunity to reconsider just what the locked-up gold ought to be without breach of historical tradition.

(MR BRAND) *Did not they fix the 260 millions on the supposition that there were a certain number of notes in circulation? Now there would be 50 millions less.* No, it is what the fiduciary issue had been. It would have been an extraordinary coincidence, if reason had led us to the conclusion that the exact amount of gold we ought to have locked up was exactly the amount which would be required as a register of stereotyping the existing position. There was the old pre-war fiduciary issue of the Bank of England under the 1844 Act. There was all the fiduciary portion of the Treasury note issue under War and post-War legislation. If you added those two together, and made a certain adjustment by reason of the fact that Ireland was detached from us, you arrived at 260 millions. That is the way it was reached.

The Treasury note issue, if the banks had paid all these notes into the Bank, would be very much less at that moment.

(PROFESSOR GREGORY) *No.* It was not the amount of the note issue at that moment. It was the amount of the fiduciary portion at that moment which determined the 260 millions.

This proposal would not alter the fiduciary position at all.

(MR BRAND) *I am not saying that it would.*

(CHAIRMAN) *The point is the fiduciary issue was fixed at a figure which would fix it, having regard to the existing practice of the banks, by which they have 6 per cent in notes.* I should not have thought it was that. It was what had been prevailing. It was not as a result of any decision as to what the locked-up amount ought to be. This gives us now an opportunity of considering what the locked-up amount of gold ought to be, without a breach of tradition.

(MR LUBBOCK) *Do you think the banks, by increasing their balances by 50 millions, really are freeing 50 millions of gold?*

(MR BRAND) *It does under the existing law.*

(MR LUBBOCK) *Does it?*

(LORD BRADBURY) *Surely it does, if you have a fiduciary issue, as at present.*

(MR LUBBOCK) *Supposing gold is taken from the Bank of England and the balances are decreased there, the banks, in order to replenish their balances, would pay in gold which they had in their vaults.*

(LORD BRADBURY) *They could do it by paying in notes, so that their balances would increase by 50 millions, so that you have transferred 50 millions from the Issue Department to the Banking Department.*

(MR LUBBOCK) *Not from their vaults?* They pay it in, and it has the effect of diminishing the active circulation in the Issue Department by 50 millions; and, therefore, the reserve is 50 millions greater.

The Issue Department is not affected. The active circulation in the Issue Department falls 50 millions.

We divide it now. The note issue to the Bank is increased, and the note issue to the public is decreased. I agree if enough gold went out, the banks would pay in notes, if the balances went down beyond a certain point; but you might easily lose 20 millions before they reached the notes. You could not, really, because that would mean they were breaking their ratios.

Something would have to happen. May I, to complete my statistics, come to the position of the Scottish banks? The Scottish banks hold about 180 millions on deposit, which is very near to my traditional guess, that it was 10 per cent of the English. Against that they hold less than one million at the Bank of England—they hold about three-quarters of a million at the Bank of England, and they hold 17 millions in notes—that is to say, not very far short of 10 per cent in notes, and nothing worth mentioning at the Bank of England. No doubt they do that because, I think I am right in saying, there is no branch of the Bank of England in Scotland.

No. So that the Scottish banks could only get notes from London; so that they keep virtually the whole of their reserves in Bank of England notes.

(PROFESSOR GREGORY) *They have to keep up more because their notes are covered by Bank of England notes.* Their total reserves are rather less than the joint stock banks. Their total reserves are under 10 per cent, whereas the joint stock banks are rather over 10 per cent.

(MR LUBBOCK) *These notes they hold are really based on their own issue of notes.* I do not know what is the amount of their note issue. That was not given in the statistics. I do not think that can be so, because it is all they hold against their deposits. If they were really held against their note issue, then they hold nothing against the deposits. The amount of the note issue was not given in the statistics.

(MR MCKENNA) *What is the liability on the note issue?* That was not given in the figures.

(CHAIRMAN) *That can easily be got.*

(PROFESSOR GREGORY) *They have a fixed fiduciary circulation.* They may hold additional notes against it.

(MR LUBBOCK) *What is their fiduciary issue—7 millions?* I am taking Mr Ismay's report, in which they shew the deposits, and they shew the cash against them. That may be open to correction; but perhaps it will do if I may take that subject to criticism on that point.

(MR MCKENNA) *How much cash is there against the 180 millions?* Three-quarters of a million at the Bank of England, and 17 millions of notes.

(CHAIRMAN) *They do not work on Bank of England balances at all.*

(MR LUBBOCK) *You must add the liability on the note issue.* I do not know if that is not allowed for. The liability on the notes is not given in the table. Perhaps Mr Ismay will find it for us. It shews what is held against deposits. This reserve is under 10 per cent, which is very near the figures of the English banks, so that I suspect these notes they hold against their deposits.

(LORD BRADBURY) *It is their total holding of notes, both cover for their own note issue and against deposits.* The important point of my argument is that the Scottish banks hold next to no balances at the Bank of England, and therefore in that sense are contributing nothing towards the upkeep of the national currency system. It appears to me that it is just as incumbent upon them to keep 7 or 8 per cent at the Bank of England as it is on any other banks. If it is owing to the absence of a Bank of England depot in Scotland that they have for their own security to keep this abnormal amount in notes—whether that is so or not we shall get later statistics about—that can easily be met by the Bank of England either having depots of its own, or appointing a bank in Scotland its agent for the purpose.

(MR LUBBOCK) *They keep a lot of money with the London banks.*

(LORD BRADBURY) *Do not they keep in fact the notes which are uncovered for their own note issue in London? They do not actually send them out of England.*

(MR MCKENNA) *Yes.*

(LORD BRADBURY) *By getting the necessary notes, they are in a position to issue their own notes to the public at a moment's notice.*

(MR MCKENNA) *Yes.*

(MR LUBBOCK) *If they would want to issue 250 million pounds of notes, they would pay us 250 millions, and we should issue 250 millions out of our vaults, and they would issue the 250 millions. That is what it comes to.* It seems to me there is a reduction of 10 millions in notes for the Bank of England to be got out of Scotland which is additional to the 50 millions for England, so that if all the banks were keeping 7 or 8 per cent of their deposits at the Bank of England, the note issue today could be reduced by something like 60 millions and the reserve of the Bank of England increased by that amount.

(LORD BRADBURY) *Do you want to make that a statutory requirement?* I am coming to that.

(SIR WALTER RAINE) *If this money is kept in London already, is not it in the hands of the joint stock banks, and it is part of what they get?* I do not know enough about the Scottish system to say. I think we must wait till we get the new figures. If they are keeping 17 millions in notes over and above what they hold against their note issue, they have this margin, whatever they do in London. They could afford to turn in 10 millions of these notes, and be in a stronger position than they are at present without any increase of expense.

(CHAIRMAN) *You are looking round for various ways for increasing the Bank of England's reserve.* At present I am trying to elucidate the statistics. It is extraordinary how little one knows about them.

(LORD BRADBURY) *The balance at the Bank of England is not the statutory basis against the Scottish note issue.* The above is on the assumption that it is not against their note issue [which subsequently turned out to be incorrect].

They have no motive for keeping Bank of England notes except against their note issue. They do not want it in England. Do not they circulate in Scotland?
Practically, no.

(CHAIRMAN) *It is against their interest to do so.*

(LORD BRADBURY) *This must be against the note issue.* What do they keep against their deposits?

Their power to issue notes on the strength of these £17 million notes, and their Bank of England balances for the time being. If that is right, it seems to me it is very wrong, and the Scottish banks ought to contribute equally with everybody else towards the upkeep of the monetary system. The resources left by the banks free of interest at the Bank of England I regard as something which is mostly left there to meet the expenses of the centralised monetary system.

(MR MCKENNA) *They have the right of issue.*

(MR LUBBOCK) *The joint stock banks in London who hold Scottish balances are putting part of them into the Bank of England.*

(MR MCKENNA) *Only one-tenth.*

(LORD BRADBURY) *If we are going to say anything particular about the Scottish banks in the Report, we ought to have further evidence on the point.* Clearly.

(MR MCKENNA) *It is very complicated with their right of note issue.*

(LORD BRADBURY) *It is very complicated indeed.*

(MR LUBBOCK) *When we get the new figures, it will be perfectly clear.*

(PROFESSOR GREGORY) *Mr Keynes is only re-echoing a point which was made some years ago by the Bank of England to the Scottish banks, who expected the Bank of England to act as their central bank and give nothing in return.* It looks to me as if there is a real grievance there. The Bank of England ought to be getting so many millions without interest as is fitting to enable them to manage the monetary system of the country and to provide facilities to the banks for disposing of their bills suddenly, and so forth. The position is that the bulk of the profits of the note issue are considered to be the perquisite of the Treasury. The revenues which the central bank has to have in order to be in a strong position are provided by the deposits which are put up by the member banks. What I am suggesting is very much like the American system, where their legal reserve consists solely of reserves at their Federal Reserve Banks. The cash in their tills is no part of their legal reserve. The actual reserve resulting from the legal ratios is a complicated one. It works out almost at the figure I am suggesting. That is about 7 per cent. On the average the member banks keep 7 per cent with the Federal Reserve Bank. That is their contribution towards the strength of the central organ. That is spread unequally as between the country banks and the banks in the large centres, because the country banks have to keep more cash. In America the banks in the large centres keep about 2 per cent in cash for their tills, and the country banks keep about 5 per cent. As an offset to that, the country banks have to keep less with the Federal Reserve Bank, and the banks in other centres have to keep more. In the United States this reserve, although it is calculated according to a complicated formula, is a statutory obligation. For reasons which will appear later, I should like to see 7 per cent made a statutory obligation here, but so far as the present part of my argument is concerned, it would be just as good if the banks would agree to keep a daily average balance of 7 per cent, so that I do not think the point I am raising now brings out in any acute form the question of the statutory obligation.

(MR LUBBOCK) *Which we want to avoid, if possible.* I hear you say so, but I do not know why.

I will not argue it now. At any rate, I think that that is expedient, whether carried out by statute or by agreement. There ought to be no difficulty in getting it by agreement, if it was thought desirable to get the whole of our desired margin for the Bank of England without touching the fiduciary issue; but I point out that, if my proposal about the Scottish banks was accepted, it might even allow us to decrease the fiduciary issue. If this proposal was carried out up to the hilt, it would reduce the locked-up gold to something not more than 50 millions, and that seems lower than I personally regard as necessary. I would be prepared to see more than 50 millions locked up.

(CHAIRMAN) *I should have thought that the public view would be this was merely a dodge to increase the fiduciary issue. It would be seen through very quickly.* It is rather an *impasse.* If you think that 110 millions to 130 millions ought to be locked up, then lock it up. If you do not think so, then it seems to me that it is illogical, first of all, to object to alter[ing] the historical system, because people have a feeling for that historical system, and then to object to finding a way out which enables you to retain the historical system. It means you can do nothing on merits.

(MR BRAND) *It all comes down to how much gold you ought to lock up.* Yes. It is strange to want to lock up 100 millions to 120 millions, and it is frightfully bad international practice in present conditions.

(LORD BRADBURY) *It turns on the question of what is the shrinkage in the note issue.* That has nothing whatever to do with it.

(MR LUBBOCK) *Because the note issue from the point of view of the public is far more than is necessary at the moment.* The note issue cannot be encashed for gold, so that there is no relation in point of risk, nor is there any relation in point of theory.

(LORD BRADBURY) *Supposing any catastrophe fell upon the world, and your internal circulation became redundant, and the outside amount required in notes was less than your fiduciary issue, what then?* It would not matter in the least.

What would happen then? The whole of your fiduciary issue would be in your reserve.

(MR MCKENNA) *Your reserve would go up.*

(MR LUBBOCK) *The Bank of England would ask the Treasury to reduce the fiduciary issue.*

(MR MCKENNA) *Thank you.* If the reserve included part of the fiduciary issue, it would not matter. I do not think there is any connection between the note circulation and the Bank's stock of gold.

(LORD BRADBURY) *The fiduciary notes coming in would increase the reserve.* It would mean that more and more gold would go into the Banking Department, but the gold would not necessarily be parted with.

(MR MCKENNA) *As the circulation goes down, the reserve goes up.*

(MR LUBBOCK) *You will see that at Christmas the reserve will go down.*

(MR MCKENNA) *The circulation is down 2, and the gold is down 1.*

(LORD BRADBURY) *Supposing the fiduciary issue is 300 millions, and the circulation 250 millions, what happens to the remaining 50 millions of fiduciary notes which are not in circulation?*

(MR LUBBOCK) *It goes into the Banking reserve.* The Bank of England's

Banking Department reserve would be greater than its gold.

(MR MCKENNA) *By 50 millions.*

(MR BRAND) *Then it may legally export its gold.* It would have free gold to the whole extent. It always has free gold to the extent of its reserves, and no more.

(PROFESSOR GREGORY) *Surely, one important thing to be considered is this. You would have in circulation notes from the fiduciary circulation. If the circulation movement is actually active, the circulation in those conditions would become more fiduciary, and the whole of the notes would be concentrated in the Banking Department of the Bank of England.*

(LORD BRADBURY) *I am referring to a situation when the actual circulation is less than the fiduciary issue.* It does not matter; you eventually transfer to the Banking Department more notes than is equal to the quantity of gold.

(MR MCKENNA) *That is all.* In theory you can go on exporting gold from the Issue Department until the reserve disappears.

(MR BRAND) *If the fiduciary issue was reduced to 50 millions, the whole gold of the Bank of England might be available for export.*

(MR MCKENNA) *And more than the whole gold; mathematically, when the minus quantity is reached, the amount of gold that the Bank of England can export is not equal to its reserve—its reserve is greater.* I want to come back to the point that this is a mere subterfuge. I do not think it is. I do not think that the world in general realises that the so-called active circulation of notes is not really an active circulation of notes.

(MR LUBBOCK) *It does not.* Those people who think there is any connection between the note issue and gold ought to be content with holding less gold against the note issue when they find that the active circulation is not as much as they had thought it was.

(MR BRAND) *I thought you started by saying that the Bank only should vary its gold between 100 millions and 150 millions.* Gold and foreign resources, but I do not think when their aggregate is down to 100 millions the reserves ought to be down to nothing. Supposing its reserve was down to 25 or 30 millions, I should be quite happy. I should not mind locking up 70 to 75 millions of gold, so that this would enable some reduction of the fiduciary issue, if my proposal was carried through up to the hilt.

(MR LUBBOCK) *Or not.* Or you could just leave the fiduciary issue as it is. *If the joint stock banks pay in 50 millions, increasing the Bank reserves to 100 millions, it does not necessarily follow that the Bank of England is letting gold go.* I do not say it should, but it could.

It would be given a discretion. It would increase our international security and credit if it was seen that our active note issue is not really as great as is made out, so that we are able without any change in our fiduciary issue to have a much larger amount of free gold than has been supposed.

(MR BRAND) *Except that the people abroad look rather at the amount of gold you have—they have got used to that way of looking at it.* Our amount of gold of 160 millions is fairly substantial.

(MR LUBBOCK) *That is one of the questions we have to talk about, whether there is that 500 millions of foreign money in London. I do not think there is.* I should like to add to it by foreign resources. I should like to see that 160 to 170 millions more like 200 millions as a normal figure, but it would be a disastrous example, I think, at the present time—circumstances might change and we might want to absorb gold, because of gold being more abundant—to try and increase our gold to 200 millions. I should leave it entirely at the discretion of the Bank of England as to the proportion it held between gold and foreign balances. One of the advantages of this system would be not only that the Bank could afford to hold less gold, when gold was scarce, but it would be in a position to sterilise gold to a certain extent at times when that was necessary.

(CHAIRMAN) *One appreciates that we should be pioneers in the financial progress of the world by seeing that we do not do things which have been historically regarded hitherto as occasions of difficulty.* It is hardly as much as that, because the Bank of France has done this on a much larger scale than I am suggesting. The Bank of Italy and the Reichsbank are doing it today on a scale comparable with that I am suggesting. We are in a weaker position for arguing for the continuance of those practices which are in a slightly precarious state at the present moment, if we do not ourselves pursue those practices. We are saying that it would be a dreadful thing if the three banks I have mentioned were to increase their gold and diminish their foreign balances. We are arguing internationally that they should maintain their foreign balances at the present figure, while we are ourselves pursuing the other policy which we say is not right.

(MR MCKENNA) *By statute the Federal Reserve Bank are compelled to hold more reserve than I suggest is necessary. I worked it out some years ago, and it worked out at about 9 per cent.* I think it is 7 per cent now.

It is a very difficult calculation. I am talking about the central bank in New York. It may be 7 per cent today. The proportion is falling owing to the increase of time deposits.

(MR BRAND) *The figure I have seen is just over 7 per cent.*

(MR MCKENNA) *I took it a year ago, and it was about 9 then.*

(PROFESSOR GREGORY) *On demand deposits it is 13 per cent in New York.* I am averaging for the whole country.

I agree it is about 7 per cent if you include demand deposits as well.

(MR MCKENNA) *You propose 7½ per cent. It is comparable to the American statutory provisions.* Yes. This is offering a bridge, if it is of importance not to touch the fiduciary issue and yet we are prepared to agree that we might have rather more of our gold freely available.

(CHAIRMAN) *Whatever be the mechanism which enables this elasticity to be achieved and the greater amount of gold to be paid out, the result in the end is, the gold stocks would be reduced.*

(MR BRAND) *No, there would be power to reduce them at times, and to increase them at other times. It only makes them free. It only makes you able to use them.*

(CHAIRMAN) *I presume the power to use them would be intended to be exercised at times.* At times.

(MR MCKENNA) *Not quite. The position today under the hard and fast system under which we are ruled is such that, although we have 160 millions of gold, we could not export anything more than a wholly insufficient amount to meet possible demands of foreign depositors.*

(MR LUBBOCK) *Without application to the Treasury. You must qualify it in that way.*

(MR MCKENNA) *I qualify it always with that, but as the system stands today, under Mr Keynes's proposal, they would be able to export sufficient gold.*

(CHAIRMAN) *A great benefit would be that there would be a substantial outflow of gold facilitated by this expedient.*

(MR MCKENNA) *But it would be a permissible outflow. It would maintain the joint stock banks' credit with their customers.*

(CHAIRMAN) *But are the other nations interested in whether it is a permissible outflow? They are not concerned with our domestic economy. They look simply at the quantity of gold we have, and the amount we have allowed to go, and they do not care a bit whether it is a permissible outflow or not.*

(MR MCKENNA) *We are not proposing to alter the total. If more gold were demanded, the Bank of England would take steps in every case to increase its quantity.*

(MR LUBBOCK) *The Bank of England's behaviour might not vary in the slightest degree, whether the reserve was increased by 50 millions or not.* It might or might not. The object would be to give it more power to vary. This is based upon it being desirable for the Bank of England to allow larger variations in its liquid assets, but that would be temporary.

(CHAIRMAN) *Would the public of the world be in the least interested with the circumstances of how you came to allow more out?* The tendency of the opinion of the world is always to be perfectly satisfied with the existing situation, and always to be upset by any change. I do not know whether that is completely true or not, but there is a certain amount of truth in it. I fancy that the disturbance to opinion only lasts a week or two. It is the intrinsic position which really matters. It in fact increases our strength if we can without any fuss export 60 millions of gold instead of 30 millions of gold, and any rational foreign banker will not take long to discern that. What the financial journalists may write about it for a week is a point I should find it hard to predict.

(MR BEVIN) *Will this give us greater elasticity in a period like we had up to 1929, which produced largely the present slump?*

(MR MCKENNA) *I think it would create greater elasticity, because your elasticity was sufficient in 1929 to enable the Bank of England to meet the demands upon it without going to the Treasury, though they were on the brink of going to the Treasury. Had the 1929 position been a little accentuated, the Bank of England would have been forced to go to the Treasury.*

(MR LUBBOCK) *That is a matter of opinion.*

(MR MCKENNA) *I think that is a true state of the position, and it is entirely undesirable.*

(MR TULLOCH) *This is going to help our internal situation.*

(MR BEVIN) *That is what I want.* That is my object.

(MR TULLOCH) *It would prevent the necessity of sometimes raising the Bank rate.* That is the whole point.

(MR TULLOCH) *The larger the outflow of gold might be, [the more] it might sometimes affect the situation abroad that you want to affect.*

(MR LUBBOCK) *We hope it may some day.* It would also obviate nervousness in the market, because the market is very often nervous when in fact nothing happens.

(LORD BRADBURY) *Is not this the position, putting it in a nutshell? There are certain conditions in which the outflow of gold will clear itself, thus enabling the Bank of England to envisage conditions abroad and take the traditional remedial measures.* That is right.

Taking temporary measures by the export of gold, which would come back when the pendulum swung back. Yes.

You get more elasticity to meet these diversions of gold that are not due to the deeper causes which require different measures. That is the point. That is the point.

(MR BRAND) *The view of foreign nations would depend on whether, when you took remedial measures, the proper results followed—whether you did get the gold back, for instance.* You always would.

(MR MCKENNA) *You can always force the gold back.*

(MR TULLOCH) *It would have a tremendous psychological effect.*

(MR LUBBOCK) *This has all been very practical.*

(CHAIRMAN) *I think it has been extraordinarily valuable and interesting. The whole question is whether inside our existing system we can make practical suggestions without upsetting the international apple-cart.*

(Adjourned till tomorrow at 4.30)

COMMITTEE ON FINANCE AND INDUSTRY

Friday 28 November 1930

Present:

The Rt Hon. Lord Macmillan (*Chairman*)

The Rt Hon. Lord Bradbury, G.C.B.	The Rt Hon. Reginald McKenna
The Hon. R. H. Brand, C.M.G.	Sir Walter Raine
Professor T. E. Gregory, D.SC.	Mr J. Frater Taylor
Mr J. M. Keynes, C.B.	Mr A. A. G. Tulloch
Mr Lennox B. Lee	Mr G. Ismay (*Secretary*)
Mr Cecil Lubbock	

Sir Frederick Leith-Ross, K.C.M.G., C.B.

(MR KEYNES) I need not add more with reference to what I was saying yesterday than just to repeat that we have here a possibility of diminishing what is called the active note circulation and, therefore, making a large transfer from the Issue Department to the Banking Department of the Bank of England, and, without changing the facts, present them in a much more favourable guise. If it is desired that the Bank of England should have more elbow room this might be a satisfactory way of giving them that without interfering with any historic tradition.

My next class of proposals has to deal with the problem of a technique having a comparatively large effect on the foreign position and a small effect on the home position. I mentioned yesterday that there is a certain automatic regulator which prevents every breath of wind from causing a movement of gold, even if the bill rate remains unchanged. That is the function of the difference between spot and forward exchange. As every movement of the spot exchange tends to affect this difference every movement of the spot exchange affects the volume of short-term arbitrage loans. That happens to work in the right direction because the nearer the spot exchange moves towards the gold export point the more attractive does London become as a recipient of such loans and *vice versa*. My suggestion is that the Bank should take more deliberate advantage of this feature of the market with the object of relying more on changes in the difference between spot and forward exchange, and less on changes in the bill rate itself for controlling movements of the international short-term loan funds. The advantage would be that there would be less unintentional interference with the domestic credit situation when the object of the Bank was not to bring about a fundamental change in the situation, but merely to tempt a little more of the international short-term loan funds to London. They could tempt them here by making the relation between spot and forward exchange more attractive instead of by raising the bill rate and leaving it to the market. I have two suggestions, one of which would only be a change of practice, the other of which would be a change of law, but they are not dependent upon one another and I am not confident how much advantage there would be in the change of practice. I think the change of law would in the long run be helpful. In regard to the change of practice I think it might be argued that the same result would be achieved by my previous proposal that the Bank of England should have a larger fund of foreign balances and be more willing to see them fluctuate.

The change of practice which I suggest. For what it is worth is, that the Bank of England should itself enter the forward exchange market and, when it wished to strengthen the spot rate, offer forward dollars at an attractive rate relatively to the spot rate. I can illustrate it by a particular case. Supposing that spot dollars are 4.86 and the Bank offers forward dollars at 4.872, that is just as effective in drawing American funds to London as would be a rise of a full one per cent in the market rate of discount for three months bills. That would effect a much larger difference between the spot and forward exchange than ordinarily exists in the market. It would be a difference of more than one cent. One quarter per cent is at present a high rate.

(MR MCKENNA) *It might be the other way?* It might be the other way.

(MR BRAND) *One cent for three months?* It would be a little more than one cent for three months. I am taking an extreme instance for the sake of arithmetical calculation. There is plenty of room for a difference of that amount within the existing gold points. The figure of 4.86 is appreciably above the export point and the figure of 4.872 is below the import point. That would be as effective as raising bill rate one per cent in attracting American money, whereas the difference of one cent between spot and forward would have practically no reaction on the internal position. The change of one per cent in bill rate could only be brought about by a change in Bank rate and a sharp readjustment of the terms of domestic credit. Therefore, it is worth considering whether when the only reason for altering the Bank rate is to attract short-term foreign money it could not be done by manipulating the forward exchange.

(MR LUBBOCK) *Assuming we have a large stock of dollars?* I had assumed that. If the Bank held no stock of dollars it would be in the nature of speculation on its part, but if the Bank normally held a stock of dollars it could use this method with perfect safety, intending probably to cover itself in three months and, therefore, in a position to retain its stock. If no convenient opportunity of covering itself occurred in the course of three months, if it did not cover itself, it would then deliver out of its stock of dollars against its purchase of sterling and sale of dollars. It is essentially a temporary expedient and it might involve the Bank in an exchange loss. The Bank would have to shoulder a responsibility which, if Bank rate were raised, would fall on other shoulders. If the spot rate at the end of three months were the same as it was at the beginning, the Bank would in effect have borne the expense of borrowing American funds at one per cent above the domestic short-term rate. That is to say, instead of raising the domestic short-term rate one per cent for everybody and some part of that increase being used to remunerate the Americans for their short-term money, the Bank of England would in practice be borrowing American funds at one per cent above the short-term domestic rate and be able by that means not to alter the domestic rate. It would involve it in expense, just as holding gold involves it in expense, and many other market operations which it performs because it considers them in the general interest. Though clearly it is a non-commercial proposition, it would not be anything unfamiliar for the Bank to do an operation of this kind, which was non-economic from the purely financial point of view. Of course, in speaking of one per cent I am taking a very extreme case for the sake of arithmetical simplicity. As I say, the actual differences in the market I do not think, have ever, in recent times, been as large as that. They fluctuate very frequently. When I was writing these notes I think the difference was one-eighth cent, and I think today it is less than that.

(MR BRAND) *For three months?* For three months.

(MR LUBBOCK) *Money rates are pretty level in both centres?* Yes, one-eighth cent, which is quite a common difference, is equivalent to an increase in the bill rate of between one-sixteenth and one-eighth per cent per annum. When I say one-eighth cent I mean the American cent, and when I am talking about the difference in bill rate I mean one per cent per annum.

(SIR WALTER RAINE) *How high would the Bank rate have to be before you took steps like that?* The actual situation today gives the American lender one-eighth cent per annum in addition to what he gets from the London bill. Assuming that he is buying a London bill at $2\frac{1}{8}$ and is at the same time entering into a forward transaction, he is making $2\frac{1}{4}$. In the same way if the Bank of England were prepared to quote him a more favourable rate, if they were prepared to quote him, say, a quarter cent instead of one-eighth cent he would then be making $2\frac{3}{8}$ per cent altogether and it would be as effective in moving international funds as a manipulation of internal credit would be which had the effect of increasing the domestic bill rate by a quarter per cent.

(CHAIRMAN) *It would localise this operation in the Bank of England?* But it would not prevent other people from doing it.

(SIR WALTER RAINE) *At what would the Bank rate have to be before you started that operation?* Whatever is the bill rate. At the moment Bank rate is rather more divorced from the bill rate than usual. Whatever the bill rate is, this would have the effect of making it a quarter per cent better for the American than it looked.

You mean this is an emergency measure to be undertaken now and again if the rates had to go up because of the domestic situation? It would be an alternative. It would be for the Bank to decide which of the alternatives they preferred.

(CHAIRMAN) *It may be that occasions will arise when the Bank wants to get the effect of the raising of the Bank rate but it may be inexpedient to do that for various reasons. Is it expedient to resort to other methods? In certain classes of circumstance where they do not want to bring about a permanent effect at home it might be wise to resort to this alternative, which would put on one market the whole shock of the change. 'The Bank's operations are sometimes directed to short-term matters, sometimes to long-term matters.' This would possibly enable them to avoid jolts from time to time.* I think one could only tell from experience how useful it would be and how far it was a profitable development. It may be that experience would show that it was not very valuable. But I think it would be worth trying. The Bank could always produce the same result by selling dollar balances spot, and the occasions when it was worth while entering into forward transactions instead of supporting spot exchange might be rare, but I think this is one of the things that we might have in our armoury.

We might state in our Report that we have considered other alternatives to raising the Bank rate. I do not know that we could actually recommend resort to that expedient. We could point out that it existed. Would that be advisable? I think it would.

(MR BRAND) *Have you any estimate of the amount of forward contracts the Bank might have to enter into? It might be rather large.* It might.

(MR FRATER TAYLOR) *Might it be, in effect, a case of asking the American banks to help our internal situation?* It would be an inducement.

(MR LUBBOCK) *It would offer them an inducement to put money here.*

(PROFESSOR GREGORY) *Would it not mean, supposing the Bank were underselling the forward market, that it would have to take on a very heavy liability. If you are offering forward dollars higher than the market is doing, you get all the market concentrated on you.* The market has some transactions which it has to do for its own sake, and for these it would then have to come to the Bank of England rate. Some people who have to sell forward dollars for their own reasons, not as an arbitrage transaction, would then have to come to the Bank of England rate. How great the scale of operations would have to be, I do not know. I do not think it would matter very much, because it would not endanger the situation as a whole; just as the counter transaction now falls into the hands of the market so it would then fall into the hands of the Bank of England. It would not affect the exchange position to a greater extent than it was attracting additional funds; apart from this it would merely be putting into the Bank business which now goes through other channels. It means borrowing American funds at a price above the bill rate, or *vice versa*, and putting the expense of that on the Bank. There was a moment not long ago when it would have been possible, I think, to have diverted the French gold drain from this country to America by transactions of this kind—perhaps on not a very important scale—in fact a little gold did go from America. It was rather touch and go a few months ago whether the French gold drain fell on the London market or on the New York market. If we had thought that for various reasons we should have liked to have seen more from the New York market, some transaction on those lines might have effected it. This is not so much a matter of theory as to how it would work out in practice; yet it is the sort of thing on which hardly anybody is an expert, so it is extremely difficult to get competent criticism.

My second point—which would need legislation—is for the widening of the gold points, a suggestion which I have mentioned in the Committee once or twice without entering into the details. I have developed this in detail in my book, Vol.ii Page 319 and following [*JMK*, Vol. VI, p. 285 and following]. I think I can make the point of this clear by this illustration: If the gold points were identical the automatic corrective which I have talked about more than once could not operate, and it would be necessary to have very frequent changes of the market rate of discount in order to prevent constant movements of gold. If the gold points were wider apart than they are there would be increased scope both for the automatic corrective and also for the deliberate use of the same feature by the Bank of England in the way we have just been discussing. On the other hand, if they were narrower, of course there would be less scope for it. Therefore I think that the appropriate gap between the gold points ought to be a matter of scientific determination. The size of gap is an historic survival—

(MR MCKENNA) *No, it is the cost*. It is made up partly of the cost, which depends on geographical propinquity, and partly upon the Bank of England's buying and selling prices for gold, which are an historic survival; it was originally based on the cost of minting, or something of that kind. It is no longer that.

It was freight insurance, handling, and loss of interest. That part of it which depends on the difference between the Bank of England buying and selling price is independent of what pair of countries you have to consider. The element of cost, on the other hand, depends upon geographical propinquity, so it is very much narrower between Paris and London than it is between London and New York. Taking everything into account, the gap between the gold points of London and Paris is about half per cent, between London and New York about three-quarters per cent. That means that when Paris wants gold the gold will come from London, unless the dollar-sterling exchange is very much in our favour. It is a tremendous bias in favour of taking it from

London. If we try and force up the sterling rate sufficiently to make the gold come from New York, we shall tend to lose short-term loan funds by the automatic corrective operating against us. So if the geographical relationships had happened to be reversed, everything else being the same, a great deal more of the Parisian gold drain would have fallen on New York, and a great deal less on London. If a larger amount of the difference depended on the Bank's buying and selling price and less on geographical propinquity the difference would be more nearly the same for each pair of countries. In my book I make the suggestion that as part of the ideal currency system of the future all countries should agree to have a wider gap between their buying and selling prices, and that they should concentrate their transactions on the B.I.S.; that is to say, every country being prepared to exchange its money either way for a balance at the B.I.S., the difference between their buying and selling prices being of the order of two per cent, as compared with the difference of $\frac{3}{4}$ per cent as between London and New York today. I think if everyone did that one could combine the advantages of an international standard with a much greater degree of domestic autonomy. It would mean that you could have a domestic bill rate which might be materially different from the international bill rate before there was a tendency for gold to move. That is to say, provided it was a short-period situation. It would not make any difference to the long-term situation.

(MR LUBBOCK) *You cannot alter our selling rate.* No, I agree. Nor do I think that it would be possible for us to have such a big change as 2 per cent. If it were done by us alone there is a slight risk of weakening ourselves as an international depository, but I think we could move a little in that direction if the change took the form not of reducing the mean gold value of sterling but of increasing it. In that case I do not see why it should do appreciable harm to our credit. My suggestion is that the Bank's selling price for gold should remain unchanged, but that its legal buying price should be reduced by, say, 3d. per ounce. equal to ·33 per cent—£3.17s.9d. to £3.17s.6d. That would have the effect of making the maximum spread between London and Paris the same as the present maximum spread between London and New York, and, I should say, about the same as between Paris and New York; so it would not make us any less attractive as a depository for bank funds.

(MR BRAND) *But it would increase the spread between London and New York?* It would increase that.

So that, so far as France is concerned, relatively we would be in the same position as now, would we not? At present we have a slight advantage over New York in that for a Parisian depositor the maximum fluctuation is less in London than in New York. At the same time we could give them back a certain amount by altering our arrangement about refined and standard gold.

It would be much better, if the Bank of England wants to have a wider spread, to do it as I suggest. The device of offering standard gold is an empirical way of doing it. It is much better not to do it that way but by altering the legal price. I would like to do that not by reducing the value of sterling but by increasing it. That means we should get no benefit, in the present stringency, from what I am proposing; it would merely mean that the next time the financial international position is in our favour we should let our exchange rise higher in terms of dollars before we began buying gold, and that would give us a wider margin for the subsequent reaction. By letting our exchange go up before we took more gold we should then have a wider spread for the automatic corrective to work in.

(MR LUBBOCK) *Has that any advantage, except to save the labour of moving gold?* Yes, the difference between spot and forward exchange could be equivalent to a larger margin in the rate of interest.

(MR BRAND) *It would make it more speculative to raise money in London.* Yes. It would make it as speculative for a Frenchman to put it in London as it is now for him to put it in New York. That would mean that the domestic interference arising from our international banking business would be minimised; we should be more seldom forced to alter the domestic bill rate in order to deal with temporary fluctuations.

(MR LUBBOCK) *Should we ever get gold?* Oh! yes; if the position is in our favour, our exchange will go to the necessary points.

But if we only give 77s.6d. for it, it would take gold a little longer to come. A little longer; not much. I would give the Bank its present power of buying a little above the legal buying price if the domestic situation warranted it.

No gold would start from the United States hoping it would get here at 77s.8d. In pre-War days it was habitual for the Bank of England to vary its buying price, and nobody ever knew what they would get until it came to the bullion market. This would only be increasing slightly the amount of possible variation.

(MR FRATER TAYLOR) *Could France and the United States nullify that by doing the same thing?* I wish they would. The maximum spread is reached by adding up the charges on both sides. I wish every country would make a two per cent difference.

(CHAIRMAN) *We could not do it alone?* I do not think we could go to that difference alone. It would be making our spread much wider than the New York spread. In the past central banks have always been wanting to have a wider spread, and have found all sorts of irregular ways of achieving it. The Bank of France did this before the War, and I dare say would do so again, by making it uncertain whether they would deliver you five franc pieces or gold coin. It was habitual in the past for certain central banks to pay out, when they did not want to let gold go, in coin that was not full weight—which again increased the spread. One could make quite a long list of ways, subterfuges, by which central banks have tried from time to time to satisfy the felt need for a wider spread. Sometimes it has been moral influence. Then again, there has been the spurious doctrine of bringing the gold points together. It has been argued that every movement of gold is bad, and yet that the gold points should be as close as possible. As a matter of fact, if the gold points were identical, international banking in the present form would be almost impossible; it would be making the movements of funds between countries as easy as it is between one clearing bank and another, without having a common reserve, and that would create an impossible situation.

I think that this proposal is a point of detail. It would not give us any immediate advantage, but I think we should have a more scientific system if we considered just how big the difference between the gold points ought to be, and if we were to move in the direction of widening them as much as our international credit allowed, and in particular if we were to use our influence for a general widening as time goes on.

(LORD BRADBURY) *Have you any scientific criterion of what the proper spread is?* Yes. You can work out how much the difference between spot and forward exchange is capable of being, relatively to changes in your Bank rate so that you can find out what is the smallest amount, so to speak, which is any good. Something which at its maximum was only equivalent to a change of $\frac{1}{16}$ per cent in the bill rate is very little good. On the other hand, anybody can form a rough estimate of what difference really interferes with long-term investment. If you had a difference of 5 per cent or 10 per cent that would clearly be a serious factor in long-term investment. I should say that a difference of 2 per cent would not be a serious factor in long-term investment and at the same time it allows for a very considerable variation in short-term rates.

(MR BRAND) *It would be a serious factor in making all international trade more speculative; the exporter would not know what he got back.* He is dealing on the forward exchange and you could combine this with the Bank of England entering the forward exchange market. If the Bank thought the forward exchange rates were too wide it could make them narrower. In practice this has no effect on trade. It does not have any effect in the American case. The gap between them and Europe is three-quarters per cent, which is what I am proposing for ourselves.

I am speaking of 5 per cent or 10 per cent. I agree if it were 5 or 10 per cent that would be a really big factor for the trader. He would not be able to cover himself. This is how I arrived at a figure of the order of 2 as being as much as you could have without bringing in other disadvantageous features. I find it extremely difficult to see quite clearly the exact effect of these measures. I do not believe anybody could. It is not a purely theoretical question. It depends a good deal on the psychology of the market and requires the sort of experience of arbitrage transactions, which is very rare, in people who take the wider view of the monetary position. This sort of transaction is done in practice by a highly specialised person who knows nothing of anything else.

Absolutely. I have never seen the opposite. This is an idea I have had in my head for many years. I have often tried to discuss it. The person who is not an arbitrage expert is in no better position than myself, and the person who is an arbitrage expert is incapable of seeing the point of the whole thing. He cannot tell you anything useful. It is a highly specialised gift which largely consists, I believe, of the power to do mental arithmetic almost instantaneously. You have to calculate so quickly that you cannot do the job if you have to sit down and work it out. You have to do it instantaneously and that power seems to be inconsistent with the possession of any other power!

(CHAIRMAN) *The calculating boy!*

(MR BRAND) *They are like jobbers; if they look ahead they will make mistakes.*

(CHAIRMAN) *Yes.* They have to look at the covering of the transaction just so, and only for the next moment. Thus this is something of which it is extremely difficult to estimate the practical value.

The third class of measures relates to the relations between the Bank of England and the joint stock banks. The evidence we have received has impressed me very strongly as to the lack of continuous and organised co-operation between the Bank of England and the joint stock banks. There seems to me to be too much dependence upon the operation of what one might call natural forces instead of getting things done on purpose, by design. The Bank of England does something or other, believing it will lead in the end to a certain result. Then it has to work itself out, with all its necessary by-products, when you might have produced the same result by indicating to the joint stock banks what was desired to occur. The worst of the natural force is that while the desired result may come about in due course, it may only come about as a by-product of other consequences which are not amongst the desired results. I think that the existing method, as I gathered from Sir Ernest Harvey's evidence, of regulating the bill rate in order to influence the international short-term loan market will continue to be a necessary expedient, whatever other devices we also employ. I gather that if the Bank of England feels that in the interest of the stability of the exchange the bill rate should be a quarter per cent higher than it is, it contracts credit until it sees the rate a quarter per cent higher, but that will only come about through a complicated process that has its reactions on all kinds of things; because if the basis of credit is contracted, since the joint stock banks divide their resources between different uses in certain proportions, the amount of money that they use in all the uses is contracted. It does not necessarily all come off bills and all have its effect on the bill market. The Committee will remember that when I was talking about the double action of the Bank rate method as a means of restoring equilibrium, its quick influence on the international short-term market, its slow influence on income levels and costs, working by means of business depression and unemployment, I emphasised how often it might be necessary to influence the international short-term loan market, and even the long-term market, when there was no desire to create unemployment. The whole use of Bank rate as a means of deliberately creating unemployment is, of course, an extraordinarily clumsy device, which we only use because in our existing society, curiously, we have no other way. If something happens to international prices and income levels and costs abroad, so that the level abroad is low relatively to the level in this country, the only way we have of restoring equilibrium is for the Bank of England to curtail credit, for the joint stock banks to pass on that curtailment to industry, for employers, after they have suffered losses as long as they feel inclined to, to throw their men out of work, and for the men, when they have been out of work as long as they feel inclined, to accept a reduction of wages. It is an extraordinary clumsy way of achieving the result, and it is a road by which you may never reach your destination, and if you do reach your destination you will only do so after a terrible amount of time, during which great harm may be done. I do not think we realise what a very peculiar way it is of bringing about the result, yet in practice it is the only way we have got, and the danger is that the Bank of England, being kindhearted, when it sees the first results of its action will lose heart, and try and mitigate the situation and relax the position again, and if a fundamental adjustment really were necessary this would only be prolonging the agony.

(MR LUBBOCK) *Might it not adjust a short-term position without having all these unfavourable consequences?* It may not get all of them because there will not have been time. It will have an incipient effect in this direction; it will have the same initial effect as it would if it was actually persisted in long enough to have the ultimate effect. Owing to the fact that business men do not discharge workers as soon as they begin to feel the loss, and that workers will not accept lower wages immediately they are out of employment, it might happen that if it was a short-period adjustment the reverse movement would come in time. I am not talking about the short period but where the Bank of England feel that a long-period adjustment is required, which is bound to be the case from time to time if the international value of money is unstable. In that case seeing that the position is adverse to us, it takes action for reasons which are not of a merely temporary character.

The Bank of England puts up Bank rate and contracts credit, it sees unemployment increase from one million to one and a half million; a great outcry arises; the Bank of England hates to see unemployment rising, it is tempted to reduce Bank rate again and so continues to keep us out of any true equilibrium. Whereas what the Governor of the Bank of England ought to be saying to himself is, that we cannot hope to get wages down until unemployment is up to (say) three or four million: What curtailment of credit, what level of Bank rate, is necessary to bring that about? and then see it through. That would be the logical way of using the existing system, but, of course, it would be very difficult in practice.

We are using a weapon which we have not the heart to use effectively, and as a result we get the worst of all worlds. When the Bank of England thinks a long period readjustment is necessary and puts up Bank rate and sees unemployment as the result, it ought to rejoice, because at any rate the first step towards the fundamental readjustment has been secured.

Does the Bank of England always curtail credit when it raises Bank rate? Not always, but often, and if its purpose is to achieve fundamental readjustment it does not help matters unless it does curtail credit. Occasions for this may arise, and I am blessed if I see what other weapon we have in our present system.

This is a little way from our present argument. I think the conclusion to draw from it is, that our present system is incompatible with large changes in the value of money in an upward direction. It is not possible for the Bank of England to carry out a policy of producing enough unemployment to bring down wages, yet there is no other way of meeting large changes in the value of money in an upward direction. Therefore, the correct conclusion is, not so much that the Bank of England ought to do what I have just suggested, but that we have got a system which simply does not work when there are large changes in the value of money in an upward direction. We must therefore avoid large changes of money in an upward direction or have quite a different system, which would involve some departure from individualistic capitalism. In fact, I venture to prophesy that if the sort of thing that has been going on in the last two or three years is to continue indefinitely, this individualistic capitalism will be superseded by some far-reaching socialistic system, because we have no instrument to bring about the necessary readjustment. We could try various subterfuges, but I doubt whether those subterfuges would be effective, or sufficiently effective if the instability in the value of money were to continue long enough.

The instrument we use for curing short-period adjustments also has an incipient tendency in this somewhat maleficient direction, even when this result is not desired at all, when there is no occasion for any long-period adjustment of incomes. It is obvious that, apart from wanting to produce a change in wages, there are all sorts of occasions for regulation of the international short-term loan market, and I think that even if the Bank of England wish to use the other methods which I have been mentioning, it will also continue to use the bill rate method.

Therefore, I come to the question—when, in addition to the other expedients I have mentioned, it is necessary to use bill rate as a means of regulating the international situation, could not that be done by some other method, rather than by a curtailment of credit? I should have thought that nothing was easier than for the Bank of England and for the joint stock banks between them to put the bill rate to whatever was suitable, not of course within very wide limits, but within certain limits, without any curtailment of credit. If the Bank of England and the joint stock banks were in one another's confidence, the bill rate could be modified within certain limits, I suggest, without its seriously re-acting on the internal volume of credit. Mr McKenna has told us how, when the Bank of England, wanting to help the internal position, has been prepared to experiment, this time not in decreasing, but in increasing the volume of credit for domestic purposes, the first effect is almost inevitably to weaken the bill market, partly because the joint stock banks need time to find other outlets for increased resources, partly because they always use a certain proportion of any increased resources in the bill market, and partly because of their own ignorance of what the wishes and intentions of the Bank are and as to the durability of the increase of credit. So that they do not care to move new money into the less liquid forms if they are not sure whether the ease of credit is only a matter of two or three weeks. The result is that this friendly experiment of the Bank of England in increasing credit weakens the bill rate, and before it has had time to produce any favourable effects on the internal situation, it affects the exchanges so as to frighten the Bank of England and cause it to retrace its steps. That all seems to me to be rather unnecessary. Would not it be better that the Bank of England and the joint stock banks should act together with a common purpose on such occasions, the Bank of England telling the joint stock banks what it was doing, and getting them to act in accordance with its intentions? It could do this by agreeing with the joint stock banks the rate which they would charge for call loans, and the rate at which the joint stock banks themselves would buy bills. It might mean that the joint stock banks would have to hold more than their usual balances at the Bank of England for a time, but as long as the joint stock banks knew what was forward, and what they had to expect, in due course they could find outlets for it without weakening the bill market. In this way the Stock Exchange and the new issue market and advances to trade could be encouraged or discouraged, or such of them could be encouraged or discouraged as it was desired to affect, without the bill market being affected in the same degree as at present. Perhaps this would be even more useful in a contracting direction than in an expanding direction. It would also mean that the Bank of England could invoke the assistance of the joint stock banks to stiffen the bill market without any curtailment of credit at a time when the Bank of England wanted to stricken the bill rate for International purposes, but did not want to contract the amount of credit for domestic purposes. At present it cannot do one thing without doing the other. In the old days, when we had innumerable banks, it would have been impracticable to get common action, but I should have supposed today, with the five big institutions ruling the roost, it ought to be rather easy to get common effective action for purposes of this sort.

(PROFESSOR GREGORY) *Is not there an agreement already between the joint stock banks as to the level of call rates and the management of call money?*

(MR MCKENNA) *There is an arrangement among the banks that they will not lend below a certain rate.*

(PROFESSOR GREGORY) *In other words, what Mr Keynes is proposing is in some sense a development of the present situation.*

(MR MCKENNA) *Yes, but we do not do it in consultation with the Bank of England.*

(PROFESSOR GREGORY) *But I mean the principle that the bill market shall in some senses be regulated by agreement is in force.* That is new, is not it?

(MR MCKENNA) *The limitation of the rate for call money is comparatively new. There is a minimum rate today, but it is not a point of very great importance. We do not regulate our rate by consultation with the Bank of England, and I am disposed to agree with Mr Keynes that it would be very desirable if we did so.*

(CHAIRMAN) *The first point is that you already have a precedent for concerted action between the joint stock banks.*

(MR MCKENNA) *Yes.*

(CHAIRMAN) *Then they could get into touch with the Bank of England in relation to your concerted action.*

(MR MCKENNA) *Yes. As a matter of fact, when the rate was limited, in the first instance, we did speak to the Governor and told him what we proposed to do, and asked him whether he would have any objection, and he had none. It might with great advantage be carried a great deal further and the rate might be fixed in consultation with the Bank of England.*

(MR LUBBOCK) *It is a very interesting suggestion.*

(MR MCKENNA) *It does affect very much now the rate we lend money at to the market.*

(CHAIRMAN) *What method of consultation do you contemplate?* (MR MCKENNA) *We now meet once in three months.* (MR LUBBOCK) *It is easily done if there is the will and the way.* (MR MCKENNA) *There is not the slightest reason why we should not meet once a week.* That is what I am suggesting. (MR MCKENNA) *Or once fortnightly, or once monthly.* I am suggesting regular routine meetings of that kind.

(PROFESSOR GREGORY) *If you want to keep up your rates to stiffen the short market, all you want is an agreement among the banks to keep the rates up and abstain from buying.*

(MR BRAND) *It is not so easy to keep the call rates up if there is too much money about. If a lot of money is left over at the end of the day, are you going to say you will not take it?* They must be prepared occasionally to lose a small amount of interest.

(MR MCKENNA) *That was the objection to our fixing the new rate when no banks would lend overnight, only at the fixed rate, so that the banks are left with a certain amount of unlent money. We have done that deliberately, because the unlent money draws the interest down ½ per cent and the bill rate could not be maintained.*

(LORD BRADBURY) *With that arrangement the position is much better, otherwise competition would make these over night rates practically nil.*

(MR MCKENNA) *And then that draws down the rate generally. I agree there might be much more organised action in the matter of the bill rate so as to prevent the Bank of England's gold from undue attack.*

(CHAIRMAN) *What Mr McKenna proposes is, on the agenda for these weekly or monthly meetings, this is one of the matters that should figure.* Yes, but it would not be much use unless they were in constant touch. I should like to see the whole attitude between the two authorities changed—that is to say, they should not be on distant terms, but they should be on terms of daily intercourse.

(MR MCKENNA) *It is only fair to say upon that point there has been a very very great change during the last few years. It has to be remembered that historically the Bank of England and the joint stock banks were competing banks, and there was not likely to be very close touch between them, neither wishing to give away its business to the other.*

(CHAIRMAN) *Indeed, until you did amalgamate, it would have been impossible.*

(MR MCKENNA) *I quite agree, but even after amalgamation, we were far more in the position of competing banks than we are today. The Bank of England has restricted its business almost entirely now to public business, and I do not think the element of competition really enters into it today. I recognise the principle on which the Bank of England acts. There is no doubt the conditions for closer action exist today, and the Bank of England has taken considerable steps to bring about a better feeling and closer action. I think the Bank of England, even if it went further, would find on our side that we were entirely willing to meet them.*

(MR BRAND) *Would that keeping up of bill rate affect adversely sometimes the rate for long loans? We want the rate of interest to fall, and if you keep up the bill rate artificially, it may sometimes interfere with that.*

(MR MCKENNA) *I do not know that what we are speaking of now would come into operation then if the rate was anything approximate to the long-term rate—it never does. The long-term rate is perhaps $5\frac{1}{2}$ per cent, or 6 per cent, and the short rate is 2 per cent and $2\frac{1}{8}$ per cent.*

(MR BRAND) *They slop over sometimes.*

(MR MCKENNA) *You might bring the short rate up to 3 per cent or $3\frac{1}{2}$ per cent, without affecting the long-term rate at all. We want the long-term rate to be down and the short-term rate raised.* Yes, at present it is extremely difficult to see how that can be done.

Very difficult. If you expand credit with the intention of bringing down the long-term credit rate, the first result is to bring down the short-term credit rate, and that forces you to retrace your steps. But if the elements in the money market acted together, you could produce results by purposive action which, if you rely upon the working of natural forces, will not come about.

(MR BRAND) *On the other hand, the very unremunerative character of bills now forces people into the long-term market.* Precisely. If the Bank of England were to say: 'We would like the bill rate at $2\frac{1}{2}$ per cent instead of $2\frac{1}{8}$ per cent. We do not want to curtail credit, because we want to see the long-term credit expand', I should think that would have a negligible effect on the long-term rate.

I daresay it would. (MR LUBBOCK) *I think it would.*

(MR MCKENNA) *The short term rate ought to be $2\frac{1}{2}$ per cent to $2\frac{1}{4}$ per cent in relation to the long-term rate at present.* I think this is not the only way in which the Bank of England and the joint stock banks might work together. If there is any sense at all in my way of approaching monetary problems, the more we develop the technique of monetary management with other objectives in view than merely the parity of foreign exchange, the more we shall find the regulation of long-term investment as well as of short-term investment falling within the purview of the monetary authorities, and that will need new weapons. One of the weapons influencing that, I think, will be the deposit rate of interest. I doubt whether there ought to be the same rule-of-thumb relationship between the Bank rate and the deposit rate at present so far as London is concerned as obtains now. The deposit rate of interest ought rather to be fixed between the Bank of England and the joint stock banks according as it is desirable to influence the public to or from non-liquid assets. When the public is too much inclined to go into non-liquid assets, then the deposit rate should be raised to tempt them into the more liquid form of investment. When the public are too reluctant to buy the less liquid assets, an attempt should be made to drive them into them by diminishing the deposit rate. If the deposit rate offered on domestic deposits was to be reduced today both in London and in the Provinces to $\frac{1}{2}$ per cent it would be one of the most useful things that could be done. It is clearly impossible for anyone of the joint stock banks to move in that direction, for competitive reasons, and it would be much easier for the Bank of England to take the initiative when it was desired to make the change on the broad ground of what it was desirable that the public should be doing with their money. It is clearly much better to get the public to move in the desired direction than that by open market operations the Bank of England should have to take up what might be in a sense rather a speculative position themselves. If they can make the public move in the direction they want, that is much better. They can do that by varying the ease and attractiveness of holding liquid funds. I think in future one of the important functions of the banking system will be to vary the volume and attractiveness of liquid funds. One of the ways in which increasing the volume of credit works, is that it offers the public more liquid funds than they want, and thereby drives them out of liquid funds, thus forcing up the price of the less liquid funds.

(CHAIRMAN) *This is all designed to control the direction in which money is finding its outlet.* Yes. I do not believe we shall rest content, as we develop the technique of all this, with concentrating so much as we have done historically on the control of the short-term rate. The most obvious ways of controlling the long-term rate are the deposit rate of interest and the volume of liquid funds which the banking system creates. One of the most hopeful expedients today would be for the principal central banks, without weakening their short-term rate for bills, gradually to saturate their domestic markets with liquid funds, completely satisfying up to the hilt the desire of their public for liquid funds, and thereby cause a certain amount of those funds to spill over into fixed investment. That would be a fundamental remedy, as I see it, for the present situation.

(MR LUBBOCK) *That assumes that good borrowers come forward.* But they will if the public is forcing up the price of existing securities high enough. The price of existing securities depends upon the relative preference of the public for liquid and non-liquid investments, and on the volume of supply available to satisfy their inclination for liquid securities. By altering the rate of interest of liquid securities, and the supply of liquid securities, I believe that the banking system can largely determine the price of non-liquid securities.

(CHAIRMAN) *If you wish to direct money towards long-term securities, the long-term security, after all, is dependent itself upon the existence of profitable enterprise in which money may be used.* Yes, but the more you raise the price of non-liquid assets, the more attractive it is to people to borrow money in order to create more long-term assets.

The ultimate psychological effect is to promote enterprise. Yes, that is what I am trying to arrive at.

(MR BRAND) *Reducing the rate of interest by raising the price.* Yes, one can express it in that way.

(MR FRATER TAYLOR) *You do not necessarily identify long-term security with non-liquid security, do you?* For present purposes to a certain extent they are not the same thing, because you may have the non-liquid asset financed by short borrowing; but as the banking system on the whole sets its face against that, that is not a very large factor in the situation. It is very hard to get a really large volume of long-term investments unless you finance it by non-liquid assets—assets effectually non-liquid. Part of this same technique of varying the relative position of liquid and non-liquid assets in order to counteract the injudicious inclination on the part of the public to go one way or the other, would be open-market operations. One way of achieving the same result would be to throw the onus on the joint stock banks by causing their proportions to fluctuate within certain limits. You see, if the Bank of England wants to expand credit, it could do it equally well by buying securities or by telling the joint stock banks that they could reduce their reserve with the Bank from 7 per cent to 6 per cent, and then leaving the joint stock banks to find an outlet for their funds. I think that second alternative in many ways preferable to open market operations by the Bank of England, because the Bank of England is so limited in the class of securities which it can properly buy. Therefore, it has to influence the market through what may be its most insensitive section. It would be much better, when the Bank of England wants to ease out credit, for the joint stock banks to embark their resources in a variety of assets which are appropriate to their activities by reducing their reserve proportion, than for the Bank of England to do it.

(MR LUBBOCK) *Do you think that the banks would be willing to do that?* I think certainly, if there was a law that 7 per cent was their ratio, and the Bank of England had power to reduce that. For you would not then find the banks keeping idle money in the Bank of England, would you? At the worst they would put it in the same sort of rather dull securities that the Bank of England would have to put it into, but they would only do that if they completely failed to find other outlets of a more profitable kind.

They would have to be prepared to publish their reserves at 9 per cent instead of 10 per cent. Yes. As my proposal of 7 per cent would be a real 7 per cent, and would be increasing their reserves above the present figure, they could reduce it to 6 per cent and be no weaker than they are now.

Not in reality. Similarly, supposing the Bank of England wants to contract the market, at present that has to be done entirely out of the Bank of England's own earning assets. If the Bank of England has to contract, it has to

229

sell earning assets on a scale which may bring its earning assets fatally low; its power is very limited indeed, because, as I shall be shewing later on, the earning assets of the Bank of England are not at any excessive figure. I suggest it would strengthen the Bank of England if it could throw the burden on the joint stock banks by, instead of contracting credit by selling securities, instructing the banks they must raise their proportion from 7 per cent to 8 per cent. The movements within those limits are very large, really, in terms of the volume of credit, and it would be very often sufficient to have a very much smaller change. Therefore, I should like to have a system by which the reserve with the Bank of England and the joint stock banks had to be such a figure between 8 per cent and 6 per cent as the Bank of England prescribed. It could move by decimal points, because in these figures decimal points amount to an extraordinary amount of money. It would be a very delicate instrument. It would not force the Bank, when it was contracting, to be hesitant in doing something that was really required for fear of running its earning assets down. On the other hand, it would not make the Bank fill itself up with securities it did not really want to have when it wished to expand.

(CHAIRMAN) *What is the range of percentage to be between?* Between 8 per cent and 6 per cent is my suggestion. The range between 8 per cent and 6 per cent gives tremendous play in the terms of actual expansion or contraction of credit. 8 per cent is not an excessive reserve for them to keep, and 6 per cent is not an unduly low one. On the point of contraction, the danger I am wanting to avoid arose very acutely in the United States after the boom of 1920. At that time it was thought to be the duty of the Federal Reserve Bank to contract, and they began contracting, and then they got to a point where, if they contracted any more, they would not be able to pay their salaries. If, simultaneously, gold was flowing in, and the Bank of England nevertheless thought it was desirable to contract—and these things might easily happen at a future date—we are now so much in the atmosphere of the opposite that we forget how things change—if the Bank of England wanted to sterilise gold, its present power of sterilising gold without reducing its earning assets to vanishing point, is really very small. If the Bank of England were to wish to increase its gold reserve by 40 millions, which in conceivable circumstances it might well want to do—it is not a very big sum in relation to what we are talking about—its earning assets would be down to 20 millions sterling, which would be totally inadequate for its requirements. Therefore, it would be a great strength to the Bank if it had this power of throwing the burden of the expansion and contraction of credit directly on the joint stock banks instead of working by this indirect way. You will notice all my proposals are directed towards increasing the power and authority of the Bank of England over the system, because it is only in that way that I think a more flexible system can be developed.

And the avoidance of the use of the Bank rate remedy except under great necessity, and in extraordinary cases. Yes. There is another feature of the open-market operations I should like to mention in this connection. I believe, without altering the volume of Bank securities, it might very often be desirable to change not their quantity but their quality; that is to say, moving backwards and forwards between long and short securities. That, properly speaking, belongs to a later section in my argument. I think willingness to do that is another development of the future. There again the co-operation of the joint stock banks might very well be invited according as it was desirable to strengthen the long-term section of the market or the short-term section as it is, the position of the long term market depends on whether the joint stock banks are buying or selling long-term securities far more than it depends on any other item. If one examines the important changes in the price of long term securities one finds that they very closely correspond with the sales and purchases of the joint stock banks. Those sales and purchases, which are a dominating factor in the market, are now done, so far as I am aware, without any consultation with the Bank of England. For these many reasons, I should like to see something like a weekly meeting between either the Governor or the Committee of Treasury and the joint stock banks for the discussion and settlement of these and probably, in course of time, many other matters. We are trying to build up a system of consultation between the governors of the central banks in order that they might meet, in a routine way, for certain specific purposes, get talking, and that good results may come from that. I should have thought that we might do something of the same kind much nearer home. By having regular occasions of consultation over matters which would not perhaps need action more than now and again, a useful link could be established which might lead to all sorts of good results other than those which one could definitely predict. The existing organisation of the Bank of England was historically designed to secure just this continuous touch between the Bank of England and the merchant bankers, and for many of the functions of the Bank of England that continuous touch must have been of the utmost utility. I should have thought today it was at least as necessary and, perhaps, more necessary for the Bank of England to have continuous touch with the Big Five just as it has had for many generations with the leading merchant bankers. I cannot see what there is in the existing system which makes it desirable for this immensely intimate touch with the merchant bankers and this comparative remoteness from the Big Five. That is the end of this section [of my] argument.

My next section can be brief, because it is something which we have discussed among ourselves to a certain extent already, namely the regulation of foreign investment. This is one of the items making up the complete picture which I have mentioned separately. I think the fact that the Bank of

England has employed unofficial embargoes from time to time, in spite of all the obvious objections to that method and its great distaste for it, is convincing proof of the necessity of something of the kind. I imagine that the practice of the big issue houses of consulting the Bank of England and being guided to a considerable extent by the Bank's views is likely to continue. How far that is a post-War practice I do not know. Was it the custom of the issue houses to consult the Bank of England in the way they do now before 1914?

(MR BRAND) *I should not have thought so. So far as my recollection goes, it was not long before the War when it started really and it was only on a comprehensive scale during the War.*

(MR LUBBOCK) *I should think that is right.*

(MR BRAND) *And particularly after the War.* It seems to me that practice of consultation is obviously most desirable and ought to be considered a permanent feature of our system. No big issue should be brought out on the London market except with the approval of the Bank of England. That is very nearly the existing system apparently; but I do not know how completely that is true.

It would not be the case with any internal issue. No, I mean external issue.

I think probably that is so. If we are making a big issue we would certainly discuss it with the Governor. Would you be mainly guided by his views?

If he expressed a strong view we would, but he very likely would say 'You must take your own line. This is my view. You must decide.' Then it is more difficult to know.

(MR LUBBOCK) *I think the Bank knows practically every foreign issue that is coming out.*

(MR BRAND) *Every foreign issue over £1,000,000.* It seems to me it ought to and provided it does one does not need to alter what is going on already. It is obvious, as has been explained to us in evidence by more than one witness, taking the foreign issue markets and especially New York, how annoying it must be to a London issue house which has refrained, in deference to the Governor's views, to take on a certain issue to see the same issue then produced in New York and offered to investors in London who within a short period may have taken up 75 per cent of the issue.

It goes further than that. When the Bank of England does agree and an international issue is made partly in London, partly in New York, and partly in Amsterdam, it is ten to one within six months London and Amsterdam have bought back nearly all the New York issue. The Americans do not hold it. They take the commission and make the issue, but they do not place it really like we do. They have a selling syndicate which holds it until they can sell it abroad very largely.

(PROFESSOR GREGORY) *In fact it amounts to underwriting.*

(MR BRAND) *It is a totally different principle. They think they have placed it but until their public like foreign issues they will not be able to place it, but they will come over here.* When foreign issues are made abroad it is not only that our issue houses lose their legitimate profits, but the Treasury suffers a serious loss, because the issue made in London produces a fairly substantial sum in stamp duty.

It is 2 per cent. I thought in addition there was a sum in composition of the transfer duty if they are in bearer form.

The ordinary one is 2 per cent. If it is bearer it is more, is not it?

No, the bearer security is 2 per cent. That drives a good many issues to New York which then are sold to London. The bonds come over here and are negotiated.

(LORD BRADBURY) *They get the stamp then.* In nine cases out of ten they do not, because the English investor buys it and continues to hold it with his New York agent.

(MR BRAND) *Very often that is so.* It is the rarest thing in the world to buy a foreign bond issued in new York and then proceed to pay the stamp on it.

I should think it is. It does not happen. My practical suggestion is that the British holders of fixed-interest securities which have not paid British stamp duty should be liable to a special income tax of perhaps a shilling in the £, or 2s. in the £, which would be collected when the coupon is collected by the paying banker exactly as the rest of the income tax is deducted.

You mean loans not issued in London. Not issued in England. (PROFFESSOR GREGORY *Not stamped here.*

(Lord Bradbury took the Chair)

(MR KEYNES) This system could take two forms. It would either be possible to allow the issue made abroad to escape the special income tax provided it paid 2 per cent on the whole issue, or it could frank itself afterwards by paying the British stamp, or it would be possible to say that they could not get out of it so easily as that, and, if it had been issued abroad, there was no way of getting round the additional income tax.

(MR LUBBOCK) *Could the additional income tax be collected?* I should have thought so very easily. It would need no new machinery beyond what exists at present. There seems to me to be a great deal to recommend this scheme. First of all, the issue made abroad escapes the stamp; secondly, the English issue house has not had the advantage of handling it. The chances of British trade getting the benefit of orders is probably less, if the whole thing has been handled in New York or Amsterdam, than if it has been handled in England.

(MR MCKENNA) *How long would the quality of a new issue attach to this class of securities?* Permanently. It might escape additional tax if at any time those responsible agreed that they would pay the stamp on the whole issue or you could have a stamp simply on the bonds handled, but I do not think that would be enough. I should like to be rather drastic about this. It would be a way of regulating foreign lending to a certain extent, while so far from injuring London as a financial centre internationally it would do the opposite.

(MR BRAND) *It would bring more issues here and you would have more strain in one way on the London market.* I am assuming that the issue houses here would not handle more than the Governor of the Bank approved of. Therefore, you would make sure that all the foreign lending which we could afford to do would take place here, and you could have effective control without this round the corner method being exploited to your disadvantage.

(SIR WALTER RAINE) *Are you referring to coupons collected in London?* Yes.

Is not there an arrangement already with the various banks by which they deduct the English income tax? Yes, I am suggesting in the case of these bonds they would be instructed to deduct the extra shilling or two shillings.

(MR MCKENNA) *On the ordinary investment in foreign securities you would not charge a special tax?* I would exclude equities, but not fixed interest securities.

If one buys an American railway bond, what about that? I would charge on all of them.

You would charge on all fixed interest securities? Yes.

On private investments through the stockbroker? Yes.

(PROFESSOR GREGORY) *On new issues or on all issues?* All issues.

(LORD BRADBURY) *On existing securities as well?* Yes. You could always mitigate it when you first introduced it by saying securities issued before a certain date were exempt if you thought it was harsh, but I see nothing harsh in this. It seems to me to be a way of raising what might be a decent amount of taxation or an amount quite worth thinking about. It might run into £3, 4, or 5 millions, or something of that order.

You could not apply it to the existing holdings of the investors who had invested in these things. Why not? We did it during the War.

That was for the purpose of forcing a sale to the Government. The French Government introduced a tax of this sort quite recently.

Taking a loan which has been issued in London and in New York at present the investors buy the New York issue if it is cheaper. Now it would have to be an extra amount cheaper for it to be worth while.

Supposing Mr Brand has bought a London issue in the past and I have bought a New York issue, as regards that investment, while I hold it, it having happened before your new legislation, there is no reason in equity surely why you should think of charging me an extra rate of taxation. Yes, you have dodged the stamp duty, and I am going to get you if I can after the event.

I took the stamp into consideration when I estimated the price of the issue. You dodged paying the revenue stamp.

I was doing something legal and something perfectly right to the best of my knowledge and belief. It seems an extraordinary thing to say as regards that investment you are going to penalise me. It is perfectly legal.

I should have thought you might have secured your object by applying the tax to all issues after the date of the legislation. It is not a very big point.

(MR MCKENNA) *Any evasion would be protected against by future amendment of the law.* (LORD BRADBURY) *There is no evasion in this case.* (MR MCKENNA) *It is avoidance.* It is legal avoidance.

(LORD BRADBURY) *There had been no avoidance of any kind. I had bought this New York security knowing I shall have to pay stamp duty if I negotiated on the London market.*

(MR MCKENNA) *Surely Mr Keynes is right. This is exactly on all fours with every legal avoidance of tax. It is a constant effort of the Revenue to close up these sort of things.*

(LORD BRADBURY) *It is hardly worth pursuing it.*

(MR BRAND) *One effect it would seem to me to have would be to depreciate the credit of those foreign countries on the New York market. I think the prices of these securities are held up in New York to a certain extent by foreign purchases. It would mean that they would not go there in future.* If New York desires to continue to be an international loan centre, it must find the funds itself. That seems to me reasonable.

(LORD BRADBURY) *Incidentally, it would be an obstacle—I do not know whether that is undesirable—to selling foreign issues to London to adjust the exchanges.* Yes; this is happening not to adjust the exchanges but to disturb them as it is. It is one large disturbance.

(MR BRAND) *It is a new form of making the foreigner pay.*

(SIR WALTER RAINE) *We are told the reason why the French system is upset is the putting on of these extra charges.* It is one of the reasons why the French are not lending so much as they ought to, but in our case we are tending to do the opposite. In the case of the French the monetary tax is not simply against issues made abroad but against all issues.

(MR BRAND) *Yes, against those made in France too.* And it is retrospective.

(MR LUBBOCK) *It was a differential tax against foreign issues, but the difference between foreign and internal now is done away with.* (MR BRAND) *It is reduced.* It was 25 per cent and 18 per cent. *It is 18 per cent.*

(MR MCKENNA) *We have no differential tax against foreign issues.*

(MR LUBBOCK) *Not here.* There is very much less disadvantage in a tax of this kind than there is in legislating against foreign issues generally. It would mean that when we buy foreign issues we should make them in London on the most favourable terms to ourselves, instead of the extreme *laissez-faire* of allowing ourselves to be deluged at any moment by any quantity of issues from the foreign market. I think it is a reasonable precaution.

(MR MCKENNA) *There is a great deal to be said for it. It is a startling proposition, and it wants thinking about.*

(MR LUBBOCK) *If we knew exactly what we were investing and how much we could invest and how much of the favourable balance is exhausted.*

(LORD BRADBURY) *It seems to me it might limit the volume of foreign investment.* No, it does not limit the volume of foreign investment, because our foreign lending will be always equal to our favourable balance of trade plus the export of gold. It is simply insisting that the foreign lending shall be made through the London machinery and not otherwise.

(PROFESSOR GREGORY) *If you exclude equities, that leaves a very wide loophole to begin with.* There is a loophole there.

It is trying to interfere with the fluidity of capital. It is an interference with *laissez-faire.* I have to admit that.

(LORD BRADBURY) *It cannot be effective, I think. You would get your foreign investments turned into equities, if you exempt the equities.* There are always a few borderline cases which will escape. That always does happen.

(PROFESSOR GREGORY) *All they need do is to form an investment trust in New York and to issue equities against bonds and so avoid the tax.* It is true of any conceivable thing you can do that there is a marginal case which can get round you. If one is against doing anything, or is against any form of regulation which would alter the existing system, all this falls to the ground; but if one is to consider what are the possibilities of control this seems to me to deserve a place on the list.

(LORD BRADBURY) *Surely the object you have in view is to prevent the volume of foreign investment, or attempted foreign investment, to use your language, from exceeding the amount of available gold.* No, it cannot. There are various means of preventing it.

(MR LUBBOCK) *Raising the Bank rate being one of them.* Yes, and persuading the issue houses not to issue is another. It seems to me that this method of producing an identical result is open to less objections than the other one. It is open to less objection than raising the Bank rate because it does not affect the internal credit situation. It is open to less objection than bullying the issue houses because it does not cause a loss of financial prestige to this country. What happens now is this. A loan for two millions is brought to a London issue house. In deference to the wishes of the Governor, they refrain from taking it. It is then issued in New York, and a million and half finds its way to London. Therefore, the next two millions which is brought to a London issue house has to be refused because the two millions that otherwise might have been available for that has been almost entirely used up in buying the previous issue from New York.

(MR BRAND) *It does not come anything like so quickly as that. If you make an*

236

issue in New York one-tenth might come back in that time. Make your time lag what you like from six months to two years, but we shall be having to refuse some other issues and so we may get into a vicious circle in which in the end comparatively little of the financing which we can afford to do goes through our hands at all. It is the feeling that that is the end of it which makes the Bank of England so hesitant to use the embargo method. It is not that the embargo method diminishes the volume of this country's foreign lendings. It is simply that it makes what foreign lending we can afford go through other channels.

(MR FRATER TAYLOR) *We have another motive and that is increasing the funds for investment at home. Is not that so?* I want to use preventives which do not discourage the home borrower. It is not so much making more funds available as making them available on easier terms, so that the competition of the foreign borrower and the methods which the Bank of England has to use to keep that within limits does not react so severely on the domestic credit situation.

(MR BRAND) *There are a great number of people who would like to have some money outside England—it is a growing amount at this moment. I suppose they would buy shares.* If this was in force we could issue in London more foreign issues to the exact extent that we keep the New York ones out, so that the supply of foreign investments for those English investors who wanted them would not be diminished by a brass farthing. It would simply be they had to pass through one channel.

(PROFESSOR GREGORY) *It is not a differential tax on all foreign investments, but such investments as pass through a foreign issuing house before coming here.*

(MR MCKENNA) *Which have not paid tax.*

(PROFESSOR GREGORY) *That is very much smaller than the amount of securities bought in New York and intended for negotiations in London subsequently, I submit.* I should say very seldom. I should prefer the larger form of this suggestion in which, if the issue had not been made in London, they could not get off the extra tax.

(PROFESSOR GREGORY) *At any time in future?* Yes.

(LORD BRADBURY) *A tax on dividend?* Yes.

(MR MCKENNA) *What quantity would be affected?* With the comparatively modest surplus we have for foreign investment of 100 millions we should desire that that 100 millions should be handled through London and bring all the indirect advantages which that brings with it.

(LORD BRADBURY) *You do not want to restrict the volume of foreign investment at all?* Why should I? Our volume of foreign lending is always equal to our favourable balance of trade.

(LORD BRADBURY) *I do not want to go into that point, but you do not want to make any attempt to make the British investor purchase more foreign securities.* I do not want to have any more prevention than there is at present. I have to prevent him from buying too many otherwise I lose gold. This is adjusting the methods of prevention. It would not have the effect of diminishing the amount he actually lends. It would be preventing him in a different way.

(LORD BRADBURY) *You do, in fact, want to prevent particular transactions.* Yes.

I quite agree that the volume will ultimately be determined by the margin.
(MR MCKENNA) *The margin plus gold.*

(LORD BRADBURY) *Except, on the other hand, that the volume of foreign investment possibly reacts on the margin.* I am sure there is no other country but ourselves which was in our position who would not have used this method years ago.

(MR MCKENNA) *It might act advantageously on the margin of trade.* It means making sure that we get for the London market all the advantages which our creditor position is capable of giving us. For us, this has become a very recent problem because on any scale purchases by English investors of foreign bonds issued abroad never occurred. I am sure if this had been going on for decades we should have come to some solution long ago, but it is a new problem.

(PROFESSOR GREGORY) *I can conceive a case in which this might be done—I do not wish to pledge myself about it—but why should you apply it to bonds and not to equities?* I am not sure that I would not extend it. My reasons for hesitating in doing so are these. It is very difficult to distinguish between equities and all kinds of British trading abroad. That is the first point. To know what you mean by an equity in this connection seems to me very difficult sometimes. Secondly, I believe it is greatly in the interest of this country that as much of our foreign lending as possible should be in the purchase of equities rather than of bonds. It is by the purchase of equities we shall share in the natural resources of the world. They are the things out of which we have made money in the past.

(MR BRAND) *Not so much by the purchase, but by the creation of equities.* By the creation of equities and their purchase. That is a form of foreign investment which I want. Therefore, I am not afraid of a factor which discriminates to some extent in favour of equities.

(PROFESSOR GREGORY) *If you are going to make it 5 per cent in income tax, it is a fairly considerable discrimination.* It is fairly large, but the equity market and the fixed interest market are to a very great extent separate. So far as it was a discrimination, I should welcome it. If we found, as a result of this, the purchase of equities which had not passed through the London issue market was getting excessive, one might have to tighten up the system and you could always do that.

I am quite certain it would lead to awful abuse in the shape of the fictitious creation of equities in New York. I do not think that is a terrible abuse.

(MR BRAND) *New York is strong enough not to rely on the London market very much.*

(PROFESSOR GREGORY) *The gravamen of this argument is that New York is a fictitious lender which relies on us.*

(MR BRAND) *In bad times they sell us their things.* My next section is one which needs some development before I reach my point.

(LORD BRADBURY) *Then perhaps we had better adjourn.*

(Adjourned to Thursday next at 4.30)

COMMITTEE ON FINANCE AND INDUSTRY

Friday 5 December 1930

Present:

The Rt Hon. Lord Macmillan (*Chairman*)

Mr Ernest Bevin The Rt Hon. Reginald McKenna
The Rt Hon. Lord Bradbury, G.C.B. Mr J. T. Walton Newbold
The Hon. R. H. Brand, C.M.G. Mr J. Frater Taylor
Professor T. E. Gregory, D.SC. Mr A. A. G. Tulloch
Mr J. M. Keynes, C.B. Mr G. Ismay (*Secretary*)
Mr Cecil Lubbock

Sir Frederick Leith-Ross, K.C.M.G., C.B.

(MR KEYNES) Mr Chairman, I should like to remind the Committee of the headings which I have dealt with. I began, first of all, by making suggestions for increasing the effective resources of the Bank of England for meeting the foreign drain. I then made some suggestions as to the use of techniques which were directed primarily to the external position and would not have such an immediate repercussion on the internal position as alterations of bill rate have. I then dealt with the question of greater and more deliberate co-operation between the Bank of England and the joint stock banks.

(CHAIRMAN) *Yes; that, I think, is extraordinarily important. I think in our drafting committee we might usefully develop ways and means more fully upon that.* Fourthly, I made some suggestions connected with restriction of the rate of foreign lending, or rather, ways of keeping foreign lending within the bounds within which it ought to be kept by methods which might be more effective than the present method.

I come now to the question of ways of increasing and strengthening the resources of the Bank of England generally, not merely their resources for meeting a foreign drain but their aggregate resources for all kinds of purposes.

239

I am very much impressed by the relatively small volume of resources at the Bank of England's disposal. The Bank is itself so used to its position, has accommodated itself to it on the whole so successfully, that I think it may overlook the absolute smallness of the figures relatively to those of other countries and of the modern world generally. At present the total assets in the Banking Department are £128,000,000, and those in the Issue Department £354,000,000, making a total of £482,000,000. If my suggestion were adopted about the joint stock banks handing in notes, but if the two Departments were nevertheless separate, that would have the effect of augmenting the assets of the Banking Department by £50,000,000 and depleting those of the Issue Department to the same amount, leaving the aggregate unchanged, at something under £500,000,000.

(MR LUBBOCK) *I do not quite follow when you say depleting?* That £50,000,000 of the assets of the Issue Department would be handed to the Banking Department.

The paying into the Banking Department of £50,000,000 of notes would not have any effect? It would not increase the aggregate reserves of the two Departments, which would remain at something under £500,000,000. The United States Federal Reserve Bank has assets of about £1,000,000,000 sterling, and that does not, as in the case of the Bank of England, comprise the whole of the note issue, because a large part of the note issue is a government note issue outside the Federal Reserve System. If you take off the notes in both cases, and the assets which are held against notes, you will find the United States Federal Reserve System left with £720,000,000 for market operations and the Bank of England with £123,000,000; that is to say, they have nearly six times the amount, apart from notes. In the case of France and Germany, of course, a much larger proportion is held against notes. The aggregate resources of the Bank of France are about £800,000,000 sterling, as against less than £500,000,000 for the Bank of England; and the Reichsbank, even in its present depleted condition today, has about £265,000,000.

(MR BRAND) *What does that last figure compare with in the Bank of England?* £482,000,000; but that is the only one which compares at all favourably; the others are all very much larger. I thought it would be useful to have the figures of the four most important institutions. This comparatively small volume of the available resources from one purpose or another is, I think, one reason for amalgamating the Departments. It may be argued that, as the Bank manages the securities in the Issue Department for the Treasury, this would not make an effective difference. But it does seem to me that, so far as the securities in the Issue Department are concerned the Bank is actually acting as trustee for the Treasury, and it is rather for it to see that the earnings of those assets are reasonably kept up. I cannot believe that it really has a perfectly free hand over the form of those assets in practice. It has to remember that those are assets the earnings on which go to a different body than itself, which is trusting it to do the best possible handling. If the payments from the Bank of England to the Treasury were to be fixed and the two Departments amalgamated the Bank would then have absolute discretion over the form of the assets. I think that may be more important in the future than it has been in the past. Until lately the rate of interest on short-term securities was quite as good as on long-term, if not better. It has not been of any great significance from the point of view of earnings whether your security was Treasury bills or Consols, but if the yield on the one becomes double that of the other, as it is now, and still more if it becomes three or four times, as it might, if we were to have the very cheap money which has happened sometimes in previous periods, I think there might be a real awkwardness. It may be said that the Treasury understands that the Bank will use those assets not with any eye as to what they earn but entirely from the point of view of the management of money, but I think that you have the possibility of difficulties between the Chancellor of the Exchequer and the Bank of England. The Chancellor of the Exchequer is actually interested in his revenue, whereas it seems to me the Bank of England, not having an enormous quantity of assets, ought to have the whole of its assets at its disposal, at its unfettered discretion, for the sole objective of the safest and best management of the monetary system, not having to earn a revenue for interests that are committed to its charge.

(CHAIRMAN) *The purpose would be to change motives?* Yes.

(LORD BRADBURY) *You think if the Bank of England had these securities as its own property, and the profit or loss on them accrued to itself, it would feel it less necessary to earn revenue than if the Treasury were interested in the earning of profit.* That is my point. I should like to make it feel that it was less necessary by framing proposals which would put it beyond doubt that the Bank of England's earning power would be always quite adequate, so that they would not be concerned to earn in any particular year any particular sum.

(SIR F. LEITH-ROSS) *Surely those securities, insofar as they are Government securities, are bringing into the Government exactly what the Government pays. From the point of view of the Government revenue it would be quite immaterial if the whole of this debt were made a non-interest-bearing debt altogether.* I do not think so. Supposing that at present—it is not the case, but for the sake of argument—they consist of five per cent War Loan, earning something approaching five per cent, and that this War Loan were then sold in the market by the Bank of England and replaced by Treasury bills purchased in the market which yielded, say, two per cent, the current revenue to the Chancellor of the Exchequer for this year would be two-fifths what it had been in the previous year.

That is assuming it was five per cent War Loan which was held. I am taking that illustration. It might be that they always had held Treasury bills, and that when the rate of Treasury bills falls from six per cent to one per cent it would not be so clear that that was the most advantageous way, from the point of view of a Chancellor of the Exchequer, of holding his earning assets against the note issue, for it seems to me that he must be governed by rather different criteria from what the Bank of England would be if they were simply considering the monetary aspect.

(PROFESSOR GREGORY) *On the assumption that the aggregate Government debt remains the same, surely what the Government gets in as additional revenue has to come out as additional expenditure?* No, because it depends on the form of the securities held by the Issue Department what the Treasury's receipts are, whereas it makes no difference to their outgoings whether the securities are held by the public or by the Issue Department.

(LORD BRADBURY) *By placing Treasury bills in the hands of the public and War Loan in the Issue Department the Government is paying the interest on so much War Loan outside the public instead of on so much Treasury bills, and, therefore, the revenue increases.* That is the point. As I say, this has not until recently been much of a question because there has not been any very great difference; in fact there has been from an earning point of view even an advantage in having short-dated securities rather than long. Quite apart from this point, that I should like to see the rather limited resources entirely at the discretion of the Bank for the purpose of capital management, I feel doubt as to whether from the point of view of future earnings the power of the Bank of England is really sufficient. It is difficult to make a good judgement on this because we all know that the full earning power of the Bank of England is not disclosed in the balance sheet, and we can only make a guess. What we do know more or less for certain is the great change in its earning power today as compared with a comparatively short time ago and the possibility of a further adverse change. It makes an enormous difference to the earning power of the Bank if in one situation it holds £30,000,000 less gold and Bank rate is 6 per cent and what the position is if it holds £30,000,000 more gold and reduces its earning assets by that amount and has a Bank rate of 2 per cent. It has actually suffered a fluctuation of this sort of amount. There was a time not long ago— if I go back further it is still more in the Bank's favour—when they had earning assets of, I think, about £100,000,000 and Bank rate was about 6 per cent. Of course, they would have some securities on which they would not get so much as 6 per cent; but say they were earning 5 per cent on the average, they would show so far as their balance sheet was concerned an annual revenue of £5,000,000 sterling. Their earning assets today have fallen to about £60,000,000 owing to their having a great deal more gold than they had at an earlier date, and the bill rate is now only a little over 2 per cent. Supposing they are now earning 3 per cent on the £60,000,000 their revenue would be at £1,800,000, that is to say, their falling off in earning power would be more than £3,000,000 sterling. If it were thought desirable for the Bank to have still more strength in the form of liquid assets which either earned nothing or very little, and if we were to have a long period of cheap money, possibly with the bill rate going considerably below the present level, so far as the published resources of the Bank of England go, they would be earning no dividend whatever. Of course, there are two unknowns. One does not know their concealed reserves, one does not know their expenses, but if the present published earning assets yield 3 per cent their total income as shown is less than £2,000,000. Their dividend costs them £1,500,000, and their expenses, even after allowing for certain services which they perform, for which they are specially paid, such as the management of the debt, must be tremendously in excess of half a million pounds. As I say, one cannot prove that they are yet in difficulty; I do not know what their concealed reserves are; supposing the concealed reserves of the Bank of England amount to £50,000,000 sterling and that those £50,000,000 sterling are earning £2,000,000 tax free, I should still say that on the face of that the prospects of the Bank of England's earnings for the next year were too much on the low side. If, on the other hand, the Bank of England has concealed reserves of £100,000,000 then I should say the position is about what it ought to be. It is a difficulty in this discussion that one does not know in the least whether £50,000,000 or £100,000,000 is the better guess for their concealed reserves, but either figure, of course, is a very large one.

(MR TULLOCH) *In what form do you think they could have the concealed reserves? It does not appear in their balance sheet.* No, nothing appears in their balance sheet. They could have it in the form of securities which they write down to nothing. I do not think the balance sheet presents any obstacle to their holding any quantity of concealed reserves. I do not know whether the order of magnitude of my guess is anywhere near right. It may surprise anybody who has not thought about it that I should suggest such large figures. I am purely guessing; I have not the faintest idea; but for all these years the Bank of England has undoubtedly been putting something by. Having regard to the tremendous profits they made during the War, of which they returned some to the Treasury, and having regard to the large sums they made while they were holding the French bills it would not surprise me if those figures were to be correct.

(MR LUBBOCK) *I do not think I am at liberty to say anything on this subject at all. I must ask that my silence is not to be construed as giving either assent or dissent.* Oh, no. But it puts us in a difficulty, because if we assume that the

Bank of England balance sheet tells the truth, they are as near as possible 'bust', and we ought to do something about it.

(LORD BRADBURY) *I think it is a safe assumption that that is not correct.* If one has to consider what sort of amount of reserve they ought to hold, one is very much in the dark.

(CHAIRMAN) *The important point is whether the reserves as disclosed justify the assumption that they are so inadequate as to embarrass the Bank of England in the pursuance of monetary policy.* Whatever the figures of the concealed reserve may be, their earnings must have been declining very greatly in recent times, so that while they may have had a sufficient margin at one time it does not seem to me certain that they might not reach a point which the Federal Reserve Bank reached some years ago, in which their policy in the management of money was really influenced by the desire to earn a given revenue. It seems to me frightfully important that in all readily conceivable circumstances the Bank of England should feel quite free not to be influenced in the slightest degree by the necessity of earning a given income.

(MR FRATER TAYLOR) *We are considering a very serious situation. Why should we be so much in the dark?* I do not know.

(PROFESSOR GREGORY) *Because it is a privately owned institution.* I think the real reason is that the Bank of England has always held that it was frightfully important for it to be very strong. It has always been afraid that if its actual profits were to be disclosed, they might be the subject of attack.

(MR NEWBOLD) *I should have imagined we might have had an estimate of the profits without knowing what the secret reserves were. There may be a reason for not disclosing the secret reserves, but there is no reason why we should not have an estimate of the profits.* You are asking for the revelation of the *arcana arcanorum.* There is a special legal provision by which the Bank of England assesses itself for tax and its true income is not disclosed to the Inland Revenue. Is that correct?

(MR LUBBOCK) *I do not think that is correct. I think the Inspector goes over our accounts.* I have heard what I have suggested, in former times.

We have to return our assessment for tax like everybody else. It is rather difficult to know on what assumption we ought to go in this matter. I think that one would with justice base a good deal upon the point that the earning assets which the Bank has had since the War have been tremendously depleted. We all know that with the arrangements that existed so long as the Bank of France had not repaid their bills the position was very profitable. We know that that has come to an end. We know that the average earnings of the short-dated assets has been greatly reduced and we know that the published earning assets of the Bank of England have been reduced and that shows, as I say, the probability of a very large diminution in earnings on a total which, anyhow, is very small. If the Bank of England were to show earning assets of all kinds of only about £60,000,000 it would be out of proportion to those of any other institution of a similar kind, and I should feel that the future was more secure if the earning assets of the Bank of England—without casting any prying eye on the amount of their concealed reserves—were £100,000,000 rather than £60,000,000. That would only be restoring it to the figure which has quite frequently prevailed in the post-War period.

How would you propose to do that?

(MR BRAND) *Is it now only £60,000,000?* At the moment it is just over £60,000,000; now that they are losing gold again it is improving a little, but a short time ago when they had a little more gold than now it was just about £60,000,000. It is creeping up above £60,000,000 with the losses of gold, every time they lose gold. Mr Ismay hands me a paper. This is the last Return.

(MR LUBBOCK) *That is mixed up with the payment of War Loan dividend.* This figure is right. At the actual date when I was preparing these notes it was £62,000,000, it was slightly more then than it had been a fortnight earlier.

(MR BRAND) *When they are losing gold their earning assets go up?* If they replace them. If they lose £30,000,000 of gold they cannot deplete the market to anything like that extent. Therefore, their earning assets will probably go up at least £25,000,000. If the view were adopted, which seems to me a very reasonable view, that the present figure of non-earning assets is dangerously low, they could easily work their earning assets down to something which is ludicrous in relation to their expenditure, their responsibilities, or even their dividends. So they would be falling back entirely on their concealed reserves. The way in which revenue is obtained for the Federal Reserve System is by requiring banks to keep non-interest-bearing deposits. I think that the central bank functions for the benefit of the whole, and the way for it to earn its upkeep is for the member banks to contribute non-interest-bearing deposits.

There are two ways of getting more for the Bank of England. The peculiarity of the British system is that only the clearing banks keep any appreciable non-interest-bearing sums at the Bank of England. I have suggested previously that the clearing banks should keep 7 per cent but that would not really alter things very much, because that would only affect the position as between the Banking Department and the Issue Department. That would not improve the earnings of the Bank of England. But supposing all banks were required to keep 7 per cent of their sterling deposits with the Bank of England it would make quite a difference. I have not precise figures, but it would add a good many millions to the Bank of England. We have already discussed the point whether the Scottish banks should get off making any contribution to the upkeep of the central institution.

(PROFESSOR GREGORY) *Anybody paying a banker's licence.* Anybody paying a banker's licence, but on his sterling deposits. Of course you could not include foreign institutions, you could not require them to keep seven per cent with the Bank of England, except on their sterling deposits, but subject to that I think it would be all for the strength of the Bank of England, and I do not see any serious objection to it. Another way would be to make the seven per cent for the clearing banks eight per cent. I think that would add £14,000,000, would it not, to the Bank's deposits.

(MR BRAND) *By adding one per cent.* By making the proportion of the clearing banks eight per cent, instead of seven per cent.

(MR LUBBOCK) *But that would mean that the banking reserves would be so much higher and the assets so much less?* Yes, the bankers' deposits would be higher in the Banking Department, and against these earning assets would be held.

The bankers when cashing those deposits in the Bank of England would pay notes. I am assuming they could not do that. If they merely did it by reducing notes I agree it would not get you any further, but the other banks have not got notes that they could pay in. My notion is that all banks should be required to keep a reserve, and that perhaps the reserves of the clearing banks at the Bank of England should be raised one per cent in relation to deposits above what they are now, which is a minute charge in relation to the whole thing, in order that the bankers' deposits should be raised by a fair number of millions.

(PROFESSOR GREGORY) *If your plan were carried out, what would it mean? Would you require merchant bankers and acceptance houses to hold a balance at the Bank of England?* Against their deposits, but I imagine they do already hold reserves. I do not know the figure; I should think it would make less difference to them than to other institutions. They all bank with the Bank of England. We have no figures of their deposits or reserves against them.

Your great accretion would probably come from the foreign banks and colonial banks in London? Yes.

(MR LUBBOCK) *They would draw a cheque on their clearing banks and pay it to us, and the present bankers' balances would be reduced.* And they would have to replenish by selling Treasury bills or Consols, and that would transfer a certain amount from the hands of the member banks to the Bank of England.

(MR BRAND) *In fact you would do what the American system does. They would be legally obliged.* They would be legally obliged.

You would tell them they must do this or they would be legally obliged.

(LORD BRADBURY) *Could you apply this to any institution accepting deposits on demand?* There are a certain number of border line cases when one tries to decide what is a bank.

(PROFESSOR GREGORY) *The legal position is very obscure. The Bankers' Institute for years has been debating this question.* You could get rid of most of the border line cases by saying that this would not apply to institutions having deposits of less than so much. The border line cases are on a very small scale. You would not include institutions like the Trustee Savings Banks.

(CHAIRMAN) *Ought the Co-operative banks to come in?* Yes.

Building societies? No. Building societies I should say not; they are not bankers, they are borrowers. They are not subject to cheque for one thing. That is a problem which I think has been faced in other countries. I do not think that it is insoluble.

(PROFESSOR GREGORY) *Things have been made so much easier in America by the fact that unless you are a joint stock bank you must not bank with the Federal Reserve System.* It might be easier to get the necessary reserves by the big banks increasing their proportion. It seems to me quite reasonable that the whole banking system should contribute to the central bank in return for this extraordinary facility of being able to keep small reserves, because you can rely on being able to turn your short-dated assets into money. It is only because of the policy of the Bank of England that the banks find themselves in this position, and I think it is legitimate that they should pay whatever is required to make the central institution strong enough to be able to serve the monetary system of the country in any conceivable emergency.

(CHAIRMAN) *The justification for this is the alleged inadequacy of the Bank's earnings?*

(MR LUBBOCK) *I was wondering whether it is a fair question to put to the Bank—'Are you satisfied that your lack of earning power now or in the future is [not] [un]likely to cramp you?'*

(CHAIRMAN) '*Do you find that the alleged inadequacy of your earning power is cramping you in the development of policies which you could otherwise develop?'* I should not have large hopes of getting a well considered answer. It is so very touchy a subject.

(MR TULLOCH) *If they had £100,000,000 of concealed reserves the question would hardly arise in relation to their earning power?* No; if they had £100,000,000 of concealed reserves I should feel that they were strong enough.

I feel that if we are to present a considered Report we should ask the Bank of England whether they do feel themselves strong enough, apart from any obligation of the banks to increase their deposits. It is a difficult question to frame. 'Suppose that it were thought desirable that your gold reserves should be £200,000,000, either in order to make the position much stronger, or because gold needed sterilising and you had to take your share, and suppose at the same time that short-dated securities were yielding something between one and two per cent, do you feel confident that your income would be adequate to your needs?'

In other words, you would impress upon them the eventuality of their income not being adequate to their needs. You would say 'This is a thing you ought to do in your own interests, to meet certain possibilities and eventualities.' The Bank of England have been exceedingly anxious to keep up the full status of a private institution, and that has made them extremely reluctant to go into any matter which would raise that issue. At the same time, they have wanted it to be quite clear that they were not going to behave as a private institution; they have always wanted to retain reserves which were reasonable assuming that they were not a private institution, while keeping the appearance of a private institution. That has put them into a position where they could not discuss anything frankly. If they were to disclose resources which I should consider adequate they would be open to the charge by some people 'What business has a private institution to be keeping all this money? It is in a privileged position.' On the other hand, if they were to disclose lesser resources and free themselves from that charge they would lay themselves open to the charge that they were running on a low margin. I think they always will be in a dilemma so long as they pretend to be what they are not—a private institution. That is the essential weakness in the Bank's position.

(MR LUBBOCK) *Do you think it is a weakness?* I think it is, because it means the Bank of England always has to pretend to be weaker than it is.

Are you speaking of the weakness of being a private institution, or, as you put it, trying to preserve the appearance of a private institution, while not behaving as one? It makes it very difficult for them, I think, to show their full strength without laying themselves open to criticism.

(MR BRAND) *On the other hand, it may have advantages, in another sense. It is more difficult to apply pressure to it than if it were a public institution.* I think they are depending on a broken reed. The fact that there are certain shareholders in the background is worth nothing. It is one of those pretences that will never stand any strain.

(MR LUBBOCK) *I think the Bank does attach very great value to the fact that its position makes it independent and free from any political pressure—or as far as possible.* I think they do, but that does not depend on the fact that they have private shareholders.

I am afraid the private shareholders are not very much considered. We should not say that our position depended on our private shareholders.

(PROFESSOR GREGORY) *I am inclined to agree with your general line of argument, Mr Keynes, but for the purpose of our Report is it really necessary to stress this aspect? I should have thought the points which it was really necessary to stress were these—first of all, that it might be necessary for the smooth working of the money market for the Bank to have larger resources, and second, that the Bank can always obtain more assets by the simple expedient of increasing the bankers' balances.* They have no power to do that. This is the only opportunity that there will be for years to come—unless we are quickly replaced by another Committee—of considering ways and means of increasing the Bank's earning assets.

I am absolutely at one with you; it is desirable. Even the legal power is not made use of. There ought to be some provision in the English legal position to increase the bankers' balances. I feel that in the discussion in our Report we should concentrate on those particular points, namely, the weakness of the published figures of the Bank of England and the necessity for an increase of their profit earning capacity. I think one can slide over one's reasons to a certain extent, provided that one has reached definite conclusions. I think one can express the conclusions without stressing the above considerations in any sort of way. The whole thing ought not to be conducted in a sort of medicine man atmosphere, in which one has to go into these matters in secret.

(MR LUBBOCK) *What you call 'the medicine man atmosphere' might be part of the system; it might be expressed in a different way and shown to have some value.*

(MR BRAND) *Are the bankers' deposits of the Bank of England almost entirely clearing bankers' deposits?* (MR LUBBOCK) *Yes.* (MR BRAND) *The non-clearing banks holding almost nothing?* (MR LUBBOCK) *No.* I think the impression I got from Sir Ernest Harvey was that there was less than £10,000,000 of bankers' deposits, in 'Other Deposits' more than £5,000,000 but less than £10,000,000.

(MR BRAND) *That covered all other banks.* It covered all other banks which come in the category of bankers' deposits. Sir Ernest Harvey's explanation was that non-English banks—which included for this purpose the Bank of Ireland—appeared in 'Other Deposits', and not 'Bankers' Deposits'. Insofar as foreign banks keep a balance at the Bank of England that is in 'Other Deposits'.

(MR LUBBOCK) *Roughly, banks doing business in England.* Yes. If one is really going seriously into the strength of the banking system and the capacity of the Bank of England to meet all eventualities, this does seem to me a subject which, though delicate, cannot be entirely overlooked.

There are one or two other points generally dealing with the question whether the Bank of England's balance sheet should get a little nearer to the facts. I feel rather strongly that the holding of what are, in effect, time deposits for foreign banks outside the Bank's Return is very unsound. We had some discussion with Sir Ernest Harvey about that. He explained that some large sums, I gathered, are invested for foreign institutions in Treasury bills or other bills, and that, while those are not called deposits, there is an arrangement by which the foreign institutions can in effect treat them as deposits, and not only as deposits, but deposits at call, provided they are prepared to sacrifice a certain amount of interest. That is to say, they are exactly, from a practical point of view, deposits at call which carry interest, but very little, and perhaps a negative interest, if the right to draw is exercised.

(CHAIRMAN) *Under which head do they appear?* Under no head at all, because the Bank hold the view that they are acting as agents.

Should not they appear under a definite head? I think they ought. The Bank would say it is not a liability because the arrangement is that they would let the foreign institution have the money at once and that any sacrifice involved in turning bills into cash would have to be borne by the institution.

(MR TULLOCH) *I did not understand there was a binding agreement, but that there was a tacit understanding that they would entertain an application in case of need. My impression was, that they were simply acting as agents, turning the money given them by a foreign institution into bills and ready at any time, if a request were made, to turn them back again.* I daresay that is how it is framed. Any joint stock bank can do that.

Are they doing more than a joint stock bank would do? I did not gather that the Bank of England are in those circumstances. You can slightly change the form of your deposits so that they do not become technically deposits. This is a way by which important transactions are concealed. Fluctuations in the amount of bills held by the Bank for a foreign institution are just as important as fluctuations in gold, and any increase in them is exactly like a decrease in the gold reserve.

From the point of view of foreign obligations, which are maturing at any time, I agree; but you were talking about the relation to foreign obligations of the Bank of England and the joint stock banks. The object of a balance sheet ought to be to disclose what essential items you can. If you like to draw it up on a legalistic basis, in which you have a very sharp definition of a deposit which must be shown and anything which does not come within that category need not, then you can easily invent some practical equivalent of a deposit which does not come under the legal designation.

(LORD BRADBURY) *These bills are discountable at the Bank of England, are they not?* Yes.

Then surely all that the Bank of England undertakes to do, if the foreign bank wants money at short notice, is to discount bills which it holds as their agent. It could discount bills equally as if they were held by an agent. (MR MCKENNA) *Is not that a liability?* (LORD BRADBURY) *It is no more a liability than the Bank is already under.* (MR BRAND) *If we get an order from a central bank to buy bills, is not that the same?* (MR LUBBOCK) *Yes.* (LORD BRADBURY) *You have exactly the same securities at the Bank of England for the bills you hold.* (MR BRAND) *We should do it through the discount market.* A good deal depends upon whether the central institution can draw against them, so to speak, by telegrams and then leave the Bank at leisure to sell the bills, or whether the bills must be liquidated first.

(MR TULLOCH) *I gather there is nothing of that kind; I seem to have formed quite a different impression from what you have formed.* I do not care what the exact form is, because I have no doubt it has been carefully framed to get round this. The view of the Bank of England has always been that, by definition, a deposit does not carry interest if it is a Bank of England deposit. When they pay interest, therefore, that is not a deposit and is not shown. That was the case during the War and afterwards, when the Bank of England took deposits from the clearing banks and allowed them interest on them, and that amounted to an enormous sum. Those figures never appeared in the balance sheet; which shows that the Bank of England was either breaking the law at that time or was availing itself of the view that anything which carries interest is by definition excluded by the Bank of England from the term 'deposit'.

(PROFESSOR GREGORY) *The official definition of that was, that they lent the money to the Government and it was not passed through the books of the Bank.* It is always true that there are entries on either side of the Bank's balance sheet, and therefore one could get to the view that there never is a deposit. All this is of the nature of subterfuge and has the effect of concealing what are really very important items. Exactly the same class of transaction is done by the United States Federal Reserve Banks, mainly the Bank of New York. They have this system by which they invest money in bills for foreign investors, and they are expressly shown in their balance sheet. They are in no sense technical deposits and they are not shown as such, but they have a statement in their monthly return showing the volume of bills purchased for foreign institutions, and that seems to me much sounder.

(MR BRAND) *You get all the advantage of publicity that way.* Yes.

(MR MCKENNA) *I cannot see the distinction between the liability of the Bank of England on deposit and the liability of the Bank of England to meet a cheque on demand if the drawer of the cheque holds bills with the Bank of England. I can see no difference between them.*

(PROFESSOR GREGORY) *Would Mr Keynes's point be met if the holding of bills on behalf of foreign correspondents were not incorporated in the balance sheet but were quite outside the balance sheet?* Oh, surely. (MR TULLOCH) *They are surely only agents.* (MR BRAND) *No joint stock bank would show such a figure.* (MR TULLOCH) *No.*

(MR LUBBOCK) *Mr McKenna, when you buy bills on behalf of your foreign clients do you show them?* (MR MCKENNA) *We should not show them, but they have no right to draw upon us in respect of these bills.*

(MR LUBBOCK) *They may ask you to discount them in the market.* (MR MCKENNA) *They may ask us to discount them in the market and if a credit balance is created they can draw upon it.*

(LORD BRADBURY) *The Bank has an obligation to discount the bills.*

(MR LUBBOCK) *I suppose there is a sort of understanding that they can always have them discounted as a matter of course at the rate of the day.*

(MR MCKENNA) *If we hold bills for a foreign customer we are under no obligation to let him draw upon us. We may or may not discount the bills for cash if he asks us. If he asked us to discount the bills we should do so in the ordinary course of business.*

(MR BRAND) *Surely if he asked you, you would do it. You could not decline to do it.*

(MR MCKENNA) *Well, in the ordinary sense of business you could not. We are under no legal obligation. We are under no obligation to cash his cheque until after we have discounted his bills and created a deposit.*

(CHAIRMAN) *Sir Ernest Harvey's reply on the point (Q 230) was:—The money is sent to the Bank of England for the purpose of being invested in bills, and the instruction will be to invest in bills acceptable by the Bank of England, and those bills they expect to be able to discount, in case of need, in exactly the same way as every other holder of acceptable bank bills in the London market expects to be able to come to the Bank of England and discount bills.*

(MR LUBBOCK) *There is the case of the foreign bank which has bills at the Bank of England and telegraphs saying 'I shall want money'.* I should say there is no difference. That does not affect the point which is the material item. What you want to get in the balance sheet is the material item. There is an analogous point to this. Until a very few years ago the joint stock banks did not publish their acceptances, I think, but now it is recognised that the acceptances are a very material item.

(MR BRAND) *Even now they do not publish the acceptances separately from guarantees or endorsements.*

(MR MCKENNA) We *do.*

(MR BRAND) *And Lloyds do, but I think some of the others do not. The important thing is not that they should publish something that exactly corresponds to a certain technical description; the important thing is that they should publish the material items.*

(MR TULLOCH) *The material item is that there are bills which they may be called upon to discount, or be asked to discount.* I should wish other institutions also would publish similar holdings as being very necessary to get a true picture of the situation. We propose to meet that by their making a joint return, and I think that might possibly provide an approach. Supposing the Bank of England published a return of bills held both by itself and by the clearing banks on foreign account, without distinguishing, that would meet my point about the substantial item, without disclosing any information peculiar to the Bank of England. That is what, in fact, has been done in the half-yearly returns sent to us. If that figure was published the material point would be met. Apart from that, I think the policy of year by year putting out a balance sheet which is more and more meaningless and less and less concerns the material items is on the whole a mistake, and from time to time the balance sheet ought to be brought up to date so as to show the really material items. The United States system is an absolute model in that way. I do not think there is any concealed item there.

(CHAIRMAN) *Sir Ernest Harvey in an answer which is before me (Q 229) said that they cannot draw on the existing deposits without discounting the bills, which is the same position as you describe in a joint stock bank.*

(PROFFESSOR GREGORY) *The essential difference between the joint stock bank and the Bank of England being that if the Bank of England discounts bills that suddenly increases the volume of money in the market.* If it is internal discounting it is in a sense a fictitious transaction. (MR MCKENNA) *It is a fictitious transaction.* (MR LUBBOCK) *No; just as Mr McKenna says, he might possibly pay the bills himself.* (MR MCKENNA) *As Professor Gregory has pointed out, that has a very different effect from the Bank of England doing it.*

(PROFESSOR GREGORY) *I should like to see the Bank of England disclose somewhere its holding of foreign bills, but I am doubtful whether that ought to go into the balance sheet. I entirely agree with Mr Keynes, though, that they ought to disclose it.* I should like to gather together these suggestions I have made for producing what, in my opinion, would be an ideal balance sheet for the Bank of England, both as regards the items shown and as regards their magnitude. I wonder if I might trouble the members of the Committee to take this down because it is the only way of making it intelligible. These are hypothetical figures produced purely for the purposes of illustration. Capital £14,500,000. Then I should like them to bring into the Rest enough of their concealed reserves while maintaining an excess sum to bring up the Rest to £50,000,000. The Rest would be shown as £50,000,000.

(CHAIRMAN) *That is adding £36,000,000.* Then public deposits £15,000,000 as a normal sort of figure. Bankers' deposits £155,000,000, brought about partly by making more classes of bankers keep deposits, and, if necessary, raising the percentage which we were discussing a moment ago. For other deposits, in order to get a round figure, say £25,500,000. That is somewhere near the present figure, I think. Then 'For account of foreign bankers'. That is the point we have been discussing.

That is a new entry? It is a new entry. It is a purely hypothetical figure, which would probably be a widely fluctuating one—£50,000,000. Then note issue £290,000,000. This is reduced, by reason of the bankers paying in some of their notes, below the present figure. That adds up to £600,000,000. Then, on the other side of the account, I should show two different gold items: First of all, reserve gold, £30,000,000. That is the excess of the note issue over the fiduciary issue, leaving the fiduciary issue at the present figure of £260,000,000. You see I have £290,000,000 in notes on the other side. Then free gold £130,000,000. Then foreign balances and bills—that means not held on foreign account, but held by the Bank of England as claims on foreign centres, or on the B.I.S., £40,000,000. Then I should rather like to show three categories below, but I am not now separating the amounts. I should like: Securities of more than three months' maturity; Securities of less than three months; and discounts and advances. The difference between the securities and discounts and advances would be exactly as Sir Ernest Harvey described to us as it is now. That is to say, securities would be assets purchased by the Bank on its own initiative, and discounts and advances would be assets coming into its possession on the initiative of its customers.

Those three items would be bunched together? Yes, and, added up together, they could come to £400,000,000, which again brings the total up to £600,000,000 on that side.

(MR MCKENNA) *Where are your holdings on account of foreign banks?* You can show them separately, if you like, but they are included in securities of less than three months. Perhaps it would be better to show them separately, and put the securities etc. at £350,000,000.

I think it would be better. Then put £350,000,000 instead of £400,000,000. Then bills on account of foreign bankers £50,000,000. I think that that both is, and appears to be, an immensely stronger position than the present one. It shows much larger liquid assets. It shows much greater strength, and it does not show the free gold as such a preposterously small proportion of the total. For example, if the free gold were to diminish by £10,000,000, that does not spoil the look of this balance sheet materially. It will be quite in the ordinary run of things to have a fluctuation of £30,000,000. If the free gold was to fall to £100,000,000, or to rise to £160,000,000, there is nothing devastating in the change in the balance sheet.

(CHAIRMAN) *It is brought into prominence in the balance sheet.* It is brought into its right proportions. At present, foreigners and the financial press, and the public, generally, attach a disproportionate importance to quite small movements of gold, because they do figure so gigantically in the Bank's balance sheet. They are also the seasonal movements. Movements of gold, which one would regard as nothing very much, have the most extraordinary effect upon the Bank of England's traditional proportion, and the whole system seems to be working on a very narrow balance. Under this I am providing the Bank with much more liquid resources to meet the foreign drain. I am providing them with much more earning assets and as regards the existing position I am showing it in a form which I think is much more truthful in substance and also fortunately much more flattering in appearance.

(MR MCKENNA) *You do not trouble about money—coin?* You can have a separate item for that. I was including that in free gold. No doubt you need a small item for silver.

(MR LUBBOCK) *Silver and coin, say £5,000,000.*

(MR MCKENNA) *That would be included in the free gold.* I ought to have put that separately. The balance sheet on the above lines would be as follows:

	£ million		£ million
Capital	14·5	Reserve gold	30·0
Rest	50·0	Free gold	125·0
Public deposits	15·0	Silver & coin	5·0
Bankers' deposits	155·0	Foreign balances or	
Other deposits	25·5	bills	40·0
For account of		Securities of more	
foreign bankers	50·0	than three months	
Note issue	290·0	maturity	
		Securities of less	350·0
		than three months	
		maturity	
		Discounts & advances	
		Bills held on account	
		of foreign bankers	50·0
	600·0		600·0

Supposing a joint stock bank draws £10,000,000 of notes from the Bank of England, the Bank's deposits will go down £10,000,000, and the note issue will go up to £300,000,000. That is right, but the right hand side of the balance sheet will remain unchanged.

(LORD BRADBURY) *Except that the reserve gold would then go up to £40,000,000.* That is quite true, and the free gold would fall to £115,000,000.

If you have a fixed fiduciary issue that follows necessarily. (MR MCKENNA) Yes. But that is not anything which is particularly disturbing to this balance sheet.

The reserves will fluctuate with the circulation. Yes.

The free gold will fluctuate with the withdrawals. I have provided against that because under this system the locked-up gold is so modest in amount that if the reserve gold was to rise from £30,000,000 to £50,000,000 I should not feel there was any ground for reasonable complaint.

(MR LUBBOCK) *All this is based on the bankers paying in notes and holding more of their cash reserves?* This is partly based on that. It is summarising the various changes I have suggested. I feel a balance sheet of that kind is much more worthy of the Bank of England than the rather miserable little affair which appears at present.

(MR MCKENNA) *We are very much more accustomed now to look at the ratio and in this balance sheet there would be no ratio. That disappears.* Yes.

(MR LUBBOCK) *Do you think that you do look at the ratio? Do not far the greater proportion of people look much more at the amount on call, and the amount of the gold? I do not care twopence about the ratio. I hate the word 'ratio', and I hope we shall never use it in this country.*

(MR MCKENNA) *We look at the reserve, but if we disregard the ratio here we have no reserve. It is the free gold which represents the reserve.* (MR LUBBOCK) *Yes. I do not like the division into reserve and free gold.*

(PROFESSOR GREGORY) *On this balance sheet £100,000,000 is purely hypothetical—£45,000,000 of it is in the Rest?* I am assuming the Bank of England has sufficient concealed reserves to bring that up to £50,000,000 and you bring in on the other side an equivalent quantity of securities.

(MR BRAND) *If you want to increase the note issue by £20,000,000, you have to add to the reserve gold and diminish the free gold.* Yes.

(LORD BRADBURY) *Unless you extend the fiduciary issue, which would mean a transfer from the reserve gold to the free gold.* There is one item I should like to dwell on for a minute and that is the hypothetical figure which I put down for foreign balances and bills. I think it would be very wise to raise the foreign bills to this figure at once by borrowing from the Federal Reserve Bank the necessary amount and then paying it off over four years at the rate of £10,000,000 a year. It would increase the liquid resources at once, whereas the business in present circumstances of building up such a reserve would be very difficult and costly and could only be done by contraction.

(MR LUBBOCK) *But that is rather a startling proposition.*

(PROFESSOR GREGORY) *You, in fact, arrive at it perfectly simply by getting the Federal Reserve Bank to put a credit in the Bank of England of £50,000,000. You could do it in that way.* That is the suggestion. If the Bank of England did anything of the sort it would be a very good thing, if it accustomed the public to seeing fairly substantial fluctuations in the free reserve which hypothetically I have put at £170,000,000. If the Bank of England allowed that to fluctuate fairly widely without troubling too much. I think the disadvantages to our domestic trade of being an international financial market would be greatly diminished. It would then only be necessary to curtail the credit for home purposes when it was really adjudged necessary to do so in the interests of long-period equilibrium.

(MR LUBBOCK) *Does it do more than that now?* I think it does.

You can put up the Bank rate without curtailing credit. It would have to, to make it effective?

It is effective—but does it work? I agree you can do it to some extent without curtailing credit, but I think to a very limited extent.

It is only short term. Putting up the Bank rate, even if it is not accompanied by anything else, affects the domestic situation by affecting the rate of interest charged for a vast number of transactions, and owing to its associations it has a very great effect on public opinion.

It has far too much effect. That is one of the things which one wants to get away from. At present, when the Bank of England puts up the Bank rate to check certain movements of gold, perhaps the great bulk of debtors fear that they will have to pay more on advances from their bankers, whereas in a very large number of cases of changes of the Bank rate the rate on advances does not move at all. But if the whole of industrial conditions are out of adjustment and there has to be a long-term squeeze it does affect it. I am afraid it affects the domestic situation not only when it is necessary to have a long-term squeeze.

It does have a greater effect because all the newspapers begin to howl and tell all the traders they are ruined, whereas to the great bulk of traders it makes no difference. The traders do not know at present whether it is a signal that they are going to be ruined, or not, because if it were to be the beginning of a long period squeeze the Bank would ostensibly do the same thing.

That is quite true. So that sometimes it is not entirely foolish for people to be upset. They do not quite know just what kind of an operation it is. (MR BEVIN) *How do you know whether it is going to be long, or short?* (MR LUBBOCK) *It is very difficult to say.* (MR BEVIN) *Is not that the trouble?*

(MR LUBBOCK) *Supposing the Bank of England did come out —the exchanges are looking very weak—with a rise of from 3 to 4 per cent, would the traders be really hurt now?* I think it would be a very serious position if the Bank rate was raised to 4 per cent today. It would affect the issue market, and it would affect people's interpretation of the situation, which is a very important factor.

Supposing we did happen to be lending a little more than we ought to lend, and whereas our trade position might be fairly good our capital movements were a little too much against us and the Bank rate was put up, how are we going to get the public mind to distinguish? Perhaps we do not know ourselves whether it is going to be a long-term squeeze, or not. I do not think you can do so on your present methods—it is very difficult anyhow.

You are suggesting if the exchanges were moving against us and £15,000,000 or £20,000,000 of gold was going we should say 'let it go'. Yes.

257

On the assumption that it will come back with a 3 per cent Bank rate. Yes, if it is due to a temporary cause. If you have misjudged the situation, then if you have adequate reserves it is not too late to correct it.

Supposing it is true that this year we have lent £30,000,000 more than our favourable foreign balances, are we going to regard that as a permanent loan, and as a permanent loss of gold, because we have invested £180,000,000 instead of £150,000,000? I should say you ought to be prepared to do that and get it back at a convenient season. It would help the world situation today very much if we were to overlend and do so at the cost of losing gold.

Can we do enough with our small gold reserves to affect the world very much? We can do something, because we can affect sentiment in other centres to a great extent.

Supposing £30,000,000 of gold went to New York would any good be done by that? I think it would because it would influence them to take earlier steps than they would otherwise, to make themselves an easier lending centre.

Supposing the Federal Reserve Bank was doing all it could to make money easy and putting money out, but there was no good foreign bond offered? If, in fact, no foreign bond was offered, no one would lend his money. The way in which foreign investment by the United States will take place in the near future, if at all, will not be by means of large volumes of new bonds of a foreign kind being placed there because as you say, there is no such large supply of those things, but it will come by cheap money in the United States producing a rise in their domestic securities and causing very low rates in their short loan market, so that a certain margin of funds is withdrawn by foreigners by the sale of their existing American assets because the American assets will come to look very unattractive. There is such an enormous amount of foreign assets that it would be sufficient if a very small percentage of them were to be withdrawn.

(MR MCKENNA) *I think Mr Keynes's view would be absolutely right if we could rely upon foreign sentiment, but I am afraid we cannot.*

(MR LUBBOCK) *That is what I think.*

(MR MCKENNA) *If we lost £30,000,000 of gold now to the United States or to France, the effect on the foreign holders of bills in this country would be to induce them to take more gold.* That is with our existing reserves, but if we had £200,000,000 and they came down to £170,000,000 it would not matter.

I agree if we had £200,000,000. That is the hypothesis of my argument. *I was supposing we had £160,000,000.* And £40,000,000 foreign bills.

(MR LUBBOCK) *Would it not be a bad example to the world if we set about deliberately trying to squeeze another £40,000,000.* Yes, but I am suggesting the implementing medium should be foreign bills.

Borrowing from the United States? Yes. *I cannot grasp it.*

(MR MCKENNA) *If we borrowed £40,000,000 from the United States I am*

258

afraid the French would take £100,000,000 from us. If the world understood the position I think your view is absolutely correct but I think they do not understand it. Then we should borrow whatever sum would enable us to repay the French. If what you say is right, then I should borrow £200,000,000 from the United States. It is a matter of opinion, but, in fact, it is much better for us to owe the money to them than to owe it to France.

(MR LUBBOCK) *Mr Keynes is talking about this outgoing £30,000,000 having all this effect on the world, but I do not know.* I am not particularly addressing myself to the present situation because the present situation is peculiar with the French drain of gold, but I am looking forward to a permanent system. It seems to me, if we are to be permanently in a situation in which a loss of £30,000,000 upsets us, there is no means of making compatible the maintenance of ourselves as an international financial centre with the interests of bought trade, and in the end trade will get its way. If you ask for too much concession as a result of being an international financial centre you will lose.

We are going to ask foreign countries to do with less gold? I am not suggesting we should hold more gold. I am proposing we should increase our liquid assets by holding more foreign bills.

(MR BRAND) *In fact, if the reserve is to be so sensitive it would be for the national interest for us to try and get in the position of France and the United States, and not to lend so much abroad for a year or two and get more gold.*

(CHAIRMAN) *It seems to me it would be necessary to institute classes on political economy for international financiers in order that they may be better able to understand their own business.* (MR MCKENNA) *It would be very desirable.* (MR NEWBOLD) *Or our view of their business—that is what it really amounts to.* (CHAIRMAN) *Yes, but that is a thing we cannot put into our Report.*

(MR LUBBOCK) *I am afraid Mr Keynes will have to introduce a great change into the mentality of our market and other markets before anything of this kind can be done.*

(MR MCKENNA) *Well, so far as the mentality of the markets is concerned, I do not think the proposal to adopt a balance sheet of this kind is at all disturbed by the fact that we might disagree on the question whether it would be desirable or not to raise the Bank rate when £30,000,000 of gold has gone.*

(CHAIRMAN) *The whole object of the new balance sheet is to enable this drain to appear less serious—to enable it to be done.*

(MR MCKENNA) *I think some gold could be taken from here with less effect on public opinion than it is likely to have on the basis of the present balance sheet. I should hesitate to say that £30,000,000 could go, but a certain considerable amount could go whereas now if £5,000,000 goes there is an immediate effect and if £10,000,000 goes it has a considerable effect. I do not think £10,000,000 would have an effect if you had the balance sheet in the way suggested, but I do not quite know that you could go up to £30,000,000. I certainly would adopt this kind of balance sheet. It is a much stronger one and would give the Bank of England greater strength.*

(CHAIRMAN) *With such a balance sheet the public would regard the withdrawal of £30,000,000 as relatively unimportant, and, therefore, would not be disturbed.*

(MR MCKENNA) *I do not think they would be disturbed here.*

(LORD BRADBURY) *Is not it rather a prior question whether the public should regard the going of £30,000,000 as unimportant?* It is very important that they should sometimes.

I am not so sure about that. If you want to upset the domestic system whenever you have an international disequilibrium the present system is admirable for the purpose, and I have no improvement to suggest.

The question is whether it is not necessary to have a certain amount of upset though I agree there are certain conceivable circumstances in which it is not necessary. There are cases which we have had frequently quite lately where the drain has been caused by a definite piece of policy on the part of a foreign central bank, or something of that kind. But then I am not sure when you have got that kind of thing whether £30,000,000 is much good. You would want a much larger amount. Supposing there was a serious attempt made to remove the French balances from here, £30,000,000 would be of no use against that.

(MR BRAND) *That is so, but would not it be better for us to do to some extent what the French are doing, and instead of having to change our Bank rate so often let us have a much larger reserve which I suppose we can get in this country if we wish to set ourselves about it.*

(LORD BRADBURY) *Then we are going into the general world scramble for gold which is undesirable.*

(MR LUBBOCK) *Or put a real embargo on any foreign lending, or on any foreign investments.* I think I am a better friend to the future of London as an international financial centre than you are, but it is a matter of opinion.

(LORD BRADBURY) *I am afraid this may be an expedient in the nature of nailing down a railway signal at safety in order to avoid a collision.*

(PROFESSOR GREGORY) *It boils down to this. One has to trust the Bank of England to discriminate between particular cases which one has to do in any case. If the Bank takes the view that £30,000,000 is incidental to the position of the French balances in London, we assume that is a different attitude on their part than if it was due to foreign lending.*

(MR LUBBOCK) *We have had variations of £45,000,000. We talk about £30,000,000, but we have seen variations of a good deal more just recently.*

(MR BRAND) *My impression is that everybody abroad is thinking that we look with great fear on gold going and have been doing so in the last few years.*

(MR LUBBOCK) *It is quite true that a great many foreigners are looking at us and saying 'What a very small amount of gold reserves these people hold for their tremendous liabilities.'*

(MR BRAND) *They always have said that.*

(MR LUBBOCK) *We are setting a very good example to the world.*

(CHAIRMAN) *I think we have the point on this part of the matter.*

(MR BRAND) *They say that because we can export so little without having to take steps owing to our peculiar system.*

(MR LUBBOCK) *With £150,000,000, or £160,000,000, or £140,000,000, and our tremendous commitments, how can we do it?*

(LORD BRADBURY) *We have not got £150,000,000. We cannot touch that.*

(MR LUBBOCK) *There is not any power to touch that at all.*

(MR BRAND) *I say there is, but Lord Bradbury says there is not.*

(LORD BRADBURY) *There is in certain circumstances.*

(MR BRAND) *You mean by going to the Chancellor?*

(LORD BRADBURY) *Yes. The majority of the Committee think it desirable that we should have a larger amount of reserve with a view to being able to lose a greater amount of gold without affecting the domestic rate. Assuming that is desirable, then it seems to me the only method of doing that consistently with not taking part in the international scramble for gold is to make a practice of holding in normal times large foreign balances as Mr Keynes suggests. We should have a larger mobile reserve obviously by keeping our existing gold reserve and adding to it in normal times £50,000,000, or £60,000,000, or even £100,000,000 of foreign balances. That seems to me to be very much the best way of securing a larger mobile reserve if a larger mobile reserve is really going to help the situation at all about which I am somewhat sceptical.*

(MR LUBBOCK) *If we have our gold and our foreign balances and bills, will the market regard the reduction in foreign balances and bills in the same way as they do gold or will it not have the same effect?* They would regard it as less ostentatious.

Is that a good thing? When it is desirable for the Bank of England to be ostentatious, they will let the gold go. I give them an alternative. I wish I could shake the complacency of the Bank of England. All my proposals under this head are directed towards caution and increasing its strength. There is a little danger—though I cannot believe it—that any suggestions for increasing the strength of the Bank of England will be taken as a criticism of its present strength, and, therefore, will be rejected because it will imply all is not well at the moment. That is not the intention of what I am suggesting. It is not intended as a sharp criticism, but it is the outcome of a very strong feeling on my part that the future contains far greater elements of danger than we are inclined to admit.

(MR MCKENNA) *This is to show strength, not to increase strength.* It is both. It is to affect opinion partly by showing strength and partly by increasing strength.

You increase strength by £40,000,000 of foreign bonds. And also by a large amount of gold being available and also by the Bank of England having a larger mass of securities by which it can enforce its will on the market. In the aggregate, I think I have enormously increased the strength of the Bank of England.

(MR LUBBOCK)*There is one rather important point you have left out, namely, what the Bank will pay to the Treasury.* I had not meant to say much about that today. I should be in favour of something like the present figure being fixed for good. I should be opposed to interesting the Treasury in any way in the profits of the Bank of England.

(MR MCKENNA) *There is no reason on these figures to change the present arrangement.*

(LORD BRADBURY) *You would have to change the formula because the Treasury now gets the actual earnings on certain securities less expenses.*

(MR MCKENNA) *You hold securities against the £260,000,000.*

(MR LUBBOCK) *We couldn't earmark them if we had one Department. I forgot what the profit has worked out at in recent years.*

(CHAIRMAN) *You propose a retaining fee for the Bank of England in effect?* Yes.

(LORD BRADBURY) *It would be fixed on the experience of the past, applying a flat percentage on the fiduciary issue.* Something like that.

Not necessarily flat—it might have to vary according to the changes in the value of money.

(MR MCKENNA) *You can easily obtain a formula which would not require the Bank of England to earmark securities against it.*

(LORD BRADBURY) *It would be quite easy to devise something.* I have now come to my last heading, and that is the increase of information at the disposal of the Bank of England and information given by it. I attach enormous importance particularly in the long period to getting rid of unnecessary secrecy and mystery of all kinds. I think, generally speaking, there must be a slight price paid in the first instance in the way of possible misunderstandings and so forth, but I think that such a price, if any, is of a very short duration. The more we get rid of unnecessary secrecy and mystery the more we can facilitate informed outside criticism. We increase the freedom with which the Bank officials can discuss the position and make use of collective wisdom. If everything is secret and everything has to be discussed in confidence the circle within which opinions can be freely exchanged is unduly narrowed. I think also that greater publicity of all kinds will lead to better understanding by the market of what the Bank's intentions are, and that will facilitate those intentions being carried into effect quicker and with more certainty. It nearly always pays the market to adapt itself to the real intentions of the Bank. So that the easier it is to interpret those, the quicker in effect will be the methods of control which the Bank uses. Publicity will also help to educate the public and the world and bring much nearer the day, which I am sure we should all welcome, when the principles of central banking will be utterly removed from popular controversy and will be regarded as a kind of beneficent technique of scientific control such as electricity or other branches of science are. At present the feeling of all of us towards banking problems represents, I think, a very primitive stage of knowledge, and if we could get into a more advanced stage of knowledge a great many of what are at present legitimate fears of wrong pressures being brought to bear, and so forth, will gradually disappear.

(MR LUBBOCK) *You are a very sanguine man.* It will, at any rate, be brought nearer by making possible a rational discussion of these subjects. The Bank of England by its mystery, I think not only retards scientific progress, but, instead of rendering itself less open to popular pressure and to dangerous charges, renders itself more open to these things.

(MR BEVIN) *Hear, hear.* That is precisely because the right defence so often cannot be made. Apart from information given by the Bank, I think the Bank has been seriously hampered by its lack of certain categories of information. It has been given to us in evidence that the Bank of England has not known what is the holding of notes by the joint stock banks. So that it has not known the actual active circulation of notes, in spite of the fact that traditionally it has been supposed to pay great attention to that as an indicator. The Bank of England has not known with any degree of accuracy the volume of foreign balances in England or their fluctuations. It has been in the position almost of a Bank with many branches which has not taken the trouble to acquire information as to how large the deposits in its branches were. It has only been able to guess at the magnitude of the liabilities against which it was holding its reserves and when there has been a strain on it it has only been able to guess as to the source from which that strain came, and which of the various items that make up our balance of trade is at fault. It is easy for us to recommend that these two phases of essential information should be regularly available to the Bank and I should hope to the public too. But, beyond that, I believe the Bank of England is well placed (and I think this is not at all out of accord with the present ideas of the Bank of England itself) for building up a very complete statistical department. It has some advantages over the public departments for that purpose. It would be most valuable if it would publish monthly figures of all monthly statistics of general or scientific interest. My belief is that it would not be very long before the Bank of England was publishing something far and away ahead of the United States *Federal Reserve Bulletin*, a document which at present is the admiration of the world, but which I believe could be easily surpassed by the resources at the disposal of the Bank of England. But I think that scientific control of the monetary system will require increasingly not merely monetary statistics. I suggest that attempts ought to be made to build up, first of all, sample statistics and eventually comprehensive statistics of such things as the volume of foreign lending in all shapes and forms, trying to make an annual balance sheet, or even a monthly balance sheet of this country, under the five or six headings which I analysed last week. We ought to know accurately our foreign favourable balance on income account and we ought to have knowledge of the fluctuations under the different headings of capital account. We ought to know the volume of physical capital investments at home to a high degree of accuracy. There is no intrinsic difficulty whatever if one builds up an organisation for the purpose in having those figures. We ought to have, as the Americans have, what they call an index of payrolls, that is to say information from a body of firms of the aggregate which they are paying out in wages each week. That is a very valuable indicator each week what the payroll for the country is as a whole. We ought to know the volume of retail sales. The Bank of England has already taken steps to secure statistics for that. We ought to know the fluctuations and absolute magnitude of the stocks of manufacturers, dealers, and retailers. We ought to have information as to business profits. It is a most extraordinary thing that this Committee has no definite information as to whether business profits in the conditions of the last six months, or even the last eighteen months are, or are not, a great deal lower than they were, say, in 1924. The available statistics suggest that perhaps they are not lower, whereas common opinion and the general impression is that they are a great deal lower. We have no check on mere impressionism in the matter.

Finally, we ought to have much better information,—something that the Board of Trade is endeavouring to do now with its index of production—on the general question of the volume of the national production. If we had all those figures, we could build up in time a true and accurate picture of the economic life of the country and the movements in that life, and we could really put our finger on what was going wrong when anything was going wrong, and see where we were. We could understand whether the fluctuations were of a fundamental character, or were not of a fundamental character. It might take five or ten years' experience to make a good job of it. Many of the tables in the early days would be open to severe criticism,—but none of the items which I have mentioned present any intrinsically impossible problem, or even a very difficult problem, particularly if in the first instance it is done by sampling rather than by attempting to be absolutely comprehensive. It is always difficult to get people to believe that you can get valuable statistics without covering absolutely the whole field, because with many fluctuations it is the changes that matter rather than the absolute figure; but if you are covering some sample area each time you can get very near the percentage fluctuations, even if you have not got the absolute figures. We should then have a means of investigating the national economic life, and we should be able to watch and control every movement in a way which today would be considered completely utopian. I am in favour, therefore, of the Bank making itself the centre of complete and scientific knowledge on all those matters which are valuable to the persons in control of the monetary management of the country. I am not in favour, I think, of the Bank indulging too much in mere expressions of opinion. I do not suggest that they should become unduly loquacious in that way, but at the present moment the Bank of England notoriously goes to the other extreme. It does seem to me there would be advantages in the Governor of the Bank, say twice a year, giving a comprehensive review of the situation. But if he had behind him the great statistical machine that I envisage, it would be more easy for him to base his survey upon facts and to say a great deal that was informative and valuable, without risking personal expressions of opinion based on mere impression- ism, which is the risk that anyone lays himself open to who does make a general statement today on the basis of the facts that he is able to command. I should have thought that it would be within the power of the Governor on such occasions to give a review which would come to be regarded throughout the world as an authoritative, scientific expression of the state of affairs.

That brings me to the end of this discourse. I feel that if our monetary system is to be managed and our economic life is to be regulated at the source, there can be no possible instrument of this except the Bank of England. In many ways the historic Bank of England, as it has evolved, seems to me to be ideal for this purpose. Without any break of continuity or traditions, everything which seems desirable to a radical thinker, like myself, can, I am sure, be achieved. I should like to see our Report centre round the magnification and evolutionary enlargements of the functions of the Bank of England. It is for that reason that I have spent a good deal of time in making suggestions which, though they have not commanded universal acceptance, were intended by me in every case to strengthen the Bank of England, and to furnish it with powers for much more securely beneficent action in the future than in the past, so that by the time her new mansion[11] is ready for her, she must be no longer the 'Old Lady of Threadneedle Street' gathering her skirts

---

[11] The Bank had started rebuilding its premises in April 1925. Work was completed in mid-1942

round her, but some new image must be thought of appropriate to the occupant of the new palace.

(CHAIRMAN) *A bright young thing?* I hardly know what—perhaps Mr Lubbock can suggest something?

(MR LUBBOCK) *Well, I am one of the old timers.*

(CHAIRMAN) *I would like to ask one question about this statistical department that you propose. Is it your view that that is the proper function of the Bank of England, because of the sources of information available to it?* I think there are one or two reasons. A good many of the figures which have to be collected are of a confidential character individually, though not in the aggregate. I think the Bank of England would be more trusted than almost any other collecting agency by those people, particularly in the early days of this system, who fear that the information they were giving might be used to their disadvantage.

This is quite a general observation. One has a sort of feeling nowadays that a vast amount of time in our country is spent in compiling documents of all sorts about every thing which goes on in this country, while the thing we are actually conducting is steadily diminishing. We are more and more compiling statistics about our affairs, many of which would not be valuable, or really are of comparatively little value. We have some historic statistics which might be dropped, but there have been so many axes wielded in the past that on the whole we err in the other direction. We are doing some very foolish things in collecting valuable statistics and economising so much on the staff that they cannot ever be published, or they are published so late as to be of little value. That is the case with the Census of Production. The staff handling the figures has been so cut down that many of them cannot be used and the date of publication is desperately late. I do not think you could accuse this country of going too far in the output of statistics if you were familiar with what is happening in the United States today. I believe that in the United States they are collecting statistics which will be of the utmost value to science. But really we are in a better position than the United States for doing this kind of thing and it is a much more manageable proposition in this country. I believe we are more capable in the long run of building this up. Also, after all, statistics cost such very trifling sums to collect in relation to the magnitude of the issues involved. If one does waste a little money and get some foolish statistics, it does not very much matter. It is a very trifling thing. Particularly in early days it is so difficult to know for certain what statistics are useful, and what are not. It is, in fact, a branch of science in which the accumulation of accurate, but odd, pieces of knowledge might come in in the most remarkable way. I think that is often the case in the United States. Their pieces of information come in useful for quite different purposes than those for which they were originally collected.

(MR BRAND) *I know for a fact that if you want in England information about companies and so forth, it is most difficult to obtain. I happen to belong to a firm which has branches in New York and Paris, and our intelligence department in France can obtain far more accurate and detailed information about industrial companies, and so forth, than they can obtain in this country.*

(PROFESSOR GREGORY) *That is partly due to the fact that the private collection of information is better organised.*

(MR BRAND) *Not in France.*

(MR NEWBOLD) *I should have thought that America had a perfect plethora of statistics, some of which were a little dubious.*

(CHAIRMAN) *I was going to say this about quite a different sphere. I have studied legal affairs in America and I have been appalled at their apparatus compared with their output. I get all kinds of reports about things like legal education. I have tried to read some of them and then I look at the lawyers they produce. I have not seen anything in my own department of science such as the apparatus I have seen in America, and I have never seen anything less impressive than the result.*

(MR BRAND) *The absence of statistics does not guarantee production.* I am prepared to scrap all the legal reports if I can have my economic statistics.

(CHAIRMAN) *I might equally say I should be happy to burn most of the works of the political economists.* Except you have precluded yourself from that conclusion by already saying that the reports you are referring to are useless on your side of science, which is not my view of those on my side.

Apart from that, the really operative point of this is that the Bank of England for its own purposes ought to be better informed, and, consequently, the information which it ought to compile for its own information should be more complete and should be made available to a larger extent to the public so that better informed criticism of its action may be brought about. That is the real point of it.

(PROFESSOR GREGORY) *May I put it rather more completely. At the moment we judge the economic position and the domestic position almost entirely from the fluctuations in the volume of unemployment. As things actually are we cannot correct our judgement by anything else [such] as the rate of physical investment, or any of these other things which we have been discussing. The result is we may be getting an entirely misleading picture of what is actually happening.*

(MR BRAND) *It is all so much based upon opinion.*

(CHAIRMAN) *I am less optimistic about the possibility of creating a better informed opinion upon these matters though you might have better technical opinion, I agree—better expert opinion.*

(MR BEVIN) *What do you mean by 'public opinion'?* (CHAIRMAN) *The kind of thing you read in the newspapers.* (MR BEVIN) *Oh, well.* (CHAIRMAN) *The public will not read statistics.* (MR BEVIN) *The public does read the unemploy-*

ment returns. (CHAIRMAN) *They read the popular articles produced by people who, having read the statistics, are not able to understand them.* (PROFESSOR GREGORY) *The public do read unemployment returns and it would be very useful if we could correct that by some information as to the rate of physical production. We have the Board of Trade index of physical production, but that is not entirely satisfactory.* (MR BEVIN) *I think all this is changing, you know.* (PROFESSOR GREGORY) *The Bank of England is already doing fairly extensive statistical work.* I do not think anything I am suggesting would be at all contrary to the trend of affairs at the Bank. I did not mean to put it in that light at all, but rather opening up vistas of the sort of thing we might expect from them, if they carry out their own ideas.

(CHAIRMAN) *So far as we have seen from the evidence from the Bank, I do not think they would be at all out of sympathy with some such proposal. They have developed a considerable intelligence department. They have recently been publishing documents which we have seen, of a statistical character.*

(MR BRAND) *Are they published?*

(CHAIRMAN) *They are not published yet, and the question might be whether they are to be published.*

(PROFESSOR GREGORY) *There is no reason why anybody in this country should not be able to buy that Bank bulletin of statistics.* I am thinking of something which will involve that.

(MR BEVIN) *There is a small public opinion which is at present badly informed on all these things and that is the people who have to handle industry. It is quite true that the ordinary man in the street reading the paper in the tube or in the bus, does not read statistics, but when you get collective bargaining, the technique that has entered into that business is far greater than it was pre-War, and it is very difficult to get the correct information. You must have discovered that when you went to Yorkshire.*

(CHAIRMAN) *Yes.* I think it is possible that some of the items which I have mentioned could be better done by Government Departments. I was not stopping at the moment to consider the exact delimitations between the two. I feel there are a good many statistics about which the Bank of England has advantages in collecting over the Government Departments, but not in all cases.

How far do you regard these matters as expert matters, and how far are they matters which are really susceptible of comprehension. There are always two spheres of knowledge. There are certain things where the general conspectus is understandable by the public but the technique of many branches of science is quite non-understandable. The work that is done by the Astronomer Royal is not work which I personally am at least able to follow. I can read all kinds of things which are instructive and which one must read as part of the general education of a person of ordinary attainments, but I do not seek, as a member of the public, to ask the Astronomer Royal to explain to me the technique of his art. It would be quite useless, because, even though he is sufficiently expert to do it, there are very few people who are in a position to criticise him, though no doubt there is a small and select circle who can. It appears to me on the question of political economy there is a sphere in which we are all interested, and on which we all ought to be informed, but there are also highly technical spheres which I feel frankly, with the most optimistic view, you will never get people to understand, and it is not their business to understand. Is not that the position? I think that is a difficult question to answer. My belief is that in the near future economics will become increasingly technical and difficult for the outsider, because the economists will be settling a number of matters among themselves and will have to discuss them in their own way, but a point may come when over a certain part of the field there will be much wider agreement. They will settle their quarrels among themselves and come to an agreement. When they have done that, they will be able to expound that part of the subject which is settled in very much simpler language, and then it will rest with the world whether it understands them. Very likely they will themselves get still more advanced on a part which is again in the technical realm, but at present the difficulty is that parts of the subject which one feels ought to be elementary are still in this disputed condition.

The thing that appals me, after listening for many days to this discussion, is this: That while the fate of everyone apparently to a large extent is determined by decisions which are taken by experts, those decisions must be taken upon knowledge and upon principles which seem to me extraordinarily recondite, extraordinarily difficult to understand, and upon which you do not find agreement among the professors of the science. I do not say that in any derogatory sense. It is because of the nature of the material you are dealing with. Yet, in many ordinary matters of life, you are capable of forming a judgement after a case has been put before you, even though you are a layman—you can form a really quite reasonable opinion upon the matter. On some political problems you can, although you may say you have not full access to information. In those cases you can form a practical opinion which is quite of value, but so many problems that we have been discussing seem to me to be wrapped up in such a degree of technical mystery that I do not know where we are getting. It is not a question of the Bank of England being mysterious, but the subject itself seems to be so difficult. Do you think it really is so difficult compared with other things? If we had been talking about physics or biology, I believe it would have been very much more difficult.

You would never ask an ordinary cultivated man to deliver an opinion on physical or biological problems. You would consult a few biologists at Oxford or Cambridge on their problem, but you would not come to me and you would not expect me to understand it. It is just the same with the quantitative theory in chemistry. I know there is such a theory, but I am not capable of explaining it, and I do not consider it is my business to do it. If I were to criticise the people to whom these things are left, I should never get on with my own business. I work my own particular business to the best of my ability and I leave these things to the people who are able to determine them. The choice of the expert is a very important thing in the modern state, but having chosen him it always seems to me the better plan is to wish him God speed at his job.

(MR MCKENNA) *Supposing we were considering here the action of the Bank of France, should we have the slightest difficulty in understanding what the Governor of the Bank of France was doing, and in recognising how wrong he was?*

(MR LUBBOCK) *I do not know what the poor man can do.*

(MR MCKENNA) *I agree he cannot help himself, but still we have no difficulty in recognising the policy he is pursuing. It is not really a difficult problem.*

(Adjourned *sine die*)

Over the winter of 1930–1 a drafting committee, consisting of Keynes, Lubbock, Gregory, Brand and the chairman set to work on the committee's Report. As expected, Keynes took an active part in the drafting committee's work. By 20 January 1931 he had prepared a framework for a possible report and drafts to fill out Parts I and IIA and B. The outline appears below.

COMMITTEE ON FINANCE AND INDUSTRY

Scheme of Draft

I   A Survey of the Problem
    A. The Disequilibrium of Prices and Costs
    B. The Problem of adjusting incomes to changes in the value of Money
II   Certain Special Questions
    A. The Adequacy of the Supply of Gold
    B. The Adequacy of the Supply of Credit for British Business
    C. The Functions of Bank Rate
III   How far is the Fall of Prices due to Monetary Causes?
IV   The Objectives of the Monetary System
    A. International
    B. Domestic
V   Proposals relating to International Monetary Action
    A. Of a permanent character
    B. To meet the present emergency

Keynes's proposed format for the report was influential, for with a division of his chapters into two broad sections, the break coming between III and IV, the drafts soon began to take the form of a first part devoted to historical and descriptive matters and a second devoted to conclusions and recommendations. This format survived in the published version of the Committee's Report.

Further drafts or parts of drafts by Keynes exist in the Keynes Papers on the following subjects: The Objectives of the Monetary System (2 February); Proposals Relating to International Monetary Action (3 February); Proposals Relating to Domestic Monetary Action: B, To Meet the Present Emergency (31 March, revised 24 April); Proposals Relating to Information and Statistics (9 April, revise undated). In addition, there are undated fragmentary drafts on The Note Issue (2 versions), The Sequence of Events since 1924 and The Recent Working of the Gold Standard. These drafts and fragments of drafts are not reprinted here.

Although drafting continued during January, February and March 1931, there was relatively little discussion, with only six meetings being recorded in Keynes's appointments book. It was only in April that discussion and re-drafting began in earnest, with Keynes's appointments book recording eleven meetings. This level of activity continued into May with thirteen meetings before the report was 'signed' on 29 May.[12] Keynes left for the United States the next day.[13]

As might be expected in a drafting committee containing the range, personalities, views and experience of Brand, Gregory, Keynes and Lubbock, agreement was not always the order of the day and disputes inevitably arose. Thus when R. H. Brand attempted to outline the coverage of a bridging chapter between the two major sections of the report, the following exchange appeared.

[12]   The published Report was signed on 23 June, while Keynes was in America.
[13]   See below, pp. 529–88.

COMMENTS ON MR BRAND'S MEMORANDUM ON THE
NEED FOR A BRIDGING CHAPTER

This memorandum brings home to me what I was beginning to forget, namely that I have nowhere introduced into my draft chapters in any clear or emphatic form what *I* believe to be the fundamental explanation of the present position. I felt, I think, when I was drafting that this was rather a personal theory of my own and that some members of the Committee might be more inclined to agree with my practical conclusions than with my fundamental reasons. Hence, what has resulted is a semi-suppression of the latter. But Brand points out in effect how lame the result is. For unless my general explanation is more or less on the right lines, it is not at all clear that it is feasible for central banks to do what I am asking them to do.

My fundamental explanation is, of course, that the rate of interest is too high,—meaning by the 'rate of interest' the complex of interest rates for all kinds of borrowing, long and short, safe and risky. A good many of Brand's factors I should accept as part of the explanation *why* interest rates are high, e.g. effects of the War, post-War instability, reparations, return to gold, mal-distribution of gold, want of confidence in debtor countries etc., etc. Now for a number of years after the War enterprise was for a variety of reasons able to support a high rate of interest. This came to an end sooner in this country than elsewhere. On the other hand, it continued longer in U.S.A. than elsewhere: also, up to 1929, one important method of borrowing in that country, namely by the issue of ordinary shares, was *cheap*. Today enterprise is not ready to pay much more than a normal pre-War rate of interest. Consequently at the current market rates of interest it is impossible to absorb the whole of the world's savings, the inevitable results of which are heavy business losses and the fall of prices. Moreover, so long as prices are falling, the rate of interest which enterprise can support drops temporarily far below even its normal rate. We cannot possibly recover normal prosperity, in my opinion, until the market rate of interest and the natural rate (meaning by this the rate at which the world's savings would be just absorbed) are brought together instead of standing a long way apart.

Next comes the question how far central banks can remedy this. In ordinary times the equilibrium rate of interest does not change quickly, so long as slump and boom conditions can be prevented from developing; and I see no insuperable difficulty in central banks controlling the position. But at the moment they are presented with an altogether abnormal problem. For it is not merely a question of reviving the natural rate to its normal long-term level, which is the usual problem in a slump; but also—so I believe—of bringing down the market rate from a level to which the world has been long accustomed. For the probable normal long-term level of the natural rate for the years to come is, I maintain, a long way below the market rate which has prevailed in recent years and much nearer to the pre-War long-term normal. The drastic reduction of the whole complex of market-rates of interest presents central banks with a problem which I do not expect them to solve unless they are prepared to employ drastic and even direct methods of influencing long-term investments which, I agree with Brand, they had better leave alone in more normal times. I have, as he says, analysed all this at considerable length in my book.

The whole matter is vastly important. I incline to believe that during the period of the economic construction of the modern world we have enjoyed, generally speaking, market rates if anything *below* the natural rate, and this has been a necessary condition of the accumulation of wealth. On the other hand, during the greater part of recorded history market rates have been, as at present, *above* the natural rate. During such periods, which have lasted for as much as 500 years at a time, economic progress and the accumulation of wealth have stood still or receded. This time we should probably abolish our existing economic system if present conditions looked like lasting indefinitely. More probably still, (that is, if I am right) we shall find the solution before things have got quite intolerable. But I should not be surprised if five years were to pass by before hard experience teaches us to get hold of the right end of the stick.

Is the Committee prepared to accept anything at all like the above? If so, this should—though of course, in quite a different form—comprise a large part of the bridging chapter. If not, then I agree with Brand that it may be difficult to make sufficiently plausible our recommendations concerning international action by central banks.

J. M. K.

7.4.31

COMMENT ON J.M.K.'S COMMENT ON R.H.B.'S MEMORANDUM RELATING TO A BRIDGING CHAPTER

1. J.M.K.'s note, and a short but significant discussion which followed upon its circulation at our meeting on Wednesday last [15 April], raised certain issues which I feel we have no right to shirk. I hope I may be permitted to submit my views upon them.

2. I certainly obtained the impression that we were being presented by an ultimatum. 'If you do not accept the explanation of the trade cycle as set forth by me, the alternative is to say that there is no explanation of the trade cycle at all: that, in fact, economic theory breaks down and we are simply faced by the *fact* of cyclical fluctuation, accentuated by factors special to the present depression.' With all due respect, I do not believe that we are faced by any such dilemma. It is not really the case that the only possible explanation lies in the direction indicated by J.M.K., whether in his discussions before the Committee or in his recent writings. Trade cycle theories have been presented by innumerable authorities, but it is sufficient to say that alternative theories, watertight within their assumptions, have been presented by Pigou and Hawtrey within recent years. The fact that economic authorities in this country have not dissented from the *Treatise on Money* is simply due to the fact that no one with any sense of responsibility will commit himself in print on so vast a subject without adequate and intensive study. In fact, if the Committee commits itself to the acceptance of the full savings/investment formula without a further hearing of prominent economic authorities, it will be simply taking on trust the statement of a very distinguished colleague: it will not necessarily be carrying with it the assent of

the British economic world. J.M.K. may be right in every one of his contentions, but *we* have no right, as it seems to me, to assume this before the economic world as a whole has expressed an opinion. We certainly have heard no evidence justifying such an attitude on our part. So far as my knowledge goes, those Continental economists who are familiar with the kind of intellectual background presupposed by J.M.K.'s recent work are not prepared, without qualification, to accept his views.

3. For my own part, I am prepared to accept the distinction between saving and investment as an important conceptual contribution to the elucidation of the trade cycle. But I do not think this carries us very far. The important matter is the explanation of why there is a divergence between the two. I think it is now generally agreed that 'hoarding' is one such explanation. 'Hoarding' I take it, is due in the main to lack of confidence in the immediate outlook, it appears to me to be almost independent of the movements of the market rate of interest, i.e. I do not think that it can be cured by reducing deposit rates of interest, but only by changes in environmental conditions. The circumstances which lead to hoarding are also the circumstances which deter investment, so that it is not easy for the banking system, even by very low rates of interest, to correct the situation. *Prima facie*, no doubt, Government could step in and carry out the investment which the entrepreneur is too scared to undertake. But, given the psychological conditions under which hoarding is likely, large-scale government intervention may deter as much or more investment indirectly as it produces directly.

4. The second relevant cause of divergence is a market rate of interest *above* the natural rate which ought to obtain at any given moment. It is here that my real differences with J.M.K. begin.

(A) Though there may be no 'insuperable difficulty in central banks controlling the position' (p.2 [above p. 273]) in normal times, in fact they have not done so in the past. I agree that higher bank rates in boom periods and lower bank rates in slump periods would help to smooth out fluctuations. In other words, I would agree that *one* cause of short-period divergencies between saving and investment has been the lack of sufficient elasticity in the movements of bank and market rates of interest. But though this truth *can* be expressed as arising out of the non-adaptation of the market to the natural rate, it is not essential to state the proposition in this way. Greater plasticity of bank and market rates has been demanded by other writers on other grounds than those stated by J.M.K.

(B) But this is not the most important proposition we are asked to commit ourselves to. We are asked to agree that the present phase is 'altogether abnormal'. (p.2 [above p. 273]) Why? The only reason assigned seems to be that stated on p. 1 (above p. 272), i.e. that 'Today enterprise is not ready to pay much more than a normal pre-War rate of interest.' No justification for this proposition is offered. And it seems to me to require a great deal of justification before it can be accepted. The fact that we are an 'old country' is surely not in itself a sufficient justification: our normal equilibrium rate may be lower than that for 'newer countries', but if important new sources of investment are opened up the equilibrium rate may still be higher than it was, though as these sources of demand are satisfied the rate will fall again, though gradually. I quite agree that 'the probable normal long-term level of the natural rate for the years to come is a long way below the market rate which has prevailed in recent years and much nearer to the pre-War long-term normal'. But this does not prove that, *in the absence of slump conditions* (and slump conditions are *not* abnormal), enterprise was not ready to pay the market rates actually ruling. It in fact did so. If by 'today' is meant here and now, the answer obviously is that here and now we have a universal depression. If the explanation of the abnormality is that natural rates have been falling *over a period of years*, and, market rates have *not*, I again ask, where is the evidence? Until the recent depression, I should have thought the evidence was rather the other way. Not only was enterprise in the U.S.A. borrowing very cheaply (thus causing the boom which entailed the slump) but so were other and far less trustworthy areas.

(C) To my mind then, it appears that if the central banks are face to face with a situation of unusual difficulty (and I think they are) the explanation lies not in the presence of abnormal *trivial* factors, but in the existence of an abnormally great *depression*, due in the main to the abnormally great preceding *boom*. To adjust market and natural rates, in consequence, *is* a task of enormous difficulty. But, whilst it may be difficult to justify the view that even now central banks by co-operative effort could combat successfully the problems of the hour, I would like to protest against the unnecessary aggravation of the task through the importation into it of J.M.K.'s main thesis.

T.E.G.

17.4.31

Again, when a majority of the drafting committee attempted to come to terms with the contents of 'Proposals Relating to Domestic Monetary Policy: B. To meet the Present Emergency', Keynes responded.

NOTES ON THE MAJORITY DRAFT OF PART II CHAPTER V

(I have thought that it may save time in discussion for me to circulate some comments in writing beforehand.   J.M.K.)

I. The argument of §§ 6 and 7 endeavours to show that equilibrium can be restored by reducing costs to correspond to the existing reduction of prices. For this purpose it is assumed that a reduction of wage costs will *not* involve a further reduction of prices, and will merely represent a transfer of purchasing power from wage earners to entrepreneurs. Sometimes this may be true, particularly where monopoly or combination exists. For example, the reduction in railway wages has not been followed by a reduction in railway charges.

But unfortunately this assumption is exactly the opposite of what is assumed everywhere else in the Chapter. For in the paragraphs dealing with our export trades, the whole point is that a reduction of our wage costs *will* involve a reduction of our prices. In so far as it is true that some reductions in wage-costs will not be reflected in prices and will merely represent a transfer from the pockets of wage earners to the pockets of entrepreneurs, a much larger reduction of wages will be needed to do our exports any good than would be necessary otherwise.

Thus the argument of §§ 6 and 7 cuts right across the argument underlying the rest of the Chapter. In fact the authors are unable to keep it up even to the end of § 7; for even in this paragraph we find it stated that a reduction of costs will bring with it an all-round fall in the cost of living, i.e., that it will after all be reflected in a further fall of prices. In the main, I believe the truth to be that an attempt to bring prices and costs back to equilibrium by cutting costs is a manoeuvre of the trying-to-catch-one's-own-tail type.

II. When the draft gets to details (last page but one of §16), we learn that it is not proposed to reduce wages in the export industries 'in which, in some instances, wages are clearly probably below the efficiency level'. The reductions are to be primarily in 'the sheltered industries of unskilled employments and of Government and municipal services'. Has the Committee considered how large such reductions would have to be to afford a given amount of relief to our export industries? Is more than 10 per cent of the cost of our exports represented by wages in the sheltered industries? Let us suppose that it is 20 per cent—which must be a very high estimate. Thus if the whole of the reduction was passed on in lower charges, a 10 per cent reduction of sheltered wages would reduce the cost of our exports by 2 per cent. But, as we have seen, not the whole of the reduction of wages would be passed on in lower charges to the export industries; and not the whole of the lower charges would be passed on in lower prices for our exports. Thus the net reduction in our export prices might be nearer 1 per cent than 2 per cent. In truth, nothing is any good along these lines except a reduction of wages in the export industries themselves, where, as it is admitted, wages are somewhat low already. No conceivable reduction of wages in the sheltered industries alone could have as favourable an effect on our balance of trade as a 10 per cent tariff on imports and corresponding advantages to exports,—which would probably help the foreign-trade industries more than would even a 40 per cent reduction of wages in the sheltered industries alone. Surely it is odd to reject a general tariff *plus* aids to export as 'impracticable', and then to propose instead, as being presumably the easier course, a reduction of money wages which to be equally efficacious would have to be on a quite gigantic scale. Even an all-round wage cut which affected wages in *all* industries would probably have to be 20 per cent to be as effective as the 10 per cent tariff *plus* export aids. I am astonished that anyone, who attaches importance to an improvement in our trade balance, should reject the tariff and then proceed to pin his hopes on wage reductions primarily in the sheltered industries. It must be that the arithmetic of the comparison has never been worked out.

III. The employment of men to make goods we now import

is in every respect an equivalent to employing men to make additional goods for export. (So also, up to a point, is increased home investment.) The draft seems quite to forget this. Yet it may be much the easier to accomplish. For example, it would be much easier not to import iron and steel than to double our exports of iron and steel. It is to live in an unreal world to ignore such things.

IV. There is also another piece of arithmetic which needs working out. Just as the majority draft expresses its extreme concern about the trade balance and then adopts the proposal which will help the trade balance least, so also it expresses extreme concern about the Budget and then adopts the proposal which will embarrass the Budget most. The steadiness in the yield from income tax hitherto is largely due to the fact that reductions in salaries etc. have not yet been made on any important scale. But a general reduction in non-contractual money incomes must, of course, reduce largely the yield of the taxes. On the other hand, a larger part of the Budget outgoings is on debt and fixed charges. It would seem probable, therefore, that the Budget would lose on balance from what is proposed. If, however, budgetary relief is expected in the ways about to be discussed, this ought to be made plain.

V. This Report is addressed to the Government. It ought to be made clear whether or not it is to be our advice to the Government to lead the way by reducing the salaries of all Government servants and schoolteachers, old-age pensions, the rate of the dole etc. For these are the only reductions of the kind desired by the majority draft which it lies within the power of the Government to effect. It might be useful, too, to give an estimate of the amount by which we should expect our exports to be increased by a cut of (say) 10 per cent in the above.

VI. The argument at the end of §17 seems to me misleading. Even the 6 per cent is out of date. But the point is—what will the gain to the rentier be *after* wages have been cut down? Nearer 20 per cent than 6 per cent, I should suppose.

VII. Finally, should not the majority draft either say much

more or much less? The policy of recapturing export trade from Germany, Belgium etc. by cutting our wages faster than they can cut theirs is not a game of pat-ball. It would require the utmost determination and ruthlessness, an iron will, and a readiness to face, almost for certain, a violent social struggle. If the Committee mean this, they should say so. But I imagine that they don't really mean anything of the kind. Their real attitude is much more negative,—indeed entirely negative. They would like to drift along much as at present—no tariff, no large-scale home investment, a steady 'nibbling' (if I may be allowed the word!) at wages, though on no great scale. I do not know whether the average reader of their Chapter will perceive what sheep they are within their wolves' clothing, or whether he will cry wolf!

J. M. K.

20.5.31

As the drafting progressed, it became clear that the members of the drafting committee—as well as members of the Full Committee—could not agree on proposals for short-term domestic monetary action that clearly fell within the Committee's terms of reference. As a result, the chairman decided to draft a fairly flat concluding note for the body of the Report and left members of the Committee to make their own proposals in the form of addenda. As a result, the final Report carried four addenda setting out the views of R. H. Brand, Professor Gregory, L. B. Lee and a group centred around Keynes.

The Keynes group document's origins are best set out in two letters.[14]

To SIR THOMAS ALLEN, *29 May 1931*

Dear Sir Thomas Allen,

As you were away from the Committee on Thursday morning [28 May] I was not able to find out whether there was any chance of your signing, with or without reserves, my draft document. You will have learned that it was decided to put in the body of the Report a few colourless sentences and then to leave different

---

[14] A third surviving letter to Sir Walter Raine, who did not sign the addendum, covers the same ground.

groups of the Committee to deal with the less monetary aspects of the domestic situation in their own way.

Mr McKenna, Mr Tulloch and Mr Frater Taylor decided that they would join with me on the basis of my draft. We therefore met this morning and fixed up a final text. I then showed this to Mr Bevin, and, subject to certain changes which I agreed with him, he agreed to sign also, subject to a reservation appended to his signature that he signed the passage relating to restriction on imports subject to provision being made, by state ownership or otherwise, for the complete protection of the public from undue charges.

The position now is, therefore, that the document will be signed, in any case, by Mr McKenna, Mr Tulloch, Mr Frater Taylor, Mr Bevin and myself. We thought that there might be quite a good chance of your feeling able to sign, or at any rate to express your agreement with a large part of it. I think that Mr Bevin is going to try to get hold of you to discuss this. I very much hope, indeed, that you will feel able to sign, for I think we are really in agreement on the substantial issues as against the others.

Mr Ismay is preparing a fair copy of the draft, and he hopes to have a print by Tuesday evening. You will therefore get the text as amended for consideration some time in the middle of next week. As I am going to America to-morrow morning I shall not be able to deal with the matter further. So I would be grateful if you would communicate your decision to Mr Ismay.

I am also sending a fair copy to some other members of the Committee, on the chance of their being disposed to sign.

Yours sincerely,
[copy initialled] J.M.K.

To L. B. LEE, *29 May 1931*

Dear Lee,

As you know, McKenna, Tulloch and Frater Taylor, as well as myself, have decided to sign, as an addendum to the Report, substantially the draft relating to domestic action which I had prepared as a minority document for the drafting committee. We settled the final text of this addendum to-day, and subsequently Bevin has agreed to sign, subject to a reservation, so far as restrictions on imports are concerned, to the effect that his signature is subject to provision being made, by state ownership or otherwise, to protect the public against undue charges. It is also quite possible, I think, that Sir Thomas Allen will sign. But I cannot speak confidently as to this since I have not yet been able to get hold of him.

Ismay is now preparing a clean copy and will have got it into print by the middle of next week. I am asking him to send it to you as soon as it is available. Will you look through it again and see whether there is any chance of your feeling able to sign it in its amended form, with or without reservations. My own feeling is that there is not really much between us. It is particularly at Bevin's suggestion that I write to you, since he was of the opinion that certain changes which we have made in the passages relating to subsidies may meet your point of view about this. Or, if they don't, this could easily be met by means of a reservation attached to your signature relating to subsidies similar to Bevin's reservation relating to tariffs; provided, that is to say, you are in sympathy on the whole with the rest of the document. It would then be a powerfully signed addendum, collecting into a common point of view representatives of a number of different interests and opinions.

As you know, I am leaving for the United States tomorrow morning, so I am afraid that I shall not be able to discuss these matters with anyone any further. If, on seeing the final version, you are at all disposed to sign all or any part of it, with or without reservations, will you let Ismay have your decision?

Yours sincerely,
[copy initialled] J. M. K.

The Addendum ran as follows:

From the Report of the Committee on Finance and Industry

ADDENDUM I

PROPOSALS RELATING TO DOMESTIC MONETARY POLICY TO MEET THE PRESENT EMERGENCY

1. We have signed the Report of the Committee without reservation.* But in our opinion it is incomplete without certain further observations. Rightly or wrongly, we conceive it our duty to consider possible methods of increasing the ability of the banking system to put into effective operation the principles of action which we have recommended above. For if the situation remains unchanged in other respects, we doubt whether it lies within the power of the banking system to restore employment to a satisfactory level.

THE EXPANSION OF CREDIT FOR DOMESTIC PURPOSES

2. The upshot of the preceding chapters may be summarised as follows. For the world as a whole the best hope of a remedy lies in a monetary policy designed to increase the volume of purchasing power, to increase the ease of borrowing if necessary by guarantees, to diminish the rate of interest long-term as well as short-term, and to stimulate in every possible way the spirit of enterprise and the volume of investment.

3. If Great Britain were, like the world, a closed system, the same monetary remedies would be equally applicable here. But unfortunately this is less true of us than of any other country. Our economic affairs are intricately bound up with an international system. Consequently the power of the Bank of England to initiate an independent policy, irrespective of what is going on abroad, is strictly limited.

* Except in the case of Sir T. Allen and Mr Bevin.

283

4. Whether it is as limited as—to judge from its policy over recent years—the Bank of England has believed, is open to debate. Mr Hawtrey has expressed in evidence most forcible and interesting views to the contrary. He urges that the power of the Bank to influence the rest of the world, and to refuse to be led by it, whilst not what it was before the War, is nevertheless great. He contends that the amount of foreign balances, which we run the risk of losing if we make money relatively cheap in London, is not so large as is commonly supposed. Whatever may have been true a little time back, we are not prepared to accept Mr Hawtrey's views as fully applicable to the present very abnormal circumstances, where confidence is liable to be disturbed; and it would, we think, be asking too much to expect the Bank of England to make an experiment of uncertain outcome in the existing environment. It is its duty to put absolute safety first. At the same time there may be much more force in Mr Hawtrey's general line of argument than is usually admitted. We do not believe that the position abroad need always prevent the Bank of England from furnishing additional credit, provided there is a real opening for its employment in increased domestic enterprise. It would be unsafe for the Bank to increase materially the total volume of credit without considering how it will be employed. But this should not be urged as an argument applicable to cases where there is a reasonable prospect of the new money finding its way into domestic enterprise.

5. Moreover the risks of expanding credit would be much diminished if the Bank of England would take the clearing banks more into its confidence, in the way in which it has traditionally confided in the leading accepting houses, and invite their co-operation. We desire to state this conclusion with some emphasis. While the quantity of money is controlled by the Bank of England, the way in which additional supplies are used can be largely directed by the clearing banks, and co-operation between these banks and the Bank of England is essential. The Committee as a whole have recommended in para. 372 that this

should be done. If this recommendation is acted upon, so that the clearing banks on their side can make it clear when they are in a position to direct additional credit into domestic channels and when they are not, and the Bank of England on its side can tell the clearing banks when an expansion or contraction of credit is intended to have its natural repercussions on the foreign short-term loan position and when it is not, it will be much easier than it is now to ensure that domestic enterprise and investment of whatever kind shall never be starved of the accommodation which it requires. In spite of some evidence to the contrary which has been offered to us, we are not convinced that this has invariably been the case in recent years.

6. Today, however, the main trouble is not a limitation on the amount of available bank credit, but the reluctance of acceptable borrowers to come forward. Thus the first step must probably be some kind of direct stimulus, for example, a considerable fall in the long-term rate of interest payable by typical borrowers, or some kind of state action. Either of these conditions here, without corresponding conditions elsewhere, can scarcely avoid putting some strain on the international position of the Bank of England. To meet this strain a strengthening of the country's surplus on the balance of trade is required. It is also true that the Bank would be in a better position to exercise its full moral influence internationally if its power to retain its gold was beyond question.

7. Thus we are led inevitably to consider whether any other measures are practicable which would restore or increase the Bank of England's ability to employ its monetary power in a constructive way—though some of these measures may seem to lead us away from monetary policy proper.

AN ANALYSIS OF THE ALTERNATIVES

8. We know no way in which the initial impetus to increased employment can be given except by (i) an increase of exports,

(ii) the substitution of home-produced goods for goods now imported, or (iii) an increase of investment at home—though once the vicious circle can be broken in any of these ways the increased purchasing power of the men put back into work will further increase employment in supplying their needs.

9. This may be put quite shortly by saying that we must either increase our favourable balance of international payments, or find an outlet for more of our savings at home, or, better still, do both. Indeed the whole problem may be made to centre round the balance of trade.* We can increase our surplus by exporting more or importing less. We can export more only if world trade revives, or if we reduce our gold costs faster than our competitors reduce theirs, or if we give the export industries some kind of special advantages. Similarly we can import less only by a relative reduction of our own costs or by some restriction on imports. Finally we can only find employment for more of our savings at home by increasing the enterprise of borrowers or by somehow subsidising the cost of borrowing.

10. In practice, therefore—putting on one side the increase of our efficiency relatively to that of our foreign competitors, the desirability of which, if we can do it, is obvious and common ground between all parties—the practical courses open to us come down to three:

(i) A reduction of salaries and wages;

(ii) Control of imports and aids to the export industries;

(iii) Domestic enterprise assisted by state action, or subsidies to private investment at home.

There is probably no serious dispute as to all these courses,

---

* For the amount of international surplus which we currently need for *net* foreign lending depends on how much of our savings is trying to find an outlet abroad. The greater the amount which finds an outlet at home, the smaller the international surplus which we require in order to be in equilibrium. Thus to restore our position and to make full employment possible, we require both to increase our surplus on the balance of trade and also to find increased outlets for our savings at home. When the excess of our total savings over that part of them which we can employ at home is equal to our surplus on the balance of trade, there need be no monetary obstacle to the full and profitable employment of all our resources of men and plant. This analysis enables us to narrow down the alternatives.

considered apart from their social and long-period consequences, having *some* effect in the right direction. The difference
between us and those who emphasise the importance of the first
might be expressed by saying that they feel on a balance of
considerations that there is not enough to be hoped for in
practice from a cautious application of (ii) and (iii) and that there
is great danger in losing sight of (i), which is more fundamental
in their judgement and in the long run 'sounder', whereas we feel
exactly the opposite, namely, that the practical results of an
attempt to reduce salaries and wages are likely to be exceedingly
disappointing. They feel that it might be dangerous to divert the
public mind from what they believe to be the ultimate necessity
of (i) by offering remedies under (ii) and (iii) which may prove
specious; whereas we believe that nothing is more likely to
produce stalemate than to concentrate public attention on (i).

11. We now proceed to consider in turn the three courses
open to us. The first and the second, let us repeat, would benefit
the situation primarily by increasing our foreign investment and
by enlarging the power of the Bank of England to pursue without
embarrassment a policy of stimulating enterprise both at home
and abroad; while the object of the third would be to increase
home investment by methods which did not run the risk of
unduly increasing at the same time the tendency to lend abroad
more than our foreign trade surplus can support.

I. A REDUCTION OF SALARIES AND WAGES

1. THE NEED FOR SOME ELASTICITY OF MONEY INCOMES

12. Certain preliminary observations are here necessary for the
avoidance of misunderstanding. So long as the standard of value
is subject to wide fluctuations in terms of consumable commodities, it is essential that there shall be a reasonable elasticity
and mobility in the level of the money incomes which workers

and others are ready to accept as equitable. If money incomes have been established at a level appropriate to a certain purchasing power of money and if purchasing power then undergoes a large increase, the fortuitous advantage which will then accrue to those whose money incomes are unchanged may be quite inappropriate to the new situation and without substantial justification. Great evils must needs result, and have resulted, from the excessive rigidity of various types of money income in such circumstances. This is just as true of the rigidity of rentiers' incomes as it is of the rigidity of wage earners' incomes. We think, therefore, that it would be quite wrong to regard the level of money incomes, with which we happen to find ourselves at any time, as sacrosanct.

13. For example, the cost of living, as measured by the Ministry of Labour index number, has fallen 18 per cent since 1925 and 12 per cent since the beginning of 1929. In so far as this is due to increased productivity, or to a movement of the terms of foreign trade in favour of this country (so that our exports are exchanged per unit for a larger quantity of imports than before), it is arguable that these advantages should be enjoyed by recipients of money incomes in the shape of increased purchasing power. But in so far as it is due to a change in the value of money for other reasons, an attempt to retain the fortuitous advantages thus accruing will involve an unjustifiable transference at the expense of the entrepreneur, which must seriously disturb the efficient working of the economic machine and be the cause of unemployment. It may be, therefore, that some downward adjustments in the quantity or value of money incomes of every kind are called for on these grounds so long as the present low level of general prices continues. A readiness to accept the fact that the value of incomes is something which must be accommodated to changing circumstances is, indeed, an essential condition of the sound working of our economic system.

2. REDUCTIONS OF SALARIES AND WAGES AS A REMEDY FOR THE INTERNATIONAL SLUMP

14. A primary reliance on reductions of salaries and wages as a means of restoring employment and of recovering our international equilibrium might, however, require much more drastic action than can be easily justified, or is likely to be accepted, merely on the grounds just given. It is impossible to calculate in advance what increase of employment could be expected from a given average reduction of wages. But the relation of the one to the other might disappoint the expectations of many people, inasmuch as a false analogy is often drawn from the obvious great advantages to an individual employer of a reduction of the wages which he has to pay. For each employer perceives quite clearly the advantages he would gain if the wages which he himself pays were to be reduced, but not so clearly the disadvantages he will suffer if the money incomes of his customers are reduced. Just as it is to the advantage of each producer that every product should be cheap except his own, similarly it is to his advantage that all costs and wages should be high except those which he himself incurs—since the demand for his product comes from the incomes which are paid out as costs by other producers.

15. On the other hand, a reduction of the costs of British manufacturers as a whole which is *not* associated with an equal reduction of the incomes of their customers, plainly benefits them. So does a reduction of costs which brings them new customers. The first applies to those of them who manufacture for export, and the second to those of them whose products, if they were cheaper, might be substituted for goods now imported. But this assumes that a reduction of costs here does not provoke a corresponding reduction by our foreign competitors. For just as a reduction of his costs only helps a domestic manufacturer if it applies to him alone and not to all his neighbours, so internationally a reduction of costs only helps

British manufacturers if it applies to them alone and not to the whole world.

16. Thus there are two subtractions which it is necessary to make from the *prima facie* advantages of general wage reductions. In the first place many purely domestic industries will only obtain secondary advantages, since what they gain in reduced costs will be offset by the diminished purchasing power of their customers; so that the greater part of the primary advantages of wage reductions would be concentrated in the foreign trade industries, i.e. those which work for export or compete with imports. In the second place, even in the foreign trade industries we cannot be certain in advance that wage reductions here will not be countered by corresponding cuts on the part of our chief competitors.

17. It might be, therefore, that an attempt to remedy unemployment by general wage reductions would require very large reductions. As an illustration, an average reduction of money wages by 10 per cent would, since it would reduce total costs by much less than 10 per cent, have much less effect on our foreign trade than a tariff of 10 per cent on all imports and a subsidy of 10 per cent on all exports. Yet it would be optimistic to expect even from the latter more than a partial remedy. The same conclusion follows from a comparison between the wages paid here and those paid by our chief continental competitors.

18. If the position had to be met by an average reduction of money wages only throughout all industries sufficient by itself to restore our foreign trade to an equilibrium position, it might have to be, in present conditions, as great as 20 to 30 per cent, though any such estimate must necessarily be liable to a wide margin of error. The corresponding reduction of real wages would not, of course, be nearly so great as this, inasmuch as there would be a substantial fall in the costs of home products and services. Nevertheless an attempt to secure any such reduction might be expected to produce social chaos and react most unfavourably on trade generally.

19. These considerations are far from intended to lead up to the conclusion that the remedy of reducing money costs in terms of gold is one which can be avoided in all circumstances. But they emphasise the grave difficulties of an approach to the problem along these lines, and they raise a doubt as to whether reductions of salaries and wages are the right way of dealing with the existing international slump. It is not easy to see how we can expect a revival in our foreign trade, on a sufficient scale to be of much value to us, by any other means than through a revival of world demand. To meet the immediate problems, arising out of the world slump, a policy intended to direct increased purchasing power into the right channels, both at home and abroad, with a view to restoring equilibrium at the *present* level of costs, would, therefore, be much wiser, in our judgement, than a policy of trying to cut our costs faster than the rest of the world can cut theirs.

3. THE ULTIMATE LEVEL OF SALARIES AND WAGES

20. Nevertheless, it is quite possible that, when the international slump is, in the maturity of time, righting itself, we shall continue to find ourselves faced with difficulties due to our money costs being still too high relatively to our neighbours. For in the long run we cannot support a level of money costs in terms of gold which is out of equilibrium with similar costs elsewhere—and this is true quite independently of our adherence to the gold standard. This, perhaps, is the fundamental reason why some would think it wise to begin at once to take steps to bring down our costs, not necessarily to the level which would be required to restore our foreign trade in slump conditions, but at least to the level which may be required to put us on equal terms with our chief competitors when the slump conditions are ended. We must, therefore, endeavour to express our views on this issue as clearly as we can.

21. There are two distinct questions on which we have to

form a judgement. First, what is the likelihood that the existing level of money wages will be beyond our capacity when the violence of the present credit cycle will have spent itself? Secondly, if in the event it does prove necessary to reduce the prevailing level of money incomes, should the reduction be a *general* one applicable to all classes of income, and by what means should it be brought about?

22. It is obvious that it is much too soon to attempt an answer to the first question. It depends on the level at which money costs expressed in terms of gold settle down in the countries which buy our goods or compete with us in producing them. This in turn depends on the success of the efforts recommended in the Report of the Committee for raising the international price level by increasing, through investment and otherwise, the effective volume of purchasing power throughout the world. It also depends on the time which will elapse before any success attends on these efforts and on the duration of the slump. For the longer the slump lasts, the more probable it is that country after country will feel itself compelled to resort to competition in wage cutting. This will be a counsel of despair, especially for debtor countries, since universal wage cutting will help no one and will merely serve to rivet on the shoulders of the debtors a heavier burden of monetary obligation. But in the downward race anyone who can get a little ahead of his neighbours will snatch a temporary advantage, and no one can afford to lag far behind under penalty of losing all his trade. For this reason we may be compelled to follow suit. Nevertheless we should not take the lead in what is so contrary to the common interest, and we should be as reluctant as our circumstances permit to press closely behind those who are leading the way in this direction.

23. If remedial measures are delayed, the pressure towards wage reductions in the rest of the world may prove overwhelming. If so, we must grapple the problem firmly on lines to be considered below. The position may change quickly. But the available statistics have not convinced us that it is, as yet, either

necessary or desirable to engage in competitive wage cutting.

24. The matter may also be looked at from another angle. Apart from competitive considerations, does the present level of wages represent an unreasonable, and in the long run an impracticable, demand on the part of labour for too large a share of the joint product of industry? No doubt, almost everyone in a country such as Great Britain is gaining advantages in the purchasing power of his income through the exceedingly low relative prices of many articles of food, which he cannot expect to retain when the international slump is over. But this is not a peculiarity of wages—it applies equally to every class of income in a country which is temporarily in a position to import large quantities of goods at distress prices. We have, therefore, postulated some rise of international prices as a necessary condition of the maintenance of the present level of British money incomes. The question whether the British worker is receiving too large a share of the British national dividend as compared with the other classes of the community is another matter. It is not proved, in our opinion, that wages have been recently a much larger proportion than formerly of the total value of the product—at any rate not up to 1929. The available statistics suggest that there has been a remarkable degree of stability in the proportionate division of the produce (see Minutes of Evidence, 47th day). Moreover there is another consideration which impresses us. If we can pay for present standards both for the employed and for the unemployed, and at the same time add to our capital wealth (as we believe to be even still the case), with nearly a quarter of our industrial resources idle, does not this suggest that we should have a comfortable margin over if we could manage to bring back into activity the whole of our resources—even after allowing substantially for the loss of our present temporary advantage from the unduly low prices of our imports?

25. Thus the problem seen in this light is one of disequilibrium rather than of excessively high standards; and the

task upon which we should concentrate is that of remedying the disequilibrium so as to bring our productive resources into full play, rather than of attempting to lower standards.

4. MEANS OF ADJUSTING MONEY INCOMES

26. Whatever efforts we may make and however high the hopes we entertain, it remains true, unfortunately, that our efforts and hopes may be defeated. It would be absurd to maintain that we can continue to adhere to the existing level of money incomes irrespective of the value of money. We have, therefore, to consider what measures we should recommend if an adjustment of money incomes becomes plainly unavoidable.

27. We are here considering, not normal wage adjustments of the kind which we have discussed at the commencement of this section, but a substantial general change, amounting to (say) 10 per cent or more, in the level of money costs and incomes, designed to remedy a position of national disequilibrium due to a change in the value of money.

28. We consider that a change of this character cannot, with equity, be concentrated on salaries and wages, but should apply to every category of income alike, including those protected by contract. The benefit of an increased value of money is just as fortuitous in the case of the *rentier* as in the case of the wage earner, and the burden on enterprise and on the Budget of having to pay the same amount of money as before to meet interest charges, though the value of money is greater, is similar in character to the burden of having to pay the same money wages as before. Moreover a great social change of this kind cannot be carried through except by general consent.

29. This view is reinforced by a consideration of the monetary history of recent years. A large part of the national debt was incurred at a price level much higher than that which now prevails. The long period of deflation which culminated in the return to gold at the pre-War parity had the effect of

increasing the burden of this debt. The fall in world prices which has occurred more recently has caused a large further aggravation of the burden. In view of the fact that the increase in the value of sterling was deliberately intended, it seems difficult to require a reduction of salaries and wages without proposing any modification of the uncovenanted blessings which accrued to the holders of the national debt and of claims on money generally and to other classes whose incomes have remained unaffected.

30. Our conclusion is, therefore, that if a substantial change should become necessary, it must be a *general* change and apply, so far as possible, to every class of income alike.

31. If this conclusion be accepted, it follows that it cannot be left to natural economic forces to bring it about by the mere pressure of events. For this would certainly not result in an equal all-round change. In Chapter XI the Committee have explained that the pressure which can be brought to bear on the economic system by a restriction of credit, whilst suitable for the purpose of effecting the comparatively small adjustments of ordinary times, is not an appropriate means for effecting large changes. Yet, in effect, it is upon this method that we have been relying hitherto. The rate of long-term interest and the volume of credit are maintained at levels which are deterrent to investment, and the unemployment which ensues is, under a *laissez-faire* system, the natural form of pressure to secure a reduction of wages. What alternative means are open to us for an orderly contraction in terms of gold of money incomes in general?

(a) Devaluation

32. Theoretically the most obvious and comprehensive method of effecting the desired object would be to leave money incomes alone but to change the monetary standard, e.g., by diminishing by 10 per cent the gold parity of sterling. This would have the advantage of bringing the direct, initial benefit to those industries which need it most, namely, to the foreign-trade

industries. It would involve no interference with contract, since debts are legally fixed in terms of sterling and not in terms of gold. It would affect every class of income without the necessity of any other special measures. For a country which was not an international banker and was not owed large sums from abroad fixed in terms of sterling, this would be the simplest solution.

33. We have already agreed, however, that for a country in the special circumstances of Great Britain the disadvantages would greatly outweigh the advantages, and we have concurred with our colleagues in rejecting it.

(b) Tariffs plus Bounties

34. Precisely the same effects as those produced by a devaluation of sterling by a given percentage could be brought about by a tariff of the same percentage on all imports together with an equal subsidy on all exports, except that this measure *would leave sterling international obligations unchanged in terms of gold*. This proposal would avoid the injury to the national credit and to our receipts from foreign loans fixed in terms of sterling which would ensue on devaluation.

35. Under existing commercial treaties, however, there would be practical difficulties in the way of a direct subsidy to exports. Nevertheless, various plans might be propounded for combining some form of restriction of imports with granting sundry indirect advantages to the export industries, which would represent an approximation of the above scheme. We consider that a plan of this kind would be so immeasurably preferable to devaluation, that it is foolish even to discuss the latter while the former remains untried.

36. It is worthwhile to remark, that, if the level of domestic money incomes is such that our international equilibrium would be restored by a reduction of money incomes or by the devaluation of sterling, then it follows that, failing the adoption of one or other of these two expedients, the optimum distri-

bution of the national resources between different uses will result, not from free trade, but from as near an approximation as is practicable to a *tariff plus bounties* measure on the above lines.

37. The avowed object of such a measure as this would be to reduce the value of a given money income; though the cost of living might be expected to rise by only a fraction of the percentage rate of duty. Its advantages would be two. In the first place it would be fair; for every description of money income would be affected equally. In the second place, it would involve no disturbance to confidence and no breach of understanding with our foreign creditors.

(c) A National Treaty

38. There remains the project of a national agreement for the general and simultaneous adjustment *of all money incomes* by a tax on incomes which, for one reason or another, are exempt from the general cut, and an adjustment of all salaries and wages and other money incomes not protected by contract. There would, inevitably, be great practical difficulties in the way of a resettlement of this kind, and we cannot say how far they could be overcome without giving more examination to the details of some such scheme than it has been possible for us to give. But in the last resort it is at least theoretically conceivable that by means of a national treaty, on some such lines as this, an escape from our currency difficulties could be found.

II. CONTROL OF IMPORTS AND AIDS TO EXPORTS

39. Proposals under this heading raise political and social issues which extend far beyond the necessities of the present emergency. A specific may be appropriate to a particular situation, and yet be rejected in obedience to wider considerations more extended in time. We do not propose to attempt any such

summing up of the final balance of advantage and disadvantage, having regard to all the relevant factors, as would be needed to justify a definite recommendation. We shall confine ourselves, therefore, to considering briefly the uses of tariffs or import boards, etc., and subsidies on articles of foreign trade regarded as an expedient to meet a situation in which a country has a large unemployed surplus of labour and of plant which it is unable to bring into use in the conditions imposed on it by its economic relations, arising out of relative rates of interest and money costs, with the rest of the world.

40. The fundamental argument for unrestricted free trade does not apply without qualification to an economic system which is neither in equilibrium nor in sight of equilibrium. For if a country's productive resources are normally fully employed, a tariff cannot increase output, but can only divert production from one direction into another, whilst there is a general presumption that the natural direction for the employment of resources, which they can reach on their merits and without being given special advantages at the expense of others, will yield a superior national dividend. But if this condition of full employment is neither fulfilled nor likely to be fulfilled for some time, then the position is totally different, since a tariff may bring about a net increase of production and not merely a diversion.

41. It appears to us, therefore, that, if imports were to be controlled, whether by a tariff with compensation for exports, or by import boards, or in some other way and home-produced goods substituted for them, there is a presumption, so long as present circumstances last, that this would mean a net increase of employment and of national productivity. Into the rate of the tariff and the classes of the articles affected we do not enter.

42. The arguments most commonly adduced on the other side—apart from long-period considerations which we are not pretending to discuss—are the following:

(i) It is said that the restriction of certain kinds of imports would curtail foreign buying power and so diminish the market for our exports. This would be true if we were to use our improved balance of trade to import gold and the consequent loss of gold by the rest of the world had the effect of causing a contraction of total credit. But if we make use of our improved balance of trade to expand investment at home with the result of increasing our imports of food and raw materials (an expansion which would have led to a *loss* of gold by us if we had attempted it without a contemporaneous restriction of imports) or to increase our foreign lending, then it need have no adverse effect on the market for our exports.

(ii) It is said that a restriction of imports would tend to increase the cost of production of our exports. This is a question of degree depending on the kind of restriction imposed. Clearly a substantial tax on imported raw materials without a rebate for exports would have a seriously adverse effect on exports. At the other extreme, it is not evident that a tax on the importation of luxury motor cars or an import board for pig products would have any appreciable consequences of this kind. It is easy to conceive both of a tariff, accompanied by appropriate rebates, and of import boards the effect of which on the cost of exports would be small compared with that of other factors. Nor is there any reason to suppose that the effect on exports need be commensurate with the effect on imports.

Nevertheless, even if these measures were so devised as to impose only a small handicap on our exports, this would be *pro tanto* an objection. The logical course, in our opinion, would be to find ways of giving equivalent advantages to the export industries. For much of the argument in favour of a restriction of imports applies equally to a subsidy to exports. A direct subsidy would be open to various practical objections. But it would not be difficult to find other ways of giving back to the export industries advantages at least equal in amount to the comparatively small disadvantages which would be imposed on them by those effects of restricting imports by a tariff or otherwise which would be individually too small and incalculable to be dealt with by means of a rebate.

(iii) The third objection, which is most commonly heard,

relates to the effect on the cost of living of the working classes. The force of this objection depends partly on the character of the tariff or other measures in view, and partly on a comparison with the effect on the cost of living of those measures to which the tariff is offered as an alternative.

For example, a given amount of revenue raised by taxing manufactured imports would probably increase the cost of living less than if it were raised by taxes on tea, sugar, beer and tobacco. Or again, if it were to diminish the necessity to reduce wages or had the effect of increasing employment at the existing wage, its effect on working-class standards would probably be favourable. We think that a scheme could be devised which would have no adverse effects on working-class standards.

43. Since many of the arguments in favour of a restriction of imports apply equally in favour of schemes of assistance to exports, some system of restricting imports, accompanied by a policy of giving advantages to the export industries, would seem to be the most practical plan of action.

44. Finally, the immediate effect of such measures in reviving business confidence and a spirit of enterprise scarcely needs to be emphasised.

45. For these reasons and also because relief would be given both to the Budget and to the balance of trade, it would seem that restrictions on imports and aids to exports would run well in double harness with the other class of remedy which we next discuss, namely, schemes of capital development. For it is obvious that the whole of the resources required for capital development at home are necessarily found within the country and as a result of our own efforts and sacrifices, except in so far as their effect is to diminish our net foreign surplus, whether by decreasing our exports or increasing our imports. Thus the 'burden' of such schemes, for which we need to make special provision is exactly measured by the burden on the balance of trade. If, therefore, we were to expand investment at home *and* control imports, we should get the favourable effects of both

schemes on domestic employment and avoid the disturbing effects of both on our international balance.

III. SCHEMES OF CAPITAL DEVELOPMENT

46. We see no reason to doubt that new capital investment at home would, in present circumstances, create additional employment—subject only to the qualifications explained below. So far from this additional employment being less than appears at first sight, it is likely to be considerably more. For in addition to the men directly employed and to the men occupied in making and transporting the materials required, there will be a further set of men put into work to supply the needs created by the additional purchasing and consuming power of the first set of men, and so on.

47. The objections which have been advanced against an unqualified acceptance of this conclusion are the following:—

(i) It has been argued that it is not possible to ensure that any particular scheme of investment will mean *additional* expenditure. It may merely cause a diversion of finance and of resources from different expenditure which would have occurred otherwise. If the national productive resources were fully occupied, this might be the case. Or if the banking system were to limit the volume of credit in a certain way, it might be the case. But in present circumstances, when the physical limit on further capital output is far from reached, there is no reason why the action of the banking system need stand in the way of additional investment, unless this investment was throwing too heavy a burden on the balance of trade—a contingency which we deal with below. For the theory that there is in any sense a fixed loan fund available to finance investment which is in all circumstances fully employed, or that the amount of the savings of the public always exactly correspond to the volume of new investment, is, we think, mistaken. At one time some such view as this appears to have influenced British policy. To a questionnaire from the International Labour Office in 1927 the British Government replied: 'The decision taken by the Government at the end of 1925 to restrict grants for relief schemes was based mainly on the view that, the supply of capital in this country being limited, it was undesirable to divert any appreciable proportion of this supply from normal trade channels.'* The Treasury White Paper, Cmd. 3331, p. 43, was also capable of interpretation in this sense. We gathered, however, from the evidence of Sir R. Hopkins that it would be a mistake to attribute this view to the Treasury at the present time.

(ii) It has been argued that, whilst investment spontaneously undertaken by private industry would help employment, there may, nevertheless, be some offsets to schemes deliberately engineered by the Government. For the effect of such schemes on the minds of business men might be such as to make them less inclined to launch out themselves. This might be true of 'unfair' Government-aided schemes, by which some private firms received assistance from which other substantially similar firms were debarred. It might also be true that business confidence would be injured if the Government were to sponsor obviously wasteful, foolish or extravagant projects. But in general, provided the schemes are wisely selected, we see no presumption in favour of the view that 'official' investment need seriously compete or interfere with 'unofficial' investment. Indeed, on the contrary, if 'official' investment is successful in restoring the volume of output and of profits, this may help to restore the business optimism which is a necessary condition of expansion. It may be that a dose of 'official' investment will be helpful in breaking the vicious circle and restoring the conditions in which we can again increase our reliance on normal 'unofficial' investment.

(iii) It has been objected that the tendency of such schemes will be in the direction of raising prices in this country and thereby hamper our export industries in their efforts to retain

* 'Unemployment and Public Works', International Labour Office, 1931, p. 30.

their hold on foreign markets. If our available plant were fully occupied, there might be much force in it. But in existing conditions, we do not doubt that output could be expanded in many directions in response to an increased demand with an insignificant increase in price. Indeed, some witnesses have gone so far as to maintain that, if output were to be increased, prices would be reduced, basing themselves upon the lower cost per unit of production when plant is fully employed.

In any case we should attach limited importance to this objection because, in so far as output cannot be increased except in response to a higher level of prices, this objection applies equally to *all* remedies for unemployment of whatever character, except those which involve a reduction of wages.

(iv) It is sometimes argued that home investment may not only embarrass our export industries for the reason just discussed, but will also put a fresh burden on our balance of trade, because it will tend to increase our imports, both to furnish raw materials and to provide for increased consumption, particularly of food, by the newly employed. This is clearly, to some extent, the case. But here again it is an objection which applies to *all* remedies for unemployment. Any increase of employment is likely to bring with it increased imports of the raw materials of our industries and of the articles of working-class consumption. But this is scarcely a reason for not providing employment. The point is to be regarded, rather, as a reason for not embarking too rashly on large-scale schemes without arranging at the same time as to how the necessary increment of imports is to be paid for.

It is at this stage that considerations which are more of a monetary character come in. It is the business of the Bank of England so to regulate our net rate of foreign lending that it does not seriously exceed our available trade balance. A recovery of domestic output must, when it occurs, present the Bank with a problem of this kind. But schemes of capital development would have to be on a larger scale and mature with greater rapidity than is at all probable, before they would present the Bank with too heavy a task, unless they were to be undertaken simultaneously with a general breakdown of confidence due to other causes. We are still a creditor country on a large scale, and it would be an overwhelming condemnation of our present methods if proposals for increasing employment were to be rejected on the ground that we cannot pay for the raw materials which the men would handle and the additional food, etc., which they would consume, if they were to be brought back into employment.

(v) It is feared that state-aided schemes are likely to put some burden on the Budget and therefore to lead to the evils of increased taxation. If, however, we lump together—as we should for the purposes of this argument—the Budget and the Unemployment Fund, we feel quite confident that the relief to the Unemployment Fund and the additional yield of taxation, resulting from the increased employment provided by the schemes in question, would materially outweigh the direct cost of the schemes to the state.

(vi) A final objection—which may, we think, have weighed with the Treasury—is based on the possible effect of loans, made or sponsored or guaranteed by the Government, on the rate of interest on British Government securities, with the result of postponing the date at which large economies can be secured by a conversion of the War debt to lower rates of interest.

This is a natural, but nevertheless dangerous, preoccupation. Over any short period it is evident that the prices of Government securities may be affected by competing issues. But it is an exact inversion of the truth about the rate of interest to suppose that it can be reduced by *refraining* from new capital investment. Apart from the short-period fluctuations around the equilibrium position, the rate of interest must tend to fall as the accumulated wealth and prosperity of the country in the shape of capital assets *increases*. The contrary view is based on some such fallacy as that 'surplus' financial resources can be gradually built up, unembodied in any physical form. It is supposed that if we 'save' a part of our current income and do not 'use up' these savings in capital schemes, we can in some way hoard them up for use at a later date and that these 'accumulated' savings will gradually strengthen our 'financial' position. These ideas are probably derived from a false analogy between the position of a particular individual or firm and that of the community as a whole. For a particular firm can clearly accumulate 'liquid' resources, un-embodied in any physical form so far as the firm itself is concerned and constituting realisable claims on the rest of the community. But a little reflection will show that the community as a whole cannot increase its 'liquid' resources by the various members of it building up claims against one another.

We have dwelt for a moment on this highly abstract point because mistaken ideas about it may be the explanation of much latent, unexpressed hostility or reluctance to the general idea of organised capital development. It is one of the cases where uninstructed common sense tends to believe exactly the opposite of the truth.

48. The main obstacle in the way of remedying unemployment by means of organised schemes of investment is probably to be found, not so much in any of these arguments, as in the practical difficulties of initiative and organisation. It is not easy to devise well-conceived plans on a large scale. It is not easy to fit them into the existing scheme of things, even when they have been conceived, without all sorts of difficulties, frictions and delays. And, finally, the period of preliminary planning and designing, which must elapse before they will provide their full quota of employment, may be somewhat lengthy. It is difficult to *improvise* good schemes. If they are to be thoroughly wise and economical, they may often need as much as two years' preliminary gestation. Yet we have seldom been ready in recent years—though subsequent experience has taught us that we ought to have been—to sit down calmly to prepare plans for the remedying of unemployment two or three years hence. This difficulty has increased with time. For by now most of the good

plans which can be quickly improvised have been used up, and the best plans still left in the cupboard are those which will yield their results most slowly.

49. If, therefore, the organised planning of capital investment is to be relied on as a remedy for our economic ills, it should, we think, be approached from now on in a somewhat different spirit from that which was natural three or four years ago. We must be prepared, that is to say, to look some way ahead, and get to work on well-conceived projects without laying too much emphasis on the rapidity with which they can be executed.

50. There is the more reason for this, in that the problem of finding an outlet at home for a substantial proportion of our current savings is likely to be with us for some time to come. We recommend, therefore, that we should now attack the task of capital development in this country in a much more systematic and far-sighted manner than hitherto. It should not be an objection to a scheme that its execution will be spread over many years or that the period of preparation will be somewhat prolonged. After several years of living from hand to mouth, a point has come when it need not be considered an imprudence to look ahead.

51. It falls outside our scope to proceed to details in a matter of this kind. But we may illustrate our argument briefly:—

(i) A considerable part of the larger towns and industrial centres of the country need rebuilding and replanning on a comprehensive scale. At present they offer neither beauty nor convenience nor health. Much of the industrial housing of the country is of an age when buildings of that character are, of necessity, only fit to be demolished. It seems an insanity to keep a large proportion of the building trade out of employment when this is the case.

(ii) Some of our staple industries need to be refitted and replanned on modern lines, at the cost of a substantial capital expenditure. In several cases, there is much to be said for replanning an industry as a whole. Apart from tariffs, and the like, we see no reason why our staple industries should wait before putting their house in order. In cases of proved necessity, we should not be opposed to measures of compulsion, in conjunction with the provision of adequate and cheap finance. It may be that we should develop an improved organisation for handling all matters of this kind. It would be outside our scope to pursue this subject in detail. But we think that efficiency and forethought might be much increased if a body were to be set up which might be designated the Board of National Investment, in the hands of which all matters relating to the deliberate guidance of schemes of long-term national investment would be concentrated. This Board might be entrusted with the duty of raising funds not only for the local authorities which now borrow through the Local Loans Fund but also for other local authorities including municipalities, for the telephones, for the roads and for such further schemes of national development as those which we have suggested above. But this is a big subject and it would lead us too far afield to develop it as it deserves.

(iii) The recommendations of the recent Committee on the Electrification of the Railway System obviously deserve the most careful consideration in this connection.

52. The fundamental objection to these expedients, in the minds of those who dissent from them, is, however, on a different plane of thought. They consider that all these devices are merely temporary shifts to enable us to postpone facing the problem, which sooner or later we shall be compelled to face, namely, that our money costs of production are too high compared with those elsewhere; whilst at the same time they are of a character which, to judge from experience, are often used unwisely and may remain as an incubus on our economic system long after their special purpose has passed away.

53. The ultimate differences between those who feel this and those who think that it is worth while to gain a breathing space are not so much matters of theory as of the practical judgement of probabilities and of what is most prudent. But we suggest that a

heavy burden of proof lies on those who cannot join with us in our plea for efforts to increase activity rather than to reduce standards. For if we can do what we are doing with nearly a quarter of our industrial resources idle, what might we not do if they were all employed? We are impressed for many reasons with what seems to us to be the greater wisdom and prudence of concentrating public attention on constructive schemes for encouraging national trade and national development rather than on efforts to drive down the general levels of salaries and wages. Let us, in conclusion, briefly recapitulate some of them:—

(i) If, at the present juncture, when we are near the bottom of a world slump of unparalleled violence, *all countries* alike were to seek equilibrium by competitive wage cuts, we should merely confirm the low level of prices and rivet on our shoulders an intolerable burden of debt fixed in terms of money.

(ii) We doubt whether it is wise to attempt fundamental adjustments, which may not be required, at a time so abnormal as the present, when similar difficulties are confronting all countries alike and when it is impossible to gauge with any accuracy the degree of adjustment which may be necessary in the long run.

(iii) We see no solution of the grave problem of social justice presented by any proposal to reduce salaries and wages whilst leaving untouched those money incomes which are protected by contract.

(iv) Even if it were desirable to secure a large all-round reduction of salaries and wages, we foresee immense practical difficulties, perhaps insuperable difficulties, in the way; whilst the social costs of an attempt which failed would be incalculable.

(v) We prefer, therefore, to pin all our hopes on a recovery of world prices, and to strain all our efforts to secure it; whilst making, immediately, a great concerted attempt to avoid the immense waste of the national productive resources now going on. If these hopes are falsified by the event, much will by then have happened in the world, which we cannot now foresee. Public opinion, both here and abroad, will be ready for many things which it would be useless to consider now. And the whole matter will have to be reviewed again.

(vi) Meanwhile, we are not convinced that we cannot in the long run, when all our productive resources are at work, continue to support permanently, and even improve, our existing working-class standards. It may well happen, if we can gain a breathing space, that the recovery of world prices, the revival of business optimism, the reorganisation of the older British industries and the steady increase of technical efficiency may eventually render unnecessary a reduction in the prevailing level of salaries and wages.

THOS. ALLEN*
ERNEST BEVIN*
J. M. KEYNES
R. McKENNA
J. FRATER TAYLOR
A. A. G. TULLOCH

From the fragments that remain in Keynes's papers, it is clear that he was responsible for drafting the following sections of the Report of the Macmillan Committee as published: paras. 118–23 (part of The Special Problems of Great Britain); 155–8, 160–74 (The Sequence of Events since 1925); 205–21 (part of The Influence of Monetary Policy on the Price Level); 243–65 (The Gold Standard); 308–16 (Proposals to Meet the Present Emergency); 320–74 (Proposals Relating to Domestic Monetary Policy) and 405–25 (Proposals Relating to Information and Statistics). Doubtless he also influenced the form of other sections, but the evidence necessary for determining which these were has not survived.

Keynes's view of the results of the Committee's work appeared in two letters—one to R. F. Kahn on his last day of work on the Report and one to Walter Gardner of the Federal Reserve Board just over three months later.

* Subject to reservation.

From a letter to R. F. KAHN, *29 May 1931*

By a miracle I finished the work of the Macmillan Committee by 2 p.m. today, after going at it practically continuously since I left Cambridge. So after all I shall get off to-morrow morning according to plan. The Report will be out, I suppose, in two or three weeks, but one never knows just how long printers, etc. will take. On the whole, I am rather happy about it, though it is a bit long-winded and has the faults of all composite documents. At any rate, I don't think its like is to be found amongst other official documents on official monetary policy.

I had a long talk with old Cassel yesterday, and found myself, as I always have on previous occasions, very fond of him. One may have one's academic quarrels with him, but when it comes to standing up against the rest of the world for some sort of sense in these matters, it is by his side that one must stand.

From WALTER GARDNER, *22 August 1931*

Dear Mr Keynes,

The enclosed summary of the Macmillan Report was prepared for use in the Division of Research and Statistics. In preparing it, I was aware of a tendency on the part of those who first read the Report to conclude that it embodied a rather naive faith in the control of central banks over prices. Personally, I felt that the Committee explored with considerable care and realism the steps by which central bank action might be expected to affect prices; indeed, they appeared none too sure that any substantial effect could be produced by central bank action in the face of a depression like the present until non-monetary developments should create sound borrowers. In summarising the Report, I have emphasised the exploration of mechanisms and the sophisticated doubts of the Committee. I am now somewhat uncertain as to whether in doing so I may not have done violence to the spirit of the Report itself. Several of us here would be much interested to know if you regard the summary as true to the intent of the Committee.

We still recall with pleasure your visit of six weeks ago.

Faithfully yours,
WALTER R. GARDNER

To WALTER GARDNER, *16 September 1931*

Dear Mr Gardner,

I have been much interested to read your summary of the Macmillan Report. The document, as is inevitable with a production of this kind which has to be signed by a number of people of somewhat different views, is to some extent a compromise document with its exact shade of opinion rather nicely balanced. It is natural, therefore, that it should be found difficult, as I gather you have found it, to observe precisely that shade of opinion in summarising. On the whole I think your summary is a fair one. But perhaps you do not emphasise quite adequately what I should say is the general upshot of the Report, which I will put shortly in the following paragraph.

The view of the Committee was, I think, that the methods of central bank monetary management deserved an adequate trial, and there was no reason to expect that they could do any harm; that they would probably do what was required of them in normal circumstances; but that it would be rash to estimate in advance what would prove possible until the policy had received an actual trial. The Commitee also recognised that in present circumstances there were unusual obstacles in the way of success of such a policy. They were most anxious, therefore, not to raise excessive hopes, and to make every reasonable concession to a natural scepticism. It is, therefore, as important to emphasise their almost unanimous recommendation that these methods should be given a thorough trial as to quote the numerous phrases in which they guard themselves from accusations of dogmatism or of claiming with too much confidence what it might prove impracticable to get. Also—to repeat what has been suggested above—many of their reserves were meant to be applicable to the extraordinary circumstances of the present position rather than to the more normal problems which face central banks.

Very truly yours,
[copy initialled] J.M.K.

Chapter 3

FIRST REACTIONS TO THE SLUMP

During the period prior to the organisation of the Economic Advisory Council, the policies undertaken by the second Labour Government had come under fire from several directions. The Government's strongest internal critic was Sir Oswald Mosley, the Chancellor of the Duchy of Lancaster and a member of the ministerial team responsible for co-ordinating unemployment policies. On 11 September 1929 Mosley proposed that the central government should take control of an enlarged road-building programme away from the local authorities traditionally responsible for road building. He also emphasised the need for a body under the Prime Minister to give continuous consideration to proposals for long-term development and reconstruction. Mosley's September memorandum and subsequent Cabinet discussions may have hastened the promotion of the Economic Advisory Council,[1] but they did not prove fast enough for Mosley, who on 16 January 1930 presented the Cabinet with a long memorandum making far-reaching proposals for future unemployment policy and its organisation. Keynes received a copy of the proposals from Mosley on 16 January. There is no indication that Keynes met with or wrote to Mosley at this stage.

Matters moved a step further on 6 February.

From SIR OSWALD MOSLEY, *6 February 1930*

Very Private

My dear Keynes,

Further to our talk on the telephone this morning, the point on which I sought your guidance relates to the whole possibility of financing public works by loan. For instance, it is clearly impossible to finance out of Revenue any scheme of the magnitude of the Liberal proposals, which involved an expenditure on roads alone amounting to £145 million in two years. It was suggested in the Liberal proposals, and also from other quarters, that a loan might be raised on the Road Fund for this purpose.

---

[1] Susan Howson and Donald Winch, *The Economic Advisory Council 1930–1939: A Study in Economic Advice during Depression and Recovery* (Cambridge, 1977), p. 20. Their volume has proved indispensable in sorting out Keynes's role in the Council's deliberations in this and the following volume.

I have in mind, as I told you, the possibility of a £200 million expenditure spread over three years divided equally between roads and the sphere which is now covered by the Unemployment Grants Committee, and is already financed by loans raised by local authorities the interest and sinking fund of which is assisted by the Exchequer.

The question with which I am now concerned is how to raise capital sums of this magnitude without undue disturbance of the market. There are natural fears in some quarters that an announcement of loans raised by the Government, or assisted by the Government, to anything like this extent would have a very disturbing effect. I want to carry through the transaction (1) with the minimum of disturbance to the money market, and (2) with the minimum charge upon the Exchequer. The latter factor, of course, must depend upon the measure of the State's generosity, and I believe you had in this connection some ideas upon possible manipulations of the local authorities' loan funds, etc.

If you could help me in this subject I should be most grateful. Anything in the form of a questionnaire with which I could elicit information on which to build a policy would in itself be most valuable. Please forgive me for troubling you, but no one can assist me in this region to anything like the extent that you can.

Yours very sincerely,

O. E. MOSLEY

On 8 February Keynes provided a brief note in reply.

To SIR OSWALD MOSLEY, *8 February 1930*

Loans from the Local Loans Fund are made at present (I think) at $5\frac{1}{4}$ per cent.

The suggestion is that for a period of one year loans, additional to those being made out of the Fund in ordinary course, should be available to local authorities, who are *bona fide* anticipating their normal programme, at a rate of interest one third below the above rate, i.e. at $3\frac{1}{2}$ per cent.

If loans were made under this arrangement—to give a purely illustrative figure—up to £40,000,000, the cost of abating the interest would be £700,000 p.a. for a number of years equal to the length of the loans (apart from loans for housing these loans are for an average duration of less than 20 years).

This charge might be placed on the Exchequer. But the

question arises whether there is not sufficient margin within the Local Loans Fund itself to make the necessary provision. The average rate of interest earned by the Local Loans Fund is now £5.3s3d per cent. The average at which the Fund has borrowed is not stated, and the following deductions may be incorrect, but it is the best which can be made on the basis of the published figures:—

Interest received by Local Loans Fund
in 1928–29   £12,538,000
Interest payable by Local Loans Stock
outstanding on March 31, 1929   11,589,000
                                                            ——————

Apparent margin   £949,000 per annum.

The only serious risk against which this margin is held—for defaults are of trifling amount—arises out of the fact that the Local Loans Stock is, imprudently, for all practical purposes irredeemable, whereas the advances made therefrom have a definite term. Thus if, hereafter, the rate of interest at which it is reasonable to lend out of the Fund falls to (say) $4\frac{1}{2}$ per cent, there would be a deficiency. The *average* rate on outstanding loans is not likely to fall to this figure for a good many years; and in this respect the future will, anyhow, have to look after itself. Besides, the risk, if deemed serious, could be met by the Consolidated Fund exchanging its liability for 5 per cent Conversion Loan with the Local Loans Commissioners for their liability for Local Loans.

There is another small source of margin, namely that the Exchequer makes at present a profit of dubious legitimacy out of the Local Loans Fund, in that the fees paid to the latter by local authorities exceed its expenses by about £100,000, which sum is bagged by the Exchequer.

Subject to the correctness of the above I conclude that the Local Loans Fund could itself finance loans to local authorities up to a certain figure at $3\frac{1}{2}$ per cent.

Any new investment and, broadly speaking, any increase of

employment in this country, whether under the auspices of the Government or not, tends to raise the rate of interest. To object to additional borrowing by the Local Loans Fund on this ground is a most desperate fallacy (see *Britain's Industrial Future*, p. 115). On the other hand, the question of how to raise large funds as cheaply as possible and with the least disturbance to the market is, of course, very important. It is mainly a technical matter. There is a good deal to be said about it and some suggestions which could be made, but it is primarily a question for inside experts. The creation of a Board of National Investment (*Britain's Industrial Future* p. 111) would probably be indispensable for the purpose.

6.2.30   [copy initialled] J.M.K.

On 19 February, Keynes discussed the unemployment situation on the BBC with Sir Josiah Stamp. An edited version appeared a week later.

From *The Listener, 26 February* 1930

UNEMPLOYMENT

KEYNES: Well, my dear Stamp, one talks in a vague way about there being something like one-and-a-half million unemployed men and women, but does that really give us a proper picture of the situation? How much unemployment is there actually?

STAMP: *No, Keynes, I do not think the bare figures are enough. There are all sorts of deceptive points about these figures. What I refer to particularly are the facts brought out by the Ministry of Labour, for example, that unemployment is mainly confined to a section of the population of about one-third of the whole. Two-thirds of the insured population, call it eleven-and-a-half millions, have been hardly touched by the problem since the War. These represent pretty stable employment mainly. Over a period of two-and-a-half years (tested) eight millions drew no unemployment pay at all. Call the one-third liable to unemployment three-and-a-half millions. Well, two-and-a-half millions of those in no single case had one*

315

hundred days in all unemployed over the period. Of course, for two-and-a-half millions to be subject or liable to seven weeks' unemployment in a year and to get into the 'million' as we call it, is in itself a pretty serious problem. So the second point is that it is not mainly a solid mass of unemployment. I believe that probably 50 per cent of those out of work at any particular moment will be in work in a month's time, but I cannot say how long for.

KEYNES: I suppose from the human point of view it helps a great deal that the unemployment should be spread over a wide field and not all concentrated on a few individuals. But does it really affect the economic problem? Is it not just as difficult to deal with 1,200,000 each unemployed for a month as with 100,000 men unemployed all the year round?

STAMP: *Well, yes, in a way, but it is very different in certain important aspects. If unemployment comes in a solid block over a long period you get disintegration of character, the gradual destruction of the morale, and what is more, you get a gradual loss of personal skill with an economic loss. If it is carried over short intervals then you have not those particular influences on character. It is a very different problem if it is a shifting set of individuals and not a solid block.*

KEYNES: After one has made every allowance for unemployment of this transitory and comparatively harmless character, what would you estimate the abnormal volume of unemployment as distinct from normal figures, which one must probably expect even at the best of times?

STAMP: *Of course, it is only a guess, but looking at the thing by and large I should think, in a country made up as ours is, we are pretty certain to have something like 300,000 to 400,000, even under the best conditions. The present problem is fluctuating between 600,000 and 700,000 and a million. Of course, it is going up rather rapidly as it is.*

KEYNES: I will take your basis as an argument. Let us take the 400,000 men who will probably be unemployed at the best of times. At the present time the problem consists of something approaching one million men and women out of work, not necessarily always the same individuals, I grant you that, and not by any means equally spread over all trades and all parts of the country. Is not the figure of average productivity of British workmen, along with the plant and productive facilities, something like £200 a year?

STAMP: *Yes, that is about the figure; perhaps a trifle more.*

KEYNES: And what is it for a woman?

STAMP: *I do not think anybody has worked it out—something like £120 or £130.*

KEYNES: On the basis, then, of this million, we have got three-quarters of a million men who might be earning £200, and we have a quarter of a million women who might earn £120; that means that the average annual loss to the country, which you agree is abnormal, is something like £180,000,000. It is a shocking figure. Is it the sort of thing that happened before the War? I suppose it did, but only for short periods.

STAMP: *Yes.*

KEYNES: I suggest to you that the explanation is to be found partly in the much greater violence of the economic fluctuations which have been experienced in recent times. Even if one leaves out the years immediately after the War, when naturally conditions were quite abnormal, and thinks only of the years since, let us say, 1924, the fluctuations of a broad economic character have been enormously more violent than they were in the twenty-five years before the War.

STAMP: *I think there can be no doubt whatever that those economic bumps have been much more violent, but we have shown a remarkable power of actual absorption since the War—there are over a million more in employment. People are always talking of unemployment, but let us think for the moment of the people in employment. When you consider the broken and unstable conditions of industry, then it seems to me very much to the credit of Britain that we have been able to achieve this task of employing 150,000 more annually. The actual task of employing 150,000 more*

317

annually will gradually slow off because of the movement of the population. There will not be so many people entering into industry in excess of those going out in future. We are entering into a period where they more or less balance, and then it ought to be easier for the industrial machine to absorb this present block of one million.

KEYNES: I do not think very much of that point. Population will probably go on increasing for at least five or six, if not ten, years more. Personally, I do not think we should have diminished our unemployment to any great extent even if the population was already stationary.

STAMP: *I agree that in the main the problem is one of industrial balance, the specialised skill, with the specialised capital, particularly in your highly specialised export industries, and it is our dependence upon this that is really our trouble. You get that if you look at the distribution of unemployment—coal mining, steel and iron, engineering and shipbuilding accounting for quite the bulk of it, so you have a geographical as well as an industrial concentration. In seventy-one industries employment has grown by one-and-a-half millions, and in twenty-nine it has decreased by 650,000. The tendency is for expansion of business in the south—where unemployment is nothing like the same problem—and contraction of business in the north.*

KEYNES: While I think that economic fluctuations have been extraordinarily violent in recent years, I am afraid one has to admit there is also another reason besides economic fluctuation. The existence of the dole undoubtedly diminishes the pressure on the individual man to accept a rate of wages or a kind of employment which is not just what he wants or what he is used to. In the old days the pressure on the unemployed was to get back somehow or other into employment, and if that was so today surely it would have more effect on the prevailing rate of wages than it has today, so that the power of industry to absorb would be much greater than we have experienced. I cannot help feeling that we must partly attribute to the dole the extraordinary fact—at present it is an extraordinary fact—that, in spite of the fall in prices, and the fall in the cost of living, and the heavy unemployment, wages have practically not fallen at all since 1924.

STAMP: *I quite admit that the dole certainly has affected the old methods of economic adjustment. It has retarded things that acted automatically in the old days. For example, in the hard times there was the necessity for taking a lower wage in another job, or the necessity for moving about.*

KEYNES: I know that is one of the difficulties now, the housing conditions. If a man were in one district he could move his family to another district, but now he has to think twice before he moves because he may be disappointed; he may not find another house in the place he goes to.

STAMP: *I quite agree that housing has a very secondary influence on mobility, but do not let us labour this aspect too much. Do you not think from the workers' point of view there is something in this lack of the old freedom to adjust economic difficulties by the employer playing about with labour, moving it and reducing its reward? After all, if he can do that easily, then he has no need to do any thinking. It is only when the matter becomes really urgent that thinking is forced upon him. You really have to address yourself to all kinds of industrial waste, lack of up-to-date machinery and ineffective management. This may prove to be a blessing in disguise.*

KEYNES: I suppose that is always true of hard times. They do get rid of a lot of dead wood, but I have never been persuaded that that is a sufficient reason for having hard times. Besides, the position is still getting worse. Bowley,[2] the only man in this country outside Whitehall who really understands the unemployment figures, tells me that what alarms him about the immediate situation is that unemployment has not only definitely increased in recent weeks, but has spread to the miscellaneous industries, many of which were previously doing comparatively well. As a matter of fact, in coal mining, which we

---

[2] A. L. Bowley, Professor of Statistics in the University of London, 1919–36.

think of as a depressed industry, there is considerably less unemployment than there was a year ago, and owing to the mild weather the seasonal depression in building is very distinctly less. But in almost every other industry, without exception, the position is worse.

STAMP: *Yes, that is very interesting, but let me go back to the point you were making about the wonderful ease with which in the Victorian days we seemed to be able to absorb any difficulty and take it in our stride. We must not set as a standard of what is possible to us today exactly what we did in the nineteenth century. For example, the accumulation of capital was on a pretty artificial basis during that period. I remember in an eloquent passage in one of your own books, in the preface, I think it was, you said that in that period men were tacitly allowed to make enormous fortunes if they turned them back into industry, so to speak, and prepared the way for greater produce in the next generation. By itself that is almost enough, but the fact that it is not done to anything like the same extent today means the almost entire slowing of industrial progress. Then, too, you had all those remarkable inventions which went to the root of industrial matters. I know we have wonderful inventions today, but perhaps not in increment comparable to those times.*

Also you have not taken account of the fact that up to the War we had a very considerable relief to the growing population in emigration, which has been very largely cut off. You must give this age, stupid as it is and out of gear, some credit for the extraordinary difficulty that it has.

KEYNES: Well, it is not so surprising as you think it. I cannot see why there should be more difficulty in employing a population of 41,000,000 than 40,000,000. After all, we live by making things for one another.

STAMP: *I quite agree. Every new man is a potential customer of every other new man. It does not matter what the size of the population is, except with regard to the relation to assets. It is a question of the degree and speed with which the change takes place. It takes time for the new ones to be arranged as customers for each other.*

KEYNES: But our population today is increasing much more slowly than it used to; indeed, I am not sure that our problem would not be easier if we were having a rapid increase of population. On the other hand, that rapid increase in the Victorian age was one of the things which kept business prosperous, when it paid employers to reduce wages. But none of these explanations seems to me to affect the main point in my mind. Is not the mere existence of general unemployment for any length of time an absurdity, a confession of failure, and a hopeless and inexcusable breakdown of the economic machine?

STAMP: *Your language is rather violent. You would not expect to put an earthquake tidy in a few minutes, would you? I object to the view that it is a confession of failure if you cannot put a complicated machine right all at once. I suppose that men are unemployed because no employer finds it worth while to employ them.*

KEYNES: I am not sure that that obvious remark helps us. If that is so, it must be because in many industries profits are low, or precarious, or non-existent. Why should that be so? Is it the difficulty of competing with lower wages abroad?

STAMP: *Well, when you come to consider the actual wages abroad—I do not mean monetary payments, but what wages will buy, the purchasing power of wages—when you think of those figures in France, Belgium and Germany you really wonder that things are not worse in this country than they are. Have you seen those figures published by the* International Labour Review? *They give them every quarter. Supposing you take an average wage in this country—what it will buy in commodities: bread, butter, cheese, shirts, boots, and everything—and call it 100, that is what the average wage-earner gets—100 units of commodities. In Berlin he would get 73, in Italy 47, and in Paris even—wonderful, prosperous France—only 57.*

If that is the cost that is entering into the product, and the product is competing in a neutral market, you can see how extraordinarily difficult it is for a man paying a higher real wage to quote a competitive price.

KEYNES: Well, now, I think, we are getting on. What you

are saying is that people are unemployed because wages are too high.

STAMP: *I would rather say that wages in some trades are higher than they ought to be in relation to others.*

KEYNES: Then there is the burden of social services. Have you got any figures about that?

STAMP: *That is a very important thing, too. I cannot give them exactly, but they are something like this: In 1911, a representative year before the War, the cost of social services—in a limited sense— was 14s. 6d. per head, whereas in 1928 it was 91s. 6d. But if you take in housing subsidies and education, then it was 32s. per head before the war and now 150s., nearly five times as much. A good deal of it must be added to the cost of production. You can see that unless there has been a similar rise in other countries in competition with us— however efficient the social services may be—there is a serious handicap.*

KEYNES: If I were a precisian I might say this is one more way of saying that wages are too high, but I do not want to press that point, because I do not think, any more than you do, that it is practicable to reduce wages, whether they are too high or not. Of course, if we are to avoid putting wages lower we must look round for some other method. What do we mean by all this talk about rationalisation if it is not an attempt to get efficient production per man up to the wage that is being paid?

STAMP: *But you must remember we have had against us all the time the run of prices, which is all against the business man; it makes him lose on stocks that he is holding; it has a bad tendency; the downward run of general prices is all against the business man.*

KEYNES: Yes, and in this country the fall of prices has been twice as great as elsewhere, because of the terms on which we returned to the gold standard. In my opinion the return to the gold standard in the way we did it set our currency system an almost impossible task, because we brought prices down without making any provision to bring costs of production down. This fall of prices all over the world is one of the most worrying things in the whole situation. If prices outside this country had been going up since 1925 that would have done something to balance the effect on this country of the return to the gold standard.

STAMP: *Hush, Maynard; I cannot bear it. Remember, I am a Director of the Bank of England.*

KEYNES: We will not say any more about that, but are there not other points? I do not believe that it is entirely foreign competition which is the trouble. Quite apart from this, I think that in our home affairs we are moving in a sort of vicious circle. The trouble is quite as much the lack of investment and enterprise at home. We are trying to invest abroad as much as we can, and our ability to do so leads to loss of gold, the Bank rate is raised, and credit is reduced. This discourages investment and enterprise at home, which leads to more unemployment and low profits. Indeed, profits have got so bad that many investors try to lend their money abroad preferably to at home, which leads to the loss of more gold, again a higher Bank rate, and we are in the vicious circle again.

STAMP: *I never can answer you when you are theorising, but is that what happens?*

KEYNES: To the best of my belief, yes. And that is not the only vicious circle we are revolving in. The low profits mean reduced yield of the taxes, so the taxes have to be raised, and that again reacts on the willingness to show enterprise and make new investments in this country. Personally, I believe one could do more for unemployment by some bold measure which would break this vicious circle than anything that one could hope from schemes of rationalisation. That is why I have been in favour for a good long time of a large programme of capital expenditure at home that would employ men and would give an outlet for our savings without putting pressure on the gold reserves of the Bank of England, as is bound to happen when the savings find their way abroad. Personally, I very much doubt, whatever we do, if we can revive our export industries to their old relative importance. Low wages and high tariffs abroad, keenness of international competition are too much for us. If that is so there is no way of reviving employment, except by increasing our investments at home.

STAMP: *Have you thought out the full implications of that? After all, what you suggest is really minimising the value of London and its financial importance in the world. I understand you would stop London being a free place for cheap foreign borrowing. After all, that foreign borrowing has been one of the most prominent factors of our export trade. The money is borrowed in London, which means that locomotives, iron, and steel are exported. You would let them go to Paris or New York. In other words, you are after a more self-contained Britain?*

KEYNES: No, not so. I am only saying we must adjust our habits to our circumstances.

STAMP: *You are certainly going to make foreign trade a lesser proportion of the total trade.*

KEYNES: Yes. Well, we must, if our exports are too dear in comparison with those abroad. I am only concluding that our export trade being less than it was, we must depend less on foreign investment as an outlet for our savings. Also I do not believe I am jeopardising the position of London. It is much more dangerous for London for us to endeavour to lend abroad beyond our capacity. This is bound, in the long run, to weaken our financial strength, to diminish our gold reserves, and to make us a dear market.

STAMP: *My dear Maynard, you would suffer like any other imperialistic Englishman, if India, Australia, or South Africa wanted money for development—say £10,000,000—and you sent them off to New York or Paris; and you forget those ancillary products of London's position in the foreign investment market we should lose, the value of many of our shipping services and our insurance services that have always followed the exports—always followed the flag. You are becoming economically more self-contained. I think you have got to realise that those foreign ships bring food supplies to our shores.*

KEYNES: I am all for encouraging these industries—shipping, or any of these things that we can have. I only say that, having expanded these industries as greatly as possible, we must then cut our investment coat to our cloth.

STAMP: *I suppose you have faced up to the fact that what in economic language we call the 'marginal return' for money at home is going to be less than for money abroad.*

KEYNES: Well, perhaps it is; but here are a million-and-a-half men doing nothing. If they could be put to work on anything moderately or reasonably useful, it would increase our national wealth. It ought not to be necessary to prove that the results of their labour would be worth five or six per cent per annum for ever. Is it not better that unemployed men should build a house, even if the house could only be let to yield three per cent on the investment? Some people seem to talk as though it were better to keep the men idle unless it could be proved for certain that the house could be let so as to yield five per cent. It is all a desperate muddle, in my opinion.

STAMP: *Would not part of the difficulty be met if we had cheaper money throughout the world?*

KEYNES: Well, perhaps; but I look upon it as being a choice between that and nothing, rather than between that and foreign investment, which is what you are suggesting. Perhaps it is inevitable.

STAMP: *It seems to me there is a tremendous amount in what you say, but it is a dangerous change for a densely populated country like ours to switch over.*

KEYNES: If we just sit tight there will be still more than a million men unemployed six months or a year hence. That is why I feel that a radical policy of some kind is worth trying, even if there are risks about it.

Two days before the broadcast with Stamp, both men had attended the first meeting of the Economic Advisory Council at 10 Downing Street. At that meeting, as well as discussing matters of organisation and procedure the

Council discussed possible areas of enquiry. The upshot was that the Council set up three committees, one, the Committee on the Economic Outlook, suggested by Keynes. Its terms of reference were 'to supervise the preparation of a memorandum indicating the principal heads of the investigation (excluding those connected with currency) which should be embraced in a diagnosis of the underlying situation'. Its members were Keynes (chairman), Sir Arthur Balfour, Sir John Cadman, Walter Citrine and G. D. H. Cole. Before the Committee met, but after preliminary discussions between Keynes and Hubert Henderson, the second meeting of the Council on 13 March at the instigation of R. H. Tawney removed the phrase in the terms of reference 'excluding those concerned with currency'. The Committee met for the first time on 21 March.

At the second meeting of the Council Keynes joined a Committee on Channel Tunnel Policy. This Committee was to review a report of a committee of the Economic Advisory Council's predecessor organisation, the Committee of Civil Research, especially as regards the building of a tunnel by private enterprise.

The Committee on the Economic Outlook met three times, on 21 March, 3 April and 1 May, 1930. It produced two reports. The first, dated 3 April, was the product of two meetings which neither Balfour nor Citrine attended. It consisted of a short note signed by Keynes, Cole and Cadman covering a memorandum on the economic situation by Henderson. At the third meeting of the full Council on 10 April, Cadman disassociated himself from the report he had signed a week earlier, saying that he did not agree with Henderson's diagnosis and did not believe that state-aided home development was a possible remedy for unemployment. The same meeting received a memorandum on the Report from Mr Snowden the Chancellor of the Exchequer effectively forbidding any discussion of monetary policy or state-aided development as being the preserve of the Macmillan Committee. This, as Keynes pointed out, was inconsistent with a suggestion of the Chancellor at the Council's first meeting and the Council's previous decision, and unhelpful given the delay expected before the Report of the Macmillan Committee became available. The Council asked Keynes's Committee to meet again with all members present to see if it could agree on more common ground. Also, in the light of Citrine's ill health, it asked Ernest Bevin to serve on the Committee in his stead.

The Committee when it met again could not agree on more common ground. Its final Report saw Keynes and Cole re-submit their previous statement without change. In it the economists said that the immediate choices before the Government were 'tariffs, bounties, import control and the like on the one hand, and a programme of productive and useful home development on the other'. Balfour and Cadman submitted a separate document suggesting that state action could not solve the problem, that wage and cost reductions were the only effective solution and that the Council should investigate the effects on unemployment and migration of increased social service expenditures. Bevin, who had replaced Citrine, signed neither document. The Keynes–Cole covering note appears below.[3]

From the Report of The Committee on Economic Outlook, April 1930

REPORT BY THE CHAIRMAN (MR J. M. KEYNES) AND MR G. D. H. COLE

1. At their first meeting the Economic Advisory Council appointed a Committee with the following terms of reference: 'To supervise the preparation of a memorandum indicating the principal heads of the investigation which should be embraced in a diagnosis of the underlying economic situation.'

.   .   .   .

3. At their second meeting the Council agreed that the Committee should be invited to consider the question of an inquiry into the desirability of more extensive state action for the purpose of increasing employment by capital expenditure by loan or otherwise, such an inquiry to include the preparation of a statement of the nature and organisation of the work to which unemployed workers might most advantageously be set.

4. We attach the memorandum which has been prepared by Mr H. D. Henderson.

5. Apart from seasonal changes, we see no hope of an immediate material decrease in unemployment, but feel, on the other hand, that there is a serious risk of a further large increase in unemployment in (say) November, which is, in any case, a bad

---

[3] The full report is available in Howson and Winch, *The Economic Advisory Council*, pp. 165–80.

month seasonally. It is against a possible background such as this that we feel that the suggested alternative remedies should be studied immediately.

6. It seems to us that, broadly speaking, there are, and can be, only three ways of increasing employment which it lies within our own power to promote, namely:

(*a*) An increase of exports, whether by a reduction of wages or by an increase of efficiency so as to put costs of production on a more competitive level, or by inter-imperial arrangements.

(*b*) A decrease of imports by tariffs, bounties, import boards or other measures.

(*c*) An increase of home capital development, whether by private enterprise or by Government aid or initiative.

7. Events in the outside world, which would help, comprise—

(*a*) a general rise of world prices;

(*b*) a reduction of tariffs by foreign countries;

(*c*) a general revival in the volume of international trade and development.

8. It will be observed that each of these external aids is correlative to one of the internal aids.

9. The desirability of greater health and prosperity in the export trades is universally accepted. But to expect an increased efficiency in these trades sufficient to absorb within a moderate period of time the bulk of the persons now unemployed, both in these industries and in other industries, would be quite unreasonable. The value of British exports in 1929 was about £730,000,000. About 20 per cent of this is represented by the value of imported raw materials, leaving a net production for export of £584,000,000. Making use of the census of production and subsequent data, the average net output per annual worker employed may be taken as about £245. We may therefore guess that somewhere about 2,400,000 workers were employed, directly or indirectly, in manufacturing for export in that year. (It would be interesting to have an accurate estimate as to what

the number was.) On these assumptions the employment of another (say) 325,000 workers on producing directly or indirectly for export would therefore mean increasing our exports (at the present price level) by about £100,000,000. We know of no improvements in the export trades likely to materialise on this scale within this year or next. Yet the present number of the unemployed is in the neighbourhood of 1,650,000.

It is a further ground for not placing too much reliance on 'rationalisation' in the export trades as a means of increasing employment, that many so-called 'rationalising' schemes are primarily devised to enable industries to produce at a level below their present capacity without the surplus capacity evoking cut-throat competition, which involves all producers alike in losses. These plans are likely for the time being to increase profits, but they are not so likely to increase exports or employment.

10. The remaining possibilities seem to be tariffs, bounties, import control and the like, on the one hand, and a programme of home development on the other. As to the merits of these two policies, we express no opinion. But we see no third alternative, so far as the near future is concerned, except a policy of inactivity in the hope of some favourable development turning up in the outside world.

11. As to what matters should be further inquired into, we think that the possible subjects of investigation fall into three groups:

(*a*) Those measures the desirability of which has been a matter of general agreement for some time past, so that no question of doubt or controversy arises.

(*b*) Those matters which are already being inquired into.

(*c*) Those suggestions, the value of which still needs clearing up, because they are either novel or controversial.

12. We report that the chief questions in group (*c*)—though one or two of them may turn out to be in group (*b*)—are, in our opinion, the following:

(1) Is there room for a material reduction of marketing and

distribution costs of consumable commodities? In particular, could economies be expected from centralised marketing methods?

(II) Have the abnormalities of the present time any important bearing on the issue of free trade, treating this issue in a broad sense so as to cover proposals for tariffs, subsidies, import boards, inter-imperial arrangements, &c.?

(III) Would a large plan of home development materially reduce unemployment? If so, what part should the state play in such a plan and what test of usefulness or 'economic productivity' should projects be expected to pass?

(IV) Is a long period of cheap money of vital importance? If so, what are the best means of securing this?

13. Of these questions (I) was dealt with at the last meeting of the Council (E.A.C., 3rd Meeting, Conclusion 4). Question (IV) should probably be included in group (*b*) above, since it is presumably being considered by the Macmillan Committee. Question (III) may also overlap, to some extent, with the work of the Macmillan Committee, but is so urgent and important as to deserve an *ad hoc* committee. Question (II) may overlap slightly with the work of the Empire Trade Committee [of the Economic Advisory Council], but also, in our opinion, deserves an *ad hoc* committee:

14. Our recommendations are as follows:

(*a*) That the Staff should be asked to prepare reports on Questions (II) and (III).

(*b*) That committees—consisting of members of the Economic Advisory Council—should consider the reports of the staff referred to in (*b*) above on Questions (II) and (III), and send them forward to the Economic Advisory Council with covering memoranda.

(*c*) That the personnel of the committee on Question (II) should overlap with that of the Empire Trade, 1930, Committee, and that the personnel of the committee on Question (III) should overlap with that of the Macmillan Committee.

15. We suggest that, in the event of there being important differences of opinion on any committee, its chairman should be asked to encourage the presentation of more than one covering memorandum so as to secure clear-cut opinions, in preference to a colourless document embodying a compromise, for compromise comes more usefully at a later stage.

In February 1930, after a discussion at the Board of Directors of the National Mutual Life Insurance Company of which Keynes was chairman, O. T. Falk circulated a memorandum suggesting that British industry was on a long-term declining trend and that investors would be wise to sell almost all U.K. industrial securities and invest the proceeds overseas, especially in North America. As usual, Falk gave his memorandum wide circulation and City editors used all or part of it as a basis for comment mentioning Falk by name without his permission, thus breaking a long-standing traditional relationship between City editors and stock exchange firms. In the light of comments in the press and elsewhere, Keynes wrote to *The Times* on 11 March.[4]

To the Editor of The Times, *11 March 1930*

Sir,

A memorandum by Mr O. T. Falk, expressing views which I have known him to hold with conviction for some time past, has been received with great hostility in the press, and was recently the subject of adverse comment in the House of Commons. I should, therefore, like to say that, while I strongly disagree with Mr Falk's view that the sale of domestic securities by individual investors and the re-investment of the proceeds abroad is at the present time in the national interest, and much doubt whether it will turn out to the interest of the individuals who do it, his behaviour in frankly stating his views seems to me to be far preferable to that of many other people who are acting on the above lines without admitting the fact publicly and without believing that it is in the national interest.

---

[4] A second letter from Falk's National Mutual colleagues, plus outsiders such as Lord Bradbury, R. H. Brand and Sir Josiah Stamp, was sent on 12 March. Both letters appeared on 13 March.

Moreover, his advocacy of *laissez-faire* in this matter, based on the conviction that what appears to the individual investor to be in his own interest will be in the long run in the national interest also, is, after all, the traditional, orthodox doctrine of the City of London. It is the principle on which practically all investment, whether corporate or private, is in fact carried on. If Mr Falk's memorandum leads to a reconsideration of this principle it may be one more demonstration of the great public advantage of frankness and of complete liberty of sincere speech. It is also full time that we faced up to the question whether, as Mr Falk thinks, we are at the beginning of a long industrial decline or, as I believe, in the middle of a painful readjustment.

Yours &c.,

J. M. KEYNES

Early in March, despite his other commitments, Keynes contributed to the columns of *The Nation* two articles somewhat removed from his current preoccupations.

From The Nation and Athenaeum, *8 and 15 March 1930*

THE DRAFT CONVENTION FOR FINANCIAL ASSISTANCE BY THE LEAGUE OF NATIONS

At the tenth Assembly of the League of Nations held last September, the so-called Draft Convention for Financial Assistance received some preliminary discussion. It is now under further consideration by Committees of the League in preparation for its being brought up again at a later date. Yet the public pays little heed. It may be that the title of this proposal arouses no expectation of anything which could have interest for the generality. But whatever the reason may be, the project has received remarkably less attention from the press than its signal importance deserves. For it represents one of the most important practical proposals which have ever come before the League of Nations. Let me, therefore, try to explain what it amounts to.

Since the conception of the League of Nations was first born, the question of what sanctions the League could employ whereby to enforce its decisions has been of vital importance. Yet it has been so difficult to suggest any convincing solution that there has been a natural inclination on the part of friends of the League—a tendency which is reflected in the terms of the Covenant itself—to push into the background this issue of how, in the last resort, the League is to enforce its will.

Some have thought that the formation of some kind of armed international force would prove, eventually, to be indispensable—a view which has found its main adherents, I fancy, in France. The English mind has turned rather to the possibility of an economic blockade, which the other members of the League would undertake to use their authority and power to enforce against a power whom the League had declared to be the aggressor.

The grave objections to an armed international force are quite obvious. Even apart from the recurrent expense involved in times of peace, it is difficult to suppose that the practical obstacles could be overcome. As for the economic blockade, it is open to the objection that it would involve on the part of members of the League, who might be but little concerned with the quarrel, a greater degree of belligerence than they would care to pledge themselves to in advance or to undertake when the time came. For in modern conditions an economic blockade, however limited in its scope, could scarcely be enforced by purely peaceful methods.

Now the great virtue of the Draft Convention for Financial Assistance is that it turns away from negative remedies to positive remedies, and, instead of endeavouring to visit punishment on the aggressor, limits itself to giving positive assistance of a purely pacific character to the injured party. Its details run as follows.

The project of financial assistance proposes that a cut and dried scheme should be drawn up beforehand whereby the Council of the League would have power and authority to offer foreign financial resources with the least possible delay to the party in a dispute which it considered to be the aggrieved party. It is an essential of the proposal that the lines on which this financial assistance is to be given should be drawn up in the most definite possible manner beforehand, so that there would be no necessity to enter into negotiations with the several guaranteeing parties when a dispute was already on the horizon, and no doubts or unnecessary delays in according the actual assistance.

The project lays it down, therefore, that the Council of the League shall be given authority to issue an international loan in the leading money markets of the world, guaranteed by the members of the League who enter into the scheme (for it is not necessary to the project that every member of the League should participate in it), in proportion to their normal contributions to the League. In order to add further to the financial security of the loan it is suggested that, in addition to the guarantees of the participant members of the League, each of which would be limited to a certain percentage of the loan, there should also be an over-riding guarantee given by the financially stronger members, each for a certain quota, so that in the event of any of the financially weaker members of the League defaulting in their guarantee the financially stronger countries would take over the liability. The League loan would therefore have, first of all, the guarantee of the borrowing party; behind this the guarantee of the various members of the League participating in the convention; and finally, in the event of emergency, an over-riding guarantee on the part of the financially strong countries. Unquestionably, therefore, the loans to be issued would be of first-class character and capable of being floated at a reasonable price even in a disturbed atmosphere.

All this having been arranged beforehand—every party to the project having agreed as to what his quota should be, and the actual form of the necessary legal documents having been drawn up to the last word so that the loan could be launched immediately upon the Council coming to a decision—the Council of the League is then to have absolute discretion to afford this assistance not only in the actual event of war, but (to quote the actual phrase) 'the financial assistance provided by the present convention shall be given in any case of war or threat of war in which the Council of the League of Nations decides that, as a measure to restore or safeguard the peace of nations, such assistance shall be accorded to a high contracting party involved in the war or threat of war'. That is to say, the contingency in which financial assistance can be granted is not linked up with any of the clauses of the Covenant, nor with any definite criteria of aggression such as were drafted in the ill-fated Protocol. The present proposal is of a wider character. Very general discretion is given to the Council to afford financial assistance to any aggrieved party under threat of war, to whom it thinks it appropriate to give it.

The main weakness of the scheme is to be found in a feature which is, I suppose, inevitable at the present stage of evolution of the whole working of the League of Nations; namely, in the provision that financial assistance can only be accorded by the Council by a unanimous vote, that is to say, unanimous apart from the parties actively interested in the dispute. From the practical point of view it would clearly be much better if such assistance could be afforded by some substantial majority, such as a two-thirds majority. For with international politics as they now are, there can never be a certainty that the parties who are actively concerned in the dispute may not have friends on the Council who may be secondarily interested and will use their position to obstruct action. Regarded as a first step, however, I daresay that the requirement of a unanimous vote may be wise, though the value of the scheme would be materially greater if action could be taken in response to a preponderating, though not unanimous, balance of world opinion.

The Draft Convention does not mention a specific figure for the amount of financial assistance up to which the Council is to have these discretionary powers. That is to be settled at a later stage. But evidently it will not be worth while to set up an elaborate machinery of the kind proposed unless some fairly substantial sum is in view. Let us discuss it on the basis of the maximum sum, disposable by the Council of the League under this convention, being of the order of £50,000,000 or $250,000,000. As we will show in a moment, this would be for practical purposes a very large sum indeed. But the actual burden which it might throw on any contributory guarantor would be extremely moderate. At 6 per cent (for interest and sinking fund) the annual service on £50,000,000 would be £3,000,000 altogether; but even in the event of the recipient countries' defaulting for the whole amount, the burden would be divided between a large number of countries—so that the actual annual amount which, at the worst, a country would have to provide which was a one-tenth contributor would amount to no more than £300,000 a year, a very trifling sum for a great power, if the provision of it is capable of making a serious difference to the prospects of war and peace. On the other hand, £50,000,000 is a very large sum indeed—I should expect that much less would be required in any ordinary circumstances—in relation to the contingencies of anything but a very great and prolonged war. Let me illustrate this by a figure which may be unfamiliar and surprising to most people, but which is, I think, convincing.

The whole of the amount borrowed by Great Britain during the late War in neutral countries—that is to say, elsewhere than in the U.S.—amounted from first to last to no more than £42,000,000. This was the aggregate of the whole amount of the loans which by all her efforts Great Britain was able to borrow in the neutral countries of Europe and elsewhere.

It is easy from this to appreciate the magnitude and the reality of the help which a provision of £50,000,000 would mean to any minor country which was threatened by war. Indeed, I venture to say that in many cases the possibility of such assistance would have a decisive effect and would compel the aggressor to bow to the will of the League of Nations.

II

As between great powers, it is probably necessary to admit the impossibility of using to much purpose any weapons of this kind, or indeed any other kind of sanction whatever. For the prevention of war between great powers we must depend mainly, or entirely, upon moral forces and forces of opinion of a different kind altogether. But whenever there is a possibility of hostilities between powers not of the first magnitude, the expectation of the Council of the League affording assistance on the scale suggested in the first part of this article might almost settle the matter. It would only be in cases in which the aggressor could overwhelm its victim by a sudden onrush, before there was time for any financial assistance to take effect, that this weapon would be of insufficient avail. Apart from such a contingency, a country of secondary size which could rely upon assistance of this magnitude would be at an overwhelming advantage as compared with a country which could not, and whose credit in the money markets of the world would be greatly diminished by the mere fact of the Council of the League having declared against it.

As between Balkan countries, for example, or minor Asiatic powers, the authority which a weapon of this kind would give to the Council of the League would be overwhelming. In the case of disputes in South America, it would probably be imprudent for the Council to take any action without the approval, or at least the acquiescence, of the United States. But this is equally the case in any dispute between South American powers. The difficulties of the position of the League of Nations in South America *vis-à-vis* the United States are in no way aggravated or further complicated by the project of financial assistance.

The proposal is therefore an extraordinarily effective way of giving greater reality to the decisions of the League. It elevates them into an atmosphere of actuality which they cannot possess so long as it is a mere question of disapproval and indefinite sanctions. It is, indeed, an immensely better way of bringing the force of the League to bear than by any such schemes as an international army or air force, or by any kind of blockade, or by any embargoes, or other discriminatory action against the aggressor. It is more spectacular. It is more practically useful to the aggrieved party. I can hardly imagine one of two minor powers really proceeding to hostilities against the other if it knew that this other was to receive financial backing on the scale proposed. Yet it is a weapon which can be put into the hands of the League at the risk of an exceedingly moderate expenditure on the part of those coming forward to contribute. Mr Rockefeller himself could put up the whole amount without feeling it. The cost is not of an order of magnitude which ought to influence for a moment any of the great powers. Indeed, those of them who have the cause of peace at heart could well afford to take more than their strict quota. I recommend this scheme of financial assistance, therefore, as one of the most solid proposals for the maintenance of peace that has been made for many years.

It is, as I have said, a more solid and important proposal than uninstructed public opinion believes it to be. For there is a general principle of war finance which is seldom fully appreciated—namely, that during a war a country must, apart from foreign assistance, maintain itself and its armaments almost entirely out of the current output of its labour during the actual period of the war. It is this which gives such extraordinary importance to the assurance of having foreign financial assistance in liquid form. Illusions as to the possibility of a country living during a war on its accummulated wealth and using up the resources which it has acquired from its past savings often lead men to overlook this. Yet, apart from foreign investments which can be sold, there is very little indeed of the accumulated wealth of the country which it can use for the purposes of war.

We often speak of a country mobilising its wealth for purposes of war. This is perfectly correct if we mean by mobilisation of wealth the disposal of a country's current productive forces so as to make them efficient for war purposes. But if it be taken to mean the utilisation of the actual accumulations of the past in order to meet current expenses, then it contains a surprisingly small amount of truth. Fortunately, perhaps, a country which is at war cannot ruin itself to the extent that it would be willing to if it was able. For the accumulated wealth of the world consists mainly in buildings, railways, roads, drainage, cultivated fields, ditches, and hedges; and very few of these things can be dissipated during a war. A country can refrain from keeping them in good repair, or can let them deteriorate a little faster than they would in peace time, but that is all. The actual liquid stocks of goods that exist in a country in the form of copper or any other important raw material are generally very small, equal at the utmost to a few weeks' normal consumption, and very little relief can be obtained merely by drawing upon these resources. Consequently, the only surplus which a country has for war is, broadly speaking, the surplus of its own current production over its own unavoidable consumption for other than war purposes, plus what it can borrow abroad. It is extraordinary, as we know from the experience of the late War, what an enormous productive activity a people is capable of developing compared with ordinary times, and it is by means of this extraordinary activity that the bulk of the services of war are furnished. But there will always be certain raw materials, food, and other necessary imports, which cannot be supplied in this way. It is therefore its foreign finance which can involve a country at war in real difficulties. It may be that the proportionate amount of the total expense of the war which has to be raised abroad is not very large, but it is a very vital amount. In the case of Great Britain during the late War something like six-sevenths of the expenditure was raised by the country during the course of the war mainly by its own current economic activity, and something like one-seventh was borrowed abroad in one way or another.

But that one-seventh was indispensable; so indispensable that it was rather strange to one connected, as I was, with the British Treasury that the acuteness of this problem of foreign finance should not have been more vivid to the imaginations of our enemies. There was a period in December 1916, a few months before America came into the War, when the British Treasury was in sight of the very gravest embarrassment. The munitions programme which had been ordered in the summer of 1916 had to be paid for, and an aggravation of circumstances was causing a terrifying drain on the foreign resources of the British Treasury. There was a moment in December 1916 when it looked as if our resources would be exhausted. The balances of the British Treasury in New York had fallen to a point, at one time, when they would only have met our requirements for a few days more. Further resources were mobilised, the drain fell off for the time being, and the trouble was surmounted. But when one comes to read the memoirs of that period from the German side it becomes clear that our extreme financial embarrassment at that date was totally unknown to the other belligerents; though surely, without any special knowledge, they might well have imagined it. The financial collapse of Great Britain in the spring of 1917 would have been extraordinarily serious, particularly in its reaction on the position of the many Allies whom we were then supporting. As it turned out, the financial problem was completely solved by the entry of the United States into the War in the spring of 1917. But by that time we had collected practically our final reserves for foreign use, and were so near to the end of our resources that it was necessary to obtain an emergency advance within a few hours of the entry of the United States into the War. Thus, from the point of view of the Allies, the financial assistance obtained from the United States in the spring of 1917 was indispensable. Yet, extraordinary as it may seem, so far as I have been able to discover, the German Government attached no particular importance to the financial significance of America's coming in. When the German authorities were considering whether or not it would be wise to introduce unrestricted U-boat warfare, the memoirs of the day show that they were well aware of running a serious risk, if not almost a certainty, of bringing the United States into the war.

340

Various aspects of that contingency they weighed, but—so far as one can judge from the memoirs—there was not one of those in the high counsels of Germany to whom it had occurred as a possibility that the British Treasury might be experiencing acute financial difficulty; that the whole network of alliances might be jeopardised by these financial difficulties; but that all such difficulty would come to an end at once as the result of the intervention of the United States.

This underestimation of financial influences in war has not only often been made in the past, but is, I think, still common. It is probably this underestimation of the importance to belligerents of foreign financial resources which has caused so little attention to be given to the Draft Convention for Financial Assistance. But it is a project on the support of which all lovers of peace should concentrate their forces.

Keynes's articles brought a letter from C. L. Lange, Secretary-General of the Inter-Parliamentary Union and Norwegian Delegate to the League Assembly. This letter attempted to get Keynes's reaction to a matter discussed extensively but without a successful resolution at the League's meetings on the Draft Convention and ignored in Keynes's articles—the extension of the plan to cases where war was merely threatened.

To the Editor of The Nation and Athenaeum, *29 March 1930*

Sir,

In writing my articles on the Draft Convention for Financial Assistance by the League of Nations, I was more concerned with the general principle involved than with the precise terms of its application. For this reason I did not enter into the controversy whether the Council ought to have the power, which the Financial Committee's Draft proposes to give them, to grant financial assistance, not only in the actual event of war, but also in the case of a 'threat of war'. But Mr Lange points out quite truly that this was the main subject of discussion before the Third Committee of the Assembly. So I was perhaps at fault in not dealing with it.

My own view is that I want as much as I can get. But I do not want to wreck the whole project by asking for more than I can get.

This applies to both of the matters most in doubt, in regard to the first of which the Financial Committee themselves made the minimum proposal, though in regard to the other they have made the maximum proposal.

The first of these points relates to the question whether the members of the Council, apart from the parties to the dispute, must be unanimous before financial assistance can be granted. I think it would be far preferable if they were allowed to act by a two-thirds majority. But the Financial Committee have recommended unanimity, and perhaps they are wise to introduce this safeguard for the timid.

The second point is that raised by Mr Lange. Here, again, it seems to me that it would be much better if the Council could use the weapon of financial assistance in advance of the actual outbreak of hostilities—which, of course, they would only do in the event of one of the parties to a dispute proving contumacious towards efforts at conciliation and negotiation. This does not seem to me an excessive power to give them, especially if the Council must be unanimous; and it might sometimes be very useful. But here also I would, without hesitation, accept the limitation which Mr Lange favours, if he is right in thinking that the whole plan would be wrecked if the wider power is asked for.

In this, as in other matters connected with the League of Nations, we must bear it in mind that we are preparing for a long period ahead, and are guiding the lines of evolution of a changing and growing organism, rather than erecting a finished mansion. Let us by all means begin with something modest if that is all we can get for the time being. Then if an actual case arises later on, and the Council finds itself hampered by the limitations on its liberty of action, that will be the time for securing a revision and for achieving those wider powers which some of us would like, if we could, to insert from the outset.

Yours, &c.,

J. M. KEYNES

The Second Labour Government came into office pledged to restore the coal miners' working day to seven hours from the eight which had followed the 1926 coal strike. In the Speech from the Throne in July 1929, the Government had, in addition, assigned a high priority to a reorganisation of the coal industry. Inevitably the Government linked the two matters together, but there was still the question of the form reorganisation would take and the extent to which the pledge on hours would be honoured.

The Government spent the summer and the autumn of 1929 trying to devise a measure which would satisfy both the miners' union and the owners, yet successfully pass through a Parliament in which the Government was in a minority position, largely dependent on the support of the Liberals who had definite views on the form reorganisation should take. The Bill that emerged on 12 December 1929 included a reduction in miners' hours to seven and a half in eight-hour areas, a National Industrial Board to protect miners' wages, a compulsory marketing levy on domestic coal to subsidise exports and a rather toothless National Committee of Investigation to protect consumers' interests. The Bill made no mention of the promotion of rationalisation or cost reductions, much less nationalisation. Yet the Liberals favoured officially sponsored amalgamations and nationalisation and were far from happy with the output restriction scheme.

The question then became one of how the Liberals would attempt to alter the Bill and whether in doing so they would be prepared to bring down the Government. At second reading stage, the Liberal leadership attacked the Bill root and branch, as did the Conservatives, but MacDonald's statement that the Government would be prepared to accept amendments at the committee stage helped it survive the second reading by eight votes, as several prominent Liberals abstained and a considerable number of Conservatives stayed away. However, this merely put off the problem, for Liberal ideas on the industry threatened the delicate compromise between the miners and the owners in the Bill. Labour could have probably passed the Bill easily in exchange for a promise of electoral reform as favoured by the Liberals, but MacDonald and his colleagues rejected this. Therefore they proceeded, against Liberal opposition, but making some concessions by withdrawing the export subsidy and its related levy and establishing a Coal Mines Reorganisation Commission to promote amalgamations. However, they stuck to their guns over the marketing scheme. On 27 February 1930 a Liberal amendment deleting the quota provisions from the Bill failed by nine votes.[5] On 20 March the Government forced another challenge in the debate on the Bill's minimum price provisions. The Liberals were opposed to it in principle and several Liberals had put their names down in support of a Conservative

---

[5] In this case four Liberals voted with the Government while eight abstained.

amendment to delete the relevant clause. The Liberals were to meet on 18 March to discuss the party's position. In these circumstances Keynes wrote to *The Manchester Guardian*.

To the Editor of The Manchester Guardian, *18 March 1930*

Sir,

May I say how very strongly I agree with the leading article in to-day's *Manchester Guardian* as to what the attitude of the Liberal party should be in Thursday's division on the Coal Bill? The Government scheme is by no means ideal, but the provisions proposed are not so wrong-headed as to justify the risk of bringing the whole Bill to naught. If Mr Graham considers that the clause in question is necessary to implement the compromise he has painfully effected, he should be allowed his way.

I write in ignorance of what the decision of this evening's party meeting is to be. But it would seem to be a case—and there may be other similar conjunctures from time to time—where abstention by the party as a whole is the right course.

Yours, &c.

J. M. KEYNES

The same day, the Government told the Liberals that it would introduce an electoral reform bill if it remained in office. The Liberals agreed to abstain and the amendment went down before a Government majority of forty-five.

On 9 April, Keynes agreed to speak to the Tuesday Club. His topic for the occasion, 'Are the Presuppositions of Free Trade Satisfied Today?', reflected his recent 'private evidence' to the Macmillan Committee and his contribution to the EAC Committee on Economic Outlook (above pp. 113–25 and 327). Seven members of the Club were present, including Sir Richard Hopkins of the Treasury and Reginald McKenna. Among the Club's guests were Sir Maurice Hankey, the Secretary to the Cabinet, and Lionel Robbins of the London School of Economics.

A month later, Keynes returned to the current economic situation in the columns of *The Nation*.

From The Nation and Athenaeum, *10 May 1930*

THE INDUSTRIAL CRISIS

Last week's concerted reductions of Bank rate took place while the central banks of Europe were represented in Brussels at a conference of the Bank for International Settlements. We may therefore regard them as the first-fruits of the co-operation which we have been led to expect from the foundation of the new Bank. Even though the motive of the reduction may have been more concerned with the prospects of the forthcoming German Reparation Loan than with wider issues, the Governors of the central banks are to be congratulated on what they have done.

It is still necessary to make the low rates thus established in Europe and the United States fully effective. In France, for example, the nominal Bank rate governs so small a proportion of the transactions, that the operative rates are still too high relatively to London. In England the rates for loans charged by the Big Five do not always follow Bank rate downwards below 5 per cent; and it is desirable that these banks should allow industry in the provinces to get the full advantage of the low rates which the Bank of England is establishing at the centre.

But whilst discount rates in the leading financial centres of the world are now cheap beyond dispute at $2\frac{1}{2}$ to 3 per cent, the results must be relative to circumstances. What would attract borrowers when prices are rising or are stable, may be far too dear when they are falling. Moreover, cheap money does very little by itself to mend matters. In the main it creates an environment in which enterprise is more likely to lift its head again. The rate of progress, therefore, will depend upon the extent to which we are able to take advantage of the environment which the co-operation of the central banks has created for us.

The fact is—a fact not yet recognised by the great public—that we are now in the depths of a very severe international slump, a slump which will take its place in history amongst the most acute ever experienced. It will require not merely passive movements of Bank rate to lift us out of a depression of this order, but a very active and determined policy.

Wholesale prices today are 12 per cent lower than they were a year ago, and 8 per cent lower than they were on January 1st. In the light of past experience such a fall of prices must be reckoned a very extreme and exceptional movement. Apart from the slump of 1921–2, one can go back seventy years without finding anything to equal it. The collapse of prices has been more rapid and has proceeded further than, for example, in 1907. In such a situation cheap money by itself may not restore prosperity for many months. We must beware of falling into the conditions of the eighteen-nineties, when Bank rate stood unchanged at 2 per cent for two years before the recovery came.

If, however, we are to use cheap money to advantage, we must understand in what conditions cheap money helps. Only, I should say, if it leads to increased enterprise and to increased capital development. Now, so far as working capital is concerned, the effect of cheap money is being more than offset at present by the influence of falling prices; and so far as fixed capital is concerned, bond prices and the new issue market are responding very slowly. In good times the stimulating effect of cheap money and abundant credit on the new issue market is exceedingly rapid. But when enterprise and confidence have collapsed to the extent that they have today, the response to what would have been in other circumstances a strong stimulus may be very reluctant.

This task of stimulating new enterprise presents a double problem—the problem of home investment and the problem of foreign investment. Now it is evident that the net amount of British foreign investment cannot increase faster than our favourable balance of trade. For if it does we must necessarily lose gold. If our loans are suitably chosen, some part of what we lend abroad should react favourably on our trade balance. But this cannot be true of more than a part of our foreign lending. Therefore we cannot move far in this direction unless our trade is also benefiting from the results of new loans made by the other leading financial centres of the world. The rate at which London lends to foreign countries must keep in step with the rate at which loans are being made elsewhere, particularly in New York and in Paris. At the moment it certainly is not London that lags behind. The drag on our ability to lend to foreign borrowers is to be found in the reluctance of New York and Paris to contribute their appropriate quota. Provided the new foreign loans which are issued are distributed between these three centres in such proportions that no gold flows from any one of them to any other, there should be no serious obstacle to a large new creation of international credit which would tend to support commodity prices and stimulate international trade. All the evidence shows that London can be relied on to increase its foreign lending fully as fast as is safe. Indeed, the danger lies in the other direction. The most important condition for the recovery of international prices and of international trade is, therefore, that New York and Paris should absorb new foreign loans up to the full extent of their capacity.

Even so, progress cannot but be slow. The would-be borrowers in the international market would readily take between them perhaps as much as £150,000,000 to-morrow. But a good many of these loans would be largely used to refund existing indebtedness. The trade position can only be improved when we have worked through those loans which are necessary to clean up the existing situation to loans which are new money in the sense that they are intended to finance new capital development. Meanwhile, one of the stupidest enterprises conceivable stands in the way, namely, the so-called mobilisation of German reparations. The bulk of this represents in effect borrowing by the French Government on the credit of her future reparation receipts from Germany—money which she does not need and for which she has no use, money for which she will have to pay a higher rate of interest than is represented by her own credit, and money which will tend merely to aggravate the existing disequilibrium by piling up still further her already redundant foreign balances. However, it is a part of the Young Plan that there should be such a loan; and we must hope that it will be got out of the way with as much dispatch and as much success as possible.

The conclusion is that until New York and Paris have taken a large volume of foreign bonds the solution of the problem through the new issue market must necessarily be retarded. Even when this difficulty has been surmounted, progress will be slow; and so far as Great Britain is concerned, it will be imprudent, in my judgement, to expect from such developments, even at the best, more than a partial solution of our present difficulties.

We shall therefore be very unwise if we concentrate too much on the foreign situation and avert our attention from the problem of stimulating capital development at home. To find in present circumstances an outlet abroad for more than one-third of our current savings would mean a development of our export trade in the near future which is in the highest degree improbable.

When, however, we turn to capital development at home, the chief obstacle is to be found in the fact that a rate of interest in the bond market, high enough to prevent our foreign lending from being excessive and to avoid a loss of gold, is too high to suit large-scale borrowers at home and is deterrent to domestic enterprise. To cure unemployment, therefore, we need either that the state should step in to supplement the lack of private enterprise, or that we should establish discriminating rates of interest for home purposes and for foreign purposes respectively, so as to maintain at the same time a rate of interest on foreign loans which keeps such lending within our capacity and a rate for home loans sufficiently low to make new domestic enterprises attractive. It is difficult to see how this could be done except by some kind of Government action, which might take the form of the Government providing money for approved enterprises at a rate of interest below the rate current in the market for long-time loans.

Such a policy could only be a stop-gap; but it would at least stop the gap. So far as the rest of this year is concerned, there seems but little prospect of any material decrease in unemployment, whilst a further increase should not surprise us. By no other means than the above can we hope to make a large improvement in the situation in the near future. If our authorities, nevertheless, prefer a passive policy, then they should not expect employment to return to normal for many months to come. I believe that the results of a passive policy, in the expense of the dole and in the loss of taxable business profits, would cost even the Treasury more than the active policy would cost them; whilst the loss to the well-being and the wealth of the community as a whole would be far greater.

Keynes sent a copy of his article to the Governor of the Bank of England. An exchange of correspondence followed.

From MONTAGU NORMAN, 20 *May* 1930

Personal

Dear Mr Keynes,

I read the article you so kindly sent me some days ago and indeed I am in the habit of reading *The Nation*.

But I think the position is more complicated than you paint it. For in some ways the effect of issuing foreign loans in Paris may mostly fall on London— as is already being seen: and apart from such domestic issues as have lately been appearing I think it would at present be hard to find many 'approved enterprises'.

I daresay you think that I am sinning against the light—perhaps because you give less weight to the international position than I do. Nor can the position be satisfactory as long as New York and Paris (and even Brussels) continue, and perhaps must continue, their acquisitive and unnecessary habits.

Believe me, with so many thanks,

Yours sincerely,

M. NORMAN

To MONTAGU NORMAN, *22 May 1930*

Dear Mr Governor,

Many thanks for your letter. I do not think that I under-estimate your international difficulties. Indeed I agree with you not only in thinking that these are the fundamental difficulties but also in doubting how much it lies in the power of this country to achieve acting alone. But that is why I twist and turn about trying to find some aid to the situation, even if only temporary, on the home front, which *is* much more in our own control.

May I, at the expense of a long letter, put the position to you as I see it?

I. FUNDAMENTALS

According to the statisticians we are saving about £9,000,000 a week—or were two or three years ago. Perhaps in these bad times it is safer to say £8,000,000.

The amount of this which we can invest abroad is strictly limited by the amount of our favourable balance of trade. For if we try to invest more *net* (short and long loans together), we lose gold and the Bank of England has to take steps to protect the position. The amount, thus limited, was about £3,000,000 a week in 1928–9, but in present circumstances—low freights, low prices for tin and rubber of which we own the producing companies, the international cyclical depression—it is probably not much above £2,000,000 a week.

That is to say, we have to find an outlet in investment at home for something like £6,000,000 a week or £1,000,000 every weekday, year in year out.

For reasons which are too long and complicated to explain here, *if* our total investment (home *plus* foreign) is *less* than the amount of our current savings (i.e. that part of their incomes which individuals do not spend on consumption), then—in my opinion—it is absolutely certain that business losses and unemployment *must* ensue. This, of course, is a difficult,

350

theoretical proposition. It is very important that a competent decision should be reached whether it is true or false. I can only say that I am ready to have my head chopped off if it is false! At any rate the rest of this argument will assume that it is true.

Now the amount of our net foreign investment, being governed by our balance of trade, depends on our gold-costs of production relatively to the complex of economic facts in the outside world. But the amount of our foreign lending does not automatically adapt itself to the limit thus set;—it has to be *kept down* to this limit by the Bank of England enforcing a rate of interest and a credit policy which will have this effect.

My fundamental diagnosis of the situation is, therefore, this. Given our present gold costs of production relatively to the foreign situation, a rate of interest, which is *high enough* to keep our foreign lending within bounds, is *too high* to permit of the absorption in home investment of the surplus of our savings over our foreign investment as thus limited. Accordingly savings exceed *total* investment. Hence *inevitably and mathematically* business losses and unemployment.

2. THE REMEDIES

There are only three possible methods (and there is no reason why we should not employ the first two of them simultaneously) of restoring equilibrium:—

(*a*) *To increase foreign investment*

(i) by increasing our exports as a result of decreasing our gold-costs of production;—this is where your rationalisation schemes come in.

(ii) by decreasing our imports either by the same means as (i) or by tariffs:—this is where safeguarding propoals come in.

(iii) by making increased loans to borrowers who are likely to expend them in part in buying more exports from us;—I return to this later, but this expedient is obviously limited by the pace at which other creditor countries are lending.

In the long run much might be effected along these lines. But in the present position of demand in the outside world, we should do wonders if we were to raise our net foreign investment to the figure of say £3,500,000 a week. Indeed, I think we shall do wonders if during this year and next we can, by these means, hold our own and avoid a further decline.

I accept the absolute necessity of rationalisation; but I think it is imprudent to exaggerate the quantitative effect of it on our exports in the next two or three years. (£100,000,000 worth of exports does not employ, at the outside, more than 400,000 men or (say) a quarter of our present unemployed; whilst rationalisation will reduce the number of men employed per unit of exports.)

(*b*) *To increase home investment*

Here I am appalled by the difficulties of absorbing our surplus savings at anything like the present rate of interest. Let me illustrate this.

The highest figure I have heard for the capital cost of a drastic rationalisation of our iron and steel industry is £50,000,000—which would absorb our surplus savings for home purposes for 50 days or about eight weeks and, once done, would be non-recurrent. The figure for the cotton industry (apart from automatic looms the large-scale introduction of which would bring more problems than it would solve) is (say) £15,000,000, or less than another three weeks' saving. And so on with other industries. I conclude that *industry* is incapable at the best of absorbing more than perhaps a quarter (£1,500,000 a week) of our available surplus—and that will take a great deal of doing.

There remain housing, transport and public utilities. At all times these have been the main absorbers of savings. But it is not surprising that their demands are not forthcoming on a large enough scale *at the present rate of interest*. We have more equipment in these respects per head today than we had in 1913. But in 1913 the gilt-edged long-term rate of interest (which is what matters to them) was 3 to $3\frac{1}{2}$ per cent. There would be nothing strange in not finding a demand in these quarters for £4,500,000 a week, year in year out, at 5 to 6 per cent interest.

I believe that the root of the trouble, both here and, more recently, throughout the world, is to be found in the long-term rate of interest being held far above its equilibrium level. (At the equilibrium level the demand for savings is equal to the supply and there is no unemployment.) This is the case for a variety of reasons—resulting partly from the War, partly from the struggle for gold ensuing on the general return to gold and aggravated by the behaviour of certain banks, and partly, at this moment, from there being a long line of distress-borrowers waiting in a queue.

(Incidentally it would be madness for the Treasury to consider conversion schemes until the long-term rate of interest has had time to fall to pre-war levels.)

(c) *To decrease saving*

If we can find *no* outlet for our savings, then it would be better to save less. But this would be a counsel of despair. I am sure that there *is* an outlet for them—at an appropriate rate of interest.

Most people think that the high long-term rate of interest is a *proof* that savings, so far from being in excess of the demand for investment, are deficient. It is natural to think this. But I am profoundly convinced that the opposite is true and that falling prices and unemployment prove the opposite to be true. It is a very difficult intellectual problem—but it is a purely scientific question and, if it is disputed, we ought to set ourselves to reach an agreed conclusion about it.

3. THE METHOD

On the monetary and banking side, therefore—as distinct from the technical, rationalising problem—the task is to produce credit conditions which will bring down the long-term rate of interest and at the same time stimulate investing enterprise.

If the governments, banks, and issue houses of all the creditor

353

countries in the world were to work together in this direction, it would present no great difficulty. For if everyone moves in step, no-one will lose gold. Moreover, if once the line of distress borrowers waiting in the queue could be satisfied and got out of the way, I believe that the long-term rate of interest could be brought down with a rush. The number of foreign borrowers at the rate now current is by no means unlimited—though it looks large at the moment.

But if Paris and New York hold back, the pace at which London can move by herself must, I agree, be slow. All we can do is to go as fast as we can, to be very brave, and not mind losing gold—which may have the effect of shaming or stimulating others into action.

So far as the international position is concerned, I see nothing else to be done; and in time, perhaps a considerable time, this will increase buying power throughout the world and restore the commodity price level. I don't think that it differs from what you are actually doing.

But when we turn to the home position, I believe that we are not doing all we could—though I admit that it is fearfully difficult to work out a practical scheme. I do not anticipate that action on the above lines will bring the rate of interest down to a level at which an adequate volume of private borrowing for home investment will come forward,—particularly in the present environment of depression and business losses.

Therefore I favour—and here I am, I know, on very controversial ground—what would be, in effect, differential rates of interest for suitable home borrowers. Otherwise I believe that our savings, unable to get out abroad because of our limited power to export and finding no users at home, will be used up and wasted in creating and then financing business losses.

What I have in mind is something like the following. (1) The Government to lend to local authorities and public boards at 3 per cent whenever guarantees are given that the work is new and will be commenced shortly. (2) The Government to put a large sum at 3 per cent at the disposal of the B.I.D.C.[6] to be handed on by them to suitable private borrowers satisfying similar conditions.

Until this, or something like this, is done, I believe that unemployment will continue.

4. THE TECHNICAL POSITION

The cheap short-term money now established was a necessary first step towards bringing down the long-term rate and stimulating investment. If it is continued long enough throughout the world, the long-term rates will in the end come down. But one would like to expedite the process.

In this country it is being held back, I think, by a flaw in the technical position. The Treasury's funding operations by which the supply of Treasury bills in the hands of the market has been reduced by at least £100,000,000, simultaneously with a fall in the face value of trade bills due to the fall in commodity prices, has caused a shortage of this particular type of security. Accordingly bill rates have been forced down until the supply of bills is replenished, one way or another, and largely by the London acceptance becoming cheaper than the New York acceptance,—with a resultant burden on our exchanges. At the same time the long-term gilt-edged market has been slightly over-supplied with stock.

The result is that there is an abnormally wide spread between long-term and short-term interest. My *recipe* would be to increase the supply of Treasury bills, so as to bring bill rate up nearly to 3 per cent, and at the same time buy long-dated

[6] Bankers' Industrial Development Company. This company was set up in April 1930 'to receive and consider schemes for the reorganisation and re-equipment of the basic industries of the country, when brought forward from within the particular industry, and, if approved, to procure the supply of the necessary financial support for carrying out the scheme'. The Bank of England subscribed a quarter of the capital, the rest came from the City. The Governor was chairman and the Bank maintained control of the new firm.

securities, thus putting the gilt-edged market good and helping new issues. I would, for example, gradually sell up to (say) £30,000,000 Treasury bills out of the Issue Department and simultaneously buy long-dated securities to replace them. This would stimulate the gilt-edged market and new issues, including foreign issues; but the strain which this would put on the foreign exchanges would be more than balanced by the favourable effect on the exchanges of the higher bill rate. In short it is now more important to stiffen the bond market than to cheapen borrowing by bill.

Further I believe that—psychologically—the quickest way of bringing Paris and New York back into the bond market will be to put bonds better. New York, in particular, is probably near the edge of considering bonds; and if they see bonds going up in price they will then want to take them from us.

At the back of my head in suggesting all this is the conviction that the present long-term rate of interest throughout the world is quite artificial, that it will move sharply downwards over the next two or three years towards the pre-war level, that the notion of there being a shortage of savings is due to an optical delusion (on the contrary it is enterprise which is flagging), and that it is good business to act on these beliefs and expectations.

We are all far too depressed—as we have good reason to be, taking the short view—whereas further ahead, if only we can row hard into the smoother water, the prospects are perfectly good.

Forgive me this impossibly long letter. Perhaps you would ask me to come round for a talk one day? Apart from these major problems, I would like to put to you beforehand some suggestions of detail which I shall be proposing to the Macmillan Committee and of which I may be asking you your opinion next time you come before us.

[copy initialled] J. M. K.

FIRST REACTIONS TO THE SLUMP

From MONTAGU NORMAN, *19 June 1930*

Personal

Dear Mr Keynes,

I have been obliged to be abroad on and off for the whole of the last month and thus have been prevented from thanking you for your letter of the 22nd May, and from availing myself of the kind suggestion contained in your last paragraph.

Next week I have to spend two days at Oxford receiving a degree and on Friday, in accordance with plans made long since, I go right away. But I want very much, if it is possible, to see you before I go. I wonder whether you would be free to call at the Bank at 11.30 or perhaps at 11 o'clock on Monday morning next. I have a meeting at 12 o'clock which I fear I cannot avoid but I think you would then be glad of the opportunity of discussion with Mr Stewart and Mr Sprague and I should be delighted if, with strength thus renewed, you would stay on to lunch at 1.30 or 1.45.

Believe me, with renewed thanks,

Yours sincerely,
M. NORMAN

Keynes saw the Governor as suggested on 23 June at 11 a.m.

Unemployment and its remedies, as well as the views of Balfour and Cadman on the Committee on Economic Outlook and Sir Alfred Lewis on the EAC itself were the subject of an exchange between Keynes and Hubert Henderson in late May and early June.

From HUBERT HENDERSON, *30 May 1930*

My dear Maynard,

I feel that I want to come closer to grips with you on certain points than it is easy to do in conversation.

1. *The need for a large new revenue to finance a large capital programme*

The argument that a large capital programme (even if unremunerative to the extent of say 50 per cent) would involve a very small annual charge on the Budget rests on the assumption that the programme can be brought to an end in a few years' time; and, of course, the case for such a programme, as a purely temporary measure, depends absolutely on the assumption that after the two

357

or three years, unemployment will be comparatively satisfactory on the basis of the ordinary commercial demand for labour. Otherwise, Sir Alfred Lewis is clearly right in contending that you will have aggravated the situation two or three years hence.

Now, in the light of your present diagnosis of unemployment, are you really satisfied that it is only a two or three years' transition that you have to consider? You tend to lay less stress nowadays on the 'jolt' conception, and more on the contention that rationalisation will increasingly displace labour. You say, for instance, consider how many weavers the automatic loom will displace in Lancashire. Now, of course, in so far as rationalisation means new machinery, the position is that it will *help* employment immediately but may injure it later on. At first engineers will be employed making the machinery. It is precisely in two or three years' time that the weavers will lose their jobs. Of course, we should both agree that the long-distance unemployment situation will turn very largely on the world's monetary trend; but we should also both agree that this is a highly speculative matter. My first shifting of opinion from my position a year or so ago, is that I am less disposed to regard (I don't say our 2 million unemployment) but our 1,200,000 unemployment as a short-period transitional problem, yielding to the treatment of a purely temporary stimulus. If I'm right there, the whole financial approach of saying—'What would be the charge on the Budget of a programme of an extra £200 millions over two years—costing the state, say, $2\frac{1}{2}$ per cent? Why, a mere £5 millions. Trifling'—is a sheer fake and fraud. A capital programme may still be right; but you must contemplate the likelihood of having to continue it for many years, turning to ever less remunerative things, to parks and playing grounds on the German model, so that your charges on the Budget will steadily mount up. If you're not prepared to contemplate that, I suspect that Sir Alfred Lewis has the better of the argument. But if you do contemplate a more or less indefinite annual programme of say an extra £100 millions (50 per cent remunerative) the real liability on the Budget is £50 millions annually, and the only really sound course is to raise that £50 millions out of revenue as you go along.

2. *Psychology*

As regards the importance of psychological factors, I have a strong belief in the following propositions:

(*a*) that where there is no real basis for an alleged psychological influence, I don't believe it is worth considering; but

(*b*) where there are solid grounds for expecting that a certain event will happen, and the grounds are of a kind which the business community can understand, then the results of that event begin to take effect in advance.

Now if you launch a large £200 millions two years' programme, proposing to place £5 millions only on the Budget, there are solid grounds at once for believing that that means that taxation is likely to be increased even higher, year by year, indefinitely; and the business community will certainly take that point. They won't believe that everything will be lovely in the garden in two years' time, and that this programme will be the last: and how, having regard to political realities, can you dispute that their scepticism will be reasonable? It won't therefore merely be a case of their *saying* they're alarmed: they *will be* alarmed. Now really doesn't that matter? I should say the alarm might quite easily serve to counteract fully the employment benefits of the programme, and you would then be in a vicious circle of requiring a still bigger programme, still more unremunerative in character, with an increasing hole in the Budget, and increasing apprehension, until you were faced with either abandoning the whole policy or facing a real panic—flight from the pound and all the rest. I doubt if this is over-alarmist.

3. *Insular socialism*

I don't believe that our unemployment and bad trade are solely attributable to monetary causes: they are due to them, in association with a trend of circumstance unfavourable to the economic position of Great Britain (that we've lost our monopoly position as manufacturers etc., etc.), which makes it difficult for us to maintain an increasing standard of life. So far I think we agree. But I'm increasingly impressed by the feeling that such a situation is fundamentally dangerous—in that a people so placed will always try to maintain its standards by one device or another to the very last, and will always tend to be too late in recognising the dangers of each device. You can keep wage rates uneconomically high for a good time: you lose trade as a result, but you lose it only gradually. The trouble is that you lose it increasingly. You (meaning you personally) have always appreciated the danger of over-high wage rates: but you have reacted by saying 'We can't increase wages. But we must go on raising the standard of living somehow. Let's press on, therefore, with social services and the taxation of the rich.' Well, that course seems to be just as dangerous in a different, but analogous way. You can tax the rich a good way for a good time without any really harmful results. But there's a danger-point, after which things go with a run; and the trouble is you can't be sure where the danger-point is, until you've passed it. And so a democracy, with its standard of life threatened, is fundamentally inclined to press things until it passes it.

That danger seems to me very real. It's like passing a water-shed, or like extracting the maximum Germany can pay. Just go a bit too far, and you get consequences which you can't easily repair. I can't help feeling that in making light of dangers of that kind, you're over-moved by a sense that it's inconsistent with your self-respect to accept anything savouring of a conservative conclusion. Anyway, don't tell me that my state of mind is shocking. I've abandoned too many orthodoxies now to be much moved by that. What are your answers, other than that Balfour and Cadman would agree with me?

Yours ever,

H. D. H.

To HUBERT HENDERSON, *4 June 1930*

My dear Hubert,

Your argument is too much of an affair to deal with in a letter. You will have to come down to Tilton for a week-end for us to thrash the whole matter out.

I do not, of course, regard the large capital programme as a solution of our difficulties which *competes* with a solution by means of wage reductions. Whether one can get a complete solution from increased investment by state agency without any reduction of wages remains to be seen. But I should not be without hope that one could.

Also, if wages are in fact not going to come down, the country will be much richer if it occupies itself with a large capital programme in the next two years than if it does not.

Of course, I agree that if the necessity for a bounty on investment or some form of differential rate of interest proves to be necessary for a long period, it would not be practicable to charge the difference between the market rate of interest and the subsidised rate on the Budget if the annual cost, apart from spreading, were to be anything like £50,000,000 a year. I should hope that the unspread cost, even in the first year or two, would be less than this, and I can also give many reasons for hoping that the necessity would not be permanent. Whether we can get on permanently with complete *laissez-faire* in foreign investment, and without some sort of discrimination between rates for home lending and rates for foreign lending, I am not sure. But if this proves to be a permanent problem, I should certainly not hope to solve it by making subsidies out of the Budget.

As regards psychology, I maintain that if I am right that a large capital programme would increase the profits of business men, this would, after the first blush, have more effect on them than anything else. Moreover, if it is true that the capital programme would increase the wealth of the country, it follows that the dangers of insular socialism would be diminished rather than increased.

I do not believe that all this regarded as a Budget problem is at all large as compared with all kinds of other issues which are likely to arise; and it might quite easily benefit the Budget on balance.

However, I do not believe we shall come to a full agreement about it until we have worked through over again the ultimate diagnosis of the whole situation and have tried to quantify the various factors.

But I take it that the main force of your argument is not that you rank lower than you did the benefits of a large capital programme, but that you rank higher than you did the dangers of financing such a thing out of the Budget, and that you are therefore inclined to make it a condition of a large capital programme that the finance of it should be found from some new source. As you know, I have no objection to this. But I should not make it a *sine qua non*. Far from it!

Yours ever,

J. M. KEYNES

We are all shattered by the Wollaston tragedy. It has been a most terrible thing—and an extraordinary story.[7]

---

[7] A. F. R. Wollaston, the Tutor of King's, was shot by a student. For Keynes's obituary note see *JMK*, vol X, pp. 347–8.

Memo

1. *If* we can translate £100,000,000 business losses into £100,000,000 capital goods yielding 2½ per cent per annum, by borrowing £100,000,000 at 5 per cent and re-lending at 2½ per cent.

    2. The Budget loses £2,500,000 p.a. over a period of years
                gains £1,125,000 p.a. over the same period in income tax

    3. If this employs 250,000 men, the Budget gains £12,500,000 on the data in the year in question

    4. This allows nothing for repercussions on employment, death duties or other revenue

    5. It is not obvious that this would not pay *as a permanency AS COMPARED WITH HAVING THE BUSINESS LOSSES AND THE MEN UNEMPLOYED.*

    1. is overstated for simplicity and to balance understatement in the other items. Probably the whole thing is overstated. But I want to bring out clearly the nature of the argument.

I suspect you of not really believing Proposition 1, even in a modified form.

J. M. K.

4.6.30

From HUBERT HENDERSON, *5 June 1930*

My dear Maynard,

Many thanks for your letter. I should be very glad to thrash the whole question out at leisure.

Essentially my position is that I am scared by the Budget position quite apart from whether capital programmes are pushed forward or not, and I want to force your attention to that question. It seems to me extraordinarily dangerous. The cost of unemployment pay is mounting up very rapidly, much more so than the numbers of unemployed. The whole system of unemployment benefit under last year's Act shows signs of developing into a scandal of the grand order. Courts of referees are apparently in some cases upholding the claims to benefit of married women who have not worked since their marriage, and the Ministry of Labour are scared that the good news will spread. Revenue must certainly be seriously affected by the state of trade and altogether we are certainly heading for another formidable Budget deficit. If that is met by raising the income tax and super tax again, I say the effects may be very serious indeed, and I can't believe you would make light of them if you considered the question really objectively and without regard to Left prepossessions. I consider therefore the two essential questions to be faced are—

    (i) the conditions and rates of unemployment pay, and

    (ii) the raising of a new source of revenue.

The way in which those two questions are handled will in my opinion affect the general economic situation far more powerfully for better or worse than any shift of policy in regard to capital expenditure which is within the bounds of practical realities.

In *practice*, as I see it here, pressing on more vigorously with capital expenditure can only mean this—that the Government will exert itself to induce local authorities to put in hand more schemes and to put them in hand more quickly, and in order to induce them to do so will undertake a larger portion of the cost. The upshot is likely to be a very slight extension of the work undertaken, but to secure this slight extension a considerable increase in the cost to the state on all local authorities' schemes including those which they would do on the present terms. That, I say, is what it is likely to mean in practice at the present juncture. It won't amount to a really large-scale thing anyway and, even if it does not aggravate the Budget situation, it will certainly leave that situation to be faced: but in practice I certainly think for the reasons given it would aggravate it to some extent.

You must, I think, take account in your budgetary calculations of the fact that subsidising capital expenditure will necessarily entail paying subsidies or larger subsidies on a good deal of work which would have been done without them, even if you go out into the general industrial sphere. But my main point is that the situation is not going to be radically affected by anything that is done under the head of capital expenditure though there may be a great atmosphere of pressing local authorities to undertake work which will be generally condemned as largely wasteful,* that on the other hand the situation will be very powerfully affected by Budget difficulties. I suggest that you are in great danger, if you persist in effect in ignoring the latter question,

---

* Not that there's not plenty of really useful work to be done. But there seems to be an unnatural law that it is the comparatively useless things which can most easily be got going quickly, e.g. it's much simpler to widen the Bath Road through Savernake Forest than to build the Maidenhead by-pass.

and implying that capital expenditure can put it right, of going down to history as the man who persuaded the British people to ruin themselves by gambling on a greater illusion than any of those which he had shattered.

Yours ever,

H. D. H.

I was appalled by the Woollaston business. He struck me as one of the nicest people I'd come across.

To HUBERT HENDERSON, *5 June 1930*

Dear Hubert,

I wonder if you became a Conservative under the influence of reading the Iron & Steel Committee Report![8] It would be quite natural.

It is an extraordinarily depressing document, not least so the utter impotence of the conclusion.

I should be inclined to say that if we wish to preserve the industry we have to choose between a tariff and a drastic reduction of wages. I see no third course which can possibly avail on a sufficient scale.

Yours ever,

J. M. K.

I am off to Spain on Friday.[9]

To HUBERT HENDERSON, *6 June 1930*

Dear Hubert,

The two matters you refer to—unemployment pay and a new source of revenue—are probably very important. If anyone can persuade the present Government to alter the terms of benefit and to put on a revenue tariff, all the better.

But what chiefly divides us, I think, is what seems to me the lack of fundamental diagnosis in your present attitude. After all, the budgetary problem is largely a by-product of unemploy-

---

[8] This Committee set up by the Committee of Civil Research and taken over by the Economic Advisory Council reported on 30 May. It recommended large regional amalgamations as essential for the industry's recovery but rejected a safeguarding tariff, which it thought might reduce the incentives to rationalisation.

[9] See below p. 367.

ment. To avoid an increase of taxation will not remedy unemployment, whilst a decrease of taxation is scarcely to be hoped for. The main question is, therefore, to diagnose unemployment.

Now there are two lines of diagnosis, both of which are sure to be partly right. The one insists on the unduly high level of real wages; the other insists on the unduly high level of the rate of interest with its resultant effect of diminishing home investment. My object has been to bring the two lines of diagnosis together by saying that the trouble is to be found—in my opinion with mathematical certainty—in an inadequate volume of *total* investment. Investment can be foreign or domestic. Foreign investment is mainly restrained by the high level of wages, and recently by the cyclical depression abroad. Domestic investment is restrained mainly by the high rate of interest, though the high rate of interest would not be so deterrent to enterprise as it is if wages were lower and if taxation were less.

Now it may be that wages are so much too high, and there is so little chance of the facts catching up the existing level of wages, that it is short-sighted to play for time and try to avoid, so far as is possible, the waste of wealth meanwhile. One ought, rather, to concentrate in an assault on wages. This is the view which I have hitherto been rejecting and still on the whole, I think, reject.

Moreover, I am rather sceptical as to whether any feasible reduction of wages or taxation would sufficiently affect the volume of our foreign investment or make much difference to the attractiveness of domestic investment.

I am therefore disposed to lay my principal stress on the difficulty of finding an adequate outlet for savings at those current rates of interest which the international situation forces us to maintain. Yet I believe that there is no possible means whatever of curing unemployment (apart from reducing savings)* except by increasing investment. Therefore I twist and turn about trying to find some reasonable means of permitting

---

* Which, however, could and probably ought to be done by temporarily suspending the sinking fund.

investment of a fairly sensible kind to take place in spite of its not yielding the current market rate of interest. The necessity for this is increased, and not diminished, by any deterrent effect on private effort which may result from high levels of taxation and of wages which are beyond remedy.

Psychological factors and high taxation probably play some part in the low level of domestic investment. But I attribute infinitely more importance to the fact that the rate of interest is 50 per cent higher than it was before the War, whereas our equipment per head in buildings and machines is greater than it was then. It does not seem to me to be surprising that we should not be able to find an adequate outlet for our savings at the present date at a rate of interest 50 per cent higher than pre-War.

Moreover, even if things are going to come more nearly right in course of time by reason of the fall in the international rate of interest, an interim policy may nevertheless increase the national wealth. Also, compared with other things, I have not yet been shown that the cost of a development programme on the Budget is not of rather trifling dimensions compared with other things.

What is your practical proposal? To try to persuade the present Government to substitute a tariff for a development programme as their means to solution, and to curtail unemployment benefit? Or to *combine* a tariff and the curtailment of unemployment pay with a scheme of capital development?

I would support you in proposing a revenue tariff and suspending the sinking fund, also in amending the Insurance Acts. But these things would not cure unemployment;—they would only make easier the application of other remedies and, perhaps, remove a possible further aggravation of the position.

I should be rather interested to know just how serious, from the point of view of prospective financial developments, the unemployment situation is capable of being. I do not carry in my head the way in which the finances of the unemployment scheme work out in relation to the Budget.

Yours ever,

[copy not initialled or signed]

Between 7 and 17 June Keynes was away from London, giving a lecture later published as 'Economic Possibilities for Our Grandchildren' (JMK, vol. IX, pp. 321–32) in Madrid. On his return he was again caught up in meetings with the Economic Advisory Council, the Macmillan Committee, Governor Norman and the Royal Economic Society. On 26 June, however, he managed to convey the 'Optimism of Economic Possibilities' in a talk to a dinner sponsored by the National Council of Women, of which his mother was president, for delegates from overseas who were returning from an international conference of such councils in Vienna.

By the end of June 1930 the Economic Advisory Council had met five times. Even at this stage, however, there was considerable dissatisfaction with its workings—particularly its overcrowded agenda and the difficulty of discussing continuously in an advisory fashion the main issues of policy in a body of such size and varied composition. Keynes and Henderson shared some of the dissatisfaction, the discussion of which occupied part of the July 1930 meeting of the Council, but both were inclined to let matters evolve naturally rather than lay down detailed procedures. However, there was one by-product of the procedural discussions. At the suggestion of Henderson the Prime Minister circulated a series of questions to members and asked for written answers for circulation before the next meeting. The questions, which were designed as the Prime Minister put it 'to enable the Council to concentrate on large questions of public policy', were as follows:

1. What in your view are the chief causes of our present industrial position?
2. What, in your view, should be the trade policy adopted by His Majesty's Government to restore trade?
3. How, in your view, can the home market be developed, and thus put people in a position to earn a living and to command effective power to consume?
4. How, in your view, can the volume of exports be increased?
5. What, in your opinion, would be the framework of a definite imperial trade policy as regards markets, tariffs, organisation for the supply and purchase of bulk produce like wheat, etc.?

Immediately after the meeting, before replying to the questions Keynes wrote a letter to the Prime Minister. He also showed a copy to Henderson and Tom Jones of the Council's Secretariat.

367

To J. RAMSAY MACDONALD, *10 July 1930*

Dear Prime Minister,

I shall be sending shortly a very brief summary of my answer to the first question in your questionnaire about the industrial position, and also a summary of my suggestions as to the answers to the second, third, fourth and fifth questions. But the proper answer to question 1 is a very difficult and lengthy matter, and I should like, therefore, to make a suggestion to you for the proper way of handling it.

It is essentially a matter of economic diagnosis, the sort of thing for which economists, if they are any good at all, should be useful. It involves the sort of analysis which professional economists are constantly attempting, but with which most business men are quite unfamiliar. I think it would be worth trying to see if a small committee, composed of leading professional economists, could agree amongst themselves sufficiently to produce an answer. The answer, when produced, ought to be submitted to the criticism of business men. But it would be contrary to the sort of notion I have in view if business men, unless they also happened to be trained economists, were members of the committee. Professional economists have a language and a method of their own, which, whether they agree or not, enables them to understand one another fairly quickly. If any member of the committee does not understand this language, endless time has to be wasted in familiarising him with it, and probably even then the attempt is unsuccessful. There is no reason why the results should not be expressed in a manner intelligible to everyone. But the process of preliminary debate and of arriving at the conclusions cannot be successfully carried on, in my judgement, by a mixed body. It may be that economics is not enough of a science to be able to produce useful fruits. But I think it might be given a trial, and that we might assume for a moment, if only as a hypothesis, that it can be treated like any other science, and ask qualified scientists in the subject to say their say. I do not feel confident that the experiment would be successful. But I think it might be worth trying.

May I indicate the sort of membership which I have in mind: Sir Josiah Stamp, Mr H. D. Henderson and myself, as representing the Economic Advisory Council; Professor Henry Clay as representing the Bank of England's new organisation for dealing with rationalisation; Professor Pigou of Cambridge, Professor L. Robbins of London, and Mr D. H. Robertson as leading academic economists.

I have selected the above as being people, all of whom are well accustomed to the most up-to-date academic methods and ways of discussing these problems, are essentially reasonable and good members of a committee, and happen to have given already a good deal of time and thought to the problem which would be set them.

I should like to ask such a body of persons to closet themselves together and try to produce, say by the end of October, an agreed diagnosis of our present problems and a reasoned list of the possible remedies. They need not be expected to commit themselves as to exactly what remedies should, on the balance of consideration, be carried into effect, nor as to the relative importance of the remedies from the practical point of view.

I should not despair of something useful emerging from an attempt on these lines.

Yours sincerely,
[copy initialled] J. M. K.

From J. RAMSAY MACDONALD, *14 July 1930*

My dear Keynes,

Thank you very much for your letter, which I am having considered.

I am inclined to agree with you myself, but I shall finally decide tomorrow.

Yours very sincerely,
J. RAMSAY MACDONALD

Keynes's answers to the Prime Minister's questions ran as follows:

ECONOMIC ADVISORY COUNCIL: THE STATE OF TRADE

Answers by Mr J. M. Keynes, C.B. to the Prime Minister's Questions [p. 367]

At the present time, as compared with, say, eight months ago, I should put in the forefront of the causes of our industrial position the worldwide international slump in prices, profits, volume of trade, employment and the output of enterprise. The trade slump which has developed since the Wall Street crash last autumn is amongst the most important which have ever occurred in modern economic history. Both the business world and the outside public are, I think, very much underestimating the magnitude of this factor. In the three chief industrial countries of the world, Great Britain, the United States and Germany, there are today more than 10,000,000 unemployed workers; and it is unlikely that the worst point has been reached. Even if we had no troubles whatever of our own, we should at this moment be suffering severely. Coming on top of our previous troubles, this has given people the impression of its being a further stage in a definite downward progression, instead of its being the downward movement of a swing—which I am quite sure it really is—to be followed in due course by an upward reaction. It might be possible, and would be serviceable, to try to make this vivid to the public mind.

Not only is the international slump now the biggest feature in the situation, but it creates an extraordinarily unfavourable environment, such as did not exist a year ago, for the application of remedies to the peculiar troubles of this country. This means, in my opinion, that we must not be in too much of a hurry to expect results. But it does not mean that we should abandon the effort to attempt to cure our local disorders, or take refuge in the international problem which is now superimposed on them as an excuse for doing nothing about the former.

So far, however, as the international problem is concerned, one is compelled to admit that the remedy does not lie to any important extent within the power of this country acting alone. The Bank of England can probably do something, behind the scenes, to accelerate the recovery. If they could act in intimate collaboration with the Federal Reserve Board of the United States they could do still more. Perhaps a more decided and sharply defined policy on their part might be possible. But I see no reason to suppose that the Bank of England lacks comprehension of the nature of the international situation or is not trying to deal with it in the right way.

If the precedents are to be believed, there is no reason to expect that the recovery will come quickly. Perhaps the greatest danger in the situation is the premature optimism in the United States, which is still looking for a substantial recovery this autumn. I think it would be more prudent to expect a bad winter, not perhaps much worse here than what we have been accustomed to, but much worse in the United States. This might pave the way, psychologically, for more determined and drastic co-operative measures to turn the tide of things next spring.

But whilst one has to estimate very high the importance of the international complications, we should only be deceiving ourselves if we were to attribute the whole of our troubles to them, and stand aside from applying reasonable cures on the ground that we have been visited by an act of God for which we are not responsible, and about which we can do nothing. Our own situation was quite bad enough a year ago. And a year ago, whilst one could find troubles in various parts of the world by looking for them, this is always the case; and we were not then entitled to refrain from action on the ground that our troubles were due to outside influences over which we had no control.

If I were asked to sum up the analysis of the fundamental difficulties, both international and local, from the technical standpoint of an economist, I should put it thus.

371

1. *International*

At the present time the expectations of new enterprise and new investment as to the returns for which they can hope are below the figure at which lenders will supply them with funds on long term; that is to say there is a gap between the rate of interest asked by lenders and the rate of profit anticipated by enterprisers. This is partly due to a depressed psychology of enterprisers occasioned by the fall of prices and other causes, but much more, in my judgement, to the very high level at which the long-term rate of interest now stands. I doubt whether there has been any period in times of peace during the last hundred years when prudent and legitimate new enterprise would have been able to support the rates of interest now charged. These rates of interest became established as the result partly of the high rates to which the War period accustomed investors; partly of the high rates which it paid enterprisers to incur for the reconstruction of the working capital of the world after the War; partly of the high rates which speculators in 'equities' were prepared to pay in Wall Street and elsewhere; and partly of there being a long line of necessitous government borrowers waiting for accommodation, who were prepared to pay almost any rate in order to satisfy their creditors, and were not, in agreeing to pay a given rate of interest, doing so as the result of any calculation that they could employ the money which they were borrowing so as to yield that rate. Nearly all the international borrowing at high rates of interest which has been oppressing the bond markets of the world in recent times has been for the purpose of paying off existing debts already incurred and not for the purpose of investment in new capital which is expected to yield an equivalent return. Thus, for the time being new real investment has been killed by the high rates established through the competition of speculators and necessitous debtors, whose borrowing does nothing whatever for enterprise or employment. By now, however, the time has passed when it pays speculators, any more than enterprisers, to incur these high rates of interest, and there are no longer more than one or two necessitous borrowers waiting for accommodation. In due course, therefore, I should expect a very great fall in the rate of interest. Not until that fall takes place will new investment recover, and not until new investment recovers will prices revive. I see no reason, however, to expect that the lenders will accommodate themselves to the ideas of the borrowers quickly. The gap will be bridged in the end, partly by a fall in the rate of interest and partly by greater optimism on the part of enterprisers when they believe that prices are grounding.

In time this is bound to happen, but many months may elapse before long-term borrowing is practicable on terms which are attractive to the borrowers. Meanwhile a vicious circle has been set up; —the excessive rates of interest in 1929 killed enterprise, the loss of enterprise killed prices, and the fall of prices has reduced what enterprises are prepared to pay far below normal and therefore still farther below what lenders have become accustomed to ask. The greater the uncertainties of the situation, the less will non-necessitous borrowers pay, yet the more will lenders ask, so as to cover the apparent risks.

At present progress towards the ultimate end is being further held back by the refusal of the French people to invest their foreign surplus funds and by the nervousness which they create in all the international markets by withdrawing gold. For the moment this is a fearfully tiresome incident. Personally I do not believe that the amount of gold which the French intend to take is unlimited, or that the present situation will last indefinitely. If, however, the amount is large, I have a suggestion below for taking care of it. In due course, both the French and the American public will be ready I believe, to buy bonds again. Bond prices will rise. This country will resell at a profit to France and New York the bonds which they have been buying lately with great courage in perhaps excessive quantities, and at long last, after the bond market has risen sufficiently, new enterprise will lift its head again.

It may be that the present industrial crisis will be recorded by future economic historians as being, in effect, the death struggle of the high rates of interest established by the War, and the re-birth of the low rates of interest which prevailed before 1914. It represents essentially a struggle of the rate of interest to get back to its equilibrium level. When the rate of interest has fought its way down to perhaps two-thirds of the present level, no one will reap more benefits than the Chancellor of the Exchequer. The day may be much nearer than most people think when 3 per cent British Government loans will be approaching par. Meanwhile he must be very patient.

2. *Local*

The surplus of our exports, visible and invisible, over our imports mainly depends on our money costs of production compared with the money costs abroad. Thus, if our wage level is comparatively high, our favourable balance is comparatively low. If, on the other hand, we reduce the level of our efficiency wages or any of the other costs of production, then we may expect our favourable balance to increase.

On the other hand, the amount of money which we endeavour to lend abroad depends on quite a different set of considerations, namely the net rate of interest, after allowing for risk which foreigners will pay, as compared with the net rate of interest which domestic enterprise feels itself able to support.

Nevertheless, we might restrain the amount of our foreign lending so as to compel it to be equal to the amount of our favourable balance. Otherwise we lose gold. To maintain exchange equilibrium with the rest of the world without setting up employment dis-equilibrium at home, we must either increase our favourable balance by lowering our gold costs, or we must decrease the pressure towards foreign lending by finding more outlets for our savings at home.

Our dilemma in recent years, as I see it, is that if we raise the rate of interest sufficiently to keep our foreign lending down to the amount of our favourable balance, we raise it too high for domestic enterprise. The consequence is that our savings can neither get abroad in the form of exports, nor be used at home for new developments here, with the result that unemployment and business losses ensue and the excess savings are in effect used up in financing the costs of unemployment and the other losses.

The discrepancy between the high foreign rate of interest and the low home rate is due, of course, to a variety of causes. The foreign rate has been abnormally high, as mentioned above, for reasons which may be transient. The rate at which large amounts of new capital can be used at home has been—not unexpectedly since we are an old country—nearer pre-war rates than post-war rates.

When we turn to our costs of production, we find that the increase of these in terms of gold brought about by the deflation and the return to the gold standard at the pre-War parity, came on the top of other difficulties, with the result of making it quite impossible for us to have more than a rather moderate favourable balance, compared with what we had formerly.

Apart from the disequilibrium which has thus come down, there is—even so—no reason to be despondent. Our favourable balance, even now, is greater than that of any other country. Even in 1929 our favourable balance available for new foreign investment was 50 per cent greater than that of the United States,—a fact not generally known. The trouble is that the excess of our savings, above what we can usefully employ at home at current rates of interest, is even greater; *hinc illae lacrimae*.

When we come to the question of remedies for the local situation as distinct from the international, the peculiarity of my position lies, perhaps, in the fact that I am in favour of practically all the remedies which have been suggested in any quarter. Some of them are better than others. But nearly all of them seem to me to tend in the right direction. The unforgivable attitude is, therefore, for me the negative one,—the repelling of each of these remedies in turn.

Accordingly, I favour an eclectic programme, making use of

375

suggestions from all quarters, not expecting too much from the application of any one of them, but hoping that they may do something in the aggregate.

Before making a list of these, I had better repeat what my touchstone is in judging of them. Nothing is any good which does not either increase our favourable foreign balance or find an increased outlet for our savings at home. The schematism adopted below automatically applies this test to each of them in turn.

A. MEANS TO INCREASE OUR FAVOURABLE FOREIGN BALANCE

I. *By decreasing our costs of production*

(i) *By the rationalisation of industry.* This is, of course, essential to prevent retrogression relatively to other countries. How much we can positively improve the position, as distinct from preventing further deterioration, is doubtful. Moreover a considerable proportion of so-called 'rationalisation' is considered to deal with the problem of surplus capacity. This may reduce losses and even restore profits, but it will not increase our foreign balance. Nevertheless, we ought without doubt to press on rationalisation by all possible means.

(ii) *By the reduction of taxation.* If this means the reduction of *aggregate* taxation, it is obviously desirable; but I do not believe that any important reduction is practicable, otherwise than by suspending the sinking fund, which I would advocate in the present emergency, except in so far as it is required to effect borrowing by the Insurance Fund. If it means the avoidance of *increased* aggregate taxation, certainly it is important. If it means the re-distribution of taxation so as to bear less hardly on industry, the question deserves careful examination. De-rating was an effort in this direction. Increased allowance for deprecia-

376

tion and renewals in respect of income tax would be another. An increased liability of the state for employers' insurance contributions would be a third (but would this be practicable without also relieving the employees?). Decreased direct taxation of profits by means of increased indirect taxation of the consumer (e.g. by a revenue tariff) would perhaps help. At the same time I believe that most business men greatly exaggerate the effect of our taxation on costs of production. On balance, our taxation system probably increases the costs of production less than that of any of the high protectionist countries.

(iii) *By the reduction of efficiency wages.* This could be effected either by reducing the actual earnings of employees, or by workers making themselves more efficient for the existing wage. The almost complete rigidity of our wage rates since 1929, in spite of the great reduction of all other price levels, is very striking to the imagination. The fact that, in spite of all adverse circumstances, we have been increasing real wages faster than ever before in our history, has undoubtedly much aggravated our other difficulties. We have been going ahead—by force of circumstances rather than by any deliberate decision—rather faster than is wise. But all the same there is now, in my judgement, a very set and deliberate determination in almost all quarters of the community not to go back on this as a general policy—though in certain cases wage reductions are inevitable and are in the interests of the workers themselves—except as an absolutely last resort.

The unwillingness of employers and associations of employers, who have appeared before the Macmillan Committee to recommend this solution has been truly remarkable. In order to test this feeling, I have often in examination pressed them to fall back on this recommendation and almost always without success.

But it does seem to me to be up to the trade unions to respond to this attitude by meeting the employers to the utmost on conditions and restrictions affecting efficiency, and that there should be a deliberate policy on the part of the workers to give greater efficiency in return for their wages. Why should not the trade unions take the initiative in approaching the employers along these lines?

II. *By protection*

Our favourable foreign balance is increased just as effectively if we diminish our imports as if we increase our exports. To employ our surplus labour making goods which we now import comes to the same result as employing it to make additional goods for export. But it is probably much easier to restrict imports than to augment exports, and—even allowing for some adverse repercussions on our existing exports—we are more likely to increase our favourable foreign balance by this means than by any other.

Protection also has other advantages, which I will summarise below.

I have, therefore, become reluctantly convinced that some protectionist measures should be introduced, but in saying this I should like to add:—

(*a*) Most protectionists enormously exaggerate the contribution which protection can make to the solution of our present difficulty. By itself it would not carry us far. Apart from existing duties, I think it is difficult to discover plausible cases, outside iron and steel, for duties which are mainly protectionist rather than revenue earning. The theoretical case for protection is in the case of Great Britain much stronger than the practical case.

(*b*) If we could get through the next ten years on free trade without suffering heavy damage and great costs of transition, we should probably be the stronger for it in the long run.

(*c*) The arguments against tariffs on the grounds of political morality, national and international, and of the invariable tendency of tariffs, once started, to be overdone and irrecoverable, are just as strong as ever they were.

All the same I am afraid of 'principle'. Ever since 1918 we, alone amongst the nations of the world, have been the slaves of 'sound' general principles regardless of particular circumstances. We have behaved as though the intermediate 'short periods' of the economist between our position of equilibrium and another really were short, whereas they can be long enough—and have been before now—to compass the decline and downfall of nations. Nearly all our difficulties have been traceable to an unfaltering service to the principles of 'sound finance' which all our neighbours have neglected. This 'long-run' policy is a grand thing in its way—unless, like the operators of systems at Monte Carlo, one has not enough resources to last through the short run. Wasn't it Lord Melbourne who said that 'No statesman ever does anything really foolish except on principle'?

The other arguments for a tariff are—

(a) Free trade is profoundly based on the assumption of equilibrium conditions and in particular that wages always fall to their strict economic level. If they do not, and if for several reasons we do not desire them to, then it is only by means of a tariff that the ideal distribution of resources between different uses, which free trade aims at, can be achieved; and there is an unanswerable theoretical case for a countervailing import duty (and also for an export bounty) equivalent to the difference between the actual wage and the economic wage.

(b) I do not believe that the Budget problem can be satisfactorily solved without a tariff, mainly for revenue on manufactured imports. This is, moreover, the only form of taxation which will positively cheer people up! Attach great importance to this argument.

(c) I am no longer a free trader—and I believe that practically no-one else is—in the old sense of the term to the extent of believing in a very high degree of national specialisation and in abandoning any industry which is unable for the time being to hold its own. Where wages are immobile, this would be an extraordinarily dangerous doctrine to follow. I believe, for example, that this country is in the long run reasonably adapted for, and ought always to have, a motor industry, a steel industry, a farming industry. If it is proved to me that in present circumstances and at present wages these industries cannot live, then I am in favour of protecting them. But a real free trader would answer without hesitation—let them go. For some months past I have been trying to find some responsible person who was in this good old traditional sense a free trader. But I have not found one. Persons calling themselves free traders nearly always retort either that the industries can thrive without a duty or even that a duty would be actually injurious to them. But such an answer has nothing whatever to do with free trade— a real free trader would not even want to know the answer to these questions; on the contrary, it is the expression of a dogmatic judgement on a purely technical matter, which the person uttering it is generally quite unqualified to give. For it is *possible* that a particular industry of a type which it is not foolish for us to maintain may benefit from a duty and may be unable to live without one. To assert the contrary is not sensible, and is no part of free trade doctrine.

(*d*) Free traders have always admitted that a tariff is likely to turn the terms of international exchanges in favour of the protected country. I believe that this factor is today quantitatively more important for us than it used to be.

III. *By import boards*

I do not yet know much about these. But I am attracted by the idea.

IV. *By arrangements with the Dominions*

I am sceptical but not hostile.

V. *By increasing world trade as a whole, in the hope of thereby increasing the absolute amount of our share of it*

This is mainly concerned with the international side of the problem which I am not enlarging on here. The steps which might be taken I summarise as follows:

(i) By a courageous and persistent policy of cheap money, even if it means losing gold. (I would at once increase the fiduciary issue of notes so as to provide for the possibility of this.)

(ii) By encouraging the bond market and new long-term loans generally up to the limit of our capacity.

(iii) By intimate co-operation with the U.S. Federal Reserve Board. If the French hold back things by obstinately demanding gold, I would arrange with the F.R.B. to borrow £50,000,000 in gold (or £100,000,000 if necessary) and feed the French with it to the teeth. This would be a perfectly sound operation; it would not diminish our wealth or increase our risks; for it would simply be the substitution of one obligation for another—we should owe the money to the U.S. instead of the French, and, as soon as the bond market revived, we should be able to repay it at a profit. I attach importance to this suggestion.

(iv) There are certain special loans which I should favour as a means of developing trade.

(*a*) I should like to take hold of the Chinese position on a big scale. I would offer them a big guaranteed loan, international if possible, (I mean like the first Austrian loan) on condition of their consolidating their existing debt and settling down quietly and sensibly—which they are all but ready to do—to peace and trade.

(*b*) I hope that we shall stretch a point if necessary to help Australia out of her difficulties, when Sir O. Niemeyer is ready with his report. She has perhaps learnt her lesson. In any case a time when wool and her exports generally are at these disastrous prices is not a time to choose for pressing her too hard. She ought to send us some more gold—say £10,000,000 to £15,000,000—

to help us with *our* problems. Subject to that we ought to meet her necessities.

(*c*) On the other hand, I should hope for very little from Russia.

B. MEANS TO INCREASE THE OUTLET FOR OUR SAVINGS AT HOME

I. *By programmes of organised home development.* I attach the greatest possible importance to this. But I have nothing more to say about it than I have said before.

II. *By subsidies to private enterprise*:

(i) By providing long-term loans for approved purposes at (say) 3 per cent.

(ii) By Trade Facilities loans.

(iii) By special income-tax allowances in respect of extensions and improvements.

These devices should all be employed up to the limit of what—when one comes down to the details of the actual projects offering—seems prudent and sensible.

III. *By making it possible for home enterprises to afford a higher rate of interest.*

(i) By decreasing the other costs of production. This is A.I over again, which thus tends to increase both the foreign balance and also home investment.

(ii) By protection. This is A.II over again.

(iii) By promoting a feeling of confidence. I return to this below.

IV. *By making lenders willing to accept a lower rate of interest from home enterprises.*

(i) By discriminating taxation against foreign loans compared with domestic loans. The possibilities of this deserve serious consideration. We used this method ourselves during the War; and it has been employed more recently by France with great success. It can take the form of higher stamp duties or of higher income tax on receipts from foreign loans.

(ii) By a partial embargo on new foreign loans. This has been used several times in recent years with partial success. The most practical form of it is for the Bank of England to use its influence with the issue houses to regulate the rate of new foreign issues.

(iii) By bringing down the world rate of interest. This is a repetition of A.V above.

(iv) By promoting a feeling of confidence. The question of confidence, which is of first-class importance in its influence on the investor when he is deciding what terms for home investment are attractive compared with what is offering abroad, is very much tied up with the Budget.

A Budget which involves increased direct taxation would be disastrous in its effect on confidence. Since the yield of the taxes is bound to be disappointing so long as trade, profits and employment are subnormal this means that:

(*a*) all expenditure on new social services, such as pensions, school-leaving and the like, should be ruthlessly postponed until better times;

(*b*) such moderate economies as are practicable should be searched out, such as remedies for the abuses of the dole;

(*c*) the one form of new taxation, namely a revenue tariff on manufactured imports which would not have a discouraging effect on industry, shall be favourably regarded; indeed I regard this as essential to a sound Budget in present circumstances.

The fact that I have given much less space to B than to A is not to be interpreted as meaning that I attach less importance to it. On the contrary, in the long run I believe that more is to be hoped from B than from A—after all we cannot be expected to go on increasing our foreign investments indefinitely. It is due, rather, to considerations of time and space and because A comes before B alphabetically.

Conclusion

All these remedies are good and touch the spot. None of them should be rejected without grave cause. Not enough can be expected from one or two of them alone. We shall do well to advance on a broad front.

21 July 1930   J. M. KEYNES

The Prime Minister's response to Keynes's letter of 10 July was revealed at the beginning of the seventh meeting of the Council, when he announced the formation of a Committee of Economists under Keynes's chairmanship. The other members of the Committee were Hubert Henderson, Professor A. C. Pigou, Professor Lionel Robbins and Sir Josiah Stamp. Its terms of reference were 'to review the present economic condition of Great Britain, to examine the causes which are responsible for it, and to indicate the conditions of recovery'. The joint secretaries of the Committee were Richard Kahn and A. F. Hemming. The work of this Committee is the subject of Chapter 4.

Keynes spent August at Tilton, putting the final touches on his *Treatise on Money* (JMK, vols. V and VI) which he dispatched to the printer for the last time on 14 September. His only contributions to public discussion took the form of two letters to the press. The first reacted to a remark by the Leader of the Opposition in a speech on 26 July.

To the Editor of The Nation and Athenaeum, *2 August 1930*

Sir,

Speaking last Saturday at a political meeting, Mr Baldwin, discussing the unemployment problem and the increase of unemployment during the past year, stated that: 'World causes will probably be heard of at the Election, but I think the country will know pretty well what answer to give to that. There are no more world causes today than there were when we were in office.'

Does Mr Baldwin really believe this statement? If so, it would seem to indicate that he is paying so little attention to the economic events which are going on in the world as to disqualify him from expressing an opinion on economic matters. For in the last year there has developed one of the greatest international slumps in prices, trade, and employment which has ever occurred in modern economic history.

Is there not some minimum standard of accuracy and sound information about economic affairs which we are entitled to expect from our leading statesmen? Mr Baldwin is apt to give himself the airs of being particularly scrupulous. But the above quotation shows that he is as capable as anyone else of darkening counsel by a reckless and ignorant statement.

Yours, &c.,

J. M. KEYNES

The second was a response to a remark by E. D. Simon to the Liberal Summer School, which Keynes did not attend, suggesting that his buying a British rather than an American car would not increase employment in Britain.

To the Editor of The Manchester Guardian, *14 August 1930*

Sir,

If Mr Simon had spent £200 on buying a British car instead of an American car, I should have supposed that in present circumstances the most probable results would be as follows.

The first effect would be to increase employment in the motor industries—the equivalent, say, of the employment of one more man for a year. This man (or his equivalent), having an increased income, would spend and consume more, and thus produce a favourable repercussion on employment in other industries; and so on. But the making of the motor car would involve the import of certain raw materials, and at each stage of improved employment some part of the increased earnings would be spent on imported food, &c. Let us guess the additional imports due to these causes at £50. Thus to this extent the import of food and raw materials would take the place of the import of an American car.

What will be the net result? Gross home output will be increased by more than £200, and home employment will be increased correspondingly. The level of consumption will be raised, partly by the import of more food. Our favourable balance of trade will be increased by £150, with the result that our foreign investments, and consequently the capital wealth of the country, will be augmented by this amount. The increased use of unemployed plant and resources will increase profits. The Treasury will benefit to the extent of more than £50 by having to pay out less in respect of the dole; it will also receive income tax on the increased profits. In short, the productivity of the country will be greater, and the equivalent of this increased output will be partly added to capital and partly used up in increased current consumption.

My figures are, of course, only approximate and illustrative—though perhaps not far out in present circumstances. Furthermore, the whole argument depends on there being unused productive resources in the country suitable for making a car and not likely to be used for the present in making anything else.

The Liberal programme of organised capital development is, in effect, a method of subsidising home investment; tariffs, in so far as they allow us to employ home productive resources of men and plant which would otherwise be unemployed, are, in effect (in present circumstances), a method of subsidising foreign investment. The principle is the same in both cases, and the immediate effect on employment and on wealth is the same. From the long-period point of view one may be better than the other; from the short-period point of view one may be more feasible than the other. The ultimate choice, as to whether to use one of these expedients or both of them or neither, must depend on a complicated balance of advantage and disadvantage.

If Sir Walter Layton really told Mr E. D. Simon that his buying a British car instead of an American one would not increase employment, meaning by this employment here and now in the year 1930, he told him what is obviously absurd. Mr

Simon certainly has ground to reproach himself if he believed it even for the time it takes to buy a car.

Yours, &c.,

J. M. KEYNES

Prior to the first meeting of the Committee of Economists, Keynes wrote two other pieces on the current situation. The first was circulated to the Economic Advisory Council prior to its meeting on 11 September.

ECONOMIC ADVISORY COUNCIL: THE PRESENT ECONOMIC POSITION

1. As I have been something of a Cassandra hitherto, I should like to record my opinion that an upward reaction may be due shortly. Commodity prices may, I think, touch their lowest point sometime this month; though at the moment prices are still falling, for example rubber to-day is 20 per cent lower than it was a week ago and the price of foreign steel in Birmingham fell about 10 per cent last week owing to the breakdown of the cartel. Whilst the absolute figures of aggregate unemployment may increase for seasonal causes, I do not think that we need expect a large further increase apart from these causes. I should be inclined to predict that this figure will not at any time exceed 2,500,000.

2. The above is based not on a belief that much progress has been made towards remedying the fundamental causes of the slump, but because a slump of this kind always has an inherent tendency to be overdone. For fundamental factors begin the slump by justifying a decline in output; and then the act of declining causes a further decline, so that the market gets into a peculiar condition of disequilibrium in which the lowness of the level reached is only justified so long as output is still in the act of declining to a still lower level. Thus the moment output ceases to

decline, the level reached at once becomes unjustifiably low; and when this generates an incipient recovery, then the mere fact that output is recovering justifies a higher level than that reached up to date, which state of affairs continues so long as output is increasing. Thus these secondary oscillations—if I have made myself clear—are self-generating and take place independently of the fundamental cause which initiated all the trouble. I believe, that is to say, that we are at or near the bottom of the secondary oscillation. (There is a complete theoretical explanation of all this, but not one which can be expressed shortly.)

3. The exaggerated character of the present slump is most marked in the United States, where the recession is far greater than in this country from the conditions of a year ago; when, of course, *we* were already at a lowish point. For example, our index of production has declined about 8 per cent in the June quarter of 1930 compared with the June quarter of 1929, whereas the corresponding American index has declined 18 per cent. But— still more striking—in July 1930 the American index had fallen below their 1925 level, whilst in this country the latest figure is still above our 1925 level. The profits of the big American corporations for the first half of this year were running 20 to 35 per cent less than the corresponding profits for last year. The available figures for this country are not so up to date, but those published in the first half of this year (which relate to 1929) showed no decline.

4. It is noticeable how closely correlated is the American decline with the falling rate of investment in fixed capital. The expenditure on new building and construction was already running lower in 1929 than in 1928 and thus preparing the way for the slump; and for the last 12 months (to the end of August 1930) the figures show a fall of about 22 per cent compared with the previous year. Turned into values, this means a reduction of about £400,000,000 in the value of fixed investment per annum. At the same time the fall in current output may be responsible for a reduction of as much as another £400,000,000 in working

capital. Thus the decline of net investment in the United States in the last 12 months may be as much as £800,000,000. Hence the decline in profits etc. But if current output merely ceases to fall further, we shall at once have a situation better than the above.

5. The Prime Minister asks if we could use some of the money now expended on unemployment benefit to stimulate employment. If, for convenience of calculation and illustration, we take the dole at £1 per head per week, it is obvious that any subsidy to employment which costs less than this is clearly beneficial, even if we can show nothing in respect of the advantage to the newly employed man himself—provided that it does not get us into bad habits for the future.

6. The objection to most schemes with this object in view are:

(a) That it is difficult to subsidise new employment without wasting money on subsidising existing employment.

(b) That, if we are successful in making this differentiation, we are in danger of subsidising the less efficient firms against the more efficient.

7. Nevertheless several of the suggestions already made to the Council are capable of surmounting this objection in greater or less degree. If we take (again for convenience of calculation) the value of the output of an employed man at £3 per week, then broadly speaking we can say that:

(a) subsidies to capital development programmes,

(b) subsidies to increased output, e.g. of such things as pigs and poultry,

(c) the cost to the consumer after deducting the gain to the Exchequer of tariffs on imports which could be produced at home pay for themselves wholly out of the dole saved, if the total amount of the subsidy or the net cost of the tariff is less than 33 per cent of the value of the additional output.

8. Where the elasticity of home supply is great—which is the case wherever there is surplus capacity—the subsidy or the net cost of the tariff may more than pay for itself out of the dole

saved, even though it applies to the existing output as well as to the new output.

J.M.K.

8 September 1930

The second was for a periodical published by the Svenska Handelsbanken.

From The Index, *September 1930*

THE FUTURE OF THE RATE OF INTEREST: PROSPECTS OF THE BOND MARKET

We are now in the middle of one of the major slumps of recent economic history. Indeed, if we measure the magnitude of events by the fall of prices from the average of the preceding three or four years, the extent and rapidity of the fall are perhaps the most severe that have ever been experienced in modern times. The prices of a large group of the world's most important staple commodities—wheat, oats, barley, sugar, coffee; cotton, wool, jute, silk; copper, tin, spelter; rubber—stood a year ago something like 50 per cent higher than they do now. In Great Britain, Germany and the United States more than 10,000,000 workers stand unemployed. In Great Britain and Germany we have become accustomed in recent years to a level of chronic unemployment far above the normal. But in America, where such occurrences are new, the extent of the collapse in industrial activity over the past year is far greater than it has been either in Germany or in Great Britain. The Standard Statistics Index of Industrial Production in the United States over the three months May, June and July 1930 was nearly 30 per cent lower than the same index for the corresponding months of 1929. Indeed, in July 1930 the index was 37 per cent below the figure for July 1929. The collapse in industrial activity has naturally caused a corresponding falling off in the demand for all kinds of raw materials, so that the producers of such materials through-

390

out the world are not only suffering from low prices, but also from inability to unload their output even at the reduced price level now ruling; and this duly reacts on their own demand for the output of the industrial countries.

Now, when calamities of this kind overwhelm the world, you may be sure that there will be many particular explanations to which different people can point with considerable plausibility. On this occasion the Wall Street slump in the autumn of 1929 is, I suppose, the primary explanation of the present position which most people would give. Others might speak of a general over-production;—though that is something in which economists do not believe. Without a doubt, the Wall Street slump, and what I should prefer to call *unbalanced* production, have played a part. But I believe that the economic historians of the future will, when they seek for an explanation, look somewhat deeper and find the ultimate cause in a series of events which have been spread over the whole of the post -War period. Let me explain, therefore, what appears to me to be, if not the root cause of what is happening, at least one of the root causes.

Perhaps one of the most striking economic changes in the post-War world compared with the pre-war world is to be found in the high level of the market rate of interest for long-term loans. As a rough generalisation, comparing securities of approximately equal risk, etc., one may say that the long-term rate of interest is nearly 50 per cent higher today than it was twenty years ago. Yet the population of the industrial countries of Central and Western Europe and of North America is not increasing as fast as formerly, and is a good deal better equipped per head with housing, transport and machines than it was. The aggregate of saving in the United States is now estimated at a prodigiously high figure, exceeding $20,000,000,000 a year, whilst at the same time that country has converted itself from being a borrowing to being a lending country. On the other hand, the volume of lending to the less advanced parts of the world is not markedly large—indeed quite the contrary, since

Russia, China and India, which include within their borders a substantial proportion of the population of the world, are able, for one reason or another, to borrow next to nothing on the international markets. It is therefore something of a paradox that the rate of long-term interest should stand at so high a level. Where are we to find the explanation of this phenomenon?

The explanation is to be found, I think, in the fact that for some years after the War sundry special causes, to be enumerated below, were operating to maintain the actual rate of interest at an exceptionally high level. And the trouble is to be found, if I am right, in the fact that whereas most of these special causes are now ceasing to operate, sundry other causes have nevertheless combined to maintain a market rate of interest which used to be appropriate to the circumstances, but is so no longer. Consequently there has now developed somewhat suddenly an unusually wide gap between the ideas of borrowers and those of lenders.

For a few years after the War there were obvious reasons why the actual rate of interest should stand for a time above its long-period normal. In particular, a very large volume of investment was required to restore the revolving fund of working capital for peace-time production. Now, the interest on working capital is not a very large part of manufacturing costs, and when the demand for manufactured goods is keen and selling prices are satisfactory, it is a matter of some indifference to manufacturers what rate of interest they pay to finance their working capital. Thus, here was an acute need requiring rapid satisfaction, which was quite ready to pay a high rate of interest. At the same time, there was war damage to be made good and arrears of housing, public utilities, etc., to be made up. Perhaps this, the first phase of the post-war decade, was coming to an end in 1924–5.

Meanwhile certain new industries were leading to large-scale investment, especially in the United States;—for example, public utilities based on the use of electricity, the motor industry, a great expansion of roads in almost all civilised countries to permit the further exploitation of the petrol engine, the cinema, and radio industries. For example, in 1904 expenditure on roads in the United States amounted to only $59,500,000, and the figure had only risen to about $240,000,000 by 1914. But in 1928 this category of investment had risen to nearly $1,660,000,000. Altogether in the United States, before the slump, somewhere about $10,000,000,000 a year was being spent on public and private fixed capital construction. The value of the projects covered by the Dodge Corporation statistics in the three years 1926–8 was about double what it had been in the three years 1919–21. These developments were probably on a greater scale in the United States than elsewhere. But in many countries something similar was happening. Thus, these forms of expansion in fixed capital enterprise served to maintain the actual rate of interest to some extent after the fund of working capital had been replenished and war damage, etc. had been made good.

I am inclined nevertheless, looking back, to think that the seeds of the recent collapse were already being sown so long ago as 1925. In spite of the various new developments to which I have just referred, it is possible that by that date the actual rate of interest outside the United States was already due for a fall. But round about that date—some of them beginning rather earlier, others rather later—there supervened two sets of events not wholly disconnected from one another which served to maintain the market rate of interest somewhat regardless of the underlying realities of what productive enterprise could really afford to pay; —namely, the general return to the gold standard and the settlement of reparations and the War debts.

For these events, though they had no bearing whatever on the real yield of new investment, were a powerful influence on the market rate of interest. Those central banks which had entered upon the new responsibility of maintaining gold parity were naturally nervous and disposed to take no risks;—some of them because they had but just emerged from currency catastrophes attended by a total loss of credit; others (especially Great Britain) because they had returned to the gold standard at a dangerously high parity which might prove inconsistent with their existing domestic equilibrium. This nervousness on the part of a number of central banks naturally tended in the direction of a degree of credit restriction, which was not truly called for by the real underlying economic facts, throughout Europe, and sympathetically in many other parts of the world. Probably London played a leading part in tightening the hold on credit during the earlier years and in urging a hurried all-round return to gold, whilst more recently the policy of the Bank of France has indirectly operated in the same direction. At this stage, indeed, that is to say in 1925 and in the years immediately following, only the United States was entirely exempt from some measure of credit restriction.

Whilst these influences towards restriction were tightening the terms of lending and stiffening the attitude of the purchasers of securities, another aspect of the same set of events was providing a supply of borrowers who were prepared to pay terms which were not based on any calculation of the probable yield of actual new investment. These borrowers were of two types. The first were the 'distress' borrowers, as we may conveniently call them, chiefly governments who were borrowing, not primarily for investment in productive enterprise, but to meet their urgent liabilities, to satisfy their creditors, and to comply with their Treaty obligations. The terms which such borrowers will pay have but little to do with the prospective returns of current investment and are dictated by the lenders. The second class were the 'banking' borrowers—sometimes governments and sometimes banks—who were borrowing, again not for investment in productive enterprise, but to build up liquid reserves, partly gold and partly foreign balances, with which to protect their newly-restored currencies. In 1927–8 we had the extraordinary situation of the United States lending on long-term at high rates of interest, largely to Europe, amounts several times greater than her favourable foreign balance, and being able to do so because these borrowers at once re-deposited with her on short term the major part of what they had just borrowed on long term at rates of interest nearly double, perhaps, those which they could obtain on short term for their re-deposits. In two or three years some £500,000,000 was thus borrowed on long term and re-deposited on short term—which inevitably had some tendency to upset the normal relations between short-term and long-term rates of interest, such as these would be if they were mainly determined, as in the long run they must be, by the ideas of those who are borrowing for actual investment.

Finally, in 1928-9 these 'artificial' borrowers on long-term—if we may so designate borrowers who are not influenced by the return on actual current investment—were reinforced by a third class of 'artificial' borrowers, this time on short-term, namely the speculative borrowers. These also were borrowing, not for investment in new productive enterprise, but in order to participate in the feverish 'bull' movement in 'equities' which was occurring most sensationally in the United States, but also in varying degrees on most of the stock exchanges of the world. Moreover, since conservative banking opinion felt it to be of the utmost importance to bring this speculative movement some-how to an end, central banks were provided with a new motive for some measure of credit restriction.

The drift of my argument is perhaps by now beginning to show itself. I am arguing that for a time high rates of interest were justified because there were outlets in genuine investment which could afford to pay a high rate. More recently, however, the high rate of interest has been maintained, not by the willingness of genuine investment to pay a high rate, but because various groups of 'artificial' borrowers were bidding up the terms of borrowing. The result was that by the middle of 1929 'genuine' borrowers—if we may so designate borrowers for purposes of actual new investment which they deem profitable on the terms offering—were already being squeezed out to a certain extent in most countries other than the United States. By the autumn the same phenomenon was appearing in the United States also; and since the Wall Street slump the retrogression of fixed investment in the United States has been on a great scale. Already in 1929 the expenditure on new construction had fallen below the 1928 figure, whilst in the first 7 months of 1930 new construction in the United States was no less than 25 per cent below its level in 1928.

It is here, therefore, that I find the most fundamental explanation of the world slump. The slump is due to a retardation of new real investment so that it is falling seriously behind the level of current saving. This is the natural and inevitable result of maintaining, year after year, a rate of interest which would have been considered high at almost any time during the nineteenth or early twentieth centuries, and is surely preposterously high in an environment so well equipped as is the contemporary world with fixed investments of every description.

Nevertheless, it may be a long and difficult process to bring the ideas of borrowers and of lenders back to their proper equilibrium. Fifteen years have now passed during which lenders have been able to obtain rates of interest which a few years earlier would have seemed to be beyond the dreams of avarice. Lenders on long term have been pampered for so long a time that they will not easily adjust themselves to the new situation. The ideas of nine people out of ten as to what it is reasonable to expect in the near future are mainly determined by what has actually happened during the past fifteen years. The reluctance of lenders to abate their terms for long-period loans has become very apparent during the recent months of exceptionally low rates of interest for short periods. Today the central banks of the world are doing what they can by means of a low discount policy to throw their influence on the side of low rates of interest. But in spite of the fact that short-term loans on the finest security do not now command more than 2 per cent in the leading financial centres of the world, the prices of long-term bonds are moving upwards with extreme slowness, and whilst they are a little higher than they were a year ago, when bank rates were high everywhere, they are no higher, in many cases, than they were in 1928. This would seem to indicate that the investing world believes that the present low short-term rates of interest are precarious and temporary, and that the prospects of the years ahead of us are for long-term rates of interest more or less on the scale that we have become accustomed to during and since the War.

Now I believe that this is a profound mistake. I see no justification for rates of interest today, after allowing for risk, etc., to be any higher than those which ruled twenty years ago. Indeed, in so far as there has been a change in basic conditions, I should have supposed that it would have been in the direction of justifying a lower, rather than a higher, rate of interest. For I see no evidence that anything has happened to the rate of saving throughout the world to counteract the other influences which I have mentioned.

I would predict, therefore, that the prospective course of the rate of interest will be steadily downwards, and the prices of first-class bonds steadily upwards. At some date, perhaps in the comparatively near future, which no one can fix beforehand with any accuracy, a belief in this tendency will suddenly seize hold of the minds of the financial world. When this happens things will move quickly. The high rates of interest obtainable for short term loans in 1929 led to very abnormal amounts of money being held in this form by persons and institutions who have no compelling reason necessarily to keep such a large volume of funds liquid. At present these persons are still continuing to lend their money at 2 per cent on short term, when they could obtain say $4\frac{1}{2}$ per cent on long term. For a time they will doubtless continue to do so. But a point will come when the steady receipt of so low a rate of interest will seem boring and unsatisfactory. Perhaps something like £1,000,000,000 is being held on short term in the leading financial centres of the world, of which not more than half need be so kept. When even a small proportion of this vast body of funds tries to switch over into first-class bonds of long date, it will be found that the surplus supply of such bonds is practically non-existent. And once the idea gets abroad that we are starting on a journey towards pre-war rates of interest, there will be a tremendous hurrying and scurrying not to miss the bus.

For the moment these developments are being held up, not only by the reluctance of lenders to change their minds, but also by the pressure of a new class of distress borrowers, namely those individuals and those governments who have been hard hit by the slump in commodity prices and in industrial output. A certain number of these distress borrowers have been already accommodated. Firms have had to sell out their liquid reserves to meet their losses; others have borrowed from their banks, not to finance new enterprise but to make good unexpected deficiencies resulting from the low level of prices. A few governments, such as Brazil, who have been gravely embarrassed by the fall in the prices of their staple exports, have found it convenient to pay whatever rate lenders demand of them. There are still other borrowers of this type waiting. So far as the London market is concerned, Australia is an outstanding instance. In New York many of the countries of South America would be glad to borrow on any reasonable terms. These loans, again, are not primarily for new productive enterprise, and the rates which the borrowers will pay will not be determined by calculations of yield or return.

I do not believe, however, that the volume of unsatisfied borrowing of this description is very great. It is most important that it should be cleared out of the way. When this has been done, issue houses may find much sooner than they expect that solvent borrowers at current rates of interest are few and far between.

Let it be clear, however, that I do not predict that the rate of interest will necessarily fall rapidly or soon. The most depressing feature of the situation, as I see it, is the probability that any such movement will be slow and gradual. I only say that it will come in the end, and that the sooner it comes the better for the ultimate revival of investment enterprise and profitable activity throughout the world. I believe that it is only a large-scale revival of investment which can restore the price level to a figure commensurate with costs of production, and I doubt whether borrowers for new real investment will come forward on a sufficient scale until there has been a very great fall in the rate of interest for sound borrowers on long term. But once there is such a fall, there must surely be an immense volume of enterprise which will be attractive to borrowers on the new terms available from lenders.

There are many lenders, doubtless, who, for many reasons, must keep their funds liquid and for whom the rate of interest obtainable is, and should be, a secondary consideration. But there are, I think, a good many others today whose permanent positions ought to be in long-term investment rather than in short-term, yet who have fallen, nevertheless, under the influence of past events, into the habit of keeping them in short-term securities. To these I venture to sound a warning note—lest they miss the bus.

Keynes's article, which attracted some attention in London financial circles, was the subject of a long discussion in *The Economist* for 11 October. In that discussion, the anonymous author questioned Keynes's suggestion that current yields were 50 per cent above pre-War and questioned his view that there had been a large fall in investment by citing figures for new issues by trade borrowers in London and New York. Keynes replied.

To the Editor of The Economist, *14 October 1930*

Sir,

There are one or two comments I should like to make on the interesting article which you published last Saturday about my views on the rate of interest.

Taking British first-class securities as the test, you show that I should have been more accurate if, instead of saying that the yields today are nearly 50 per cent higher than twenty years ago, I had said that they were more than 40 per cent higher. But I was speaking in round figures.

I also accept the point that the fall in the yield of those bonds which are much affected by political considerations must lag behind. For I was dealing with the rate of interest after allowing for any unusual risk. But if many borrowers are ineligible in the opinion of lenders, this may accelerate the rate at which the yield on really prime securities will fall.

My main point relates, however, to the figures you adduce to show that there has not recently been any falling off in investment. I cannot accept the figures of new capital issues which you quote as having any direct bearing on the question. For by 'investment' I meant, as perhaps I should have explained more clearly, 'physical investment', that is to say the net increment of capital goods. It would be convenient if new issues were a satisfactory guide to this, but unluckily so many corrections have to be made that they are, in my judgement, nearly useless for this purpose.

In the United States other, more direct, evidence is available as to the rate of physical investment. This shows that such investment began to decline in 1929, some months before the Wall Street slump, and is now at least 20 per cent, and perhaps a good deal more, below the level of 1928. In other countries comparable statistics are not available. I only wish they were. But from indirect indications my judgement is that, taking the world as a whole, the rate of physical investment, in the broadest sense of the term, began to fall away earlier than in the United States.

Behind all this lies, of course, my general view (which you quote) that 'the slump is due to a retardation of new real investment so that it is falling seriously behind the level of current saving'. But it would need a long argument to justify this statement. I have done my best to do so in my forthcoming *Treatise on Money*.

Yours etc.,
J. M. KEYNES

Chapter 4

THE COMMITTEE OF ECONOMISTS

As noted above (p. 384) the formation of the Committee of Economists was announced at the 24 July meeting of the Economic Advisory Council. Its terms of reference were 'To review the present economic condition of Great Britain, to examine the causes which are responsible for it, and to indicate the conditions of recovery'. After informal discussions with its members over holiday arrangements and the like, on 13 August Keynes suggested a possible plan of attack.

To L. C. ROBBINS, *13 August 1930*

Dear Robbins,

My proposals for the procedure of the Economists' Committee of the Economic Advisory Council are as follows.

1. To meet at 11 o'clock on Thursday, September 11, at the offices of the Economic Advisory Council in Whitehall Gardens; to consider at this meeting a list of topics prepared beforehand by the Secretary; to amend and approve this list; to consider on what matters we are all of us *prima facie* in agreement; to divide between us the task of writing short memoranda on the matters where we agree; to elucidate the issues where we appear to have some disagreement amongst ourselves, either in principle or quantitatively; and to divide up the task of preparing memoranda merely for the purposes of our own discussions, and not for publication, which would aim at bringing to a head the precise character of our disagreements where they seem to exist.

2. To occupy the next week or fortnight writing memoranda as determined above.

3. To meet together for a long weekend, either September 19th to 22nd or September 26th to 29th, whichever may suit

most people best, to examine and discuss the memoranda and to get as far forward towards a Report as we can.

I conceive that a Committee of this kind ought to be able to do a reasonable amount of its work on paper, and that it would be easier for most of us to find opportunity to give uninterrupted thought to the duties of the Committee in September than if we put off until October. As regards the long weekend, I think I can just manage to put up all the members of the Committee and the Secretaries at my house at the above address[1] if, when we meet on September 11, we find that this would be mutually convenient.

Will you let me know whether the above would fit in with your plans, and which of the two weekends you would prefer? If you have any time to give to the matter before September 11, and can send suggestions to the Secretary about the main headings of topics, it would be helpful.

I am sending a similar letter to the other members of the Committee.

Yours sincerely,
[copy not signed or initialled]

Both Robbins and Professor Pigou thought that Keynes's plans were over-ambitious. Robbins suggested that 'Ten days is not a long time to cogitate about ultimate differences of principle—if any such exist'. Pigou thought that 'the members shall be genii if we get an agreed report out of terms of reference like that'. Ultimately the Committee did meet more often—on 10 and 11 September (a meeting of the E.A.C. having put paid to Keynes's original idea of a long meeting on 11 September); 26–28 September at Stamp's home at Shortlands in Kent; 7, 8, 15 and 16 October in London; 18–19 October at King's College, Cambridge and 22 and 23 October in London. The Committee's report was signed on 24 October, although a few minor loose ends remained to be tidied up.

Before the first meeting of the Committee, Keynes circulated various E.A.C. memoranda, including some of the replies to the Prime Minister's questions of 10 July, to non-E.A.C. members of the Committee. On 31

[1] Tilton.

August, Robbins sent Keynes a list of topics that he thought should be covered in the Committee's discussions. His covering letter continued:

I have just been glancing through the bundle of memoranda submitted by various members of the Economic Advisory Council which you have circulated. It occurs to me that, although it would be superfluous to call English witnesses, our deliberations might be very materially assisted if we could have the views of three or four foreign economists (*a*) on the world slump, (*b*) on the British position as it appears to an outsider. Formal evidence would not help very much and moreover would take too long to procure, but informal conversation might prove very helpful and could be arranged without delay. I should suggest young men; we know what the aged major prophets (Cassel e.g.) are thinking—exactly what they thought twenty years ago. If I were asked for nominations I should name Jacob Viner for America (he is in Geneva this autumn and, therefore, near at hand), Röpke for Germany, Ohlin for Scandinavia and Hayek for Central Europe. As usual the French wouldn't help much.

When the members of the Committee met for the first time on 10 September, they had already received four more documents: Keynes's letter 'Buying a British Car' (above pp. 385–7), Pigou's heads of evidence for the Committee on Finance and Industry, a set of draft heads of discussion prepared by R. F. Kahn (one of the Committee's joint Secretaries), and Robbins' 'Possible Topics for Discussion'. At this meeting they agreed to ask for the circulation of the Macmillan Committee evidence of Sir Josiah Stamp, Dennis Robertson, and Professor A. L. Bowley. They also agreed to defer the question of hearing the opinion of foreign economists until after they had prepared a first draft of their report. They then spent the rest of the meeting, and the meeting on the following day, generally discussing the lines upon which they should approach the problem set them in their terms of reference. At the end of the second day of discussion, the members of the Committee agreed that before the next weekend meeting at Shortlands each of them would circulate written answers to a short questionnaire prepared by Keynes during the course of the meeting. Keynes's questionnaire ran as follows:

THE COMMITTEE OF ECONOMISTS

ECONOMIC ADVISORY COUNCIL
COMMITTEE OF ECONOMISTS
QUESTIONNAIRE PREPARED BY THE CHAIRMAN

I

In what way would
(*a*) British employment
(*b*) British prices
(*c*) British real wages
be affected by
(i) an increase of investment (*a*) in the world at large; (*b*) in Great Britain
(ii) a tariff
(iii) a reduction of British money wages (*a*) all round; (*b*) in the relatively highly paid industries?

II

How much too high (in order of magnitude) are
(*a*) real wages
(*b*) money wages at the existing level of world prices?
What is your estimate of the increase
(*a*) of real wages
(*b*) of productivity per head since 1910–14?
If your estimate of the excess of real wages is greater than your estimate of the increase in real wages per unit of productivity, how do you explain this?

At its meeting of 26–29 September at Shortlands the Committee had before it the replies to Keynes's questions. Keynes's own replies appear in *JMK*, vol. XIII (pp. 178–200). In the early stages of the weekend, Keynes also circulated four other papers for discussion.

405

ECONOMIC ADVISORY COUNCIL
COMMITTEE OF ECONOMISTS

REAL WAGES COMPARED WITH PHYSICAL
PRODUCTIVITY PER HEAD

What I have said in my Memorandum under this head may give rise to some confusion as compared with what Mr Henderson and Professor Robbins have said, owing to my not being clear enough as to the period I was dealing with. The comparison which I intended to make was not with pre-War, but over the period 1924–9.

On page 2 [*JMK*, vol. XIII, p. 179] of my Memorandum I state that real wages up to 1929 'had not increased appreciably faster than physical output per head'. On page 24 [*JMK*, vol. XIII, p. 198] I estimate the reduction of real wages on the 1929 basis to bring real wages and productivity together at not more than $2\frac{1}{2}$ per cent.

Mr Henderson (p. 7) estimates that real wages have run 20 per cent ahead of productivity.

Professor Robbins (p. 2) gives reasons for thinking that in 1924 real wages had run 10 per cent ahead of productivity as compared with pre-War; that from 1924 to 1929 real wages increased 5 per cent and productivity also about 5 per cent, i.e. that from 1924 to 1929 there was no material change in real wages relatively to productivity.

Thus as regards 1924 to 1929 I agree substantially with Professor Robbins. As regards the pre-War comparison I also agree with Professor Robbins. Some part of the discrepancy, but not all, between Professor Robbins' 10 per cent and Mr Henderson's 20 per cent may be due to Mr Henderson having in mind 1930 as his year of comparison and not 1929 (apparently Professor Robbins' figure for June 1920 [1930?] compared with pre-War might be somewhere round $12\frac{1}{2}$ per cent).

The comparison with pre-War helps to bring out the force of

the terms of trade argument. The fact that in 1924 and afterwards real wages could be maintained at so high a level per unit of physical productivity at home relatively to pre-War was surely due to the very great improvement in the terms of trade which had taken place in the meantime. Mr D. H. Robertson in his evidence [to the Macmillan Committee] estimated this at 18 per cent.

In 1924 the actual terms of trade may not have been very far from the equilibrium terms of trade, though no doubt somewhat in excess of them, and it was these favourable actual terms of trade which permitted so high a level of real wages to be established. The increased trouble since 1924 is due, not to real wages having increased appreciably faster than physical productivity per head, but to a widening between the actual terms of trade and the equilibrium terms of trade. One could express it as follows:

(i) Present real wages are only possible with actual present terms of trade.

(ii) Present actual terms of trade are only compatible in equilibrium with foreign lending on a modest scale.

(iii) The existing volume of our savings, minus the demands upon them for home investment at the rate of interest set by world conditions, is greater than the modest scale of foreign lending permitted by (ii).

(iv) Thus if we are to return to the old scale of foreign lending, we must return to something nearer the old terms of trade, which would mean a serious reduction in the real wages we could afford to pay, unless we take other measures to improve the equilibrium terms of trade.

J.M.K.

25 September 1930

ECONOMIC ADVISORY COUNCIL
COMMITTEE OF ECONOMISTS

THE RELATION BETWEEN A GIVEN CHANGE IN MONEY
WAGES AND THE ASSOCIATED CHANGE IN REAL WAGES

J.C.S. estimates changes in real wages greater than those in money wages.

H.D.H. implies (top of page 4) that a reduction in money wages would cause an equal reduction in real wages.

J.M.K. estimates reduction in money wages at nearly double that in real wages, namely, 175 per cent.

A.C.P. estimates reduction in money wages not more than double reduction in real wages.

	Per cent reduction	
	Money wages	Real wages
J.C.S.	10	12
H.D.H.	10	10
J.M.K.	10	5.7
A.C.P.	10	5+

J.M.K.

25 September 1930

ECONOMIC ADVISORY COUNCIL
COMMITTEE OF ECONOMISTS

RELATIVE QUANTITIES

The following notes of relative quantities may be useful.

I deduce as the result of certain calculations made by the Staff of the Economic Advisory Council that about 60 per cent of the gross value of exports is wages cost, and that about 20 per cent of this wages cost is in sheltered industries. That is to say, about 12 per cent of the gross value of exports is wages cost in sheltered industries. So that a reduction of 10 per cent in the latter, leaving unsheltered wages alone, would reduce the price of exports 1·2 per cent.

If 70 per cent of the price of goods produced for the home market is wages cost, and if 70 per cent of this wages cost is in sheltered industries (I think that both these estimates are not far out) it follows that a 10 per cent reduction of wages in sheltered industries, leaving unsheltered alone, would reduce the price of goods produced for home use by about 5 per cent (equal, in effect, in the case of investments such as houses, to a reduction in the rate of interest from 5 per cent to $4\frac{3}{4}$ per cent).

If about 40 per cent of wage-earners are in unsheltered industries and 60 per cent in sheltered industries, a 10 per cent reduction in the wages of the latter would be equivalent to a 6 per cent average reduction in money wages and (say) a 3 per cent average reduction in real wages.

J. M. K.

25 September 1930

ECONOMIC ADVISORY COUNCIL

COMMITTEE OF ECONOMISTS

NOTES ON PROFESSOR A. C. PIGOU'S MEMORANDUM

(The references are to the paragraphs in Professor A. C. pigou's Memorandum.[2] I have thought it better to put in writing beforehand the questions which I want to ask Professor A. C. Pigou.   J.M.K.)

I. (3) I agree with this analysis of the causes determining real wages, except that there is no explicit mention of the influence of the pressure towards foreign lending on the terms of trade. Presumably this is intended to be included in the top paragraph of page 2. But it is so much covered up that it does not obviously follow to the reader, from what Pigou says, that, for example, the building of battleships out of a loan, or out of taxation which is at

[2]   Not printed.

the expense of savings, would enable a higher real wage to be paid. Or, again, that an earthquake in London would raise equilibrium real wages. In fact, the real wages method of approach, whilst applicable to a closed system, does not bring out clearly enough the complications attendant upon membership of an international system.

1. (4) Does Pigou hold that, if items (1) (2) and (3) of § 3 and the terms of trade are unchanged, the amount of employment is uniquely determined by the level of real wages?

I deny this proposition. It would only be correct if for 'amount of employment' we substitute 'amount of employment on the production of consumption goods'.

1. (6) Could Pigou give an example of an increase in investment of the kind that does *not* raise prices?

1. (7) Am I right in taking the last sentence to mean that it is the *amount* of the fall in the rate of interest which matters from the point of view of employment, and not the *amount* of increased investment associated with it? When I say that it is the increased investment which increases employment, and regard any attendant fall in the rate of interest as a secondary phenomenon, I mean (1) that increased investment would increase employment even if there were no fall in the rate of interest; and (2) a fall of $\frac{1}{2}$ per cent in the rate of interest associated with £50,000,000 increased investment would help employment more than a fall of 1 per cent in the rate of interest associated with £25,000,000 increased investment. I take Pigou to mean the opposite in this paragraph, namely that he would expect a fall of 1 per cent to do more for employment than a fall of $\frac{1}{2}$ per cent even if the former was associated with less increased investment than the latter.

1. (8) I do not clearly understand the force of the words 'but is a monetary affair'. Is the latter part of the sentence intended to

mean that the extra amount of employment resulting from an increase of investment, due to a change in the policy or behaviour of the banking system, would be associated with the same reduction of real wages as if the same amount of additional employment were to be brought about by any other method? If so, I suggest that the differences between a closed system and an international system are being overlooked.

II. (1) Why should not the result of the tariff be to cause a fall in the rate of interest? Gold will only flow if the banking system refuses to let the rate of interest fall. In order to understand the effects of a tariff it is necessary to follow up the course of events which would ensue if the result of the check on imports is to allow the rate of interest to fall without any movement of gold.

II. (2) When members of the Committee are talking about demand being 'probably elastic', or 'probably inelastic', there is, I think, room for a certain confusion. I gather that when Pigou says that demand is probably elastic, he means that the elasticity of demand is probably greater than 1 rather than less than 1. When I have used this expression, on the other hand, I have meant by 'not elastic' what I ought, perhaps, to have expressed by saying 'not very elastic'; that is to say, I have meant that elasticity is not several times greater than 1.

This question arises very acutely in the passage under comment. I assume Pigou to mean by his statement that 'the foreign real demand for English exports is probably elastic', that the percentage increase in the volume of British exports demanded in response to a fall in their price relatively to the price of our imports is greater than the percentage fall of relative price with which it is associated. I should not deny this. But what matters for restoring equilibrium is, not shipping out a given *volume* of exports, but shipping out exports having a given *value* in excess of the value of the correlative imports; and in order that the aggregate surplus value may increase substantially when the price is moderately reduced, it is necessary either that the percentage increase in quantity demanded should be several times the percentage reduction in price, or that the *fact* of our reducing the price of our exports brings about a reduction in the price of our imports.*

For example, if the elasticity of the foreign real demand for English exports was only a little more than unity, and if the price of our imports is not materially affected by our reducing the price of our exports, no reduction in the price of British exports, however great, could materially increase our foreign balance. Even if the percentage increase in quantity demanded were double the percentage decrease in price asked, there is no conceivable reduction in British costs which would increase the aggregate value of our exports by more than $12\frac{1}{2}$ per cent; and a greater reduction than this in our costs would *reduce* the aggregate value of our exports. If, on the other hand, the percentage increase in quantity demanded were to be, say, ten times the percentage reduction in price asked, then of course it would be quite a different story.

My feeling is that the elasticity is greater for a large reduction in price than for a small reduction, and greater over a long period than over a short period. But I am not satisfied that a reduction of 10 per cent in average money wages would greatly increase the money value of our aggregate exports within the next three years. Nor do I think that it would reduce the price of our imports—unless it were to set a fashion of cutting wages all over the world, which is just what we don't want, since it would render nugatory the reduction in the price of our exports. Perhaps the greatest relief to the balance of trade ensuing on a reduction of wages would be due to the reduction of working class consumption of foreign goods resulting from their reduced standard of life. But that has nothing to do with the 'elasticity' argument.

---

* This is not the same thing as a fall in the price of our imports due to other causes altering the amount of our exports demanded at a given price.

It is important, therefore, to know exactly what Pigou means by 'probably elastic' in the above context.

II. (4) I think there is a danger of the term 'bounty' being extended rather too widely for convenience, so as to include almost any kind of transfer. If there were to be a rise in the world price level, would Pigou explain that the reason why this would increase the real wages payable would be because it would involve a bounty to wage earners at the expense of *rentiers*?

Moreover, has Pigou allowed for the fact that the capital wealth of non wage earners would be increased by much more than the amount of the so-called bounty?

IV. (5) Does this paragraph mean that the fact mentioned makes it likely that a small reduction in real wages would do the trick over the short period, i.e. that a small reduction in cotton or coal wages would cause a large increase in employment? Is there not a possible confusion between the statement that there could be a large increase in the quantity supplied in response to a small stimulus of price, and the statement that there would be a large increase in the quantity demanded in response to a small stimulus of price? Pigou seems to suggest the latter, though perhaps I misunderstand him. But it is the former which seems to me to follow as a consequence of the existence of surplus capacity. Or is it that he is stating a proposition only true in a closed system?

IV. (7) This is another example of the ambiguity as to what one means by elasticity being large or small. Pigou here explicitly explains that when he says demand is elastic he means merely that it is not less than 1. I would underline the point that if he cannot hold out better hopes than this, and if he is right, as I think he is, that a given reduction in money wages means not much more than half that reduction in real wages, then in order to cure the existing unemployment—which approaches 20 per cent—merely by reducing money wages, unaided by any other contrivances, the reduction in money wages would have to be about 40 per cent. I do not say that this is untrue. But if it is true, it emphasises the importance of seeking methods other than mere reductions of money wages,—in particular, methods which are calculated to improve the equilibrium terms of trade.

In general. The main difference of bias between Pigou's analysis and my own seems to me to be as follows:

He argues that, although we belong to an international system, the facts are such that things work out much the same as if we were in a closed system; and he then proceeds with the greater part of his argument the same as it would be if we were in a closed system.

I, on the other hand, find the main explanation of the vagaries of recent years in the fact of our belonging to an international system. As a bye-product of this difference of diagnosis, I find the real wages method of approach less helpful, and the money wages method more helpful, than he does.

Moreover, if the terms of trade are elastic in the sense that a small adverse movement in them would enable us to increase largely the volume of our exports, I cannot understand why a large reduction of money wages should be necessary to cure unemployment. It seems to me, that if they were elastic, it would follow that a small reduction would be sufficient.

Finally, will Pigou say what reduction of money wages would be necessary to cause a given reduction of real wages if we were a closed system, assuming the rate of interest to be unchanged?

I think one clue to the source of our differences may be the following:

(1) If we were a closed system, a given reduction of real wages (*cet. par.*) would, I agree, increase employment.

(2) The proposed way of reducing real wages is presumably to reduce money wages.

(3) My view is that, if we were a closed system, the requisite

414

reduction of money wages to restore employment subject to the above assumptions, would have to be simply enormous; but that, as we are not a closed system, a reduction of money wages would have cured most of the existing unemployment, via international trade *before* this reduction was large enough to have made more than quite a small effect in improving employment for the reasons which would be operative in a closed system.

The above points to an omission in my own memorandum, p. 12 [*JMK*, vol. XIII, p. 188]. I should have added a third source of employment, namely the increase of employment ensuing on the reduction of the money wages cost of home products relatively to their total money cost (otherwise than through an increase of the foreign balance as a result of the absolute reduction in money wages cost). What I should have said is that the reduction of money wages required to make this of a significant amount is so large that it is not of practical importance within the range of change of money wages which it is necessary to contemplate in order to cure unemployment in our actual environment of an international system.

(4) If we were, in fact, a closed system, then in my view employment could be mainly restored not by a fall in money wages, but by a fall in the rate of interest—a fall which is impracticable in existing circumstances because the rate of interest has to conform to world conditions. Pigou seems to conceive a situation in which neither the foreign balance nor the rate of interest is greatly changed, but in which, for the reasons which would operate in a closed system, unemployment is nevertheless remedied by a fall in real wages. Perhaps his failure on the top of page 2 to mention the size of the foreign balance as affecting the terms of trade is due to his not conceiving a change in the size of the foreign balance as a material factor in the situation.

I, on the other hand, regard the size of the foreign balance as one of the fundamental factors, because every change in its size automatically affects the value of foreign investment by an equal amount and is, therefore, a concomitant of primary employment on a scale corresponding to the change.

J.M.K.

25.9.30

At the meeting of 26 September, Keynes informed the Committee that the Prime Minister had expressed the hope that its report would be available for full consideration by the Government before the opening of Parliament on 28 October. This set the Committee a target deadline of 20 October.

In the course of the next three days the Committee spent almost eighteen hours in formal discussions, and doubtless more hours informally. For the Sunday morning session Keynes presented another paper for discussion— one that was to have important repercussions in the case of Robbins in particular.

ECONOMIC ADVISORY COUNCIL
COMMITTEE OF ECONOMISTS

A PROPOSAL FOR TARIFFS PLUS BOUNTIES

The general effect on my mind of reading the various memoranda is to make me very much in favour of the following proposal. It has not got the advantages which might ensue from interferences with *laissez-faire* as between home and foreign investment. But I seem to be the only member of the Committee who stresses this, and any advantages to be got from the methods along these lines which I favour could be superimposed on the advantages of the following proposal.

1. My proposal is for a uniform tariff of, say, 10 per cent on all imports whatsoever, including food, and a bounty of the same amount on all exports whatsoever.

2. The effect of such an arrangement on international trade would be to restore the conditions which would exist under free trade if money costs were reduced 10 per cent.

3. It has, in effect, the same result as devaluation, except that it leaves sterling international obligations unchanged in terms of gold. There are, obviously, very great advantages in this from the point of view of the national credit. Moreover, since we are a

creditor nation in terms of sterling, and our imports exceed our exports, there is actually a pecuniary benefit to us in leaving the gold value of sterling alone.

4. It is much fairer than a reduction of money wages, since it reduces the value of all incomes, etc., fixed in terms of money, to the same extent and does not discriminate against wage earners.

5. It diminishes the real burden of the internal national debt as compared with wage reductions, since the service of the national debt is a smaller percentage of the national income in terms of money than it would be if money wages were reduced.

6. It brings £40,000,000 into the Exchequer.

7. It involves no interference with contract.

8. It can be brought about by a single act of legislation of a kind not likely to be particularly unpopular; at any rate, much less unpopular than reductions of money wages concentrated on the working classes, the position of all other recipients of money incomes being left untouched. Moreover, even if we recommend that money wages be reduced and the Cabinet accept the recommendation as well advised, it is not obvious what legislative or other steps could possibly be taken to carry the recommendation into effect.

9. Since the tariff or the bounty, as the case might be, would apply to *all* exports and *all* imports (ships for this purpose would have to be regarded as an export), no rebates or complications of any kind would be required. Imported raw materials would pay the tariff, but when they were worked up into exports they would get the money back in the shape of the bounty. The only point that could possibly arise in the case of manufacture for export would be the interest on the import duty paid during the period of manufacture, which might be met by some sort of deferred system of discharging the duty out of the subsequent proceeds of the bounty.

10. It turns the terms of trade against us less than if the same result on the foreign balance were produced in reducing money wages.

11. It would tend to have an equalising effect as between sheltered and unsheltered industries, since it would be the unsheltered industries which would benefit directly and in the first instance. If the amount of the tariff–bounty were to be a little greater than would be required to restore equilibrium at the present level of money wages, so that average money wages could be allowed to rise, equilibrium could be restored by a rise in money wages in the unsheltered industries, which is what would tend to happen naturally, so as to bring them up to a proper level with money wages in sheltered industries.

12. The system would be capable of being adjusted from time to time with the changing value of money. Indeed, it might be laid down from the outset that the rate of the tariff–bounty would be annually increased or decreased according to the international price level. Thus if international prices were to fall another 5 per cent the tariff–bounty could be increased 5 per cent. On the other hand, if they rise by an adequate amount it could be abolished. Indeed, it is a method of rendering us to some extent independent of external instability in the value of money without interfering with the position of London as an international financial centre and as a depository of short-loan funds. Indeed, the tendency to increase tariffs everywhere in the last few years may be interpreted as an instinctive act of self-protection against the instability of the external value of gold. Unless some way can be found of making money wages habitually mobile it is difficult to see how we can do without such a device in the event of the world value of gold being highly fluctuating.

13. It would not help if every other country followed suit. But this is equally true of a reduction of money wages.

14. I should be inclined to estimate that a 10 per cent tariff–bounty would cause a fall of real wages not exceeding say 4 per cent on the 1930 position, i.e. would bring us back to the position of 1928–9, which practically no one would regard as harsh or unjust. At the same time the bounty, quite apart from the tariff, would have as much effect on the trade balance as, say,

a 13 per cent decline in money wages. Altogether, the effect on the foreign balance might be as great as could be obtained by a 20 per cent average reduction of money wages under conditions of *laissez-faire*.

15. The argument that the effect of the tariff on the cost of living would cause trade unions to demand an increase of money wages does not seem to me a valid objection if advanced by those who are proposing as an alternative a very large all-round reduction of money wages. For it is obvious that both the desire and the power of trade unions to resist the tariff–bounty proposal, or to negative it by changes in money wages, would be enormously less than their power to prevent a 20 per cent all-round reduction of money wages.

16. I repeat that this proposal does not have those advantages, which I estimate high, of turning the equilibrium terms of trade in our favour, which would, in my opinion, result from a judicious interference with *laissez-faire* in the realm of lending and investment. I do not put it forward, therefore, as an alternative to this, but only as an alternative to a reduction of money wages and other measures aiming at the same effective results as such a reduction might be expected to have.

17. Nor does it have the advantages to employment, which I estimate low, from a reduction of the money wages cost of production *relatively* to the money total cost of production, as distinct from the consequences of a reduction of the total money cost of production.

18. I would also repeat, what I have stated above, namely that a great advantage of this method is that it is capable of being put into force by legislative enactment, whereas a reduction of money wages cannot be enforced in this way, but only as a result of a sort of civil war or guerilla warfare carried on, industry by industry, all over the country, which would be a hideous and disastrous prospect.

J. M. K.

25.9.30

Throughout the weekend, the level of discussion appears to have been quite high. R. F. Kahn's 'Relation between Primary and Secondary Employment', an early version of part XI of his 'The Relation between Home Investment and Unemployment'[3] was one of the papers circulated and subject to comment. Another example of the form and level of discussion came in an exchange between Pigou and Keynes.

From A. C. PIGOU, *26 September 1930*

INVESTMENT, SAVINGS, PRICES AND EMPLOYMENT

1. If people, while spending the same on consumable goods, (i.e. saving the same) invest more (i.e. spent more on services that do not at once yield a product; that is, all services except direct services not mediated through any commodity), the recipients of the extra money so invested spend it. It enters into the money income stream and this stream is *pro tanto* increased. Meanwhile the real income stream is unchanged, i.e. the stream against which the money income stream is exchanged and therefore the price level rises.

2. The price level that thus rises is the price level of *things bought with money income*. Of course, it is true that in the conditions contemplated the price level of consumable goods also rises in practice; but it is theoretically conceivable that it should not, i.e. if all the new money income were spent on machines. But the logical point remains that the real income stream to be set against the money income stream is *not* the flow of consumable goods but the flow of things purchased with income. There is no case for excluding machines and including pianos. Properly speaking, direct services ought also to be included. On the other hand things (e.g. land and securities) the making of which brings in money that is counted as *capital receipts*, not income receipts, are excluded. They could only be logically included if we consider the receipts for them rather as money income.

3. It follows from what has been said that, the flow of real income being given and the amount of money savings being given, the only way in which the *price level* can be raised is by increased investment of money. But it does *not* follow that this is the only way in which employment can be increased. Employment—money wage rates being given—*will* be increased by increased investment, but it can also be increased otherwise. Thus, suppose that I save £100 by buying £100 worth of less eatables and invest by hiring labour to paint a house or build a factory, and suppose that the men spend the £100 on buying the very same eatables that I do not now buy. I have saved £100 and also invested £100; there has been no excess of investment over saving. (It is a quibble and spoils the whole thing to reply at the next stage the

---

[3] *Economic Journal*, June 1931.

newly employed men 'dissave' £100. They have been called into employment and employment has been increased before there can be [any] quantity of this 'dissaving'.)

4. The explanation of this is perfectly simple. The money stock becomes money income more frequently in such a way that the money income is £100 more. But against this money income are set the services of the workmen who painted the house or built the factory. Thus, there is no more money income stream to balance against the flow of real income, although there is absolutely more money income stream and with it more employment.

5. The failure of Keynes' method to lead to a perception of this point (it is directly denied in his memorandum) leads also in my view to confusion about primary and secondary employment. There is no secondary employment when primary employment is brought about in this way.

6. It is necessary to my purpose to follow through this analysis further. But it should be noted that, owing to the need of the newly employed to build up balances, the higher level of the money income stream brought about in the way described above can only be maintained if the banks emit bank notes without consequently reducing the amount of deposits.

A. C. P.

26 September 1930

From A. C. PIGOU, *27 September 1930*

BUSINESS LOSSES

Suppose I decide to save £1000 instead of spending it on commodities or capital goods. I am then no richer than before unless what I would have bought would have perished. To avoid this case, suppose that I would have bought pianos or machines. I am then no richer than before but I have a *claim to £1000* instead of a piano.

Since £1000 less money is spent on goods, it is obvious that the sellers of goods (business men called shopkeepers) have £1000 less money than they would have had—on the assumption that the interval of my saving is too short to allow changes in their policy. But they have not necessarily made losses. If the price level is held over the interval, they sell £1000 worth less goods than they would have done. Thus they end up with £1000 more goods and £1000 less money—which balances. If, on the other hand, the price level is not held but falls at once to the new theoretical level, the sellers sell the same *amount* of things in exchange for £1000 less money. Hence they *do* make £1000 loss which is offset by the £1000 worth of extra goods which buyers get for the same money.

A. C. P.

27 September 1930

To A. C. PIGOU, *27 September 1930*

AN ADDITIONAL WAY OF INCREASING EMPLOYMENT
NOTE ON PROFESSOR PIGOU'S ARGUMENT

Pigou's example has nothing to do with investment and saving. Nor—I think—has it anything to do with wage earners and non wage earners. It is an example of a more general proposition, as follows:

If the balance of saving and investment is unchanged, and if wages are unchanged, a shift of demand from articles of relatively inelastic supply to articles of relatively elastic supply will increase employment provided the proportion to labour is the same in both cases.

It was an omission on my part not to mention this as a way of increasing employment. It ought to have occurred to me, thinking along my own lines. For, according to my theory, the excess of saving over investment causes a determinate loss to entrepreneurs but not a determinate amount of unemployment. The amount of unemployment depends on how much employers curtail output in response to a given fall in price, i.e. on their elasticity of supply. Thus, whenever demand is shifted from those products for which the supply is relatively inelastic to those for which it is relatively elastic, there will be an increase of employment.

When foreign trade comes in, the elasticity of supply of foreign products depends, subject to the above assumptions, on the terms of trade. Thus, there is a presumption (I think) of inelasticity of supply. Accordingly, every shift of consumption from foreign goods to home goods will increase employment.

This is one of the arguments for a tariff. A tariff, which left real wages, terms of trade, and size of foreign balance unchanged, might nevertheless increase employment.

For similar reasons, an increase of home investment at the expense of foreign investment, without any net increase in investment, can increase employment.

All these examples turn on the fact that when there is unemployment and surplus capacity at home, there are many home-produced articles of highly elastic supply.

I overlooked this cause of employment, because when investment is equal to saving, it largely evaporates (except in fancy cases). For it does not diminish the aggregate loss to entrepreneurs; it simply redistributes it between different classes of entrepreneurs so as to diminish the amount of unemployment caused by a given excess of saving over investment.

J. M. K.

27 September 1930

At the end of the weekend's discussions, the Committee asked the Chairman to prepare a draft embodying the sense of the meetings. It also agreed to meet again on 7 and 8 October. Before the first meeting Keynes circulated a substantial portion of the draft report. Further sections followed for the next day's session; while at the meeting itself Keynes circulated an outline of what was to follow.

ECONOMIC ADVISORY COUNCIL

COMMITTEE OF ECONOMISTS

DRAFT REPORT

(EXCLUDING INTRODUCTORY SECTION)

I

Between 1924 and September 1929 world gold prices of staple commodities had fallen 6 per cent. (Owing to the return to gold in 1925 the fall in sterling prices of the same class of commodities amounted to X per cent during this period.) In the year which has elapsed since the end of September 1929 these prices have fallen further by the catastrophic amount of 18 per cent. In the great depression of the eighteen-nineties prices fell about 18 per cent altogether, spread over a period of 6 years. Apart from the

423

slump of 1921, when the fall was from an exceptional level out of relation to established costs of production, there is no recorded case in recent economic history of so violent and rapid a collapse in the prices of staple commodities.

The effect of this fall on a country such as Great Britain, which is primarily a consumer rather than a producer of such commodities, is double in character. On the one hand, we benefit from the cheapness so long as the price of manufactured goods has fallen to a lesser extent, and also, apart from this, because we are a creditor nation in terms of money. But, on the other hand, it deprives us of markets, since it causes great financial distress to a large proportion of our best overseas customers, and injures the credit of those who are our debtors.

The beneficial side of the fall in prices is reflected in a decrease in the cost of living, so that the existing money wages of our workers purchase more than before. Its injurious side is reflected in unemployment owing to the greatly diminished volume of our exports. It is more correct to say that the increase in real wages, due to cheaper imports, and the unemployment in export industries are effects of the same cause than that the former is the direct cause of the latter.

It is not to be expected, however, that the fall in the cost of living will be so great as the fall in the prices of staple commodities, since, by the time goods reach the consumer, a considerable part of the price represents home costs of one kind or another, including manufacturing, distribution and retailing costs, which do not fall so long as our own level of money wages is maintained except at the expense of normal business returns. Actually, the cost of living fell $6\frac{1}{2}$ per cent between 1924 and September 1929 and has fallen only a further $3\frac{1}{2}$ per cent during the past year. It may be that the more recent of these figures does not yet reflect the full effect of the fall which has already occurred in staple commodities owing to time lags, frictions, etc. But, on the other hand, it is possible that the cost of living index, which is now somewhat seriously out of date, does not allow quite sufficiently for the cost of house rents which have not materially declined.

As against this very large fall in the prices of staple commodities (X per cent since 1924 in terms of sterling) and the substantial fall in the cost of living (10 per cent since 1924), British money wages have remained virtually unchanged. Between 1924 and September 1929 wages fell 1 per cent, whilst during the past year they have fallen by less than another 1 per cent.

II

The causes of the collapse of world prices are complex and are not a matter either of easy analysis or of general agreement. But its effects are evident. All economic arrangements made in terms of gold standard money are becoming seriously and perhaps disastrously inappropriate.

Outstanding examples of this are the following:—

(i) The effective burden of inter-governmental debts arising out of the War is very greatly increased. In the case of German reparations, for example, it is probable that the whole of the concessions made to Germany by the Young Plan as compared with the Dawes Plan have been obliterated by the fall in prices which has occurred subsequently.

(ii) The same is true of the internal national debts. It is not easy at this stage to calculate the amount of this increased burden, since the level of money incomes at home has not yet adjusted itself to the external price level. If, however, it becomes necessary to adjust the general level of money incomes to the fall in world prices, the increase in the effective burden of the national debt, that is to say, the proportion which its service will bear to the income of the community will have been increased by X per cent, or *nearly one-third*, since 1924.

The same argument applies, of course, to all other forms of bonded debt expressed in terms of money. In the case of industry or the railways, for example, the percentage of the gross receipts required to meet debenture and preference interest is seriously increased.

(iii) The same considerations apply to many other Government obligations which are fixed in terms of money—even when the arrangements governing them are not so unalterable as those governing the national debt—so long as no measures are taken by Act of Parliament to alter these obligations in terms of money. This applies, for example, to all pensions, and, in particular, to unemployment relief which happens to have been fixed when the cost of living was particularly high (in fact, X per cent above the present level); so that by mere accident and without any expressed intention on the part of Parliament or the country the value of unemployment relief has been increased X per cent.

(iv) Money wages and money incomes generally, other than business profits which are entitled to the residue, also become seriously inappropriate to the new situation unless they are altered. In these cases, the obstacle to a change is for the most part neither law nor contract, but a strong social resistance to changes which, for the very reason that they would have to take place piecemeal and without any ordered plan, are likely to be open to charges of inequity and injustice. But it is the inevitable result of so many of the items of production costs remaining fixed in terms of money that the residue which forms the inducement to the business man is reduced to vanishing point.

The result of all this is that money costs interpreted in the widest sense are out of line with money prices. Consequently, producers lose money; they are unable to maintain their former labour forces; and unemployment ensues on a colossal scale.

III

Most of the above considerations apply to all the chief manufacturing countries of the world, but the degree to which they are affected is not necessarily the same. In our own case, we returned to the gold standard at a parity which probably required some reduction of the money wages then existing in order to restore equilibrium. France, on the other hand, returned to the gold standard at a parity which probably left money wages too low for equilibrium. Thus, we started with less than no margin to meet the subsequent fall in world prices, whereas France found herself with a substantial margin in hand. The parity at which Germany returned to the gold standard was probably intermediate, in its relation to the level of money wages ruling, between those adopted by Great Britain and France respectively. Another reason why countries have been affected unequally is explained by the varying proportion of their international trade to their total national commerce. There is a very great difference in this respect between the position of the United States and the position of Great Britain. The part which exports play in the American national economy is relatively so small compared with the part which they play in Great Britain that the existence of external dis-equilibrium is of much less significance.

There are also other respects in which the difficulties of Great Britain arising out of external events have been further aggravated.

(a) By 1924 we had already raised our level of real wages so substantially as to absorb practically the whole, and perhaps more than the whole, of the fruits of all the technical progress made since pre-War days, as well as those of the advantage resulting from the fact that we have since the War been exchanging our own goods more favourably in terms of foreign goods.

(b) The loss, possibly inevitable, of our former international pre-eminence in certain staple industries.

(c) The burden of heavy taxation, due in part to the fact that we, alone among the European countries, not only maintained the unabated value of the money in which our War debts were contracted, but in fact increased it to a level higher than that in which the debts were contracted.

(d) The steady growth of restrictions of various kinds, limiting the efficiency of labour below what it might be in less rigid conditions.

(*e*) The obstacles which have grown up to the movement of labour between different industries resulting in a serious want of balance between relative wage rates.

Thus, we started out with no margin in hand to provide against a long process of falling world prices unaccompanied by falling home wages.

IV

If we leave out the fall of prices in 1921–3 as mainly representing a reaction from the previous boom, our business men have suffered a series of blows since that date in the shape of a reduction in the selling prices of their goods without a corresponding reduction in their money costs. Up to 1924–5 there was the fall of prices attendant upon the deflation preparatory to the return to gold. In 1925–6 came the further fall of prices, especially of exports, associated with the return to gold at the pre-war parity. More recently there has ensued, on the top of these price falls, the further and much greater subsequent fall of world prices affecting all countries alike.

Nor do we think it prudent to assume that there may not be a further fall of world prices. We should expect some recovery from the present exceptionally low level at a date which may be near at hand. But it is not certain that this rise of prices will go far enough to mend the situation or that it may not be followed by a further sagging tendency in the price level continued over a long period. The existing international situation as it affects credit, rates of interest, the state of international confidence and the use of gold in bank reserves has not necessarily done its worst. For the same reasons that it has been producing a fall of prices hitherto, its mere continuance may provoke a further fall for some little time to come.

We would wish to affirm with all the emphasis at our command the disastrous consequences which are to be expected

428

if this fear were to be fulfilled. All money settlements of every kind, upon which the stability and prosperity of modern life, organised as it is, so profoundly depend would become, hopelessly inappropriate,—international settlements and national debts not less than money wages.

V

Nothing can be a remedy or even a palliative for the evils set forth above which does not restore business returns to a more normal level, increase the inducement to entrepreneurs to engage labour, and bring the value of what the employment of additional workers can produce back to equality with the wages which they expect to receive.

Remedies for unemployment can be classified according as they seek to restore this equilibrium:—

A. By increasing our ability to pay the present money wage otherwise than by materially raising the price level.

B. By raising the domestic price level relatively to the money wage.

C. By methods intermediate between A and B in character.

D. By reducing the money wage relatively to the domestic price level, or, as it might be expressed, by a straightforward reduction of money wages.

Some actual remedies which may be proposed do not, of course, fall precisely into any one class; and, whilst producing their major effects along one of these lines, they may also have secondary effects falling into one or more of the other categories.

In the case of Class D, it is important to emphasise at once the fact that, if money wages are reduced, real wages are not likely to fall to an equal extent. The principal part of the reason why the cost of living has not fallen so fast as wholesale prices is precisely because money wages have not fallen. Thus, if money wages were to fall, it would be reasonable to expect an important offset to this in a reduction in the cost of living; though so long as rents

429

remain at their present level the amount of this offset may be disappointing. We would estimate that something between one-third and one-half of any reduction in money wages might be offset by a fall in the cost of living. Unfortunately, neither the exact amount of the compensating fall nor the interval of time which would elapse before it would be realised can be predicted with confidence; so that in asking the working classes to submit to a reduction of money wages it is not possible to make a definite promise as to the consequent effect on the cost of living even though the effect may be actually expected with some considerable degree of confidence.

Remedies of Class A are clearly preferable to other types of remedy in so far as they are available. This is also true of remedies of Class C in so far as they share the characteristics of Class A. Furthermore, other things being equal, remedies of Class B are probably preferable in general to remedies of Class D, unless they are inadvisable in other respects,

(i) because they apply to all money incomes equally and not merely to money wages and are therefore fairer and more commendable to public opinion;

(ii) because they are likely, for the reason that they are spread over a wide area, to involve a less reduction in real wages (rents being the most important item in this connection for the working class, but the relief to taxation being also of first-rate importance for the community as a whole);

(iii) because they are likely to provoke less social resistance than a reduction of money wages which involves the same reduction of real wages; inasmuch as for all sorts of human reasons men cling to the level of money wages which they have won for themselves, and will not readily believe promises of future compensating benefits from an increase in the purchasing power of money, even though these promises are well founded;

(iv) because a change of Class B effects its results automatically over the whole field, whereas there is no way of bringing about changes of Class D except piecemeal by a series of separate conflicts, which are likely to result unequally in accordance with the bargaining strength of the different groups concerned.

VI. REMEDIES OF CLASS A

1. We are convinced that there are many ways in which the efficiency of labour could be increased without any change in its actual skill, in the sense of becoming more valuable to the employer and therefore more worth the existing wage, merely by the removal of artificial restrictions. We know that trade unions attach great importance to restrictive provisions, which have often been hardly won and represent a real contribution to the amenities of working conditions. But such restrictions may easily become out of date and inappropriate to new techniques, so that they are much more of a nuisance to the employer than a benefit to the man.

If the trade unions would agree to re-open the whole question of restrictions all along the line and consider afresh with an open mind what it is really reasonable and desirable to enforce in the actual conditions of today, there might be a surprising increase in the effective output of labour and, consequently, in the ability of the employer to offer increased employment at the existing wage.

2. The same applies to the obstacles to the mobility of labour between industries, which result in an excessive relative wage in certain industries and, in a few cases, in an actual shortage of available labour of certain types alongside superabundance of other types.

The obstacles are sometimes increased by trade union rules which today operate unfairly as between labour employed in the sheltered industries and labour employed in the unsheltered industries, although this may have been no part of the original intention of the rules. But we attribute primary importance in this connection to the manner in which the system of unemployment benefit is now operating. This system tends to immobilise workers where they happen to find themselves and hinders their transfer to quarters where the future prospects of employment may be more promising. Offers of employment which is actually available today at the customary wage for the type of employment in question, and of employment which could easily be called into existence if a supply of labour were forthcoming, may go begging merely because the potential employers are immobilised elsewhere in a state of subsidised unemployment.

A drastic amendment of the conditions of eligibility for unemployment benefit is, therefore, urgently called for.

3. The introduction by employers of methods of greater technical efficiency and the pruning away of occasions of waste and extravagance come under this head; particularly those improvements which represent a belated use by us of methods already operating elsewhere, since these bring a definite increase in our relative efficiency, which is not true of entirely new techniques the use of which by everyone leaves relative efficiencies unchanged. But it is necessary to point out that not all the changes, which are included to-day under the vague term 'rationalisation', are calculated to increase employment. For not all the kinds of changes which diminish the losses or increase the profits of business men necessarily increase their incentive to offer an increased volume of employment,—at any rate for the time being. This is true, in particular, of so-called 'rationalising' schemes the main purpose of which is to organise semi-monopolies to arrange an orderly contraction of output in a declining industry with a minimum of financial loss to the firms concerned. Nor is the introduction of labour-saving devices, possibly provoked by the apparent rigidity of money wages, calculated to increase the volume of employment offering at the present wage, except in so far as labour is required during the period of transition for the manufacture of the labour-saving devices.

4 October 1930

(1) Page 1. [above, p. 423] Sterling prices fell 18·3 per cent in this period. Sterling was depreciated to an extent averaging 9·2 per cent over year 1924: but in that year British prices appear to have been rather higher than would be suggested by a purchasing-power-parity theory of the exchange rate, while since 1925 British prices have fallen with significantly greater velocity than world prices.

(2) Page 2. [above, p. 425] 30 per cent on Board of Trade Index, 34 per cent on Statist, say '30 to 35 per cent'.

(3) Page 3. [above, p. 425] The service of the U.S. debt had to be met out of the national income in 1924: now it is covered by receipts from allied debts and reparations. Confining ourselves to internal debt and excluding sinking fund we have (£m.):

	1924	1929	1930
Wages	1600	1700	1620
Profits and salaries	2200	2320*	2100 †
Social (net) income	3800	4020	3720
Debt service	295	305	295
% of social income	7·8	7·6	7·9

The rise in money value of the net income assessed to taxation between 1924 and 1928 is seen from Table 43 of the last Inland Revenue report. There was a rise in all schedules except B, but the largest rises were in E and A.

Thus the service of the debt in terms of commodities at wholesale has risen 30 per cent or more, in terms of commodities at retail 10 per cent, in terms of labour 2 per cent, as a percentage of the social income 1 per cent, in terms of rent or salaried labour apparently fallen.

(4) Page 4. [above, p. 426] For a single man benefit was fixed at 15/- by the Act of August 1920 (value 25/- at present cost of living). This figure however was altered twice in 1921, raised to 18/- in 1924, lowered to 17/- in 1927, raised again to 18/- in 1930. Dependants' benefits have been increased during this period. It is hard to say whether the 'expressed intention' of Parliament had in view changes in the cost of living at the time of the 1924, 1927 and 1930 Acts.

C. G. C[lark]

* Based on income tax assessments.
† Assuming 20 per cent fall in profits of industry, stationary profits in services.

ECONOMIC ADVISORY COUNCIL
COMMITTEE OF ECONOMISTS

DRAFT REPORT
SECTION VII—REMEDIES OF CLASS B

Since we have attributed a large part of the existing dis-equilibrium to the fall in prices (i.e. to the rise in the value of money), it follows that a reversal of this tendency might be expected to go a long way towards effecting a cure.

If prices generally were to be restored to the level of (say) 1924 and if money wages were to remain at their present level, real wages also might be expected to fall back towards the same level as obtained in 1924, subject to such improvements above this level as might be permitted by the increase of efficiency in the meantime. But it would be wrong to conclude that this would be disadvantageous to the working classes on balance. Security of employment must be given an important place in calculating the net advantages of the conditions of employment as a whole; and it cannot be to the interests of the workers to fix wage conditions which must have the effect of causing a large and ever-increasing volume of unemployment. Nor do we believe that the working classes would resent a return of prices to their former level, even if it somewhat increased the cost of living, provided that all classes in receipt of money incomes were affected equally and that the prospects of employment were restored to normal.

Thus it is not a *prime facie* objection to a remedy that it is calculated to raise prices;—on the contrary, this is in itself, in present circumstances, a recommendation. The kind of rise of prices which would be open to objection would be a rise of British prices relatively to foreign prices of such a character that it tended to affect adversely our foreign trade balance.

The criterion of choice between different remedies should be, therefore, not so much their effect on prices taken as an isolated fact, as the proportion in which they are calculated to increase employment compared with the proportion in which they are calculated to diminish real wages, having regard to the situation as a whole. Thus those remedies are to be preferred, unless they are inadvisable on other grounds, which are likely to have a large effect on employment and a relatively small effect on real wages.

(1) The most clearly desirable remedy falling into Class B would be a general recovery of gold prices throughout the world.

Some recovery may be expected in the comparatively near future merely by the working out of the extreme phase of the credit cycle by the lapse of time. But the prospects of a sufficient recovery and of a maintenance of the higher price level are not good, so long as the central banks of the world pursue their recent practices in regard to the use of gold and the regulation of credit.

The facts as to the current supply of gold and the distribution of the existing stocks are well known. The fault is not chiefly due to the policy or the practice of this country. Nevertheless we can exert an important influence—and we have no reason to suppose that the Bank of England is not doing what lies in its power—in the right direction.

We conceive that the way in which the maldistribution of gold works its consequences is, in the first instance, through the rate of interest. Central banks are driven, in their effort to maintain their gold reserves at what they consider an adequate level, to enforce a higher rate of interest and permit a smaller volume of credit than would be the equilibrium rate and volume if the resources of the world are to be fully employed with a prospect of selling their output at prices commensurate with existing money costs of production. The difficulties they introduced in the way of free international lending at a rate of interest appropriate to the prospects of new investments and the restrictive influence on the rate of new capital development throughout the world produce the appearance of an over-production of raw materials (inasmuch as there are no buyers for the materials which would have been used in the new capital construction or for the goods which would have been consumed by those employed in this construction), so that the prices of these materials fall; and the producers of such materials are also in their turn prevented from making their normal purchases.

Since the end of 1929 central banks have been able to reduce the short-term rates of interest, but the lack of confidence throughout the world has prevented this from being sufficiently reflected in the long-term rates of interest, which are still very high on any pre-War standard.

Anything, which tends to restore confidence in new investment or which makes it easier and cheaper to borrow on long term to finance such investment, operates, therefore, in the right direction.

It follows that an intensification of the cheapness and abundance of bank credit, measures to increase confidence in the continuance of such conditions, and any technical management which would have the effect of raising the price of bonds etc., and of diverting financial resources from short-term to long-term securities, are calculated to help the general situation.

There are strict limits to the extent to which any one central bank can safely move in this direction acting alone. But if some of the more important central banks act together, then there is a great deal which could be usefully accomplished. If even the Bank of England and the Federal Reserve Board of the United States were to act in full collaboration, and if any abnormal demands for gold were to be freely met from the redundant reserves of the latter, it might be possible definitely to reverse the sagging tendency of the price level.

As a minor measure, we suggest that it would be useful if the joint stock banks of this country and the member banks of the United States were to reduce to a nominal amount the rate of interest which they allow on deposits.

(2) We cannot greatly alter the price level in this country relatively to the rest of the world (apart from remedies to be discussed in VIII below), except by altering the gold value of sterling, i.e. by devaluation.

The obvious objections to this course should, however, carry very great weight; and we are not prepared to recommend it. In the next section we offer for discussion an alternative remedy which would produce the same results in some respects without being open to the same objections, though it may be open to other objections.

6 October 1930

ECONOMIC ADVISORY COUNCIL
COMMITTEE OF ECONOMISTS

DRAFT REPORT
SECTION VIII. REMEDIES OF CLASS C

We come now to a class of remedies, capable of being applied by this country acting alone, which, whilst they are likely to be accompanied in most cases by some rise of prices, produce their primary effect on employment otherwise than as a result of the rise of prices. This is true, broadly speaking, of all those remedies which aim at increasing employment by increasing the amount of new capital investment which is being produced out of the current output of British labour.

The total of new investment is made up of the new net investment at home plus the new net investment abroad. The first depends on the amount of new capital works (roads, buildings, plant and the like) and increased stock, finished or unfinished, in the hands of manufacturers, merchants and retailers, within the country. The latter depends, in effect, on our favourable foreign balance on income account (i.e. the excess of our exports, visible and invisible, over our imports); for we cannot acquire wealth abroad to a *net* amount in excess of this, except to the extent that we diminish our stock of gold.

Now, when there exists surplus labour and equipment capable of being employed on output the production of which would increase net investment (e.g. investment goods at home, increased exports, or goods of any kind produced at home which replace imports), an increase of such investment will, if it takes place, mean a corresponding increase of employment, which it is convenient to call *primary* employment. This increased employment, even if it is associated with some increase in the prices of particular commodities, does not depend on this rise of prices to bring it into existence;—it depends on some change in the state of demand for output which will result in investment (interpreted in the wide sense).

The increase in demand for output which will result in investment, as an expedient for increasing output and employment is obviously one which only works so long as there exists surplus capacity of equipment and labour of a suitable kind. When there is no longer any suitable surplus capacity, a change on the side of demand can only bring about the substitution of one kind of output for another. But it is important to emphasise this, because what we have been accustomed to believe has often been based on the assumption either that there is no surplus capacity or that, if there is any, it will be brought into use within so short a period by the operation of normal forces that it would be unwise to allow the thought of it to influence considered principles of policy. Thus those arguments against means of remedying unemployment by increasing investment, which are based on the idea that such remedies will mainly cause a mere substitution for existing output of other output (which is likely to be inferior in utility, because artificial in origin), are sometimes inadvertently assuming that there is no unemployment to remedy. For this reason, namely that they are based on the assumption that there is no chronic unemployment, some of the arguments against Government stimulus of home investment (on the ground that it will mainly divert the channels of existing output) or against tariffs (on the ground that a reduction of imports will lead to a corresponding reduction of exports and so fail to increase aggregate employment except for a brief transitional period) are not as convincing as they might be in other circumstances.

But, apart from the primary employment which increased investment is capable of providing, there is or may be a further source of *secondary* employment, as we may call it, additional to the amount of primary employment associated with the actual production of the output which will result in investment. For the newly employed men and others whose receipts are increased as a result of the new investment may spend these receipts (or part of them) on increasing their own consumption, with the effect of increasing employment in industries producing consumption goods; and those engaged in these consumption industries will also have more to spend; and so the ripple of increased demand will spread over the whole pool of employment.

The answers to the questions whether primary employment will also bring secondary employment with it, how great the secondary employment is likely to be, and whether it is likely to involve a serious increase in the cost of living, are, however, somewhat difficult and complicated. We attempt an outline analysis as follows.

(1) If the increased investment is financed out of new additional savings from income previously spent on consumption or (e.g.) out of taxation which has the effect of reducing the taxpayer's own consumption, then there will be no secondary employment. For the expenditure on consumption goods of the newly employed factors of production will merely take the place of the previous consumption of those whose consumption is now reduced because they are saving more or paying more in taxes. (This argument assumes that the new consumption follows the same lines as the old consumption; otherwise the following out of the consequences is more intricate.)

(2) But if the increased investment is financed from other sources than the above, then secondary employment may duly ensue. These 'other sources' (apart from increased imports) are the saving on the dole (which we deal with below) and the change in the net receipts of business men. For when business men are making losses, some part of current savings is required to make

good these losses. Thus if business men make smaller losses or larger profits, new resources come into existence which are available to finance the increased investment.

The increased investment may in itself bring to business men a part of the receipts needed to finance it, since producers of the goods required for the new investment are likely to make more profits than before, both because they have an increased output at the old price level, and, if prices go up, an increased receipt per unit both of their old output and of their new (the extent to which the prices of such goods go up, if at all, depending on the ease with which output can expand in response to increased demand).

But, however this may be, the expenditure of the newly employed and of others whose receipts are increased by the new investment will swell business receipts over a wide field of industries producing consumption goods. Here again, the amount by which prices rise will depend on the ease with which the output of the goods required can expand in response to increased demand.

To sum up, the increased consumption of the newly employed will be provided partly by imports, partly by new output of consumption goods and partly at the expense of other con-sumers, the last item being large or small according as it requires a large or a small rise of prices to stimulate an increased output of consumption goods.

(3) There are two cases worth distinguishing. If we start from a state of affairs where prices have fallen below the normal costs of production so that entrepreneurs are making a loss (in the sense that they are making less than their normal returns), then the effect of the increased investment is to diminish these losses, and so to release current savings from having to be used to finance business losses and to restore them to their proper use of financing new investment. So long as this is a correct account of what is happening, the effect of the increased investment may be called 'anti-deflationary' and is, surely, wholly desirable, since

we cannot hope to restore employment so long as employers find themselves unable to produce without a loss.

But when the amount of investment has been sufficiently increased to restore business receipts to a normal level, then a further increase of investment takes on a new character. For the further rise of prices, which will be associated with it, will bring windfall profits to the business world at the expense of consumers who have to pay prices exceeding the costs of production. In fact we shall have produced a situation which is correctly described as 'inflationary'. If there is still unemployment, inflationary measures may contrive to reduce it, just as anti-deflationary measures had previously; but there are now important disadvantages due to the social and other repercussions of inflationary conditions to be weighed on the other side. Thus inflationary methods of remedying unemployment would be open to objections which do not apply to anti-deflationary methods.

In present circumstances, however, it is safe to assume that increased investment, even if it is unaccompanied by increased savings and is not financed out of taxation, would be 'anti-deflationary' and not 'inflationary' in character.

(4) There may be some cases where output can be increased without any material stimulus in the shape of higher prices and merely in response to increased demand at the existing price level. But, where home-produced goods are concerned, it is more probable in general that increased demand will mean *some* increase in prices. Thus the consumption of the newly employed will be partly at the expense of other consumers, the purchasing power of whose income will be diminished by the rise in prices; and partly out of the new increased output brought into existence by the stimulus of better prices. How much comes from the one source and how much from the other depends on the responsiveness of the volume of output to the stimulus of a small change in price. In existing circumstances, however, it is reasonable to hope—having regard to the

surplus capacity which now exists for the production of almost every class of goods—that a fairly large increase of output could be obtained in response to a fairly small improvement in prices.

In this case the secondary employment might not involve any serious increase in the cost of living.

(5) The *amount* of secondary employment caused by a given amount of anti-deflationary primary employment cannot be calculated without making a number of assumptions.

It depends (i) on how much of the increased expenditure is directed to home produced goods; (ii) on how much of the price of the goods they buy is represented by wages cost and how much by other costs; and (iii) on how much prices have to rise to stimulate output—for the greater the necessary rise in price, the greater is the extent to which the increased consumption of the newly employed is merely a diversion of previous consumption, and the less is the extent to which it is satisfied out of new output requiring secondary employment.

Perhaps the most plausible guess which can be made applicable to present circumstances in Great Britain—though we would not commit ourselves to the accuracy of this—would be to the effect that the secondary employment might be not much less in amount than the primary employment. In this case, if the expenditure of £200 on increased investment employed one man for a year, directly or indirectly, in producing and transporting the goods required for this investment, then it would also, as the result of a series of repercussions, call into secondary employment for a year nearly another man engaged in producing goods to satisfy the increased demand for consumption.

(6) In present circumstances, the possible saving on the dole is a vital factor in the situation. If £200 worth of increased investment will create primary employment for one man and secondary employment for another, half of the new investment can be financed out of the loans which now go to the payment of the dole; though the effect of this is to make the amount of the

secondary employment less than it would be if the whole of the wages received, instead of the excess of the wages over the dole previously received, were being added to the income and expenditure of the newly employed.

(7) It must not be forgotten that, quite apart from its effect on employment, the result of increased investment is to increase the capital wealth of the country by the value of the investment assets thus created; for it avoids the *waste* as well as the expense of unemployed resources.

The class of beneficial results outlined above are the consequence—as we have expressed it above—of 'some change in the state of demand for output which will result in investment'.

Such changes of demand can be classified under two heads according as they increase home investment or as they increase foreign investment, the latter being the same thing as an increase of the favourable foreign balance, which may be effected either by increasing exports or by diminishing imports.

6 October 1930

ECONOMIC ADVISORY COUNCIL
COMMITEE OF ECONOMISTS

DRAFT REPORT
1. HOME INVESTMENT

The above being the results of increased investment, we have to consider how, in practice, increased investment can be brought about.

(i) So far as home investment is concerned, we would put in the forefront the restoration and maintenance of a state of business confidence. For this is the most natural, normal and permanently efficacious means of restoring home development to a more satisfactory scale.

The best means of restoring business confidence is a

443

psychological problem on which the opinion of this Committee is not likely to be specially valuable. In the long run we do not see how business confidence is likely to be maintained otherwise than by an actual recovery of business profits. This means that if business and employment improve for other reasons, then the effect of this improvement on business confidence may be cumulative;—which is, indeed, a part of the justification for emergency measures of a temporary character. For the effect of judicious emergency measures might be to improve business confidence, after which business confidence might take the place of the emergency measures as providing the necessary stimulus.

The ways of restoring business confidence which have been recommended in one quarter or another and seem to us to have some plausibility may be catalogued as follows, without our expressing any opinion as to the quantitative effects to be expected from them or as to their general desirability regarded merely as stimuli:—

(*a*) A solution of the Budget problem satisfactory to business sentiment—in particular, the avoidance of increased direct taxation, the avoidance of any serious reduction of the sinking fund, the avoidance of increased expenditure.

(*b*) A drastic reform of the system of the dole. It is widely felt that, if Parliament can suffer the present monstrous anomalies of the dole—as they seem to be to the general consensus of public opinion—without trying to do away with them, this would be symptomatic of a general unwholesomeness in the body politic. A far-reaching reform might cause a great revulsion of feeling as showing those fears to be groundless.

(*c*) A tariff on manufactured imports is recommended in some quarters partly on the ground that it would supply just the stimulus (or, as others would contend, the dope) which business needs after the depression caused by losses partly due to forces, such as the return to gold and the fall of world prices, beyond its own control. With the general question of a tariff we deal later.

(*d*) In general, any of the remedies which we discuss under

444

headings A, B, C and D, which would improve the prospect of earning profits, might also be classified, of course, as producing their results through their effect on business confidence.

We would add that an improved state of confidence would, if it were brought about, help home investment in two ways;—it would raise the terms on which borrowers would think it worth while to borrow, and it would lower the terms on which lenders would be ready to accommodate British enterprise.

(ii) The next group of suggestions covers those which aim at increasing the amount of home investment by easing the terms on which borrowers for such purposes can be accommodated, either by lowering the rate of interest or improving the facilities in other ways.

(a) The most general effect in this direction would be produced by a credit policy on the part of the Bank of England to make bank credit as cheap and abundant as possible. The difficulty is, of course, that the Bank of England cannot, under gold-standard limitations, move far in this direction, unless other central banks are doing the same. Some of us consider that an important cause of existing unemployment is to be found in the fact that world conditions in combination with the requirements of the gold standard have enforced on the Bank of England in recent years a credit policy which has kept the volume of domestic investment below what it would otherwise have been.

In recent months short-term rates of interest have fallen to a low level. Probably we have not yet experienced the full benefits of this; for capital projects take a long time to mature and the amount of those actually afoot is still under the influence of the abnormally high rates of 1929. But it is particularly noticeable that, so far, the reduction of short-term rates of interest is only very slightly reflected in long-term rates—which are of much greater significance to borrowers for fixed investment.

We consider that a policy on the part of the Treasury and the Bank of England intended to bring down long-term rates of interest, even if it meant some raising of short-term rates, would be useful on balance as facilitating an increase of long-term investment.

(*b*) The effect of a high world rate of interest in raising the domestic rate of interest above the rate which new domestic investment can support, might be mitigated by measures which discriminated against foreign lending, so as to establish a differential in favour of lending to domestic borrowers as against lending abroad. The control exercised by the Bank of England over the rate of new foreign issues may operate to some slight extent in this direction. But a much more important effect could be produced by measures of discriminatory taxation, such as are in force in France and elsewhere and were in force in this country during the War. This might take the form of increased stamp duty on foreign issues or, better, perhaps, a higher rate of income tax on interest derived from foreign bonds and other fixed interest securities. It is questionable how far such measures would be compatible with the policy which this country has advocated hitherto towards double taxation. Nevertheless, measures of this kind should not be left out of consideration. They would have the added advantage of bringing in additional revenue, perhaps a substantial amount, to the Treasury. For example, an extra income tax of 2/- in the £ on, say, £100,000,000, of interest from abroad would bring in a revenue of £10,000,000, quite apart from its widening the difference between the home and foreign rate of interest in favour of home investment by about a half per cent.

(*c*) Another method would be to subsidise approved forms of home investment, as, for example, by the state advancing sums for approved purposes at a rate of interest which is below what would have to be paid for such borrowing in the open market. This was the principle underlying the Trade Facilities loans and also many recent advances which have been made with Treasury authority to railway companies, public authorities and others.

We consider that subsidies of this kind are fully justified on theoretical grounds whenever suitable projects for assistance can be found. Indeed, the mere saving in respect of unemployment benefit is sufficient to justify a very high rate of subsidy. It may, perhaps, be that in selecting projects to receive assistance too high a standard has sometimes been set up and that a larger subsidy than those hitherto given might be justified in the public interest. In cases where it is clear that the projects would not be entered upon without a subsidy, it would be easy, generally speaking, to justify a subsidy amounting to fully one-third of the interest cost. Indeed, on certain assumptions as to the amount of secondary employment, a subsidy up to a half of the interest cost which would have to be paid in the open market would be justified.

We think, therefore, that any projects, of which the prospective yield reaches $2\frac{1}{2}$ to 3 per cent, are worthy of assistance in present circumstances, and ought to be facilitated, whenever this is possible without unfairness to the subsidised enterprise of a comparable character.

(*d*) There remain schemes of capital development carried out under the direct auspices of the Government, central and local. Most of what has been written above as applicable to subsidies to capital schemes applies here also. We believe that these schemes, wherever suitable projects are available, are a genuine and important contribution to remedying unemployment in respect both of the primary employment and of the secondary employment which they create. We do not accept the view that such schemes must necessarily cause a diversion from other employment or that there is in any sense a fixed limit, which is always reached and can never be passed, to the amount of employment on development schemes, which can be offered in any given situation of the national credit.

We should dwell on this remedy at greater length if it were not for the fact that the advantages of such schemes are now generally accepted and that the obstacle to pushing this remedy still further is to be found, not so much in theoretical views, as in the difficulty of finding suitable schemes to assist. If, however, it be the case that this remedy has not been pushed to its limit, or if the standards of eligibility hitherto in force have been higher and the maximum rate of assistance smaller than can be justified by reference to the unemployment benefit saved, then there is every reason why this policy should be pursued further with the greatest energy and with the greatest confidence as to its efficacy in creating more employment.

6 October 1930

OUTLINE OF PARTS OF DRAFT REPORT NOT YET
PREPARED BY THE CHAIRMAN
SECTION VIII (*contd.*)

C. 2. *Means of Increasing Foreign Investment* (i.e. means other than reductions of money costs due to Class A improvements or to reductions of money wages under Class D).
(ii) Development of inter-imperial trade.
(iii) Special devices such as export credits of the linking up of
(iii) Special devices such as export credits or the linking up of
loans with orders.
(iv) A tariff.
C. 3. *The Tariff–Bounty Proposal.*

SECTION IX. REMEDIES OF CLASS D

D. 1. *Reductions of money wages* mainly concentrated on the higher paid groups.
D. 2. *An all-round reduction of money wages.*
(i) Advantages to employment ensuing from a reduction of wage costs relatively to other costs, which do not ensue, e.g. from remedies which raise prices or from such expedients as the tariff–bounty proposal.

448

(ii) Probable effect on real wages.

(iii) Probable effect on exports.

(iv) Objection that it leaves all other types of money income untouched.

(v) How is a reduction to be brought about?

SECTION X. GENERAL OBSERVATIONS

Dangers of near outlook. Reason for caution over the next few months. Importance, just now, of *appearances* as well as realities. Improved prospect of the efficacy of special remedies, when the world slump has turned the corner, so that we are rowing with the stream and not against it.

Grounds for optimism looking a little further ahead. Immense absolute strength of this country compared with others, though we may not be able to maintain the whole of our former relative superiority. Some international comparisons.

SECTION XI. SUMMARY OF RECOMMENDATIONS

Summary of remedies about which there is substantial agreement not only as to their being remedies but also as to their being preferable, so far as they are practicable, to the other expedients next to be considered.

Having dealt with these, there remain two questions for the Committee—

(i) Can the above remedies be put into effect in a sufficient degree for there to be a reasonable prospect of their bringing adequate alleviation to the present position? If not, it is necessary to consider the second-line expedients.

(ii) In this case, we are practically reduced to choosing between (*a*) some measure of reduction of money wages, and (*b*) some measure of tariffs or tariff bounties.

In settling this choice wider considerations of policy must necessarily come in than those merely of economic cause and effect. As to the balance of advantage, when account is taken of these wider considerations, economists, like other people, differ amongst themselves.

Some of us are of the opinion that the first-line expedients taken by themselves are not likely to prove adequate and that the immediate introduction of some measure of tariffs or tariff bounties is advisable.

Statistical Appendix [To be added later]

In the course of the meetings of 7 and 8 October, the Committee discussed Keynes's draft and agreed that Henderson should re-draft the section on rationalisation (above pp. 431–2); that Pigou should re-draft the sections dealing with remedies of classes B and C (above pp. 434–43); and to make some smaller verbal amendments. It also agreed on 8 October that Professor Robbins, by this time in deep disagreement with Keynes, should prepare before the meeting in Cambridge on 18–19 October a statement setting out the matters in which he was in disagreement, with such explanatory notes as he thought necessary. (Robbins, even by this stage, expected that this disagreement would carry through to the final report, for he was inquiring as to the precedents for means of expressing his dissent to such a report.)

When the Committee met again on 15 October, with Robbins' statement in hand, it attempted to continue drafting as far as possible on the basis of Keynes's draft and the Pigou–Henderson amendments. The next day, Keynes stated that on considering Robbins' draft, he found it possible to include large portions of it in a re-cast report. As a result Robbins did not press for the discussion of another note of his written after the previous day's meeting. The note, however, indicates something of the Committee's problems.

NOTE ON THE PRESENT POSITION OF OUR DISCUSSIONS

My impression of yesterday's discussion is that after all our theoretical wrangling we do not yet know where we severally stand on the main practical problems to be decided. Because I have afflicted them with a voluminous statement, members of the Committee may know where I stand: I confess I am still in ignorance about the position of some of my fellow members. I suggest, therefore, that, before we do anything else, we should each attempt (always, of course, without prejudice to future action) to give a simple yes or no to the following fundamental questions.

(1) Apart from possible differences about the effects of the gold standard, is the diagnosis of the *pre-slump* position in my draft roughly acceptable?

(2) Now that the slump has come, do we believe that prices will recover to anything near their 1928 position, or that the chance of their doing so is good enough to justify sitting tight?

(3) Do we hope for any early substantial results from what international action in the monetary sphere is possible in existing conditions?

(4) Do we consider that a substantial volume of exports is essential for Great Britain?

(5) Do we consider that we can safely rely on preferential markets, to ensure us a sufficient volume of exports?

(6) Do we consider that we can hope to retain over a long period any substantial volume of exports in non-preferential markets, unless our selling prices are somewhere near equilibrium with the selling prices of competing countries?

(7) If not, do we agree that wage adjustments are necessary?

(8) Do we wish in present circumstances to impose restrictions on foreign lending?

(9) Do we believe that the *methods* open are *desirable*

(10) or likely to be *effective*?

(11) Do we disagree with the *formal* criteria of extraordinary public expenditure as set forth in my draft?

(12) Do we believe that, in the present crisis, *more* extraordinary public expenditure is desirable and practical?

(13) Do we disagree with the *long-period* case for free trade?

(14) Do we believe that a moderate tariff under present circumstances would materially improve the immediate economic situation?

(15) Do we believe that, in the short period, a tariff would not hit the export trades?

(16) Do we believe that the tariff bounty scheme is feasible?

(17) Do we believe that there is the ghost of a possibility of a 'scientific' tariff surviving party politics?

(18) Do we believe that if the tariff is imposed it can easily be removed?

(19) Do we believe that it will not seriously corrupt politics?

(20) Are we willing to accept the international repercussions?

L. C. R.

16 October 1930

Three days earlier Hubert Henderson had written in a similar manner.

ECONOMIC ADVISORY COUNCIL
COMMITTEE OF ECONOMISTS
MEMORANDUM BY MR H. D. HENDERSON ON THE DRIFT OF THE
DRAFT REPORT

I understand that the Draft Report is to be reshaped from the point of view of securing a more acceptable form of exposition. But I find myself in such serious disagreement with its practical gist and tenor (as conveyed not merely by the drafted sections but also by the skeleton outline of the undrafted sections) that I think it desirable to make my attitude clear at once. So that the issue may no longer be blurred under partial but inadequate agreement, I will make my criticisms sharp, and very possibly unfair. If unfair in their interpretation of the intention of the Draft Report, they may none the less be useful as serving to crystallise issues which I feel have still to be thrashed out.

The broad effect produced on my mind is that the central argument of the Report is lacking in sense. It seems to me to run away, under cover of complex sophistication, from the plain moral of the situation which it diagnoses; namely, that in view of the turn which world prices have taken and the extreme slenderness of the chance of substantial recovery, in view of the fact that before the slump began our costs were not properly competitive and we were faced even then with the danger of a steady erosion of our export trade, in view of the overwhelming probability that we shall now be faced with sharper international competition at reduced prices, in view finally of the highly dangerous touch-and-go position we have reached in regard to the public finances and the public credit, we have no alternative now but to face up to the disagreeable reactionary necessity of cutting costs (including wages) in industry and cutting expenditure in public affairs, acting generally in short as Sir Otto Niemeyer advises the Australians to act, and as any similar competent impartial outsider would certainly advise us to act.

That I say is the plain moral of the situation, as plain as a pikestaff. It is of course extremely disagreeable in itself. Furthermore, it is the moral drawn by the ordinary, conservative, unintellectual businessman; and some may find it still more disagreeable to admit that the ordinary businessman can possibly be right. But, if we allow ourselves to be swayed by such distaste we run a danger of making applicable the Duke of Wellington's description of another controversy: 'All the clever fellows were on the one side, and all the damned fools were on the other; and, by God! all the damned fools were right.'

The Draft Report, as it seems to me, after half-recognising the truth of the

452

foregoing, runs right away from it, and proceeds to twist and wriggle and turn in a desperate attempt to evade the logic of the situation. Its practical drift is that we may with luck be able to evade the necessity for reducing costs by adopting a series of expedients of the most different kinds, which are all labelled 'Remedies for Unemployment', but some of which, whether they deserve that description or not, are in no sense remedies for but rather aggravations of the fundamental maladjustment which has got to be put right. I infer from the skeleton outline of the undrafted sections that the ground on which this policy of evasion is justified is nothing more or less than the expression of a hope that matters will right themselves in a few years in the ordinary course. Now I share, as I think we all do, the bias against pursuing so disagreeable a path as that of wage reductions and public retrenchment, until it has become clearly imperative that we should so do; and I have accordingly in recent years supported recourse to temporary expedients and makeshifts in the hope that trade conditions would gradually improve. But in the light of the world slump I find it quite impossible to maintain such an attitude any longer. The necessity which I have been reluctant to admit seems to me now to be proven beyond a reasonable doubt. I should still support pressing forward with roads within the limits of transport requirements, and useful public works generally, by way of a recognised palliative for unemployment in time of depression, (though I should be opposed to grandiose schemes under this head, having regard to what I have termed the touch-and-go position of the public credit, such that while, on the one hand, we may hope, if confidence is not disturbed, to secure a valuable lowering of the interest rates at which the British Government can borrow, it would not take much, on the other, to reduce British Government securities to the rank of second-class bonds). But to describe the undertaking of such work as an *alternative remedy* for the situation in which we find ourselves, i.e. as something we may reasonably turn to in order to avoid the necessity for reducing costs is so misleading as to make the whole treatment of this question in the Draft Report entirely unacceptable to me.

The only ground on which the policy of evasion appears to be justified is, as I have said, the expression of a hope that, if we put off the evil day a little longer, something will turn up after all. But I don't think that Keynes is really very confident of that; and from a question he has put to me more than once in the course of the discussions, I fancy the difference between us is really of another character. He has asked me whether it would really matter so very much if there was a flight from the pound, and a real *dégringolade* of British currency and credit. Well, of course, it is quite true that we could still hope in that contingency to restore, after a period of confusion and horror, some sort of economic stability, as Germany and Austria have done, doubtless with the benevolent assistance of American finance. It is equally true in my judgement that the process would entail an important degree of permanent impoverishment, the final loss, for example, of London's position as the leading financial centre, and that the restoration of stability would entail the acceptance of a decidedly lower standard of living than would be entailed by facing up to our difficulties now. It is clear to me in short that the danger of such a development is one to be avoided very anxiously. I was completely mystified at the time as to why Keynes put this question. It has since occurred to me that the explanation was this: that he, for his part, is in favour of pursuing a course which he recognises to be dangerous, except on the assumption of an early recovery of world prices to their 1928 level, that he is conscious that the chance of this is not at all a good one, but none the less he is prepared to gamble on this chance, because he doesn't think it would matter very much if the pound should go the way of the mark and the rouble.

This seems to me like advising a man who is suffering from toothache not to go to the dentist but to take some whisky instead, in the hope that the pain will pass off, and when the pain gets worse advising him to take a stronger dose of whisky, and when he says 'But I'm afraid if I don't go to the dentist soon, I'll get an abscess', replying easily, 'Well, what if you do? An abscess won't kill you'. I use the language of metaphor, rather than of economic analysis, deliberately, because it seems to me that the really important issues which divide the Committee are of a broad and almost temperamental nature and are merely obscured by disputes about investment and secondary employment or even about the increase in physical productivity since 1913. My position is that we've been taking whisky for some days in the hope that the pain would pass off, that it hasn't passed off but has got worse, and that the time has come when it won't do to put off going to the dentist any longer. I should like to know how many of the Committee disagree with me that this fairly sums up the position, because this seems to me the main essential issue.

It remains true, of course, that it will not be an easy matter to effect wage reductions; that, on the contrary, the process will be an extremely difficult and painful one, involving a vast amount of social friction and class feeling. Altogether something odious. I don't suggest for a moment that we should treat it lightly, with a sort of intellectual gaiety of demonstration. On the contrary, it's entirely proper that we should urge the desirability that directors' fees, managers' salaries, etc., should be cut *pari passu* with wages (a suggestion which seems to me more in place than that of a special tax on bonds, which raises other very doubtful issues). But the essential point under this head is not what we recommend. The attempt to reduce wages is going to be made anyway by employers in particular trades. The essential point is whether the effect of our Report is, on the one hand, to amount to a censure on employers who make the attempt and an encouragement to the Government to blame them and to the workers to resist them, or, on the other hand, to encourage the view that the tendency is really essential and that the workers will be well-advised to make reasonable concessions.

Of course, again, it may prove impossible to get wages down appreciably, or, if world prices continue to fall, the problem may become too big to be capable of solution by cutting our money costs. In that case, there is only one adequate solution, namely devaluation. It is clearly, I think, too soon to prejudge whether resort to so extreme a measure will be necessary; but perhaps it is not too soon for us to contemplate the possibilities that are open if the contingency materialises. In default, for example, of any headway with international co-operation for stabilising the purchasing power of gold, we might conceivably induce other countries which are equally embarrassed by falling prices to enter into an international convention to reduce the gold content of their currencies in common in accordance with the movement of gold prices. Such an arrangement might greatly diminish the damage to our credit of an independent measure of devaluation. I have no considered view as to whether it would really be wise to canvas such contingent possibilities in our Report. I am clear that this is the sort of thing on which we must fall back if it proves impossible to restore equilibrium by reducing our money costs. I am equally clear that the attempt to reduce money costs must be made first.

I have said nothing so far as regards tariffs. I do not regard them as belonging to the category of unsound devices which must be condemned as tending necessarily to aggravate the situation. From a long-period stand-point, there are various considerations which make me think that it may become unwise for us to adhere to our traditional free trade policy in a world of growing tariffs. If, for example, we are more and more deprived of our traditional export markets, it may really be our wisest national policy to enter into a satisfactory arrangement with the Dominions, though I see no possibility of negotiating an arrangement I would regard as satisfactory just now. With such possibilities ahead, I can see no adequate reason for depriving ourselves, at a very critical time, of the great relief which a moderate general tariff would afford in many ways—relief to the Budget position, relief to the exchange position, some slight direct assistance to employment, and a much-needed stimulus to business confidence. However, it is not my present purpose to argue the case for a tariff. The point I wish now to make is that, though I support a tariff, I do not consider that a tariff can by itself provide a solution of our problem of maladjustment, and that the necessity for reducing our costs remains in my judgement, whether we adopt a tariff or not, though not perhaps in as large a degree in the former case as in the latter.

Let me briefly sum up what seems to me the ineluctable problem. The prices of primary products have recently fallen heavily. The prices of manufactured goods have not fallen in anything like the same degree. There is a big disparity between the two, the correction of which is a prior condition of world trade revival. Unless agricultural prices recover quickly (which is almost out of the question), the prices of manufactured goods must fall and will fall. They will fall as the result of a process of price-cutting competition, accompanied by wage reductions, between competing manufacturing countries. It is idle to suppose that we can avert that tendency by refusing to take part in it, and building roads instead. The forces making for lower manufacturing costs are too deep-seated in the need for the correction of the disparity between manufacturing and primary prices to be held in check so easily as that. Under the conditions which obtain, it is a case of woe to the manufacturing country which is the last to reduce its costs.

I ask that the statement of the problem set out in the above paragraph should be considered seriously by the Committee.

I append, with reference to the secondary employment controversy, the note which I handed round at the last meeting, revised and expanded so as to make clearer my essential criticism.[4]

H.D.H.

13 October 1930

At the end of the meeting of 16 October, Keynes circulated a memorandum for consideration prior to the Cambridge meetings planned for the coming weekend.

ECONOMIC ADVISORY COUNCIL
COMMITTEE OF ECONOMISTS

MEMORANDUM ON SAVINGS AND INVESTMENT BY THE
CHAIRMAN (*all figures illustrative*)

Case I. (Money wages assumed unchanged Cases I–IV)

Domestic current output ($=100$) divided as follows (on the basis of cost of production):

20	Sold as exports
6	Home capital goods
74	Balance of consumption goods available for home consumption

100

---
[4] Not printed.

To get total domestic income (= 113) we have to add

6	Interest on foreign investments and other net favourable invisible balance
7	Rents, etc.

13

Domestic income utilised as follows:

21	Imports
11	Savings
7	Rents, etc.
74	Home consumption goods

113

This is a position of equilibrium with full employment and normal profits.

Case II

Now suppose that imports fall in price relatively to exports and home-produced goods, but that the quantity imported increases in the same proportion as the price falls and that exports are unaffected.

Real wages (and the value of all other money incomes) rise, but equilibrium is undisturbed.

Case III

But suppose that the quantity of imports increases more than in proportion to the fall of price, and also that exports fall off as a result of the lower prices abroad. Then the result of the above fall may be as follows:

Domestic current output divided as follows:

17	Exports
6	Home capital goods
77	Home consumption goods
100	

Domestic income utilised as follows:

22	Imports
11	Savings
7	Rents, etc.
73	Home consumption goods
113	

Thus the cost of production of current output is 100 but the money spent on buying it is only 96; so that *entrepreneurs* must either keep their goods unsold or sell them at a loss of 4. In this case savings are utilised as follows:

1 (17+6−22)	Foreign investment
6	Home investment
4	Financing entrepreneurs' losses
11	

Case IV

Entrepreneurs realising this situation curtail output and employment. If the lessened consumption of the unemployed factors of production comes entirely off home consumption goods, they are no further forward. For example if they curtail output 10 per cent, the result is:

17	Exports
6	Home capital goods
67	Home consumption goods
90	

And domestic income is utilised as follows:

22	Imports
11	Savings
7	Rents
63	Home consumption goods
103	

So that the loss of the entrepreneurs is exactly as great as it was before, namely 4.

Case V

But suppose some of the lessened consumption is at the expense of imports and rents, let us say 30 per cent of it at the expense of imports and 10 per cent of rents. Then domestic income is utilised as follows:

19	Imports
11	Savings
6	Rents
67	Home consumption goods
———	
103	
———	

In this case by curtailing employment 10 per cent, the entrepreneurs have restored profit equilibrium.

Case VI

If the entrepreneurs instead of curtailing output reduce prices and if this raises exports to 18 and reduces imports to 21·5, the result is:

Cost of Output		
	18	Exports
	6	Home capital goods
	76	Home consumption goods
	———	
	100	
	———	

and Distribution of Income is—

21·5	Imports
11	Savings
7	Rents
73·5	Home consumption goods
———	
113	
———	

Thus entrepreneurs lose 2·5 (instead of 4) and the savings are utilised:

2·5 Foreign investment
6 Home investment
2·5 Financing entrepreneur's losses
———
11
———

The actual case of this country seems to me to be intermediate between Case V and Case VI, so that the fall of foreign prices relatively to home incomes shows itself partly in unemployment and partly in business losses.

Case VII

If the entrepreneurs instead of curtailing output, reduce wages by an amount which represents 10 per cent of the total cost of production, and reduce prices 10 per cent; then if this has no effect on the value of exports or home investment (i.e. if the elasticity of demand for them is 1) and no effect on savings (because savings are done by a different class of people), and if wage earners have to economise entirely at the expense of their consumption of home-produced goods (because their expenditure on rents and imports is on necessaries), then our tables become:

Cost of output 17 Exports
6 Home capital goods
67 Home consumption goods
———
90
———

Distribution
of income

22	Imports
11	Savings
7	Rents
63	Home consumption goods

103

Thus entrepreneurs' losses are exactly as great as before, namely 4.

Conclusion

If the disequilibrium is of this character, reductions of wages can only do good in so far as they (1) increase the foreign balance; (2) increase home investment; (3) diminish saving.

Apart from these influences, however much wages are reduced, there will continue to be business losses and unemployment.

On the other hand, if (1), (2) and (3) can be sufficiently changed without altering wages, equilibrium both of profits and of employment will be restored at the original wage level. If the excess of saving over (foreign balance *plus* home investment) is large or if it is going to be large, and if domestic rates of interest are determined by world conditions, then a point comes at which a reduction of wages, etc., is the only means of sufficiently increasing total investment and diminishing saving so as to bring them together.

16 October 1930

Thus by the time the Committee held its Cambridge meeting on 18 and 19 October, it was in some disarray. Despite its problems, it still managed to produce a report with few signs of unresolved conflicts other than over aspects of tariff policy and Robbins's separate report. The Report was very much a composite document bearing the marks of Keynes, Henderson, Pigou and Robbins in particular. As the report has recently been republished elsewhere with a detailed discussion of the draftmanship of particular sections,[5] we do not print it here.

The meetings of 22 and 23 October forced the question of what to do with Professor Robbins, who had said on 19 October that he would probably be unable to sign the report and had later expressed his desire to make a dissenting report. On 22 October Keynes set out his position to A. F. Hemming who was to inquire of Sir Maurice Hankey of the Cabinet Office as to precedents.

To A. F. HEMMING, *22 October 1930*

Dear Hemming,

I think it will be proper for me, as Chairman, to give you a statement of Robbins' position, as it seems to me, for you to put before those whom you may consult on the point of procedure which has been raised.

1. It seems clearly desirable, as a general rule, that Committees of the Economic Advisory Council should adopt the rule of Royal Commissions as to Minority Reports.

2. The Economists' Committee is a Committee of a rather unusual kind, and there might be good reason, therefore, for stretching points of procedure in this particular case, in order to allow members full latitude in the expression of their views.

3. I am afraid, however, that this particular consideration cannot really be urged in the present case. Robbins has taken part in all the deliberations of the Committee, many compromises have been effected to meet his views and a substantial part of the final version of the Report is actually from his pen. Moreover, he has drafted his reservations in a form which seems to me, as Chairman, entirely suitable for incorporation in a note of dissent. There is nothing in what he has written which I should rule as being out of order in a minute of dissent.

---

[5] See Howson and Winch, *The Economic Advisory Council*, pp. 180–243. The discussion of draftmanship is on pp. 71–2, while the discussion of the Committee's work occupies pp. 46–81. For other discussions see R. F. Harrod, *The Life of John Maynard Keynes* (London, 1951), pp. 426–7; R. Skidelsky, *Politicians and the Slump: The Labour Government of 1929–1931* (London, 1967), pp. 203–15 and Lord Robbins, *Autobiography of an Economist* (London, 1971), pp. 150–6.

4. The point which really arises, therefore, is of a different character from what might have been expected, and is indeed rather peculiar. The point is a purely formal one. Robbins has a scruple of conscience about which he has worked himself up to a high degree of emotional feeling. This scruple of conscience stands in the way of his signing a Report which contains something to which he greatly objects, even though his signature is appended subject to a minute of dissent dissociating himself root and branch from the thing he objects to. That is to say, the question in dispute does not relate in any way to the content of what he desires to append to the Majority Report, but solely to the question of the half-dozen formal words with which his document commences.

5. I think there is no doubt that Robbins entertains a genuine scruple of conscience, and there is a general presumption in favour of giving way to such scruples if no serious harm results. The question is, I think, whether it might not be right to allow an exceptional latitude to Robbins as to the form of words he uses in order to respect this scruple, without creating any precedent applicable to other cases not similar to his in this peculiar respect.

6. Perhaps the only substantial reason against this which ought to be weighed for what it is worth on the other side arises out of the fact that he cannot both be a signatory to the main Report and not a signatory. If he drops out of the main Report entirely, the balance of opinion as represented in that Report is seriously disturbed, and a rather unfair position is created for those who are signing the main Report but nevertheless agree with Robbins on some important issues, rather than with the majority.

Yours sincerely,
[copy initialled] J. M. K.

464

At the meeting of 23 October Hemming reported that Hankey and his colleague R. B. Howorth were unable to find precedents for a minority report by a single member. He also gave Robbins a form of words drafted in the light of the Cabinet Office discussion for his consideration. Robbins then said he was unable to sign the Report. The Committee then accepted Robbins' statement of his disagreements subject to certain drafting changes. However, it still took some days of negotiation to get a form of words satisfactory to all concerned, as the following letter indicates. Keynes's pencilled comments appear as footnotes.

From A. F. HEMMING, *27 October 1930*

Dear Keynes,

Robbins was lecturing until seven o'clock, and it was not till then that I was able to get him on the telephone. I put to him the revised draft which you dictated to me on the telephone this afternoon, which he definitely rejected. I tried to suggest alternative forms of words which I thought you might be willing to accept and which might have been acceptable to him, but without success. Half way through the conversation I got Henderson to talk to him on the telephone but he was as unsuccessful as I had been.

Finally, he said that he would be willing to modify the words he had proposed so that they should read as follows: 'I am informed, however, by the Chairman* that he is unable to discover any precedent for † a Minority Report signed by a single member. I am, therefore, compelled to adopt the procedure that I have followed.' We pressed him to modify the last sentence but he is unwilling to do so.

We both told Robbins that our only interest in the matter at this stage was to secure an agreed form of words which would enable us to submit the document to the Government, and we undertook to submit his revised formula for your consideration.

There is one point which was not raised by Robbins himself which I think would go a long way towards meeting his difficulties, and it is one which I recommend that you should adopt. It is this. That his document should be printed as Appendix I, that is to say, that it should precede Clark's statistical tables. (This would be in accordance with the procedure followed in the case of Lord Ebbisham's Minute of Dissent, although the case is not on all fours,

---

* This is not accurate. I have not examined the precedents. I informed Prof. Robbins, on the authority of Sir M. Hankey and the assistant sec^y of the Cabinet, that the practices of procedure etc. In order, however, that Prof. Robbins should not be prevented by this from expressing his views, the Com^ee agreed that Prof. Robbins' statement should be printed as an appendix to this report.

† The practices of procedure do not permit of

as Lord Ebbisham did sign the Report.) Nevertheless, I do think that this re-arrangement is one which could properly be made. Henderson and I both hope that you will agree to this.

I hope that you will receive this letter early tomorrow and I will ring you up to get your further directions.

Yours sincerely,
A. F. HEMMING

Robbins, in the end was allowed a separate report.

The full Economic Advisory Council discussed the Report at its meetings of November and December 1930 and March and April 1931.[6] The discussion cannot be regarded as a success, for it was diffuse and inconclusive. The Cabinet also gave the report some consideration before officially burying it. The report resurfaced briefly during the 1931 financial crisis, in connection with Keynes's tariff campaign (see below pp. 487 ff).[7]

[6] Discussion was planned for the 12 February meeting, but deferred when it turned out that Keynes was absent owing to influenza, and that Stamp was also unable to attend.
[7] For a summary of subsequent discussion, see Howson and Winch, *The Economic Advisory Council*, pp. 73–81.

Chapter 5

UNEMPLOYMENT AND PROTECTION

The deliberations of the Committee of Economists coincided with the final stages of publication of *A Treatise on Money* (*JMK*, vols. v and vi) which appeared on 31 October. On 11 and 18 October Keynes also published 'Economic Possibilities for Our Grandchildren' (*JMK*, vol. IX, pp. 321–32) in *The Nation*. A week later a letter from Francis White of North Harrow appeared in that journal deploring Keynes's statement that 'For at least another hundred years we must pretend to ourselves and everyone, that fair is foul and foul is fair; for foul is useful and fair is not.' Keynes replied for the next issue.

To the Editor of The Nation and Athenaeum, *24 October 1930*

Sir,

Your correspondent, Mr Francis J. White, may not have detected every element of the ironic which may have been present in my article. But anyhow, I am in good company in wishing to postpone (until we can afford them) the application of those 'most sure and certain principles of religion and virtue', relating to the pursuit of gain, to which I was referring. I am not aware that even archbishops would be in favour of putting them into force immediately.

Moreover, is it not the highest virtue to 'do evil that good may come'? For is this not what we mean by 'doing good' as distinct from 'being good'? 'Doing good', as I understand the phrase, means to forgo the best oneself in order that others may have an opportunity to be good, which is the completest form of self-sacrifice. That is the choice which has to be made. For it is given to very few in this awkward world both to do good and to be

467

good. Or is it true that to do good is the only way to be good? I ask questions, both *num and nonne*.

Yours, &c.,

J. M. KEYNES

At the end of October, Keynes also had an exchange with Sir Frederick Leith-Ross, the Treasury observer at the Macmillan Committee's proceedings.

From SIR FREDERICK LEITH-ROSS, *24 October 1930*

My dear Keynes,

In the discussions about the fall in world prices, the argument is constantly advanced that a fall in the price of one commodity should be accompanied by increase of prices elsewhere, and that as the recent fall of prices is general it can only be accounted for by monetary causes.

It seems to me that this argument is very unconvincing. In the first place when there is a surplus of a commodity like wheat, in the production of which a large proportion of the population of the world is interested, a jolt in purchasing power is created which is not compensated for elsewhere. I estimate in round figures that the recent drop in wheat prices represents a reduction in the value of the last wheat crop, as compared with last year, of £400 millions. The agricultural population having to reduce their demand for the goods they normally require a depression must inevitably be created in the country supplying these goods which spreads the fall in prices and does not counteract it.

But apart from this specific argument, it seems to me questionable whether we are justified in speaking about a general fall in prices. The existence of a general fall of prices is assumed from an index which consists of a comparatively small selection of primary commodities, and does not by any means cover the sum of things produced or consumed. In particular, it does not give any accurate reflection to the changing volume and character of consumption. For example, during the last ten years there has been an immense increase in the demand for highly manufactured goods such as motor cars which require comparatively little raw material, but which absorb a great deal of the purchasing power of the country. If the money spent on motor cars had been invested in railways, the demand for steel products would have been much greater and the index would have been different. Surely so long as the index used is so incomplete, there is no justification for

468

the view that a general fall in the particular commodities included in the index is conclusive evidence that monetary factors are operating.

I wish you could tell me some time your reaction to these doubts.

Yours sincerely,

F. W. LEITH-ROSS

To SIR FREDERICK LEITH-ROSS, *29 October 1930*

My dear Leith-Ross,

You ask me questions which it is frightfully difficult to answer satisfactorily in a letter.

The worst of economics is that it really is a technical and complicated subject. One can make approximate statements in a common-sense sort of way which may appear superficially satisfactory. But if someone begins to ask one intelligent and penetrating questions it is only possible to deal with them by means of something much more complicated.

It is really impossible to deal with the particular questions you ask except by getting you first of all to make a professional study of the whole subject. But I might say this much. As regards the first question, if we assume that aggregate incomes are unchanged, then if the price of wheat falls and if the amount of saving is unchanged, it is evident that there will be more money to spend on other articles and that their price must therefore go up. Whether or not this will happen in practice will of course depend upon whether incomes are or are not changed, and what is going on simultaneously in regard to saving and investment, and above all, what the behaviour of the banking system is. The statement I made the other day[1] followed from the assumption that the banking system was not doing anything to alter the preexisting relationship between saving and investment and was supplying enough money for the industrial circulation to maintain aggregate incomes at the same level as before.

To your second question the short answer is that one may

---

[1] At one of the Macmillan Committee's informal discussions on 23 October.

mean various things by the phrase 'a general fall in prices', and that one is not justified in speaking of such a thing unless one has explained which meaning one has in mind. From the practical point of view perhaps the two most important and usual meanings are : (1) the wholesale prices of primary commodities; and (2) the price of consumption goods. It is quite true that these two price levels do not necessarily move together. You will find a chapter or two about that in my book. As regards monetary factors, both sets of price levels are, I should say, subject to monetary factors in the sense that at any given time either of them will be different from what it is if the monetary factors are different. That is to say, monetary factors are capable of changing either of the price levels. But different changes in the monetary factors will be required to stabilise one of these price levels from what would be required to stabilise the other.

But, as I began by saying, if you are going to ask intelligent questions on this subject there will be no answering you unless you first of all immerse yourself deeply in the whole subject!

Yours sincerely,
[copy initialled] J. M. K.

In December Keynes became involved in a controversy with Sir Herbert Samuel in *The Times*. On 1 December Samuel, attempting to explain the co-existence of depression in the basic industries and high unemployment on the one hand and high and growing working-class savings and no sign of distress over the greater part of the country on the other, suggested that the fall in prices had resulted in reductions in household expenditure on traditional items and a rise in saving and expenditures on other items, thus creating employment. He also suggested that a protective tariff, then a subject of widespread discussion owing to Lord Beaverbrook's Empire Free Trade scheme, by raising the cost of living would reduce this additional employment. Keynes replied.

To the Editor of The Times, *1 December 1930*

Sir,

In a letter which you publish today, Sir Herbert Samuel calculates that the prices of the articles on which half the national income is spent have fallen on the average by about 10 per cent since 1925. By releasing purchasing power this has the result, he says, of 'providing additional employment for at least 500,000 workpeople'. He suggests that a further fall of prices would provide still more employment, so that—presumably—when prices had fallen another 40 per cent every one would be employed. He recognises that the fall of world prices injures our foreign trade, but he thinks that the greater cheapness of home goods to home consumers provides this important offset.

He does not suggest that his result is due to an increase of efficiency. His conclusion seems to be reached by assuming (correctly) that the money incomes of those working men who are not yet out of work and of those recipients of fixed incomes from securities of which the interest is not yet in default will, being substantially unchanged, purchase more goods, and *forgetting* that the fall of prices will *reduce* the receipts, and hence the purchasing power of the other sections of the community. If it were not for foreign trade, this reduction of purchasing power would exactly offset Sir Herbert's increase. In so far as the prices of imports have fallen more than those of exports (including sea-freights), and in so far as the net interest due to us from abroad is fixed in terms of money (and is not defaulted), we obtain a real benefit. But our benefit is limited to this: and even this benefit is, as Sir Herbert agrees, largely or entirely offset by the ruin which the fall of prices has brought on agriculturists and other producers of raw materials all over the world, and the consequent destruction of the purchasing power of our best customers. In any case such net benefit, if any, would be due, not to the fall in British prices, but to the exact contrary—namely, to their having *risen* relatively to foreign prices.

What an extraordinary thing that Sir Herbert should claim advantages to employment from the excess of production costs over sale proceeds, which ensues when wages and interest charges are unchanged, but prices fall! For it is that very excess which causes business losses. Yet it is only the expectation of reasonable profit which causes offers of employment, whilst the fear of business loss causes the withdrawal of such offers.

It is shocking to read that he ventures to launch the fragile barque of free trade on the treacherous waters of such an argument. For it is not merely that there is no increase of purchasing power for the community as a whole as a result of falling prices (except such as arises from foreign prices falling more than British prices after allowing for the adverse effect on British exports). It is much worse than this. The offer of employment depends, as I have said, on the expectation of some margin of profit for the employer. A transfer from producers to consumers which is large enough to destroy this margin destroys at the same time the possibility of employment. If, instead of arguing that a fall of British prices by 10 per cent, unaccompanied by a fall of wages, increases employment by 500,000, he were to argue that such a fall increases unemployment by 1,000,000, he would be nearer the truth.

Yours, &c.,

J. M. KEYNES

Samuel replied that Keynes had misunderstood his argument and ignored his statement that the additional employment caused by the effect of falling prices on consumers' saving and expenditure was only a partial offset to the unemployment caused initially by the 'catastrophic fall in commodity prices'. Keynes carried the argument further.

To the Editor of The Times, *5 December 1930*

Sir,

Certain passages in Sir Herbert Samuel's first letter led me to suppose that he saw advantages to employment in falling prices and disadvantages in a reversal of the tendency. I am glad to learn that this is not so and that he recognises the fall of prices as 'a main cause for the existing unemployment'. But I venture to say that he will only confuse the minds of your readers if he tries to analyse the effect of any proposal on unemployment by the obscure and difficult route of studying the effect of price

472

changes on the distribution of consumers' purchasing power.

The simple truth is that nothing in the world can increase employment which does not create in the minds of manufacturers and contractors the expectation of an improved margin of profit. Let him, as the Russians say, 'screw that on his moustaches'.

Yours, &c.,

J. M. KEYNES

In December 1930, Sir Oswald Mosley, who had resigned from the Cabinet on 20 May after his proposals for government reorganisation and economic expansion were rejected, and had unsuccessfully tried to win both the Parliamentary Labour Party and the Labour Party conference over to his views, published a manifesto, signed by A. J. Cook and 17 Labour M.P.s. Keynes discussed it in *The Nation*.

From The Nation and Athenaeum, *13 December 1930*

SIR OSWALD MOSLEY'S MANIFESTO

Sir Oswald Mosley's manifesto deserves attention. There are matters in it which an academic economist is bound to criticise. The mere payment by an industry of higher wages than are paid by its foreign competitors is a very bad criterion for imposing a tariff, and quite incompatible with promises to the consumer not to raise prices against him. Indeed, the manifesto seems to me to stand insecurely between promises of advantage to the producer and of cheapness to the consumer. It would be better today to take a firm stand for the former in the first instance as the sole possible condition of increased employment, and to promise no more to the consumer than that no monopoly shall take unreasonable advantage of him or curtail his full share—he can ask no more—of the maximum output of which the country is capable.

But I like the spirit which informs the document. A scheme of national economic planning to achieve a right, or at least a better, balance of our industries between the old and the new, between agriculture and manufacture, between output for export and output for home consumption, between home development and foreign investment; and wide executive powers to carry out the details of such a scheme. That is what it amounts to. The question for us is not whether the signatories to the manifesto have thought out correctly the details of such a plan in all their particulars; but whether or not it is desirable to have a plan. If it *is* desirable, the manifesto offers us a starting point for thought and action.

For the important question today which we have to face individually and collectively is the question whether those are right who think that the course of prudence and proved wisdom is to trust to time and natural forces to lead us with an invisible hand to the economic harmonies; or those who fear that there is no design but our own, and that the invisible hand is merely our own bleeding feet moving through pain and loss to an uncertain and unprofitable destination.

Or to be more particular;—there are three possible views of policy today. The first is to trust to the operation of natural forces; to abstain from action so far as public opinion will permit, for fear lest action may interrupt the healing virtues of time; and meanwhile to grin and bear it. Such—with whatever disguises—is, under the influence of Mr Snowden, the policy of the present Government. It is difficult to maintain this position with equanimity unless supported by the hope that the waiting period will not be long—three months, perhaps, or six at the most. I see no firm foundation, in fact, for such a hope. But time will show.

The second is to hasten the operation of natural forces by accentuating what appear to be their tendencies. This means, in the main, efforts to reduce the level of money wages. For this, apparently, is what the natural forces—interrupted in this country by the social conscience, the trade unions, and the dole—seem to be trying to do all over the world. Perhaps there is more to be said for the second view than for the first.

The third is to substitute for the operation of natural forces a scheme of collective planning. The Liberal programme of the last General Election approached this problem from one angle, namely, the planning of capital development at home. Mr Lloyd George's more recent agricultural programme approaches it from another angle, namely, the planning of output as between the home and the foreign market. So, in a sense, though by a crude and dubious technique, does the protectionism of Mr Baldwin. The signatories of the Mosley manifesto, dismayed by the difficulties of carrying through anything by existing methods, seek to free us from the limitations which stand at present in the way of any drastic action, in the hope that this will allow us to employ improved techniques.

It will shock—it must do so—the many good citizens of this country, including, I expect, some readers of *The Nation*, who have *laissez-faire* in their craniums, their consciences, and their bones. These will continue to do service by criticising honestly and acidly the projects of the planners. But how anyone professing and calling himself a socialist can keep away from the manifesto is a more obscure matter.

Whether or not anything comes of it in the near future will almost entirely depend on the pressure of events—on the natural forces themselves. If the optimists are right who look for a substantial and lasting recovery of employment within six months, we shall slide back, not unhappily, into our old ways. If not, the Mosleyites will, at the least, find their planks purloined. For the choice will be ever more openly and obviously set between forcing a reduction of wages and a scheme of national planning. But, however this may be, looking further ahead I do not see what practical socialism can mean for our generation in England, unless it makes much of the manifesto its own—this peculiar British socialism, bred out of liberal humanitarianism, big-business psychology, and the tradition of public service.

There are, in truth, only three political parties today deserving of serious consideration. (1) The party of—shall we say?—Mr Lloyd George, Mr Ramsay MacDonald, Mr Bevin, and Sir Oswald Mosley. For, assuredly, if we think their temperaments back twenty years or imagine them occupying positions of 'more freedom and less responsibility', Mr Lloyd George and Mr Ramsay MacDonald would be where Mosley is. Let them not, then, look too schoolmasterlike on his ebullience. (2) The party of Sir Herbert Samuel and Mr Snowden. (3) The party of Lord Beaverbrook, the late Lord Birkenhead, and (in spite of 'humbug') Mr J. H. Thomas. It would be very convenient to be able to call these three parties the Socialist, the Liberal, and the Conservative parties;—and they would be fine parties too, corresponding to the things that matter. I would gladly entrust the fortunes of this country sometimes to one of them and sometimes to another, according to the appropriate pace and immediate direction of progress. But so long as party organisation and personal loyalties cut across the fundamental differences of opinion, the public life of this country will continue to suffer from a creeping paralysis. We should be grateful to Sir Oswald Mosley for an effort to clear the air.

On 20 and 29 December Keynes published a two part article, entitled 'The Great Slump of 1930' in *The Nation* (*JMK*, vol. IX, pp. 126–34). Well before publication, he appears to have sent a proof to the Governor of the Bank of England.

From MONTAGU NORMAN, *18 November 1930*

Personal

Dear Mr Keynes,

I do not exactly know what bold scheme you have in mind for the two or three central banks: but having talked with Sprague about the proof you kindly sent me I am glad to hear from him that you are coming here some time—perhaps lunch now and then and a talk.

Besides the slump there are a good many questions to be thought about; the B.I.S. if you please, but for the moment

I am,

Yours sincerely,

M. NORMAN

Keynes visited the Bank on 21 November. Thereafter, his contacts with senior officials at the Bank, if one is to judge from his appointments books, became more frequent than they had been in the past.

On 12 January 1931 Keynes gave the second talk in a BBC series entitled 'The Problem of Unemployment'. It appeared in *The Listener* under that title on 14 January and later under the title 'Saving and Spending' in *Essays in Persuasion* (*JMK*, vol. IX, pp. 135–41). The talk caused widespread press comment.

On 6 February he lectured at the Royal Institution under the title 'The Internal Mechanics of the Trade Slump'. Prior to the lecture he issued an abstract of his remarks.

THE INTERNAL MECHANICS OF THE TRADE SLUMP

The subject of economics is at a stage of development at which it is difficult to expound it to laymen. Not so much because of its intrinsic difficulty as because it is in a transitional stage. However, I will do my best.

I

The slump is characterised by falling prices and unemployment. These two phenomena are naturally connected. For the first means a general loss of profit for entrepreneurs as a whole, so that their willingness and ability to provide employment is diminished; just as in a boom entrepreneurs as a whole secure abnormal profits. In other words, the total receipts of producers are less than their total outgoings. This can only happen if some part of current income is being spent *neither* on current consumption *nor* on the production of durable goods.

I express this by saying that saving exceeds investment. It used to be assumed that the two were always exactly equal. This was due to one or other of two confusions. The first confusion arose out of regarding windfall losses as negative saving and windfall profits as positive saving, which is permissible as a use

477

of language but tends to obscure what is happening and leads to the paradox, that an increase in expenditure on consumption can occur with no reduction of saving. But the confusion is also partly due to the fact that saving and investment *are* equal in *equilibrium*. For saving has the effect of releasing productive resources which become unemployed. These resources are assumed to fall in price until a demand springs up to employ them in new investment. But in disequilibrium this does not occur. The resources released by saving are not absorbed in the production of new durable goods and remain unemployed.

What happens in this case to the savings? They are used up in financing the unsold stocks of the entrepreneurs or in financing their losses if they sell these stocks for what they will fetch.

II

This is the first point I seek to establish—a possible inequality of saving and investment and the emergence of loss to the entrepreneurs if the former exceeds the latter.

Let us next consider how the vicious circle of a slump is developed. We start with equilibrium, something then occurs to diminish the volume of new investment. For example, the tremendous scale of current expenditure on building and construction in the United States which characterised 1928 was for various reasons coming to an end by the middle of 1929. The result of the decline in investment is a fall in prices and a decline in profits. The decline in profits by discouraging the expansion of business causes a further decline in investment and consequently a further fall in prices. There ensues an extreme disinclination to embark on new enterprise and a loss of credit and insolvency for many entrepreneurs. Finally, perhaps, the ruin is completed by the development of a thrift campaign, on the false analogy of what is the proper behaviour of an individual in financial distress. For a thrift campaign by increasing saving widens still further the gap between saving and investment, and therefore causes a further fall in prices, increased business losses, and greater unemployment.

Meanwhile unemployment only reaches its maximum gradually. For producers are disinclined to produce output so long as their receipts exceed their prime costs, and only when they are convinced that the set-back is more than quite temporary.

Thus it is apparent what a vicious circle it is. So long as no profit is being earned there is no incentive to lend or to borrow. But until someone is able and willing to borrow for the purpose of new investment, no profit can be earned.

What will bring the slump to an end? Apart from a reduction of saving nothing can bring it to an end except an increase in investment. In course of time an increase of investment may come about from the new stimulus given by (a) the ordinary course of invention and progress; (b) from existing capital wearing out; (c) a fall in the rate of interest; (d) the deliberate development of investment schemes by government; or (e) war.

In taking active steps to end a slump, there are, however, serious limitations to what can be done by a single country which belongs to a world system. For some part of all expenditure dribbles abroad. This sets a limit to what one country can effect by itself unless other countries move in step. But once the tide turns and prices begin to rise, speculative efforts to get in at the bottom may cause the movement upwards to develop rapidly.

III

We are now in the midst of one of the most violent slumps which have ever occurred. The most parallel case is that of the 1890's after the great age of railway expansion had passed its point of greatest activity and when Great Britain was disinclined for various reasons to lend abroad, just as France and the United States are disinclined today. In that case it took six years before recovery came.

The collapse in the scale of investment in 1930 was on an

unexampled scale. Naturally there were all sorts of *reasons* for this collapse, but the main point to appreciate is that the collapse of investment was the cause of the depression. In the United States, in particular, the net investment last year may have been not much more than half what it was two years ago, which represents a reduction approaching £1,000,000,000 in amount.

This reduced expenditure by entrepreneurs was not balanced by an increased expenditure on the part of consumers. For, unluckily, each individual is impelled by his paper losses or profits to do precisely the opposite of what is desirable in the general interest; that is to say, he saves too little in the boom and too much in the slump.

At the same time, lending by creditor countries for investment in debtor countries may have been reduced, perhaps, by some £300,000,000. These figures are guesses, but the order of magnitude is probably not far wrong.

The problem of recovery is chiefly a problem of increasing the volume of investment. It is, however, at the present time unusually difficult to do this. The collapse of the credit of debtor countries makes them bad or doubtful borrowers. In the United States the great construction boom which ended in 1929 has taken the cream off the business for the time being. Until recently new inventions such as the motor car and the motor lorry and the new roads which they require, new cinema developments, and wireless instruments, have played a big part in maintaining prosperity, but there seems at the moment a lull in new inventions. At the same time the rate of interest is higher than pre-War standards; and the nervousness of investors tends to keep up these rates.

In the long run I rely on a fall in the long-term rate of interest more than on any other factor. But this may not come about in an adequate degree for a long time. In the meanwhile the foundations of capitalist society are being shaken. For these foundations are the expectation of normal profit to the individual as an incentive to enterprise and the sacredness of contract.

Countries are being divided into two groups, the debtor countries and the creditor countries. Inside each country also its citizens are divided into two groups, those whose incomes are protected by contract and those whose incomes are not so protected.

It does not facilitate a solution that the nature of the trouble should be completely misunderstood in most quarters.

(The argument of this discourse has been developed in greater detail in the author's lately published *Treatise on Money*.)

J. M. K.

When *The Manchester Guardian* misreported his remarks at the Royal Institution, Keynes wrote to the Editor.

To the Editor of The Manchester Guardian, *7 February 1931*

Sir,

In the first sentence of your brief account of my remarks at the Royal Institution on Friday night your reporter has misunderstood my meaning. He reports me as saying 'that however much money was spent on consumption, there was no diminution in saving'. This sentence was, however, part of a *reductio ad absurdum* by me of the views held by my critics, my own view being, of course, just the opposite. My point was that the above absurd conclusion would follow if the term 'savings' were used in a sense which would make true the conventional view that savings always correspond to an increment of the community's capital wealth.

Anyone who is interested in the point will find that it is dealt with in my *Treatise on Money*, vol. I [*JMK*, vol. V], chaps. 9–12.

Yours, &c.,
J. M. KEYNES

Late January also brought a request from Sir Oswald Mosley to examine a draft of a pamphlet *A National Policy*, prepared by some of his supporters, John Strachey, W. J. Brown, Aneurin Bevan and Allan Young. The document was published at the end of February 1931.

To SIR OSWALD MOSLEY, *2 February 1931*

My dear Mosley,

I find it rather difficult to criticise the enclosed. Not many specific criticisms have occurred to me, but I may mention the following small points.

1. On page 7 I do not see how it is easier for America to sell her exports at a loss because her exports are a smaller proportion of her total production. The answer would depend rather on how far marketing is monopolised.

2. Page 8. The references here to dumping seem to me to go much beyond the evidence.

3. The same remark applies in the middle of page 15. So far from the American Farm Board having dumped wheat, it has retired entirely from the market, is holding up its wheat and is selling nothing, or next to nothing, overseas.

Apart from details, on the general effect of the whole, if you ask me for a relentless criticism I should make two. The first is, that the document, particularly in its latter part, seems to me rather wordy and does not grip the reader's attention. This is also due perhaps to a certain feeling of 'old hat' which I get when I read it. It sometimes has an air [of] putting forward something new, but in fact what is being said is something which we have got tired of hearing, however sound it may be in fact.

I expect this is related to my second criticism. I feel that the document dates rather,—that it is perhaps a year old in feeling. It does not seem to me to be addressed to the immediate crisis of 1931 and so tends to fall between being a long period policy and being a fully realistic one expressly designed for the immediate facts of the moment.

As regards the form of the drastic changes in the method of

government which are required, I am rather attracted by some part of Mrs Sidney Webb's proposals.

All the above does not mean that I do not agree with a great deal of the document.

Yours sincerely,
[copy initialled] J. M. K.

Keynes's public utterances and writings brought him a letter from Hubert Henderson on 14 February. There is no record as to whether Keynes replied, but the letter is of some considerable interest as an indication of mood.

From HUBERT HENDERSON, *14 February 1931*

My dear Maynard,

You will remember that during the Economists' Committee, we left it as interesting speculation whether British Government securities would rank in a year or two as a first-class or a second-class bond. Present developments show that the latter is a very likely contingency; indeed what I've always been afraid of seems to be now blowing up—namely, that there will be sufficient repudiation talk to increase the costs of Government borrowing quite considerably, without of course doing a ha'porth of good to the Budget or anything else, and, quite possibly, the talk may reach a point which will imperil sterling and cause large-scale withdrawals of funds.

Now in that atmosphere do you really want to encourage Ll[oyd] G[eorge] to make speeches like his one the other night?[1] Because what is their practical significance in effect? The Labour Party takes him as saying, 'It's ridiculous to be worried about all these financial dangers: don't you pay any attention to what the City says. They are always warning you of the danger of doing this or that, and it's always bunkum. I didn't let myself be frightened of them, and if you've any spunk you won't either.' And the Labour Party cheer him uproariously and apply the moral not merely to development but to any sort of expenditure. They feel that Ll.G. has supplied the answer to the whole contention that the financial situation is serious, that the dole must be dealt with somehow, and that generally you really must be careful how much you spend. The main result is to weaken Snowden within the Cabinet and in the Labour Party, not upon development schemes where there is no real issue,

---

[1] On 12 February in the House of Commons, Lloyd George had unleashed a ferocious attack on the City and its views on economic policy.

but in resisting standing for a responsible approach to the whole financial position.

My complaint against the tenor of all your public writings or utterances in the last year or so is that in not a single one of them has there been a trace of a suggestion that the Budget situation is one which is really very serious and must be treated seriously. On the contrary, over and over again you have implied that it doesn't matter a bit, that expenditure is a thing you want to press on with, whether by the Government or by anybody else, and that the question of whether it involves a Budget charge is a minor matter which is hardly worth considering. The notion that this is the right emphasis just now, the thing that most needs stressing, seems to me wildly false. The effect is to convey the impression to all people, however intelligent and open-minded, who have some appreciation of the financial difficulties, that you have gone completely crazy, and impairing all the influence you have with them, while pleasing and encouraging only those who say that you mustn't lay a finger on the dole.

Of course at the root of it lies the fact that you do in your own mind regard the Budget problem not indeed as the negligible thing you seem in public to suggest, but still far too lightly. It is quite true that we have in the tariff a very substantial source of revenue still untapped. None the less, it is a limited one, sufficient to secure Snowden's next Budget but really not much more, and the rate at which expenditure is destined at existing legislation to increase over future years would startle you if you could see the figures. The notion that there is any parallel between 1909 and 1931 simply won't do. Of course silly people will always cry 'wolf' too soon: but the argument that there can't be a wolf now because there wasn't in 1909 is one I should be sorry to see you endorse. In Ll.G.'s mind, of course, there is the old complex which you came across during the War, that no financial or monetary thing ever does matter, and of course if he had his head what he would really do in the present situation wouldn't be to get any more desirable schemes going on any scale that would count, but merely to pour money down the agricultural drain. I think what really ought to happen is that you should be made Chancellor of the Exchequer in a Government where Ll.G. was Lord Privy Seal.

Yours ever,

H. D. HENDERSON

A week later Keynes gave Walter Case, a New York investment banker,[2] his view of the situation that had been behind Henderson's letter.

---

[2] For Keynes's obituary notice for Case see *JMK*, vol. X, pp. 326–7.

UNEMPLOYMENT AND PROTECTION

From a letter to WALTER CASE, *21 February 1931*

As you will have been aware there has been an extraordinary nervosity about in the London market during the last week. Indeed, much more than I ever remember to have experienced before. It has been attended, of course, by a fall in gilt-edged securities, and some people have been much upset by the fact that the forward rates for dollar and franc exchange have represented a point appreciably below gold export point, so that the rates charged represent in part a payment of a premium against the risk of the Bank of England ceasing to part with gold on the present terms.

This has been accompanied also for the first time in my experience, by a good deal of more or less open talk about devaluation of sterling and the abandonment of [the] gold standard, at any rate from the present parity. Quite a number of people have been expressing themselves as actually in favour of such a course, and the sort of people who would have said no such thing a short time ago. They are taking up the attitude that it is obviously quite hopeless to reduce wages, and with money at its present value it is quite hopeless for Gt. Britain alone to go on trying to pay 20/- in the £ at the old value. Therefore they are inclined to say we had better face up to the position without further delay. I have been surprised at the sort of people who have been disposed to take this view.

I suppose that this state of mind has been partly precipitated by Snowden's pessimistic speeches, by recent revelations as to the finances of the Unemployment Fund (though this contained nothing that was not quite well known long ago) and by Lloyd George's attack on the City—the money Barons and the Penguins. But to a large extent I diagnose it as a lot of talk which one has known to have been going on for some time past on the Continent and America having at last reached London.

On the basis of all this I fancy that quite an appreciable bear position is being built up in respect of sterling securities, though it is seldom that a bear position in London ever reaches the size

485

which you in New York would consider worth mentioning.

My own view is that all this pessimistic prognosis is complete moonshine so far as the near future is concerned. The real crisis, if there is going to be one, is much more likely to be some appreciable way off. If world prices were to settle down anywhere near their present level I should think it not at all unlikely to find our present exchange position untenable. But in that case I should expect the change to take the form of endeavouring to establish some sort of new currency embracing the whole of the Empire and possibly many other countries which would find themselves in the same boat, leaving France and the United States to amuse themselves as best they may with the existing standard.

But all this is obviously comparatively remote. I think that the bears are overlooking many resources which have not yet been brought into play. In particular, apart from slightly raising rates, the Bank of England has not as yet lifted more than a finger in defence of the situation and has all its powder dry.

The situation is, therefore, capable, in my opinion, of turning round quite suddenly. The introduction of a tariff which is a resource both for the Budget and for general business confidence which we still have up our sleeves, a change of Government, or a thousand and one other factors which one cannot foresee at the moment may quite suddenly reverse sentiment when it will be discovered that the market is completely bare of stock.

I suppose it is true that one ought not to feel absolute confidence as to the impossibility of a really serious crisis in the next three or four months, but I consider this most unlikely.

In view of the strong undercurrents which do not appear in newspapers, I have thought you might perhaps like to have this appreciation of the situation. I may add that it is not by any means off the map for the present Labour Government to have recourse to a revenue tariff.

By early March, however, he was more optimistic.

From a letter to WALTER CASE, *9 March 1931*

The minor crisis of confidence about which I wrote to you a week or two ago has almost completely blown over for reasons perhaps no more solid than those which brought it on. British Government securities which had fallen 5 points have now regained nearly 4 points. This corresponds to an equally marked change in sentiment. This is partly based on increased hopes of a tariff, partly to satisfaction over the truce in India and the Naval Agreement with Italy, partly to feeling that financial relations with France are distinctly easier, and partly to mere reaction from a previous state of mind which was not very well founded and was anyhow seriously overdone. As you know, my own views are that in conceivable circumstances there are considerable troubles ahead of this country. But if they arise in any dangerous manner it will not be in the near future but at some date after various efforts have been made and experiments have been tried which are still in reserve.

In his letter to Case, Keynes had spoken of 'increased hopes of a tariff'. These hopes may have had some connection with his own activities, for his private advocacy of the previous year was becoming public. Its first appearance came in a foreword to a pamphlet by Rupert Trouton, *Unemployment: Its Causes and their Remedies*, which appeared in the Hogarth Press's series of 'Day to Day Pamphlets'. His foreword ran as follows.

From Unemployment: Its Causes and their Remedies *(1931)*

FOREWORD

Mr Trouton has here set forth something approaching a complete collection of the chief categories of remedy for unemployment. Anyone who really wants or hopes to cure the malady must make a selection from Mr Trouton's Pharmacopoeia.

I must not be taken to agree with all his arguments or all his proposals. But broadly speaking I think that he is right. He delineates correctly the *general character* of what can be usefully done. And even if he has sometimes passed rather lightly over practical and human difficulties which stand in the way of carrying his schemes into operation, he is nevertheless doing a service by emphasising without too much qualification that these schemes, if we would and could accept them, would do the trick.

I commend particularly to the reader's attention Mr Trouton's proposal for a duty on all imports combined with a rebate or bounty on all exports. An unprejudiced person—if there is one—will find increasing attractions in this idea the more he thinks about it.

It is also important to notice how well a scheme for capital development at home would marry with a scheme for import duties. For the bad effects of the former on business confidence and on the foreign exchanges would be offset by the good effects of the latter; whilst both would increase employment. But it is, unfortunately, a marriage which neither of the mothers-in-law elect will permit; whilst the Countess Gruffanuff at No. 11 will have neither—indeed nothing.

At the end of 1930, following several years of losses, Keynes proposed to his fellow directors of *The Nation and Athenaeum* that that journal come to an arrangement with *The New Statesman* whereby the two weeklies would form a new concern to publish *The New Statesman and Nation*. The directors approved and negotiations proceeded successfully in the course of January 1931. The first issue of the merged paper appeared on 28 February under the editorship of Kingsley Martin.[3]

On 1 March Keynes sent Martin his first contribution to the new weekly. Entitled 'Proposals for a Revenue Tariff' (*JMK*, vol. IX, pp. 231–42), it brought out into the clear light of day suggestions Keynes had been adumbrating in more restricted circles over the previous year or so. Prior to publication on 7 March, Keynes sent proofs of the article to prominent politicians such as the Prime Minister and the Chancellor of the Exchequer. Their replies, or in the Chancellor's case his wife's, are of interest.

---

[3] For the rest of his life Keynes kept up a lively correspondence with Martin on the newspaper's editorial policy and attitudes. The correspondence appears in *JMK*, vol. XXVIII.

From J. RAMSAY MACDONALD, *9 March 1931*

Private

My dear Keynes,

Thank you so much for your letter with the enclosed article. The position is getting a very critical one and the illness of the Chancellor has enormously increased my difficulties. It will be a fortnight or three weeks before I can see him to exchange views on the Budget.

Yours very sincerely,

J. RAMSAY MACDONALD

From ETHEL SNOWDEN, *7 March 1931*

Private

Dear Mr Keynes,

I grieve to have to return your article unread by my husband, but he is really too ill to give his mind to anything. I am not immediately anxious, though I realise that great care must be continuously exercised, and doctors and nurse are keeping a watchful eye on him. A specialist is expected to report tomorrow.

I have read your article, and will tell him the contents when he is able to listen. I dare say he will feel as sad as I do that you should think it necessary to take this line, for we are as strongly convinced that it is wrong (taking a long view) as you are that it is right.

Sincerely yours,

ETHEL SNOWDEN

As Keynes expected, the article created a sensation. Keynes, at the request of the editor of *The Daily Mail*, moved to increase its impact with a more popular version.[4]

From The Daily Mail, *13 March 1931*

PUT THE BUDGET ON A SOUND BASIS:
A PLEA TO LIFELONG FREE TRADERS

I have been asked to develop a proposal for a revenue tariff which I put forward last week in an article contributed to *The New Statesman and Nation*. I do so from the point of view of one who believes that tariffs are dangerous. If we were in our usual

---

[4] The paragraphing here follows Keynes's transcript rather than the *Daily Mail's*.

economic equilibrium with the rest of the world, I should be opposed to such an expedient. But the world slump and a fall of wholesale prices of a quite unprecedented severity, coming on the top of other difficulties, have created a position of great anxiety, when one must be ready to consider extraordinary remedies. Unqualified free trade is part of an austere philosophy which depends, and indeed insists, on things being allowed to find their own levels without interference. But if economic changes are very violent and very rapid, human nature makes it impossible for some things to find their proper levels quick enough. In particular, we all know that it is not practical politics (whether we like it or not) to bring down wages generally— though some money wages ought to come down somewhat and probably will—to an extent corresponding to the fall in prices. When a free trader argues that a tariff cannot increase employment but can only divert employment from one industry to another, he is tacitly assuming that a man who loses his employment in one direction will lower the wage rate which he is willing to accept until he finds employment in another direction. When small changes only are in question, there may be much long-run truth in this. But in present circumstances it is sheer nonsense.

Nevertheless, even so, I should be afraid of the long-run effects of introducing the whole apparatus of discriminating protection. It would be much wiser to keep to a measure of a general all-round character, dictated by the requirements of the present emergency, and to employ other measures for the assistance of particular industries which make out a case for special assistance. That is why I propose a general revenue tariff, though a somewhat stiff one—namely, 15 per cent on all manufactured and semi-manufactured goods and 5 per cent on foodstuffs and some raw materials.

No taxes are good in themselves. But a tax of this kind at least has the advantage that it brings down several desirable birds with one stone. What are the troubles in our way? There is a lack of confidence—that subtle, intangible, priceless quiddity—at home and abroad. There is a pressure on our foreign exchanges, a tendency for what we lend abroad to exceed the surplus that we have to lend, which makes us nervous and uncomfortable. There is a lack of profit for home producers. And because of this lack of profit men are unemployed who are capable of producing goods which we are now importing. Above all, we have an unbalanced Budget. Yet we need not only to balance the Budget by means which will not upset business confidence or put new burdens on industry, but to provide ourselves with a financial margin under cover of which we can make progressive, constructive plans for more far-reaching remedies to improve the demand for our products. Then we should reduce business losses and un-employment without serious detriment to our standards of life.

Observe how appropriate a revenue tariff is to all these objects. Assuredly there is no other tax which, so far from diminishing confidence, will actually increase it. At the same time a tariff of 15 per cent on all manufactured and partly manufactured goods will keep out some goods which we now import and cause home-produced goods to be substituted for them. In so far as this happens, the pressure on our exchanges will be relieved, while profits and employment will be increased in the industries which are thus enabled to supply the home market. And finally, from the revenue levied on the goods which would still be imported—some part of which might, in the exceptional conditions of today, be paid in effect by the foreign exporter—we could put the Budget on a thoroughly sound basis. I regard a revenue tariff as a high card in hand which we have not yet played. What other country in the world is there which could face the burdens of our national debt and of our social services—or even the half of them—without such assistance? Direct taxes have reached their limit so long as profits remain below normal. Some additional indirect taxes we must have.

Can the weight of these arguments be denied? I beg lifelong

free traders to think twice before they reject these counsels of expediency called forth by an exceptional emergency. The ideal of the free play of natural forces simply cannot be pursued to-day—the contrary forces are too strong. Yet to leave some forces free when other forces cannot be free may become unwise. I do not deny the likelihood of some increase in the cost of living. But I should expect it to be small compared with the downward changes of recent months. Prices are now artificially low and almost any remedy will have to raise them. A purely negative policy may mean a slow sapping of our national strength, an inevitable reduction of our standards of life attended by strikes and social unrest, and a fatal loss of our financial prestige in the eyes of the world.

Liberals and Socialists are coming to appreciate this. For this reason many members of both parties sympathise with what I am here saying. It is to those who are still hesitating that I was primarily addressing myself in my *Statesman and Nation* article.

On the other hand the wealth and financial strength and productive capacity of this country are enormous, if we can pull ourselves together, cast fear aside, bring into employment our wasted resources, and re-assume that financial leadership of the world which is properly ours. For this we need a breathing space. I see no other way of getting one.

Comments on Keynes's revenue tariff proposals led to further contributions to the press by Keynes. The most extensive of these came in *The New Statesman and Nation* where the controversy generated by the original article rumbled on until mid-April.

The week after Keynes's original article, *The New Statesman* published a reply by Lionel Robbins and critical letters from, among others, Sir William Beveridge, G. W. Daniels, T. E. Gregory, Arnold Plant and G. L. Schwartz. The next week, amidst further critical letters from E. D. Simon, Ramsay Muir and E. F. M. Durbin, Keynes made his first comment.

UNEMPLOYMENT AND PROTECTION

To the Editor of The New Statesman and Nation, *16 March 1931*

Sir,

I shall hardly know where to end in commenting on the contributions to last week's *New Statesman and Nation* concerning my proposals for a revenue tariff. But I must begin by admitting a fault. I have no doubt that my critics are right in arguing that in practice the yield from a tariff at the levels I suggested would be less, rather than more, than £50,000,000. Mr G. L. Schwartz's useful letter last week provides the necessary data for an estimate, though he may have let his imagination run away with him towards the end. The most difficult thing to estimate in advance is the amount of goods now imported which would be kept out by a 15 per cent tariff. Mr Schwartz, I gather, thinks that nearly £70,000,000 of goods would be kept out. *The Economist*, which is not likely to over-estimate the advantages of a tariff, thinks that the effect in restricting imports would be 'considerable'. I hope that these optimistic forecasts are correct. For the saving on the dole and the gains from income tax, etc., resulting from the substitution of home-produced goods for goods now imported, will much outweigh the loss of tariff revenue. The Budget will gain more from the results of keeping goods out, than it would have gained from the tariff on them if they were still coming in. Mr Schwartz allows nothing, moreover, for the substitution of one kind of import for another, as the result of more employment and activity at home. If the unemployed are set to work making £70,000,000 of goods now imported, the indirect result of this will certainly be to increase the imports of food and raw materials. But, taking one thing with another, I am prepared to accept Professor Robbins' upper limit of £40,000,000 as a safer and more cautious estimate than my own.

It has been interesting to see what a large proportion of the limited space at their disposal my free trade critics (whether in *The New Statesman and Nation*, *The Economist* or elsewhere) have devoted to the question whether I had exaggerated the probable yield of the tariff and whether it might not prove more effective than I had claimed in increasing employment by substituting home-produced goods for imports. There could be no better indication of how little steam there is in the opposition. Not a single critic has denied that we need to increase business confidence, to relieve the balance of trade, to raise revenue, and to stimulate employment; and not one has denied that my proposal would have a tendency to do all these things. Yet surely the truth of these suggestions is of much greater importance to the nation in making up its mind, than whether the revenue raised would be £40,000,000 or £50,000,000. *The Economist* agrees that indirect taxation must be increased, but demands that it be placed 'on commodities which we are fairly certain will continue to come into the country', so that the effect on confidence, the balance of trade and employment will be as small as possible. This immediately follows, moreover, on a criticism of my proposal on the ground that it will raise the cost of living. That is to say—apparently—taxes concentrated on beer, tobacco and petrol will *not* raise the cost of living. I notice that Mr A. V. Alexander has criticised a revenue tariff as being a back-door attack on the standard of living, a criticism which is often made. This is, I think, a dangerous and misleading argument to use. For example, it would apply equally well to a policy designed to raise the international price level, which almost every one agrees would be highly desirable. In the second place, it is a question of a *choice* between alternatives, none of which are attractive in themselves. In calculating the effect on the standard of living, should not Mr Alexander allow for the effect on employment and compare the results of the *alternatives* which are open to us? I should not expect my own proposal to raise the cost of living by so much as 2 per cent, whilst a tariff limited to manufactured and semi-manufactured goods would probably be less open to Mr Alexander's criticism than any other practicable indirect tax. Perhaps, therefore, his criticism was limited to my proposed tax on food.

I am more nearly touched by Professor Robbins' contention that a tariff, once put on, will never be taken off when the special circumstances which called for it have passed away. I know that there is a risk that this may be so. But it is a risk which circumstances demand that we should take. Nor do I rate the risk so high as he does. Several critics have asked me point blank whether there is any known case of a protective duty being taken off. That is easily answered. All the chief protective measures of my time in this country—the Hicks–Beach duty on wheat, the McKenna Duties and the Safeguarding Duties—have been repealed, though one of them was subsequently reimposed. It depends above everything on what happens to the price level. A tariff is the natural reaction, and in my judgement a sensible reaction, to an external price level which is falling at a rate to which internal costs and incomes cannot adjust themselves. I believe that Joseph Chamberlain's campaign was engendered in the falling price level of the 'nineties and was entombed in the rising price level of the nineteen-hundreds. When prices are falling, we all welcome a measure which will hold some of them up; and when they are rising we all welcome what will cause a reduction. A return to the price level of two or three years ago will make a world of difference to the national sentiment. If prices rise to their former level, and if unqualified free trade turns out to be as much in the interests of this country in the conditions of the twentieth century as it certainly was in the conditions of the nineteenth century, then I believe that the tariff will be taken off again. But if I look into the bottom of my own heart, the feeling which I find there is, rather, that a tariff is a crude departure from *laisser-faire*, which we have to adopt because we have at present no better weapon in our hands, but that it will be superseded in time, not by a return to *laisser-faire*, but by some more comprehensive scheme of national planning.

Sir William Beveridge, in his cautious comments, points out quite truly that my article of March 7th fell into two parts, and that the second, which proposed a revenue tariff, was exceedingly compressed. I cannot, I am afraid, in the compass of a letter express all the economic arguments, which are at the back of my head, in the degree of detail which Sir William Beveridge would properly require from me before he makes up his mind. But I do not agree with him that the connection was small between the two parts of my article. In my own mind the connection was very close indeed. My article was addressed primarily to those who have accepted the desirability of what I called an 'expansionist' policy, that is to say, to the members of the Liberal and Labour Parties, both of which have accepted this programme—the programme which was well summarised in the four-fold objects of policy set forth in the leading article of last week's *New Statesman and Nation*. My point was that there are strong, perhaps overwhelming arguments, against the feasibility of such a programme unless we secure for ourselves the breathing space which the revenue tariff would give. None of my critics have tackled this issue. Indeed some of them have no need to, inasmuch as they are 'contractionists', in my sense of this term. For example, *The Economist*, in an article which follows that from which I have quoted, calls for 'an all round 10–15 per cent cut in every sheltered wage', and laments how far short of this the recent railway wage settlement has fallen. If such 'half-hearted compromise', *The Economist* continues, is repeated elsewhere, 'the restoration of equilibrium and the revival of British prosperity will be tardy'. I should also include Professor Robbins in this category. For he wants what he euphemistically calls 'increased elasticity of local wage costs' and a 'readjustment of wages and removal of hindrances to efficiency' which means in plain English, I suppose, a reduction of average wages (or does he mean a greater readiness of some wages to rise?) and the abolition of trade union restrictions. So, in individual cases, do I, but not on a scale which I should expect to solve our problem. Now free trade, combined with great mobility of wage rates, is a tenable intellectual position—though it presents a problem of justice so long as many types of money income are protected by contract and cannot be mobile. The practical reason against it, which must suffice for the moment, whether we like it or not, is that it is not one of the alternatives between which we are in a position to choose. We are not offered it. It does not exist outside the field of pure hypothesis. The actual alternative is the policy of Negation. The question which I should like to put to those of the readers of *The New Statesman and Nation*, who believe a large reduction of money wages to be impracticable or undesirable and accept in a general way the 'expansionist' policy of the Liberal and Labour Parties, [is] whether they consider that it would be safe, or indeed possible, to proceed with such a policy without the support of a revenue tariff.

Professor Robbins taunts me in conclusion with abandoning 'the service of high and worthy ideals in international relations' for 'the service of the mean and petty devices of economic nationalism'. I know that he sincerely feels this, and that for him, as for many others, free trade stands as a banner and as a symbol of fundamental reason and decency between nations. Free trade unbesmirched invokes old loyalties, and recalls one of the greatest triumphs of reason in politics which adorns our history. It is a poor retort, perhaps, to this, to say that one must not let one's sense of the past grow stronger than one's sense of the present and of the future, or sacrifice the substance to the symbol. But I can at least say that my practical aims are to avoid a disastrous process of competitive international wage cutting, and the social strife which this would bring; to enable this country to resume the financial leadership of the world which we alone are capable of using in the general interest; and to prevent a domestic political reaction which might delay progress towards international peace and interrupt our policy in India.

Yours, etc.,

J. M. KEYNES

After reading the correspondence columns of *The New Statesman* for 21 March, Keynes proposed to Kingsley Martin that, rather than reply to individual letters, he write a series of short articles on specific points, often raised by more than one contributor. He asked Martin to reply by Monday morning, as that was the only day he had time for writing the first piece. It and two successors appeared in the course of the next three weeks.

From The New Statesman and Nation, *28 March, 4 and 11 April 1931*

ECONOMIC NOTES ON FREE TRADE

I. *The export industries*

The correspondence columns of *The New Statesman and Nation* indicate a tremendous reawakened interest in the question of tariffs. The comments on my article proposing a revenue tariff have opened up such a wide range of problems that I cannot deal with them all at once. But I will do my best to give my frank opinion about the more important in some separate notes. I must not be accused of being a spoil-sport if I admit that there is much to be said on both sides. I have reached my own conclusions as the result of continuous reflection over many months, without enthusiasm, and as the result of the gradual elimination of the practicable alternatives as being even more undesirable. Nor do I suppose for one moment that a revenue tariff by itself will see us out of our troubles. Indeed, I mainly support it because it will give us a margin of resources and a breathing space, under cover of which we can do other things.

I begin this week with one of the weakest points of a tariff—its effect on the export industries. Mr E. D. Simon called attention in last week's *New Statesman and Nation* to the great decline in our exports, and asked me whether I had forgotten these trades and what a tariff would do for them. I think that the answer is clearly that which he himself suggests, namely, that a general tariff cannot be expected to give any direct benefit to our exports and will probably tend to increase manufacturing costs rather than otherwise, though I should expect this increase to be small and almost negligible compared with the other factors of cost. I find, however, a balance of advantage in the fact that industries which compete with imports would be benefited altogether out of proportion to the effect on export industries, and that the international influence of this country would be increased for promoting other measures which might help the export industries. I would put it like this. I believe that it would be of great advantage to the international equilibrium of this country if we could increase our favourable balance of trade by, say, £50,000,000; and that it will be much easier to do this by checking imports to this amount than by increasing exports.

For how are we to increase our exports? Mr Simon tells us that he would have to reduce his wages by 20 per cent in order to be on level terms with Germany, and I have no doubt that he is right. Has he any prospect of doing this? If he could, does he feel sure that Germany would not reply with a further reduction of her wages, seeing that we have bound her by treaty under dire penalties to compete successfully with ourselves and (in effect), however much we reduce our wages, to reduce hers by more? Does he expect that the free trade Budget, outlined in this week's *Economist*, including taxes on beer, tobacco, tea and sugar, and 3d. per week extra insurance contributions, will predispose his workpeople to accept in addition a cut of 20 per cent in their wages?

I do not see much positive hope for our exports along these lines. Indeed, I doubt if there is anything material which we can do for them directly, unless it be by subsidies, in the present state of world trade. A revival of world trade is their only hope. It will come in time. When it comes, we shall have a true measure of the magnitude of the permanent problem confronting us, if we are to maintain a sufficient volume of exports. Meanwhile, the best we can do is to strengthen the financial position and prestige of London, so as to restore to us our full weight of influence in propounding plans for international co-operation. This brings

499

me back to the revenue tariff, which would, in my belief, contribute to this end.

If I knew of a concrete, practicable proposal for stimulating our export trades, I should welcome it. Knowing none, I fall back on a restriction of imports to support our balance of trade and to provide employment. Moreover, even if we were to agree that we cannot recover a sufficient volume of exports without a large cut in wages, what exactly one is to do about it I do not know. I wish that someone, who relies on this alternative, would tell me.

II. *A revenue tariff and the cost of living*

Free traders have been long accustomed to use as an argument against a tariff its effect on the cost of living. In ordinary times there is no purpose, quite the contrary, in raising prices. But before making this objection in present circumstances, we must be quite sure that it is properly applicable today and is not just parrot talk from the past.

It is generally admitted that the root of our present troubles is to be found in the disparity between costs and prices, with the result that output cannot be sold, or men employed, at a profit. Does any sensible person believe that there can be a remedy which does not either diminish costs or raise prices? If so, it is not in itself an objection to a proposal that it does the one or the other. If our desire is to further the interests of the working class, we must compare the consequences of one kind of remedy with the consequences of another.

When *The Economist* complains against a revenue tariff that it will increase the cost of living of the working classes, I know that these are crocodile's tears. For in the same breath they propose alternative means of raising the same amount of revenue by taxes on beer, tobacco, sugar and tea, and demand a reduction of 10 to 15 per cent in the level of wages. Several, however, of the correspondents to *The New Statesman and Nation* have not provided in their letters sufficient evidence to permit of a diagnosis. For example, would Mr Ramsay Muir deplore a rise in world prices? Is he opposed to all indirect taxes on articles of working-class consumption? Is he hostile to every reduction of wages, such as the railwaymen have just suffered? If not, it is a question, not of discussing a particular proposal in isolation, but of making comparisons.

Obviously a rise in world prices or a reduction of British wages would, if we could get them, be much better than a tariff for our export industries. But this belongs to a different branch of the argument and must be treated as such. If we are to take as our test the effect on working-class standards, my proposal of a revenue tariff comes out very favourably, I maintain, as compared with the alternatives. Its exact effect greatly depends, of course, upon whether or not it includes taxes on imported food. My proposal, which included such taxes, would be most unlikely, in my estimation, to raise the cost of living by so much as 2 per cent, and if food taxes were left out and the tariff were to apply only to manufactured and semi-manufactured goods, it would be unlikely to raise it by so much as 1 per cent. I consider these effects to be no greater than those of other indirect taxes and negligible compared with wage reductions. In former controversies the comparison was between a tariff and an increase of direct taxation, whilst wage reductions were not in question. Today it is different. If the other advantages which I claim for a revenue tariff—its favourable effects on employment, on business confidence, on the balance of trade and on the Budget—are well founded, then its reaction on working-class standards, so far from being objectionable, can be claimed as a further advantage, because it is so small compared with those of the alternatives.

I appeal for a reconsideration of the whole matter with a fresh head, and a clear one. It is easy to go on repeating what one has been accustomed to repeat, unaccompanied by any new process of cerebration. Yet the conditions of the problem are so different from what they used to be that one has—at least, so I have found—to think it out all over again with a new apparatus of thought. For never before have we had to consider what it is best to do in face of an enduring and a large-scale disequilibrium. We have generally been concerned, not with the problem of how to get out of a very tight place, but with what will be the best long-run policy *assuming conditions of equilibrium*. May I also register a mild complaint against the undercurrent of moral reprobation which I detect in some quarters? I seem to see the elder parrots sitting round and saying: 'You can *rely* upon us. Every day for thirty years, regardless of the weather, we have said "What a lovely morning!" But this is a bad bird. He says one thing one day, and something else the next.'

III. *The reaction of imports on exports*

The course of the present controversy seems to indicate that a large proportion of free traders hold their faith, not as the outcome of a nice balancing of advantages against disadvantages, but believing it to be an obvious inference from a simple truth. If you keep out an import, then 'since imports and exports pay for one another' it follows mathematically—so it is believed—that you will lose an export after an interval of time so short as not to matter. This doctrine has even been supported by high authority. It has appeared, in one form or another, in several communications to *The New Statesman and Nation*; Professor Robbins, though he would not, I imagine, go the whole hog, has lent colour to it in an article published in *Economica* (February, 1931, pp. 54, 55) where, under the designation of 'the *pons asinorum* of international trade theory' he employs an argument against a tariff as a means of increasing employment which would apply equally against a reduction of wages or an increase of efficiency; and Sir William Beveridge, in *The Times* newspaper,[5] has produced the doctrine in its full purity, asserting that

[5] See below, p. 511.

it makes no difference to employment in this country whether I buy an American car or a British car, or whether our costs of manufacturing iron and steel are reduced to a competitive basis with foreign costs. No, not quite in its full purity! For Sir William's credulity falters at a critical point; whilst he believes that a reduction in our imports would cause a reduction in our exports, he does *not* believe that an increase in our imports would cause an increase in our exports.

Now, if all this were true—if a reduction of imports causes almost at once a more or less equal reduction of exports—obviously a tariff (and many other things) would be completely futile for the purposes of augmenting employment or of increasing the balance of trade in our favour. But, of course, it is not true! To believe it is to fly in the face of common sense and of experience, and cannot be supported by argument. It would only be true in a hypothetical economic system possessing such an inherent capacity for stable equilibrium, that not only were both the initial and the final positions in equilibrium, but the elasticity of the system was such that any disturbance was responded to so immediately that the system was incapable of ever departing appreciably from equilibrium. At any rate, I am sure that the assumptions required for the conclusion are far remote from contemporary facts; and in the proof along these lines, that a tariff cannot diminish unemployment, one of the inappropriate assumptions which has tacitly slipped in is, I suggest, that there is no unemployment to diminish! Nor does it help to make the qualification that exports, though not necessarily diminished at once, will be diminished sooner or later. The ultimate effect of keeping out particular imports may be, sooner or later, to increase other imports.

On the contrary, whilst the position of every element in the economic system is, in a sense, dependent on that of every other, there is not, according to my view of the subject, any direct and simple relationship between the volume of exports and the volume of imports. A change in imports, due to the interposition of a new factor such as a tariff, sets up a series of complex reactions on the economic body, which are likely, indeed, before they have completely worked themselves out, to have *some* effect on almost every factor in the situation. But the nature of this effect depends profoundly (amongst other things) *upon whether the initial position was one of equilibrium*. Let me indicate briefly, by an example, the sort of considerations of which one has to take account. If our imports are reduced by a tariff or in some other way, in the first instance the Bank of England has a choice between importing more gold or lowering the Bank rate. In so far as it imports more gold, the countries losing the gold may or may not contract their domestic credit. In so far as it lowers its Bank rate, this may be expected to cause us immediately to lend more abroad (or to borrow less) and to expand credit at home. The expansion of credit at home may be expected to cause us both to import more and to increase our own output. How far an increase in our output will involve an increase in the price of this output, will depend upon whether we have a surplus capacity for production and upon how far this surplus capacity can be brought into use at approximately the same money rate of remuneration per unit of efficiency as the productive plant and labour already in use. In so far, however, as the surplus capacity can only be brought into employment at the expense of an increased cost per unit, this will apply equally to many other remedies for unemployment, and will not be a peculiarity of the case, where the initial impulse comes from a tariff. What the net effect of all this will be on the value of our exports, as compared with the effect of alternative remedies for unemployment, cannot be answered merely on *a priori* considerations, but must be determined by applying a sound theoretical apparatus to a knowledge of many current facts, and an estimation by the practical judgement of the probabilities suggested by this application. I can imagine cases where the final result would be actually to *increase* our exports and other cases where I should expect exports to be decreased. In any case, it could only be by an improbable and extraordinary coincidence that the net effect on the value of our exports would be *equal* to the change in the value of our imports. In the present instance, I believe that there is an opportunity for a tariff to produce a net favourable effect on employment; firstly, because the Bank of England is having to exert pressure by maintaining a rate of discount artificially, indeed unprecedentedly, high relatively to the rates in France and the United States, and has been more or less in this position for a considerable time past, in order to prevent us from lending too much abroad, so that a relaxation of the pressure on the foreign exchanges might be expected to increase forthwith our foreign lending; and secondly, because we have a large surplus capacity of men and plant, so that a substantial increase of output for use at home might be possible without the reaction on the price of our exports which might be expected if we had no surplus capacity.

Perhaps controversy with one's friends and colleagues is an essentially barren thing. But I come to the end of my attempt to deal with the controversy which I have provoked in the pages of *The New Statesman and Nation* with an unusually arid flavour in my mouth. There is a great deal to be said on both sides about this tariff question. It is a difficult decision. But in this discussion we have not been reaching more than the fringe of what are for me the real problems. As Professor Bellerby pointed out in his letter last week, my critics have not taken any notice of, or shown the slightest interest in, the analysis of our present state, which occupied most of my original article and led up to my tariff proposal in the last paragraph. Is it the fault of the *odium theologicum* attaching to free trade? Is it that economics is a queer subject or in a queer state? Whatever may be the reason, new paths of thought have no appeal to the fundamentalists of free trade. They have been forcing me to chew over again a lot of stale mutton, dragging me along a route I have known all about as long as I have known anything, which cannot, as I have discovered by many attempts, lead one to a solution of our present difficulties—a peregrination of the catacombs with a guttering candle.

Discussion of Keynes's proposals was not, of course, confined to the *New Statesman*. Nor were Keynes's replies to critics. On 20 March, *The Times* published a letter from Cyril Asquith suggesting that Keynes had seriously over estimated the possible yield from his proposals. Asquith also asked why, if the proposals were for revenue purposes, Keynes did not propose countervailing excise duties on domestic output, for without these Keynes's revenue tariff was higher than Joseph Chamberlain's protective tariff proposals of 1903–5. Keynes replied the same day.

To the Editor of The Times, *20 March 1931*

Sir,

You publish today a letter from Mr Cyril Asquith criticising my estimate of the possible yield from a revenue tariff. It happens that I have dealt with this point at some length in to-day's issue of *The New Statesman and Nation* [above p. 493]. But I will, if I may, say a word in direct response to Mr Asquith.

In the article on which he comments I proposed a revenue tariff which aimed at 'a substantial revenue, not less than £50,000,000, and, if possible, £75,000,000', I then went on to give, 'for example', the sort of tariff I had in mind. I did not attempt any close estimate of the yield. Indeed, it is difficult to do so. For one cannot easily predict what goods will be kept out or what quantities of other imports will be substituted as a result of the increased activity and employment in making goods to replace the imports kept out. But in this week's *New Statesman and Nation* I have admitted a fault in not being more exact, and am prepared to agree, if only for the sake of getting on with more fundamental aspects of the matter, that, after allowing for various deductions which might have to be made in practice from the *prima facie* gross yield, £40,000,000 would be a more cautious estimate. With that admission, may I assume that Mr Asquith is satisfied?

But Mr Asquith is, I am afraid, thinking me a better free trader than I am in existing conditions when he assumes that revenue is my only object, and asks why I have not mentioned countervailing excise duties. I believe that the greater the quantity of goods kept out by a moderate general tariff the greater from one source or another will be the benefit to the Budget. For it is my opinion that if, for example, such a tariff were to cause £50,000,000 home-produced goods to be substituted for £50,000,000 imports, this would mean in present circumstances an appreciable reduction of unemployment. The most important question for free traders to consider is the truth of this assertion. For this, together with the favourable effect on business confidence and on the balance of trade, is my reason for preferring this particular type of indirect tax to a policy of balancing the Budget by increased taxes on, say, beer, tobacco, and petrol.

In ordinary circumstances, when abnormal unemployment is expected to be quite temporary, it is impossible to justify a tariff by reference to its effect on employment. For when the productive resources of the country are likely to be almost fully employed in most directions, a tariff means a diversion of output, not a net increase. I have often argued the free trade case on these lines, and would do so again in the appropriate circumstances. But at present the necessary conditions are not fulfilled. The unemployment of men and plant is so large and so widespread, has lasted so long, and looks like lasting so much longer, that I should expect a tariff to increase employment now, and for some time to come; while the advantages to business confidence, the balance of trade, and the Budget are too obvious to need emphasis. Uncompromising free traders are entitled to claim that they are taking a long view but they are on weak ground when they deny the immediate advantages of a tariff. My own view of our position is so pessimistic that I am afraid to forgo advantages at a time when we greatly need a breathing space. I believe that opponents of a tariff are rash in relying on a large reduction of money wages, or in expecting this to happen by mere force of circumstances if only they stand pat. Nor am I sufficiently confident that the more distant future will repeat the *laissez-faire* economic organisation of the nineteenth century, to be ready to stake much on it.

Yours, &c.,

J. M. KEYNES

Keynes's reply to Asquith brought a letter to *The Times* on 25 March from Sir William Beveridge who suggested that a reduction of imports caused by a tariff would lead to a reduction in British exports; so that the net result would be a shift in activity from export industries to import substitution. Keynes replied.

To the Editor of The Times, *26 March 1931*

Sir,

Sir William Beveridge believes—subject to two exceptions which he mentions only to dismiss them as not applicable to present circumstances—that a restriction of our imports will lead at once to a more or less corresponding reduction of our exports, because it will mean 'a reduction of the power of foreigners to buy in Britain'. It will help me to clear up what appears to be a deep-seated difference of opinion if I may be allowed to ask him some questions.

(1) Does he believe that it makes no difference to the amount of employment in this country if I decide to buy a British car instead of an American car? For it seems, clearly, to follow from his argument that the reduction last year in the imports of foreign cars must have injured our export industries to the same extent that it benefited our motor car industry. I say that our difference of opinion must be profound, for to me such a conclusion seems quite silly.

(2) Does he believe that an *increase* in our imports would at once increase our exports also, by providing 'an increase of the power of foreigners to buy in Britain'? For example, I have always thought that it was a difficulty in the way of home development schemes that they might lead to increased imports of raw materials and also of food to meet the increased consumption of the newly employed, since this, by weakening

our trade balance, might lead to a loss of gold. But according to Sir W. Beveridge this would, apparently, be an extra advantage in favour of such schemes, because, by increasing our imports, they would increase our exports and hence augment employment in the export industries as well as in the home construction industries. Is this right? And if not, why not?

(3) Suppose that our imports were to fall off as the result of a lowering of our own costs of production in the iron and steel industry so that our own producers could compete more successfully with Continental producers. Does Sir W. Beveridge hold that this would do nothing for employment, because 'by reducing the power of foreigners to buy in Britain' it would increase unemployment in the export industries by an amount equal to the improvement in the iron and steel industry? I see nothing in Sir W. Beveridge's argument which would not apply just as forcibly to a reduction of our imports caused by a diminution in our own costs as to a reduction caused by a tariff. Moreover, even if it did not have this effect, we should be just as much in the soup according to Sir William. For, in the event of our balance of trade becoming more favourable, he holds it 'unproved that an increase of lending abroad could take place without harmful contraction of lending at home'.

When I know Sir William's answers to these questions I can, if necessary, pursue the matter further. With some of my free trade friends my differences of opinion are due, not to a different logical analysis, but to a different judgement of the balance of advantage and disadvantage, having regard to the probable reactions of a tariff on the future policy of Parliament and politicians. But Sir William's defence of free trade is, I submit, the result of pure intellectual error, due to a complete misunderstanding of the theory of equilibrium in international trade—an error which it is worth while to extirpate if one can, because it is shared, I fancy, by a multitude of less eminent free traders.

Yours, &c.,

J. M. KEYNES

The Times of 30 March contained Beveridge's attempts to answer Keynes's three questions. In his letter Beveridge then continued:

Mr Keynes has made no attempt to answer my letter or to explain his own position. He has tried instead to entangle me in rather elementary dialectical difficulties, of the kind put to first-year students of economics, in order to teach them the differences between barter and money economy, and between static and dynamic equilibrium. He must not mind if I recall to him an equally elementary consideration which is indicated in my last answer and is fundamental to the issue, but is tending to drop out in his present approach to it. The test of economic progress is not the maximising of employment, but the maximising of wealth in relation to effort; that, according to the nearly universal opinion of all economists since Adam Smith, means the use of the natural resources of each country in the ways determined by experience under free conditions to be most economical and not their use as distorted by tariffs. Does Mr Keynes differ from this?

Having tried to answer his questions, may I put to him one or two of my own? Does he think that the ability of (say) the Argentine to take exports from us is unaffected by what we take from them? Could we cut off all imports from that (or any other) country without reducing our exports? Could we, without that consequence, cut off any imports, and, if so, how much and why so much and no more, and in what circumstances and for how long, and what ground has he for saying that those circumstances exist to-day? I have sufficient respect for Mr Keynes's intelligence to think that I know his answers to the first two questions. But I am really interested in knowing his reasons and not merely his conclusions on the last group of questions. Won't he, writing at far more length than even your hospitable columns allow, now drop both dialetic and *pronunciamento* and give, in book or pamphlet, the reasons for his new faith? Won't he also tell us what in the world all this has to do with a tariff for revenue?

The issue of 31 March also contained a letter signed Mercator setting out the complexities of balance-of-payments adjustment he thought Sir William Beveridge had ignored and questioning his view that home and foreign investment were substitutes. Then, turning to Keynes's proposals, he said he thought that, if protection was really needed, something more than 15 per cent would probably be necessary. However, he did not think that a tariff was necessarily advantageous at the present time, for it would reduce the pressures on British industry to adopt its economic organisation to world conditions, would be open to sectional and popular pressures and would be unlikely to disappear even if world prices reached Keynes's target level. Keynes touched on both letters when he replied the next day.

To the Editor of The Times, *1 April 1931*

Sir,

Sir William Beveridge has answered my three questions quite clearly:

(1) He thinks that it makes no difference to the amount of employment in this country, 'for any length of time that matters', whether I buy an American car or a British car.

(2) While he believes that a reduction of our imports would lead to a reduction of our exports, he does not believe that an increase of our imports would lead to an increase of our exports.

(3) If we were to reduce our costs of manufacturing iron and steel, he thinks that this would tend to affect the 'quality' but not the quantity of employment in this country—which would be a discouraging thought, if anyone could be found to believe it.

I could not hope in my previous letter to expound my own theory of international equilibrium in the space at my disposal. It seemed, therefore, that the best hope of bringing the issue to a head within a reasonable compass was to invite Sir William to tread the path of the *reductio ad absurdum*. I must leave it, in the main, to your readers to decide whether I am right in believing that he has done so. But I should like to call particular attention to the effect of the first of his three answers taken in conjunction with the second. Sir William believes (answer 1) that if I buy a British car instead of buying an American car this causes a diminution in our exports, but (answer 2) that if I buy an American car instead of buying a British car this will not cause an increase in our exports—'which hideous it would be if true', since, if I sometimes buy an American car and sometimes a British car, it seems to follow that British exports will gradually sink towards zero! Of course, Sir William is right that we cannot increase our exports merely by increasing our imports. I had hoped that this would lead him gently to the perception that his first answer might not be correct.

Sir William complains, reasonably enough, about my not having expounded my own theory of international equilibrium in this correspondence. If my theory was as simple as his, I would certainly do so. But there is, in my opinion, no simple or direct relationship between the volume of imports and the volume of exports, and it is a complicated business, beyond the scope of a letter, to analyse the various reactions, domestic and international, which would be set up by a reduction of our imports, and the possible ultimate effects of these on our exports. I have done my best to explain the underlying theory in my recently published *Treatise on Money*. I will try to apply it in a particular case in a forthcoming note, to appear in *The New Statesman and Nation*, supplementary to the article which first evoked Sir William's comments [above p. 502]. Meanwhile 'Mercator's' letter in your issue of yesterday furnished him with an answer on broad lines of experience and common sense, with which I entirely agree.

I do not, however, agree with 'Mercator' that a tariff of 15 per cent on manufactured and semi-manufactured imports would not have much effect. Of course, one cannot tell for certain until one tries. But in the modern world 15 per cent is a fairly wide margin for a manufacturer. Apart from slump conditions, I see no reason to believe that our manufacturing disequilibrium with the rest of the world exceeds this figure. *The Economist*, which is not likely to exaggerate the advantages of a tariff, has prophesied that the effect would be 'considerable'. In other quarters it has been estimated that it might cause the substitution of home-produced goods to the value of £50,000,000. This strikes me as being a reasonable guess.

Yours, &c.,

J. M. KEYNES

Keynes's controversy with Beveridge in *The Times* coincided with a private exchange on the subject which echoed some of the points made in public. The origins of this exchange lay in the events of the previous autumn, most notably in Lionel Robbins's controversy with Keynes over tariffs in the Committee of Economists, but also in other contemporary pressures for protection. In response to these Sir William Beveridge, Henry Clay, John Hicks, Walter Layton, Arnold Plant, Robbins and a few others joined together under Beveridge's chairmanship to produce a defence of the free trade position. Originally designed for a popular audience, the defence took a more academic turn as the authors recognised they would also have to deal with professional economists such as Keynes and Stamp. On 19 March 1931 Beveridge sent Keynes the proofs of the first six chapters of the resulting book, ultimately published as *Tariffs: The Case Examined*. On reading them Keynes replied.

To SIR WILLIAM BEVERIDGE, *23 March 1931*

My dear Beveridge,

Many thanks for your proofs, which I have looked through. There is naturally a very great deal with which I agree. But apart from the last of the chapters which you send me—Chapter 6—I do not find enough attempt to answer what seem to me the awkward and pressing questions. I would express my main criticisms as follows.

Most of these chapters seem to me like an attempt to give a very elementary rendering, addressed to entirely ignorant persons, of some well-established and accepted truths. Then in Chapter 6 you jump to a very advanced discussion of subtle matters. It seems to me there would have been room for a great deal of work of an intermediate degree of complexity. When I read the elementary exposition I find myself wanting to know what your answer is to certain questions. But when I get to the advanced matter, I find myself again asking the same questions, and hindered in following the argument through the absence of such prior explanations.

Let me give an example. I find no discussion anywhere as to the precise train of causation by means of which reduction of exports is expected by you to result, sooner or later, in reduction of imports. I do not find any discussion of what one might call the inverse proposition. For example, it would seem to follow from your argument that one need not be afraid of Lloyd Georgian expansionist schemes, on the ground that they might cause an increase of imports, because on your argument this would be balanced by an increase of exports. Do you hold this? If not, it needs explaining.

I find no account of what does determine the balance of trade. I find no account of how far the optimum distribution of resources, at which free trade aims, depends on the mobility of money wages. And I could go on mentioning many other things of the same sort which have escaped discussion.

In short, apart from Chapter 6 which is a serious discussion of a difficult matter—though I naturally have my own views as to its validity—this scarcely seems to me a grown-up discussion of the matters at issue.

Yours sincerely,
[copy initialled] J. M. K.

On 10 March *The Financial News* commented on Keynes's proposals in an editorial which suggested that there were other less disruptive and harmful means of obtaining revenue than a tariff. To this Keynes replied in a letter that was never sent.

To the Editor of The Financial News, *10 March 1931*

Sir,

In your interesting references today to an article of mine, you overlook one part of my argument. I agree with you that taxes other than a revenue tariff might be found. I also agree with you that the *direct* effect of such a tariff on the profits of business, though important and valuable, would not be enough by itself. The advantages of a revenue tariff, as compared with alternative taxes, which have impressed themselves on me, are the following:

(1) It would have a very favourable effect on business confidence.

(2) In so far as it caused home-produced goods to be substituted for imported goods, it would relieve the foreign exchanges and increase profit and employment at home. (I do not understand how you can deny this so far as concerns the present and the near future.)

(3) Enough resources could be raised, in conjunction with other unobjectionable methods, to give us a financial margin which would further revive confidence and give us courage to embark on a considered plan at home and abroad, which would further increase profits and employment.

Can you tell me another tax which will at the same time restore business confidence, relieve the pressure on the exchanges, increase profits and employment, and provide the Chancellor of the Exchequer with a margin of resources? If you can, you should not keep it to yourself.

Yours, etc.,

J. M. KEYNES

Keynes also took his case to the Currency Group of Labour M.P.s at a meeting on 24 March. For this occasion, he did not prepare a set speech but answered questions and used his *New Statesman* article as the basis for a general discussion.

On 12 April Keynes made a brief broadcast on the slump for the American CBS network. His script ran as follows.

This talk of mine follows on addresses from Sir Josiah Stamp and Lord D'Abernon. They have told you in different ways how the behaviour of the financial system and the banking system is capable of suddenly going off the rails, so to speak, and interfering with everyone's prosperity for obscure and complicated reasons which are difficult to understand and probably impossible to explain in a popular way. It is a matter which ought to be left to the experts. *They* ought to understand the machine. And *they* ought to be able to mend it when it goes wrong. It is hopeless to expect the man in the street even to discover what is amiss; far less to put matters right. Unhappily, however, the machine is not well understood by anyone. In a sense there are no experts. Some of those representing themselves as such seem to me to talk much greater rubbish than an ordinary man could ever be capable of. And I daresay there are people—I am sure there are—who will say the same about me and my ideas. In other words, the science of economics, of banking, of finance is in a backward state. Yes, but I believe it is progressing very far all the same. Far enough, perhaps, to deal with the next slump. But I doubt whether the *present* one is going to be cured by these experts, if there are any, who really understand the machine, being asked in and allowed a free hand to mend it. We shall muddle along, just as we used to do when there was something wrong with our own insides, until time and nature and, perhaps, some happy accident work a cure by themselves.

The chances are at least two to one, more probably ten to one, that this is what we have to look forward to.

I should like, then, to use my time this afternoon to make a few observations about this prospect. And just as, when you are hearing an opera, you are prepared to believe for the time being that the voice of the tenor to whom you are listening comes from a golden-haired and god-like man with a spare and muscular figure, so, I beg you, persuade yourselves for the next quarter of an hour that the voice you are hearing is the voice of an expert.

Well, first of all, what a shameful and paradoxical thing it is that we should be suffering economic distress at all! Ten years ago when much the same thing happened, we had not so much reason to be surprised. For then it came as a natural reaction from a short-lived belief that we could ignore the effects of the War and live as though we had not been blowing our wealth away for several years. It was natural to believe that the slump of 1920–1 came as a reminder that we could not live as though the Great War and the unwise peace which followed it had never occurred. But today, ten years later, there can be no such excuse. We have accumulated far more material wealth than we have ever possessed before. The United States which has been building up its material possessions on an unparalleled scale is as hard hit as other countries which are not so wealthy. The improvement in manufacturing technique has been going on faster than ever before. Three men in a factory today can do on the average what before the war would have occupied four men. Moreover, agriculture and mining have not lagged behind. The power of the soil to render up its riches has been so vastly augmented by science and by organisation, that the improvement there is comparable with the improvements in the factory. In the United States and Western Europe population has been increasing more slowly than formerly; so that we have not the same strain on our resources that we used to have in providing the newcomers with upbringing, houses and equipment.

Yet in the midst of this plenty—perhaps even because of it— we have millions of men standing idle, unable to earn a decent week's living. How can this be? It is not the engineers or the technicians who have failed us. It is—I venture to assert— nothing but a breakdown of the mysterious co-ordinating power of banking and finance. How shall I put it? This co-ordinating power has failed to co-ordinate. It has failed to create the environment in which our energies can find their appropriate outlet. We have produced our activities too far in certain directions compared with others. We have an unbalanced position. But this want of balance is not of a single character. It is not that we are making too many motor cars when we ought to be making more radio sets or more aeroplanes; or making too many agricultural machines when we ought to be making more machine tools; or building too many houses when we ought to be making more cars; or that we are growing too much wheat when we ought to be growing more corn or cotton; or that we are minting too much copper when we ought to be minting more lead. There appears to be a surplus capacity in every direction at once. How can that be? I believe that the explanation is, after all, simple; though I shall not be able to make it appear so. I believe that we are withholding from consumption a larger part of our incomes than is able to find an outlet in new constructive enterprises, or in anything which will serve to increase our accumulated capital. Or, as I like to express it, individuals are

517

saving more of their incomes than the business world is able to find an outlet for in new investments, that is to say in new construction of one kind or another. For reasons which I shall not try to explain, a want of balance of this sort is capable of stopping the proper action of the whole economic machine.

It follows that there can be only two remedies—to save less, or to construct more. If we had all the buildings and constructions for which we had any sensible use, obviously the right solution would be to save less. In a time such as the present, when constructive enterprise is lagging behind, the common-sense view that free spending by individual citizens is good for employment is perfectly correct. When I broadcast in England a few weeks ago, I shocked many good people by saying this. Yet I am afraid it is quite true. But of course it would be much better that savings should be absorbed by new capital enterprise. For we are, surely, far short of having all the durable goods and equipment which we could possess to our advantage. So long as rents, for example, are so high as they are—so long as the current cost of occupying a house is more than let us say two per cent of the cost of constructing it, so long as the rent of a $5,000 house or flat is more than $100 a year, which of course it is,—far more—it is impossible to say that we have all the house room we could use. No, the truth is—and this is my secret, my remedy, my patent cure—that the rate of interest for most kinds of loans is much too high, and that is—one way or another—the fault of the banking and financial system. For example, we have all the houses which we can afford at the present levels of rents. But the rents are largely fixed by the rate of interest. If the rate of interest were to come down, rents would fall and we should then want more house room. In other words, too high a price is being asked for use of savings—and the consequence is that savings are being wasted. For a time the financial world became over-excited and believed that it was worth while to pay almost any rate to obtain a command over savings. Since then the short-term rate of interest has come down with a rush. But not the long-term rate. The long-term rate is still higher than it used to be before the War, in spite of the enormous increase of wealth since that time. We have to get back to the pre-war rate of interest for loans of every kind, and perhaps much lower than that, before we shall have a well-balanced economic system. The resistance to such a change will be enormous. It will be a heavy job, indeed, to bring it about.

And this brings me to my last observation. If we trust for a cure—as we are trusting—to time, and nature and a happy accident, we have no right to expect this cure *soon*. Ups and downs, of course, there will be. False starts and apparent recoveries and a few weeks' excitement in Wall Street. But the real remedy—the day when business will be booming, when everyone fit to be employed will have a well-paid job, and when profits will again be the reward of energy and enterprise—that, it seems to me, may be a long way off. And we shall get good warning before it comes.

The spokesmen of the business world—though they are not so gay and foolish as they were a year ago—seem to me to be still far too optimistic and to have no sound basis for their optimistic talk. They predict a business recovery six months or a year hence for no better reason, so far as I can discover, than that so many months are surely long enough for something to happen and, anyway, that is a sufficient time ahead for people to have forgotten what the prophets had been saying before they are proved wrong. For myself, I make no prediction, except that I think we shall have long warning, in the shape of some marked change in fundamental conditions, before a genuine recovery manifests itself, and I see no such warning at present. But, to judge from past experience, there would be nothing strange if anything from two to five years were to pass by before the high tide of prosperity visits us again. The present collapse, judged by the fall of prices or by many other indicators, is one of the most violent which have ever occurred in economic history. The problem of the recovery will be correspondingly severe. We may, as I have said, have to effect a tremendous change in the price of capital. These things do not happen easily or suddenly. From what I hear, I doubt if the people of the United States are yet appreciating the full gravity of the economic problem, with which they and the rest of the world are being faced.

When Philip Snowden introduced the 1931 Budget, Keynes provided a discussion of its provisions which *The Evening Standard* published under the title 'The Budget that Wastes Time' on 28 April. Below we reprint Keynes's manuscript version of the article rather than the newspaper version. The only changes were those of paragraphing.

MR SNOWDEN'S BUDGET

The main impression which Mr Snowden produces is quite clear. He is speculating on an early revival of trade and prosperity. If this prospect were justified, there would be much in favour of the shifts by which he proposes to deal with the immediate situation. But he gave no reasons for his hope. Nor are there any.

Mr Snowden's speculative optimism permeates every part of his Budget. He begins by providing no recurrent revenue except the increase in the petrol duty. For £30,000,000 out of £37,500,000 he depends on special receipts which cannot be repeated. But this is not all. In estimating his receipts from present taxes he has proceeded on what appears to be a rosy view. The Inland Revenue department have so fine a record of accurate estimating that one hesitates to criticise their figures. But to take one item—stamp duties—the stock exchange will be surprised, I think, to learn that Mr Snowden expects them to enjoy more activity and a larger money turnover in 1931–2 than they did in 1930–1. Next, he provides no margin of revenue to cover the inevitable Supplementary Estimates, which are likely to arise either out of the cost of maintaining the unemployed or out of attempts to employ them, as well as in other unforeseen ways. It would be safe, I should say, to bet ten to one that this Budget will end up a year hence with a realised deficit.

Broadly speaking, then, it will probably be found in practice that Mr Snowden has solved his problem mainly by a handsome raid on the sinking fund. For this is the result of a realised deficit. It is also the result of his expedient of taking £20,000,000 out of the so-called Exchange Account. There is, by the way, a good deal of misunderstanding about this Account. It is unlikely that the sum which he is taking from it exists in the shape of dollars in New York, for the fact that it is no longer needed for buying dollars is the reason for raiding it. It is doubtless already advanced to the Treasury by a book-keeping transaction, against Treasury bills or Ways and Means Advances. Thus the return of this sum to the Exchequer will merely mean the cancellation of these advances and will furnish no new resources for the purpose of reducing the *net* national debt. Mr Snowden's expedient is, therefore, no more than a polite way, not so inconsistent in form with his previous professions, of diminishing the allocation to the sinking fund.

Now, I know one ought to regard any reduction of the effective sinking fund as very shocking. That is not my view. At a time when other outlets for the money which would be released by the redemption of debt appear to be lacking, it is much better to postpone repayment. Repayment of debt should not be made at a level annual rate regardless of changing circumstances. On the contrary, it should be on a large scale when investment is brisk and business needs more funds and on a small scale when investment is slack and ample funds are already lying idle. I approve, therefore, of Mr Snowden's practice in this matter more than I approve his precepts. Since so many of Mr Snowden's 'principles' are misguided, it is a comfort that he is ready to abate one at least of them in action.

But when we turn from his expedients for avoiding taxation to the taxes which he has nevertheless to impose, I find less reason to applaud. His adjustment of the dates of payment for certain classes of income tax payers is, of course, an increase of tax for those affected. The money does not come from nowhere. It does not reduce receipts in subsequent years. For these income tax payers it is an additional payment which they, as a class, will never be able to recoup. I see several objections to getting the money in this way. The earned incomes of farmers and of individuals under Schedule D are, one would have thought, the last class of income to be singled out for special burdens at the present time, when prices are low and profits exiguous. Nor is there any reason to put a new burden on salaried persons and not on *rentiers*. Moreover I share the view that an increase of indirect taxation would be better today than an increase of direct taxation. But worst of all, this source of revenue is non-recurrent. In so far as we are raising more tax revenue this year, it should be recurrent taxation which will alleviate next year's problem. We already know almost for certain that the yield of income tax and surtax will be substantially less in 1932–3 than in 1931–2. Mr Snowden will leave an appalling legacy to next year's Chancellor.

Mr Snowden's resort to the petrol tax has its curious side. When he finds himself compelled to put on a tax which must, as one of its effects, somewhat increase business costs, Mr Snowden's 'principles' require that he should make sure that it will have no useful bye-products in the shape of providing increased employment for British labour. But this is no surprise. Mr Snowden told the House of Commons that he will never be a party to a revenue tariff, and no-one supposed that he would. He has, however, done the next thing to it. By providing so little recurrent revenue for next year, he has done as much as possible to ensure that it will be impracticable for the Chancellor of the Exchequer to solve next year's Budget problem without recourse to a tariff.

Mr Snowden's Budget does no more than mark time. It solves nothing. It faces up to nothing. He relapses into the unreasoning hopefulness which has marked so many of his speeches since he became Chancellor. With this difference, however,—that, whereas he appeared a year or less ago to believe his own cheery forecasts, there are several passages in his speech of yesterday which indicate that today he does not really place much more reliance than I do in his gamble in hope.

This Budget marks time. But it also wastes time. Things will not come right by themselves, however much the intensely negative mind of our Chancellor wishes they would. Nothing has occurred in recent months—quite the contrary—to modify my belief that a tariff is a necessary ingredient in any constructive policy and that events will force us in this direction, whether we like it or not. But a constructive policy, alas! is far from our Chancellor's heart. The first Socialist Chancellor is also the last adherent of true blue *laissez-faire*. And this is not the only paradox. For whilst hardly anyone in any party agrees with all Mr Snowden's 'principles' or thinks him wise and right in opposing every conceivable way out of the mess we are in, yet there is no-one in public life whose character and personality the country respects and loves more than his.

Two days later Keynes provided an amplification of his comments on the Chancellor's income tax changes.

From The Evening Standard, *30 April 1931*

Many people differ from Mr J. M. Keynes, the economist, who, discussing in *The Evening Standard* the plan of Mr Snowden for income-tax payers to pay three-quarters instead of half the tax next January, maintained that it meant that taxpayers would pay more.

Mr Keynes wrote:

His (Mr Snowden's) adjustment of the dates of payment for certain classes of income-tax payers is, of course, an increase of tax for those affected. The money does not come from nowhere. It does not reduce receipts in subsequent years. For these income tax payers it is an additional payment which they, as a class, will never be able to recoup.

This view has been disputed, and to-day Mr Keynes amplified his statement.

Whether the income tax payer pays more as a result of Mr Snowden's alteration of the date of payment is the sort of question which one can argue until all is blue. But it ought not to be beyond the wit of man to make it quite plain. I will try to do so.

Here is the explanation in Mr Keynes's own words:

Take the first year. The income tax payer pays a quarter of his tax six months sooner. In every subsequent year he will do the same so long as he earns his income, and when his place is taken by his successor that successor will do the same.

Thus income tax payers *as a class* will advance the sum in question without interest for half of each year in perpetuity. This is exactly equal to imposing on them as a single net additional payment half the sum brought by the Chancellor into this year's Budget.

So far as individual people are concerned, the division of the present value of the burden of this sum between them and their successors depends on how long they continue to earn their present incomes. Thus, to be quite accurate, I should have said that *half* these additional receipts fall on the income-tax-paying class as a net addition.

Where does the other half come in?

The other half is a net addition to the national debt, for, in subsequent years, the date of part of the Chancellor's receipts will be six months later. During this six months a corresponding additional amount will have to be outstanding in the shape of Treasury bills or Ways and Means Advances. Thus, the national debt outstanding in subsequent years on the average of the year will be increased by the amount of the other half of the additional receipts which the Chancellor has brought into this year's Budget.

Mr Keynes paused.

Then he added with a smile:

Well, have I made it plain? I wonder. It is as good as a bridge problem; indeed, it is better, for the stakes are higher.

Another aspect of the Budget brought a letter from Keynes and G. M. Trevelyan to *The New Statesman*.

To the Editor of The New Statesman and Nation, *9 May 1931*

Sir,

A short time ago some of us took part in a correspondence in *The Nation* on the subject of Land Taxation and Rural Amenities. Most of the letters and the editorial article took the view that, unless certain conditions were observed, a tax on land values would speed up the pace of road-ribboning and the destruction of natural beauty. The C.P.R.E. elsewhere expressed the same view. It would, unfortunately, appear that the proposals that are being presented to Parliament pay no regard to these considerations.

Agricultural land that has no other value is to be exempt. But (so far as we know at this moment) woodlands and playgrounds, unless municipally held, are to be subject to the new tax. And certainly agricultural land that has any further value as building land is to pay on that further value. No exemption, so far as we have learnt, is to be given to land beside roads and lanes; its owners will, therefore, be put under the pressure of the tax to sell it for building. 'Ribboning', therefore, will receive a great impetus, as well as the sale of 'beauty-spots' coveted by the jerry-builder. Moreover, the new tax has not been adjusted to the town planning schemes encouraged by the Government in another of its measures. In many places, moreover, there is no town planning scheme, for town planning has not been made universal and compulsory. In such places the new tax may have some very bad results indeed.

The present proposal is limited to a penny in the pound. But neither the Chancellor of the Exchequer as such, nor Socialists and Radicals as such, will be able to resist the temptation to raise it. So much is already confessed. If, therefore, we put the tax on the wrong lands now, the results must ultimately be disastrous.

There are many people all over the country who are preserving, as agricultural lands or woodlands, certain sites which they might sell for building; they are doing so for love of beauty and for love of their neighbours. These people are now to be penalised by taxation until the bungalow-builder and estate-breaker can have their way. If the state is going to use taxation as a means of forcing land into the market, it ought to decide what lands should in the public interest be built upon and what should not. The plea of advantage to the community in the preservation of a site as agricultural land or woodland ought in many cases to be admitted on the ground of amenity. If the state, by taxation, deprives the private owner of the ability to preserve land unbuilt upon, then the state ought in his stead to take the responsibility of making the decision on that point. But if the state will not save natural beauty itself it ought to leave private owners in a position to do so.

We are not opposed to the principle of taxing building-value—far from it. But Mr Snowden's proposed tax seems to be based on an obsolete order of ideas. Most modern reformers consider that betterment levies should be the central feature of any scheme for the taxation of building-value; and we hope that it is not too late to satisfy Mr Snowden's radicalism by stiffening up the Government's town planning measure, rather than by cutting across betterment levies with a flat tax on building-value, whether or not the owner is exploiting this value and whether or not the community desires him to do so.

We may all feel gratitude to the present Government for those things which it has done for amenities. The Prime Minister's appointment of the National Parks Committee, Mr Lansbury's excellent Ancient Monuments Bill, the Town Planning Bill, and Mr Snowden's proposal to exempt the lands of the National Trust from the land value tax, are evidence of such good will. It is to be hoped that Liberals also care about natural beauty, as well as about the taxation of land values. Unless their respective claims can be fairly adjusted, we are in danger of a great catastrophe to the weaker, but not the least precious, of these two causes.

Yours, etc.,

G. M. TREVELYAN

J. M. KEYNES

The rest of May saw Keynes heavily involved in the final stages of the Macmillan Report, and no further contributions to the press appeared. However, at the end of the month he did make one break when the honorary secretary of the National League of Young Liberals informed him on 20 May that he had been re-elected a vice-president, and asked him to contribute funds to the League.

To AUBREY HERBERT, *21 May 1931*

Dear Mr Herbert,

Thank you for your letter of May 20 about my Vice-Presidency of the National League of Young Liberals. In view, however, of my present heretical state of mind, I think that perhaps it would be better if I did not appear in this capacity. Apart from my well-known heresies, I am much shocked at the moment that the Party should be supporting this reactionary and, I should have supposed, unworkable Land Tax, cutting right across the Betterment Tax, in which I had believed all modern reformers to put their faith.

I am sorry. But as you have raised the matter, to leave my name in your list might, I think, imply sounder Party opinions on my part than I hold just at this moment.

Yours very truly,
[copy initialled] J.M.K.

The correspondence continued.

From AUBREY HERBERT, *29 May 1931*

Dear Mr Keynes,

I was very sorry to hear that you feel you cannot continue to be a Vice-President of this League.

I think I ought to say that the Annual Conference was very anxious that our list of Vice-Presidents should include all sorts and kinds of Liberals of distinction, and as I suppose whatever may be your views about revenue tariffs, you remain in general agreement with the Radical Liberal Party, I feel you will forgive me if I ask you to re-consider your decision and to help us in the future as you have in the past.

Yours sincerely,
AUBREY HERBERT

To AUBREY HERBERT, *29 May 1931*

Dear Mr Herbert,

I appreciate your letter. I should still call myself a Radical. But I feel, all the same, that my appearing as Vice-President of an official Liberal body may lead to misunderstanding. I am keener than ever on schemes of home development, and indeed on much of the Yellow Book. But with the Party's present concentration on the cries of the past, such as free trade, quite regardless of circumstances, and a Land Tax fifty years out of date, I feel that life has gone out of it—which I did not at all feel when the ideas of the Yellow Book were in the forefront. With these explanations, I am prepared to leave myself in your hands.

Yours sincerely,
[copy initialled] J.M.K.

Chapter 6

AN AMERICAN VISIT

On 30 May Keynes set sail for the United States. The major purpose of his visit was to give lectures in Chicago on the Harris Foundation on the subject 'An Economic Analysis of Unemployment' (*JMK*, vol. XIII, pp. 343–67). In addition to giving his three lectures on that subject and taking part in other discussion groups, he introduced a discussion on the subject 'Is it Possible for Governments and Central Banks to Do Anything on Purpose to Remedy Unemployment?' on 1 July.

From Unemployment as a World Problem: Reports of Round Tables (1931), *volume* II.

HARRIS FOUNDATION INSTITUTE ROUND TABLES

1 July 1931, 7.30 p.m.

Is it Possible for Governments and Central Banks to Do Anything on Purpose to Remedy Unemployment?

John Maynard Keynes, Discussion Leader

Government Action

(*a*) Public works: difficulties and objections practical rather than theoretical

(*b*) Special financing and purchasing bodies

(*c*) Measures to assist business confidence and business profits: e.g., relief from taxation, concession of high rates to railroads

(*d*) Measures to relieve unbalanced international situation

Central Bank Action

(*a*) Cheap money—discount rate and buying rate for acceptances

(*b*) Enlarging basis of credit—purchases of governments,

contrasts between American and British conditions, difficulties of American technique

(c) Promoting confidence in duration of cheap money

(d) Persuading member banks and savings banks to reduce rate of interest allowed on deposits

(e) Participation in international schemes designed to remedy international loan position

(f) Generally speaking, cooperation with other central banks

Unlikelihood of any one method or any one line of approach proving practical on a sufficient scale, and importance, therefore, of attacking problem on a broad front, trying simultaneously every plausible means.

Possibility that the present depression is constituted by a combination of a normal cyclical depression with a transition from post-war long-term rates of interest back to pre-war rates or lower, and necessity, in this case, of very determined, obstinate and drastic action by central banks.

MR JOHN MAYNARD KEYNES: The emphasis here is 'on purpose'. I chose this title before I had seen the titles of the other Round Tables. As a matter of fact, on Monday we had a Round Table on public works, which I think covered a great deal of the ground of what governments could do, and with the leave of the Round Table I propose that I pass over that, and I will concentrate on central bank action. I believe we shall find enough to talk about in central bank action to occupy us.

I should like to speak rather briefly, and leave other matters to subsequent conversation, and dwell rather upon certain of the difficulties which have come to my notice in various talks here. It obviously isn't quite such a simple matter as one might have supposed, in the actual technical situation of this country, to force money into the bond market. In Great Britain it would be much easier, and the first respect in which it would be easier is raised by my first heading. In Great Britain the market is not normally indebted to the Bank of England at all. The Bank of

England rate is normally above the market rate, so nobody takes a bill to the Bank to be discounted in the ordinary way. The market is only indebted to the Bank of England seasonally or when they have been taken by surprise, or over the end of the year, for instance, or when something has happened to throw them out of their calculations. They may then for a very short time take some bills to the Bank, but the normal position is that they are not indebted. At the present moment I should be surprised if the market owed the Bank of England more than two or three million [pounds] sterling.

The consequence is that when the Bank of England itself goes into the market and buys Treasury bills or government securities, there is nothing that the market has ready to pay off. It necessarily means that the basis of credit is increased by the amount of the Bank of England's purchases. But in this country the market, in the form of member banks, is normally indebted to the Federal Reserve System. The indebtedness happens to be abnormally low at the present time, because discounts do not represent a very big factor, but as I understand it, acceptances have drifted to much the same position as discounts; that is to say, the Federal Reserve Bank has a buying rate just as it has a discount rate, and the amount of acceptances which come to it is determined by the initiative of the market, how much the market cares to sell to them at that rate. The only difference between the acceptance rate and the discount rate is that the acceptance rate is varied more frequently by smaller amounts.

On the other hand, the Federal Reserve Banks go into the market for their foreign correspondents, and buy acceptances, in whatever volume they wish, at whatever the market price is. That would be an open market operation, but the only strictly-speaking market operation at present open to the Federal Reserve Bank is the buying of governments, and that may always be countered by the market using funds thus becoming available either to diminish their discounts or to hold acceptances away from the Federal Reserve System; therefore there is no certainty when the Federal Reserve Banks buy governments that credit will be increased by that amount. Consequently they may have to buy a fearful lot before they produce a given effect, which also may lead to their having a rather unbalanced position, which might be open to criticism. At the present time it is possible that if the Federal Reserve Banks buy governments the market will use the funds to hold acceptances which otherwise would have found their way to the Federal Reserve Banks; so the Federal Reserve Banks, in order to maintain the basis of credit, will have to keep on buying governments until finally a rather excessive portion of its earning assets would be in that form.

I believe that that sometimes causes the Federal Reserve System to hesitate more than they otherwise would. For example, if they have to buy very large quantities of governments, their action, I believe, may affect the price very much, and therefore bring in sales from various quarters. The whole thing is not so automatic as it is in England.

It has occurred to me that perhaps the present way of dealing with acceptances may be a bit divergent from the original intention. I think that the Federal Reserve System is rather diverted from the London practice in the first instance by its desire to foster the acceptance market. In present conditions it seems to me it might be desirable for the Federal Reserve Banks to buy acceptances, much in the same way as they buy governments or acceptances from their own correspondents. They would decide they wanted a certain quantity, and would go and buy that quantity at whatever the market would surrender it at. They then get a little away from the automatic system.

I think it is a weakness of the practice here that the market is normally indebted to the system, and therefore normally has funds which it can pay off. Exactly the same difficulty exists when there is a risk of an inflation, that the member banks can themselves bring about an inflation of credit by discounting unless the Federal Reserve Banks have a large supply of ammunition in the shape of governments that they can sell. In

England that is impossible, because as long as the Bank of England assumes its traditional practice of keeping its rates above the market rate, there is no possibility of the market itself increasing the basis of credit. The changes take place on the initiative of the Bank of England.

I mention that as one cause, it seems to me, of why the Federal Reserve Bank is rather nervous in operating, because in order to produce its end, it may have to operate on such a fearfully large scale, or thinks it might have to.

Then a second difficulty which might arise is that in exceptional conditions member banks might not make use of the additional credit put at their disposal. It might be that they would simply maintain larger balances than they require. That again would mean that the Federal Reserve System would have to act on a larger scale than would otherwise be required. I should be glad to get opinions as to whether that is a risk. In England it is an absolutely negligible risk. The clearing banks never maintain with the Bank of England more than their minimum reserves, and whenever they are supplied by the Bank with more than that quantity, they use it, so an inflation at the base is transmitted to the main banking fabric almost invariably. It has been suggested to me that it is not equally certain that that would happen here.

That again seems to me to be a difference of degree rather than of anything else, because they won't go on holding idle balances up to any quantity. If you inflate their balances, you are also inflating their deposits, even if they don't multiply them by nine or ten. When the Federal Reserve System buys governments, it means the public has increased deposits, and they can't afford to accumulate non-interest-bearing assets beyond a certain point. But it does mean that the scale of operations may be rather uncomfortably large in order to produce consequences.

I have sometimes thought that a good way of working this would be to have a variable reserve ratio for the member banks; that is to say, a ratio variable at the instance of the Federal

Reserve System. Of course, you have a complicated reserve system, but assume for the sake of argument that it works out normally at ten per cent over all. I am simplifying it in order to be able to talk in terms of one ratio instead of the several different ratios you have. Suppose the normal ratio is ten per cent. It might be convenient if the Federal Reserve System had the liberty to decree that the ten per cent should be raised to 10·5 per cent, or 11 per cent when it wanted to contract credit, or reduced to 9·0 per cent or 9·5 per cent when it wanted to expand credit, leaving it then to the member banks to make use of this additional facility. That would relieve the Federal Reserve Banks of any risk of not having enough ammunition. Instead of having to buy or sell governments on a large scale, they would simply alter the legal ratio, and where it was an upward move, the law would force the member banks to comply. When it was a downward movement, self-interest could be relied upon to make them comply.

I think we may hereafter come to think that the method of buying or selling governments is a rather unnecessarily indirect way of causing the banking system as a whole to expand or contract. At any rate, it is worth trying out as an adjunct.

You could also have the variation by a very small amount. You could move from a 10 per cent ratio to a 10·1 per cent ratio. In that case the Federal Reserve System would have its two weapons of discount rate and reserve rate, and it could alter them as it wished. Also, in this country, you would have different reserve rates for different reserve banks, so if you wanted to stiffen up or relax a particular part of the country, you could do it by altering the ratio instead of by the method of governments, which is a nation-wide phenomenon and very difficult to localise. I think the thing might be worth considering.

My conclusion, after hearing various grounds for hesitation, is that even in this country there is no reason to suppose that buying and selling governments will not expand or contract the basis of credit, but I do have to concede that it works more slowly than it does in Great Britain, and it might have to be on a larger scale.

There is a further point perhaps connected with that, or connected with these two methods. I think the enlargement of the basis of credit is an almost necessary part of your technique, and that you cannot produce all of your results merely by lowering the discount rate. When you have the discount rate down to a certain extent, you have exhausted that method.

There is a particular reason why the discount rate method, I think, is of limited applicability, and that is this: the discount rate represents the pure rate of interest. The number of borrowers who are entitled to the pure rate of interest is very few. The average borrower has to pay some premium over and above the pure rate of interest, partly to cover risk. The business of collecting deposits and lending them out again is an expensive business. Banks must necessarily charge their borrowing clients more than the pure rate of interest to cover expenses. When banks are charging their customers 6 per cent it may be that 3 per cent of that is pure rate of interest, 1 per cent is protection against risk, and 2 per cent is expenses. Well, that 1 per cent and 2 per cent do not go down with the pure rate of interest, so even if you reduce the pure rate of interest to naught, it might still be reasonable for banks to be charging their customers three per cent. Therefore the amount of reduction to the average borrower which you can bring about by a reduction of discount rate is limited, and he may still be paying a faily high rate even when the pure rate of interest has reached almost the vanishing point.

I do not know whether bankers would agree, but I feel that in putting expense at 2 per cent I am not putting it by any means too high. Consequently the range of borrowers whom you can meet merely by cheap money is not sufficiently great, apart from the fact that the short-term rate is not necessarily quickly transmitted to the long-term rate. On the other hand, when you enlarge the basis of credit, the field of your influence is very greatly extended. The governments which the System buys may come from anywhere, and if the banks themselves begin making use of the extended basis of credit to buy bonds, the influence of the cheaper rates is spread over a very much wider field and you reach a very much larger range of potential borrowers. There-fore, I think the enlargement of the basis of credit by means of affecting the bond market not only transmits the lower rates of interest to long terms as distinct from the short, but also to a much greater range of persons than a mere alteration of the short-term pure rate of interest is capable of doing.

On the next point I do not know that I have very much to put forward. Obviously one of the reasons why short-term rates are not quickly transmitted to long-term rates is a lack of confidence in the probable duration of cheap short-term rates. You can see very quickly that unless the disparity between long- and short-term rates is going to persist, you can lose in depreciation on the long term more than you gained in interest, so it is quite prudent not to worry very much about the difference in the rates of interest. You ought to be convinced that the thing is going to last long enough so that it won't be necessary to worry about any depreciation of the interest rate you are after.

Is there any way, in times like this, for the banks to create confidence? I am very doubtful. They have to retain their freedom of action, but one suggestion I heard (it isn't my own) which I think is worth considering is this: suppose the Federal Reserve Banks were to announce that for eighteen months they would not allow their stock of governments to fall below the figure at which it stood for the past six months, so that confidence was felt that the bond market would not be attacked suddenly by sales of governments by the Federal Reserve System. Might that not help banks to feel confidence that they would not be risking writing off depreciations? I think we are at a stage where we are justified in using abnormal methods, because the market is in a state of abnormal psychology, unusually nervous, unusually afraid of suffering depreciation in some shape or form.

There is a certain point where almost everybody in charge of funds reaches the stage of what I call 'abnormal psychology'. In an ordinary way, any kind of financial institution has a certain cushion of some kind, reserves and margins, and is prepared to run reasonable risks, prepared to be sensible on the evidence, but when those margins run down to a certain point they get into a state of mind where they are not prepared to run even an actuarial risk or better than an actuarial risk. They just won't run any risk at all, because they have got to the end of their margins. If they would run any risk at all, and it was to go wrong, they would be in a horrid situation, and as credit and security is their total stock in trade, they get into a state of mind where they won't run a sound risk.

That morbid psychology, though quite intelligible and natural, is a tremendous obstacle to a right development of affairs when it exists. There is an element of that morbid psychology present today; there are financial institutions and individuals who want to safeguard themselves against any possibility of future loss, and are therefore unwilling to run sound risks. Willingness to run sound risks is the [only] possible basis for all progress, and in order to restore a normal state of mind, to get rid of the abnormal psychology, it may be quite right to use methods of comforting which would be unsound in any ordinary conditions.

As I began by saying, I haven't much to suggest in that situation, but I think it is worth considering whether banking systems could not think out working means of comfort with the idea of restoring a normal psychology toward sound risks.

My next heading relates to the rate of interest allowed on deposits. I attach first-rate importance to that from several points of view. I might begin with the point of view which is not the most important. There has been a surprising amount of opposition, so far as I can gather, on the part of prominent bankers to a very easy money policy on the part of the Federal Reserve System. Various plausible or unplausible economic reasons are adduced for that opposition, but I cannot help coming, the more and more I have heard it argued, to the opinion that these plausible or unplausible arguments are really

537

vamped up, and the most important thing at the bottom of it is that very cheap money doesn't suit the banks. It makes it more and more difficult for them to earn their expenses. They are short-sighted about it. They don't realise that enlarging the basis of credit and getting things right is to their advantage more than earning interest. They don't want to see rates of interest too low, for it means their earning power is going to be seriously impaired. That is partly due to the fact that their expenses are so large a proportion of their total receipts, but I think it is also due to the fact that for competitive reasons they have got into the habit of paying so much too much on their deposits. If the banks could be persuaded to agree on some common action which would bring down deposit rates very greatly, I am inclined to believe that that would mitigate their opposition to cheap money policies. It would not be such a desperate business for them to have cheap money if their expenses were being kept down on the other side to a somewhat proportional extent.

I know that the deposit rates have been cut and are being cut, and in the long run, that is going to be very important, but it is going on fearfully slowly, and what I say of the United States in this respect is just as true of Great Britain. Our banks are allowing rates of deposit interest which make it really impossible for them to cover their expenses with pure rates of interest as low as they are now in London. They have got into a thoroughly rotten position about it.

Not only does that operate in opposition to cheap money; it also necessarily keeps up their lending rates, and it also, I think, operates viciously in another way, and that is what I attribute major importance to. It makes the holding of deposits far too attractive to the public, and causes the public to invest much too much of their money via the banking system instead of direct. One of the troubles in this country, as I see it, is that the volume of deposits is far too great, partly owing to the strong financial position of many large corporations. The short-term commercial and industrial financing required of the banking system is not nearly so large as it was at one time. On the other hand the attractive terms of deposit have drawn in sums which otherwise might have been directly invested.

Either the amount of deposits has to be curtailed, or if the volume of these deposits is allowed to expand to a figure which does not represent deflation, it means the member banks get themselves tied up far too much in long-term securities, simply because there aren't enough short-term securities to go around. It would be much better if the volume of time deposits was much less, and if a great part of the bonds held by the member banks against their time deposits were held by the owners of the time deposits instead, without the banking system intervening. The more I hear about the situation here, the more I attach importance to this. I think one of the occasions of the excessive lending by banks imprudently against real estate is the fact that the volume of their deposits is so large in relation to the quantity of short-term sound assets that there are to go around that they are driven to the investment not entirely suitable for a banking system.

Also, this makes the whole community much more vulnerable to a change in the value of money, because you have a whole lot of people owing a whole lot of other people very large sums of money, and then holding assets against those, instead of there being a direct investment by the public in the assets; if you got the direct holding, if the ultimate owners of wealth would hold the direct assets themselves, changes in the value of money would not be so dangerous, but if the ultimate owners of the wealth have it in terms of money, and somebody owes them that money and buys assets against it, then any change in the value of money sets up an appalling strain and it is a very dangerous position.

A thing I have failed to find in published books is a really good account of what terms the average depositor in member banks all over the country gets, but I have formed the impression that they were quite outrageously favourable. it is quite easy to get interest on demand deposits as well as time deposits. The banks charge very little for service rendered; the rates on time money are very high, and even now on savings deposits they are very high; so that in a rather dubious world like this, where there is a risk in anything, if you can get three or four per cent by having your money at a month's notice, and if you have been getting that or better for years and years together, you, a cautious person, naturally, being one not interested greatly in appreciation or depreciation, but interested in income, will form the deposit habit, and form the deposit habit on a dangerously large scale. I fancy that is one of the root troubles.

We want to drive depositors off deposits into bonds, and buy from the banks great amounts of bonds which the banks now have, and very likely ultimately have less credit outstanding than you have now, although there would be more effective credit. I am sure that is the thing on which you people ought to concentrate. It is such a technical problem that I am not qualified to say very much about it, but I throw it out as one of the lines worth exploration.

Then I have put down here two other headings relating to the international action. The first one relates to the international loan position. I am afraid that the raising of prices of raw commodities will not happen quickly enough to save the credit of a great many of the debtor countries. I think the debtor countries may be driven into defaults, partial or complete, owing to a fall in the prices of the products they export, and these defaults will interrupt the normal process of international lending, and by the time that the recovery of prices comes, people will be so disgusted with foreign bonds that they will have nothing to do with them, so the unbalanced international financial position may be prolonged through far too great a period. If one could do something to save the position for the moment so as to prevent the defaults and allow enough time to elapse for prices to rise, hoping for other methods of attack to eventually equalise the prices, it might prevent a serious debacle. It would be to the interest of the creditor countries to do this, for once it becomes a habit to default, it is a very catching and attractive habit. It is worthwhile for creditor nations to try to prevent that habit from growing, and apart from that, I think for quite a number of years yet the international loans will have to form a very important part of our financial organisation. If that gets jammed, combined with the universal disgust with foreign loans, the whole scheme of progress will be delayed. If that problem can be protected by some sort of a pool of credit under the auspices of leading financial houses in all countries, or possibly under the auspices of central banks, by which somebody could step in between the lender and the borrower and give some kind of guarantee to the lender and special assistance to borrowers who were doing all that was reasonably in their power to do, I think it would be a very sound thing if every country which does not wish to default and is doing its best not to default were assisted to maintain its solvency.

That isn't the kind of risk the private investor takes. It isn't the sort of thing that can be done without some sort of organisation. I believe it is worth while for those in authority to consider whether some system could be worked out for making sure that any country which is doing its best to keep from defaulting, which is put into a hopeless position by the present prices of its produce, should be helped out, possibly even by the formation of a central pool for buying its products.

I don't know. It isn't a matter on the detail of which the economist as such has any particular facility of speech.

Finally—a matter of very great importance—is cooperation between the central banks. The pure rate of interest is an international phenomenon, and altogether the rate of interest is a much more international factor than the rate of wages. Consequently, except for countries which have free gold reserves, it is not easy for anything to be done on the lines I was discussing earlier, unless all countries keep in step. When one is discussing these subjects in Great Britain, this plays a very leading part.

You find people ready to agree with the first part of the argument, but they say 'if we move an inch ahead of the other people, we shall lose gold'. One doesn't find that so important here, because if gold were lost, many people would welcome it.

In any event, I think these policies will be far more successful if the various countries concerned work together and keep step. You will then avoid any large international movements of gold, and the thing will go forward in a much more orderly way. Even if the cooperation were limited to London and New York it would, I believe, be very helpful. If we had a concerted policy of going forward on these things, if it were definitely agreed between the Federal Reserve System and the Bank of England that we want to reduce rates, if that is the way to get investment going, and they would have a real drive against interest rates, and they were to do it together, by homeopathic doses, keeping step step by step all the time, it would work out more successfully than if any particular individual bank were to rush in unaided by the others.

Those are the suggestions I have to put before you. I should like to see all of them having anything in them adopted simultaneously. I would move forward on a broad front, with as much cooperation between different countries and different classes of institutions as possible. A good many of these devices are devices that can't be pressed on the member banks by the central banks, or pressed by the Bank of England on the clearing banks. Therefore it is important, I think, that leading member banks should get together and agree on a concerted policy. That particularly applies to deposit rates. Although you in this country have such a gigantic number of banks, you haven't such an enormous number of really influential institutions. If the really influential institutions in the country got together, they could probably dominate the situation.

I think it is therefore a question of a lack of united conviction. I cannot help thinking that if everybody agreed with my general desires, they would find a way of carrying them out. The technical difficulties are large when people are really raising those technical difficulties against you because they do not thoroughly agree with your thesis, and when people do not thoroughly agree with your thesis, there are thousands of technical difficulties that a knowledgeable and ingenious man can raise against you.

Finally, I think we ought to be prepared to take this position exceptionally seriously. I need not add much here to what I have said on other occasions in the last week. As you know, my diagnosis of this is that we have a normal credit cycle, perhaps abnormally severe, but of normal type, superimposed on a transition back from the high rates of interest established by the War and post-war periods to a lower rate of interest comparable to the pre-war rate, and, owing to the increment of the world's wealth in the meantime and the slower rate of the growth of population in the wealthy countries, to a much lower than the pre-war rate of interest.

An ordinary credit cycle is one in which you start and end with the rate of interest, say, at 5 per cent. During the credit cycle confidence is shattered, and for various reasons people won't pay anything like 5 per cent. They will pay almost nothing, perhaps. Once confidence is restored, the 5 per cent which was about right at the beginning of the slump is about right at the end of the slump. You have merely to get people back into their stride.

On this occasion you have not merely to get people back into their stride, but you may have to reduce your 5 per cent ratio perhaps to a 3 per cent rate before you are in equilibrium. That means that the problem is enormously more difficult, and you are liable to a series of false starts. Something would have happened which would have overcome a normal credit cycle, but owing to the fact that the rate of interest, which is equal to the equilibrium rate, is not the rate you are assuming, the whole system deteriorates again.

We may have before us a long period of subnormal activity,

interspersed with false starts, some of which go quite a way. I fancy we shall have plenty of time to think about this problem. We shan't find our thoughts becoming out of date, even if they are not quickly adopted. Another false start will make people much more ready to consider novel methods of diagnosis in attacking the problem.

Keynes's visit to the United States in 1931 was his first since 1917 (*JMK*, vol. XVI, pp. 264–5). The trip thus provided him with an opportunity to renew old acquaintances and to acquire new information as well as to impart it. He spent his time in New York meeting central bankers, including Eugene Meyer, Governor of the Federal Reserve Board, private bankers, stock-brokers and members of various advisory services. Also in New York, at the request of Alvin Johnson, he gave two lectures on 15 and 18 June to the New School for Social Research. His notes appear below.

I. DO WE WANT PRICES TO RISE?

Dr Sprague made recently an address in London which attracted much attention. He declared it to be preferable 'that manu-factured costs and prices should come down to an equilibrium level with agricultural prices, rather than that we should try to get agricultural prices up to an equilibrium level with the higher prices of manufactured goods'. This declaration attracted attention not merely because of the authority with which Dr Sprague speaks on his own account and from his position as economic adviser to the Bank of England; but also because he went out of his way to approach with his view those responsible for the great central banks. His words distinctly implied that he was speaking the mind of the Bank of England and the Federal Reserve Bank of New York. That he was justified in this implication, I am not at all sure. But that is a matter of secondary interest. For there can be no doubt as to the extraordinary importance of the substantial issue which Dr Sprague has raised. I suggest that these are the questions before the central banks of the world today with which they must grapple at close quarters and about which they must come to clear-cut decisions as quickly as they can.

The first question is—Do they want prices to rise?—average prices, the index number of prices, that is to say. Do they, in that agree or disagree with Dr Sprague?

The second question is—Does it lie within their power to do anything effective to influence this price level? And if so, what?

My experience in London tells me—I do not know what the position may be in New York; one of the reasons I have come over is to find out—that those in authority would wish prices to rise, in fact that they do not really agree with Dr Sprague, though they may not feel this with the strong conviction one could wish; but, on the other hand, they have reached no other conclusions in their own minds as to what effective action to try and it lies within their power to make.

May I pursue these two questions? I should like, if I could, to provoke a vehement controversy, in the hope that out of the daze of minds something useful might emerge. For I feel that we are drifting disastrously without clear intentions.

Do we *want* prices to rise back to a parity with what, a few months ago, we considered to be the established levels of our salaries, wages and income generally? Or do we want to reduce our income to a parity with the existing level of the prices of English commodities? Please notice that I emphasise the word *want*. For we shall confuse the argument unless we keep distinct what we want from what we think we can get.

My own conclusion is that there are certain fundamental reasons of overwhelming force, quite distinct from the technical considerations tending in the same direction to which I shall come later, for wishing prices to rise.

The first reason is on the ground of social stability and concord. Will not the social resistance to a drastic downward readjustment of salaries and wages be an ugly and a dangerous thing? I am told sometimes that these changes present comparatively little difficulty in a country such as the United States where economic rigidity has not yet set in. I find it difficult to believe this. But it is for you, not me, to say. I know that in my own country a really large cut of money wages, a cut at all of the same order of magnitude as the fall in wholesale prices, is simply an impossibility. To attempt it would be to shake the social order to its foundation. There is scarcely one responsible person in Great Britain prepared to recommend it openly. And if, for the world as a whole, such a thing could be accomplished, we should be no further forward than if we had sought a return to equilibrium by the path of raising prices. If, under the pressure of compelling reason, we are to launch all our efforts on a crusade of unpopular public duty, let it be for larger results than this.

I have said that we should be no further forward. But in fact even when we had accomplished the reduction of salaries and wages, we should be far worse off. For the second reason for wishing prices to rise is on grounds of social justice and expediency because of the burden of indebtedness fixed in terms of money. If we reach a new equilibrium by lowering the level of salaries and wages, we increase proportionately the burden of monetary indebtedness. In doing this we should be [a line of the typescript is missing at this point]. For the burden of monetary indebtedness in the world is already so heavy that any material addition would render it intolerable. This burden takes different forms in different countries. In my own country it is the national debt raised for the purposes of the War which bulks largest. In Germany it is the weight of reparation payments fixed in terms of money. For creditor and debtor countries there is the risk of rendering the charges on the debtor countries so insupportable that they abandon a hopeless task and walk the pathway of general default. In the United States the main problem would be, I suppose, the mortgages of the farmer and loans on real estate generally. This is, in fact what, in a most instructive essay, Prof. Alvin Robinson has called the Farmers' Indemnity. The notion that you solve the farmers' problem by bringing down manufacturing costs so that their own produce will exchange for the same quantity of manufactured goods as formerly is to mistake the situation altogether. For you would, in effect, have doubled the farmers' burden of mortgages where [it] was already too high. Or take another case,—loans against buildings. If the cost of new building was to fall to a parity with the price of raw materials, what would become of the security for existing loans?

Thus national debts, war debts, obligations between the creditor and debtor nations, farm mortgages, real estate mortgages;—all this financial structure would be deranged by the adoption of Dr Sprague's proposal. A widespread bankruptcy, default and repudiation of bonds would necessarily ensue. Banks would be in jeopardy. I need not continue the catalogue. And what would be the advantage of having caused so much ruin? I do not know. Dr Sprague did not tell us that.

But there is also a technical reason, the validity of which is not so generally recognised, for believing that the results of attempting to achieve equilibrium by reducing salaries and wages might prove exceedingly disappointing. If our object is to remedy unemployment, it is obvious that we have first of all to make business more profitable. In other words, the problem is to cause business receipts to rise relatively to business costs. So it is—as long as we forget that business costs are the same thing as the incomes of those whom business employs, and that business receipts are partly the result of spending those incomes. Thus if a reduction of business costs means cutting down business receipts by an equal amount, business will be no more profitable than it was before. This will not necessarily be the case; for if people's incomes are cut down they may save less, i.e. their expenditures may not fall off as much as their incomes. But this is likely to be a small factor in the situation. Broadly, in my opinion, Mr [Henry] Ford is right.

For the main reason why business receipts are insufficient in comparison with business costs is quite a different one. If an individual cuts his costs, he gains at the expense of other individuals; if a country cuts its costs, its entrepreneurs gain at the expense of the entrepreneurs of other countries. But if every individual producer in every country cuts his costs equally, no one will be any better off than before. What then is the quite different direction in which the main part of the explanation is to be sought? I find it in the fact that business receipts are made up of two strands—the flow of direct expenditures on consumption out of the incomes of the public and the flow of expenditures on investment diverted and set in motion by the financial machine. I find, in present circumstances, the reason for the deficiency in business receipts, not in the excessive level of business costs, but in the great falling off in the flow of expenditures on investment. There is no means—if I am right—of improving business receipts to a better level compared with business costs except by stimulating expenditures on investment.

If anyone disputes this conclusion, I fear that I cannot convince him within the compass of this lecture. But for those who accept it—and I am saying nothing very paradoxical in asserting that only a revival of investment and business enterprise can put things right—there is this further technical argument for preferring a rise of prices to a fall, namely that rising prices and the restoration of business profits are both manifestations of the same process—the revival of investment.

The cumulative argument for wishing prices to rise appears to me, therefore, to be overwhelming—as I hope it does to you. Fortunately most people agree with this view. You may feel that I have been wasting time in emphasising it so vehemently. But I do not think that I have been wasting time. For whilst most people probably accept this view, I doubt if they feel it with sufficient intensity. I wish to take precautions beforehand against anyone asking—when I come to the second and constructive part of my argument—whether, after all, it is so essential that prices should rise; is it not better that liquidation should take its course?; should we not be then all the healthier for liquidation, which is their polite phrase for general bank-ruptcy, when it is complete?

II. WHAT CAN WE DO TO MAKE PRICES RISE?

Our conclusion, so far, is, then, that we need to find some way to stimulate investment. This—I am prepared to argue—must necessarily have the effect of raising the prices of consumption goods and raw materials.

Obviously there can be only one way of raising the prices of such articles, namely by increasing the demand for them in the [amount] of the purchasing power directed toward them without increasing their supply to an equal extent. But there are, broadly speaking, two methods through which demand can be increased. The one is by increasing consumers' expenditure for example, by individuals saving less, by direct advances to the consumer such as your recent Veterans' Bonus, by the dole as in Great Britain, even by raising wages, though that would have the same disadvantage as reducing wages, namely that it would alter business costs to an almost equal extent as business receipts so that profits would be no better than before. It is evident that there are obvious objections to this method if we can find an alternative. And there is an alternative. The alternative is to increase demand by directing more expenditure to capital construction, that is to say to what I have called investment.

For expenditure on capital construction means an increased pay-roll which the recipients will expand on consumption and also an increased expenditure on all kinds of raw commodities and materials; whilst at the same time it will do nothing (at any rate, nothing at once and perhaps not much in the long run if the capital construction is directed to housebuilding, transports and public utilities) to augment the supply of these articles. And that is just what we need in order to raise prices, to increase profits to normal and so to renew the motive to increase output and employment. For if we increase the demand for consumption goods and raw materials without, in the first instance, increasing their supply, their prices must necessarily rise.

Our argument is now a stage further on. In order to raise

prices, we must stimulate investment. How can we do that?

The impediment comes, we are plausibly told, not from any shortage of credit or of loanable funds but from a lack of sound borrowers. We are in a vicious circle. So long as business profits are low, it is worth no-one's while to borrow; and so long as it is worth no-one's while to borrow, business profits will be low. How are we to break the vicious circle?

It might be that there would be no way to break it within a reasonable space of time except direct Government intervention, a sort of Five Years' Plan—or Five Months' Plan, perhaps. In Great Britain I am an advocate of such measures. Whether they are appropriate here, I do not venture to say. But I am convinced that in principle they are sound. If your own attempts in this direction have appeared to fail, it has not been, I am sure, from any lack of soundness in the idea, but simply that the scale of operations, though doing good in proportion, has not been sufficient relatively to the scale of the collapse of other kinds of investment to produce convincing results. Government intervention, however, is not my theme today. Let us assume that it is, for one reason or another ruled out; or if not ruled out, at least—what is undoubtedly true—that it would need supplementing from other quarters.

I assume, then, that the problem is to stimulate increased capital construction through the agency of private, non-governmental enterprise. What can the banking system do to promote this? My answer can only be the obvious and familiar one—to increase the quantity and reduce the cost of banking credit.

There is no novelty in this. Consequently I know beforehand what the critics of such a policy are likely to say. I shall not be able in what time remains to me to explore this controversy to its inward parts. I should like to see staged a full-dress debate between the advocates and the opponents of such a policy. Let us argue it down to the bottom. It is important enough to deserve it. Meanwhile I will say what I have time to say.

The critics are likely, I think, to advance two contradictory objections, so that one is fighting, as it were, on two fronts at once. Some of them will contend that in present circumstances an intensification of the cheap money policy would produce practically no effects, that it would be negative, that it is obvious to the meanest intelligence that credit is already as cheap and as abundant as anyone could wish. But others will warn us that the measures proposed are inflationary in character, that they are replete with the usual dangers of inflation, that it would be dangerous to fool us into thinking that we can get through without taking our proper medicine, and that a heavy penalty would have to be paid later on for trying to dodge by such means the necessary 'liquidation'.

The austere view that we must continue to live in a deflation because anything else would be an inflation, I will leave on one side in this address; not because it is not held with simple conviction by some authorities whose views are entitled to respect, but because it is neither so scientifically interesting or so practically important as the other objection, namely the view that we have got already any advantages that are to be found in an easy credit policy and that the effects of any further intensification of this policy would be of trifling significance.

I do not share this view. My argument for holding the contrary is in three stages. In the first place I do not think that it is yet time to say that the terms of borrowing are cheap. In the second place, I do not agree that it would make no significant difference to the volume of capital construction if the terms for borrowing were made cheaper. In the third place, I believe that there is something which the banking system can still do.

What is our criterion of cheapness of borrowing? It should I suggest, be based on pre-war standards and not on the abnormally high rates which ensued in the War and which were maintained by various temporary influences for some years after the War. I mean by low rates of interest for typical bonds or mortgages or other forms of loans, rates which we should have considered to be low before the War.

For what classes of borrowers are rates of interest low in this sense of the term? For exceedingly few, I should say. In fact only for certain classes of borrowers on very short-term—cash-money and first-class acceptances and for the very highest class of borrower on bonds, such as the Government, which comprises practically no privately-owned concerns whatever, not even railroads or public utility concerns. Indeed for the average first-class industrial borrower, the terms are probably a good deal stiffer than they were before the slump came, if we consider how cheap it was during the boom to borrow by new issues of common stock. For bank borrowers up and down the country, for borrowers on mortgage, for the vast majority of borrowers by bonds or preferred stocks, the rate of interest is still exceedingly high. I am astonished when I look through the stock market lists to see what high yields can be obtained to-day on apparently unexceptionable security. First-class American bonds stood at higher prices thirty years or so ago than they stand at today—when America was a creditor country, when her population was increasing much faster and her savings much slower than is the case today, when the vast construction programmes lately undertaken still lay in the future. Why should this be? In the light of past experience, the rate of interest in the U.S. to-day is, it seems to me, absurdly, incredibly high—sufficient by itself to explain the slump in which we are labouring. And when one comes to the Foreign bond market, there can be no two opinions that the yields obtaining today are beyond all reason, beyond what any individual or any country can possibly hope to earn over the average of years, injurious in the extreme.

Would it make any significant difference if the rate of interest for large, typical classes of borrowers were to come down? Here I am prepared to make two concessions. I do not think it would make much difference to purely industrial borrowers for the purpose of extending manufacturers' plants. That class of experience can only come *after* business profits have revived, not before. In the second place, I am not confident that a *small* reduction in the rate of interest would remedy the situation. The prevailing rates of interest today seem to me to be so very high that they may be far above what large-scale new expansion can possibly support, with the result that a small reduction would still leave them out of gear. But we cannot give a sure answer to this until we try. One of the reasons why I think that the present depression may prove to be one of the longest on record is my fear that the rate of interest may need to be driven down a great way before we recover. But this is no reason for not beginning the task:—it is, rather, a reason for pushing on. Our task is to bring down the rate of interest to whatever extent is necessary to bring about an equilibrium balance in demand for loans and the supply of current savings.

If, however, the rate of interest can be brought down sufficiently, then I do feel confident that the demand for loans will in due course develop for buildings, for transport and for public utilities. For these are three big sources for borrowing. Manufacturing enterprise is never capable of absorbing any large proportion of current savings. It is above all of building that we must think, and after that of public utilities, when we are considering how to stimulate investment.

Before Keynes left London, what later became known as the 1931 financial crisis had already started with the failure of the Credit-Anstalt in Vienna on 11 May. During May and early June, central bankers and governments moved slowly to aid the Austrian authorities who were suffering from large withdrawals of short-term funds, largely as a result of incomplete information as to the magnitude of the potential problems involved and of political difficulties arising from Austria's relations with Germany. Late in May, the crisis of confidence spread to Germany as well and the Reichsbank lost $250 million in international reserves during the first three weeks of June. While in New York, Keynes picked up information on German developments and passed it back to London to Hubert Henderson, who passed it on to the Prime Minister and the Treasury.[1]

On 20 June, in response to the growing European crisis, President Hoover proposed a one-year moratorium on reparation and war debt payments. On

[1] This material appears in *JMK*, vol. XVIII, pp. 352–5.

22 June, before beginning his first lecture to the Harris Foundation, Keynes made a few brief remarks on the President's proposals. His press summary appears below.

Summary of remarks to the Harris Foundation, 22 June 1931

Before beginning his lecture Mr Keynes made a few opening remarks on the subject of President Hoover's proposal dealing with war debts. He declared that this represented a fine piece of policy, though in his judgement not the best possible. It would undoubtedly exercise an immediately favourable influence on the situation, provided that it was accepted by the other interested parties; and it would provide a breathing space for a more thorough discussion of the whole problem as it had now disclosed itself. But there were two rather obvious comments which had to be made.

The proposal involves substantial sacrifice on the part of the United States, but it also calls for a substantial sacrifice on the part of France. In round figures, France receives under the present scheme $200,000,000, and pays out $100,000,000. Suspension, therefore, involves her for the time being in a loss of no less than $100,000,000. Doubtless she will begin by resisting such a sacrifice, even though the public opinion of the world may ultimately induce her to accept it. And in making this resistance she will be entitled to some measure of sympathy. She may be expected to retort that the Young Plan provided for any concessions which might be made by the United States to be passed on to Germany, and if the Plan does not provide for concessions made just in the form in which the President has offered them, it could easily be adapted to this offer. Thus, France will doubtless be prepared to accept the plan to the extent of handing on to Germany the equivalent of the concessions made by the United States, but it does not follow that she will be prepared herself to make so large a sacrifice as that for which the President's plan calls.

President Hoover, therefore, will soon be faced with the question of whether or not he is prepared to modify his plan to meet the French point of view. If France makes some counter-proposal nearer to the Young Plan than this is, and involving some continued payments by Germany to France, he will be faced, I think, with a diplomatic problem of some considerable difficulty. For if he makes any material concessions, his plan will easily be spoilt and become quite inadequate to the situation.

The second question relates to what is to happen after the expiration of a year. President Hoover has not made it clear whether the postponement he has in mind is for a period of one year, so that Germany and everyone else would have to pay a double dose in 1932–3, or whether the whole scheme of payments is to be pushed forward one year, with the result of not increasing the payments in any future year, but only of extending by one year the total duration of payments. In the first case the problem as to what is to happen at the end of the year arises in acute form. It will obviously do little or no good, if Germany has to look forward to double payments a year hence, which would obviously prove impossible for her to make. Perhaps we may assume, therefore, that President Hoover either means already, or shortly will mean, the second interpretation of his plan which I offer above. But even then it is unlikely that a year will be sufficient to solve the problems of Europe; that is, unless there is a considerable rise in the level of commodity prices. I should say, therefore, that the President deceives himself if he supposes that matters can stop at the point to which he has advanced them. But this is so obvious that he may be assumed to be well aware of it himself. He has taken a *first* step of the greatest practical value to the immediate situation.

The same day as he gave his first Harris Foundation lecture, Keynes also reported to Hubert Henderson on the American banking situation.

To HUBERT HENDERSON, *22 June 1931*

Dear Hubert,

Quite apart from the immediate situations, German or other, the effect on the situation here which I had most underestimated before I came was the position of many banks in the country.

A very great proportion of the member banks, measured in number, and a fairly substantial proportion, measured in assets (perhaps as much as 10 per cent) are probably not solvent to-day, if their assets were to be valued strictly. They have purchased great quantities of second-grade bonds which have depreciated and their advances to farmers and against real estate are inadequately secured. Their position on paper is only maintained by their being allowed to reckon at par advances, the security against which is unrealisable and probably bad, and by allowing them in the case of bonds which have a marked fluctuation to write off only one-quarter of the amount of depreciation actually suffered. I believe it has been an actual instruction to the examiners of the Federal Reserve system to accept valuation of bonds which are only below their cost price by a quarter of the actual depreciation.

Owing to the number of banks which have actually failed there is great unrest amongst depositors. There is a possibility at any moment of bank runs breaking out in different parts of the country, similar to what was lately experienced at Chicago. The consequence is that depositors not infrequently take their money out in cash and keep it in a safe deposit box. This has been particularly marked in recent weeks in the Chicago district, where safe deposit boxes are no longer obtainable. Everyone agrees that there must be at least $400,000,000 to $500,000,000 being actually hoarded by the public in the shape of currency in boxes. The same movement which has been occurring in Chicago might break out at any time in the Middle West if suspicions as to the position of the banks were to increase.

This means that the banks in their turn are extraordinarily nervous, even those which are perfectly solvent, since they never know when they may have to support a run from their depositors. Accordingly they have an absolute mania for liquidity. They put pressure on their customers to repay loans, since loans and advances are non-liquid in an emergency. Generally speaking, they turn all the assets they can into a fairly

556

liquid form and in some cases keep an abnormally large amount of till money.

As long as this mentality exists on the part of depositors and banks, and it is obvious that in the circumstances it is entirely intelligible, since many banks are in fact not safe, whilst the members of the general public cannot tell which the dangerous ones are, it overshadows the whole situation. It is a large part of the explanation of the failure of the bond market to make more progress. Whenever the less saleable bonds improve a little in price and become more saleable, some bank takes the opportunity to get more liquid. It is indeed a vicious circle. The anxiety of the banks to get liquid keeps the bond market weak (I mean the bond market for second-grade bonds) and so long as the bond market is weak the position of the banks remains precarious.

Moreover, quite apart from bonds, the real estate position is undoubtedly extraordinarily bad. Many classes of properties are almost unsaleable and many mortgages are badly secured. As regards the position of loans, the farmers' difficulties do not need rubbing in.

It is the weakness of the banking system all over the country which primarily stands in the way of the usual remedy, cheap and abundant credit, failing to take effect. It will be difficult to make much progress until there is a change in this mentality.

I would emphasise, however, that this is only one isolated element in the total situation. I shall try to draw a more complete picture on my way home. The position is so complex that one can only build it up out of a variety of factors.

Yours ever,
J. M. KEYNES

On 1 July, his last full day in Chicago, Keynes returned to the international situation at a luncheon of the Chicago Council on Foreign Relations.

Remarks to the Chicago Council on Foreign Relations, 1 July 1931

When I was kindly invited by you to this luncheon I did not know that the foreign situation would be so interesting as it is today. Indeed, perhaps the situation has reached its most interesting moment. This morning's news confirms what was perhaps obvious from the beginning, that it is not all plain sailing. From the outset of the negotiations [on the Hoover Moratorium] I have been ready to predict that the stage of apparent deadlock now reached would have to come some time. But at this point, unluckily, my powers of prophecy give out! I am not prepared to predict the further outcome. What, therefore, I should like to try to do today is to analyse some of the essential elements of the situation as I see them.

One's first impulse was to rejoice so genuinely at your President's move as not to criticise or to inquire; and whatever the outcome may be this feeling will persist. For the American President to step down and talk reparations with European governments is an enormous step forward. It had to happen some day and we must rejoice, and continue to rejoice, that the day has come. But when we examine the exact form which the proposal has taken there are surely several comments to be made.

Let us begin by trying to do justice to the French point of view. Relative to her financial strength France is asked to make a larger concession than the United States. In the case of the rest of us, in the case of Great Britain for example, this is not so. But France is being asked to acquiesce in an act of considerable generosity which she had not herself contemplated at peril, if she refuses, of isolation from the public opinion of the rest of the world. It is easy to see that this is not altogether a fair position in which to place her. But this is not all. For some time past the

[1] July had been the original date for the beginning of the Hoover Moratorium, still the subject of negotiations in Paris between American and French representatives.

558

underlying idea of French policy towards reparations has been the vital distinction between the conditional payments under the Young Plan and the unconditional payments. For some time she has contemplated, I imagine, that by an act of American generosity, or in some other way, the conditional payments would be cleared out of the way and the permanent solution would consist of payment of the unconditional sums by Germany, which would probably be well within her capacity, the greater part of which would accrue to France. But Mr Hoover's plan strikes right across this; and yet it does not point the way to any final solution.

This dilemma partly arises from there being a large element of unreality in the President's proposal. On the one hand his plan is assuredly but little use unless it be regarded as a first step to a general revision; and in fact we all believe that it is such a first step. On the other hand the spokesmen of the White House are voluble to the effect that it is no such thing. Thus the proposal in the actual form in which it has been made is iced over with a curtain of unreality; though we are all so pleased that the President has done anything that every one is reluctant to make such a comment.

Has the President a perfectly clear idea in his own mind as to what his next step is to be? No one knows. Or, rather, *I* don't know. Does he really think that after one year Germany will resume payments and will be ready to go forward with the Young plan unrevised? If he believes this he believes, to put it mildly, what is exceedingly improbable. If he does not believe it ought he to think it entirely unreasonable on the part of the French Government to be reluctant to give up what has been the essence of their recent policy without being given any rational idea of where it is leading them? Why, year after year, month in month out, in cold weather and in hot weather, should we be forever condemned on this subject of reparations to silence and to pretence, never talking to one another like sane and rational people?

At the same time it may well be that public opinion in this country is not yet ripe for the final step and that it is real political wisdom on the part of the President to propose at this stage some kind of a stop-gap arrangement to hold the immediate situation. Granting this, however, it is arguable to suggest that there is a much better stop-gap proposal that he might have made, namely, that all War debt payments should be cut down by half for a period of say five years. There would be several advantages in such a plan. It really would gain for the world breathing space. In five years there will be a new situation, of which we can take account; with [a] one-year moratorium we shall have to begin reconsidering the situation long before there is anything new of which to take account. Moreover it would be free from a premature suggestion of total cancellation and it might well contain within it the seeds of a permanent solution. Finally it would during the transitional period be fitted much better into the Young Plan than the President's actual scheme. For the President's actual scheme is one which it is very difficult to compromise without spoiling it. If Mr Hoover had made the five year proposal which I suggest, I believe that an adjustment of different interests and points of view would have been much easier.

It is now 12 years almost to a day when, in somewhat of a frenzy of mind, I began writing the first pages of *The Economic Consequences of the Peace*. I thought then, as I think now, that there was good reason—good reason in an extraordinary degree—to feel a mingled indignation, mingled because it was directed almost equally against what was stupid and against what was wrong. Mr Hoover was there in Paris in those days and I believe that he was not far off from sharing these sentiments of mine. He had played a noble part during the War and he did nothing ignoble during the transactions of the peace. I cannot believe that he and I think very differently about these things at the bottom of our hearts.

In these 12 years there has been, it is true, a continual

progressive movement towards sense and decency. But 12 years is a long time to wait before the last sentence is written of a shameful chapter in the history of civilisation. Twelve years is a long time. A German in the prime of life today, who is now 30 years old, was a young school boy of 13 when the War broke out. A new generation has grown up. This means—naturally and properly and inevitably—that a new factor has entered the problem, of which statesmen will do well to take account. It is no longer entirely a question of Germany's capacity to pay. It is a question of her state of mind and of what she will choose to endure.

Mr Hoover—in spite of all that I have said and that I have found to criticise—has taken a vital first step. One catches a glimpse of the Hoover of former days. Let him be large minded and with imagination in planning his future course.

Keynes left Chicago on 2 July and travelled east to Boston. He then went on to Washington where he met the President and Eugene Meyer. He reached New York on 8 July. Keynes sailed for London on 11 July.

During his Atlantic crossing he prepared a memorandum on economic conditions in the United States. When he reached London, he circulated it to members of the Economic Advisory Council, to Sir Charles Addis, Sir Ernest Harvey and Cecil Lubbock of the Bank of England, and to Sir Walter Layton of *The Economist* and to Francis Rodd of the Bank for International Settlements.

ECONOMIC ADVISORY COUNCIL

A NOTE ON ECONOMIC CONDITIONS IN THE UNITED STATES

(Circulated by direction of the Prime Minister)

I. THE POLICY OF THE FEDERAL RESERVE SYSTEM

I saw, in the course of five weeks in the United States, a good deal of the responsible authorities of the New York Federal Reserve Bank and of the Federal Reserve Board, especially of Mr Eugene Meyer, the Governor of the latter, and had some thorough-going discussions. I also had a discussion with the chiefs of the Chicago Reserve Bank. The question of their prospective policy has to be discussed under three, partly separate, headings, namely—

(i) The policy which Governors Meyer and Harrison would pursue on its merits.

(ii) The limitations on their complete freedom of action, since they have no such despotic powers as the Bank of England possesses.

(iii) The limitations in the present American environment on the efficacy of any steps which it lies within their power to take.

(i) It would not be true to say that the heads of the Reserve System in New York and Washington are as confident and whole-hearted adherents of the so-called 'monetary' school as, for example, I am myself. But they lean very decidedly to that side of the fence, and their qualifications would relate, not to the objectives to be aimed at, but to the likelihood of attaining them by monetary expedients. That is to say, they are, at any rate, definitely not of the party of the 'equilibriumists' (whom I discuss below). They want to raise commodity prices as much and as soon as they can; they want to reduce the long-term rate of interest by any means in their power; and they believe that a revival of the construction industries is probably a necessary condition of the recovery of industry in general.

Consequently they are quite in favour of trying the experiment of cheap money and abundant credit carried *à outrance*, convinced that at the worst it can do no harm and that it must be of a right tendency in present conditions, and only doubtful (and I share their doubts) as to how substantial the practical results will prove to be in the *near* future.

I should say that those parts of the Macmillan Committee Report which concern them are almost entirely sympathetic to them, and that they will assuredly co-operate along these lines to the best of their ability.*

---

* I supplied an early copy to the New York Reserve Bank, where it created interest and, so far as I could gather, approval.

(ii) It is necessary for the leaders of the Reserve System to carry banking opinion with them. 'Open-market' operations can only be carried out by authority from a Committee of the twelve Reserve Banks which in turn are dominated by representatives of the member banks. Until recently average banking opinion has been opposed to large-scale 'open-market' operations. Their motives have been mixed. Partly a deflationary bias such as is common enough among bankers in bad times (unluckily, by a perverse dispensation, the opposite is generally true in booming times) as we know from our own experience. But also, and perhaps more decisively, from certain calculations of supposed (though, I should say, short-sighted) self-interest;—in the first place, it does not suit the banks that money should be too cheap and abundant, since this reacts unfavourably on their earning power, and in the second place they are afraid of being forced, from lack of alternative outlets for their funds, into buying bonds at rising prices on which they will subsequently suffer a depreciation when at some later date the Reserve System reverses its policy, this motive being specially strong because this is just what happened on the last occasion (in 1927) when the Reserve System intervened with large purchases of 'governments'.

These underlying motives have been reinforced by the fact that most of the so-called 'economists' attached to the leading New York banks have erected, quite sincerely, an intellectual façade in front of them. For most of these economists adhere in varying degrees to what is now called in New York the 'equilibriumist' theory. This is the theory which Dr Sprague has made familiar in London, to the effect that our troubles are essentially due to a disparity between manufactured prices and raw material prices, and that equilibrium can only be restored by depressing the prices of the former to the level of the latter by means of wage reductions and otherwise. (I discovered, however, not the slightest foundation for Dr Sprague's suggestion that his views were shared by the authorities of the Federal Reserve System—quite the contrary.)

Nevertheless it seemed clear to me whilst I was in New York that the influence of this way of thinking was rapidly waning. Bankers were beginning to see how suicidal from their own point of view would be the establishment of a new equilibrium at a level of prices and incomes so low as to render the superstructure of financial and banking indebtedness fixed in terms of money altogether insupportable to the debtor. Prominent opponents of 'open-market operations' even got to the point of admitting that, at the worst, the experiment could not do harm in present circumstances. Moreover, Governor Eugene Meyer was handling the members of his Reserve Board and Reserve Banks with great skill and discretion. Thus open-market purchases did actually take place on quite a substantial scale before I left New York, though they were partly under cover of special circumstances which happened to make it easier to justify them to the hesitant.

Nevertheless, whilst there need be no doubt as to the right-mindedness of the Federal Reserve authorities, it is not certain whether they will be able to pursue their policy far enough or whether it may not again arouse criticism before it has had time to justify itself by success. For no magical results are to be expected in the near future—for the reasons to be given below.

(iii) The objective of ultra-cheap money and an expansion of the basis of credit by open-market purchases is to facilitate and encourage borrowing for new capital enterprise both by lowering the long-term rate of interest (as a result of raising the price of bonds) and in other ways. But in existing American conditions it is much more difficult to attain this objective than it would be in England if we were free to go ahead without regard to possible repercussions on the foreign exchanges.

In the first place there is the vital distinction between our central banking methods, that in London the clearing banks and the money market are not normally indebted to the Bank of England except on a trifling scale, so that they cannot use surplus funds put at their disposal to repay their indebtedness at the central institution; whereas in the United States the member banks can offset the effect of purchases of Government securities by the Reserve System by reducing the System's holdings or discounts and acceptances. This has actually occurred in recent weeks. Fortunately the total volume of discounts and acceptances is at the present time abnormally low as a result of the enormous gold holdings. Nevertheless the Reserve System may have to purchase a very large volume of Government securities to make its immediate purpose effective, and in the course of doing this it may lose nearly all its bill holdings—both of which developments may tend to evoke hampering criticism and give a handle to the deflationist party. I should expect that in the effort to retain bills the New York Reserve Bank is likely in the near future to lower its buying rate for acceptances (which will be helpful to cheap money policy in London), whilst leaving its discount rate unchanged.

There are also two other reasons why open-market purchases may have to take place on an inconveniently large scale before they are effective. Bank nervousness in the United States is causing a most dangerous tendency to hoard currency. This has already, most unfortunately, offset the large gold imports, and it might partly offset future purchases of Government securities. It is possible that some $500,000,000 of actual currency is being hoarded by nervous depositors or as extra till money by nervous banks. I return in the next section to this weakness of the member banks which I regard as a matter of first-class importance. For the same reason, namely the extreme nervousness of the member banks, they may, for a time, actually refuse to make use of the additional reserves put at their disposal by the Reserve System, i.e. they may maintain idle reserves in excess of their legal requirements, a thing which is almost unthinkable in London and has never previously occurred in New York. It still seems safe to assume that the member banks will not hold excess reserves beyond a certain point or for more than a certain time. When I left New York, this question was still unresolved. But at that date the New York member banks were in fact holding substantial excess reserves, and the inter-bank rate of interest on what are known as 'Federal Funds', i.e. loans of balances at the Reserve Bank between member banks, had sunk to zero. These observations will serve to show the difficulties of the Reserve System in making their will effective by means of operations which are not so large as to alarm uninstructed public opinion.

But even when the Reserve System has persuaded the member banks to expand their assets, only the first step will have been taken. The most probable course of events would seem to be the following. Certain banks will be induced to sell their Government securities at rising prices and to replace these with other bonds of not quite so prime a quality. Moreover if the banks use their surplus reserves, the bonds bought will, for the System as a whole, be for a much larger amount than the governments sold. This will cause a rising bond market all along the line, and will enable many of the country banks to liquidate bonds they now hold at a price which does not show a loss on what they paid for them, which will enable them to satisfy their desire for greater liquidity without putting pressure on their commercial customers. Obviously bonds will have to rise in price until some holders choose to part with them and prefer to hold bank deposits instead. At this point it is impossible to predict further without assumptions as to popular psychology. On the most favourable assumption, the sight of a rising bond market might actually stimulate depositors to take money off deposit to buy bonds, thus accelerating the upward movement to a point at which borrowers for new enterprise are encouraged to come forward. On the most unfavourable assumption depositors, distrusting the high prices of bonds and fearing subsequent depreciation, will prefer deposits to bonds (or other securities) before the latter have risen high enough to prove attractive to new borrowers. It seems to me reasonable to act on the former assumption until it is disproved by experience. But one has to remember that there is no guarantee that the ideas of borrowers and lenders can be brought into harmony. The lenders may distrust the price of bonds before this price has risen high enough to be attractive to the borrowers. With the special reasons for fearing this in existing conditions in the United States I deal in Section III below.

The other route along which ultra-cheap money can operate is by forcing American banks to reduce the interest rates which they allow on deposits with the effect, in course of time, of causing some transference by depositors from bank deposits to bonds. Deposit rates are falling, but they are still far too high. For example, savings deposits can still earn 3 per cent or more in most districts. The movement and the tendency are in the right direction, but, as a consequence of competition between the banks and the difficulties in the way of securing co-ordinated action, a long time is likely to elapse before the movement will have proceeded far enough.

At present the cost of long-term borrowing to the ordinary borrower is higher than it was before the slump began. I attach a chart of bond movements.

I conclude that the Federal Reserve System will endeavour to operate along what are, to my way of thinking, the right lines,

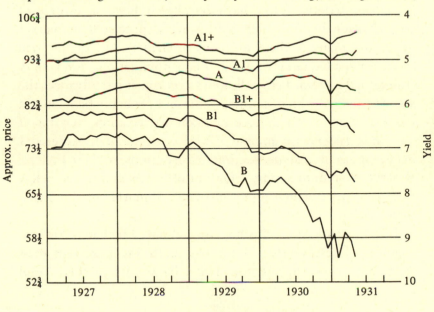

but that there are certain serious obstacles to its carrying this policy to a decisive conclusion, except with the exercise of obstinacy and determination, after the lapse of considerable time, and unless extraneous help comes from circumstances outside the ambit of the banking system. Two of these obstacles are so important that I have reserved them for separate treatment to which I now proceed, namely the weakness of certain member banks and the lack of opportunity for new construction enterprise on an adequate scale.

II. THE WEAKNESS OF THE AMERICAN BANKS

The anxiety of many banks and of many depositors throughout the country is a dominating factor, the importance of which I had not fully estimated before visiting the United States. It is, I think, one of the biggest obstacles overhanging the situation, in the way of the normal process of recovery.

A considerable number of the member banks and a fairly substantial proportion, measured in assets (perhaps as much as 10 per cent), are probably not solvent today, if their assets were to be valued strictly. They have purchased large quantities of second-grade bonds which have since depreciated in market price, and many of their advances to farmers and against real estate are inadequately secured. Their nominal position is only maintained by their being allowed to reckon at par advances the security against which is unrealisable and probably bad, and, in the case of bonds which have a market depreciation, to write off only one quarter of the amount of depreciation actually suffered. I believe it has been an instruction to the examiners of the Federal Reserve System to accept valuation of bonds at a figure below their cost price which represents only a quarter of the actual depreciation.

It is easy to see how this has come about. The banks' ratio of capital and reserves to liabilities is often small, so that even moderate losses wipe it out. Yet a large part of their bond holdings have depreciated by 10 per cent or more. And real estate, against which they have lent money, has fallen to 50 or 60 per cent of its former value and is often entirely unrealisable. In many parts of the country the farmers, who have been heavy borrowers, are quite unable to repay what they owe with their produce at present prices.

The inevitable result is an absolute mania for liquidity wherever liquidity is possible. Bonds saleable at a reasonable price are sold; borrowers against good stock exchange collateral are pressed to liquidate; and new loans are not readily accorded. Thus for many ordinary people in small towns up and down the country, it is a travesty of the case to suggest that credit is easy.

Here is to be found a large part of the explanation of the weakness of the bond market and of the failure of cheap short-money to produce its normal reaction on the long-term rate of interest. When the less saleable bonds improve a little in price and become more saleable, some bank takes the opportunity to get more liquid. It is, indeed, a vicious circle. The anxiety of the banks to get liquid keeps the second-grade bond market weak, and so long as the bond market is weak the position of the banks remains precarious.

This atmosphere affects perfectly good banks as well as the bad ones. For no small up-country bank knows when it may not have to stand a run by its depositors. Moreover I fancy that the great New York institutions have more skeletons in their cupboards than anyone yet knows about for certain, and that their concealed anxieties cramp their action more than is admitted. The American banking system, by and large, is not prepared today to take even a good actuarial risk in the financing of new large-scale enterprise. The readiness to withdraw deposits from Germany was a reflection of their unwillingness to run any avoidable risk.

Owing to the number of banks which have actually failed already, there is great unrest amongst depositors. There is a possibility at any moment of bank runs breaking out in different parts of the country, similar to what was lately experienced at Chicago. The consequence is that depositors not infrequently take their money out in cash and keep it in a safe deposit box. There must be at the present time at least $400,000,000 to $500,000,000 being actually hoarded by the public in the shape of currency in boxes. This has been particularly marked in recent weeks in the Chicago district, where safe deposit boxes are no longer obtainable. The same movement which has been occurring in Chicago might break out at any time in the Middle West if suspicions as to the position of the banks were to increase.

The position can be well illustrated from what has recently happened in Chicago where I discussed the details with several of the leading bankers. The total deposits in this neighbourhood stood at the prodigious figure of $2,500 million, of which about two-thirds was held by three or four very large banks in the centre of the town, and one-third (about $800 million) by 260 small outlying institutions. No bank in Chicago is allowed a branch establishment even within the City, whilst Chicago stretches about 30 miles from end to end, so that many ordinary people have naturally banked with mushroom suburban establishments, many of which were little better than collecting agencies for funds with which to support real estate operations. In the last two months fifty of these banks have suspended payment, ten to twenty more are likely to do so, and fifty which were solvent but not liquid have been taken over by stronger institutions. Many of the banks have put off suspending payment until the last possible moment and have tried to restore confidence by not requiring the notices of withdrawal to which they were entitled. I was told of banks which had paid out more than 60 per cent of their deposits, which is a considerable accomplishment for any bank, before putting up their shutters. Nevertheless the effect of these practices on confidence has been the reverse of favourable; for the dividends remaining for the 40 per cent of the depositors who have not withdrawn have been distressingly small, and the principle of 'first come, first served', rather than early suspension and an equal distribution for everyone, has stimulated the practice, by justifying the prudence, of early withdrawals. It is believed by the local bankers that in Chicago alone at least $150,000,000 of actual currency is now held by the public in safe deposit boxes.

The Chicago situation is largely a reflection of a quite appalling real estate collapse from which it may take years to recover. The centre of Chicago is now a vast medley of skyscrapers which are quite a colourable imitation of New York. Almost everything in sight of more than a moderate height has been put up within the last five years; a good deal of it is unlet; little of it is valued even nominally above 50 or 60 per cent of its first cost, and is often unsaleable at any price; and most of it has been erected with borrowed money. It is an amusing complication that the mortgage laws of Illinois have been designed for the protection of the farmer, who is allowed to gamble on the chance of the next harvest being good before he is actually turned out. Thus the skyscrapers of Chicago are treated before the law as if they were farms, so that the lender, when he forecloses, cannot obtain actual possession or begin to clear up the position until after the expiry of fifteen months!

The truth is that the financial structure of the United States is no more able than that of the rest of the world to support so terrific a change in the value of money. The vast growth of bank deposits and of bonded indebtedness in that country interposes a money contract between the real asset on the one hand and the ultimate owner of wealth on the other. A depreciation in the money value of the real asset, sufficient to cause margins to run off, necessarily tends to burst up the whole structure of money contract, particularly those short-term contracts represented by bank deposits.

I think it would be true to say that the first preoccupation of Governor Meyer is to restore solvency and liquidity to his member banks and that the objective of restoring the level of

571

output to normal is at present remote. In seeking to put the bond market better by open-market operations, he is thinking of restoring the value of the bonds held by the banks rather than of stimulating new enterprise. In discussing plans to form a great industrial trust to purchase real estate, his object is to restore some confidence to this market and so bring market values nearer to the former mortgage valuation, rather than to encourage new building. In seeking to raise the prices of wheat and cotton, it is, again, the solvency of the farmer which he has in view. These problems have to be solved first, before it is useful to consider seriously large programmes of new construction.

After observing this background, I understand much better than I did part of what lies behind Dr Sprague's attitude, his feeling that no good can come until insolvencies have progressed much further and a large amount of monetary indebtedness wiped out. But if we are to proceed along these lines, how much of the financial structure would be left standing when we were done, I do not know. To counsel this way out seems to me to be, even for a philosopher, a counsel of despair; whilst for one attached to a central bank, it is suicidal, because it means sacrificing what central banks exist to safeguard. But whilst we ought, in my judgement, to bend every effort to move the course of events in the opposite direction to that which Dr Sprague recommends, it is not wise to underestimate the extraordinary difficulties of doing so.

III. THE OBSTACLES IN THE WAY OF NEW CONSTRUCTION

To my mind the proofs are overwhelming that the slump is primarily a slump in construction. I attach a chart of the twelve months' moving average. It is difficult to see how there can be a real recovery without renewed construction enterprise on a large scale. But I have been greatly depressed by perceiving more clearly than before the many obstacles in the way of increased construction.

INDEX OF VALUE OF BUILDING ACTIVITY
(3 Months Moving Averages Placed on Last Month, Seasonal Variation Eliminated).
COMPARED WITH INDUSTRIAL PRODUCTION.

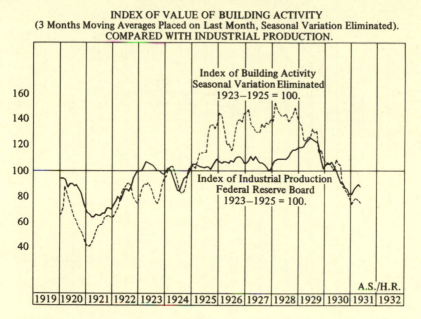

(i) Looking back it seems to me that one important peculiarity of the 1927–9 boom was the readiness to neglect the rate of interest and to agree to pay rates which, cautious calculation should have shown, could not be earned by the enterprise. Thus quite apart from the facts that population is no longer increasing rapidly and that the cream has been taken by now off most of the new construction business, etc., etc., the rates of interest which were being paid before the slump were already too high. Rates of interest may have to fall a tremendous way before it will pay on a cool calculation to repeat the enterprise of 1927–9.

(ii) In the leading manufacturing industries, such as steel, motors and many others, it is certain that no new plant will be required for a long time to come.

(iii) There is a good deal of renewal and reconstruction which the railways might do. But the great falling off in their revenues, more severe than in Great Britain, has broken their spirit and destroyed their credit.

(iv) The condition of the real estate market and the opportu-

573

INDEX OF VALUE OF BUILDING ACTIVITY
(12 Months Moving Totals Placed on Last Month)
COMPARED WITH INDUSTRIAL PRODUCTION

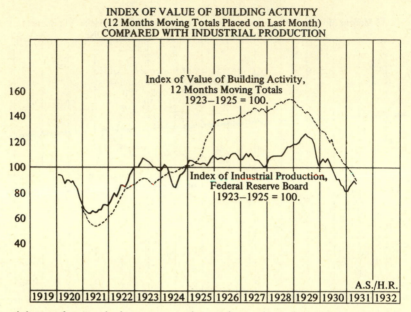

nities to buy existing properties at bargain prices must stand in the way of new building.

(v) An enormous amount remains to be done in improving the housing of the common man. But it is a vicious circle. With his present reduced earning power he cannot pay a higher rent. If the rate of interest fell by half, it would, of course, be quite another matter.

(vi) There is a marked absence of new inventions, and it may be necessary, again, for a very great fall in the rate of interest before enough new techniques based on existing knowledge will be brought within the payable zone.

(vii) But just when it is so important to bring about a really drastic reduction in the long-term rate of interest, the extreme nervousness of lenders and their recent unhappy experiences conspire to keep the rate up.

(viii) There are severe limitations on the possibilities of new construction expenditure by public authorities, though very large expenditures on roads are still proceeding. Many local authorities are near the maximum that they are allowed to borrow under the law. The activities which fall within the direct purview of the state itself are restricted in character.

The position as regards state-directed public works is almost exactly the same as it is in Great Britain. The Administration, that is to say, is heavily committed to being in favour of them in principle. Enthusiasts outside Government Offices declare that there is much ready to be undertaken. One individual, who struck me as being well informed, declared that there was $1,000m worth of projects which could be executed within a year. But the President told me that he had just gone over the figures again, that they had already shot their bolt, and that there was not above $150m worth of projects still to be done over and above the normal programmes. Cynics say that the Administration is keeping some schemes up its sleeve with a view to launching them so as to produce their effects nearer the date of the elections (November 1932).

Whilst I was in America I spent much time pleading the cause of new construction. But I came to the conclusion that an adequate recovery is really out of the question pending the elapse of time and a great fall in the long-term rate of interest.

IV. WAGES AND EMPLOYMENT

To judge from dinner party conversation or Wall Street gossip, wage-cuts in the United states are already widespread and large in amount, not always by cuts in the standard rate, but by various devices and subterfuges which have greatly impressed the popular imagination so that one is told about them again and again. It is exceptionally difficult to bring this general impression to a statistical test; but those who follow statistics, such as pay-rolls, etc., tend to tell a somewhat different story. The facts as near as I could get at them by tackling a variety of sources of information are as follows.

Farm wages have fallen heavily. There is an official index which shows an average drop of 21 per cent for April 1931 as compared with a year previously. It is reasonable to suppose that with the present appallingly low prices for farm products they are falling still further today in the areas producing wheat, corn and cotton. This has led to extraordinary wage anomalies. A cotton picker in the South, for example, does not now get above $1 to $1.50 a day, whereas a building labourer in New York may get $13 a day, though, generally speaking, $3 to $4 a day (or, say, $20 a week) is now a typical wage for unskilled labour in manufacturing industry, and $4.50 to $5.50 a day (or, say, $26.50 a week) for skilled labour. Agricultural wages can easily fall to the barest level of subsistence, as they have already in Cuba.

In large-scale industry, however, my conclusion is that hourly wage rates have not been affected very much more than in England. In certain large groups, such as the railways, the building trade (subject to the qualifications given below), General Motors, United States Steel, there has been no reduction at all. In May the Industrial Conference Board (an organisation which has been set up by big business for information and research duties) took a sample, described to me by those who did the work as being a thoroughly good and satisfactory sample of large-scale manufacture, from the manufacturing concerns with which they are in touch, of actual payments covering 625,000 workers. This showed a reduction in hourly rates per head of 3·4 per cent, compared with September 1929, nearly all the reduction having occurred since September 1930. They told me that, as a broad generalisation, this resulted from a cut of about 10 per cent in one-third of industry and no cut at all in the other two-thirds. Owing, however, to the prevalence of short-time the reduction in average weekly receipts was far greater, namely, 17·6 per cent. The common impression about wages cuts may, I think, be partly due to a confusion between hourly rates and weekly receipts. This related to big business. In little concerns up and down the country larger cuts would probably be found.

The position and prospects can be further illustrated by

reference to the particular cases of railways, building, and United States Steel.

The railways are now asking the United States Commerce Commission for leave to raise their rates. Behind this there is a tacit threat to attack wages—which the Administration does not at all want—if they are refused, and a tacit understanding to leave wages alone if their request is allowed. Thus the railways have, after great discussion and acute controversy amongst themselves, definitely decided to prefer rate raising to wage cutting as a solution of their present difficulties.

The building situation is very confused. It is to this industry that the stories of special wage-cuts and of the men's business agents accepting subterfuges, such as less in the pay envelope than is stated outside, chiefly relate. It is clear that in country districts or with non-union labour or with small contracts this is often true. It is also true that for all classes of contracts there has been a substantial fall in costs. One could rely on letting a building contract to-day some 20 per cent below the level of 1929, whereas the published indexes show a fall in building costs of only some 5 per cent. But I am told that in the case of a large contract with union labour in a big centre this would not be due to any cut in wage rates, whether admitted or concealed, but to a reduced cost of materials, to a lower margin of profit and to a greater efficiency of labour. The less efficient workers have been discharged, men will agree to work harder to enable their employer to get a contract and so keep them employed, and, generally speaking, vexatious union restrictions have given way more readily than wage rates have.

I am not sure that more illumination is not thrown on the present position and prospects of wages in American manufacturing industries by the reasons given to me by a prominent director of the United States Steel Corporation why they have *not* reduced wages, than by anything else I heard. The problem is particularly acute in this case because several of the smaller steel concerns have cut both wages and the prices of their products, and because there is a strong school of opinion in favour of the view that a reduction in the prices of construction materials must be the first step towards a recovery. Accordingly the general question of reducing wages is discussed at every Board meeting, and the reasons why the answer has been so far in the negative are, I was told, the following:—

(i) The steel trust employs somewhere around 250,000 workers. So far they have discharged no efficient individual, the numbers on their books have been reduced by only 8,000 as a result of natural wastage not replaced. But the majority of these 250,000 workers are only employed and are only paid for 2 days a week. With their present wage rates and by drawing on their savings, etc., they can just live on 2 days' earnings. But if their wages were to be cut by an important percentage, this would be impossible. Thus it would be necessary to discharge many workers, so as to be able to give the others 3 days' work a week. In the absence of any unemployed relief this would be a very serious step to take. This reason was given me, first and foremost.

(ii) The steel trust is specially reluctant to discharge workers, because, having always insisted on non-union labour, they feel a special obligation to their workers to protect their conditions of life.

(iii) Their managers have figured out that they could not sell an appreciably increased quantity of steel products as a result of the rather modest price reductions which would be made possible by any practicable wage cut.

(iv) If they are going to have to reduce wages, this is not the time of the year to do it. In the hot summer months the workers—cost them what it might—would refuse to accept a wage cut but would prefer to lie in a hammock or drift off into the country. By October, however, this would have ceased to be true. The workers would have to accept whatever they are offered. Thus the winter is the time, if any, to abandon ideals and consider wage reductions seriously.

(v) Finally the industry is riddled with price and rate agreements of one kind or another, both between producers and with consumers, which it might be tiresome or unwise to upset by the price reductions which would have to ensue on wage reductions.

I believe that short time *plus* high wage rates has been a very important offset to the absence of unemployment relief. If wage rates are cut, this method of mitigation will be less feasible.

The social risks of wage-cutting in the United States take, I think, a different form from that which they take in Great Britain. First, it is not so much a question of strikes and lockouts as of direct social disorder, looting and other forms of lawlessness in that naturally lawless country. The Administration, as is well known, has set its face strongly against wage reductions. Doubtless obvious political considerations with an election in sight come in; in addition it must weigh with them that, for the reasons just given, wage reductions would not be easily compatible with the absence of unemployed relief, against which the Administration has also set its face. But when I discussed this question with President Hoover personally I was interested that the reason which he put in the forefront was the maintenance of law and order. He claimed that on the whole industrial wage rates had been maintained and that it was owing to this that they had got through the slump so far without any really troublesome occasion for calling out the police or the militia, which he regarded as a remarkable achievement. He declared it to be his conviction that any general assault on wages would be followed, not by strikes or lockouts, but by a widespread tendency towards lawlessness. I had not heard this point emphasised either in Wall Street or amongst academic economists, but the opinion of the Administration on such a point must be entitled to some respect.

And this view is, moreover, extremely plausible in a country where there is no organised relief to the unemployed, if it is true, as I believe it to be, that the percentage of unemployment in the United States is not far short of what it is in Great Britain, and quite likely, greater. On the best informed estimates I could obtain there has been no improvement, apart from seasonal changes, during the first half of this year, and the percentage of unemployed industrial workers is somewhere round 21 per cent today, which is very near out figure. But the number of those on short time may be nearly as many again. Moreover, many of the unemployed are individually not unemployed continuously, and it is their spasmodic earnings at a rate of hourly wages, which is better than it has ever been after allowing for the fall in the cost of living, which makes it possible for them to get along without a dole. But if wages were cut, on the top of the existing unemployment, more than a third of the industrial population might be in acute distress, over and above the troubles of the agriculturalists.

I heard the question of the advisability of wage reductions discussed in a large gathering of academic economists. The voice of the 'equilibriumists' (whom I have discussed above) was heard, but I think it would be true to say that the balance of opinion was decidedly in favour of the view that the immediate advantages to employment from wage reductions would not be large and were outweighed by other considerations (social and the effect on the price level in relation to monetary indebtedness). In business and Wall Street circles there are many people in New York, as in London, who plead wage reductions as the solution. But these opinions are often 'academic' in the bad sense of the word. The real forces on the other side are those which I have indicated.

As regards 'white-collared' workers, an elaborate inquiry recently conducted by an official of the Metropolitan Life shows that up to the end of 1930 unemployment was very heavy but salary reductions very small. I believe that the same is true to-day. In banks, insurance offices and the like salaries have not yet been cut, and the reductions are mainly confined to the salaried employees of industrial concerns where a cut (of say 10 per cent in the typical case of such reductions) has been made to correspond to a cut in wage rates.

V. THE PROSPECTS OF RECOVERY

As stated above, the figures indicate beyond question that this depression, in strong contradistinction to the depression of 1921, is a construction slump. It is a characteristic of a construction slump that it is likely, failing some special stimulus, to be of much longer duration than a slump which is due to a reaction from a boom in consumption goods. In this particular case it is difficult to see how recovery can come without a revival of construction; for an intermediate revival in the market for consumption goods could not be expected by itself to carry us very far.

I held this view before I went to the United States, and discovered nothing there to lead me to modify it. Indeed, just the contrary; but, as explained above, I became much more pessimistic than before as to the prospects of a revival in construction. Nor did I discover a single responsible or intelligent authority in the United States who differed from this view. Many of them were, in effect, more pessimistic than I was, because I was generally arguing in favour of possible remedies, urging that *something* could be done to mend matters and to hasten recovery, whereas a common view there was that matters must be allowed to take their course—which no one expected to be a quick one. I do not think that a vestige of a reason can be found for supposing that anything approaching a genuine recovery is in sight.

The possibility of an intermediate recovery, a temporary upward movement within the main depression which Wall Street might mistake for the genuine article is, however, quite a different question and a much more difficult one, about which my opinion fluctuated from time to time. I had better set forth the pros and cons, beginning with the favourable symptoms.

(i) There is some evidence that the rate of consumption of goods may have been greater than the rate of their production, so that invisible stocks are very low.

(ii) Motor cars are certainly wearing out faster than new cars are being purchased, so that a replacement demand is being built up.

(iii) A point has come, or will soon come, when repayments in respect of previous instalment purchases will cease to exceed the amount of new purchases, so that this particular source of excessive and unwanted, but more or less compulsory, saving will come to an end.

(iv) Raw materials and foodstuffs have certainly suffered hitherto more than their share of the aggregate loss of producers as a whole, due to their being for various reasons in a specially vulnerable position. The consequent curtailment of output now is, or soon will be, in many cases sufficient to allow the producers of such goods better to protect themselves. Quite apart, therefore, from a revival in demand, it is reasonable to expect some recovery during the ensuing months in the wholesale index number. This will exercise a stimulating influence in more ways than one, in particular by stimulating retarded demand and leading to a building up of normal invisible stocks, and by putting a stop to inventory losses and thus enabling many manufacturing and retailing concerns to put a better face on their published profits. Perhaps this has been in the past the most reliable stimulus to recovery in the case of slumps more moderate and more normal than this one.

(v) In general, every slump tends on the downward phase to overdo itself and to proceed further than the fundamental conditions justify. Thus it contains within itself, and without the assistance of any material improvement in the fundamentals, the seeds of a partial recovery.

On the other side, however, the following considerations can be adduced:

(i) The argument about under production of consumption goods may be already out of date and may have spent itself in the spring recovery, which it may have partly caused. For example, the recent level of output of the textile and boot and shoe industry in the United States has been decidedly on the high side, much higher in the last six months than in the preceding six months. When one comes to details, it is not easy, I think, to find an important consumption industry which appears to be lagging behind unduly.

(ii) The argument about a replacement demand for motor cars may be, on the other hand, premature. Some day it will be true. But the possibilities of making even an American car 'do', when money is short, for a far longer period than formerly must be far from exhausted. Moreover American roads are much better than they were. This is an argument which will have much more force eighteen months or two years hence than it has today.

(iii) The instalment argument has some force, though the excellent trade in refrigerators in recent months has partly offset declines in motor cars, etc. But there is another factor on the other side which deserves very great emphasis and may perhaps outweigh a whole bunch of the favourable factors, namely that markets must have already had the main part of the benefit of the Veterans' Bonus. During the four months ending on June 30th the Veterans' Bureau paid out the enormous sum of $1,150,000,000, or at the rate of about $10,000,000 a day. It is to be assumed that an important part of these sums were taken for the purpose of new expenditure of one kind or another, though some deduction is necessary for amounts used to pay off bank loans, where banks were pressing (there was during this period a very substantial reduction of bank loans). The aggregate anticipated has been already largely exceeded and the payments may be expected to peter out before long. Allowing for a time lag of (say) three months, purchasing power will be deprived by the autumn of this large volume of support, comparable in amount to our own dole but not so permanent. It is also possible that public works may have partly spent their force and be from now on a declining, rather than an increasing force. But I could obtain no clear or decisive evidence as to this.

(iv) The expectation of some recovery in commodity prices is probably legitimate. But when one comes down to details, there is, so far as the United States is concerned, a good deal to be said on both sides. Let us take wheat, cotton, corn, copper and oil as typical, important commodities produced in the United States. Without stopping to give reasons which would take a long time, the evidence shows, I should say, that wheat and oil* may well be at the turning point. But in the case of copper organised control is breaking down and prices should go lower; in the case of corn there is a prospect of a greatly increased crop with the risk of still lower prices; and in the case of cotton it is doubtful whether this year's acreage cut is sufficient to hold the price unless boll-weevil comes to the rescue (which, however, it quite well may) and whether we must not wait until next year before there is a rally under the stimulus of a still greater cut in acreage.

Moreover, even if there is quite a considerable rally in prices, farmers will nevertheless go through the selling season with prices far below anything they have ever previously experienced. One must not forget that this year's prices for grains represent, even compared with last year's prices, a first-class calamity for the farmers. Wheat is only a trifle above 50 cents at Chicago compared with round 90 cents this time last year and round 90 cents in 1913. This means 35 cents or less on the farm, i.e. about 12s a quarter—a desperate price; and the prices of the other cereals are just as bad or worse. These prices on the farm are not much more than *half* the worst prices that the American farmer has ever previously experienced at harvest. Thus, even if, as may be hoped, there is some recovery in the course of the next three months, the farmer's position will still be desperate. The disturbance to the American price structure taken in relation to the burden of monetary indebtedness is of formidable dimensions. I see no background here even for an intermediate recovery.

(v) Against the general principle of the see-saw within the framework of the main depression, there is nothing to be said

* Oil has been given away recently in Texas which must represent about bed-rock for prices.

except the possibility that we shall perceive when we look backwards from a greater distance, that we have already had the intermediate up-swing last spring.

My first impression after looking at the American position at close quarters was to expect, on a balance of considerations, some moderate improvement this autumn. My last impression, however, was to doubt it. I still consider that it is a possibility but, on the whole, a bad bet. A negative attitude is the wisest. How closely Wall Street will follow trade, it is impossible to predict. When I reached New York early in June, it was evident that the market wanted to move upwards—there were too many bears waiting to take profits. Mr Hoover's announcement came when the market was already better and had the effect of releasing a spring which was almost ready to release itself. But Wall Street's intermediate movements mean very little of fundamental importance. It seems to me to represent at the present time, and likely to continue to do so for the rest of this year, a game of see-saw between professional bears working at suitable moments on the basis of poor current earnings, impaired margins and general nervousness and, on the other hand, a crowd of hungry losers standing on the side-lines (as it was expressed to me) still desperately hoping to recoup on the bull tack what they have lost on the bull [bear?] tack.

On the one hand, there are very large amounts of liquid investible reserves which will not, presumably, be kept liquid forever. On the other hand, the leading stocks are still by no means undervalued on the basis of present earnings and look dear compared with some British securities. For example, steel shares, copper shares, motor shares, radio, General Electric etc. are capable of meeting severer disappointments yet, and might well suffer heavy further falls. Very few market leaders (except General Motors) yield more than $5\frac{1}{2}$ on current dividends at current prices. Naturally I discussed this question of stock-market prospects with all sorts of people, but found no-one who even thought that his opinion was worth two-pence. When the elements of bluff and skilled market manipulation and mass psychology and pure chance are added to the intrinsic difficulties of forecasting the courses of the credit cycle itself, the case is hopeless. But I should say that the wisest and weightiest opinion was to the effect that *if* the classes of shares which I have mentioned above were to rise 15 per cent, during the course of the next two or three months, it would be a golden opportunity for the bear.

Before I went to the United States I was disposed to hold with some confidence that the first impetus to recovery in the rest of the world would have to come from America. I held this view so firmly that it was some time before I even questioned it. But eventually it was put to me point-blank in discussion that perhaps the opposite was true. And in the end I came to wonder whether this might not be the more probable opinion. We may have to drag along what seems an endless period until something happens to stir the dry bones elsewhere than in North America. But a complete and durable relaxation of credit conditions, due to a reversal of the present direction of tension between debtor and creditor countries, must be the necessary preliminary to this.

Meanwhile there are certain, of course, to be plenty of intermediate swings and false starts.

VI. THE WAR DEBTS[2]

My impressions regarding the American attitude to this question can be summed up briefly:—

(1) Mr Hoover's pronouncement was an unqualified success in *all* quarters. I did not discover anywhere a shadow of opposition even to the prospects of the 'next step' which everyone assumed must follow. The papers which had previously been intransigent concealed or discarded their opinions

---

[2] This section also appears in *JMK*, vol. XVIII, pp. 355–7.

in response to the obvious popular feeling—except the Hearst papers, and Mr Hearst was, I think, out of the country at the time. It seemed to me clear that popular opinion is entirely purged of its former passions and will readily accept whatever the Administration may propose.

(2) Indeed it is not going too far to say that this is the most popular thing the President has yet done. When I arrived, his stock stood incredibly low. There was not a soul who would say a good word for him. But this 'constructive' step changed the whole situation. With the elections in sight the Democrats would doubtless be willing to work up the old feelings. But two things restrain them. Partly the obvious change in public sentiment. Chiefly, perhaps, that they are just as dependent on Wall Street for funds as the Republicans are, and Wall Street is unanimous in desiring a solution, indeed they cannot possibly afford that there should not be one. It is the slump, as well as the lapse of time and the inherent reasonableness of Americans, which is partly to be thanked for the change in mind.

(3) Quite apart from political considerations, social or other-wise, the immense short-term indebtness of Berlin to New York (and indeed to American member banks all over the country) made some action by the President almost imperative. The total indebtedness of Berlin to American banks before the run began, was estimated at £200,000,000, and the five largest New York banks were owed, I was told, an average of £20,000,000 each— sums far larger than they could afford to see in jeopardy on the top of their other troubles. Thus the pressure of big finance on the Federal Reserve System, and of the Reserve System on the Treasury and the President, was overwhelming. If Mr Hoover had refused to move, that, on the top of his previous extreme unpopularity, might well have ruined him. He acted at the very last moment when he had practically no other choice left him. I was convinced that this was so a week before he actually moved.

(4) But now that a move has been made, it is of first-class importance that the main architects should have been the

President, Mr [Andrew] Mellon and Mr Ogden Mills, and that they should have got great credit out of it. For these are the individuals who have been hitherto the great stumbling-blocks. Now, however, they are somewhat committed to seeing it through, and will probably themselves wish to make, if they can, a good job of what they have put their hands to. I do not think that anyone in Washington is so foolish as to conceal from himself that what has been done is only a beginning.

(5) The two chief dangers in the situation are these. There was an *extreme* irritation in Washington against the French— and I am speaking of a date before their latest exploits as engineers of ruin. Both the President and Mr Ogden Mills, the Acting Secretary of the Treasury, spoke of them in my presence with extraordinary bitterness. The other danger is lest Germany should tumble down altogether on reparations *before* the time has come for the Americans to make their further concessions. It might, paradoxically enough, be more difficult for the United States to make concessions which overtly benefited their former Associates only than concessions which were associated with a voluntary reduction of what these Associates are demanding from Germany.

(6) The scheme of a large long-term loan to Germany— though here I may be speaking rashly and without enough knowledge of the immediate diplomatic circumstances—seems to me to be quite chimerical, having regard to what America is likely to, and is able to do constitutionally, as well as a bad idea from our own point of view.

J. M. K.

Chapter 7

THE 1931 FINANCIAL CRISIS

On 13 July, while Keynes was on the high seas, sterling came under pressure on the foreign exchanges, as the financial crisis which had affected Austria, Germany and Central Europe made its effects felt on London.[1] The same day, the Report of the Macmillan Committee on Finance and Industry with its estimates of Britain's large short-term net debtor position appeared. The Bank of England lost gold until 23 July without changing Bank rate, which it then moved to $3\frac{1}{2}$ per cent. A week later, with the agreement of credits to the Bank of England from the Bank of France and the Federal Reserve System of $125 million, Bank rate rose to $4\frac{1}{2}$ per cent. The same day Parliament adjourned without discussing the Report of the Committee on National Expenditure chaired by Sir George May. The May Committee, formed by the Government the previous February, forecast a Budget deficit of £120 million and recommended cuts of £97 million in Government expenditure, including a reduction in the unemployment benefit of 20 per cent.

On the following Sunday the Prime Minister, who had retired to his home at Lossiemouth, wrote to Keynes.

From J. RAMSAY MACDONALD, *2 August 1931*

My dear Keynes,

I am up here a little bit isolated, but I shall be exceedingly grateful to you if you will send me anything that you may write on the [May] Economy Committee's Report, as I should like very much to have your views for my guidance.

I hope you are going to have a good holiday,

And am,

Yours very sincerely,

J. RAMSAY MACDONALD

---

[1] The same day the Danat Bank failed in Germany and the German authorities declared a two-day bank holiday.

Keynes replied on 5 August.

To J. RAMSAY MACDONALD, *5 August 1931*

Dear Prime Minister,

I do not propose to publish anything about the Report of the Economy Committee, because my views are not fit for publication;—they are not even fit for corculation to the E.A.C., but I welcome very much the opportunity, in response to your letter, to tell you personally what is in my mind.

One could criticise the Committee's recommendations in detail, but I would prefer to consider them on very broad lines, because their recommendations are a quite logical outcome of a general point of view which many responsible and authoritative people hold—or have held up till recently.

The Committee's recommendations obviously represent in substance and broad effect an effort to make the existing deflation effective by bringing incomes down towards the level of prices. They are part and parcel of the policy of seeking equilibrium by *general* reductions of wages and salaries and they would indeed, if they were taken in isolation, be a most gross perversion of social justice. To select the school teachers as solitary victims is surely unthinkable. The effect, therefore, on my mind is to be hard up against a prompt and definite decision whether I am in favour of making deflation effective, or whether I prefer to seek another exit. This is the question which we now have to face, because the adoption of the Committee's recommendations as an isolated act and not as part of a much larger policy on the same lines would, I am sure, be useless.

My advice is that we do *not* attempt to make the deflation effective, because, apart from the question whether it is intrinsically desirable, I am convinced for the following reasons that an attempt made now would be both futile and disastrous.

1. The *first* effect of adopting the proposals of the Economy Committee and analogous measures would certainly be a further decline in business profits and a substantial increase of un-

employment, because economies which are not balanced by reduced taxation must necessarily reduce demand relatively to supply,—the buying power of those immediately affected would be diminished, whilst no one else's buying power would be increased. Thus there would be no initial success from adopting the policy to give us the necessary courage to persevere and take strong doses.

2. The cut in money incomes which would be required to reach equilibrium by this route would be more than those concerned would submit to. It might well be 30 per cent. Indeed there might be no feasible cut which would be sufficient, because of the reaction of what we might do on what would be done abroad.

3. It would be impossible to obtain the public consent to such measures unless bondholders, etc., were treated in the same way. I know no practical means to ensure this or to secure even a modicum of social justice.

4. But above all—and this is the new fact within the last two months—it is now nearly *certain* that we shall go off the existing gold parity at no distant date. Whatever may have been the case some time ago, it is now too late to avoid this. We can put off the date for a time, if we are so foolish as to borrow in terms of francs and dollars and so allow a proportion of what are now sterling liabilities to be converted into franc and dollar liabilities, thus giving a preference to those of our creditors who are the quickest to sell. But when doubts as to the prosperity of a currency, such as now exist about sterling, have come into existence, the game's up; for there is no object to foreigners in keeping sterling balances if there is any appreciable doubt about their value. It is conceivable that we might have avoided this if we had been more clear-sighted. But we cannot avoid it now.

It will be difficult for the City to give clear guidance at the present time. The accepting houses, who constitute the major part of the Court of the Bank of England, are many of them more or less insolvent. The Governor is probably near the end of his nervous resources.[2] It is now a problem for the Government rather than for the City. I suggest that you should consult a Committee consisting of all living ex-Chancellors of the Exchequer, whether they believe that deflation *à outrance* is possible and are in favour of attempting it, or whether we should not at once suspend gold convertibility and then take collective thought as to the next step.

We might, I think, try to convert disaster into success. We should remember that most of the rest of the world is suffering much as we are. I should seek forthwith to win the hegemony of a new Currency Union by inviting all Empire countries to join us in adhering to a new currency unit. I believe they would all, including Canada, accept, with the possible exception of South Africa. I should further have it in mind to invite also at some stage all South America, Asia, Central Europe, Italy and Spain—indeed anyone who felt inclined to come in.

The new currency unit might be a gold unit, obtained by devaluing existing units by not less than 25 per cent. It is *vital* that the change should not be smaller than this, and preferably greater. But it would be much better that its value should not be permanently fixed in gold—at least in the first instance—but should be allowed to depend on the future behaviour of the countries still remaining on the gold standard. Do not forget that the initial effect of these measures would be more or less to destroy the export trade of these gold standard countries. Having thus put exchange difficulties behind us, we should then proceed to organise activity and prosperity at home and abroad along the boldest possible lines.

I believe that many people, even in the City, far more than might be expected—very likely the Governor of the Bank of England himself, for example—are now in favour of something of this sort at the bottom of their hearts. It might quite well be taken by the country as a whole, not as a disaster, but with an

[2] The Governor had, in fact, collapsed on 29 July. He was out of action until after the crisis was over.

extraordinary sense of relief and of hope. The 'inner opinion'—what everyone believes at the bottom of his heart but never realises until the last moment—is a mighty force in this country.
5.8.31   [copy initialled] J. M. K.

A week later, having changed his mind about writing on the Economy Report, Keynes wrote to MacDonald. His article 'Some Consequences of the Economy Report' (*JMK*, vol. IX, pp. 141–5) appeared in *The New Statesman* for 15 August.

On 16 August, *The Liverpool Echo* commended Keynes's *New Statesman* article to its readers in an editorial. This produced a letter from a correspondent, who signed himself 'Sammy Smiles' and suggested, using the analogy of a person in a tight financial corner, that the sensible solution appeared to involve reducing expenditures to balance the income available. Keynes replied.

To the Editor of The Liverpool Echo, *27 August 1931.*

I have read the letter from 'Sammy Smiles' about 'True and False Economy'. When he is out of work and consequently hard up, does he suppose that he betters himself by 'economising' on the things he does for himself?

Does he give up shaving, and does Mrs. Sammy Smiles give up cleaning the house, on the ground that being out of work and consequently hard up, he cannot afford these things? For that is the true analogy for the effect of the community as a whole economising when already insufficiently employed on the things it does for itself.—J. M. KEYNES.

To J. RAMSAY MACDONALD, *12 August 1931*

Dear Prime Minister,

I am after all writing an article on an aspect (but only one) of the Economy Report for next Saturday's *New Statesman and Nation*. So I enclose* a proof of it for you.

* Not attached.

I feel, however, that this article has little enough bearing on the immediate situation. Indeed I rather feel this about the Economy Report as a whole. I still feel that the probabilities of the situation, if left to themselves, are at least as bad as I suggested in my previous letter. I should expect that we should have to make a big decision one way or another within a few weeks. If we decide to try and patch the situation up, it probably still lies within our power to do so; but only by means of drastic action of a kind which has been scarcely discussed so far, and of which the Economy Report, if it formed any part at all, would be nothing more than trimming for psychological purposes.

Yours sincerely,
J. M. KEYNES

P.S. The impressions I have collected today[3] persuade me that there will be a crisis within a month unless the most drastic and sensational action is taken. I believe that it is still possible for us to keep on the gold standard if we deliberately decide to do so, but in this case we should have to conform our whole policy accordingly. Personally I should support for the time being whichever policy was made, provided the decision was accompanied by action sufficiently drastic to make it effective. But I should only *favour* the gold standard policy if it were part of a general scheme for restoring credit everywhere—which it probably would not be.

I am staying in London until tomorrow and will be visiting H. D. Henderson at the Cabinet Offices in the morning.

The next day he wrote to Richard Kahn.

To R. F. KAHN, *13 August 1931*

The foreigners are taking their money away as fast as they can. We should be off, I should say, within a month unless heroic

---

[3] That day he had been at meetings of the National Mutual and Provincial insurance companies and seen R. H. Brand and Francis Rodd.

measures are taken. Perhaps they will be, perhaps they won't.
Betting slightly on.
13.8.31   J. M. K.

Although the Government had hoped to consider the Report of the May
Committee at leisure in time for the return of Parliament in October, events
pushed the timetable forward. On 11 August, summoned by the Chancellor
of the Exchequer, the Prime Minister returned to London. The Cabinet's
Economy Committee met four times in the next week before the full Cabinet
assembled to discuss the proposed Budget changes. Over the next four
days the Cabinet attempted to agree on a package of expenditure cuts
and tax increases that would prove satisfactory to financial opinion so that
the Government could raise additional loans in New York and Paris to
support sterling. The Cabinet failed to agree on a suitable package, including
a cut of 10 per cent in the unemployment benefit; and MacDonald agreed
to head a National Government on 24 August. The new Government agreed
to a programme of cuts on 27 August. Two days later the Government
raised loans totalling £85 million in New York and Paris.

Keynes commented on the new proposals in *The New Statesman* for 29
August. Two days earlier he wrote to Sir Josiah Stamp.

From a letter to SIR JOSIAH STAMP, *27 August 1931*

I feel very unhappy about the whole course of developments. It
seems to me that the question of adhering to the gold standard is
going through the same sort of stages as reparations.

We are now, if I understand rightly, about to raise what one
might call the Dawes Loan. It remains to be seen whether we shall
be content with this or whether we shall have to raise a Young
Loan, and then at long last we shall have to face the real question
(again like the Germans) whether we are going to have a large
reduction of wages or in the end go off gold. But why do we
always have to go through these dilatory and disastrous stages
before facing up to anything? As you know, I have been putting
off facing up to the position so long as there was a chance of any
other exit. But the other exits are now closed.

The enclosed, which will appear in Saturday's *Statesman and
Nation*, reflects my feelings.

The next day, Keynes wrote to his mother.

From a letter to MRS F. A. KEYNES, *28 August 1931*

You will have seen something of what I feel about the political situation in this week's *N.S. & N.* But the more I reflect, the worse I feel about the way things have developed. One's hopes were always precarious and now they have disappeared. The country has been stampeded into an attempt to make this deflation effective, and heaven knows how it will end.

From The New Statesman and Nation, *29 August 1931*

NOTES ON THE SITUATION

1. It is true that drastic reductions in the Budget had become a *sine qua non* of the maintenance of the gold parity of sterling.

2. It is probable that public opinion is not ready for devaluation, whether or not devaluation is desirable on its merits. This is so for several reasons. As it is a matter very difficult to debate in public with candour, opinion is unprepared. The idea of devaluation carries with it for the ordinary man all the exaggerated terrors of something the consequences of which are unknown to him. National pride is deeply involved. In any case the decision involves a difficult balance of advantage and disadvantage which most people feel themselves incompetent to make.

3. Thus it is natural that very strong forces should insist that one more struggle be made to retain gold parity. If the effort is to be made, it should be made with energy and decision.

4. Consequently it is not for those who doubt the wisdom of the decision or hesitate before all that it implies and symbolises to attempt to carry it out. If they believe that for various reasons it is inevitable that the attempt be made, then it is for them to make way for those who fully believe both in the policy itself and in its necessary consequences. Thus if the Labour Government were not prepared (as they were not) deliberately to abandon the present gold standard, it was their duty to resign. That it was

open to them to do so, is one of the advantages of the party system, especially in present circumstances when a majority could be found for a new Government without a General Election.

5. This is particularly true in the present case. For though some parts of the Economy Programme, including the cut in the dole, may be in themselves justifiable, they stand, in actual practice, for a point of view which is unacceptable. The reasons for 'economy' which weigh heavily with those who are enthusiastic for it are mixed reasons. Those who like deflation and those who dislike state action get their innings. Thus anyone who actively participates in enforcing the economy necessarily becomes involved in these points of view. In particular, the abandonment of state-directed or state-assisted capital development schemes, and the postponement of a tariff, mean a sole reliance on competitive wage reductions as a means of remedying unemployment.

6. The actual results of 'economy' will be disappointing for the reasons which I have recently explained in *The New Statesman and Nation*. In some directions its immediate effect will be to make matters worse and it may be expected (unless it is accompanied by a tariff) to aggravate unemployment.

7. Whilst the 'economy' Budget is a *sine qua non* of maintaining gold parity, it is unlikely that it will be sufficient by itself. As a result of recent events, we are probably faced, or soon will be, with the definite choice between devaluation and a heavy reduction of all kinds of money incomes—which was by no means certain even three months ago. But not all those who are now supporting 'economy' realise this, or that 'economy' is logically only the first step in a far-reaching policy to make deflation effective. If the effort is successful without too much stress and strain, too many insolvencies or too great social injustice, well and good. But if not, or if the public, when they discover what deflation involves, refuse to give all the support which will be necessary, it is well that there should be some

organised political force to which they can turn. After a perplexed and anxious fashion, issue has now been joined on a matter of great importance, both in itself and because of its implications, about which opinions can differ for the sort of deep reasons, difficult to express adequately, which genuinely divide us.

On 10 September Keynes returned to the crisis in an article in *The Evening Standard* entitled 'We Must Restrict Our Imports' (*J M K*, Vol. IX, pp. 238–42).

On 12 September, Keynes provided an unsigned article for *The New Statesman*, later identified as his in their half yearly index.

From The New Statesman and Nation, *12 September 1931.*

A GOLD CONFERENCE

There is one criticism which all those who are opposed to the present Government's policy must squarely meet. Whatever the rights and wrongs of the past, whatever the long-distance effects of the policy of economy, one thing, it is argued, is certain—that a state of emergency existed, and still exists, and that there is consequently no alternative to the course which the Government is now proposing. Thus if resignation had not been open to Mr [Arthur] Henderson and his colleagues, they would have been compelled to do just what the Coalition is now doing. Is this true?

The government's own policy is, in truth, no policy at all. They have submitted to the conditions of foreign lenders as to the manner in which we should balance our budget, in order to obtain a short-term loan expressed in foreign currencies which will enable us to repay short-term loans expressed in sterling. But this does not get us far, and the funds thus obtained may not last us long. For it does not touch the ultimate causes of our discomfiture. It would be ridiculous to pretend that cutting the dole and school teachers' salaries and increasing the burden of taxation will restore either the confidence of investors or the balance of trade. The 'economy' policy can only delay, it cannot prevent, a recurrence of another crisis similar to that through which we have just passed. We have to ask ourselves, therefore, whether there is not an alternative policy of a more fundamental character, which—unlike the present Government's policy—would, if it were successful, open up some vista of hope for the future.

We suggest that there was, and still is, an alternative emergency policy open to the Government, however difficult it may have become as a result of the blunders of the past few weeks. The first step is for the Government of Great Britain to announce to the world that it intends to maintain a stable currency, but that it cannot and will not work the international gold standard if the other creditor countries do not play the 'rules of the game'. It should thereupon demand an international conference of the gold standard countries at which the issues can be plainly discussed and faced, and a decision arrived at as to whether it is in the interests of the world economy either that matters should continue as at present or that Great Britain should be forced off the gold standard. As emergency measures pending the meeting of this international conference, the Government should announce that it proposes to prohibit the export of domestic capital as far as measures can be devised to this end, and to restrict dealings in foreign exchange. At the same time it should declare that it does not intend to raise any further credits abroad for the protection of sterling, and that it is prepared to submit to a further drain of gold, allowing the amount of the fiduciary note circulation to be increased, though not the total note circulation in the country, but that this is to be the last effort to preserve the gold parity of the sterling exchange. If it were clearly shown that our policy was not one of destroying the value of our currency or of allowing sterling to fall to a fraction of its present parity, as was done by France in revaluing the franc at 2d., and that if we were forced off the gold standard this would only follow because the other creditor countries refused to play the rules of the game, then there is good warrant for believing that the financial prestige of Great Britain would be more surely restored than by the present policy of drift or by any other course open to us.

The whole world is heartily sick of the selfishness and folly with which the international gold standard is being worked. Instead of being a means of facilitating international trade, the gold standard has become a curse laid upon the economic life of the world. It is not necessary to go into academic questions as to how far the fall in the world level of prices has been brought about by a world shortage of gold. It is only necessary to look at the present distribution of the world's gold supplies. Half the world's gold stocks are now held by America. Between December, 1929, and December, 1930, the American gold stocks rose from £880,000,000 to £944,000,000 and the French from £336,000,000 to £431,000,000. At the present time the American gold stock is about £1,000,000,000 and the French £471,000,000. The reason for this concentration of gold in America and France is that these countries have not lent their surplus balance on international account as Great Britain used to do in the past. France appears to have employed virtually the whole of her international surplus during the last three or four years in the purchase of gold and short-term liquid claims instead of embarking on long-term investments abroad. The attitude towards long-term foreign investments of investors in the United States has varied but has been generally unfavourable, except in periods of boom when American issuing houses have lost their heads. It was the opinion of the Macmillan Committee that the disposition of these creditor countries to employ their international balances in the purchase of liquid claims, including gold, had been primarily responsible for the disastrous fall in the level of world prices. Yet it is one of the objects of the gold standard to maintain stability of the international price level.

Consider the game from the point of view of the debtor

countries. as the Macmillan Committee pointed out, the sole practical use of a gold reserve, seeing that gold coin has been withdrawn from circulation, is to serve as a medium for meeting a deficit on the balance of international payments until steps have been taken to bring it again to equilibrium. To quote from their report:

Today the position of debtor countries is apt to deteriorate rather than improve as a result of their having to export gold. For it is usually beyond their power to adjust their balance of payments so rapidly and completely as to permit a complete cessation of borrowing; yet, in so far as they export gold, their credit as borrowers suffers. Thus, having lost their gold and not being able to borrow, they are forced off the gold standard.

Thus we see the great primary producers of South America and Australia unable to borrow and unable to buy, and endeavouring to balance their international accounts by restricting their imports and perpetuating the slump in the manufacturing countries.

Great Britain itself is now being forced into the position of a debtor country. its surplus balance on international account fell last year from £138,000,000 to £39,000,000, and according to Professor Clay is now non-existent. (Why then did the Bank of England allow £44,000,000 of overseas loans to be raised in the London capital market in the first six months of this year? What is their 'unofficial embargo' worth if the Bank of England makes blunders of this sort?) Yet the steps which have been taken by Great Britain to bring her balance of international payments into equilibrium have proved ineffective. Bank rate has been raised to $4\frac{1}{2}$ per cent, but this has not attracted foreign funds to London because there is lack of confidence. Nor has it increased the confidence of the domestic capitalist. The more foreign credits are engineered to support the pound sterling, the greater opportunity is given to nervous patriots to transfer their capital abroad without loss. The domestic flight from sterling is still going on, as is shown in our City page, and until a sane economic and financial policy for this country is devised, confidence at home is not likely to be restored. To raise further foreign credits in these circumstances is futile. The pound sterling will never be saved by such panic measures.

If an international conference of the gold standard countries is called, as we suggest, there would be some chance—and without it there is almost no chance—of saving the financial structure of the whole world. This gold conference has to be put forward to America and France as an act of common sense and prudence, as a means of saving the economic world from the disaster which will surely overtake it if the slump is to be prolonged by a universal deflation policy. Its object would be a far wider one than to stabilise London's position. It would be unsuccessful unless it were to reverse the whole trend of international deflation. There is probably no means of securing this except by the threat that otherwise Great Britain will leave the existing gold standard system. For, if we do so, we shall not be alone. We could make ourselves the centre of a new currency system to which the Empire, and indeed half the world, whose need for a change is even greater than ours, would gladly adhere.

If the countries of the world are all bound together by a network of credit, it is to the interest of all to preserve the centre, which is London. Professor Clay put it thus in his broadcast address on Monday:

The banking systems of all other countries keep a portion of their funds in London. . . . You can guess, therefore, what a shattering blow to credit throughout the world any fall in the value of sterling would inflict. All the other monetary centres of Europe would find their resources suddenly diminished and their stability undermined. Depositors in every country would become nervous, banks in every country . . . subjected to a run. A breakdown of the economic life of half the countries in Europe would not be an unlikely result.

If the gold parity of the pound sterling is so vital to the rest of the world, we may surely count upon full attendance at a conference of the gold standard countries. We must make it plain to our friends on the gold standard that, if they refuse to play the game according to the rules, this is not to be made a compelling reason for reducing the standard of life in this country for a generation. If, as a result of the conference's failure, we were to leave the gold standard system, this would be preferable to the deflation policy with which the Coalition Government intends to launch this country in the race for economic suicide.

Two days later, on 14 September, Keynes summed up the situation for Walter Case in New York.

To WALTER CASE, *14 September 1931*

My dear Case,

It is difficult to know what to say about the present situation here and in the world at large. I am utterly depressed, and rack my brains as I may, I find it almost impossible, even by way of a day-dream, to conceive a way out now that matters have been allowed to develop as they have. I wonder how you and Stewart[4] are feeling about it. Make him write a letter if there is any force on earth which can do that.

To read the newspapers just now is to see Bedlam let loose.

---

[4]   Walter Stewart, formerly Economic Adviser to the Bank of England.

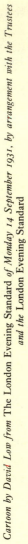

AND SO TO BED.

Cartoon by David Low from The London Evening Standard of Monday 14 September 1931, by arrangement with the Trustees and the London Evening Standard

Every person in the country of super asinine propensities, everyone who hates social progress and loves deflation, feels that his hour has come, and triumphantly announces how, by refraining from every form of economic activity we can all become very prosperous again. Many of the things which are being done by the Government are of course necessary and unavoidable. But the spirit which actuates them is, to my way of thinking, quite appalling. They also have the disadvantage that they only touch the fringe of our real problem.

There is, as you will have gathered, a sort of hysterical outburst for economy of every description, not only Governmental, but municipal and personal. We shall soon all be unemployed from refusal to purchase one another's services. But whilst cutting ourselves with knives in this way, we are leaving totally unattacked the real problem of the balance of trade.

It is quite clear that at the point which things have now reached, our choice lies between devaluation, a tariff (which though a mitigation might be by itself very far from a cure) and a drastic reduction of all salaries and incomes in terms of money. It is useless to gamble any longer on a rise of world prices, which was what I was still hoping up to last May.

But an extraordinary feature of the situation is that our so-called National Government has been formed on the basis of the members of it promising one another not to adopt any of the three remedies. Sacrifice being the order of the day, everyone has agreed to sacrifice what he himself believes to be the only possible remedy for the situation. Furthermore, the Labour Party, which now forms the Opposition, is really exactly in the same boat as the National Government. They also refuse to adopt any of the three possible alternatives. So I suppose we shall drift along from the last crisis to the next, and what the date of the next will be you can probably say better than I can, since it will largely depend upon what happens to the American bank money in London, which is still estimated at around £100,000,000. The minor countries, as distinct from the United States and France, have probably withdrawn by now the bulk of what they could withdraw. Very pessimistic figures are going round as to the amount of our unfavourable balance of trade. I think they may be over-pessimistic, but I suppose the figure must be above £50,000,000 and might reach £100,000,000 owing to the decline in the receipts from our foreign investments.

The chief matter of political discussion is whether or not there is to be an early general election. Originally the idea was to have an election not later than October, and it is still probable that the business now in hand can be got through quickly enough to make this possible. Also there is immense pressure from Conservatives, not in the Government, for an election with a view to an immediate tariff, [and] a purely Conservative adminis-tration. On the other hand, I have no doubt that the financial authorities will advise that an early election may throw too great a strain on the exchanges, and must at all costs be avoided. The question will then arise whether the free traders in the present Government will make concessions to their tariff colleagues. Possibly some compromise may be patched up. A short time ago I thought an early election more probable; today I feel that I really do not know. Indeed nobody knows. It will be the course of events in the next few weeks, and particularly the strain on the Bank of England, that will settle the matter.

For my own part I have now come quite clearly to the belief that devaluation is the solution for this country and am publishing that opinion shortly. In private there are many who agree with me in their hearts, but I am almost alone in openly saying so. At present there is a vast wave of so-called patriotic propaganda to the contrary, which is trying to frighten the people with most fantastic accounts of what would happen if we slipped our anchor.

[copy initialled] J. M. K.

My belief is that the undercurrent of opinion tends to the ultimate inevitability of devaluation. But this may not be for a bit yet. For I am sure we shall try a stiff tariff first.

On 16 September, at the invitation of a small group of M.P.s, including Norman Angell, John Buchan, Oswald Mosley and Eleanor Rathbone, Keynes addressed a meeting of M.P.s interested in the economic situation. This was the first of a pair of such talks; Henry Clay of the Bank of England was to speak the next day. Keynes's notes for the meeting have survived.

Notes for a speech to Members of Parliament, 16 September 1931

1. The significance of Economy
2. The effects of the Budget
3. The question of the balance of trade

1. False analogy with private individual.
Why false?
Mainly because most of the individual's expenditure is in the nature of foreign trade.
It would be absurd if I was already out of work, to refuse to do, for reasons of economy, the things I do for myself.
For example for an unemployed man not to shave himself or his wife not to clean the house.
This is a good example because he would save the shaving soap and his wife would save the household soap.
Our own economy is like that. We do save imports equal to a small proportion of the total amount by which our wealth is diminished. If the only object is to buy less in the shops, the obvious way is to economise on those activities a large proportion of the price of which is represented by outside expenditure.
What are the rational purposes of economy?
    Either to buy less from abroad
    Or to release resources for other purposes
Now practically none of the resources which economy will release are needed, or will be used, for any other purpose.
Thus economy will do no good except in so far as it leads to reduced imports.
If extreme free traders were right, even this would do no good.
2. Now all this relates to the aggregate expenditure. From the point of view of employment etc. it makes no difference on what

it is spent. But from a larger point of view it is obviously desirable that it should be as useful as possible.

Also for quite different reasons, connected with future budgetary problems when we have returned to more normal conditions, the deficit incurred for current purposes should be kept as small as possible consistently with not exacting a great increase in unemployment.

I might sum up in this way. It is desirable, in the interests of employment that the expenditure of the Gov^t. of one kind or another should somewhat exceed its income. I should estimate the appropriate excess in present crisis at more than £50,000,000. But this expenditure should be as much as possible on things which have some utility such as education, public health, and public works and as little as possible on things wholly useless in themselves such as the dole.

But the way to reduce expenditure on the dole is to reduce the number of unemployed. And the way to do this is to spend *more* not less on education, public health and public works.

As for the balance of trade that needs attacking along different lines.

2. *The Budget and the Economy Bill*
Its objects should be (1) to improve the balance of trade, (2) to increase employment, (3) to do these things without running contrary to social justice.

This Budget fails on every test. In my opinion the Gov^t.'s programme is one of the most wrong and foolish things which Parliament has deliberately perpetrated in my lifetime.

I should like to say a word first of all on social justice. Can scarcely trust myself to speak. The attacks on the schoolteachers seem to me to be a most foul iniquity. The well-to-do suffer 3 or 4 per cent, the schoolteachers 15. There can be no plea of necessity. £6,000,000 saving. Sinking fund. Tea and sugar. But apart from the figures, the whole principle of attacking Gov^t. employees as such when other people are to be left alone seems utterly wrong.

Of course this may be a prelude to a general attack on wages. But I do not believe it is.

The Gov^t. must surely have mentioned it by now if this had been their intention.

As regards employment every single effect adverse.

It does nothing to decrease costs of production because those salaries which Govt^t. controls have least effect in this direction.

Cutting schoolteachers' salaries will not help us recapture lost markets.

In order to prove perfectly mad, increase of industrial contribution. Stop housing, roads, telephone expansion—simply insane.

Flagellate ourselves so that foreigners will say at any rate these Britons take their problems seriously—we might lend them some money.

Certain that the Budget will increase the number of unemployed by more than 10 per cent by Christmas. [The] dole is cut [by 10 per cent], so that total expenditure on the dole itself (I am now excluding savings on transitional benefit) will be increased by the Budget.

Reasonable to expect that the Budget by the time it has produced its full effect will directly increase unemployment by somewhere in the neighbourhood of 400,000 men. We shall, in other words, have 'economised' the services of this number of men.

There remains the balance of trade.

The Budget only helps this in so far as men who are thrown out of work or otherwise impoverished will reduce their expenditure on imported food and the like.

But what an extraordinarily roundabout and extravagant way of reducing our imports of food!

3. This brings me to the third part of my discourse.

Our international balance of payments.

Apart from foreign withdrawals and the flight from sterling by British citizens I agree that our actual balance of trade on income account is now unfavourable and may be seriously unfavourable, *due to falling off of our invisibles.*

What can we do to fight this underlying disequilibrium which is far more serious than the Budget?

Three possible lines of policy

a. Tariffs and bounties

b. British wage reductions

c. Devaluation

I first of all rule out wage reductions (i.e. 30 per cent) as being not now a serious alternative.

Tariffs and bounties are obviously the middle means and should be tried. But I no longer feel certain that devaluation can be avoided.

The aim of tariffs to-day must be primarily the exclusion of imports. I would plead strongly that an important part of the proceeds should be directed to helping exports.

Discussed in Macmillan Report.

In present conditions tariffs *plus* bounties necessary to restore free trade conditions

It seems to me unwise to delay measures of this kind.

They would also supply internal stimulus and, unlike the Budget, increase employment.

c. *Devaluation*

But this will do nothing for external situation.

I believe choice lies between a large rise of world prices and Devaluation. There is no other means of handling the problem of the internal debt and the relative wage level.

We should, therefore, give the world the choice.

I should proceed at once, before we have spent all our £80,000,000, to control the exchanges and prohibit the movement of capital and of foreign balances, whilst for the time being allowing approved transactions on the present basis.

I should then summon an international conference at which I should propose

(1) Cancellation of war debts and reparations

(2) Funding of debts of all debtor countries expressed in foreign currencies for 3 years

(3) Large pool of international credit to finance improvements

(4) Cheap money everywhere

(5) Every Gov^t. to undertake large public works programme.

If this programme not accepted, I should invite those countries prepared to accept it to join us in a new currency and credit system centred on London based on a commodity standard.

If all this is too much and bold for our weak imaginations and feeble wits, then let us try a stiff tariff and if and when that fails, as it quite likely would, slide off gold as peacefully as we can. The idea that sterling would sink to nothing like the German mark is of course rubbish. The C. of E.'s remarks about this struck me as quite balmy.

I speak from a full heart. The course of policy pursued so far has reduced us to a point of humiliation one could not have conceived. During the last 12 years I have had very little influence, if any, on policy. But in the role of a Cassandra, I have had a considerable success as a prophet. I declare to you, and I will stake on it any reputation I have, that we have been making in the last few weeks as dreadful errors of policy as deluded statesmen have ever been guilty of.

Although Keynes expected devaluation would occur in the fairly near future, he did nothing to arrange his own financial affairs appropriately. When O. T. Falk suggested that the Independent Investment Trust, of which they were both directors, replace a dollar loan with a sterling loan—the company already was in financial difficulties—Keynes replied.

From a letter to O. T. FALK, *18 September 1931*

What you suggest amounts in the present circumstances to a frank bear speculation against sterling. I admit that I am not clear that this would be against the national interest; for it may be better that the special credits should be used up by Englishmen than by foreigners. All the same I am clear that an institution has no business to do such a thing at the present time. I should like to see exchange dealings controlled so as to take away the opportunity of choice. But meanwhile, one is not entitled to take matters into one's own hands. One has to fall in with the collective decision whether one agrees with it or not. I am confident that this would be the wish of our shareholders if we could consult them.

18.9.31   J. M. K.

The Company did not switch its financing and the resulting loss to the firm was over £40,000.

The New Statesman for 19 September contained an article by Keynes commenting on the Budget and Economy Bill introduced by the National Government on 10 and 11 September (*JMK*, vol. IX, pp. 145–9). However, after the Government had spent the day fruitlessly trying to obtain additional credits to give it time to pass whatever measures might be necessary to keep sterling on gold, the Bank of England reported to the Government on 18 September that it could no longer hold the exchange rate beyond the close of trading on Saturday morning. The weekend was spent preparing the Gold Standard (Amendment) Bill, which was introduced and passed on Monday, 21 September. During the weekend, Keynes was involved in discussions at the Treasury on exchange control. Only a few temporary restrictions were imposed when sterling left gold.

Just prior to sterling's fall from gold, the Committee on Economic Information of the Economic Advisory Council held its first meeting. The Prime Minister set up this Committee on 14 July 1931 'to supervise the preparation of monthly reports to the Economic Advisory Council and to advise as to the continuous study of economic development'. The Committee's initial members were Sir Josiah Stamp (chairman), W. M. Citrine, G. D. H. Cole, Keynes and Sir Alfred Lewis. Its secretaries were H. D. Henderson and A. F. Hemming.

The Committee's first subject was not unnaturally the balance of payments, on which it issued its first report on 25 September 1931, nine days after the first meeting. On the day sterling left gold Keynes's draft conclusions to the report were circulated.

ECONOMIC ADVISORY COUNCIL
COMMITTEE ON ECONOMIC INFORMATION

THE BALANCE OF INTERNATIONAL PAYMENTS
DRAFT REPORT: CONCLUDING PARAGRAPHS

The above calculations, which lead up to the conclusion that this country has in present circumstances a substantial adverse trade balance on income account, make no allowance for the probability that our invisible income from the fixed interest portion of our foreign investments may wilt away under the continuance of the existing international situation. In 1930 our income from fixed interest foreign investments was estimated at £135,000,000 and the income from the variable income investments at £115,000,000. The latter has been already greatly reduced, but so far the reduction of the former has been quite small, so slight that we have only reduced it to £130,000,000 for the current year and believe that even this modest reduction is on the safe side. Nevertheless, looking forward into 1932–3 we believe that these receipts must be regarded as in the highest degree precarious unless there is an early and complete reversal of the international position. Moreover, even now it is impossible to regard this sum as a net receipt, because the continuance of some part of it (the interest on Indian loans, for example) is contingent on our lending the equivalent to the debtor country. Without a great change in external conditions we believe that a large part of this source of income might quite quickly disappear, though it would of course be mere guess-work to attempt to estimate exactly how much within any given three-monthly interest.

This brings us to a few observations, which will not be out of place, on a hidden danger which may escape the careful attention it deserves at a time when we are necessarily so much concentrated on our own affairs. A restoration of confidence in the British position might stem the withdrawal of foreign balances and the flight from sterling. Domestic measures to improve the balance of trade might go a long way to make good the adverse balance estimated in the first part of this Report. But if at the same time our income from fixed interest investments abroad was fading away, this would render all our other measures of no avail. Yet it is unfortunately true that most of the steps which we can take to help ourselves not only do nothing helpful to the outside world but may be actually injurious. These measures to right our own position by decreasing our imports or increasing our exports—whether they take the form of tariffs, bounties, wage reductions, or the devaluation of our currency— must have the effect of increasing unemployment elsewhere and of making it still more difficult for debtor countries to meet their obligations. Thus what we do to improve our visible balance of trade may have a serious adverse reaction on our invisible balance. Indeed it is, in our opinion, virtually certain that if we concentrate on domestic measures alone, our efforts will be brought to nought by the wilting of our invisible income from debtor countries.

At present our power of international initiative is paralysed by our anxiety to prevent or provide for foreign withdrawals of balances and the British flight from sterling. Yet unless we recover this initiative in some measure, the drift of international events will overwhelm us. We conclude, therefore, as a result of our examination of the balance of trade position as a whole, that it is urgently necessary to terminate the present phase of un-controlled exchanges in which anyone in command of sterling balances is at liberty to use them how he chooses. We think that all dealings in foreign exchange should be forthwith centralised and that transactions for approved purposes only should be permitted. It would be wise to take this step before our foreign credits are further exhausted. It would, of course, entail many consequential measures into which we need not enter in this Report.

Such a situation would be obviously of a purely temporary character—to free us from immediate pressing anxieties and to allow us to take stock of the situation in a calmer atmosphere.

Having done this, there would be two lines of thought we could pursue. One of these would be a partial departure from the international monetary system in the direction of barter. Having controlled our imports and our exchanges, we might enter into a series of individual transactions with various countries. For example we might take shipments of goods, reckoned at more reasonable prices (say 25 per cent higher) than present world prices, from such countries as India, Australia, Canada, Argentina, Germany etc., the proceeds to be credited against the interest dues of these countries in London. These few sentences are probably sufficient to indicate the line of thought.

The second alternative would be to summon an International Currency Conference with a view to very drastic steps in the interests of world solvency, with the threat lying behind that, in the event of the results of the Conference being inadequate, we should invite the Dominions and any other countries like-minded with ourselves to join us in a new currency and credit system. But here again the detailed suggestions would go beyond the proper scope of this Report.

21 September 1931   J. M. K.

Two days later, he revised his draft in the light of what had happened.

ECONOMIC ADVISORY COUNCIL
COMMITTEE ON ECONOMIC INFORMATION

THE BALANCE OF INTERNATIONAL PAYMENTS
DRAFT REPORT: CONCLUDING PARAGRAPHS

The above calculations, which lead up to the conclusion that this country has in present circumstances a substantial adverse trade balance on income account, make no allowance for the probability that our invisible income from the fixed interest portion of our foreign investments may wilt away under the continuance of the existing international situation. In 1930 our income from fixed interest foreign investments was estimated at £135,000,000 and the income from the variable income investments at £115,000,000. The latter has been already greatly reduced, but so far the reduction of the former has been quite small, so slight that we have only reduced it to £130,000,000 for the current year and believe that even this modest reduction is on the safe side. Nevertheless, looking forward into 1932–3 we believe that these receipts must be regarded as in the highest degree precarious unless there is an early and complete reversal of the international position. Moreover, even now it is impossible to regard this sum as a net receipt, because the continuance of some part of it (the interest on Indian loans, for example) is contingent on our lending the equivalent to the debtor country. Without a great change in external conditions we believe that a large part of this source of income might quite quickly disappear, though it would of course be mere guesswork to attempt to estimate exactly how much within any given three-monthly interest.

This brings us to a few observations, which will not be out of place, on a hidden danger which may escape the careful attention it deserves at a time when we are necessarily so much concentrated on our own affairs. Domestic measures to improve the balance of trade, whether in the shape of a devaluated exchange or of a tariff, might go a long way to make good the adverse balance estimated in the first part of this Report. But if at the same time our income from fixed interest investments abroad was fading away, this would render these measures of insufficient avail. Yet it is unfortunately true that the steps which we take to help ourselves may not only not help the outside world but may be actually injurious. Measures to right our own position by decreasing our imports or increasing our exports— whether they take the form of tariffs, bounties, wage reductions, or the devaluation of our currency—are liable to have the effect of increasing unemployment elsewhere and of making it still more difficult for debtor countries to meet their obligations. Thus what we do to improve our visible balance of trade may have a serious adverse reaction on our invisible balance. We fear, therefore, that if we concentrate on domestic measures alone, our efforts may be defeated by the loss of invisible income from debtor countries.

Until lately our power of international initiative was paralysed by our anxiety to prevent or provide for foreign withdrawals of balances and the British flight from sterling. But now that we have recovered this initiative, we should consider most carefully how best to use it.

It seems possible that many other countries will be constrained to follow our example. This opens up to us opportunities of financial leadership, by using which we might hope to save the value of our existing foreign investments, though detailed suggestions, would lie outside the scope of this Report.
23 September 1931   J. M. K.

The Sunday after Britain's departure from gold, *The Sunday Express* printed Keynes's first public comment under the title 'The Future of the World'. Keynes's own title had been 'The World Influence of England's Decision', but when he reprinted the article in *Essays in Persuasion* he called it 'The End of the Gold Standard' (*JMK*, vol. IX, pp. 245–9). The next day, 28 September, Keynes wrote a letter to *The Times* suggesting that the immediate question for consideration was the currency question and that its settlement, with its implications for Britain's competitive position, must precede any discussion of tariffs (*JMK*, vol. IX, pp. 243–4).

After the suspension there was much talk of a general election. Keynes wrote letters on the subject to both the Prime Minister and Lloyd George. He also saw both men on Sunday, 4 October.

To J. RAMSAY MACDONALD, *30 September 1931*

Dear Prime Minister,

I wonder if those who are pressing you towards a general election appreciate the rapid developments towards an unprecedented banking crisis which are proceeding in the rest of the world. It seems to me that there are now two alternative courses which events may take in the near future. The first would be for country after country to tumble off gold parity. The second would be a general banking moratorium outside this country, but including France and the U.S.A. I think the latter may be perhaps the more probable because whereas in our case it was primarily a balance of payments crisis and not a banking crisis at all, elsewhere it is primarily a banking crisis. Further developments would necessarily lead up to a world conference, in which we—almost alone in the world in having a solvent banking system—would have the strong position.

The time factor is the most dangerous thing about which to prophesy. But these things might happen quickly. It seems to me that it would be too foolish to be caught by them in the middle of a general election fought on largely irrelevant issues. Great events are pending, and we need to be thinking out with undivided attention various lines of policy which it is open to us to pursue. For the problems are largely new and very difficult.

I know that you are far from disagreeing from this sort of attitude to the surrounding problems, and I only write because, if one is to believe the newspapers, you need all the support you can get for putting first things first. In any case might it not be worth while to have the possible alternatives brought on to the tapis and examined in a preliminary way by a small Joint Committee of the E.A.C., the Treasury and the Bank of England.

Yours sincerely,
[copy initialled] J. M. K.

To J. RAMSAY MACDONALD, *1 October 1931*

Dear Prime Minister,

It will save your time if I put in writing a point which I should have liked to mention to you if the Cabinet Meeting this evening had not interfered.

It quite beats me how a programme can be agreed by members of the different parties to cover the lifetime of the new

Parliament. But on the other hand it happens partly by chance that the matters which ought to be occupying everyone's attention for the next six months or so are exceptionally non-party in character. I mean three things. The currency question, the Indian Conference, and the Disarmament Conference. Here is enough to occupy the energy and attention of Ministers. At the same time they raise nothing acute between the parties. I would suggest that the obvious course is to put these three questions in the foreground, to have no Parliamentary programme of new legislation whatever, and to employ the House of Commons on little more than routine business whilst the three great topics above are concentrated upon. When these issues are out of the way the arguments both against an election and against a return to party allegiances will have disappeared.

Yours sincerely,
[copy initialled] J. M. K.

From J. RAMSAY MACDONALD, *2 October 1931*

My dear Keynes,

Thank you so much for your letter this morning. The question of whether we shall have an early election or one about the middle of winter is rather a complicated problem, which I should like very much to have discussed with you. I am just leaving Town and shall not be back until to-morrow. Do you happen to be free for lunch on Sunday at Chequers? If so, I would be very glad indeed to see you. If you came at one o'clock we could have half-an-hour's talk before lunch, as I shall have to leave you not later than 2.45 p.m.

Yours very sincerely,
J. RAMSAY MACDONALD

To DAVID LLOYD GEORGE, *1 October 1931*

Dear Mr Lloyd George,

I should like to write and say how enthusiastically I agree with the line you are taking up if common report be true, and how much I hope that if this ridiculous Government does force things to an election in any shape or form, you will lead the

Liberal Party—or what is left of it—into the fight in an honourable alliance with Labour. Both the national issue and the personal issue would conspire I am sure to make such a project feasible and fruitful in a way it never could have been in the past. I have seen something of the Labour people lately and judge them to be exceedingly desolate and anxious for assistance where they can get it. I also have a strong impression that the personal feeling in relation to you is totally different from what it was, and that the obstacles to friendly relations are disappearing with extraordinary rapidity.

Anyhow, it seems to me quite mad to suppose that Liberals and Conservatives can possibly consort in any common programme which could occupy the life of a new Parliament,—though they might be able to do so for a temporary period of 6 or 12 months to deal with the immediate problems. But apart from all this it would be insensate to have a general election now wholly on issues quite irrelevant to the pressing matters. It happens that all the matters about which we ought to be occupying ourselves at this juncture are more or less of a non-party character. There is the currency question which is most urgent and terrifically important. There is the Indian Conference. And there is the Disarmament Conference a short way ahead. These are quite enough to occupy the attention of Ministers in the Cabinet for several months and there is no purpose at this moment in having any particular Parliamentary Programme of legislation. It seems to me that the right line to take is that the present Government should handle these three issues, and that after that the several parties should depart into their own tents.

I do not think that those who are pressing for an election probably realise the extraordinarily critical character at this moment of the international financial situation. Our own problems are more or less solved for the moment. The reports I hear about the stimulus to British exports and the buzz of business which is going on are quite extraordinary. But abroad things are still crashing to destruction. I doubt if there is now a solvent bank in the whole of the United States. Some considerable disasters cannot be far off, and they are bound to lead up pretty quickly to a first-class international situation.

[copy initialled] J. M. K.

He also wrote to Sir Josiah Stamp, enclosing his first letter to MacDonald.

To SIR JOSIAH STAMP, *30 September 1931*

My dear Stamp,

Would it not be a good plan for the Bank of England to fix up a definite arrangement with the South African mines to buy their entire output of gold on the basis of the dollar quotation on the date of delivery? It seems to me that a moderate accession of resources coming to the Bank by a sort of routine, regardless of the exact level of the exchange, would be a sound arrangement.

I have a feeling that a banking crisis in Europe and the United States is moving forward very fast. There are two lines which the course of events may take. One is for various countries to tumble off gold parity. The other is a general banking crisis ending in moratoriums. I incline to the view that the latter is now becoming the more likely. I should not be surprised to see in the ensuing weeks a general banking moratorium extending even to the United States, and then the summoning of a general conference to deal with the whole business.

These are the important urgent matters which are afoot. It would be too silly if they were to come on us in the middle of an election. I am writing a letter to the Prime Minister to this general effect.

Yours ever,
[copy initialled] J. M. K.

From SIR JOSIAH STAMP, *1 October 1931*

My dear Maynard,

Thanks for sending me your letter, which I return. I am so glad that you are helping to keep him up to the essentials; he has so many who are distracting him. I agree also about dollar resources.

I am going away for a few days as I have had great pressure upon me lately.

Yours ever,

J. C. S.

However, by this time a new range of policy options were coming to the forefront in discussions. As if to mark the change, almost immediately after 21 September Keynes decided to collect together a selection of his writings from the previous twelve years in a volume entitled 'Essays in Prophecy'. On 3 October he proposed the book to Macmillan, who agreed to take it two days later. On 16 October Keynes sent Macmillan copy for the entire book, then called 'Essays in Prophecy and Persuasion'. By 22 October, however, he had settled on the title *Essays in Persuasion*. The book appeared in England on 27 November and two months later in America. By then Keynes was deeply involved in new exercises in persuasion. These will be the subject of the next volume.

DOCUMENTS REPRODUCED
IN THIS VOLUME

Where documents come from the Public Record Office, their call numbers
appear before the date.

MINUTES OF EVIDENCE

SPEECHES AND BROADCASTS

Acknowledgements

We whould like to thank the Humanities and Social Science Research Council of Canada for financial assistance, Professors Susan Howson and Donald Winch for advice, Gary Dobinson for help with the proofs, and Lady Henderson for copies of certain letters.

Crown copyright material appears with the permission of the Controller of Her Majesty's Stationery Office.

INDEX

Abnormal phase, 273, 284, 308, 330; JMK's assumption questioned, 275–6

Acceptances on foreign account, 184–7 *passim*, 252, 355; buying rate by central banks, 529, 531–2; in U.S., 531–2, 552, 565

acceptance houses, 187, 246, 284, 591

Accumulation of wealth, 273, 338–9, 516

Addis, Sir Charles, Bank of England, 561

Advertising, 140

Agriculture

fall of prices, 456, 468, 471; in U.S., 569, 576, 580

land, 339, 525–6

Lloyd George's agricultural programme, 475, 484

and manufactures, 473–4, 544

Minister of, 28

progress, 517

wages, 67; in U.S., 576

Alexander, A. V., 494

Allen, Sir Thomas, member, Macmillan Committee on Finance and Industry, 17, 38, 44, 47, 48, 50, 51–2, 57, 66, 67, 94, 97, 101, 105, 106, 119, 122, 124–5, 148, 152, 153, 155; letter to, on proposals for short-term domestic monetary action, 280–1; signs JMK's Addendum, with reservations, 282, 309; reservation on Report, 283n

Allies, in World War I, 340–1; repayment of debts, 433

see also War debts

Amalgamations, 343, 364 n8

America, discovery of, 64

American

edition, *Essays in Persuasion*, 622

efficiency, 58

funds in London, 214; bank money, 605

securities sold in London, 188, 190–1; purchase of British securities, 188

American Farm Board, 482

Amsterdam: as financial centre, 187, 188, 190, 191; foreign issues, 232–3

Analogies, 83; false, 305, 478, 593, 607

Ancient Monuments Bill, 526

Angell, Norman, M.P., 607

Anglo-American securities, 2

Arbitrage: loans, and gold movements, 181–3, 187, 213; transactions, 216, 221

Argentine, 151, 615; railways, 85

Arithmetic, 214, 215, 221, 278, 279

Armaments, 338

Ashfield, Lord, 113

Asia, 337, 592

Asquith, Cyril, letter to *The Times*, answered, 506–7

Assets

American, 258; of American banks, 568–9

Bank of England, 134, 197, 211, 240–1, 242–5, 248–9

capital, 128, 304

foreign, 39–40, 141–2

liquid, and non-liquid, 227–9, 259

long-term, 190; short-dated, 247

in relation to population, 320

Assumptions, 45, 50–1, 54, 83, 117, 130

Australia

bank crash in '90s, 56

gold from, 381–2

Government loans raised in Britain, 186, 324, 398; aid for, 381–2

as primary producer, 601; Prime Minister on wheat prices, 152; advised to cut her costs, 452; barter arrangements, proposal for, 615

wages: and prices, 105; and unemployment, 50

Austria, 453

financial crisis of 1931, 553, 589

loan to, 381

Automatic looms, 352, 358

Automatic mechanisms, 131, 310, 430

arbitrage, 181–2, 213

631

Business (*cont.*)
  on, of Bank rate, 46, 80, 81–2, 96; in
  Depression of 90s, 56; investment from
  profits, 73–4, 97, 129–32, 439–40, 547–8;
  reform of business organization, 167;
  capital development schemes, 174, alarm
  at public schemes, 302, 358–9; effect on,
  of fall in prices, 322, of production costs
  fixed in money terms, 426; signs of
  revival (October 1931), 620
  in U.S., 67, 519
Businessmen, 19
  in classical and modern theory, 5–7
  and economists, 368
  Henderson on the ordinary . . . businessman, 452
  and taxation, 12–13
'Buying a British Car', 385–7, 404

Cabinet, 466, 473, 483, 620; Cabinet Meeting,
  618
  Cabinet Office, 465
  Cabinet Secretariat, 25
Cadman, Sir John, member, Committee on
  the Economic Outlook, 326, 327, 357,
  360
  member, Economic Advisory Council, 28
Call rates (money), 224, 225–6
Cambridge, 165, 269, 310, 450, 462
Campbell-Bannerman, Sir Henry, 104
Can Lloyd George Do It? (JMK and H. D.
  Henderson), 167
Canada, 105, 116, 592, 615; wheat, 153
Capital, 44, 479
  accumulation, 118, 320, 517
  in Bank of England balance sheet, 302
  as factor of production, 45, 147
  fixed, 346
  for home rather than abroad, 51, 57, 144,
  149, for rationalisation, 115; limited
  supplies, 302
  management, 242
  in U.S., 58
  tendency to flow abroad, 11
Capital development schemes
  in Addendum to Macmillan Report, 300,
  301–9
  to break the vicious circle, 323
  Government schemes, JMK's proposals,
  144–7; Lord Privy Seal's programme,
  173–4
  Labour Party views, 483
  Liberal programme, 'We Can Conquer
  Unemployment', 386; criticised in

Treasury Memorandum, 166–9; Sir
  Richard Hopkins cross-examined on,
  169–79
  proposals of Economic Advisory Council
  Committee of Economists, 437–43,
  447–8, Henderson's view, 456
  in Report of Committee on the Economic
  Outlook, 327, 328, 330
  subsidies for, 389, 446–7
  in U.S., 564
  as way out of the Great Slump, 346, 347,
  348, 488, 518, 549; difference with Henderson on, 357–66
  world-wide development, need for, 153,
  435
Capital goods, 74, 75, 362, or physical investment, 400; capital assets, 128
Capital market, *see* London
Capital movements, 257; in the financial
  crisis, 599, 601, 610; fluctuations in task
  of Bank of England, 180–9
  net outward capital movements equal
  income surplus, 180
Capital transactions, 182–3; distinguished
  from income transactions, 39–40
Capital wealth, 73, 293, 443
Capitalism, 223, 480
  capitalists, 8, 9, 15
Carnegie, Colonel David, 22 n 2
Cartels, 78, 110
Cascara, 83
Case, Walter, New York banker, 484, 603–6
  list of letters, 626
Cassel, Gustav, 310, 404
Census
  of manufacturers, U.S., 67–8
  of production, U.K., 98, 266, 328
Central banks
  Bank rate policy, 2, need for concerted
  action to lower, 151, 272–6; reduction
  agreed on at Brussels Conference, 345,
  396–7, 436; further cooperation on interest rates needed, 541–2
  buying and selling prices of gold, 219–30;
  need to reduce legal ratio of gold, 152;
  function in the gold standard game, 42;
  responsibility for maldistribution of
  gold, 435–6
  capital development, need to encourage,
  153; provision of liquid funds for domestic market, 228; credit restriction following return to gold standard, 393–4, cheap
  and abundant credit needed, 445
  consultation between governors, 231

Quantification, 361
Quarries, 169
Quotas, 108, 334, 338

Radical Liberal Party, 527
Radicals, 525; JMK still calls himself a
Radical, 527; radical policy on unemployment, 325
Radio industry, 393, 480, 585
Railways, 21, 44, 78, 103, 168, 339
Electrification of the Railway System,
Committee on, 307
exports of locomotives, 324
investment in, nineteenth century, 63, 85
losses, 98
railway bonds, 426; American, 234, 552
railwaymen, 61; wages, 67, 98, 277, 496,
reductions, 501
relief for: derating, 107; Treasury advances, 145, 446; development schemes,
174
a sheltered industry, 71, 98
tube railways, 145; underground, 112–13,
145
in U.S., 85, 529, 573, 576, 577
Raine, Sir Walter, member, Macmillan Committee on Finance and Industry, 17, 38,
44, 47, 60, 66, 86, 94, 97–8, 103, 114, 116,
119–21, 125, 127, 148, 179, 206, 213, 215,
232–3, 280 n 14
Ramsay, Frank, 28
Rand Mines, 89, 161
Rate of interest
meaning of term, 40, 272; included in term
'bank lending', 41; relation to Bank rate,
41, 46, 148–9, 257, or 'pure rate', 535,
538
capital transactions dependent on, 40, 95;
income balance and capital balance governed by, 40–1, 43
in a closed community, 79–80, 98; in an
international system, 79–80, 290, 415,
428, 446
and costs of production, business losses
determined by, 136–7
on deposits, 227–8, 530, 537–40
equilibrium rate, 43, 273, 276, 353; long
rate held above, 353, 374, 530; investment in a state of disequilibrium, 138,
150
and gold points, 217
and hoarding, 275
too high, JMK's fundamental explanation,
272–4, 285, 353–4, 356, 365–6, 372–4,
391–9, 480, 518, 551–3, 574, 575

for home investment, 352, 382–3, 446; rates
correct for foreign, deterrent to home,
95, 139, 348, 351, 374–5, 446; proposed
discriminatory rates, 143, 144–7, 348,
354, 360, 446
in investment schemes, Treasury view,
174–8
on Local Loans, 145, 313–15; on Government securities, 304
market and natural rate, 273, 275–6
and new investment or employment,
314–15, 410, 415, 479
and prices, 229
raised by maldistribution of gold, 435
regulation by joint-stock banks, 225–8
short and long-term, 227–8, 241, 283, 355,
396–7, 535–6; long-term, 295, 530; fall
in short, not in long, 445–6, 518–19;
movements of short money governed by,
40
in U.S., 569, 573; aim to reduce, 562, 564,
567
in the vicious circle, 373
and the Wall Street crash, 2
see also Bank rate; Interest
Rates, 103, 145; derating measures, 106–7,
376
Rathbone, Eleanor, M.P., 607
Rationalisation: or productive efficiency, 322;
JMK's fourth remedy, 109–13; of steel,
115; rationalisation loans, 145–6;
schemes for, 19–20, 176, 323, 358, 364
n 8, 432, for export industries, 329, 351,
352, none for coal, 343; to decrease cost
of production, 376; mixed effect on
employment, 432; in Report of Economists' Committee, 450
Raw material, 73, 339
fall of prices, 44, 471, 540–1, 549
imports, 48, 132, 299, 303–4, 328, 339, 385,
417, 493, 508
international index numbers of, 151
in the slump, 390–1, 435–6, 582
tariff on, 495, 508
Real estate, in U.S., 539, 571–2, 573; skyscrapers in Chicago, 571
Reconstruction, 57, 146
Refrigerators, 583
Reichsbank, 210, 240
'Relative Quantities', 408–9
Relief schemes, grants for, 302
Religion, 467
Remedies for disequilibrium, 66, 133, 504
four remedies, 82, 99, 125; 1st, revaluation
of gold, 99–102; 2nd, income reduction,